The Farm Ho...

HOLI...

IN

ENGLAND, WALES & IRELAND

& THE CHANNEL ISLANDS

1997

COLOUR SECTION

Please note all advertisers in this colour section
also have a full review in the classified section
under the relevant county.

SELF-CATERING

THAMES VALLEY HOLIDAY HOMES
Two country holiday homes overlooking the Thames Valley

Overleigh sleeps 2-6 people. Underleigh sleeps 1-4 people. Both properties are fully equipped – central heating, colour TV, telephone, pretty gardens/orchard, plenty of parking. Situated in a picturesque village a short distance from the famous Cliveden Estate, within easy reach of London (25 miles) and Windsor (10 miles). Registered with Tourist Board.

For further information see classified entry under Wooburn Green, Bucks.

Send for free colour brochure: Mrs E.G. Griffin

MYOSOTIS, WIDMOOR, WOOBURN GREEN, BUCKS HP10 0JG
Tel: 01628 521594 Fax: 01628 850471

BOARD

CENTRAL LIZARD PENINSULA
TREGADDRA FARM
ETB ❦❦❦ Highly Commended AA QQQQ Selected

Unwind in this beautifully furnished 18th century farmhouse on working farm. Pretty en suite bedrooms (two have balconies, one romantic four-poster). Heated outdoor swimming pool and lovely garden with views of peaceful rolling countryside for a 15 mile radius. Beaches, sailing, coastal walks, horse riding, art galleries, etc, nearby. Activities arranged for cycling, golf, fishing and walking. Lots of information and ideas, storage and drying facilities! Open all year, including out of season breaks with candle-lit farmhouse dinners and open log fires for chilly evenings and, of course, the mammoth Tregaddra breakfast. Individual attention and warm family hospitality guaranteed. **Send for colour brochure and local information.**

Mrs. J. Lugg, Tregaddra Farm, Cury Cross Lanes, Helston, Cornwall TR12 7BB
Telephone/Fax: (01326) 240235

SELF-CATERING

Picturesque group of 17th century cottages overlooking beautiful National Trust Valley, some with sea views. All our cottages are individually furnished and equipped to a very high standard. All have colour TV etc. Cottages are warm and comfortable and are open all year. Wonderful walks, peace and quiet and unspoilt beaches nearby.
English Tourist Board Member. 2-4 Keys Commended.
Please write or phone for our free colour brochure.

Mr & Mrs D. Clough, Courtyard Farm, Lesnewth, Near Boscastle, Cornwall PL35 0HR. Telephone 01840 261256.

BOARD

Crantock Plains Farmhouse
1990, 1991 & 1992 WINNERS OF 'NEWQUAY IN BLOOM'

Relax in this charming character farmhouse in peaceful countryside and combine comfort, home cooking and personal service for an enjoyable holiday. Crantock Plains Farm is situated two and a half miles from Newquay and half a mile off the A3075 Newquay-Redruth road. Picturesque village of Crantock with Post Office, village stores, tea rooms, two pubs and beautiful sandy beach is nearby, as are riding stables and many sporting activities. Four doubles (one twin en-suite), two family rooms, one family en-suite. Ground floor bedrooms are available. Shower room; two toilets, bathroom; sittingroom; central heating, log fire. Electric blankets for chilly nights. Table licence. Home grown vegetables when available. No pets. Open all year. Please send SAE for brochure with details of prices. Non-smoking establishment. Tourist Board and H.A.S.S. Registered. Cream Tea Award.

Mr and Mrs Rowlands, Crantock Plains Farm, Near Newquay, Cornwall. Tel: Crantock (01637) 830253

A REAL COUNTRY HOUSE HOTEL JUST OUTSIDE OF FALMOUTH

👑 👑 👑 COMMENDED

THE HOME
PENJERRICK, FALMOUTH

Telephone: Falmouth (STD 01326) 250427 and 250143

Situated in lovely unspoilt countryside, yet only 2½ miles from Falmouth. Ideal for lovers of the country, yet within 18 minutes' walk of Maenporth Beach.

An Ashley Courtenay Highly Recommended Hotel

Our house, in its large garden, has lovely views over tree-clad countryside to Maenporth and the bay. Close to the Helford River with its beautiful walks and boating facilities. Ideal base for touring. Majority of bedrooms now completely refurbished with full ensuite facilities, TV and tea/coffee making facilities and heating. Our home is graciously furnished and carpeted to a high standard. All beds are modern divans. Central heating. Our elegant dining room has separate tables. Large lounge with colour TV. In addition there is a spacious sun lounge overlooking the garden.

★

TABLE LICENCE   GOOD ENCLOSED CAR PARK   BUS SERVICE

★

Mr & Mrs P. Tremayne have welcomed guests to their lovely house for the past 31 years

★

Dinner, Room and Breakfast from £160 per week, including 17.5% VAT.

Illustrated brochure from: Mrs. T. P. Tremayne

We are of a farming family and our visitors' book is blushingly complimentary over the home-cooked food and its presentation. This is our home and as such we welcome you to it and hope you will enjoy it as much as we do.

Also Self-Catering Furnished Farmhouse at Constantine, Falmouth

Tregurrian Hotel

AA** ETB ♥♥♥

LES ROUTIERS

**Watergate Bay, Near Newquay
Cornwall TR8 4AB
Tel: St. Mawgan (01637) 860280**
100 yards from this glorious sandy beach and
spectacular Atlantic coastline. Peaceful
position between Newquay and Padstow.

* 27 rooms with radio/listening, tea makers, heaters, most
  en suite – TV all rooms. Car park.
* Heated pool and sun patio, Games room, Solarium
* Licensed Bar, Sauna, Jacuzzi
* Family run, children welcome at reduced rates
  (some free offers off-season)
* Central for touring all of Cornwall
* Parties and coaches by arrangement
* Open Easter to November
* Spring and Autumn Breaks
* Dinner, Bed and Breakfast £144 to £230 (inclusive of VAT)

Brochure from resident proprietors, Marian and Derrick Molloy.

SELF-CATERING

"Halwyn"

Manaccan, Near Helston,
Cornwall TR12 6ER
Tel: 01326 280359

John and Sharon Darling

Delightful cottages, fully equipped in
naturally beautiful surroundings.

Indoor swimming pool, sauna and solarium.

For full details see SELF CATERING
SECTION – CORNWALL – HELSTON.

BOARD

MANOR FARM

FARMHOUSE
BED & BREAKFAST

Come and stay on our family-run Dairy Farm set
amidst 450 acres of Cornish countryside. Our Grade II
listed Georgian farmhouse offers en suite and family
en suite facilities with colour TV, tea/coffee in all rooms.
Relax in the spacious gardens with camellias and
rhododendrons; or roam around the fields and nearby
woodland. Manor Farm is centrally located for exploring
the character of Cornwall's unique countryside and
coastline. Tariff from £17. Please contact

**Suzanne Manuell, Manor Farm,
Burngallow, St. Austell PL26 7TQ.
Telephone/Fax: 01726 72242**

BOARD

Dalswinton Country House Hotel

AA ★★
ENGLISH TOURIST BOARD ✹✹✹

St. Mawgan, Near Newquay, Cornwall TR8 4EZ
Telephone: St. Mawgan (01637) 860385

- All rooms en suite
- Full central heating
- Colour TV in rooms
- Tea/coffee facilities
- Residential and Restaurant Licence
- 5 course Dinner – choice of menu
- Log fires in lounge and bar
- Heated swimming pool

OPEN for CHRISTMAS & NEW YEAR

Approached by its own private 200 yard drive, The Dalswinton is an old Cornish house of immense character in 1½ acres of superbly landscaped gardens. Overlooking the beautiful valley of Lanherne with views to the sea. Ideally situated between Newquay and Padstow, reputed to be the finest coastline in Europe. The Hotel has been completely refurbished and offers superb cooking in a comfortable, friendly atmosphere. Excellent beaches and coves within one and a half miles with many picturesque coastal walks. Some of the best coarse fishing in Cornwall, two new golf courses plus horse riding are all available locally. Bed and Breakfast from £18 per night. Weekly from £112.50. Dinner, Bed and Breakfast from £157.50. Bargain Breaks available. Colour brochure on request.

BOARD

AA★★
RAC★★

Rosemundy House Hotel

ETB
✹✹✹
Commended

Telephone St. Agnes (01872) 552101

Rosemundy House is a delightful Georgian residence set in its own sheltered and attractive grounds in the village of St. Agnes and within a mile of Trevaunance Cove beach. Rosemundy is family owned and run and we take pride in the quality of food, service and accommodation we offer. St. Agnes is an unspoilt village on the north Cornish coast between St. Ives and Newquay and is an ideal centre for touring.

* Family-run Hotel
* Attractive licensed bar
* Good home cooking
* Colour TV lounge
* 44 ensuite bedrooms

* Colour TV in all bedrooms
* Tea/coffee making facilities in all bedrooms
* Large car park
* 45ft heated swimming pool

* Games room with table tennis, pool, snooker, darts, etc
* Badminton, Croquet, Putting
* Horse riding, golf, tennis, surfing, gliding, fishing nearby

Dinner, Bed and Breakfast from £180 to £265 per week (including VAT)
Bed and Breakfast from £155 to £240 per week (including VAT). We make no service charge.
Rosemundy House Hotel, Rosemundy, St. Agnes, Cornwall TR5 0UF

Bossiney House Hotel
Tintagel, Cornwall PL34 0AX

At Bossiney House Hotel emphasis is on good cooking with excellent choice and variation throughout the menus, and a wine list designed to provide a selection of attractive wines at reasonable prices. A very personally run hotel, the resident proprietors and their family, together with their staff, work as a dedicated team to make your stay a really comfortable one. A holiday at Bossiney House Hotel can be one of complete rest and relaxation, but equally for the energetic, there is ample scope – a wide variety of walks, or for the really serious golfer the championship courses at St. Enodoc and St. Mellion are only a short distance away. Within our spacious grounds, where guests can laze the afternoon away, we have an interesting putting green and an attractive Scandinavian log chalet with indoor heated swimming pool, sauna and solarium.

Bossiney House, standing in two and a half acres above Bossiney and Benoath Coves and a half mile from Tintagel, overlooks one of the finest stretches of coastline in Great Britain. The diningroom is modern and comfortable and overlooks the front and rear gardens. All the bedrooms have country or sea views, are tastefully furnished and have either ensuite or private facilities. We have one family suite plus two family rooms in addition to the sixteen other twin/double bedrooms, all of which benefit from colour television, hair drying and tea/coffee making facilities.

Tintagel, is in fact an ideal springboard for touring Cornwall and Devon. Numerous beauty spots and places of interest are within easy driving distance. Cornwall with its mild climate, is ideal for either an early or late holiday, and prospective guests with freedom of choice, are invited to consider lower terms at either end of the season.

Situated on the B3263 Tintagel to Boscastle coast road, the Bossiney House Hotel offers the best of both worlds – a holiday in the country *and* by the sea.

AA
★★
RAC

For Reservations and/or Brochure
please contact
Ian or Heather Graham
Tel: 01840 770240; Fax. 01840 770501
ASHLEY COURTENAY RECOMMENDED

ETB
👑👑👑
APPROVED

BOARD

ST. MARGARET'S HOLIDAY PARK
Tel: (01726) 74283 Fax (01726) 71680

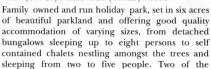

Family owned and run holiday park, set in six acres of beautiful parkland and offering good quality accommodation of varying sizes, from detached bungalows sleeping up to eight persons to self contained chalets nestling amongst the trees and sleeping from two to five people. Two of the bungalows are suitable for disabled persons. All property is well equipped including colour TV and microwave ovens. Launderette and pay phone on park. St. Austell golf course is 400 yards away and the Polgooth shops and inn are conveniently near. Well controlled pets allowed. Special rates early/late season or for two persons. Open March to December. Terms and colour brochure from: Mrs M. King, St. Margaret's Holiday Park, Polgooth, St. Austell, Cornwall PL26 7AX.

Linda & Alan Bleasdale
Borwick Lodge
Outgate, Hawkshead, Ambleside, Cumbria LA22 0PU
Tel: Hawkshead (015394) 36332

Three times winners of the AWARD for "Accommodation of the Highest Standards of Comfort, Amenity and Hospitality". Delightful 17th century country house nestling in 3 acres of secluded gardens. Breathtaking panoramic lake and mountain views. Ideally situated. Close to Hawkshead village with good choice of restaurants and inns. Beautiful ensuite rooms with colour TV and tea-making facilities. King-size four-poster rooms. Prize-winning home-made breads. Tourist Board "Two Crown Highly Commended". Somewhere special in this most beautiful corner of England. Ample parking. NON-SMOKING THROUGHOUT. Bed and Breakfast from £18. May we send our brochure? See Board Section – Ambleside, Cumbria.

CHARACTER COTTAGES AND PINE LODGES

Fringe of Lake District, National Park. 3 lodges peacefully situated in our grounds in picturesque hamlet. Views over farmland to Caldbeck Fells, 30 minutes Lake Ullswater, Keswick or Gretna Green.

* 3 cottages, 1 heavily beamed with wood burning stove
* 1/2/3 Bedrooms (sleep 2/7)
* Shower/bath, second WC in 3-bedroom properties
* Heaters in all properties
* Colour TVs
* Microwaves
* Laundry
* Open all year, Winter Breaks
* Warm for your arrival
* Excellent quality throughout
* Direct dial telephones
* ♛♛♛ / ♛♛♛♛ up to Highly Commended

Featured in Good Holiday Cottage Guide. Terms £145-£480. Winter Breaks from £95. For details and brochure:
Mrs Ivinson (FHG), Green View, Welton, Near Dalston, Carlisle CA5 7ES
Telephone: 016974 76230 Fax: 016974 76523

ETB 4 Keys Commended

PETS WELCOME
Fishing, Walking, Pure Escapism
Tranquil quality cottages overlooking two modest lakes amid Lakeland's beautiful Eden Valley countryside, only 30 minutes' drive *equidistant* from Ullswater, North Pennines, Hadrian's Wall and Scottish Borders. You will find beds freshly made up for your arrival, tranquillity and freedom in your surroundings, and good coarse and game fishing at hand. Accommodation is guaranteed clean, well equipped and maintained; laundry area; **PETS WELCOME.** Exceptional wildlife and walking area. **NO SILLY RULES.** Relax and escape to **YOUR** home in the country – why settle for less! Telephone or SAE for details.

Crossfield Cottages, Kirkoswald, Penrith CA10 1EU. 7 day 8am-10pm Tel: 01768 896275 (Fax available)
24 hour Brochure Line: 01768 898711 (manned most Saturdays).

Patterdale Hall Estate

GLENRIDDING • PENRITH • CUMBRIA • CA11 0PJ
Telephone & Fax: Glenridding (017684) 82308 (24 hours)

SELF-CATERING

In a magnificent mountain setting at the southern end of Ullswater, Patterdale Hall Estate is ideally situated for holidays and outdoor activities. Its spacious wooded grounds reach from the shores of the lake to the lower slopes of the Helvellyn range. The 300 acres contains a working hill farm, own private section of foreshore and 100 acres of private woodland and gardens. Sailing, fishing, canoeing, windsurfing and steamer trips on Ullswater, and the Estate makes an ideal base for touring the whole of the Lake District.

There are 16 self-catering units in various parts of the Estate.

Three	Two	Six	Two	Three
English Tourist Board COMMENDED	English Tourist Board APPROVED	English Tourist Board COMMENDED	English Tourist Board COMMENDED	English Tourist Board COMMENDED
Apartments	Cottages	Cedar Chalets	Pine Lodges	Dairy & Bothies

Terms are from £112 to £381 per week including central heating and one tank of hot water per day. Other electricity metered. Linen hire available. Children welcome. Pets by arrangement in some accommodation. Colour TV in all units. Launderette on site.

"Short Breaks" available.
Telephone for detailed brochure.

HOWSCALES
COTTAGES FOR NON-SMOKERS
Nestle in the beautiful, tranquil countryside of the Eden Valley.

Originally built as a working farm in the late 17th century, made of local sandstone set around a central courtyard. Our well equiped, warm, centrally heated cottages painstakenly converted from the farm buildings and keeping many of the original features, make an ideal place in which to relax and unwind or a base from which to explore the Lake District, Borders, Yorkshire Dales and Pennines.

ETB 3 and 4 key, highly commended. FOR MORE DETAILS SEE CUMBRIA SELF-CATERING SECTION.

For our colour brochure and price list, please ring or fax Mike or Toni Parsons.
Tel: 01768 898666. Fax: 01768 898710

The Beaumont Hotel
Holly Road, Windermere, Cumbria LA23 2AF
Telephone and Fax: (015394) 47075

Opened Easter 1992, this elegant Victorian House Hotel lends itself to all the Grace & Charm of its time combined with all the comforts of today. Ideally situated for Windermere and Bowness and a perfect location for touring the Lakes. All 10 luxury bedrooms are ensuite with tea making facilities, TV and hairdryers. Some ground floor rooms.

Two Four-Poster rooms are available for that Special Occasion and a 'Romantic Presentation' of wine, chocolates, fruit and flowers may be ordered. The Beaumont has very quickly gained a reputation for quality and excellent value. Please ring for room availability. Standards are high, Breakfasts are hearty and the Hospitality is warm and sincere. Prices from £23. Private parking.

AA QQQQ Selected. RAC Highly Acclaimed.

 Highly Commended

GLENCREE
Lake Road, Windermere
Cumbria LA23 2EQ

*Coveted
AA QQQQ Selected
RAC Highly Acclaimed*

Warm and friendly hospitality welcomes you to our small hotel which has, over the years, earned an enviable reputation as one of the best in The Lake District. **GLENCREE** is beautifully and tastefully furnished and decorated throughout with your comfort in mind. Super ensuite rooms, some with King-size beds, all have Colour TV and Tea/Coffee Trays, and most overlook pretty private woodland. Delicious English Breakfast, cooked to perfection, will set you off in happy mood on your explorations. **GLENCREE** is well recommended by major prestigious tourist guides for quality and value for money. Tariff: According to Season of the year and duration of stay – From £18.50 per person, low season, (Two sharing). SAE for brochure. All the information you need is here, so make your reservation with confidence by

Telephoning us on 015394 45822
ACCESS/VISA   Proprietors: Julie & Rip Butler

For the widest choice of cottages in Devon ....

... and the best value you'll find anywhere!

Contact us now for a free copy of our guide to the 500 best value cottages around Devon's unspoilt National Trust Coast. Spring and Autumn breaks in delightful Exmoor farm cottages from only £69 to luxury beachside homes with swimming pools at over £690 p.w. in Summer. All are regularly inspected and guaranteed to offer first class value.

Free leisure guide and £75 worth of discount shopping vouchers with every booking. Cottages for sale details and free hotel accommodation also available.

North Devon Holiday Homes
19 Cross Street, Barnstaple, EX31 1BD
Tel: 01271 76322 (24 hrs) Fax: 01271 46544

SELF-CATERING

SELF-CATERING

There's no better way to experience the charms of North Devon than from the comfort and luxury of a Marsdens holiday cottage.

Our acclaimed full colour brochure includes properties each personally inspected by our staff, as well as graded by the Tourist Board, and most are commended for quality.

Romantic whitewashed cottages nestling in the heart of North Devon's idyllic countryside and Exmoor... secluded beach houses just a stone's throw away from some of Britain's most spectacular and unspoilt coastlines..... whatever your idea of a perfect holiday, we can help make it a reality.

And, as an extra bonus, our prices will come as a pleasant surprise too. Little wonder, then, that so many of our customers come back for more. For more details, call or write today for your free brochure. We look forward to making your holiday unforgettable.

MARSDENS
COTTAGE HOLIDAYS
01271 813777
for a colour brochure
Fax:(01271) 813664 email address:
holidays@marsdens. demon.co.uk
Department 13, 2 The Square, Braunton,
North Devon, EX33 2JB.
http://www. rom. net/marsdens

Denham Farm

North Buckland, Braunton, North Devon
Telephone or Fax: 01271 890297

♟♟♟♟ COMMENDED ♨♨♨ COMMENDED

In the heart of a small unspoilt hamlet, Denham offers you the best of accommodation whether Bed & Breakfast or Self Catering. Where nowhere is far away and everywhere inviting. A children's paradise with play area and games room. A walker's dream with country lanes and farm trail. Tempting home cooking. Delicious desserts, peace and tranquillity. **Denham**, a place you can rely on.

Self Catering with a Difference

Enjoy the freedom of self catering with friendly 5 star service. Beautiful gardens surround watermill and pretty cottages, lovely Exmoor views, near superb beaches. Inclusive indoor pool, fitness room, maid service, linen, flowers, four poster beds, log fires. Plus central heating, dishwashers, home baking, sauna, tennis with tuition, garden visits. Families welcome. Prices from £180-£840 per week. Off peak short break holidays available.

Wheel Farm Country Cottages
Berrydown 9, Combe Martin, Devon EX34 0NT

Tel: 01271 882100

Compton Pool Farm, South Devon

★ *Heated indoor swimming pool* ★ *Toddlers' and Children's play area*
★ *Fishing lakes* ★ *Tennis court* ★ *Games barn* ★ *Sauna*
★ *Family holidays* ★ *Ponies and farm animals* ★ *Lots to do*

Nestling in a sheltered sunny valley, surrounded by red Devon hills, the nine tastefully converted, comfortably furnished stone cottages are grouped around a central courtyard and fish pond. All cottages are attractively decorated and fully equipped. The farm is kept tidy and the gardens colourful. Torquay and the sea are nearby and Dartmoor is close at hand.

JOHN & MARGARET PHIPPS, COMPTON POOL FARM,
COMPTON, DEVON TQ3 1TA.
Tel: 01803 872241 Fax: 01803 874012

SMALLACOMBE FARM

Aller Valley, Dawlish, Devon EX7 0PS
Telephone 01626 862536 ♨♨ Commended

Off the beaten track, yet only two miles from Dawlish and the beach. Enjoy the best of both worlds, 'country and coast'. Children play freely with no fear of busy roads. Meet our 3 friendly dogs. Relax in the peaceful surroundings and homely atmosphere. 2 double rooms, 1 twin room, family unit available, en suite. Fridges in bedrooms. Reductions for children, weekly discounts. Bed and Breakfast from £15-£17. Evening Meal from £8.50. Ring or write for brochure. Open all year.

RADFORDS
DAWLISH

In beautiful unspoilt countryside not too far from the beach

Chosen by the independent 'Peaudouce Guide' to Hotels as the very best
Hotel for Children that they visited.

FOR THE PERFECT FAMILY HOLIDAY

Come and relax at Radfords in one of our chintzy old world lounges, our comfortable bar or our six acres of lovely garden – or come and enjoy an active action-packed holiday swimming in our heated indoor pools, playing badminton outdoors or enjoying a game of table tennis or skittles or one of the many other games in our large indoor games room. Squash, indoor badminton, golf, tennis, fishing and horse riding are all available close by. We have our own solarium for that essential sun tan.

We have family bedrooms or two room family suites available, all with a private bathroom, to accommodate a total of about thirty families. All bedrooms have tea/coffee making facilities.

THE CHILDREN will love their special heated indoor pool, the outdoor playground, the freedom of our large gardens and the assorted ponies there are to talk to. In the evenings they can look forward to a swimming gala, live entertainment, a party and their own cartoon show etc. Large well equipped indoor playroom.

THE ADULTS can look forward to superb food lovingly cooked and served and the various entertainments we arrange for them – from skittle tournaments to live entertainers. We also have a fully equipped launderette and an evening babysitter to help make your holiday as relaxing as possible. We have a playgroup several mornings a week. Mothers can bring babies and small children here with every confidence. Radfords has been featured on TV by Judith Chalmers and holds the Farm Holiday Guide Diploma.

MEMBER WEST COUNTRY TOURIST BOARD.
Please telephone or send for an illustrated brochure to:

Mr and Mrs T. C. Crump, MHCI
RADFORDS, DAWLISH, SOUTH DEVON EX7 0QN
Tel: 01626 863322   Fax: 01626 888515

SELF-CATERING

SMYTHEN FARM
COASTAL COTTAGES

The cottages are set in an area of natural beauty, with unspoilt views over the beautiful Sterridge Valley to the sea and the coast of Wales beyond. Heated swimming pool in a suntrap enclosure. Spacious lawns and gardens. Children's play area with treehouse, swings and slide. Garden furniture and barbecue. 14 acre recreation field. Games room. Laundry room. Pay phone. Central for sandy beaches and touring Exmoor. The village of Berrynarbor is just two miles, with stores, an inn and many quality eating places. The area is well blessed with tourist attractions, from surfing and fishing to golf and pony trekking.

ETB ♦♦♦♦ Commended and Highly Commended

For brochure and terms apply to: J. Elstone, Smythen House, Sterridge Valley, Berrynarbor, Ilfracombe, Devon EX34 9TB. Telephone: Combe Martin (01271) 882875

BOARD

SEAWOOD HOTEL

North Walk, Lynton EX35 6HJ. Telephone 01598 752272.

Seawood Hotel is set in its own grounds overlooking the sea with breathtaking views of Lynmouth Bay and Exmoor. The Peacock family make guests very welcome in their charming old-world house.
Five-course dinners with imaginative home cooking, for which great praise is received. Both lounges, diningroom and all bedrooms enjoy sea views. The latter all have ensuite bathroom and/or shower/WC, colour TV and tea/coffee making facilities. Four-posters are also available. Full central heating. Residential licence. Pets welcome. Colour brochure on request. Open March to November.

RAC * (Special Award for Hospitality, Service & Comfort)   AA*   ♛♛♛ Highly Commended

BOARD / SELF-CATERING

MAELCOMBE HOUSE

A small coastal working farm nestling beneath wooded cliffs overlooking Lannacombe Bay. Beach one minute from comfortable farmhouse which is nearly the most southerly in Devon. Choice of family, double or single rooms. Excellent food, much being produced on farm; freshly caught seafood is a speciality. Activities include fishing, tennis (new hard court), bathing, spectacular walking, exploring, climbing or just relaxing in the gardens. Prices from £119.50 per week for Bed & Breakfast or £169.50 for Bed, Breakfast & Evening Meal, with special reductions for children. Also two self-catering flats to sleep 6; limited camping facilities are provided. Telephone or write for colour brochure.

Mr and Mrs C. M. Davies, Maelcombe House, East Prawle, Near Kingsbridge, Devon TQ7 2DA (Chivelstone (01548) 511300).

SELF-CATERING

Mrs Bealey, Week Farm, Torrington, Devon EX38 7HU
Telephone: (01805 623354)

Excellent accommodation (enjoyed by many) in our farmhouse flat, scenic views and beautiful surroundings. Well equipped kitchen/diner; lounge with colour TV. One room with double bed, one with twin beds; covertable bed and cot if required. Bathroom with WC. Electric cooker and heaters, spindryer; automatic washing machine and tumble dryer available in farm laundry room. Linen for hire. Electricity metered. Advance orders. No pets. No smoking. Children welcome. One mile from Great Torrington with heated swimming pool, tennis, golf, Dartington Glass factory and R.H.S. Rosemoor Gardens, Tarka Trail. Easy reach beaches, Exmoor, Dartmoor.

English Tourist Board
COMMENDED
♦♦♦♦

Terms from £95 to £210 weekly.
SAE please, or telephone.

HEMSFORD
'A Country Holiday for All Seasons'

Hemsford is ideally situated in the heart of South Devon, with Torbay, Dartmoor and the excellent beaches of the South Hams only a short drive away. Our 16 comfortable and well appointed cottages accommodate 2-10 people. All have night store heating and are available throughout the year. Own riding stables, heated indoor pool, sauna, solarium, games room, licensed bar, two all-weather tennis courts, 9-hole approach golf and children's play area. Full colour brochure on request. Regret no pets. ETB ♙♙♙ / ♙♙♙♙ **Commended.**

**Hemsford Country Holidays,
Hemsford, Littlehempston,
Totnes, Devon TQ9 6NE
Telephone: 01803 762637**

West Pusehill Farm Cottages
For the very best in self-catering

A small group of picturesque stone-built country cottages accommodating 2-8. Set in an area of outstanding natural beauty, only one mile from the coast. Prices £108-£590. Swimming pool, sauna, games room plus family-run country inn/restaurant, all set in 20 acres of tranquil gardens and farmland. For full colour brochure write to John & Gill Violet.

**West Pusehill Farm, Westward Ho!, North Devon
Tel: Bideford (01237) 475638**

MANOR FARM HOLIDAY CENTRE
CHARMOUTH, BRIDPORT, DORSET

Situated in rural valley of outstanding natural beauty, Manor Farm has all the requisite amenities for an exciting yet carefree holiday. Shop, launderette, licensed bar with family room, swimming pool and children's pool, play area. Ten minutes' level walk to beach, safe for bathing and famous for its fossils. Golf, riding, tennis, fishing and boating all nearby. Accommodation in 3 bedroomed bungalow, 2 and 3 bedroomed houses, and luxury caravans. All units sleep 4/6, and are equipped with colour TV; parking.

**SAE to Mr. R. B. Loosmore
or Telephone 01297-560226**

MARSHWOOD MANOR

ꕥ ꕥ ꕥ Commended
**Near Bridport, Near Charmouth,
Dorset DT6 5NS
Tel. Broadwinsor (01308) 868442**

Five tastefully furnished ensuite rooms. Close to Chalmont and Lyme Regis. Bed and Breakfast, Evening Meal on request. Speciality home cooking. Weekly or Short Breaks available. Brochure on request. AA Listed. For full details see

Board Section – 'Bridport', Dorset

BOARD

Cheltenham (Cotswolds)

Heart of England Tourist Board ❦❦ Commended

Mrs A. E. Hughes, Ham Hill Farm,
Whittington, Cheltenham, Gloucestershire GL54 4EZ
Telephone 01242 584415; Fax: 01242 222535

This 160 acre farm has farmhouse built in 1983 in true traditional style, with panoramic views. Two miles from the town of Cheltenham. Leisure activities nearby are horse riding, golf and walking the Cotswold Way. The tastefully decorated and comfortable en suite bedrooms all have colour TV, tea/coffee facilities. Two doubles, two twin, one family and one single. Two comfortable lounges, with maps and information about the area.
EXCELLENT FARMHOUSE BREAKFAST; NON-SMOKING; OPEN ALL YEAR ROUND.

Bed & Breakfast from £20 to £23.50 per person.
Colour brochure on request.

BOARD

ORMONDE HOUSE

Southampton Road, Lyndhurst,
Hampshire SO43 7BT

Telephone: 01703 282806
Fax: 01703 282004

Ormonde House, in the heart of the New Forest, offers elegant, luxury accommodation at affordable prices, all rooms ensuite, CTV, phone, beverage facilities. Luxury rooms are spacious with bath and shower, sofas and remote CTV. Comfort extends throughout the lounge and conservatory overlooking the flower filled gardens. Your host, Paul, who has been a leading restauranteur, offers freshly prepared traditional English dinners. Bordering the south coast and famous for its ponies, the New Forest can be reached in under $1^{1}/_{2}$ hours from London. Close to Beaulieu Motor Museum and Exbury Gardens. Special Break details on request. Rover welcome! B&B £20-£35 pppn. Freephone 0500 240140.

NEW FOREST *TOURISM*   AA QQQQ *Selected*

BOARD

Mrs Tessa Plummer, ROSE COTTAGE,
Woonton, Hereford HR3 6QW
Telephone 01544 340459

ROSE COTTAGE

Located 13 miles north west of Hereford, **Rose Cottage** is situated down a quiet, country lane within easy reach of the Black Mountains, Hay-on-Wye, Worcester and The Cotswolds. One twin-bedded room with en suite bathroom and one double room with private bathroom. Cosy beamed sittingroom with colour TV. Log fires in winter. Generous Breakfasts. Reductions for stays of five nights or more. Bed and Breakfast £20-£22.50 per person (£18 per person per night January, February, November and December). No smoking. Brochure available on request.

ETB ❦❦ Highly Commended

Withy Grove Farm

Come and enjoy a relaxing and friendly holiday 'Down on the Farm' set in beautiful Somerset countryside. Peaceful rural setting adjoining River Huntspill, famed for its coarse fishing. The farm is ideally situated for visiting many local attractions including Cheddar Gorge, Glastonbury, Weston-super-Mare and the lovely sandy beach of Burnham-on-Sea. Self-catering barns and cottages are tastefully converted, sleeping 4/6. Fully equipped with colour TV.

★ Heated Swimming Pool
★ Licensed Bar and Entertainment (*in high season*)
★ Games Room   ★ Skittle Alley   ★ Reasonable Rates

For more information please contact: **Mrs Wendy Baker, Withy Grove Farm, East Huntspill, Near Burnham-on-Sea, Somerset TA9 3NP.   Telephone: (01278) 784471.**

Higher Dipford Farm

ETB ♛♛♛ **Commended   AA QQQQ**

This dairy farm is situated two and half miles from Taunton, and the accommodation is in the 600 year old farmhouse. There are many exposed elm beams and inglenook fireplaces. All bedrooms have ensuite showers/bathrooms. Home cooking is our speciality with fresh produce from the farm and garden all helped down by a jug of local cider.

Higher Dipford Farm, Trull, Taunton, Somerset TA3 7NU
Mrs Maureen Fewings. Telephone 01823 275770.

WOOD ADVENT FARM
EXMOOR NATIONAL PARK

You have to experience the peace and tranquillity of our majestic farmhouse set in 350 acres of glorious working farmland. Four ensuite bedrooms with hospitality tray, TV and radio for your convenience. Reception rooms and diningroom heated with log fires and central heating. Savour the delights of delicious dishes prepared here using local produce. Lose yourself in the vast gardens, enjoy the grass tennis court or the heated swimming pool. Many well marked walks.

Recommended by the 'Holiday Which' Guide. AA QQQQ Selected. ETB ♛♛♛ Commended.
John and Diana Brewer, Wood Advent Farm, Roadwater, Somerset TA23 0RR
Telephone/Fax: 01984 640920

When making enquiries please mention FHG Publications.

Please remember a stamped addressed envelope with enquiries.

BOARD

moorlands

· MENDIP · COUNTRY · GUEST HOUSE ·

HUTTON
Nr. WESTON-SUPER-MARE

This attractive Georgian House stands in extensive grounds with peaceful views of nearby wooded hills. The pretty village of Hutton is just four miles from Weston's centre.

Moorlands is personally run by the family; our daughter is a trained pâtisserie chef. Children are most welcome; we offer reduced rates and pony rides. Some rooms have en-suite facilities, one of which is a ground floor room suitable for the less mobile. We are open from early January to early November. Write or phone for a brochure from:

GOOD ROOM AWARD

MARGARET AND DAVID HOLT, MOORLANDS, HUTTON, Nr WESTON-SUPER-MARE BS24 9QH. TEL: (01934) 812283.

* RESIDENTIAL LICENCE   * ETB ♥♥♥ COMMENDED

BOARD

'Langber Country Guest House'

Ingleton, 'Beauty Spot of the North', in the National Parks area. Renowned for waterfalls, glens, underground caves, magnificent scenery and Ingleboro' mountain – 2,373 ft. An excellent centre for touring Dales, Lakes and coast. 'Langber', a detached country house, is set amidst beautiful scenery with $4\frac{1}{2}$ acres of fields and gardens. There are three family, three double or twin and one single bedrooms, some ensuite. Central heating, comfortably furnished throughout. Fire precautions. Babysitting offered. Open all year except Christmas and New Year. AA and RAC Listed. Tourist Board registered. Reductions for children under 13 sharing parents' room. Good food and a warm welcome. SAE please.

Mrs Mollie Bell, Langber Country Guest House, Ingleton, North Yorkshire LA6 3DT. Tel: (015242) 41587 ♥♥

BOARD

Ryedale House *Coach Road, Sleights, near Whitby YO22 5EQ (01947 810534). Mrs Pat Beale.*

Welcoming non-smoking Yorkshire house of charm and character at the foot of the moors, National Park and 'Heartbeat' country, 3½ miles from Whitby. Rich in history, magnificent scenery, picturesque harbours, cliffs,

beaches, scenic railways, superb walking. 3 double/twin beautifully appointed bedrooms with private facilities. Guests' lounge and diningroom (separate tables) with breathtaking views over Eskdale. Enjoy our large sun terrace and gardens, relax, we're ready to pamper you! Long established. Delicious Yorkshire fare – extensive breakfast and snacks menus, picnics (traditional and vegetarian). Recommended local inns and restaurants. Parking, near public transport. Regret no pets. B&B £16.50 - £18 per person, min. 2 nights. Weekly reductions, special breaks Spring and October. Member Yorkshire & Humberside Tourist Board since 1985.

KILLARNEY LAKELAND COTTAGES

Muckross, Killarney,
Co. Kerry, Ireland

Superb complex of traditional and modern cottages situated on **O'SHEA'S** Farm on 12 acres of landscaped parkland on the edge of the Killarney National Park, providing an ideal base for touring in South-West Ireland.

❖ 2, 3 and 4 bedroomed cottages (sleep 4/8)
❖ Colour TV; multi-channel TV
❖ Dishwasher ❖ Direct Dial Telephones
❖ Laundry Service ❖ Full Central Heating
❖ Two tennis courts, games room and children's play equipment on site
❖ Available locally: Nature Walks, Golf, Fishing, Boating, Horse Riding, Hill Walking, Access to Leisure Centre at reduced rates.

IRISH TOURIST BOARD APPROVED
Telephone or Fax for colour brochure:
Tel: 00-353 6431538   Fax: 00-353 6434113
Email: boshea@killarneycottages.iol.ie   http://www.iol.ie/lakeland

West's Holiday Park
Killarney Road, Killorglin, Ring of Kerry, County Kerry
FREEPHONE 0800 374424 (from Britain)
Telephone 00 353 66 61240
*Fully equipped caravan holiday homes for hire
*A perfect touring location in an area of outstanding beauty
*Kiddies indoor pool, tennis, and fishing on Park & golf, sandy beaches, and hillwalking nearby on the Ring of Kerry
*Near Killarney National Park, Dingle Peninsula and Dolphin, Skellig Rock. Babysitters available.
Pubs, traditional music, restaurants, one mile.
Special Ferry package from Britain

Mobile Home including Ferry crossing from only £299 per family.
Freephone 0800 374424 NOW! for details

Please note all advertisers in this colour section also have a full review in the classified section under the relevant county.

BOARD

Tyddyn Du Farm Holidays

Gellilydan, Ffestiniog, Porthmadog, Gwynedd LL41 4RB

Telephone and Fax: 01766 590281

**WALES
TOURIST BOARD**
♛ ♛ ♛
HIGHLY COMMENDED

This enchanting 17th century historic farmhouse is situated amidst spectacular scenery in the **heart of Snowdonia National Park**. It is an excellent central location base for the numerous attractions, beaches and walks of North Wales. Old World farmhouse has a relaxed homely atmosphere, charm and character with a massive stone inglenook fireplace, antique furniture, exposed beams and stonework. Superb private ground floor cottage suite, with solid fuel stove, sleeps up to four (meals served in farmhouse). All bedrooms have colour TV, beverage trays and most are ensuite.

Payphone for guests' use. Delicious candlelight dinners are served using fresh local produce, with home-made soups and buns. Vegetarians welcome. Packed lunches available. Breakfast menu with seven choices, plus porridge! Non-smoking areas in farmhouse. You are welcome to bottle feed pet lambs, collect the eggs, feed the ducks on our mill pond and fuss over Polly the pony. We are easy to find – 300 yards off the A470, near the village of Gellilydan. Open all year. Bed and Breakfast from £17-£21, Dinner £10, Weekly Dinner, Bed and Breakfast from £165-£200.

Stamp for brochure please to Mrs P. F. Williams (2).

SELF-CATERING

BETWS-BACH & RHOS-DHU

Ynys, Criccieth, Gwynedd LL52 0PB
WALES TOURIST BOARD GRADE 5

A truly romantic, memorable and special place to stay and relax in comfort. Old world farmhouse and period country cottage. Situated just off the B4411 road in tranquil surroundings. Equipped to WTB Grade 5 standard with washing/drying machines, dishwashers, microwaves, freezers, colour TV, old oak beams, inglenook with log fires, full central heating. Snooker table, pitch n' putt, romantic four poster bed, sauna and jacuzzi. Open all year – Winter weekends welcomed. Ideal for couples. Sleep two/six plus cot. Own fishing and shooting rights, wonderful walks, peace and quiet with Snowdonia and unspoilt beaches on our doorstep. For friendly personal service please phone, fax or write to Mrs Anwen Jones.

Tel / Fax: 01758 720047; 01766 810295

SELF-CATERING

**Open all year including for Short Breaks.
BROCHURE SENT WITH PLEASURE.**

BRYN BRAS
—CASTLE—

**LLANRUG, Nr. CAERNARFON, NORTH WALES LL55 4RE
Tel & Fax Llanberis (01286) 870210**

This romantic neo-Romanesque Castle is set in the gentle Snowdonian foothills near north Wales' mountains, beaches, resorts and heritage. Built in 1830, on an earlier structure, the Regency castle reflects peace not war ... it stands in 32 acres of tranquil gardens, with views. Bryn Bras offers distinctive and individual apartments, for 2-4 persons within the castle, each having spacious rooms radiating comfort, warmth and tranquillity and providing freedom and independence. All highest grade.

Many inns and restaurants nearby. This welcoming castle, still a family home, particularly appeals to romantic couples.

DE LUXE

Mrs. M. Jones
Lochmeyler Farm

AA selected RAC
RAC Guest House
Highly of the Year
Acclaimed 1993

AWARD

WEEKLY RATES
B&B from £140
Dinner, B&B £210

DAILY RATES
B&B from £20
Optional Dinner £12.50

A warm Welsh welcome awaits you at Lochmeyler, a dairy farm at the centre of the St David's peninsula. Luxury facilities including some four poster beds for those romantic breaks. Vegetarian and traditional Pembrokeshire farmhouse fare served using home cooked local produce. Children welcome. Smoking and non-smoking lounges – sorry no smoking in bedrooms. National Park Activity Packs provided in each bedroom – to help you to explore our beautiful coastline and countryside. Credit cards accepted. For full information pack and brochure please let us have your address. Open Christmas and New Year.

Llandeloy, Pen-y-Cwm, Nr. Solva, Haverfordwest, Dyfed SA62 6LL
Tel: 01348 837724   Fax: 01348 837622

SELF-CATERING

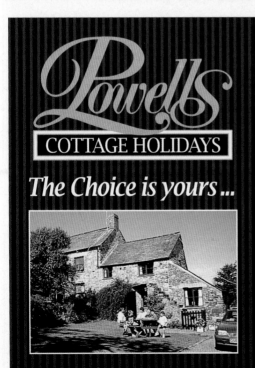

Powells

COTTAGE HOLIDAYS

The Choice is yours ...

... discover the freedom of Cottage Holidays.

- Superb collection of top quality holiday accommodation
- West Country, West Wales, Cotswolds and the Heart of England.
- Excellent value Mini Breaks in all areas.
- **Pets welcome at many of our properties**

Powells Cottage Holidays,
51 High Street, Saundersfoot,
Pembrokeshire
SA69 9EJ.

FREE
100 PAGE COLOUR BROCHURE
FREEPHONE
0800 378771

SELF-CATERING

· MYDROILYN ·

Stone farm buildings, recently converted into 4 cottages, providing modern standard of comfort in traditional setting. Sleep 2/3 (terms £90-£180) or 4/8 (terms £145-£300). Gas, electricity, linen included. All have shower room; fully equipped kitchen; colour TV; shared laundry room; facilities for children. Secluded rural area, abundant with wildlife and flowers; 5 miles from sandy beaches, picturesque harbours of Cardigan Bay, National Trust coastal paths; breathtaking mountain scenery; birdwatching, fishing, pony trekking, steam railway nearby.

WTB and AA Approved.   Open Easter to October.
Gil & Mike Kearney, Blaenllanarth Holiday Cottages, Mydroilyn, Lampeter, Ceredigion SA48 7RJ. Telephone: Lampeter (01570) 470374.

BOARD / SELF-CATERING

FRIENDLY FARMHOUSE HOSPITALITY

A warm welcome awaits you in our
Cottages – Self catering or Bed & Breakfast

Upper Genfford Guest House, Talgarth, Brecon LD3 0EN
Tel: Talgarth (01874) 711360

Mrs Prosser has been nominated one of the top 20 proprietors selected from the AA Bed & Breakfast Guide, reaching the finals of the AA Landlady of the Year competition in 1996. She is also one of the two FHG Publications Diploma Winners chosen from Wales for 1996.

The cottages are situated amongst the most spectacular scenery of the Brecon Beacons National Park. An excellent location for walking and exploring the Brecon Beacons, Black Mountains and Wye Valley. An area of outstanding natural beauty rich in historical and archaeological interest. The cottages are beautifully furnished with fitted carpets, oil-fired Rayburns, oak-beamed lounges, antique furniture, open log fires, Calor gas heaters and colour TVs; fridge freezers and tumble dryers.
In Bed and Breakfast cottage, bedrooms are ensuite with colour TV and beverage trays. Tea and home-made cakes are served on arrival at both cottages. Pets welcome and linen provided.
A warm, friendly welcome awaits you. Children enjoy our friendly pony 'Topsy'.
Terms: B&B from £16 p.p. per night; self-catering £160 per week.
Weekend Breaks available. Highly Commended.

AA Recommended QQQ   WTB Award   FHG Diploma
Please write or phone to Mrs Bronwen Prosser for further details.
Also caravan to let.

SELF-CATERING

RED HOUSE
Trefeglwys, Caersws,
Montgomeryshire SY17 5PN
Tel: 01686 430285

A highly furnished, self-contained part of the farmhouse, situated on a mixed working family farm. With panoramic views, unspoilt scenery and the tranquillity of the Trannon Valley it makes an ideal, convenient base for touring mid-Wales attractions and recreational pursuits – Llanidloes 6 miles and Clywedog reservoir, Powys Castle and the coast all close at hand. A fully equipped kitchen plus washing machine, refurbished bathroom and tea served on arrival all ensure guests' comfort is the main priority and extras include log fire, oak beams, garden furniture, ample parking and wildlife, so come to Red House and enjoy a refreshing change. Bed linen included. Open all year. SAE for brochure. Terms from £100–£250 per week. OS Map ref SN992 899.

GRADE
1 2 3 4 5

Farm Holiday Guide

ENGLAND, WALES & IRELAND
AND THE CHANNEL ISLANDS

1997

The Farm Holiday Guide to
HOLIDAYS
IN
ENGLAND, WALES & IRELAND
AND THE CHANNEL ISLANDS

Farms, guest houses and country hotels
Cottages, flats and chalets
Caravans and camping
Activity Holidays
Country Inns

FHG

Other FHG Publications

Recommended Short Break Holidays
Recommended Country Hotels of Britain
Recommended Wayside & Country Inns of Britain
Pets Welcome!
Bed and Breakfast in Britain
The Golf Guide: Where to Play/Where to Stay
Farm Holiday Guide Scotland
Self-Catering Holidays in Britain
Britain's Best Holidays
Guide to Caravan and Camping Holidays
Bed and Breakfast Stops
Children Welcome! Family Holiday & Attractions Guide
Scottish Welcome

ISBN 1 85055 212 6 © FHG Publications Ltd. 1997
Cover photograph: supplied by Mirror Syndication International.
Design by Cyan Creative Consultants, Glasgow

Please note: owing to recent boundary changes
the following counties no longer exist:
England
Avon — see under Gloucestershire and Somerset
Cleveland — see under Durham
Humberside — see under Yorkshire (East) and Lincolnshire
In **Wales** the changes have been more extensive
and we have arranged that section as follows:
North Wales — formerly Clwyd and Gwynedd
Dyfed
Powys
South Wales — formerly Glamorgan and Gwent

Typeset by RD Composition Ltd., Glasgow.
Printed and bound by Benham's Ltd., Colchester.

Distribution – **Book Trade**: WLM, Downing Road, West Meadows Ind. Est., Derby DE21 6HA
(Tel: 01332 343332. Fax: 01332 340464).
News Trade: USM Distribution Ltd, 86 Newman Street, London W1P 3LD
(Tel: 0171-396 8000. Fax: 0171-396 8002).
E-mail:usm.co.uk

Published by FHG Publications Ltd.,
Abbey Mill Business Centre, Seedhill, Paisley PA1 1TJ (0141-887 0428. Fax: 0141-889 7204).

US ISBN 1-55650-763-1
Distributed in the United States by
Hunter Publishing Inc., 300 Raritan Center Parkway CN94,
Edison, N.J., 08818, USA

FOREWORD

The Farm Holiday Guide to
Holidays in
ENGLAND, WALES
IRELAND & THE CHANNEL ISLANDS 1997

Welcome to the fiftieth edition of *Farm Holiday Guide*!

The first *Farm Holiday Guide* was planned and published in the same year as the opening of Heathrow Airport and the inaugural meeting of the United Nations Assembly. In the same year, 1946, the 'bikini' swimsuit made its appearance and women in Italy got the vote. Holidays abroad were almost unknown and even holidays in Britain were restricted affairs because of rationing and difficult travelling conditions. These fifty years have seen enormous changes – and the next fifty will no doubt see even more. Given the loyalty of many of our readers and many of the holiday entries, however, it's quite likely that the *Farm Holiday Guide* will still be around then, in some form or another!

We are pleased to offer for the 1997 holiday season, an interesting range of holiday opportunities of all sorts throughout Scotland, including a separate section exclusive to the Association of Scotland's Self-Caterers. Full board, bed and breakfast, self-catering; hotels, farms, guest houses, caravan parks and camping sites, not forgetting inns and activity entries . . . in the country, by the sea . . . for short breaks or annual holidays . . . the variety of choice and the quality of hospitality available in the following pages are as much the hallmark of this latest *Farm Holiday Guide* as of its predecessors for the past fifty years! And as usual we hope that readers will find the few following words of advice helpful.

ENQUIRIES AND BOOKINGS. Give full details of dates (with an alternative), numbers and any special requirements. Ask about any points in the holiday description which are not clear and make sure that prices and conditions are clearly explained. You should receive confirmation in writing and a receipt for any deposit or advance payment. If you book your holiday well in advance, especially self-catering, confirm your arrival details nearer the time. Some proprietors, especially for self-catering, request full payment in advance but a reasonable deposit is more normal.

CANCELLATIONS. A holiday booking is a form of contract with obligations on both sides. If you have to cancel, give as much notice as possible. The longer the notice the better the chance that your host can replace your booking and therefore refund any payments. If the proprietor cancels in such a way that causes serious inconvenience, he may have obligations to you which have not been properly honoured. Take advice if necessary from such organisations as the Citizen's Advice Bureau, Consumer's Association, Trading Standards Office, Local Tourist Office, etc., or your own solicitor.

COMPLAINTS. It's best if any problems can be sorted out at the start of your holiday. If the problem is not solved, you can contact the organisations mentioned above. You can also write to us. We will follow up the complaint with the advertiser – but we cannot act as intermediaries or accept responsibility for holiday arrangements.

FHG Publications Ltd. do not inspect accommodation and an entry in our guides does not imply a recommendation. However our advertisers have signed their agreement to work for the holidaymaker's best interests and as their customer, you have the right to expect appropriate attention and service.

HOLIDAY INSURANCE. It is possible to insure against holiday cancellation. Brokers and insurance companies can advise you about this.

Don't forget our **Farm Holiday Guide Diploma**. Every year we award a small number of Diplomas to holiday proprietors who have been specially recommended to us by readers. The names of our 1996 Diploma winners are listed in several places throughout this book and we will be happy to receive your recommendations for 1997.

You will also see our Voucher/Coupons for free or reduced rate entry to a range of popular holiday attractions if you turn a few pages forward. We hope that these will add to your holiday enjoyment.

We would be grateful if you would mention the name of *Farm Holiday Guide* when you make enquiries and bookings. May this Golden Anniversary edition bring you holidays to remember and hopefully the pleasure of new places to explore and new company to enjoy.

Peter Clark
Publishing Director

CONTENTS

READERS' OFFER VOUCHERS 36–50

ENGLAND

BOARD

LONDON.............................51
BEDFORDSHIRE 53
BERKSHIRE 54
BUCKINGHAMSHIRE 54
CAMBRIDGESHIRE 55
CHESHIRE...........................56
CORNWALL...........................59
CUMBRIA 78
DERBYSHIRE.........................98
DEVON 104
DORSET 127
DURHAM 135
ESSEX 136
GLOUCESTERSHIRE 137
HAMPSHIRE 146
HEREFORD & WORCESTER 150
HERTFORDSHIRE..................... 156
KENT............................. 157
LANCASHIRE 162
LEICESTERSHIRE................... 164
LINCOLNSHIRE..................... 166
NORFOLK 167
NORTHAMPTONSHIRE................. 173
NORTHUMBERLAND 174
NOTTINGHAMSHIRE 178
OXFORDSHIRE 180
SHROPSHIRE 182
SOMERSET 188
STAFFORDSHIRE.................... 200
SUFFOLK.......................... 202
SURREY 206
SUSSEX (EAST) 207
SUSSEX (WEST) 211
WARWICKSHIRE..................... 214
WILTSHIRE........................ 221
YORKSHIRE 224
ISLE OF WIGHT 242

ENGLAND

SELF-CATERING

BEDFORDSHIRE 247
BERKSHIRE 247
BUCKINGHAMSHIRE 248
CAMBRIDGESHIRE 248
CORNWALL......................... 249
CUMBRIA 265
DERBYSHIRE....................... 278
DEVON 283
DORSET 299
DURHAM 306
GLOUCESTERSHIRE 307
HAMPSHIRE 309
HEREFORD & WORCESTER 310
KENT............................. 315
LANCASHIRE 315
LINCOLNSHIRE..................... 315
NORFOLK 316
NORTHAMPTONSHIRE................. 320
NORTHUMBERLAND 321
OXFORDSHIRE 324
SHROPSHIRE 325
SOMERSET 326
STAFFORDSHIRE.................... 335
SUFFOLK 336
SUSSEX (EAST) 337
SUSSEX (WEST) 339
WARWICKSHIRE 340
WILTSHIRE........................ 341
YORKSHIRE 342
ISLE OF WIGHT 350
CHANNEL ISLANDS 351

COUNTRY INNS......................... 243
CARAVAN AND CAMPING........ 353
ACTIVITY HOLIDAYS................. 365

FHG

CONTENTS

WALES

BOARD
NORTH WALES.............................367
DYFED 376
POWYS 381
SOUTH WALES 385

SELF-CATERING
NORTH WALES............................388
DYFED 397
POWYS 403
SOUTH WALES 405

CARAVAN AND CAMPING........406
ACTIVITY HOLIDAYS................409

NORTHERN IRELAND

BOARD
ANTRIM.......................................410
C. DOWN 411
FERMANAGH 411
LONDONDERRY 413

SELF-CATERING
C. DOWN 414
FERMANAGH 414

REPUBLIC OF IRELAND

BOARD
CARLOW 415
CLARE 415
CORK..416
KERRY..416
TIPPERARAY................................417
WATERFORD 417

SELF-CATERING
CORK..418
KERRY..419
LEITRIM.......................................420

CARAVAN AND CAMPING........421

WALES

IRELAND

England and Wales

Counties, unitary authorities and council areas

1. HARTLEPOOL
2. STOCKTON-ON-TEES
3. MIDDLESBROUGH
4. REDCAR & CLEVELAND
5. ABERCONWY & COLWYN
6. DENBIGHSHIRE
7. FLINTSHIRE
8. WREXHAM
9. NORTH LINCOLNSHIRE
10. KINGSTON UPON HULL
11. NORTH EAST LINCOLNSHIRE
12. SWANSEA
13. NEATH & PORT TALBOT
14. RHONDDA CYNON TAFF
15. MERTHYR TYDFIL
16. CAERPHILLY
17. BLAENAU GWENT
18. TORFAEN
19. MONMOUTHSHIRE
20. BRIDGEND
21. VALE OF GLAMORGAN
22. CARDIFF
23. NEWPORT
24. NORTH WEST SOMERSET
25. BRISTOL
26. SOUTH GLOUCESTERSHIRE
27. BATH & NORTH EAST SOMERSET

NORTHUMBERLAND

TYNE & WEAR

DURHAM

CUMBRIA

ISLE OF MAN

NORTH YORKSHIRE

YORK

EAST RIDING OF YORKSHIRE

LANCASHIRE

WEST YORKSHIRE

GREATER MANCHESTER

SOUTH YORKSHIRE

MERSEYSIDE

CHESHIRE

DERBYSHIRE

NOTTS.

LINCOLNSHIRE

ANGLESEY

GWYNEDD

STAFFS.

LEICESTERSHIRE

NORFOLK

SHROPSHIRE

WEST MIDLANDS

CARDIGANSHIRE

POWYS

HEREFORD AND WORCESTER

WARKS.

NORTHANTS.

CAMBRIDGE-SHIRE

SUFFOLK

PEMBROKESHIRE

CARMARTHEN-SHIRE

BEDS.

BUCKS.

GLOUCESTER-SHIRE

OXFORD-SHIRE

HERTS.

ESSEX

GREATER LONDON

BERKSHIRE

WILTSHIRE

KENT

SURREY

SOMERSET

HAMPSHIRE

WEST SUSSEX

EAST SUSSEX

DEVON

DORSET

ISLE OF WIGHT

CORNWALL

CHANNEL ISLANDS

SCILLY ISLES

© GEOprojects (UK) Ltd
© Crown Copyright

England and Wales

Towns and Main Roads

Scale 1:4 300 000

© GEOprojects (UK) Ltd
© Crown Copyright

THE FHG DIPLOMA

HELP IMPROVE
BRITISH TOURIST STANDARDS

You are choosing holiday accommodation from our very popular FHG Publications. Whether it be a hotel, guest house, farmhouse or self-catering accommodation, we think you will find it hospitable, comfortable and clean, and your host and hostess friendly and helpful.

Why not write and tell us about it?

As a recognition of the generally well-run and excellent holiday accommodation reviewed in our publications, we at FHG Publications Ltd. present a diploma to proprietors who receive the highest recommendation from their guests who are also readers of our Guides. If you care to write to us praising the holiday you have booked through FHG Publications Ltd. – whether this be board, self-catering accommodation, a sporting or a caravan holiday, what you say will be evaluated and the proprietors who reach our final list will be contacted.

The winning proprietor will receive an attractive framed diploma to display on his premises as recognition of a high standard of comfort, amenity and hospitality. FHG Publications Ltd. offer this diploma as a contribution towards the improvement of standards in tourist accommodation in Britain. Help your excellent host or hostess to win it!

FHG DIPLOMA

We nominate ....

....

Because

Name ....

Address ....

.... Telephone No. ....

FOR THE
MUTUAL GUIDANCE OF
GUEST AND HOST

Every year literally thousands of holidays, short-breaks and overnight stops are arranged through our guides, the vast majority without any problems at all. In a handful of cases, however, difficulties do arise about bookings, which often could have been prevented from the outset.

It is important to remember that when accommodation has been booked, both parties — guests and hosts — have entered into a form of contract. We hope that the following points will provide helpful guidance.

GUESTS: When enquiring.about accommodation, be as precise as possible. Give exact dates, numbers in your party and the ages of any children. State the number and type of rooms wanted and also what catering you require — bed and breakfast, full board, etc. Make sure that the position about evening meals is clear — and about pets, reductions for children or any other special points.

Read our reviews carefully to ensure that the proprietors you are going to contact can supply what you want. Ask for a letter confirming all arrangements, if possible.

If you have to cancel, do so as soon as possible. Proprietors do have the right to retain deposits and under certain circumstances to charge for cancelled holidays if adequate notice is not given and they cannot re-let the accommodation.

HOSTS: Give details about your facilities and about any special conditions. Explain your deposit system clearly and arrangements for cancellations, charges, etc, and whether or not your terms include VAT.

If for any reason you are unable to fulfill an agreed booking without adequate notice, you may be under an obligation to arrange alternative suitable accommodation or to make some form of compensation.

While every effort is made to ensure accuracy, we regret that FHG Publications cannot accept responsibility for errors, omissions or misrepresentation in our entries or any consequences thereof. Prices in particular should be checked because we go to press early. We will follow up complaints but cannot act as arbiters or agents for either party.

Farm Holiday Guide
ENGLAND, WALES & IRELAND
1997

READERS OFFER VOUCHERS

On the following pages you will find vouchers which offer free and/or reduced rate entry to a selection of Visitor Attractions in Scotland.

Readers should simply cut out the coupons and present them if they are visiting any of the attractions concerned.

Please let us know if you have any difficulty.

FHG READERS' OFFER 1997 VALID during 1997

Sacrewell Farm and Country Centre

Thornhaugh, Peterborough, Cambridgeshire PE8 6HJ Tel: (01780) 782254

GROUP RATE ADMISSION for all members of party

NOT TO BE USED IN CONJUNCTION WITH ANY OTHER OFFER

FHG READERS' OFFER 1997 VALID during 1997

DAIRYLAND FARM WORLD

Summercourt, Near Newquay, Cornwall TR8 5AA Tel: 01872 510246

One child FREE when accompanied by adult paying full admission price

NOT TO BE USED IN CONJUNCTION WITH ANY OTHER OFFER

FHG READERS' OFFER 1997 VALID Easter to October 1997

Tamar Valley Donkey Park

St Anns Chapel, Gunnislake, Cornwall PL18 9HW Tel: 01822 834072

10% OFF admission price for up to 6 people, free donkey ride for children included

NOT TO BE USED IN CONJUNCTION WITH ANY OTHER OFFER

FHG READERS' OFFER 1997 VALID during 1997

COARSE FISHING AT CROSSFIELD

Crossfield, Staffield, Kirkoswald, Cumbria CA10 1EU Tel: 01768 898711

ADMIT two children for the price of one; three adults for the price of two

NOT TO BE USED IN CONJUNCTION WITH ANY OTHER OFFER

FHG READERS' OFFER 1997 VALID during 1997

THE CUMBERLAND TOY AND MODEL MUSEUM

Banks Court, Market Place, Cockermouth, Cumbria CA13 9NG Tel: 01900 827606

One person FREE per full paying adult

NOT TO BE USED IN CONJUNCTION WITH ANY OTHER OFFER

The fascinating story of farming and country life with working watermill, gardens, collections of bygones, farm and nature trails. Excellent for young children. Campers and Caravanners welcome.

DIRECTIONS: Junction A1/A47, 8 miles west of Peterborough.

OPEN: daily all year.

FHG PUBLICATIONS, ABBEY MILL BUSINESS CENTRE, PAISLEY PA1 1TJ

Britain's premier farm attraction - milking parlour, Heritage Centre, Farmpark and playground. Daily events include bottle feeding, "Pat-a-Pet" and rally karts.

DIRECTIONS: 4 miles from Newquay on the A3058 Newquay to St Austell road.

OPEN: from early April to end October 10.30am to 5pm. Also open from early December to Christmas Eve 12-5pm daily.

FHG PUBLICATIONS, ABBEY MILL BUSINESS CENTRE, PAISLEY PA1 1TJ

Donkey and donkey cart rides for children. Feed and cuddle tame lambs, goats, rabbits and donkeys. Playgrounds, cafe, gifts.

DIRECTIONS: just off A390 Tavistock to Callington road at village of St Anns Chapel

OPEN: Easter to end October 10am to 5pm

FHG PUBLICATIONS, ABBEY MILL BUSINESS CENTRE, PAISLEY PA1 1TJ

Relax, escape and enjoy a great day out - Carp, Rudd, Tench, Bream, Crucians, Ide, Roach and (for fly) Rainbow and Brown Trout

DIRECTIONS: from Kirkoswald follow signs for Staffield, turn right (signposted Dale/Blunderfield); Crossfield is 200m up narrow road via cattle grid.

OPEN: flexible — please telephone to book your fishing

FHG PUBLICATIONS, ABBEY MILL BUSINESS CENTRE, PAISLEY PA1 1TJ

Winner of the 1995 National Heritage Shoestring Award. 100 years of mainly British toys including working tinplate Hornby trains, Scalextric cars, Lego etc. Free quiz.

DIRECTIONS: just off the market place in Cockermouth

OPEN: daily 10am to 5pm from 1st February to 30th November

FHG PUBLICATIONS, ABBEY MILL BUSINESS CENTRE, PAISLEY PA1 1TJ

Water-driven working corn mill; displays of milling and papermaking through the centuries. Occasional demonstrations of hand-making of paper.

DIRECTIONS: one mile south of Milnthorpe off A6, follow brown tourist signs. Exit 35 off M6, north on A6 to Beetham, follow tourist signs

OPEN: 1st April to end Sep: Tuesdays to Sundays plus Bank Holiday Mondays

FHG PUBLICATIONS, ABBEY MILL BUSINESS CENTRE, PAISLEY PA1 1TJ

Attractions, rides, adventure play areas, circus and wildlife, all set in undulating parkland amidst beautiful scenery, make Lowther the Lake District's premier all-day attraction.

DIRECTIONS: travelling North leave M6 at J39, follow brown signs; travelling South leave at J40, follow brown signs. A6 Shap Road, 6 miles south Penrith.

OPEN: March/April to September 10am to 5/6pm.

FHG PUBLICATIONS, ABBEY MILL BUSINESS CENTRE, PAISLEY PA1 1TJ

Cable car return journey plus two famous show caverns. Tree Top Visitor Centre with restaurant, coffee and gift shops; nature trails and children's play areas.

DIRECTIONS: signposted from all nearby major trunk roads.On A6 at Matlock Bath.

OPEN: daily Easter to end October 10am to 5pm (later in High Season).

FHG PUBLICATIONS, ABBEY MILL BUSINESS CENTRE, PAISLEY PA1 1TJ

"England for Excellence" award-winning rural attraction combining traditional rural crafts with hilarious novelties such as sheep racing and duck trialling.

DIRECTIONS: on A39 North Devon link road, 2 miles west of Bideford Bridge

OPEN: daily all year, 10am to 6pm

FHG PUBLICATIONS, ABBEY MILL BUSINESS CENTRE, PAISLEY PA1 1TJ

Award-winning centre sited on Plymouth's famous Hoe telling the story of the city, from the epic voyages of Drake, Cook and the Mayflower Pilgrims to the devastation of the Blitz. A must for all the family

DIRECTIONS: follow signs from Plymouth City Centre to the Hoe and seafront

OPEN: daily all year (Smeaton's Tower closed October to Easter)

FHG PUBLICATIONS, ABBEY MILL BUSINESS CENTRE, PAISLEY PA1 1TJ

FHG | **READERS' OFFER 1997** | VALID Easter to end Oct. 1997

Dorset Heavy Horse Centre

Edmondsham, Verwood, Dorset BH21 5RJ Telephone: 01202 824040

Admit one adult **FREE** when accompanied by one full-paying adult

NOT TO BE USED IN CONJUNCTION WITH ANY OTHER OFFER

FHG | **READERS' OFFER 1997** | VALID April to October 1997

Killhope Lead Mining Centre

Cowshill, Upper Weardale, Co. Durham DL13 1AR Tel: 01388 537505

Admit one child **FREE** with full-paying adult (not valid for Park Level Mine)

NOT TO BE USED IN CONJUNCTION WITH ANY OTHER OFFER

FHG | **READERS' OFFER 1997** | VALID during 1997

Cotswold Farm Park

Guiting Power, Near Stow-on-the-Wold, Gloucestershire GL54 5UG Tel: 01451 850307

Admit one child **FREE** with an adult paying full entrance fee

NOT TO BE USED IN CONJUNCTION WITH ANY OTHER OFFER

FHG | **READERS' OFFER 1997** | VALID during 1997

NATIONAL WATERWAYS MUSEUM

Llanthony Warehouse, Gloucester Docks, Gloucester GL1 2EH Tel: 01452 318054

20% off all tickets (Single or Family)

NOT TO BE USED IN CONJUNCTION WITH ANY OTHER OFFER

FHG | **READERS' OFFER 1997** | VALID during 1997

BEAULIEU

Near Brockenhurst, Hampshire SO42 7ZN Tel: 01590 612345

£4.00 off adult ticket when accompanied by adult paying full admission.
(Not valid on Bank Holidays or for special events; not valid in conjunction with Family Ticket)

NOT TO BE USED IN CONJUNCTION WITH ANY OTHER OFFER

Heavy horse and pony centre, also Icelandic riding stables. Cafe, gift shop.
Facilities for disabled visitors.

DIRECTIONS: signposted from the centre of Verwood, which is on the B3081

OPEN: Easter to end October 10am to 5pm

FHG PUBLICATIONS, ABBEY MILL BUSINESS CENTRE, PAISLEY PA1 1TJ

Britain's best preserved lead mining site — and a great day out for all the family,
with lots to see and do. Underground Experience — Park Level Mine now open.

DIRECTIONS: alongside A689, midway between Stanhope and Alston
in the heart of the North Pennines.

OPEN: April 1st to October 31st 10.30am to 5pm daily

FHG PUBLICATIONS, ABBEY MILL BUSINESS CENTRE, PAISLEY PA1 1TJ

The home of rare breeds conservation, with over 50 breeding flocks and herds of rare
farm animals. Adventure playground, pets' corners, picnic area, farm nature trail,
Touch barn, Woodland Walk and viewing tower
DIRECTIONS: M5 Junction 9, off B4077 Stow-on-the-Wold road.
5 miles from Bourton-on-the-Water.
OPEN: daily 10.30am to 5pm April to September (to 6pm Sundays, Bank Holidays
and daily in July and August).

FHG PUBLICATIONS, ABBEY MILL BUSINESS CENTRE, PAISLEY PA1 1TJ

---

3 floors of a Listed 7-storey Victorian warehouse telling 200 years of inland waterway
history by means of video film, working exhibits with 2 quaysides of floating exhibits.
Special school holiday activities.
DIRECTIONS: Junction 11 or 12 off M5 — follow brown signs for Historic Docks.
Railway and bus station 10 minute walk. Free coach parking.
OPEN: Summer 10am to 6pm; Winter 10am to 5pm. Closed Christmas Day.

FHG PUBLICATIONS, ABBEY MILL BUSINESS CENTRE, PAISLEY PA1 1TJ

Beaulieu offers a fascinating day out for all the family. In the National Motor Museum there
are over 250 vehicles from the earliest days of motoring; within the Palace House many
Montagu family treasures can be viewed. Plus a host of rides and drives to enjoy.

DIRECTIONS: off Junction 2 of M27, then follow brown tourist signs.

OPEN: daily 10am to 5pm (Easter to September to 6pm). Closed Christmas Day

FHG PUBLICATIONS, ABBEY MILL BUSINESS CENTRE, PAISLEY PA1 1TJ

READERS' OFFER 1997   VALID during 1997

Isle of Wight Rare Breeds and Waterfowl Park

St Lawrence, Ventnor, Isle of Wight PO38 1UW Tel: 01983 852582

Admit one child **FREE** with full-paying adult

NOT TO BE USED IN CONJUNCTION WITH ANY OTHER OFFER

 READERS' OFFER 1997   VALID from Easter to end 1997

White Cliffs Experience

Market Square, Dover, Kent CT16 1PB Tel: 01304 210101

One adult/child **FREE** with one full paying adult

NOT TO BE USED IN CONJUNCTION WITH ANY OTHER OFFER

 READERS' OFFER 1997   VALID during 1997

SNIBSTON DISCOVERY PARK

Ashby Road, Coalville, Leicestershire LE67 3LN Telephone: 01530 510851

Admit one child **FREE** with full-paying adult

NOT TO BE USED IN CONJUNCTION WITH ANY OTHER OFFER

 READERS' OFFER 1997   VALID during 1997

The Incredibly Fantastic Old Toy Show

26 Westgate, Lincoln, Lincs LN1 3ED Tel: 01522 520534

One child **FREE** (age 5-16 incl) with accompanying adult

NOT TO BE USED IN CONJUNCTION WITH ANY OTHER OFFER

 READERS' OFFER 1997   VALID during 1997 except Bank Holidays

Southport Zoo and Conservation Trust

Princes Park, Southport, Merseyside PR8 1RX Telephone: 01704 538102

Admit one child **FREE** with two full paying adults

NOT TO BE USED IN CONJUNCTION WITH ANY OTHER OFFER

One of the UK's largest collections of rare farm animals, plus deer, llamas, miniature horses, waterfowl and poultry in 30 beautiful coastal acres.

DIRECTIONS: on main south coast road A3055 between Ventnor and Niton.

OPEN: Easter to end October open daily 10am to 5.30pm;
Winter open weekends only 10am to 4pm

FHG PUBLICATIONS, ABBEY MILL BUSINESS CENTRE, PAISLEY PA1 1TJ

Over 2000 years of Britain's history is vividly re-created
at this award-winning attraction

DIRECTIONS: signposted on entry into Dover from M20/A20 and M2/A2

OPEN: Easter to end October 10am to 5pm;
November to end December 10am to3pm. Closed Christmas and Boxing Day.

FHG PUBLICATIONS, ABBEY MILL BUSINESS CENTRE, PAISLEY PA1 1TJ

Award-winning science and industry museum. Fascinating colliery tours and "hands-on" displays including holograms, tornado and virtual reality.

DIRECTIONS: 10 minutes from Junction 22 M1 and Junction 13 M42/A42.
Well signposted along the A50.

OPEN: April to Oct.10am to 6pm; Nov. to March 10am to 5pm. Closed 25/26 Dec.

FHG PUBLICATIONS, ABBEY MILL BUSINESS CENTRE, PAISLEY PA1 1TJ

A marvellous collection of toys dating from the 1780s. Nostalgia and fun for all ages, with push-buttons, old pier-end machines, silly mirrors, videos of moving toys, music and lights

DIRECTIONS: approach Lincoln via A46, A15, A57 or A158. Opposite large car park at foot of castle walls

OPEN: Easter to end Sep: daily except Mon (unless Bank Hol); Oct to Christmas weekends and school holidays only. Groups by arrangement.

FHG PUBLICATIONS, ABBEY MILL BUSINESS CENTRE, PAISLEY PA1 1TJ

Lions, snow leopards, chimpanzees, penguins, reptiles, aquarium and lots more, set amidst landscaped gardens.

DIRECTIONS: on the coast 16 miles north of Liverpool; follow the brown tourist signs.

OPEN: daily except Christmas Day. Summer 10am to 6pm; Winter 10am to 4pm.

FHG PUBLICATIONS, ABBEY MILL BUSINESS CENTRE, PAISLEY PA1 1TJ

Beautiful walled garden with nearly 900 types of herbs, woodland walk, nursery, shop. Guide dogs only.

DIRECTIONS: 6 miles north of Hexham, next to Chesters Roman Fort.

OPEN: daily March to October/November.

FHG PUBLICATIONS, ABBEY MILL BUSINESS CENTRE, PAISLEY PA1 1TJ

A modern working farm with over 3000 animals including ducklings, deer, bees, rheas, piglets, snails, lambs (all year). New pet centre.

DIRECTIONS: off the A614 at Farnsfield, 12 miles north of Nottingham. From M1 Junction 27 follow "Robin Hood" signs for 10 miles.

OPEN: daily all year round.

FHG PUBLICATIONS, ABBEY MILL BUSINESS CENTRE, PAISLEY PA1 1TJ

Leading naval aviation museum with over 40 aircraft on display — Concorde 002 and "Carrier". Based on an operational naval air station.

DIRECTIONS: just off A303/A37 on B3151 at Ilchester. Yeovil rail station 10 miles.

OPEN: April to October 10am to 5.30pm; November to March 10am to 4.30pm

FHG PUBLICATIONS, ABBEY MILL BUSINESS CENTRE, PAISLEY PA1 1TJ

---

* Britain's most spectacular caves * Traditional paper-making * Fairground Memories * * Penny Arcade * Magical Mirror Maze *

DIRECTIONS: from M5 Junction 22 follow brown-and-white signs via A38 and A371. Wookey Hole is just 2 miles from Wells.

OPEN: Summer 9.30am to 5.30pm; Winter 10.30am to 4.30pm. Closed 17-25 Dec.

FHG PUBLICATIONS, ABBEY MILL BUSINESS CENTRE, PAISLEY PA1 1TJ

Planet Earth and Dinosaur Museum, Botanic Garden, model village, playland park, garden centre and coffee shop

DIRECTIONS: signposted "Garden Paradise" off A26 and A259

OPEN: all year, except Christmas Day and Boxing Day.

FHG PUBLICATIONS, ABBEY MILL BUSINESS CENTRE, PAISLEY PA1 1TJ

 READERS' OFFER 1997 VALID during 1997

Wilderness Wood

Hadlow Down, Near Uckfield, East Sussex TN22 4HJ Tel: 01825 830509

One **FREE** entry with full-paying adult (only one voucher per group)

Not valid Bank Holidays or special events

NOT TO BE USED IN CONJUNCTION WITH ANY OTHER OFFER

 READERS' OFFER 1997 VALID during 1997

Cadeby Steam and Brass Rubbing Centre

Nuneaton, Warwickshire CV13 0AS Telephone: 01455 290462

Train ride for **TWO**, and **TWO** cream teas or similar

NOT TO BE USED IN CONJUNCTION WITH ANY OTHER OFFER

READERS' OFFER 1997 VALID during 1997

HATTON COUNTRY WORLD

Dark Lane, Hatton, Near Warwick, Warwickshire CV35 8XA Tel: 01926 843411

Admit **TWO** for the price of one (not valid weekends or Bank Holidays)

NOT TO BE USED IN CONJUNCTION WITH ANY OTHER OFFER

READERS' OFFER 1997 VALID until 31/12/1997

Eureka! The Museum for Children

Discovery Road, Halifax, West Yorkshire HX1 2NE Tel: 01422 330069

One child **FREE** with two adults paying full price

NOT TO BE USED IN CONJUNCTION WITH ANY OTHER OFFER

READERS' OFFER 1997 VALID during 1997

Furever Feline

Windhill Manor, Leeds Road, Shipley, West Yorkshire BD18 1BP Tel: 01274 531122

One child **FREE** with two full paying adults (not valid Bank Holidays)

NOT TO BE USED IN CONJUNCTION WITH ANY OTHER OFFER

See woodland with new eyes at this family-run working wood — fascinating and fun for all the family. Trails, adventure playground, exhibition, picnic areas, BBQs for hire, teas.

DIRECTIONS: on main A272 in Hadlow Down village, 5 miles north east of Uckfield

OPEN: daily all year

FHG PUBLICATIONS, ABBEY MILL BUSINESS CENTRE, PAISLEY PA1 1TJ

Working narrow gauge steam railway, railway museum and over 70 replica brasses to rub.

DIRECTIONS: on the A447 six miles north of Hinckley.

OPEN: second Saturday each month

FHG PUBLICATIONS, ABBEY MILL BUSINESS CENTRE, PAISLEY PA1 1TJ

England's largest craft village, factory shops, butcher's and farm shops, antiques centre; restaurant, cafe and bar (no entrance charge). Rare breeds farm, pets' corner, nature trail, guinea pig village, falconry and farming displays and soft play centre

DIRECTIONS: 3 miles north of Warwick, 5 miles south of Knowle, just off Junction 15 of M40 via A46 (Coventry), A4177

OPEN: daily 10am to 5.30pm

FHG PUBLICATIONS, ABBEY MILL BUSINESS CENTRE, PAISLEY PA1 1TJ

Britain's first hands-on museum designed specifically for children 4-12 years old, where they can make hundreds of fascinating discoveries about themselves and the world around them.

DIRECTIONS: next to Halifax railway Station 5 minutes from Junction 24 M62

OPEN: daily 10am to 5pm (closed 24-26 December)

FHG PUBLICATIONS, ABBEY MILL BUSINESS CENTRE, PAISLEY PA1 1TJ

An unusual attraction of animated cat characters in log cabins. Humorous repartee and educational scripts; meet "Robbie" the singing bobcat.

DIRECTIONS: on the A657 500 yards from Shipley centre on left side of road.

OPEN: weekdays 12.30pm to 4pm; weekends and school holidays 11am to 4.30pm.

FHG PUBLICATIONS, ABBEY MILL BUSINESS CENTRE, PAISLEY PA1 1TJ

FHG

READERS' OFFER 1997

VALID during 1997

Alice in Wonderland Centre

3/4 Trinity Square, Llandudno, North Wales LL30 2PY Tel: 01492 860082

One child **FREE** with two paying adults

NOT TO BE USED IN CONJUNCTION WITH ANY OTHER OFFER

FHG

READERS' OFFER 1997

VALID during 1997

Llanberis Lake Railway

Llanberis, Gwynedd LL55 4TY Telephone: 01286 870549

One child travels **FREE** with two full fare-paying adults

NOT TO BE USED IN CONJUNCTION WITH ANY OTHER OFFER

FHG

READERS' OFFER 1997

VALID March to October 1997

PILI PALAS – BUTTERFLY PALACE

Menai Bridge, Isle of Anglesey LL59 5RP Tel: 01248 712474

One child **FREE** with two adults paying full entry price

NOT TO BE USED IN CONJUNCTION WITH ANY OTHER OFFER

FHG

READERS' OFFER 1997

VALID during 1997

CENTRE FOR ALTERNATIVE TECHNOLOGY

Machynlleth, Powys SY20 9AZ Telephone: 01654 702400

One child **FREE** when accompanied by paying adult (one per party only)

NOT TO BE USED IN CONJUNCTION WITH ANY OTHER OFFER

FHG

READERS' OFFER 1997

VALID July to Dec 1997

Techniquest

Stuart Street, Cardiff Bay, South Wales CF1 6BW Tel: 01222 475475

One child **FREE** with full-paying adult

NOT TO BE USED IN CONJUNCTION WITH ANY OTHER OFFER

Walk through the Rabbit Hole to the colourful scenes of Lewis Carroll's classic story set in beautiful life-size displays. Recorded commentaries and transcripts available in several languages.

DIRECTIONS: situated just off the main street, 250 yards from coach and rail stations

OPEN: 10am to 5pm daily Easter to November; closed Sundays November to Easter

FHG PUBLICATIONS, ABBEY MILL BUSINESS CENTRE, PAISLEY PA1 1TJ

A 40-minute ride on a quaint historic steam train along the shore of Llyn Padarn. Spectacular views of the mountains of Snowdonia.

DIRECTIONS: just off the A4086 Caernarfon to Capel Curig road. Follow the "Padarn Country Park" signs.

OPEN: most days Easter to October. Free timetable available from Railway.

FHG PUBLICATIONS, ABBEY MILL BUSINESS CENTRE, PAISLEY PA1 1TJ

Visit Wales' top Butterfly House, with Bird House, Snake House, Ant Avenue, Creepy Crawly Cavern, shop, cafe, adventure playground, picnic area, nature trail etc.

DIRECTIONS: follow brown-and-white signs when crossing to Anglesey; one-and-a-half miles from the Bridge.

OPEN: March to end October 10am to 5pm daily; November/December 11am to 3pm.

FHG PUBLICATIONS, ABBEY MILL BUSINESS CENTRE, PAISLEY PA1 1TJ

Europe's leading Eco-Centre. Water-powered cliff railway, interactive renewable energy displays, beautiful organic gardens, animals; vegetarian restaurant.

DIRECTIONS: three miles north of Machynlleth on the A487 towards Dolgellau.

OPEN: from 10am every day all year (last entry 5pm); times may vary when cliff railway closed ie November to Easter.

FHG PUBLICATIONS, ABBEY MILL BUSINESS CENTRE, PAISLEY PA1 1TJ

Science Discovery Centre with 160 interactive exhibits, Planetarium, Science Theatre and Discovery Room. Fun for all!

DIRECTIONS: A4232 from Juntion 33 of M4. Follow brown tourist signs to Cardiff Bay and Techiquest (10 minutes)

OPEN: weekdays 9.30am to 4.30pm; weekends and Bank Holidays 10.30am to 5pm

FHG PUBLICATIONS, ABBEY MILL BUSINESS CENTRE, PAISLEY PA1 1TJ

LONDON

HARROW. Mrs M. Fitzgerald, 47 Hindes Road, Harrow HA1 1SQ (0181-861 1248). Private family guest house built at the turn of the century, offering very clean, comfortable accommodation. Situated within five minutes of Harrow town centre, Harrow bus and train stations. Wembley Stadium and Conference Centre six minutes away. Central London 17 minutes. 20 minutes M1, M25 and M40 motorways. Accommodation comprises single, double, twin and family rooms, all with central heating, washbasins, tea/coffee making facilities and colour TV. Sorry, no pets. Terms from £16 per person per night.

LONDON. Kirness House, 29 Belgrave Road, Victoria SW1V 1RB (0171-834 0030). A small friendly guest house, please try us. Situated close to Victoria Station. All European languages spoken, satisfaction guaranteed. Single £25, Double £35. Stay five nights, pay for four.

FOR THE MUTUAL GUIDANCE OF GUEST AND HOST

Every year literally thousands of holidays, short-breaks and overnight stops are arranged through our guides, the vast majority without any problems at all. In a handful of cases, however, difficulties do arise about bookings, which often could have been prevented from the outset.

It is important to remember that when accommodation has been booked, both parties — guests and hosts — have entered into a form of contract. We hope that the following points will provide helpful guidance.

GUESTS: When enquiring about accommodation, be as precise as possible. Give exact dates, numbers in your party and the ages of any children. State the number and type of rooms wanted and also what catering you require — bed and breakfast, full board, etc. Make sure that the position about evening meals is clear — and about pets, reductions for children or any other special points.

Read our reviews carefully to ensure that the proprietors you are going to contact can supply what you want. Ask for a letter confirming all arrangements, if possible.

If you have to cancel, do so as soon as possible. Proprietors do have the right to retain deposits and under certain circumstances to charge for cancelled holidays if adequate notice is not given and they cannot re-let the accommodation.

HOSTS: Give details about your facilities and about any special conditions. Explain your deposit system clearly and arrangements for cancellations, charges, etc, and whether or not your terms include VAT.

If for any reason you are unable to fulfil an agreed booking without adequate notice, you may be under an obligation to arrange alternative suitable accommodation or to make some form of compensation.

While every effort is made to ensure accuracy, we regret that FHG Publications cannot accept responsibility for errors, omissions or misrepresentation in our entries or any consequences thereof. Prices in particular should be checked because we go to press early. We will follow up complaints but cannot act as arbiters or agents for either party.

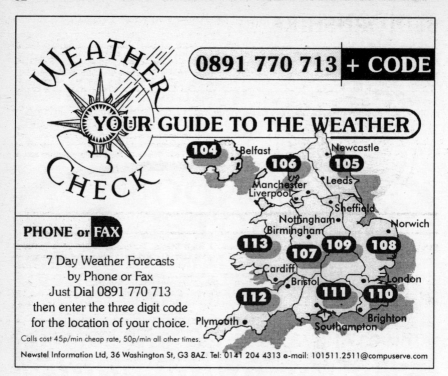

BEDFORDSHIRE

BEDFORD. Mrs Sheila Mousley, Lea Cottage, Old Harrowden Road, Bedford MK42 0TB (01234 740182). Members of the Bedfordshire Farm and Country Accommodation Group can offer a selection of Bed and Breakfast and Self Catering accommodation in rural areas. Thirteen properties offering Bed and Breakfast with prices from £15 per person per night; nine self catering units with prices from £90 to £310 per week. Easily accessible by road or rail and offering a variety of country pursuits such as walking, cycling, fishing, golfing and watersports. Only 50 miles north of London. All accommodation in our brochure is inspected annually by the Tourist Board. Further information and a colour brochure on application.

PULLOXHILL. Phil and Judy Tookey, Pond Farm, 7 High Street, Pulloxhill MK45 5HA (01525 712316). ETB Listed. Pond Farm is situated opposite the village green in Pulloxhill. Three miles from the A6 and five miles from the M1 Junction 12. We are within easy reach of Woburn Abbey and Safari Park, Whipsnade Zoo, the Shuttleworth Collection of Historic Aircraft at Old Warden and 11 miles from Luton Airport. Flitwick mainline station is only three miles away and 45 minutes by train to London. Pond Farm, built in the 17th century, is mainly arable although we have horses grazing on the meadowland. We also have a resident Great Dane. All bedrooms have tea/coffee facilities, washbasins and colour TV as no guest lounge is available; one toilet and washbasin, one shower room with toilet and washbasin and one bathroom. Price from £15. Evening Meals at local inn.

SANDY. Mrs M. Codd, Highfield Farm, Great North Road, Sandy SG19 2AQ (01767 682332). 🖤🖤 *HIGHLY COMMENDED.* Tranquil welcoming atmosphere on attractive arable farm. Set well back off A1 giving quiet, peaceful seclusion yet within easy reach of the RSPB, the Shuttleworth Collection, the Greensand Ridge Walk, Grafham Water and Woburn Abbey. Cambridge 22 miles, London 50 miles. All rooms have tea/coffee facilities, most have bathrooms en-suite and two are on the ground floor. There is a separate guests' sittingroom with TV. Family room. Dogs welcome by arrangement. No smoking. Guestaccom "Good Room" Award. Most guests return! Prices from £17.50 per person per night.

STAGSDEN. Mrs Pam Hutcheon, Firs Farm, Stagsden MK43 8TB (01234 822344). 🖤🖤 *COMMENDED.* Firs Farm is a family-run arable farm set in quiet surroundings quarter of a mile south of A422. The farmhouse is timber framed and set in a large garden with swimming pool. Accommodation consists of double or twin rooms (one en suite) with tea/coffee making facilities and guests' lounge with colour TV. Many local tourist attractions. Open all year. Children and pets welcome. Bed and Breakfast from £15 to £20.

PLEASE SEND A STAMPED ADDRESSED ENVELOPE WITH ENQUIRIES

BERKSHIRE

MAIDENHEAD near. Mrs G. Reynolds, Moor Farm, Holyport, Near Maidenhead SL6 2HY (Tel & Fax: 01628 33761). 🐦🐦 *HIGHLY COMMENDED.* In the

pretty village of Holyport, Moor Farm is four miles from Windsor in a lovely country garden setting. The farmhouse is a timber-framed 700 year old listed manor with charming en suite rooms, furnished with antiques. Well placed for touring the Thames Valley and visiting London. Children welcome. Open all year. Bed and Breakfast from £19.50 to £24 (based on two people sharing). Also self catering cottages available, graded 4 KEYS Highly Commended, sleeping two to four persons from £225 to £425 per week.

MAIDENHEAD Near. Mrs J. Power, Woodpecker Cottage, Warren Row, Near Maidenhead RG10 8QS (01628 822772; Fax: 01628 822125). Woodpecker

Cottage was part of Woodpecker Farm until 40 years ago when the two houses, surrounded by bluebell woods, were sold separately. Set in an acre of pretty gardens, Woodpecker Cottage is unbelievably rural and yet within half an hour of Heathrow, Windsor, M4, M40 and M25. London (Paddington) is 35 minutes from nearby Maidenhead (four miles). The three comfortable ground floor rooms have TV and tea/coffee making facilities. The large double-bedded room and the single room are both en suite and the twin-bedded room has a private bathroom opposite. There is a cosy sitting room, with open fireplace. The full English breakfast includes home-made bread and jams. Bed and Breakfast from £20. Open all year. Non-smoking house.

BUCKINGHAMSHIRE

AYLESBURY. Binnie Pickford, New Farm, Oxford Road, Oakley, Aylesbury HP18 9UR (01844 237360). Tourist Board Listed *COMMENDED.* Friendly

atmosphere in fully modernised farmhouse. Good food, comfortable bedrooms, views over 163 acres devoted to sheep, beef, arable. Situated on Oxfordshire/Buckinghamshire boundary in peaceful surroundings. Walks in adjacent Bernwood Forest Nature Reserve. Golf course one and a quarter miles; seven miles Oxford, close to Waterperry Gardens, Waddesdon Manor, Quainton Railway Centre, Blenheim Palace and M40. Pubs and restaurants nearby. Children over six years welcome. Open all year except Christmas. Bed and Breakfast from £17; Evening Meal from £10.

PUBLISHER'S NOTE

While every effort is made to ensure accuracy, we regret that FHG Publications cannot accept responsibility for errors, omissions or misrepresentation in our entries or any consequences thereof. Prices in particular should be checked because we go to press early. We will follow up complaints but cannot act as arbiters or agents for either party.

CAMBRIDGESHIRE

CAMBRIDGE. Mrs M. Quintana, Segovia Lodge, 2 Barton Road, Cambridge CB3 9JZ (01223 354105/323011). ♨♨ Within walking distance of the city centre and colleges. Members of the English Tourist Board and East Anglia Tourist Office. Rooms with private facilities. Double room: minimum £35 and maximum £42. By A603, close to M11 Junction 12; A45, A604. Children welcome; sorry no dogs and no smokers.

CAMBRIDGE. Mrs Jean Wright, White Horse Cottage, 28 West Street, Comberton, Cambridge CB3 7DS (01223 262914). A 17th century cottage with all modern conveniences situated in a charming village four miles south-west of Cambridge. Junction 12 off M11 — A603 from Cambridge, or A428 turn off at Hardwick Turning. Accommodation includes one double room, twin and family rooms. Own sitting room with colour TV; tea/coffee making facilities. Full central heating; parking. Excellent touring centre for many interesting places including Cambridge colleges, Wimpole Hall, Anglesey Abbey, Ely Cathedral, Imperial War Museum at Duxford, and many more. Bed and Breakfast from £17 per person. Children welcome.

CAMBRIDGE near. Vicki Hatley, Manor Farm, Landbeach, Cambridge CB4 4ED (01223 860165). ♨♨ *COMMENDED.* Five miles from Cambridge and 10 miles from Ely. Vicki welcomes you to her carefully modernised Grade II Listed farmhouse, which is located next to the church in this attractive village. All rooms are either en suite or have private bathroom and are individually decorated. TV, clock radios and tea/coffee making facilities are provided in double, twin or family rooms. There is ample parking and guests are welcome to enjoy the secluded walled gardens. Bed and Breakfast from £17.50 per person double, and £22 single.

CAMBRIDGE near. Mrs J.L. Bygraves, Elms Farm, 52 Main Road, Little Gransden SG19 3DL (01767 677459). Situated south west of Cambridge on B1046 from Junction 12 on the M11 or from A1 at St. Neots. Excellent touring centre for Cambridge, Duxford War Museum, Wimpole Hall, Woburn Abbey, Audley End House, Ely Cathedral, etc. Working arable farm with rural views and country walks around picturesque village. Recently renovated farmhouse offering a friendly atmosphere. Accommodation comprises one double, one twin with en suite facilities and one single bedrooms, all with colour TV, tea/coffee making facilities and central heating. Four pubs nearby for evening meals. Bed and Breakfast from £17 per person. No smoking.

ELY. Mrs Margaret Sicard, The Laurels, 104 Victoria Street, Littleport, Ely CB6 1LZ (01353 861972; 0850 199299 mobile). A large, attractive Victorian House in a quiet location offering excellent accommodation and farmhouse breakfast. Set in pretty, old-fashioned garden, 200 yards from riverside pub. Situated on the Norfolk/Suffolk/Cambridge borders, four miles from Ely Cathedral; Wildfowl and Wetlands Trust, Cambridge's ornate colleges and famous Backs 30 minutes, Sandringham one hour. Superior twin/double en suite rooms, one suitable for partially disabled visitors, with easy chairs, tea/coffee facilities, radio, colour TV, door locks and central heating. Diningroom leading to sub-tropical garden room. Evening Meal. Cot/high chair, Z-bed. Private parking with security lights. Non smoking guests only. Bed with full bath or shower en suite and Breakfast from £16.

SANDY. Mrs S. Barlow, Model Farm, Little Gransden, Sandy, Bedfordshire SG19 3EA (01767 677361). A warm welcome awaits visitors to this traditional 1870s farmhouse situated on a working family farm. The farmhouse, providing comfortable and quiet accommodation with lovely views, is set in open countryside between the villages of Little Gransden and Longstowe. Guests are welcome to walk around the farm and garden. Model Farm is an ideal base for visiting Cambridge, Ely, Duxford Imperial War Museum, Shuttleworth (vintage aircraft and cars), Wimpole Hall and Farm (National Trust) and the RSBP at Sandy. M11, A1, A14 are all within 20 minutes' drive. Please write or telephone for further details.

WICKEN. Mrs Valerie Fuller, Spinney Abbey, Wicken, Ely CB7 5XQ (01353 720971). 🏵🏵 *COMMENDED.* **Working farm.** Spinney Abbey is a spacious Georgian farmhouse. A Grade II Listed building of historical interest, rebuilt from the former priory in 1775. It stands in a large garden with tennis court adjacent to our dairy farm which borders the National Trust Nature Reserve "Wicken Fen". The accommodation comprises two double en suite rooms and a twin-bedded room with private bathroom, all with TV and tea/coffee tray. Guests' sittingroom. Central heating and electric blankets for colder months. Regret no pets and no smoking upstairs. Bed and Breakfast from £19 per person. Situated just off the A1123 half a mile west of Wicken. Open all year.

CHESHIRE

CHESTER. Audrey Charmley, Ford Farm, Nenton Lane, Tattenhall, Chester CH3 9NE (01829 770307). ETB Listed *COMMENDED.* A friendly welcome to our dairy farm set in beautiful countryside with views of Beeston and Peckforton Castles. Close to ice cream farm and Cheshire workshops and many tourist attractions. Chester seven miles, Oulton Park eight miles. Guests' own lounge and dining room with TV. One double and one twin room, tea/coffee making facilities; bathroom with shower. Open all year. Children and pets welcome. Bed and Breakfast from £14 to £15.

Terms quoted in this publication may be subject to increase if rises in costs necessitate

CONGLETON. Mrs Sheila Kidd, Yew Tree Farm, North Rode, Congleton CW12 2PF (01260 223569). ETB Listed *COMMENDED.*

This working farm has a peaceful village setting with scenic country walks on our doorstep. It is central for the Peak District, Potteries, Alton Towers and the historic houses of Cheshire. Just 20 minutes from the M6. You can be assured of a warm welcome, a cosy atmosphere and good food. One double en-suite room and two twin rooms. Lounge with open log fire. Children are welcome and guests are invited to look around the farm and get to know the animals and wide range of pets. Bed and substantial cooked Breakfast from £17; optional Evening Meal £10. Write or phone for brochure.

HYDE, Near Manchester. Mrs Charlotte R. Walsh, Needhams Farm, Uplands Road, Werneth Low, Gee Cross, Near Hyde SK14 3AQ (0161-368 4610). 👑 👑 👑 *COMMENDED.* **Working farm.**

A cosy 16th century farmhouse set in peaceful, picturesque surroundings by Werneth Low Country Park and the Etherow Valley, which lie between Glossop and Manchester. The farm is ideally situated for holidaymakers and businessmen, especially those who enjoy peace and quiet, walking and rambling, golfing and riding, as these activities are all close by. At Needhams Farm everyone, including children and pets, receives a warm welcome. Good wholesome meals available in the evenings. Residential licence and Fire Certificate held. Open all year. Bed and Breakfast from £18 single minimum and £32 double maximum; Evening Meal £7. AA Listed, RAC Acclaimed.

MACCLESFIELD. Mrs M.M. Birch, High Low Farm, Langley, Macclesfield SK11 0NE (01260 252230). 👑

Built in 1645, tastefully modernised and still run as a sheep farm. A friendly welcome awaits you at our country home situated between Langley and the 1000 acre Macclesfield Forest with its herd of wild deer. Adjacent to Teggs Nose Country Park and on the edge of the Peak National Park it is the ideal spot for tourist or walker. One family/twin and one double with washbasins. Guests own bathroom. Separate toilet. Own dining and sitting room with colour TV. Fully centrally heated. Ample parking. Bed and Breakfast from £16 to £17. Brochure available.

MACCLESFIELD. Mrs P.O. Worth, Rough Hey Farm, Leek Road, Gawsworth, Macclesfield SK11 0JQ (01260 252296). 👑 👑

Delightfully situated overlooking the Cheshire Plain and on the edge of the Peak National Park, Rough Hey is an historic former hunting lodge dating from before the 16th century, tastefully modernised yet retaining its old world character. This 300 acre sheep farm consists of wooded valleys and hills with plenty of wildlife and lovely walks. In the locality there are numerous old halls and villages to visit. Double room en suite, twin room en suite and two single rooms, all with washbasins, TV and tea/coffee making facilities. Large comfortable lounge with TV. A warm and friendly welcome is assured. Terms from £18.

MALPAS. Chris and Angela Smith, Mill House, Higher Wych, Malpas SY14 7JR (01948 780362). 👑 👑 👑 *HIGHLY COMMENDED.*

Modernised Mill House on the Cheshire/Clwyd border in a quiet valley, convenient for visiting Chester, Shrewsbury and North Wales. The house is centrally heated and has an open log fire in the lounge. Bedrooms have washbasins, radios and tea making facilities. One bedroom has an en suite shower and WC. Reductions for children and Senior Citizens. Open January to November. Bed and Breakfast from £16; Evening Meal from £8.

NANTWICH. Mrs Jean E. Callwood, Lea Farm, Wrinehill Road, Wybunbury, Nantwich CW5 7NS (01270 841429). ❦❦ COMMENDED. Working farm, join in. A charming farmhouse set in landscaped gardens, where peacocks roam, on 150 acre dairy farm. Spacious bedrooms with washbasins, colour TV, electric blankets, radio alarm and tea/coffee making facilities. Family, double and twin bedrooms, en suite facilities. Luxury lounge, diningroom overlooking gardens. Pool/snooker; fishing in well stocked pool in beautiful surroundings. Bird watching. Children welcome, also dogs if kept under control. Help feed the birds and animals and see the cows being milked. Near to Stapeley Water Gardens, Bridgemere Garden World. Also Nantwich, Crewe, Chester, the Potteries and Alton Towers. Bed and Breakfast from £14.50 per person; Evening Meal from £9. Children half price. Weekly terms available.

NANTWICH. Caroline Hocknell, Poole Bank Farm, Wettenhall Road, Poole, Nantwich CW5 6AL (01270 625169). ❦ COMMENDED. A charming 17th century timbered farmhouse on 360 acre dairy farm set in quiet countryside two miles from the historic town of Nantwich. Ideal base for discovering the beautiful Cheshire countryside. Central for Chester and the Potteries. Comfortable and attractive rooms, all with period furnishings. TV and tea/coffee making facilities. A warm welcome and an excellent breakfast are assured. Children welcome. Open all year. Bed and Breakfast from £15 to £18.

FREE and REDUCED RATE Holiday Visits!
See our READERS' OFFER VOUCHER for details!

Key to
Tourist Board Ratings

The Crown Scheme
(England, Scotland & Wales)

Covering hotels, motels, private hotels, guesthouses, inns, bed & breakfast, farmhouses. Every Crown classified place to stay is inspected annually. *The classification:* Listed then 1-5 Crown indicates the range of facilities and services. Higher quality standards are indicated by the terms APPROVED, COMMENDED, HIGHLY COMMENDED and DELUXE.

The Key Scheme
(also operates in Scotland using a Crown symbol)

Covering self-catering in cottages, bungalows, flats, houseboats, houses, chalets, etc. Every Key classified holiday home is inspected annually. *The classification:* 1-5 Key indicates the range of facilities and equipment. Higher quality standards are indicated by the terms APPROVED, COMMENDED, HIGHLY COMMENDED and DELUXE.

The Q Scheme
(England, Scotland & Wales)

Covering holiday, caravan, chalet and camping parks. Every Q rated park is inspected annually for its quality standards. The more √ in the Q – up to 5 – the higher the standard of what is provided.

CORNWALL

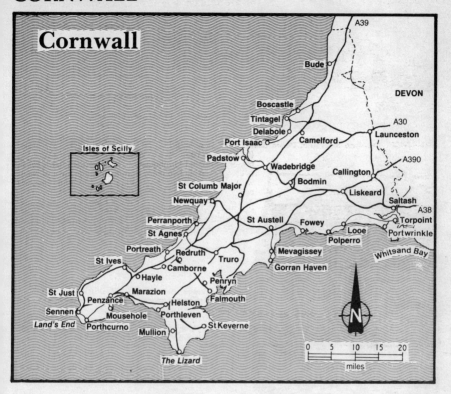

Cornwall

BODMIN. Mrs Jill Cleave, Tregellist Farm, Tregellist, St. Kew, Bodmin PL30 3HG (01208 880537).

🌟🌟 COMMENDED. Tregellist Farm is a 125 acre working family-run farm set in pleasant countryside with wonderful views. The house offers spacious and comfortable accommodation in twin, double and family rooms, all en suite and having colour TV and beverage trays. Central heating. Ideally situated for touring the North Cornwall beaches for surfing and swimming and the Moors. Close to several golf courses and the Camel Trail. Good home cooking using home produce when available. Children welcome, cot and high chair available. Sorry, no pets. Bed and Breakfast from £19; Bed, Breakfast and Evening Meal available.

BODMIN. Mrs Jenny Bass, Trehannick Farm, St. Teath, Bodmin PL30 3JW (01208 850312).

Working farm. First mentioned in the Domesday Book in 1086, Trehannick is a 180-acre family farm situated in the beautiful Allen Valley. Safe sandy beaches, coastal walks, golf, sailing, surfing and fishing are all within easy reach of this peaceful farmhouse. Two double rooms, one with en suite bathroom and one with washbasin, plus family room with double and twin beds and washbasin; bathroom; lounge with colour TV (log fires when needed). Good home cooking using own farm produce when available. Car essential. Sorry, no pets. Reductions for children sharing parents' room. "Glorious views", "lovely peaceful atmosphere", "a very happy stopover" "magical" — some of the comments made by my 1996 guests. Come and see and enjoy for yourself the relaxing surroundings at Trehannick Farm. Bed and Breakfast, or Bed, Breakfast and Evening Meal. SAE please or telephone for terms and further details.

BODMIN. Mrs Joy Rackham, High Cross Farm, Lanivet, Near Bodmin PL30 5JR (01208 831341).

Cornwall Tourist Board *APPROVED.* **Working farm.** High Cross is a 91 acre working dairy farm situated in the village of Lanivet which is the geographical centre of Cornwall and therefore central to beaches on the North and South coast and the moor. Riding, fishing and cycle tracks available in the area. The bedrooms have washbasins; separate lounge and dining room for guests. Bed and Breakfast £13 daily; Evening Meal optional. SAE please or telephone.

BODMIN. Mrs S. Menhinick, Loskeyie Farm, St. Tudy, Bodmin PL30 3PW (01208 851005). ❦

COMMENDED. Loskeyle is a working dairy farm in the Duchy of Cornwall where a warm welcome awaits you. Relax and enjoy the peace and tranquillity of farm life here where you can watch the milking, feed the hens, collect eggs or enjoy leisurely walks through open fields. Children especially welcome with reduced rates. Delicious farmhouse cooking using fresh local produce. Pretty bedrooms with tea/coffee facilities and vanity units. Ideal base for north/south coasts. Golf, Camel Trail nearby, also pony trekking over the moors only a stone's throw away. Bed and Breakfast from £15; Evening Meal £8.

BOSCASTLE. Mrs Sarah James, Trehane Farm, Trevalga, Boscastle PL35 0EB (01840 250510).

❦❦ *COMMENDED.* Welcome to Trehane, a dairy farm on the spectacular North Cornwall Heritage coast. Farmhouse set in magnificent position overlooking sea, superb coastal views. We offer a comfortable friendly atmosphere and wholesome nourishing food using fresh farm produce and home baked bread. Enjoy fine walks along the coast or inland on to Bodmin Moor. And you can learn to spin in this very lovely place. We can accommodate six guests. Children welcome, pets by arrangement. Bed and Breakfast from £17.00.

BOSCASTLE. Mrs Cheryl Nicholls, Trerosewill Farm, Paradise, Boscastle PL35 0DL (01840

250545). Working farm. ❦❦❦ *HIGHLY COMMENDED.* AA QQQQ Selected. Bed and Breakfast accommodation in modern farmhouse on working farm, only short walk from the picturesque village of Boscastle. Rooms have spectacular coastal and rural views, all en suite with tea making facilities. Colour TVs and telephones available if required. Four-posters, mineral water and bath robes. Licensed. Centrally heated. Seasonal log fires. Large gardens. Traditional farmhouse fayre. Feed the calves. Superb coastal and countryside walks. Specially negotiated rates for nearby golf and pony trekking. One way walks arranged. Packed lunches available. Spring and Autumn breaks. Strictly no smokers. Bed and Breakfast from £16. FHG Diploma Award 1995.

BOSCASTLE. Mr J. Perfili, Trefoil Farm, New Road, Boscastle PL35 0AD (01840 250606). Trefoil Farm is situated on the boundary of Boscastle, overlooking the harbour, valley and ocean. On the farm we breed and show pedigree Suffolk sheep, and we have large gardens for you to sit and relax in. Accommodation comprises family and double rooms, fully en suite and having colour TV and tea/coffee making facilities. Full central heating, TV, lounge, seasonal log fires. Full English breakfast, evening meal optional — traditional farmhouse fayre. There are superb coastal and countryside walks, and one-way walks can be arranged. Leisure facilities, sandy beaches nearby. Spring and Autumn Breaks. No pets. No smoking in the house. Bed and Breakfast from £15.

WHEN MAKING ENQUIRIES PLEASE MENTION
FARM HOLIDAY GUIDES

BUDE. Mrs Rosina Joyner, Penrose, Dizzard, St. Gennys, Bude EX23 0NX (01840 230318). Penrose

is a delightful 17th century cottage with beamed ceilings and inglenook fireplaces. Tastefully modernised, yet retaining all its Olde Worlde charm. Set in one and a half acres of lawns and gardens within the National Trust area close to the coastal path, it is ideal for those seeking peace and quiet. Nearby is the beautiful beach of Widemouth Bay. The views from the cottage are extensive. All rooms have washbasins, TV and tea/coffee making facilities; two rooms with double four-poster beds (one with shower). One bedroom with king-size bed with canopy, en suite and with sea views; ground floor suitable for disabled guests. Good English breakfast; optional Evening Meal. Also available is a mobile home and self-catering cottage annexe, both sleep six; prices range from £150 per week low season to £375 high season. SAE for booking form and brochure, or telephone. Bed and Breakfast from £17.50 per night.

BUDE. Michael and Christine Nancekivell, Dolsdon Farm, Boyton, Launceston PL15 8NT (01288

341264). Dolsdon was once a 17th century coaching inn, now modernised, situated on the Launceston to Bude road within easy reach of sandy beaches, surfing, Tamar Otter Park, leisure centre with heated swimming pool, golf courses, fishing, tennis and horse riding. Ideal for touring Cornwall and Devon. Guests are welcome to wander round the 260 acre working farm. All bedrooms have washbasins and tea making facilities (en suite family room available). Comfortably furnished lounge has colour TV. Plenty of good home cooking assured — full English breakfast, four-course evening dinner (optional). Parking. Bed and Breakfast from £13; reductions for children. Brochure available.

BUDE. Michael and Pearl Hopper, West Nethercott Farm, Whitstone, Holsworthy (Devon) EX22

6LD (01288 341394). Working farm, join in. A warm welcome awaits you on this dairy and sheep farm. Watch the cows being milked, help with the animals. Free pony rides, scenic farm walks. Short distance from sandy beaches, surfing and the rugged North Cornwall coast. Ideal base for visiting any part of Devon or Cornwall. We are located in Cornwall though our postal address is Devon. The traditional farmhouse has washbasins and TV in bedrooms; diningroom and separate lounge with colour TV. Plenty of excellent home cooking. Access to the house at anytime. Bed and Breakfast from £12, four-course Evening Meal available. Children under 12 years reduced rates. Weekly terms available.

BUDE. Mrs Sylvia Lucas, Elm Park, Bridgerule, Holsworthy EX22 7EL (01288 381231). 👑👑

APPROVED. Elm Park is a 205 acre dairy, beef, sheep farm six miles from surfing beaches at Bude and ideal for touring Devon/Cornwall. Children are especially welcomed with pony rides and a tractor and trailer ride around the farm. There are spacious family rooms (two en-suite) and a twin-bedded room, all with colour TV and tea/coffee making facilities. Ample four-course dinners with freshly produced fare and delicious sweets. Games room with snooker, table skittles, darts, etc, and golf putting. Bed, Breakfast and Evening Meal, reasonable terms. Reductions for children and everyone is made welcome and comfortable. Brochure available.

BUDE. Penhalt Farm, Widemouth Bay, Bude EX23 0DG (01288 361210). Working farm. Panoramic

sea and country views from all rooms of Penhalt Farmhouse. 120 acre beef and sheep farm situated off the Heritage Coastal footpath, ideal for walking or touring and splendid sandy beaches at Widemouth Bay and nearby Bude. Two double bedrooms, one with shower and one with separate private cloak/shower room, one twin room with wash basin. Separate bathroom and toilet. Lounge with TV and video. Dining room. Good farmhouse breakfast provided in friendly comfortable surroundings. Well behaved pets welcome. Outside children's play area and telephone. Bed and Breakfast from £25.00 for a double room. Also self-catering accommodation available (♛♛♛♛ COMMENDED).

CAMBORNE. Mrs Christine Peerless, Highdowns, Blackrock, Praze-an-Beeble, Camborne TR14

9PD (01209 831442). Highdowns is a comfortable, quiet and ideally situated base from which to explore the beautiful Cornish countryside and magnificent coastline. It is set on a south-west-facing hillside with extensive country views towards St. Ives Bay. We offer traditional home made and varied meals using fresh home grown and local produce whenever available; vegetarian and special diets catered for. All bedrooms en suite with tea/coffee making facilities. TV lounge. Easy parking. Fire Certificate. No smoking. Bed and Breakfast from £16 per night; Evening Meal £8.

CAMBORNE/TROON. Mrs S. Leonard, Sea View Farm Guesthouse, Troon, Near Camborne TR14 9JH (01209 831260). Farmhouse on small horticultural holding, one mile from Troon village. Six double, one single and three family bedrooms, all with individual heating, washbasins etc. Large lounge with colour TV; bathroom, two shower rooms, three toilets; diningroom. Good home cooking. Residential licence. Heated swimming pool. Well recommended by previous guests. Cot, high chair, babysitting and reduced rates for children. Pets permitted. Panoramic views from some bedrooms. Within easy reach of north and south coasts, only 15 minutes by car. Open all year round for Bed and Breakfast from £75 weekly; Dinner £8 per night. AA Approved.

FALMOUTH. Anne Durrant, Blue Haze Guest House, 7 Gyllyngvase Terrace, Falmouth TR11 4DL

(01326 313132). ♨♨ Ideally situated in a quiet terrace two minutes' walk from the safe golden beaches. We are conveniently placed near the town, railway station and public entertainments; courtesy car from coach and train stations if required. All bedrooms have washbasins and are centrally heated. Guests have free access to their rooms and TV lounge at all times. We enjoy good food and hope to please your appetites! The dining room has separate tables and a licensed bar; special diets catered for. Packed lunches available at small additional charge. We regret no pets except guide dogs. Please write or telephone for our brochure.

See also Colour Display Advertisement

FALMOUTH. Mrs T.P. Tremayne, The Home, Penjerrick, Falmouth (01326 250427 and 250143). ♨♨♨ *COMMENDED.* A real Country House Hotel just outside Falmouth. Our house, in its large garden, has lovely views over tree-clad countryside to Maenporth and the bay, close to the Helford River with its beautiful walks and boating facilities. Ideal base for touring. Majority of bedrooms now completely refurbished with full en suite facilities, TV and tea/coffee making facilities and heating. Our home is graciously furnished and carpeted to a high standard. Our elegant dining room has separate tables; there is a large lounge with colour TV and in addition there is a spacious sun lounge overlooking the garden. Table licence. Good enclosed car park. Bus service. Dinner, Room and Breakfast from £160 per week. Illustrated brochure available for full details.

FALMOUTH. Celia and Ian Carruthers, Harbour House, 1 Harbour Terrace, Falmouth TR11 2AN (01326 311344). AA Recommended QQQ. Enjoy quality bed and breakfast accommodation with some of the most fantastic harbour views in Cornwall. Clean, comfortable, tastefully decorated bedrooms with TVs and hot drink making facilities, half en suite. Delicious home cooking with a generous and varied menu. Close to idyllic walks, secluded coves, creekside pubs, watersports, ancient castles and country houses. Two minutes' walk into town. Private car parking. Drying and storage facilities for sailing, diving, walking gear, etc. Bed and Breakfast from a very reasonable £14. We welcome guests for short or long stays, almost all year. Please call for a brochure or to check availability.

HELSTON. Mrs Maureen Dale, Polgarth Farm, Crowntown, Helston TR13 0AA (01326 572115). ♨♨ *APPROVED.* **Working farm.** Polgarth Farm is central for touring West Cornwall, three miles from the market town of Helston (home of the famous Furry Dance — 8th May) on the main Helston-Camborne road (B3303). Market gardening. Maureen Dale, having cooked at The London Dairy Show, Ideal Home Exhibition, on TV, and broadcast on local radio, takes great pleasure in producing sumptuous meals for all her guests and, with her husband, welcomes you to their home. Standard and en suite rooms available. Pets welcome by prior arrangement. Open January to end of November. SAE for terms.

HELSTON. Gillian Lawrence, Longstone Farm, Trenear, Helston TR13 0HG (01326 572483). ✿✿

COMMENDED. A warm welcome awaits you at Longstone Farm, situated in the centre of West Cornwall's peaceful countryside. Ideal for touring both coasts and holiday attractions including Flambards. Traditional farmhouse fayre served and leisure facilities nearby. All bedrooms en suite or private facilities. Accommodation suitable for disabled visitors. Ample room to relax and make yourself at home in our TV lounge and sun lounge/play area. Children and pets welcome. Open February to November. Bed and Breakfast from £16 to £19; Evening Meal from £8.

See also Colour Display Advertisement **HELSTON. Mrs J. Lugg, Tregaddra Farm, Cury Cross Lanes, Helston TR12 7BB (Tel & Fax: 01326 240235).** ✿✿✿

COMMENDED. **Working farm.** AA QQQQ Selected. Tregaddra is an early 18th century farmhouse set in half-an-acre of well-kept gardens. Ideally situated in the centre of The Lizard Peninsula with views of peaceful rolling countryside for a 15 mile radius. Pretty, large en suite bedrooms; inglenook fireplace in lounge, farmhouse Aga cooking and local produce used. Out of season breaks with candlelit dining room and open log fires for chilly evenings. Coastal walks, sailing, sandy beaches, horse riding, golf all nearby. Drying facilities for walking boots, etc. A warm welcome and family hospitality guaranteed. Send for colour brochure and local information.

HELSTON. Mrs Margaret Jenkin, Boderloggan Farm, Wendron, Helston TR13 0ES (01326 572148). Working farm. "Boderloggan" is a 120-acre dairy farm, ideally situated for touring the main towns and beauty spots of South and West Cornwall. Within easy reach of the coast, Newquay, Falmouth, St. Ives, Penzance, Truro; Helston three miles. Also well situated for visiting holiday attractions and National Trust properties and gardens in the area. Two double (family) bedrooms with washbasins and tea/coffee making facilities; bathroom; beamed dining room/lounge with colour TV. Mrs Jenkin will give her guests a value-for-money holiday with plenty of fresh vegetables, clotted cream, with a three-course Evening Meal. English Breakfast. Friendly homely atmosphere, children welcome. Food Hygiene Certificate. FHG Diploma Winner. Bed and Breakfast or Bed, Breakfast and Evening Meal.

HELSTON. Mrs P. Roberts, Hendra Farm, Wendron, Helston TR13 0NR (01326 340470). Hendra

Farm, just off the main Helston/Falmouth road, is an ideal centre for touring Cornwall; three miles to Helston, eight to both Redruth and Falmouth. Safe sandy beaches within easy reach — five miles to the sea. Beautiful views from the farmhouse of the 60-acre beef farm. Two double, one single, and one family bedrooms; bathroom and toilets; sittingroom and two diningrooms. Cot, babysitting and reduced rates offered for children. No objection to pets. Car necessary, parking space. Enjoy good cooking with roast beef, pork, lamb, chicken, genuine Cornish pasties, fish and delicious sweets and cream. Open all year except Christmas. Evening Dinner, Bed and Breakfast from £110 per week which includes cooked breakfast, three course evening dinner, tea and homemade cake before bed. Bed and Breakfast only from £12 per night also available.

HELSTON near. Mrs D.J. Hill, Rocklands, The Lizard, Near Helston TR12 7NX (01326 290339).

Rocklands is situated overlooking part of Cornwall's superb coastline and enjoys uninterrupted sea views. The Lizard is well known for its lovely picturesque scenery, coastal walks and enchanting coves and beaches, as well as the famous Serpentine Stone which is quarried and sold locally. Open Easter to October. The Hill family have been catering for visitors on the Lizard since the 1850's. Three bedrooms with sea views, tea/coffee making facilities and electric heaters; sitting room with TV and video; sun lounge; dining room with separate tables. Bed and Breakfast weekly terms from £126 per person. NO VAT. Children and well trained pets welcome.

LAUNCESTON. Mrs A. E. Werren, Waterloo Farm, North Petherwin, Launceston PL15 8LL (01566

785386). A warm welcome awaits on our working farm set amid peaceful countryside overlooking the beautiful Ottery Valley. Riverside walks along ancient county boundary and one and a half miles good trout fishing. Nearby pub and Otter Sanctuary, rural town of Launceston four and a half miles, coastal resort of Bude nine miles. Excellent farmhouse cooking and relaxed, comfortable atmosphere make Waterloo Farm an ideal touring centre for moors and coasts of Devon and Cornwall. Visitors' lounge with TV, elegant dining room, private bathroom; one double, one family room with washbasins, tea/coffee making facilities. Bed and Breakfast £15 per night; Evening Meal optional. Reductions for children. SAE please.

LAUNCESTON. Mrs A. Strout, Bradridge Farm, Boyton, Launceston PL15 9RL (01409 271264).

You'll get a real country welcome at Bradridge, a working mixed farm of 400 acres set in wonderful countryside right on the border between Cornwall and Devon, ideal for touring both counties! Guests are welcome to see the animals and to enjoy the walks and tranquillity. Good farmhouse cooking with home-grown produce. The beach and golf course are close by and there is excellent fishing on the River Tamar bordering the farm. All bedrooms have washbasins and tea/coffee making facilities. Guests' own bathroom. Log fires late and early in season. Bed and Breakfast from £14. Evening meals extra. Brochure available.

Peacefully situated on the Devon/Cornwall border just two miles from historic Launceston with its Norman Castle, leisure centre, golf course, horse riding and lots of eating places. Ideal base for touring. Enjoy the start to the day with a hearty breakfast in a 17th century farmhouse with a warm, friendly atmosphere. Choose between double/family en suite or double with private bathroom. Both bedrooms have tea, coffee, drinking chocolate and biscuits. In the large guest lounge there is colour TV and a log burner which is lit on cold evenings. Browse through the file of tourist information. Sorry, no smoking. ✿✿ **Commended.**

Bed & Breakfast per person per night: £17.50 en suite, with private bathroom £15.00.
Self catering also available. ♥♥♥♥ **Commended.**

Mrs K.W. Broad, Lower Dutson Farm, Launceston, Cornwall PL15 9SP   Telephone 01566 776456

LAUNCESTON near. Mr and Mrs J. Turner, Lanzion Farmhouse, Egloskerry, Launceston PL15 8RZ (01566 781678/781509). Comfortable accommodation in our former farmhouse with good home cooking and friendly, personal attention. Ideal as a stopover if you are en route to the west of the county (10 minutes A30), or for touring North Cornwall. Quiet, rural location amongst farmland ideally situated for coastal walks, horse riding, moors and beaches which are all within easy reach. 18 hole golf course at Launceston. Accommodation comprises one family room (sleeps four); beverage tray; guests' own bathroom; TV lounge. Evening meal optional. Bed and Breakfast £15 per person per night, family room £40 per night. Longer stay reductions available on request.

LAUNCESTON. Mary Rich, "Nathania", Altarnun, Launceston PL15 7SL (01566 86426). Christian couple offer Bed, Breakfast and Evening Meal accommodation on a small farm on Bodmin Moor within easy reach of coast, moors, towns, lakes and fishing. Visit King Arthur country — Tintagel, Dozmary Pool, famous Jamaica Inn, Wesley Cottage and cathedral of the moors. Double and twin rooms with en suite bathroom and tea making facilities. Conservatory and lounge for quiet relaxation. Please telephone, or write, for details — SAE, thank you.

LISKEARD. Mrs Lindsay M. Pendray, Caduscott, East Taphouse, Liskeard PL14 4NG (Tel & Fax: 01579 320262). ETB Listed *APPROVED.* **Working farm.** Down the lane where the wild flowers nod in passing to relax and unwind in attractive 17th century listed farmhouse peeping over the valley where streams converge to make the 10 mile journey to the sea at Looe. Double room (en-suite toilet/shower), adjoining twin-bedded room. Traditional Bed and Breakfast with Evening Meal served in a large lounge/diningroom where a log fire assures you of a warm welcome, also central heating. Children especially welcome; cot, high chair and open spaces to play in with swing and climbing frame. Bed and Breakfast from £15 to £19 per person per night. No smoking. The Pendray family have farmed Caduscott for over 70 years and will make every effort to ensure that you discover Cornwall.

LISKEARD. Mrs Stephanie Rowe, Tregondale Farm, Menheniot, Liskeard PL14 3RG (Tel & Fax: 01579 342407). ✿✿ *HIGHLY COMMENDED.* **Working farm, join in.** Feeling like a break near the coast? Come and relax, join our family with the peace of the countryside — breathtaking in Spring — on a 200 acre mixed farm, situated near Looe between A38 and A390. See pedigree South Devon cattle and sheep naturally reared, explore the new woodland farm trail amidst wildlife and flowers. This stylish character-istic farmhouse, which dates back to the Domesday Book, as featured in the Daily Telegraph, Cream of Cornwall, provides exceptional comfort with quality en suite bedrooms all with colour TV, tea/coffee facilities, lounge, dining room with log fires. A conservatory to enjoy each day's warmth capturing a beautiful view over the farm. Set in original walled garden including picnic table, tennis court and play area. Special activities can be arranged — golf, fishing, cycling and walking. Home produce a speciality, full English breakfast; four-course optional evening meal from £10.00. Bed and Breakfast from £18.00. AA QQQQ. Open all year. Self catering character cottage also available (4 KEYS HIGHLY COMMENDED). A warm welcome awaits you to discover the beauty of Cornwall. Please phone for a brochure and discuss your requirements.

LISKEARD. Mrs E.R. Elford, Tresulgan Farm, Near Menheniot, Liskeard PL14 3PU (01503 240268).

👑👑 *HIGHLY COMMENDED*. **Working farm, join in.** Tresulgan is a 115-acre arable mixed farm where picturesque views can be seen from the 17th century farmhouse, attractive garden and patio area. Delicious home-cooked meals are served in our original oak-beamed dining room. Three en suite bedrooms are tastefully decorated to a high standard throughout, with colour TV and drinks facilities. Set in the countryside, yet within easy reach of the numerous attractions, sandy beaches and inviting coastline of this beautiful part of Cornwall. Always a warm welcome. SAE for brochure and terms please. FHB Member.

LIZARD PENINSULA. Mrs G. Rowe, Trethvas Farm, The Lizard, Helston TR12 7AR (01326 290720).

Trethvas is a family-run 300 acre dairy farm with large farmhouse standing in countryside with sea views. Half a mile from the Lizard village, footpaths through the farm lead to the Coastal Path, Cadgwith and the Lizard. Nearby are the beaches of Kynance and Kennack Sands. One double en suite bedroom with shower and TV, one room with double and single beds and washbasin, one twin or triple with washbasin; tea/coffee facilities in all rooms. Bathroom, shower room and separate toilet; comfortable lounge with colour TV. Ample parking. Sorry, no pets. Bed and Breakfast only. Open April to October.

LOOE. Mrs J. Kitto, Treveria Farm, Widegates, Looe PL13 1QR (01503 240237). 👑👑 *COMMENDED*.

Charming Victorian Manor House set in the grounds of a large garden offering superb accommodation. Beautiful colour co-ordinated en suite rooms, all with colour TV and beverage facilities. Romantic four-poster room also available. Many excellent places to eat in the area. Open Easter to November. Prices from £18 to £20.

LOOE. Mrs Angela Eastley, Little Larnick Farm, Pelynt, Looe PL13 2NB (01503 262837). 👑👑 Get

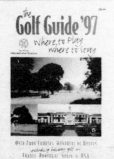

away from it all at Little Larnick, a dairy, beef and sheep farm in the beautiful Looe Valley, four miles from picturesque Looe and Polperro where we welcome guests from February to November. The character farmhouse offers twin, double and family rooms, all en suite. The rooms are spacious and have comfy armchairs, colour TV, tea/coffee facilities, electric blankets and heating. The family room is in a downstairs annexe overlooking the garden. There is a sitting room with colour TV and log fires on cold evenings and the beamed dining room has separate tables. Bed and Breakfast from £17. No smoking.

LOOE. Mrs Lynda Wills, Polgover Farm, Widegates, Looe PL13 1PY (01503 240248). Working

farm. Polgover Farm is situated in picturesque countryside, four miles from Looe on the B3252 and ideally situated to explore Cornwall and South Devon. Local attractions include horse riding, golf, fishing, water sports, Monkey Sanctuary and many beaches. There is always a warm welcome at Polgover's spacious 16th century Listed farmhouse, where you can have a peaceful and relaxing holiday. There are three tastefully decorated bedrooms, all with washbasins and tea/coffee facilities. Guests' bathroom. Lounge with colour TV incorporating breakfast room with separate tables. Sorry, no pets. Open Easter to October. Ample parking. Bed and Breakfast from £14. Weekly and child reductions. Brochure available. Also modern, six-berth fully equipped self catering caravan in its own garden available at the farm.

LOOE. Mrs D. Eastley, Bake Farm, Pelynt, Looe PL13 2QQ (01503 220244). Working farm. This is an

old farmhouse, bearing the Trelawnay Coat of Arms (1610), situated midway between Looe and Fowey. There are three double bedrooms all with washbasins and night storage heaters; bathroom/toilet; shower room/toilet; combined sitting/diningroom. Children welcome at reduced rates, babysitting available. Sorry, no pets. Open from May to October. Plenty of fresh farm food, a lot of home produce including Cornish clotted cream and an abundance of roasts. A car is essential for touring the area, ample parking. There is much to see and do here — horse riding four miles, golf seven. The sea is only five miles away and there is shark fishing at Looe. SAE, please for terms for Evening Meal, Bed and Breakfast. Cleanliness guaranteed.

LOOE. Mrs Jean Henly, Bucklawren Farm, St. Martin, Looe PL13 1NZ (01503 240738; Fax: 01503

240481). 🦚🦚🦚 *HIGHLY COMMENDED.* **Working farm.** Bucklawren is situated deep in the unspoilt countryside yet only one mile from the beach, two and a half miles from Looe and only one mile from the Woolly Monkey Sanctuary. It is mentioned in the Domesday Book, but the manor house is now replaced by a 19th century spacious farmhouse, which has a large garden and beautiful sea views. We offer excellent accommodation in en suite and family rooms, with farmhouse cooking in a friendly relaxed atmosphere. There is ample parking. Open all year. Reduced rates for children. Bed and Breakfast from £17 to £19 per person per night; Evening Meal £9 (optional). Brochure on request. Farm Holiday Bureau member.

Bucklawren Farm

LOOE. Mrs J.M. Gill, Cleese Farm, Nomansland, Looe PL13 1PB (01503 240224). Cleese Farm is a

dairy farm, just off the main B3253 Looe Road, in an ideal position for touring Cornwall. Sandy beach at Looe one and a half miles, Monkey Sanctuary, golf course, horse riding, water sports within five minutes' drive. Also relaxing woodland walks on farm. Set in beautiful unspoilt countryside. All rooms have sea and valley views, washbasins and tea/coffee making facilities. We offer a friendly atmosphere, babysitting, ample parking. Pets welcome. Garden furniture available. Bed and Breakfast from £13.50.

If you've found
FARM HOLIDAY GUIDES
of service please tell your friends

LOOE near. Jane and Barry Wynn, Harescombe Lodge, Watergate, Near Looe PL13 2NE (01503 263158). Harescombe Lodge is a country guest house situated 'twixt Looe and Polperro in the secluded picturesque hamlet of Watergate. Once the shooting lodge of the Trelawne Estate, home of the Trelawney family. Beautiful river views and walks with interesting wildlife. Peaceful surroundings, idyllic location appealing to the discerning visitor to South East Cornwall. All bedrooms comfortably furnished with en suite facilities and tea/coffee making. Ample off-road parking. Open all year. Unsuitable for children under 12 years. Bed and Breakfast from £17; Evening Meal optional. AA QQQQ.

MARAZION near. Jenny Birchall, Mount View House, Varfell, Ludgvan, Penzance TR20 8AW (01736 710179). Mount View House is a Victorian former farmhouse standing in half an acre of gardens overlooking St. Michael's Mount. The house is furnished in traditional style and offers one room with sea views and another with rural views. Rooms have washbasins, central heating and tea/coffee making facilities. Guests' WC and shower room; sitting/dining room with open fire. Children welcome, cot available. Situated approximately three miles from Penzance and five miles from St. Ives. We are the ideal touring stopover. Our close proximity to the heliport (one mile) makes us ideal stopover en route to the Scilly Isles. Bed and Breakfast from £14 per person per night. Self catering accommodation also available, please telephone for details.

MEVAGISSEY. Mrs Jane Youlden, Steep House, Portmellon Cove, Mevagissey PL26 2PH (01726 843732). ♥ ♥ Steep House stands in an acre of ground by the sea, in a natural cove which has a safe, sandy beach 20 yards from the large garden. Comfortable, centrally heated double bedrooms with washbasins and sea or beach views, colour TV and tea/coffee maker; some en suite. English Breakfast served overlooking Portmellon Cove. Covered summertime swimming pool. Guests welcome all year. Modest prices, special weekly and winter break rates. Residential drinks licence. Private parking. Fire Certificate. All enquiries welcomed.

MEVAGISSEY. Mrs Anne Hennah, Treleaven Farm, Mevagissey PL26 6RZ (01726 842413). Working farm. Treleaven Farm is situated in quiet, pleasant surroundings overlooking the village and the sea. The 200-acre mixed farm is well placed for visitors to enjoy the many attractions of Mevagissey with its quaint narrow streets and lovely shops. Fishing and boat trips are available and very popular. The house offers a warm and friendly welcome with the emphasis on comfort, cleanliness and good food using local produce. A licensed bar and solar heated swimming pool add to your holiday enjoyment, together with a games room and putting green. Tastefully furnished throughout, with central heating, there are five double bedrooms and one family bedroom, all en suite with tea/coffee making facilities and TV; bathroom, two toilets. Sittingroom and diningroom. Open February to November for Evening Dinner, Bed and Breakfast from £28; Bed and Breakfast from £17. Sorry, no pets. SAE, please, for particulars or telephone.

CORNISH CUISINE!

The traditional Cornish Pasty was originally the tin-miners' portable lunch — shaped like a torpedo to fit in his pocket! The filling is usually mutton mixed with potatoes and swedes, and is enclosed in pastry pinched high along its entire length. Another Cornish speciality is Stargazey Pie, where pilchards are arranged in a dish like the spokes of a wheel, the pastry cover being cut to allow the eyes to gaze out. And to finish off — a clotted cream tea with scones and strawberry jam!

MEVAGISSEY. Mrs Dawn Rundle, Lancallan Farm, Mevagissey, St. Austell PL26 6EW (01726 842284). Lancallan is a large 17th century farmhouse on a working 200 acre dairy and beef farm in a beautiful rural setting, one mile from Mevagissey and surrounded by lovely coastal walks and sandy beaches. We are well situated for day trips throughout Cornwall. Enjoy a traditional farmhouse breakfast in a warm and friendly atmosphere. Accommodation comprises one family room, one double room; bathroom; lounge with colour TV and tea-making facilities. Terms available on request, reductions for children. SAE please.

MEVAGISSEY. Mrs Linda Hennah, Kerryanna Country House, Treleaven Farm, Mevagissey PL26 6RZ (01726 843558). 🌸🌸🌸 *HIGHLY COMMENDED.* **Working farm.** AA QQQQ Selected; FHB Member. Kerryanna Country House enjoys a superb position overlooking the quaint fishing village of Mevagissey surrounded by rambling farmland, abundant wildlife and flowers. You are welcome to meet our goats, ponies and assorted chickens. Swim in our beautiful outdoor pool — heated May to September — or try your skills in the games barn or putting green. All rooms are en-suite with colour TV and tea/coffee facilities. Large lounge with open fire and there is a cocktail bar in our plant-filled conservatory. Local fish, vegetables and meat used daily in our lovingly prepared dishes with plenty of choice. Bed and Breakfast or Bed, Breakfast and Dinner. Colour brochure.

MULLION. Mrs Joan Hyde, Campden House, The Commons, Mullion TR12 7HZ (01326 240365). Campden House offers comfortable accommodation in a peaceful setting with large gardens and a beautiful sea view. It is within easy reach of Mullion, Polurrian and Poldhu Coves, and is ideally situated for exploring the beautiful coast and countryside of the Lizard. Mullion golf course is less than one mile away. All eight bedrooms have handbasins with hot and cold water and comfortable beds; some rooms have en suite showers. There is a large sun lounge, TV lounge with colour TV and a large dining room and bar. Guests have access to the lounges, bedrooms and gardens at all times. Children and pets welcome. Bed and Breakfast £15.

MULLION. Margaret Hobday, Gweal an Drea Guesthouse, Polurrian Cove, Mullion, Near Helston TR12 7HB (01326 240341; Fax: 01326 240039). Mullion is a pretty village on the unspoilt, picturesque Lizard Peninsula, the warmest, most southerly point on mainland Britain. Recommended guesthouse next to secluded sandy beach and within walking distance of village pubs. Surrounded by beautiful National Trust coastline. Tea/coffee facilities and TV in spacious en suite rooms. Large comfortable lounge with open fire. Separate lounge with video and book library. Pets welcome. Non-smoking. Bed and Breakfast £17 to £22 per day. Reduced rates October to March. Evening Meals available. Lizard Peninsula Tourism Association recommended. "Wonderful — a real find!" "Great hospitality and perfect location."

NEWQUAY. Mike and Doris Mortimer, Pensalda, 98 Henver Road, Newquay TR7 3BL (01637 874601). Tourist Board Listed. Take a break in the "Heart of Cornwall". An ideal location from which to explore and enjoy the finest coastline and beaches in Europe. A warm and friendly welcome awaits you at our family-run guest house, situated on the main A3058 approximately half a mile from town and close to beaches and amenities. Accommodation available in one twin, one single, two double and two family bedrooms including two chalets situated in pleasant and peaceful garden surroundings. En suite rooms available. All have colour TV, tea making facilities. We have an excellent reputation for serving good freshly prepared food with choice of menu. Hot and cold snacks and packed lunches available on request. Licensed bar. Central heating. Parking on premises. Fire Certificate. Bed and Breakfast from £13; Bed, Breakfast and Evening Dinner from £17 per day. Special weekly terms, Bargain Breaks and reduced rates for Senior Citizens early and late season available. Brochure on request or phone for details.

NEWQUAY. Mrs B.L. Oakes, Shepherds Farm, Fiddlers Green, St. Newlyn East, Newquay TR8 5NW
(01872 540502). 🐾 🐾 *HIGHLY COMMENDED.* **Working**

farm, join in. A warm welcome awaits you on our family-run 700 acre mixed working farm. Come and share our warm and friendly atmosphere with first class service in affordable quality accommodation. Cleanliness guaranteed. All rooms en suite and have colour TV and tea making facilities. Large garden. Central location, ideal for touring. The farm is set in rural, small hamlet of Fiddlers Green three miles from beautiful Cornish coastline, five miles from Newquay; 20 minutes from south coast. Glorious sandy beaches, ideal for surfing, little rivers for the very young. Beautiful breathtaking views and walks along scenic clifftops. One and a half miles from National Trust property of Trerice. Good pub food close by. Come and join us! Bed and Breakfast from £15 to £17. Free horse riding seasonal.

LANTERN COTTAGE
Trebudannon, Newquay, Cornwall TR8 4LP

Lovely old farm cottage, with beamed ceilings, leaded double glazed windows, log fire and central heating. Situated in the tiny hamlet of Trebudannon, secluded yet close enough to town and beach entertainments. A car is essential to take you down the picturesque country lanes. Sheep and horses graze nearby. Three bedrooms, bathroom, large lounge/dining room. Ample parking. Bed linen supplied. £1 meter. SAE for further details:

Mrs Joy Weldhen, 'Panorama', Trebudannon, Newquay, Cornwall TR8 4LP
Telephone 01637 880346

NEWQUAY. Porth Enodoc Hotel, 4 Esplanade Road, Pentire, Newquay TR7 1PY (01637 872372).

🐾 🐾 🐾 Standing in its own grounds overlooking Fistral Beach and Newquay Golf Course this delightful hotel offers a warm friendly welcome. Family owned and managed. Delicious home cooking. There are 15 well appointed bedrooms, most with sea views, all with en suite facilities, colour TV, radio/intercom/child listening, tea/coffee making and central heating. There is a comfortable bar and the lounge and dining room have panoramic views over the Bay. Parking space for all within the hotel grounds. Bed and Breakfast from £15 daily; Dinner, Bed and Breakfast from £129 to £185 per week including VAT. Short Breaks available throughout the year. AA QQQQ, RAC Highly Acclaimed. Self catering cottage also available.

See also Colour Display Advertisement **NEWQUAY near. Mr and Mrs Rowlands, Crantock Plains Farm, Near Newquay TR8 5PH (01637 830253).** Charming character farmhouse in peaceful countryside. Comfort, home cooking and personal service combine to make an enjoyable, relaxing holiday. Crantock Plains Farm is situated two and a half miles from Newquay and half a mile off the A3075 Newquay-Redruth road. One and a half miles to the village of Crantock with Post Office, village stores, two pubs and beautiful sandy beach. Riding stables and many sporting activities nearby. Choice of four doubles (one twin en-suite), two family bedrooms; ground floor bedrooms are available; shower room, toilets. Electric blankets for your comfort on chilly nights. Sittingroom and diningroom. Home grown vegetables where available. Table licence. Sorry, no pets. Bed, Breakfast and Evening Meal or Bed and Breakfast. Terms and brochure on request with SAE please. Non-smoking establishment. Cream Tea Award. Award winners of "Newquay in Bloom" 1990, 1991 and 1992.

See also Colour Display Advertisement **NEWQUAY near. Marian and Derrick Molloy, Tregurrian Hotel, Watergate Bay, Near Newquay TR8 4AB (01637 860280).** Peaceful position between Newquay and Padstow — 100 yards from glorious sandy beach and spectacular Atlantic coastline. Open Easter to November, 27 rooms (most en-suite) have tea makers, radio/listening, heaters and colour TV. Heated pool sun patio, games room, solarium. Licensed. Central for touring Cornwall; parties and coaches by arrangement. Spring and Autumn Breaks. Dinner, Bed and Breakfast £120 to £230 inclusive. Children welcome at reduced rates. Brochure from resident proprietors **Marian and Derrick Molloy.**

See also Colour Display Advertisement NEWQUAY near. **Dalswinton Country House Hotel, St. Mawgan, Near Newquay TR8 4EZ (01637 860385).** ♛♛♛ An old Cornish house of immense character in one and a half acres of secluded grounds, overlooking the beautiful Valley of Lanherne with views to the sea. Ideally situated between Newquay and Padstow, reputed to be the finest coastline in Europe. Excellent beaches and coves within one and a half miles with many picturesque walks. Some of the best coarse fishing in Cornwall, two new golf courses, plus horse riding are all available locally. The Hotel offers superb cooking in a comfortable, friendly atmosphere. Bed and Breakfast from £17.50 per night, weekly from £110; Dinner, Bed and Breakfast from £155. Bargain Breaks available. Open all year including Christmas and New Year. Colour brochure on request.

PADSTOW. **Mrs A. Woosman-Mills, Mother Ivey Cottage, Trevose Head, Padstow PL28 8SL (Tel & Fax: 01841 520329).** Mother Ivey Cottage is an old tradi-

tionally built Cornish house, furnished with antiques and having stunning sea views. The area is renowned for swimming, fishing and surfing. There is also a Championship Golf Course nearby. Bedrooms have en suite bathrooms and twin beds. There is a TV and sitting room for guests' use and evening meals are available with notice. There is easy access for many National Trust properties, historic fishing villages and the working harbour at Padstow. Car essential, ample parking. Bed and Breakfast from £20.

PADSTOW. **Andrew and Sue Hamilton, Trevone Bay Hotel, Trevone, Near Padstow PL28 8QS (01841 520243; Fax: 01841 521195).** ♛♛♛

COMMENDED. On arrival relax with a pot of tea then stroll through the tranquil village to the beautiful sandy bay. Follow the coast path along rocky bay then back across the fields to your comfortable Hotel. Does this tempt you? How about an excellent home cooked meal, coffee watching the sunset and an evening socialising in the bar. Our hotel is non-smoking throughout. All bedrooms en suite. Ideal for walking, touring, bird watching or relaxing on the beach. From £29 for Dinner, Bed and Breakfast. Open Easter to October. If this sounds like your sort of holiday write or phone for brochure.

PAR. **Jeremy and Jill Rowe, Tregaminion Farm, Menabilly, Par PL24 2TL (01726 812442).** En suite Bed and Breakfast accommodation with or without Evening Meal throughout the year in a traditional Cornish Farmhouse.

Nestling in the hollows of the South Cornish Coast, eight miles from St. Austell and three miles from the ancient Port of Fowey. The farmhouse is set deep within Du Maurier countryside and can offer you peaceful accommodation on a typical working farm. It lies on both the major footpaths of Cornwall, the Saints Way and the South Cornish Coastal Path, and is also within easy walking distance of the private beach of Polkerris where you can also find the Rashleigh Inn Pub, open all year for excellent pub food. Well behaved pets welcome. Please write or telephone for further information.

PENZANCE. Mrs Monica Olds, Mulfra Farm, Newmill, Penzance TR20 8XP (01736 63940). Superb accommodation is offered on this 50 acre hill farm high on the Penwith moors. The 17th century stone built farmhouse has far reaching views, is attractively furnished and offers two double en suite bedrooms with tea/coffee trays and TV. The comfortable lounge with inglenook fireplace and Cornish stone oven has a good selection of books and TV. Diningroom with separate tables, sun lounge and good food. Car essential, ample parking. Ideal centre for exploring West Cornwall's beaches and places of historic interest. We even have our own Iron Age village, as well as cows, calves and horses. Warm friendly atmosphere. Beautiful walking country. Penzance three miles, St. Ives nine miles. Bed, Breakfast and Evening Meal from £125 per week. Further details sent with pleasure.

PENZANCE. Mrs Penny Lally, Rose Farm, Chyanhal, Buryas Bridge, Penzance TR19 6AN (01736 731808). 🐾🐾 *COMMENDED.* Rose Farm is a small working farm in a little hamlet close to the picturesque fishing villages of Mousehole and Newlyn and seven miles from Lands End. The 200-year-old granite farmhouse is cosy with pretty, en suite rooms. One double, one family suite and a romantic 15th century four-poster room in barn annexe. We have all manner of animals, from pedigree cattle to pot-bellied pigs! Open all year (closed Christmas).

PORT ISAAC. Chris and Liz Bolton, Trewetha Farm, Port Isaac PL29 3RU (01208 880256). 18th century traditional Cornish Farmhouse with 20 acres of grazing land in "Betjeman country", on the Heritage Coast. Superb sea and countryside views. Sheep, miniature Shetland ponies kept. Ideal area for water sports, beaches, fishing, bird watching and walking; footpath to beach from the farm. Wadebridge is nine miles and has sports facilities and cycling along old railway track to Padstow. Separate dining room and sittingroom with colour TV. Access to house throughout day. Tea-making facilities. Reductions for children. Bed and Breakfast; Vegetarians welcome. Fire Certificate held. Also available, self catering cottages. Member of the Cornwall Tourist Board.

ROSELAND PENINSULA. Mrs Shirley E. Pascoe, Court Farm, Philleigh, Truro TR2 5NB (01872 580313). Working farm, join in. Situated in the heart of the Roseland Peninsula at Philleigh, with its lovely Norman church and 17th century Roseland Inn, this spacious and attractive old farmhouse, set in over an acre of garden, offers Bed and Breakfast accommodation. There are double, single and family bedrooms with washbasins and tea making facilities; bathroom, separate toilet; large comfortable lounge with colour TV. Enjoy a full English breakfast in the traditional farmhouse kitchen. Children welcome, cot, high chair, babysitting available. Sorry, no pets indoors. Car essential — ample parking. The family livestock and arable farm includes 50 acres of woodlands which border the beautiful Fal Estuary providing superb walking, picnic areas and bird-watching opportunities, while the nearest beaches are just over two miles away. Please write or telephone for brochure and terms.

CORNWALL – FUN FOR ALL THE FAMILY

Colliford Lake Park, Bolventor, Bodmin; Flambards Triple Theme Park, near Helston; Goonhilly Satellite Earth Station, near Helston; Lappa Valley Railway and Leisure Park, Newquay; Merlin's Magic Land, Lelant, St. Ives; Paradise Park, Hayle; Poldark Mine, Helston; St. Michael's Mount, Marazion; Tamar Otter Park, near Launceston; Tunnels Through Time, Newquay; Tropical Bird Gardens, Padstow; World of Model Railways, Mevagissey.

SALTASH. Peter and Violet Batten, Burcombe Farm, St. Dominick, Saltash PL12 6SH (01579 350217; Fax: 01579 350105). 🐦🐦 *APPROVED.*

Burcombe Farm extends to 160 acres, mainly arable, corn and beef cattle with a history that dates back to 1722. It is an ideal spot for a quiet holiday with many walks in this scenic area of Cornwall. The farmhouse is large with wonderful views across the River Tamar to Plymouth and as far as the eye can see. Bedrooms are en suite and have colour TV and hot drink making facilities; lounge with colour TV, dining room. Car parking space. Sorry no children. Bed and full English Breakfast £20 per person per night, two or more nights £17.50. Brochure giving full details available on request.

ST. AGNES. Cleaderscroft Hotel, 16 British Road, St. Agnes TR5 0TZ (01872 552349). This small,

detached, family-run Victorian hotel stands in the heart of the picturesque village of St. Agnes, convenient for many outstanding country and coastal walks. Set in mature gardens and having a separate children's play area we can offer peace and relaxation after visits to the beach, which is approximately half a mile away. Accommodation is provided in generous sized rooms, mostly en suite with colour TV. Public rooms comprise lounge, bar, dining rooms and games room. Non smoking and smoking areas. Private parking. Bed and Breakfast from £20.00 with discounts for children sharing. Evening set menu available. We also offer a self-contained flat, details on request.

See also Colour Display Advertisement **ST. AGNES. Mr S. Manico, Rosemundy House Hotel, St. Agnes TR5 0UF (01872 552101).** 🐦🐦🐦 *COMMENDED.* Rosemundy House Hotel occupies a most sheltered and secluded position in the village of St. Agnes and within a mile of Trevaunance Cove beach. Built around 1780, Rosemundy has been tastefully extended to provide a charming diningroom and many bedrooms with en-suite facilities. Our amenities include an attractive licensed bar, 45ft outdoor heated swimming pool and a large games room with table tennis, pool, snooker, darts, etc. The informal grounds comprise some four acres of gardens and woodland secluding the property and making Rosemundy ideal for a restful holiday. Badminton, croquet and putting may be enjoyed in the grounds. Our hotel boasts a warm and friendly atmosphere with good English home cooking. Dinner, Bed and Breakfast from £165 to £265 per week, Bed and Breakfast from £140 to £240 weekly (including VAT).

ST. AGNES. Dorothy Gill-Carey, Penkerris, Penwinnick Road, St. Agnes TR5 0PA (01872 552262). 🐦🐦 An enchanting Edwardian residence in garden with large lawn in unspoilt Cornish village. AA, RAC and Les Routiers Recommended. Penkerris has fields on one side yet there are pubs, shops, etc only 150 yards away on the other side. Attractive dining room, lounge with colour TV, video, piano and log fires in winter. Bedrooms with washbasins, TV, kettles, shaver points, radios; en suite if required. There is a shower room as well as bathrooms. Delicious meals, traditional roasts, fresh vegetables and home made fruit tarts. Beaches, swimming, surfing, gliding and magnificent cliff walks nearby. From £15 per night Bed and Breakfast and from £22.50 with Dinner. Open all year.

PUBLISHER'S NOTE

While every effort is made to ensure accuracy, we regret that FHG Publications cannot accept responsibility for errors, omissions or misrepresentation in our entries or any consequences thereof. Prices in particular should be checked because we go to press early. We will follow up complaints but cannot act as arbiters or agents for either party.

ST. AUSTELL. Mrs Liz Berryman, Polgreen Farm, London Apprentice, St. Austell PL26 7AP (01726

75151). Polgreen is a family-run dairy farm nestling in the Pentewan Valley in an Area of Outstanding Natural Beauty. One mile from the coast and four miles from the picturesque fishing village of Mevagissey. A perfect location for a relaxing holiday in the glorious Cornish countryside. Centrally situated, Polgreen is ideally placed for touring all of Cornwall's many attractions. Pentewan Valley Leisure Trail adjoining, Lost Gardens of Heligan three miles. Bed and Breakfast accommodation includes en suite rooms, colour TV in bedrooms, tea/coffee facilities, guests' lounge. Children welcome. Terms from £15 per night, £98 per week.

See also Colour Display Advertisement **ST. AUSTELL. Suzanne Manuell, Manor Farm, Burngullow, St. Austell PL26 7TQ (Tel & Fax: 01726 72242).** Come and stay on our family-run dairy farm set amidst 450 acres of Cornish countryside. Our Grade II Listed Georgian farmhouse offers en suite and family en suite facilities with colour TV, tea/coffee in all rooms. Relax in the spacious gardens with camelias and rhododendrons or roam around the fields and nearby woodland. Manor Farm is centrally located for exploring the character of Cornwall's unique countryside and coastline. Tariff from £17.

ST. BURYAN. Mrs Julia Hosking, Boskenna Home Farm, St. Buryan, Penzance TR19 6DQ (Tel &

Fax: 01736 810705). ETB Listed *APPROVED.* A warm welcome awaits you at Boskenna Home Farm, a working dairy farm situated on the south coast five miles from Land's End. Why not relax on one of the many beautiful beaches, visit the legendary picturesque coves or take advantage of the striking coastal walks. Enjoy the friendly atmosphere and excellent farmhouse breakfast. Bed and Breakfast from £15 per person with reductions for children. Two double rooms and one twin-bedded room with tea/coffee facilities, washbasins and heating; lounge with TV; separate dining room. Large garden for guests to relax. Please ask for brochure. Sorry no smoking.

ST. IVES. Mrs N.I. Mann, Trewey Farm, Zennor, St. Ives TR26 3DA (01736 796936). Working farm. On the main St Ives to Land's End road, this attractive granite-built farmhouse stands among gorse and heather-clad hills, half-a-mile from the sea and five miles from St Ives. The mixed farm covers 300 acres, with Guernsey cattle and fine views of the sea; lovely cliff and hill walks. Guests will be warmly welcomed and find a friendly atmosphere. Five double, one single and three family bedrooms (all with washbasins); bathroom, toilets; sittingroom, diningroom. Cot, high chair and babysitting available. Pets allowed. Car essential — parking. Open all year. Electric heating. Bed and Breakfast only. SAE for terms, please.

ST. IVES. Mrs C.E. Blewett, Menwidden Farm, Ludgvan, Penzance TR20 8BN (01736 740415). ETB

Listed *APPROVED.* Menwidden Farm is centrally situated in west Cornwall four miles from St. Ives (north coast) and three miles from Marazion (south coast). Within easy reach of Land's End and The Lizard. Comfortable bedrooms and good home cooking including roast meats, pasties and Cornish cream. Two double, one twin, one family and one single bedrooms, one with washbasin; bathroom, shower room and toilet; sittingroom, diningroom. Cot, high chair, reduced rates for children. Pets allowed. Open March to October. Car essential — parking. Lots of interesting places nearby including many beaches and coves, St Michael's Mount, Bird Paradise. Fire Certificate held. AA Listed and past winner of Farm Holiday Guide Diploma. Evening Meal, Bed and Breakfast from £120 per week or Bed and Breakfast from £15 per night.

ST. IVES. Mrs Meg O'Connor, Little Trink, St Ives TR26 3JG (01736 740376). Little Trink is situated on the slopes of Trink Hill in a peaceful rural position, with wonderful views across the surrounding countryside from all the bedrooms. Ideal for moorland, country and coastal walking, beaches and horse riding. Approximately three miles from St Ives, three miles from Hayle and seven miles from Penzance. Accommodation comprises two double bedded rooms and one twin bedded room, all with washbasins. Shared bathroom. Separate lounge with TV. Sorry, no smoking. Ample parking. Bed and Breakfast from £12.00 per person per night.

ST. IVES. Miss B. Delbridge, Bella Vista Guest House, St. Ives Road, Carbis Bay, St. Ives TR26 2SF

(01736 796063). ✿ First class accommodation, highly recommended, satisfaction guaranteed. Extensive views of sea and coastline. Washbasins in all rooms. Colour TV. Central heating. Own keys to rooms. Free parking on premises. Personal supervision. Fresh farm produce. Radio intercom and baby listening service in all rooms. Fire Certificate held. Bed and Breakfast from £15. Open all year. Non-smokers welcome. SAE for brochure.

ST. MAWES/TRURO. Mrs A. Palmer, Trenestrall Farm, Ruan High Lanes, Truro TR2 5LX (01872

TRENESTRALL FARM

Ruanhighlanes
Truro, Cornwall

501259). Working farm, join in. A tastefully restored 200 year old barn, now a farmhouse offering comfortable accommodation on a 300 acre mixed farm. Situated on beautiful Roseland Peninsula, within easy reach of St. Mawes and Truro. Close to safe beaches and beautiful Fal estuary for sailing, bird watching etc. Accommodation consists of double or twin rooms with washbasins and tea/coffee facilities, own sittingroom with TV, bathroom and shower room. Amenities include private fishing lake and snooker room, table tennis and pony riding. Pride taken with presentation of food using home produce whenever possible. Children welcome, babysitting service. Pets accepted. Phone or write for details of Bed and Breakfast from £14 per person per night.

See also Colour Display Advertisement **TINTAGEL. Bossiney House Hotel, Tintagel PL34 0AX (01840**

770240; Fax: 01840 770501). ✿✿✿ An ideal base to tour and explore an area packed with interest and beauty. Bossiney House is situated about half a mile from Tintagel on the cliffs overlooking a magnificent stretch of coastline. Nearly all of the 19 bedrooms have sea or country views, colour TV, hair dryers and tea/coffee making facilities. Spacious diningroom and cocktail bar; coffee lounge. Good English cooking with excellent choice of menu. Personal attention. Indoor heated pool, sauna, solarium. Nearby activities include surfing, riding, golf, squash, pony trekking and shark fishing. Reductions for children. Open Easter to end of October.

TINTAGEL. Mrs Ann Jones, Grange Cottage, Bossiney, Tintagel PL34 0AX (01840 770487). A

warm, friendly atmosphere greets you at Grange Cottage. Built of stone and slate, the original cottage is approximately 400 years old. Close to the coastal footpath and rugged cliffs and within easy walking dostance to Tintagel Castle and sandy cove. The comfortable accommodation has full central heating and comprises two large double/family bedrooms with colour TV and tea making, and a small single bedroom. All rooms have washbasins. Dining room has a character granite fireplace and beamed ceiling; traditional English or vegetarian breakfast served. Ideal location for walking or touring. Comfort and cleanliness assured. Open Easter to October. Bed and Breakfast from £15 per person. Non smoking. Cornwall Registered Acccommodation.

CORNWALL

There's much more to Cornwall than just sand and sea. Take time to explore the traces of the past at Chysauster Ancient Village, near Penzance, a collection of huge stone houses dating from prehistoric times, and Pendennis Castle, Falmouth, built by Henry VIII to guard against invasion. The legend of King Arthur lives on at Tintagel Castle and at Dozmary Pool, Bodmin Moor, reputed to be where he threw back the sword, Excalibur.

TRURO. Mrs J.C. Gartner, Laniley House, Near Trispen, Truro TR4 9AU (01872 75201). Laniley

House, a Gentleman's Residence built in 1830, stands in two acres of gardens amidst beautiful, unspoilt countryside, yet only three miles from the Cathedral city of Truro. Ideally situated for discovering Cornwall and close to major towns, beaches and National Trust properties, Laniley offer unequalled privacy and peace. Our aim is to make you feel at home, giving each person individual attention; only six guests at any one time. Accommodation consists of three large double bedrooms, two with washbasins, one with en suite bathroom; separate breakfast room; lounge with colour TV. All rooms with TV, radio and Teasmaid. Regret unable to accommodate children under 13 years, also no pets. Bed and Breakfast from £17 per person. SAE, please. Highly recommended accommodation.

TRURO. Mrs S. Hicks, Pengelly Farm, St. Erme, Truro TR4 9BG (Tel & Fax: 01872 510245).

Working farm. Pengelly Farm is a working dairy farm set in 230 acres, situated 10 minutes' drive from Truro and central for both the north and south coasts of Cornwall. The farmhouse has been traditionally restored and offers both ensuite bedrooms and bedrooms with hot and cold running water with shared bathroom facilities. We specialise in Bed and Breakfast accommodation and you will find several local pubs and restaurants within 10 minutes' drive that provide excellent food at reasonable prices. Children are always welcome. Bed and Breakfast from £15. For further details please write or telephone. Also self catering unit available.

TRURO. Mrs Margaret Retallack, Treberrick Farm, Tregony, Truro TR2 5SP (01872 530247).

Working farm. Treberrick is a 250 acre working farm situated on the edge of the Roseland Peninsula and two miles from unspoilt beaches at Carhays and Portholland and six miles from Mevagissey. Most parts of Cornwall reached by car within one hour. Guests are welcome to walk around the farm. Spacious house, bedrooms have washbasin and tea-making facilities. Diningroom with separate tables, lounge with TV always available. Guests can expect traditional home cooked food using own produce where possible. Maximum number of guests six. Sorry no smoking. Bed and Breakfast from £15; Evening Meal available. Near Heligon Manor Gardens — Restoration Project. Please telephone or write for brochure.

CUMBRIA — including "The Lakes"

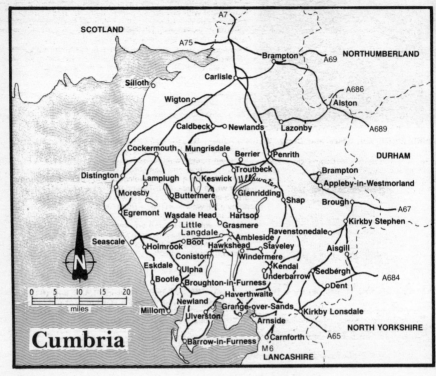

AMBLESIDE. Peter and Anne Hart, Bracken Fell, Outgate, Ambleside LA22 0NH (015394 36289).

Bracken Fell

👑🐝 *COMMENDED.* Bracken Fell is situated in beautiful open countryside between Ambleside and Hawkshead, in the picturesque hamlet of Outgate. Ideally positioned for exploring the Lake District and within easy reach of Coniston, Windermere, Ambleside, Grasmere and Keswick. All major outdoor activities are catered for nearby including windsurfing, sailing, fishing, pony trekking, etc. All six bedrooms have private facilities, complimentary tea/coffee making and outstanding views. There is central heating throughout, a comfortable lounge and diningroom, together with ample parking and two acres of gardens. Fire Certificate. Open all year. Bed and Breakfast from £20. Non-smoking. Self catering accommodation is also available. Write or phone for brochure and tariff.

AMBLESIDE. Mike and Gill Dixon, The Howes, Stockghyll Brow, Ambleside LA22 0QZ (015394 32444). ETB Listed *COMMENDED.* The Howes is a modern

detached house situated in a very quiet and peaceful area of Ambleside with ample parking. Two minutes from Stockghyll waterfalls and five minutes from village centre. The rooms are all on the ground floor, purpose built and of a very high standard. En suite, colour TV, tea/coffee making facilities and, as an added luxury, your breakfast will be served in your room. The Howes is an ideal centre for walkers and touring guests, we know you will appreciate the comfort and friendly service provided. Bed and Breakfast £17.50 to £22.50. Non-smoking.

AMBLESIDE. Helen and Chris Green, Lyndhurst Hotel, Wansfell Road, Ambleside LA22 0EG

(015394 32421). ❦❦ COMMENDED. RAC Acclaimed, AA Listed. Attractive Victorian Lakeland stone built, family-run small hotel with private car park, quietly situated in its own gardens. Lovely bedrooms, all en suite and with colour TV, tea/coffee trays. Four-poster bedroom for that special occasion. Scrumptious food, friendly service. Full central heating for all-year comfort. Cosy bar. Winter and Summer Breaks. A delightful base from which to explore the Lakes either by car or as a walker. Bed and Breakfast from £17.50 per person per night. Phone or write for colour brochure, please.

AMBLESIDE. Liz, Mary and Craig, Wanslea Guest House, Lake Road, Ambleside LA22 0DB

(015394 33884). ❦❦❦ Wanslea is a spacious family-run Victorian guest house with fine views, situated just a stroll from the village and lake shore with walks beginning at the door. We offer a friendly welcome and comfortable rooms, all of which have colour TV and tea/coffee trays. Most rooms are en suite. A good breakfast will start your day before you enjoy a fell walk or maybe a more leisurely stroll by the lake. Relax in our licensed residents' lounge with a real fire on winter evenings. Children are welcome and pets by arrangement. Bed and Breakfast from £16 per person. Evening Meal can be provided. Autumn, Winter, Spring Breaks at reduced rates. Brochure available.

AMBLESIDE. Mrs S. Briggs, High Wray Farm, High Wray, Near Ambleside LA22 0JE (015394

32280). Tourist Board Listed. Working farm. Charming 17th century olde worlde farmhouse once owned by Beatrix Potter. Original oak beams, cosy lounge with log burning fire, pretty colour co-ordinated bedrooms, one with en suite facilities. Heating and tea/coffee trays are in all rooms. Situated in a quiet unspoilt location, panoramic views and lake shore walks close by. A warm welcome awaits all who visit us, where comfort, cleanliness and personal attention are assured. Follow the B5286 from Ambleside towards Hawkshead then turn left for Wray. Follow road to High Wray, the farm is on the right. Families welcome. Terms from £15.50. FHG Diploma Winner.

AMBLESIDE. Anthony Marsden, Betty Fold, Hawkshead Hill, Ambleside LA22 0PS (015394

36611). ❦❦ HIGHLY COMMENDED. Betty Fold is a large country house in its own spacious grounds, rich in fauna and flora, with magnificent views and set in the heart of the Lake District National Park. Hawkshead, Coniston and Ambleside are all within easy reach and the beauty spot Tarn Hows is 20 minutes' walk away. This privately licensed guest house, run by the resident owner, offers Bed, Breakfast, Evening Meals and Packed Lunches. All bedrooms are en suite. Children are welcome, cots are available and babysitting can be arranged. Parties are particularly welcome from November to Easter. We regret, no pets in the guest house. Open all year. Terms approximately £34 per night for Bed, Breakfast and Evening Dinner. See also advertisement in SELF CATERING section of the guide.

AMBLESIDE. Mrs E. Culbert, Kingswood, Old Lake Road, Ambleside LA22 0AE (015394 34081). Kingswood is ideally situated near the town centre, yet off the main road. Ample car parking. Well equipped and comfortable bedrooms with washbasins and tea/coffee making facilities. Colour TV. Central heating. Single, double, twin and family rooms. Pets welcome. Open most of the year, with special bargain breaks off season. Non-smoking. Write or phone for rates and details.

AMBLESIDE. Jim and Joyce Ormesher, Rothay House, Rothay Road, Ambleside LA22 0EE

(015394 32434). Rothay House is an attractive modern detached Guest House, set in pleasant gardens with views of the surrounding fells. All bedrooms are comfortable and well furnished with en suite facilities, colour TV, tea and coffee trays. Our visitors are assured of warm and friendly service in attractive surroundings. The house is within easy walking distance of the village centre. Ambleside has a variety of interesting shops and restaurants and makes an ideal base for walking, touring or enjoying sailing, watersports and angling on Lake Windermere. Car not essential, but ample parking space in the grounds. Open all year. Bed and Breakfast from £18 to £22. Children welcome. Sorry, no pets. Winter Weekend Breaks available.

APPLEBY. Mrs Diana Dakin, Morningside, Morland, Penrith CA10 3AZ (01931 714393). Morn-

ingside is idyllically situated in the pretty village of Morland midway between Appleby and Penrith, in the beautiful Eden Valley. Convenient for touring all of Cumbria and only 10 miles from Ullswater, it is perfect for a relaxing break. Friendly, personal service is assured in the beautifully appointed ground floor twin-bedded room with en suite shower room, colour TV, hot drinks facilities plus the advantage of own entrance from private patio. A delicious breakfast is served in the bedroom overlooking the garden and village views. Central heating. Parking. Bed and Breakfast from £16 per person. No smoking please.

APPLETHWAITE. Mrs Rosalind Hunter, Croft House, Applethwaite, Near Keswick CA12 4PN

(017687 73693). Beautifully situated house, enjoying magnificent views of Lakeland mountains, in a lovely quiet village at the foot of Skiddaw, one-and-a-half miles from Keswick. An excellent base for touring all parts of the Lake District, walking, pony trekking and all Lakeland pursuits. A warm welcome is assured and good home cooking a speciality. The comfortable accommodation in our non-smoking house comprises three double, two single and two family rooms en-suite, all with washbasins and showers. Lounge, dining-room. Children welcome. Well-behaved pets accepted. Ample private parking. SAE, please, or telephone for terms for Bed and Full English Breakfast. Open all year.

BRAMPTON. Mrs Una Armstrong, Town Head Farm, Walton, Brampton CA8 2DJ (016977 2730).

Tourist Board Listed COMMENDED. Town Head offers comfortable and pleasant accommodation. Our 100 acre dairy/sheep farm is situated in the peaceful village of Walton overlooking the village green and commanding scenic views of the Pennines and Lakeland hills. An ideal base for touring the Lakes, Hadrian's Wall and Scottish Borders; three miles from Brampton, 10 miles from Carlisle — leave M6 at Junction 43. One double, one twin or family bedrooms with tea making facilities and TV; lounge/dining room. Children welcome. Open all year except Christmas and New Year. Bed and Breakfast from £14. Reduced rate for children and Short Breaks.

BRAMPTON. Mrs S. Graham, Miller Hill, Banks, Brampton CA6 7DE (016977 47298). Miller Hill is a beef and sheep stock rearing farm situated on Hadrian's Wall. For the sightseeing tourist it is steeped in history with Lanercost Priory only three and a half miles, Birdoswald Roman Fort only two and a half miles; Naworth Castle is also nearby. Alston the highest market town in England, Gretna Green, Bewcastle Cross, the Lakes and Scotland are all within easy reach. A warm welcome awaits guests at all times. One of the main attractions of our farmhouse are the house walls which are 52 inches thick. We offer a family room and a double room. Children welcome. Dogs by arrangement. Terms on request.

Terms quoted in this publication may be subject to increase if rises in costs necessitate

Peace and Seclusion at the
Fish
Hotel

ETB

The Fish Hotel, personally run by the proprietors,
Jean and John Richardson who are on hand at all times to ensure that
guests receive the warmest of welcomes and attention.
The Hotel is ideally situated in one of Lakeland's most beautiful valleys
between the two Lakes, Buttermere and Crummock Water
(five minutes' walk from each). The delightful village of Buttermere lies
at the foot of Honister Pass and Newlands Hause.

There are eleven pleasant rooms all of which have their own private
facilities and tea/coffee machine, direct dial telephones, radio alarms.
Children are welcome and have a 30% reduction if sharing a family
room. A comfortable lounge is at residents' disposal, and a separate
residents' lounge bar. A delightful restaurant renowned for serving
excellent food. The Hotel is fully centrally heated. Once the home of the
famous Mary Robinson, the Beauty of Buttermere, whose life story has
recently been the subject of a best selling novel. A Free House serving
traditional and cask conditioned ales and cider.

Members of British and English Lakes Tourist Boards.
Weekly rates from £200 for Dinner, Bed and Breakfast.
Nightly rates from £30.00 for Dinner, Bed and Breakfast.

MR & MRS JOHN RICHARDSON,
THE FISH HOTEL, BUTTERMERE,
VIA COCKERMOUTH, CUMBRIA CA13 9XA.
TELEPHONE BUTTERMERE (017687) 70253.

BRAMPTON. Mrs Ann Thompson, Low Rigg Farm, Walton, Brampton CA8 2DX (016977 3233).

Tourist Board Listed *COMMENDED.* We are a family-run dairy farm in beautiful Hadrian's Wall country, three miles Brampton, nine miles Carlisle. Conveniently situated for the Scottish Borders, Northumberland and the Lake District. The farmhouse is comfortably furnished with guests' own lounge, dining room. The bedrooms have king-size beds, tea/coffee facilities and clock radios. Free range eggs, homemade bread rolls and preserves are served for breakfast. Evening meals are available by arrangement. There is a large garden and ample parking space. Guests are welcome to view the farm activities including milking. Bed and Breakfast from £16; Evening Meals from £10. Reductions for children and more than one night's stay.

BRAMPTON near. Mrs Annabel Forster, High Nook Farm, Low Row, Brampton CA8 2LU (016977 46273). Tourist Board Listed. Working farm. Friendly

farmhouse with relaxing atmosphere and good home cooking. Situated one mile from Low Row village and four miles from Brampton in peaceful Irthing Valley. Beef cattle, sheep, goats and poultry are kept and visitors are allowed to wander around the farm. Conveniently situated for touring Northumberland, Lake District and Scottish Borders and only a few miles from Roman Wall, Lanercost Priory and Talkin Tarn. Accommodation comprises one double and one family room, lounge, TV; diningroom. Bed and Breakfast from £12. Light snacks available. Reductions for children under 12 years. Packed lunches available. Well controlled dogs accepted.

Swaledale Watch

Ours is a mixed farm of 300 acres situated in beautiful countryside within the Lake District National Park. Easy reach of Scottish Borders, Roman Wall, Eden Valley. Primarily a sheep farm (everyone loves lambing time), with 60 dairy cattle. Visitors are welcome to see farm animals and activities. Many interesting walks nearby or roam the peaceful fells where John Peel hunted. Enjoyed by many Cumbrian Way walkers. Very comfortable accommodation with excellent home cooking. All rooms have private facilities. Central heating. Tea making facilities. **Registered with the English Tourist Board 👑👑 Highly Commended. AA QQQQ Selected.** We are a friendly Cumbrian farming family and make you very welcome. Bed and Breakfast from £17.00 to £19.00; Evening Meal £10.00.

Mr & Mrs A. Savage, Swaledale Watch, Whelpo, Caldbeck CA7 8HQ   Tel: (016974) 78409

CARLISLE. Mrs Georgina Elwen, New Pallyards, Hethersgill, Carlisle CA6 6HZ (01228 577 308).

👑👑👑 *COMMENDED.* **Working farm, join in.** GOLD AWARD WINNER. Farmhouse filmed for BBC TV. Relax and see beautiful North Cumbria and the Borders. A warm welcome awaits you in our country farmhouse tucked away in the Cumbrian countryside, yet easily accessible from M6 Junction 44. In addition to the surrounding attractions there is plenty to enjoy, including hill walking, peaceful forests or sea trout/salmon fishing or just nestle down and relax with nature. Two double en suite, two family en suite rooms and one twin/single bedroom, all with tea/coffee making equipment. Bed and Breakfast from £20 per person, Dinner £13; Dinner, Bed and Breakfast weekly rates from £160 to £170. Menu choice. Self catering offered. Disabled facilities. We are proud to have won a National Salon Culinaire Award for the "Best Breakfast in Britain".

CARLISLE. Mrs M.N. Nichol, Croft End, Hurst, Ivegill, Carlisle CA4 0NL (017684 84362). Tourist Board Listed *COMMENDED.* **Working farm.** Comfortable Bed and Breakfast midway between Carlisle and Penrith, three miles west of Southwaite Service area; M6 Junction 41 and 42 just 10 minutes. Two double bedrooms. Children welcome. Sorry no pets. Bed and Breakfast from £15 to £16.

CARLISLE. Mrs Dorothy Nicholson, Gill Farm, Blackford, Carlisle (01228 75326). 🐾 In a delightful

setting on a beef and sheep farm, this Georgian style farmhouse dated 1740 offers a friendly welcome to all guests breaking journeys to or from Scotland or having a holiday in our beautiful countryside. Near Hadrian's Wall, Borders and Lake District. Golf, fishing, swimming and large agricultural auction market all nearby. Accommodation is in one double, one family and one twin or single bedrooms, all with washbasins, shaver points and tea/coffee making facilities; two bathrooms, shower; lounge with colour TV; separate diningroom. Open all year. Reductions for children; cot and babysitting available. Central heating. Car essential, good parking. Pets permitted. Telephone for further details.

CARLISLE. Marchmain Guest House, 151 Warwick Road, Carlisle CA1 2LU (01228 29551). 🐾

COMMENDED. A lovely Victorian house of character offering comfort and warm hospitality, central heating, vanity suite, shaver point, colour TV, hair dryer and welcome tray in ever room. Choice of single, double, twin and family accommodation. All guests have their own key for access at all times. Within easy reach of beautiful Lake District and only a few minutes' walk from Carlisle's historic city centre and cathedral; sports facilities available at Sands Leisure Centre and shopping in the picturesque Lanes. Easy access from M6 Junction 43. Full English breakfast, home cooked evening meals by arrangement. Well recommended by guests. From £16 per person per night.

CARLISLE. Mrs Elizabeth Woodmass, Howard House Farm, Gilsland, Carlisle CA6 7AJ (016977 47285). 🐾🐾 HIGHLY COMMENDED. **Working farm, join**

in. A 250 acre mixed farm with a 19th century stone-built farmhouse situated in a rural area overlooking the Irthing Valley on the Cumbria/Northumbria border. Half a mile from Gilsland village and Roman Wall; Haltwhistle five miles and the M6 at Carlisle, 18 miles. Good base for touring — Roman Wall, Lakes and Scottish Borders. Trout fishing on farm. Guests' lounge with colour TV where you can relax anytime in comfort. Diningroom. One double room en-suite, one twin and one family room with washbasins, bath or shower. All bedrooms have tea/coffee making facilities. Bathroom with shower, toilet. Children welcome at reduced rates. Sorry, no pets. Car essential — parking. Open January to December for Bed and Breakfast from £17 to £20; Evening Meal optional. Weekly terms available. SAE or telephone for brochure.

CARLISLE. Mrs Harrison, Clift House Farm, Carlisle CA6 6DE (01228 75237). Set on the "cliff"

overlooking the River Lyne "Clift House" offers Bed and Breakfast on a working farm. We are centrally situated for exploring historic Carlisle, South West Scotland, the Borders, Roman Wall Country, the Lakes, the Solway Coast and the Eden Valley. Five well appointed bedrooms with separate residents' lounge. Traditional full English breakfast. Beautiful walks and abundant wildlife. Good inns and restaurants nearby offering local fayre.

CHAPEL STILE. Mrs J. Rowand, Baysbrown Farm, Chapel Stile, Great Langdale, Ambleside LA22

9JZ (015394 37300). Working farm, join in. Baysbrown Farm is set at the beginning of the Langdale Valley. It has Herdwick sheep and beef cows with 835 acres of land. It is a good "stopping off" place for Cumbrian Way walkers and within easy reach of Ambleside (five miles), Windermere (nine miles), Coniston (six miles) and Hawkshead (nine miles). Enjoy a relaxing evening in front of an open log fire after a home cooked meal. Accommodation comprises one family, one twin room, one double room, all with tea/coffee making facilities. Reductions for children, cot provided. Non-smoking accommodation available. Pets welcome. Open February to October. Bed and Breakfast from £17.50; Evening Meal £9. ELDHCA Award.

COCKERMOUTH. Mrs Dorothy E. Richardson, Pardshaw Hall, Cockermouth CA13 0SP (01900 822607). Old farmhouse in small, quiet village, three and a half miles from Cockermouth with views to the fells. Children most welcome, cot, highchair and babysitting available, also large garden to play in. Pardshaw Hall is ideally situated for touring the Lakes and children delight in the miniature railway at Ravenglass; there are some lovely walks. Good home cooking with fresh produce. Accommodation in one double, one single and one family or twin rooms, most with washbasins. Log fires. Open all year. Sorry, no pets in house. Car essential, parking. Bed and Breakfast from £14; Evening Meal optional. Reduced rates for children.

CONISTON. Mrs M. Aldridge, Thwaite Cottage, Waterhead, Coniston LA21 8AJ (015394 41367).

COMMENDED. Thwaite Cottage is a beautiful 17th century former Lakeland farmhouse, half a mile east of Coniston Village and about 200 yards from the Lake (OS Ref: SD311977). It stands 100 yards from the road in a peaceful wooded garden. The cottage is centrally heated with log fires in Winter. There is a guests sittingroom with TV and tea/coffee. We let a double bedroom with en suite shower, a double with a private bathroom and a twin/triple room with private bathroom and shower. Ample parking. Non-smoking. Sorry no pets. Closed Christmas Day and Boxing Day. Rates from £17 to £20 per adult Bed and Breakfast.

DENT (Yorkshire Dales/Cumbria). Mrs Mary Ferguson, Scow Cottage, Cowgill, Near Dent, Sedbergh LA10 5RN (015396 25445). Scow was built

approximately 1750, situated at the head of Dentdale surrounded by hills and trees and alongside the River Dee; fishing permits can be obtained locally. Ideal for touring the Lake District and the Yorkshire Dales, near to the village of Dent famous for the "terrible Knitters of Dent", Adam Sedgwick, and narrow cobbled streets. Guests are accommodated in large beautifully decorated and comfortably furnished rooms with washbasins and central heating; bathroom and separate toilet; lounge. Lovely landscaped gardens in which to relax and enjoy Dentdale's peace and quiet. Bed and Breakfast £14; Evening Meal £8. Further details on request.

EDENHALL. Mrs Jane Metcalfe, Home Farm, Edenhall, Penrith CA11 8SS (01768 881203). Working farm. A warm welcome awaits you at Home Farm,

situated on the outskirts of the peaceful village of Edenhall three miles east of Penrith. This a a working farm and is ideally situated for seeing the Eden Valley, North Pennines, Hadrian's Wall and is conveniently located for the Lake District or en route to/from Scotland. Full English Breakfast, evening meals obtainable locally. Accommodation comprises double, family or twin rooms. Reduced rates for children. Bed and Breakfast from £16 per person.

ENNERDALE. Mrs E. Loxham, Beckfoot Farm, Ennerdale, Cleator CA23 3AU (01946 861235). Jim

and Liz would like to welcome you to their homely, comfortable NO SMOKING guest house standing on the northern shore of Ennerdale Lake, in one of Lakeland's quiet and spectacular valleys. Guests' lounge with colour TV, guide books, games and tea/coffee making facilities; two double bedrooms and one twin-bedded room, all with washbasins, continental quilts, electric underblankets and lake and mountain views. Central heating. Superb home cooking with quality, variety and quantity being our aim. Bed and BIG Breakfast (with choice of menu) £15.50 to £17.50. Three-course candlelit Evening Dinner plus coffee and mints and complimentary glass of wine £10.50. Please telephone for further details or a leaflet.

FAR SAWREY. Irene Forbes, West Vale Country Guest House, Far Sawrey, Hawkshead, Ambleside LA22 0LQ (015394 42817). 🏆🏆🏆 *HIGHLY COMMEN-*

DED. Superbly situated on the edge of the village of Far Sawrey with fine views, West Vale offers you personal service and home-cooked food in a warm, friendly atmosphere. We have full central heating, and log fire and TV in one lounge. All bedrooms have private facilities en-suite and tea and coffee making facilities. Residential licence. Free trout and coarse fishing. AA QQQQ Selected and RAC Highly Acclaimed. Bed and Breakfast from £22.50; Half Board from £33 per day. Weekly terms £217. Children under 11 years two thirds. For further details please send for brochure to Resident Proprietor — Irene Forbes.

GRANGE-OVER-SANDS. Mrs Jean Jackson, Templand Farm, Allithwaite, Grange-over-Sands LA11 7QX (015395 33129). Working farm, join in. Though built in 1687, Templand offers comfortable and quiet accommodation with all modern conveniences. This 100 acre mixed farm is close to the Grange-over-Sands/Cartmel road and is within easy reach of the Lake District. Under two miles to the sea. Fishing and hill walking, swimming pool, golf and tennis at Grange. Superb 12th century Priory at Cartmel. One double, one single and one family bedrooms; bathroom, toilet; lounge and diningroom. Children welcome — cot, high chair and babysitting available. Car not essential but parking provided. Open 1st March to 31st October. SAE brings prompt reply. Terms for Evening Dinner/Meal, Bed and Breakfast from £17 or Bed and Breakfast from £10. Half price for children. No pets.

HAWESWATER/ULLSWATER. Anne and Rob Hunt, Holywell Country Guest House, Helton, Penrith CA10 2QA (01931 712231). Fed up? Tired? Need a Break? Look no further, we have the perfect tonic — so we warmly invite you to sample Cumbrian hospitality in our superbly situated non-smoking country house in the least discovered part of the National Park. Guests are amazed at the commanding views from all rooms and appreciative of the peace and quiet that surrounds them. Tastefully furnished throughout. Own cosy sitting room and dining room. En suite, private facilities. Central heating. Convenient en route to and from Scotland. Hearty breakfast. Enthusiastic advice on pursuits and activities. No pets. Good pubs locally. Bed and Breakfast from £20 per person. Open February to November. Brochure.

See also Colour Display Advertisement

HAWKSHEAD. Linda and Alan Bleasdale, Borwick Lodge, Outgate, Hawkshead, Ambleside LA22 0PU (015394 36332). 🌟🌟 *HIGHLY COMMENDED.* Three times winners of the AWARD for "Accommodation of the Highest Standards". A leafy driveway entices you to the most enchantingly situated house in the Lake District, a rather special 17th century country lodge with magnificent panoramic lake and mountain views, quietly secluded in beautiful gardens. Ideally placed in the heart of the Lakes and close to Hawkshead village with its good choice of restaurants and inns. Beautiful en suite bedrooms with colour TVs and tea/coffee facilities, including "Special Occasions" and "Romantic Breaks" — two king-size four-poster rooms. Prize-winning home-made breads. Linda and Alan welcome you to their "haven of peace and tranquillity" in this most beautiful corner of England. Ample parking. Non-smoking throughout. Bed and Breakfast from £18. May we send our brochure?

HAWKSHEAD. Peter and Anne Hart, Bracken Fell, Outgate, Ambleside LA22 0NH (015394 36289). 🌟🌟 *COMMENDED.* Bracken Fell is situated in beautiful open countryside between Ambleside and Hawkshead in the picturesque hamlet of Outgate. Ideally positioned for exploring the Lake District and within easy reach of Coniston, Windermere, Ambleside, Grasmere and Keswick. All major outdoor activities are catered for nearby including wind surfing, sailing, fishing, pony trekking, etc. All six bedrooms have private facilities, complimentary tea/coffee making and outstanding views. There is central heating throughout, a comfortable lounge and dining room together with ample private parking and two acres of gardens. Fire Certificate. Open all year. Bed and Breakfast from £20. Non-smoking. Self catering accommodation also available. Write or phone for brochure and tariff.

Bracken Fell

HAWKSHEAD. Veronica and Donald Brindle, High Grassings, Sunny Brow, Outgate, Hawkshead, Near Ambleside LA22 0PU (015394 36484). Here is one of the most tranquil settings in the heart of the Lakes. The house nestles against a Woodland Trust coppice and has seven acres of grounds inhabited by deer and red squirrels, with views over fields and woods which are the haunt of curlews to majestic mountain ranges. Walk by bridle path to the pub or take a short drive into the quaint village of Hawkshead with its wide variety of pubs and restaurants. Enjoy log fires in the beamed lounge and take a leisurely breakfast in our spacious conservatory. If you would like to escape from life's hustle and crowds rest at High Grassings for a while. All rooms en suite with tea/coffee facilities. Ample parking. Bed and Breakfast from £22.50 per person.

FUN FOR ALL THE FAMILY IN CUMBRIA

Muncaster Mill, near Ravenglass; World of Beatrix Potter, Bowness-on-Windermere; Carlisle Castle; Wordsworth Museum, Dove Cottage, Grasmere; Appleby Castle Conservation Centre; Cumberland Toy and Model Museum, Cockermouth; Wildlife Oasis, near Milnthorpe; Brockhole National Park Centre, near Windermere; Cumberland Pencil Museum, Keswick; Windermere Steamboat Museum.

HAWKSHEAD. David and Jane Vaughan, Ivy House Hotel, Hawkshead, Near Ambleside LA22 0NS (015394 36204; Freephone: 0500 657876). ♥♥♥ *COMMENDED.* AA QQQ, RAC Highly Acclaimed. Ivy House is a fine Grade II Listed Georgian house full of great charm and character. As a family-run hotel we take much pride in our reputation for providing comfortable accommodation and good English cooking in a friendly informal atmosphere. We have six bedrooms in the main house and five in Mere Lodge situated just across the drive. All bedrooms have en suite facilities, hot drinks tray and are centrally heated. Children are most welcome, cot and high chairs can be provided. Dogs welcome free of charge. For further information and tariff please send for our brochure. We look forward to welcoming you — soon!

HAWKSHEAD. Edward and Judith Ireton, Holmeshead Farm, Skelwith Fold, Ambleside, Hawkshead LA22 0HU (015394 33048). Working farm. A warm, comfortable 17th century farmhouse nestling between Ambleside and Hawkshead, just outside the hamlet of Skelwith Fold. The Drunken Duck Inn is within easy walking distance (one mile). Family, twin and double rooms, all with washbasin, colour TV and tea/coffee making facilities. Cosy lounge/dining room. Central heating, log fire in winter. Full breakfast, traditional and vegetarian. Home-made Evening Meals. Bed and Breakfast. Terms on request. Open all year. An ideal base for all outdoor activities. Walkers' paradise.

See Also Colour Display Advertisement

AMBLESIDE. Linda & Alan Bleasdale, Borwick Lodge, Outgate, Hawkshead, Ambleside LA22 0PU.
Telephone: Hawkshead (015394) 36332.

Three times winners of the AWARD for "Accommodation of the Highest Standards". A leafy driveway entices you to the most enchantingly situated house in the Lake District, a very special 17th century country lodge with magnificent panoramic lake and mountain views, quietly secluded in beautiful gardens. Ideally placed in the heart of the Lakes and close to Hawkshead village with its good choice of restaurants and inns. Beautiful ensuite bedrooms with colour televisions and tea/coffee facilities including 'Special Occasions' and 'Romantic Breaks', two king-size four-poster rooms. Prize-winning homemade breads. Tourist Board 'Two Crown Highly Commended'. Linda and Alan welcome you to their 'haven of peace and tranquillity' in this most beautiful corner of England. Ample parking. NON-SMOKING THROUGHOUT. Bed and Breakfast from £18. May we send our brochure?

HAWKSHEAD. Lynda and James Johnson, Borwick Fold, Outgate, Near Ambleside LA22 0PU (Tel & Fax: 015394 36742). Tourist Board Listed. 17th century farmhouse on the edge of the Fell. Glorious views over the Hawkshead Valley and the High Fells. Large garden, orchard, walks from the door, plus three friendly Elkhounds, two aloof cats, and geese roaming the field. A house full of character and comfort, lovely old furniture, delightful sitting-room full of books/pictures for unwinding, log fire for chilly evenings, central heating. Bedrooms have tea/coffee facilities and TVs. Cooking a pleasure with full English breakfast, freshly baked fruit muffins, home made bread and marmalade. A haven of tranquillity, one mile from Hawkshead village and country inns for bar meals/dinner. Warm welcome. Ample parking. Brochure. Bed and Breakfast £22 per person from Easter 1997.

WHEN MAKING ENQUIRIES PLEASE MENTION
FARM HOLIDAY GUIDES

HIGH WRAY. Mrs P. Benson, Tock How Farm, High Wray, Ambleside (015394 36481). A beautiful

Lakeland farm giving the visitor an opportunity to sample the peaceful life of a Lake District farmer. It is set in idyllic surroundings overlooking Blelham Tarn with magnificent panoramic views of the Langdale Pikes, Coniston Old Man, the Troutbeck Fells and Lake Windermere. High Wray is a quiet unspoilt hamlet set between Ambleside and Hawkshead making this an ideal base for walking or touring. Visitors can expect to taste at breakfast the culinary delights of a working farmhouse kitchen. Sky TV and tea/coffee making facilities are provided in all rooms, together with washbasin and towels. Please write or phone for terms and further details.

KENDAL. Mrs Anne Knowles, Myers Farm, Docker, Grayrigg, Kendal LA8 0DF (01539 824610). A

mixed farm of 220 acres with sheep and dairy cows. Children are welcome to see the working of the farm. The house is over 250 years old with oak beams and a beautiful partition in the lounge/dining room where a log fire burns. Two double and one twin bedrooms; bathroom, shower and toilet; homely and friendly accommodation. Peaceful, scenic countryside, beautiful area for walking locally and further afield yet close to Kendal amenities. Two and a half miles from Junction 37 of the M6, good half way stop en route to Scotland and within easy reach of the Lake District, Dales National Park and the coast. Central heating. Reduced rates for children under 11 years with high chair and babysitting available. Open from March to November for Bed and Breakfast from £15.50. Car essential, parking. SAE please.

**KENDAL. Mrs A.E. Bell, Hill Fold Farm, Burneside, Kendal LA8 9AU (01539 722574). Working
farm.** Situated three miles north of Kendal close to rolling

hills of Potter Fell, with many quiet walks and within easy reach of lakes and sea. Genuine working farm of over 1000 acres; beef and sheep. Three double rooms with washbasins, heaters, TV, shaving points and tea/coffee making facilities. Sittingroom; diningroom; bathroom, toilet. Cot and babysitting; reduced rates for children under 12 years. Wholesome meals served. Car essential, parking. Open January to December (including Christmas and New Year). Sorry, no pets. Terms on request.

**KENDAL. Mrs Jean Bindloss, Grayrigg Hall, Grayrigg, Near Kendal LA8 9BU (01539 824689).
Working farm.** Comfortable, peaceful, 18th century farm-

house set in a beautiful country location, ideal for touring the Lakes and famous Yorkshire Dales. We run a beef and sheep farm only four and a half miles from Kendal and with easy access to M6 motorway, Junction 38. Guests are assured of the finest accommodation and a friendly welcome. One spacious family room and one double bedroom; tasteful lounge/diningroom with colour TV; bathroom. Children most welcome; cot, babysitting if required. Open March to November. Tourist Board registered and inspected. Bed and Breakfast from £14 per person, with Evening Meal on request. Good home-made meals using local produce from £5 to £7. Further information gladly supplied.

**KENDAL. Mrs Val Sunter, Higher House Farm, Oxenholme Lane, Natland, Kendal LA9 7QH
(015395 61177; Fax: 015395 61520).** ❀ ❀

COMMENDED. In a peaceful village south of Kendal, this 17th century beamed farmhouse offers comfortable bed and breakfast accommodation with delicious breakfast. Two double and one twin bedroom, each with private bathroom. Four-poster bed, TV, hair dryer and coffee/tea making facilities in all bedrooms. Residents' lounge with colour TV. Central heating throughout. Pay phone in hall. Overlooking the Lakeland Fells, convenient for the M6 and Oxenholme station. Golf, riding, historic visits nearby. Bed and Breakfast from £18 to £22 per person. Pets welcome. AA QQQQ Selected. Self catering accommodation also available.

KENDAL. Mrs D.M. Swindlehurst, Tranthwaite Hall, Underbarrow, Near Kendal LA8 8HG (015395 68285). Working farm. Commended and AA Selected for

excellent standards of comfort and quality. Tranthwaite Hall is said to date back to 1186. A charming olde world farmhouse with beautiful oak beams, doors and rare black iron fire range. This working dairy/sheep farm has an idyllic setting half a mile up an unspoilt country lane where deer can be seen, herons fishing in the stream and lots of wild flowers. This is a very peaceful and quiet retreat yet only minutes from all Lakes and local attractions. Attractive bedrooms, all are en suite and have tea/coffee making facilities, hair dryer, radio and full central heating. Lounge with colour TV. Full English breakfast is served with milk and eggs from our farm and home made jam and marmalade. We like guests to enjoy our home and garden as much as we do. Walking, pony trekking, golf and many good country pubs and inns nearby. Bed and Breakfast £18 to £20.

KENDAL. Mrs Sylvia Beaty, Garnett House Farm, Burneside, Kendal LA9 5SF (01539 724542).

♛ ♛ *COMMENDED.* **Working farm.** This is an AA QQQ and RAC Acclaimed 15th century farmhouse on large dairy/sheep farm situated half a mile from A591 Kendal/Windermere road. Accommodation comprises two double, one twin and two family bedrooms, (some en suite), all with washbasins; colour TV, shaver points and tea making facilities. In the lounge the 4ft thick walls have 16th century panelling. Excellent home cooking is provided at separate tables in the dining room. Full English breakfast and five-course evening dinner available using home produced beef and lamb; meringues, trifles, gateaux, etc, also served. Reductions for children; cot, high chair and babysitting facilities available. Good parking but car not essential. Shops, inn, bus stops and station within walking distance. Fire Certificate. Scrabble players welcome. Open all year for Bed and Breakfast and Dinner. Special offer November to mid-March: three nights Bed and Breakfast £45, en suite £50. SAE for prompt reply and brochure. Featured in "The Times".

KENDAL near. Mrs Olive M. Knowles, Cragg Farm, New Hutton, Near Kendal LA8 0BA (01539 721760). Working farm. Tourist Board Listed. Cragg

Farm is a delightful 17th century oak-beamed farmhouse which retains its character yet has all modern comforts. This 280 acre working dairy/sheep farm is set in peaceful countryside and ideally positioned for exploring the Lake District and Yorkshire Dales. Located four miles from Kendal on A684 road, and three miles M6 Junction 37. This makes an ideal stopover between England and Scotland. We have one double, one family and one single bedrooms, all with tea/coffee facilities; bathroom with shower and toilet; lounge/dining room with colour TV. Full central heating. Full English breakfast served. Families are welcome. Open March to November. Bed and Breakfast from £15. Self catering caravan also available.

KESWICK. Colin and Lesley Smith, Mosedale House, Mosedale, Mungrisdale CA11 0XQ (017687 79371). ♛ ♛ ♛ *COMMENDED.* Traditional 1862 built, Lake-

land farmhouse. Listed building. A smallholding with sheep, ducks and hens, it enjoys a magnificent position, nestling at the foot of Carrock Fell, overlooking open fields, the River Caldew and Bowscale Fell. Off the beaten track, yet only three and a half miles to the A66 Keswick to Penrith road. Vegetarians welcome. Home baked bread, farm produce — our own free-range eggs. Packed lunches. Non-smoking establishment. Central heating. Open all year. Most bedrooms have en suite facilities. Visitors' diningroom and lounge. Excellent facilities for disabled guests — ground floor twin-bedded room with en-suite bathroom; no steps throughout. Bed and Breakfast from £20 per person. Also self catering cottage in adjacent barn.

KESWICK. Mrs E.M. Richardson, Fold Head Farm, Watendlath, Borrowdale, Keswick CA12 5UW (017687 77255). Working farm. Fold Head Farmhouse is a white Lakeland farmhouse situated on the banks of Watendlath Tarn in this picturesque hamlet. It is a 3000 acre sheep farm and an ideal centre for touring, climbing, fell walking and fishing. Fly-fishing for rainbow trout at Watendlath Tarn; permits available. Guests are accommodated in two double bedrooms and one twin bedroom, with washbasins; bathroom, two toilets; sittingroom; diningroom. Full central heating; separate TV lounge. Pets are allowed free. Open from February to December. Car essential; parking. Sir Hugh Walpole used this farmhouse in his book "Judith Paris" as the home of Judith Paris. Evening Dinner, Bed and Breakfast or Bed and Breakfast. Terms on request.

KESWICK. Mrs M.E. Harryman, Keskadale Farm, Newlands, Keswick CA12 5TS (017687 78544).

Bed and Breakfast at a traditional Lakeland farm. Pleasantly and peacefully situated in the lovely Newlands Valley surrounded by mountains and countryside. Excellent area for walking or touring Buttermere two and a half miles, Braithwaite four miles, Keswick six miles. A warm welcome awaits you. Our old world farmhouse has two double bedrooms and one twin bedded room, all with washbasins, central heating and tea-making facilities. Lounge with open log fire early and late season, colour TV; dining room; shower room with toilet. Bed and Breakfast from £16.00. Sorry no pets. Open March to late November. Also self catering holiday flat and luxury caravan. SAE for details.

KESWICK. Mr and Mrs P.H. Smith, Goodwin House, 29 Southey Street, Keswick CA12 4EE (017687 74634).

👑👑 Goodwin House is a detached imposing three storey residence with central hall and staircase of solid pine with verandah on first landing. It affords easy access to parks and town shopping centre and is an ideal base for walks and drives to fells and lakes. All rooms have central heating, washbasin, tea making facilities and colour TV. There are en suite rooms and guests have own front door keys. They can enjoy delicious home cooking. Bed and Breakfast from £15. Weekly terms by arrangement. Reduced rates for children. Open all year. AA Approved.

KESWICK. I. and M. Atkinson, "Dancing Beck", Underskiddaw, Keswick CA12 4PY (017687 73800).

Large Lakeland country house two and a half miles from Keswick just off A591 Carlisle road, signposted Millbeck. Situated in its own elevated, spacious grounds with summerhouse. Magnificent views of Derwent Valley and surrounding mountains. Walks onto Skiddaw Mountain are possible from the grounds of "Dancing Beck". All rooms are centrally heated. Bedrooms have private facilities and tea/coffee facilities. Children welcome. Car essential. Bed and Breakfast from £19. Weekly terms available. Open Spring to November. A pleasant welcome assured. A self catering cottage also available.

KESWICK. Mr and Mrs G. Turnbull, Rickerby Grange, Portinscale, Keswick CA12 5RH (017687 72344).

👑👑👑 COMMENDED. Quiet location in the pretty village of Portinscale, three-quarters of a mile west of Keswick. Ideal base for explorers of the Lakes, by foot or car. Family-run 12 bedroom hotel (most en-suite), all with tea/coffee making facilities, colour TV and central heating. Three ground floor bedrooms, and four-poster available. The lounge and cosy bar offer a relaxing atmosphere before a delicious five course meal in the elegant diningroom. Private car park. Bed and Breakfast £26; Dinner, Bed and Breakfast from £36.50 per person. RAC Acclaimed, AA QQQ. Non-smoking available. Write or phone for brochure.

OUT AND ABOUT IN CUMBRIA

Take a trip back in time on a narrow-gauge railway: The Lakeside and Haverthwaite runs through the beautiful Leven Valley, Ravenglass and Eskdale travels 7 miles from the coast up into the fells, and the South Tynedale Railway offers a journey through a beautiful North Pennine Valley.

The perfect way to appreciate the magnificent Lakeland scenery is on a leisurely Lake cruiser — Ullswater, Coniston, Derwentwater all have scheduled services daily in season.

KESWICK near. Muriel Bond, Thornthwaite Hall, Thornthwaite, Near Keswick CA12 5SA (Tel & Fax: 017687 78424). 👑👑👑 *APPROVED.*

Thornthwaite Hall is a traditional 17th century farmhouse, modernised and converted into a very comfortable guesthouse. All rooms are en-suite with TV, tea/coffee making facilities. Catering includes good home cooking, residential licence. The Hall lies in an acre of grounds complete with a lovely garden. Thornthwaite is a lovely quiet hamlet three miles west of Keswick. There are numerous walks from Thornthwaite, with a different feel to other parts of the Lake District. Climbing in pine forest locations on the numerous paths and forest trails, spectacular views rewarding those who climb to the tops of Barf, Lords Seat, Seat How. Dogs and children most welcome. Open all year, except Christmas. Bed and Breakfast from £21 to £24; Dinner, Bed and Breakfast from £30.50. Send for brochure, please.

KESWICK. Mrs D. Mattinson, Bassenthwaite Hall Farm, Keswick CA12 4QP (017687 76279). Cumbrian Tourist Board Listed. Working farm. A sheep and cattle farm in Bassenthwaite Village, with beautiful views of the Skiddaw Range on the front and the river rippling past at the rear. Flower garden and lawn. Ample parking. Open April to November, the four bedrooms all have washbasins; one room en suite. Bath/shower room, two toilets. Living/diningroom with colour TV. Coal/log fires when needed. Home cooking and hospitality. Children and pets welcome. Golf, riding and fishing nearby. Bed and Breakfast from £16, en suite from £20. AA Listed.

KESWICK. Mrs M.M. Beaty, Birkrigg Farm, Newlands, Keswick CA12 5TS (017687 78278). Tourist

Board Listed *APPROVED.* **Working farm.** Birkrigg is a working dairy and sheep farm, very pleasantly and peacefully situated, with an excellent outlook in the lovely Newlands Valley. Five miles from Keswick between Braithwaite and Buttermere. Being in a beautiful mountainous area makes this an ideal place to stay especially for those wishing to walk or climb. Centrally located for touring the many beauty spots in the Lake District. Clean, comfortable accommodation awaits you. A good breakfast is offered at 8.30am, evening tea at 9.30pm. Packed lunches available. Sorry no evening meals. Local inns all provide good food, two to four miles away. Open March to December.

KESWICK (Newlands). Mrs Christine Simpson, Uzzicar Farm, Newlands, Keswick CA12 5TS (017687 78367).

A warm welcome awaits you at Uzzicar Farm situated in the peaceful Newlands Valley, only three miles from Keswick with magnificent views of the surrounding fells. Being within 30 minutes of the M6 Junction 40 makes this the ideal place for a holiday in the Lake District or a break in your journey when travelling north or south. Well located for touring by car and the comfortable farmhouse makes a particularly good base for fell walking and sailing. Fishing, swimming, golf and pony trekking are all relatively close. All bedrooms have washbasins, central heating, tea/coffee making facilities and shaver points. There is a separate sittingroom and dining room, toilet and bathroom with toilet. Sorry no smoking. Open February to December. Ample parking. Bed and Breakfast £14 to £16 per person. Please write or phone for further details.

KIRKBY STEPHEN. Mrs Sylvia Capstick, Duckintree House, Kaber, Kirkby Stephen CA17 4ER (017683 71073).

Duckintree is a working family farm set in the quiet Eden Valley countryside just off the A685 Kirkby Stephen to Brough road. Easy access to the Lakes and Yorkshire Dales or ideal for breaking your journey from the South of England/Midlands to Scotland. Car essential, ample parking. The rooms comprise family, double and twin (cot available) with tea/coffee making facilities. Lounge/diningroom with colour TV. All rooms overlook a large garden and countryside. Bed and Breakfast from £15. Reductions for children under 12 years. Pets welcome by arrangement. Evening Meal can be provided. Open from March to October. Write or phone for details.

PLEASE SEND A STAMPED ADDRESSED ENVELOPE WITH ENQUIRIES

KIRKBY STEPHEN near. Mrs B.M. Boustead, Tranna Hill, Newbiggin-on-Lune, Near Kirkby Stephen

CA17 4NY (015396 23227). Tranna Hill offers a relaxing and friendly atmosphere in a non-smoking environment. Five miles from M6 (Junction 38), beautifully situated on fringe of Newbiggin-on-Lune village, ideal base for country lovers and walkers with nature reserve and Sunbiggin Tarn nearby. Well placed for touring the Lake District, Yorkshire, Durham, Dales and for breaking your journey. Relax in guests' lounge with TV and then have a good night's sleep in en suite rooms with tea making facilities, central heating and beautiful views, followed by a delicious breakfast. RIPHH Certificate. Bed and Breakfast from £16.

LAKESIDE/NEWBY BRIDGE. Brian and Sylvia Slingsby, Landing Cottage, Lakeside, Newby Bridge,

Ulverston LA12 8AS (015395 31719). ♚♚ Traditional Lakeland stone cottage built about 1870, situated at the southern tip of Lake Windermere, about 100 yards from the Lake Steamer and Lakeside/Haverthwaite Steam Railway terminals. Conveniently located as a touring base to all the Lakes, places of interest and the Morecambe Bay coast. The cottage has en suite, standard double and family bedrooms with pretty, colour co-ordinated decor, tea/coffee making facilities. Whole of the ground floor is non-smoking including en suite bedroom. Just starting our 13th year, we shall be extending a warm welcome to all our new and returning guests. Good home cooking, packed lunches available on request. Complimentary pot of tea/coffee on arrival. Car parking. Open all year. Bed and Breakfast £17 to £19.50. Brochure on request.

LANGDALE VALLEY. Mrs Jean Rowand, Stool End Farm, Great Langdale, Ambleside LA22 9JU

(015394 37615). Working farm. A working farm with sheep, cows, shire horses, goats and sheep dogs. In Great Langdale, with splendid views of the Langdale Pikes, at the foot of the Band (the path up to Bowfell). Ideal for walking or rock climbing. Lakes Coniston, Grasmere and Windermere are a short drive away. Other places to visit include the houses of Beatrix Potter, William Wordsworth and John Ruskin, and the Ravenglass and Eskdale narrow gauge railway. A warm welcome awaits all at this 17th century farmhouse which is owned by the National Trust. The sitting/dining room has a log fire and TV. There is a family room with en suite facilities and a double bedroom with wash-basin; separate bathroom and shower. Bed and big farmhouse Breakfast from £16 per person per day.

MARYPORT. Mrs W.B. Carruthers, East Farm, Crosscanonby, Maryport CA15 6SJ (01900

812153). ETB Listed *COMMENDED.* Enjoy a warm welcome to our dairy farm on the fringe of the Lake District. Situated between Maryport and Allonby with beautiful views over the Solway Firth to Scotland; Cockermouth is nine miles away and Keswick 20 miles. Beach, golf course, windsurfing, pony rides and leisure centre with swimming pool nearby. Comfortable TV lounge wth separate dining room overlooking pleasant garden. Full central heating. Peaceful, comfortable, spacious bedrooms with tea making facilities: one family, one double. Children welcome, reduced rates. Traditional farmhouse breakfast served, evening meals available locally. Sorry, no pets in house. Ample parking.

MILNTHORPE. Mrs Lynn Green, "Springlea", Heversham, Milnthorpe LA7 7EE (015395 64026).

Situated in South Lakeland, Springlea faces rolling farmland framed by woods and stone walls with the Kent estuary glinting between the trees. It is ideally positioned for the Lakes, Yorkshire Dales and the Morecambe Bay resorts. Historic houses, nature reserves and many other centres of attraction are within easy reach. Local pubs and restaurants serve good food at reasonable prices. There are twin and double en-suite rooms with central heating, TV and tea/coffee making facilities. A lounge, sunroom and terrace are available as is safe off-road parking. Bed and Breakfast or Bed, Breakfast with Evening Meal. Open all year. Terms from £14.50 per person per night. AA QQQ Recommended.

NEAR SAWREY. Mrs Elizabeth Mallett, Esthwaite How Farmhouse, Near Sawrey, Ambleside LA22 0LB (015394 36450). A warm and friendly welcome awaits you at Esthwaite How Farmhouse, situated in this lovely village where Beatrix Potter wrote her books. Beautiful views of the countryside and the lake (where part of the television film about her life was made) can be seen from bedrooms and the diningroom. Ideal for walking, fishing and touring. Accommodation comprises one double and one family bedrooms with washbasins; bathroom with shower; dining/sitting room with open log fire, central heating. Children welcome; babysitting can be arranged. Open all year. Car essential, parking for two cars. Bed and Breakfast from £12; Bed, Breakfast and Evening Meal from £18. Half rates for children sharing room.

NEAR SAWREY. Miss Gillian Fletcher, High Green Gate Guest House, Near Sawrey, Ambleside LA22 0LF (015394 36296). ☙☙ The Guest House is a converted 17th-century farmhouse in the quiet hamlet where Beatrix Potter lived and wrote. Her house, owned by the National Trust, is close by and open to the public. The area abounds with pleasant easy walks and is a good centre for the Southern Lakes. Open from March to October. Good food and service under the personal attention of the owner. Spacious diningroom, lounge and separate TV lounge. All bedrooms have hot and cold water and individual heating in addition to central heating. Rooms with private facilities available. Reduced rates for children sharing with parents. Cot and highchair are available and babysitting can be arranged. Dogs welcome. A car is desirable and there is parking for seven cars. AA Approved/Listed, RAC Acclaimed. Bed and Breakfast from £20 per night; Bed, Breakfast and Evening Meal from £30 per night (£179 weekly).

NEWBY BRIDGE near. Mr and Mrs F. Cervetti, Lightwood Farmhouse, Cartmel Fell, Grange-over-Sands LA11 6NP (015395 31454). ☙☙ *COMMENDED.* This 17th century farmhouse with original oak beams is in a two acre garden with streams. Situated two miles from southern end of Lake Windermere, just off the A592, near Bowland Bridge. Tea making facilities. Eight rooms are en suite. Guests' own sittingroom with colour TV and log fire. Offering personal, friendly attention at all times. Bed and Breakfast from £22, half price for children under 12 years when sharing.

NEWLANDS. Mrs M.A. Relph, Littletown Farm, Newlands, Keswick CA12 5TU (017687 78353). **Working farm.** Littletown has all the facilities of a small hotel and most bedrooms are en-suite. Situated in a peaceful part of the beautiful Newlands Valley, with surrounding hills providing excellent walking and climbing. Market towns of Keswick and Cockermouth, Lakes Derwentwater and Bassenthwaite all within easy distance. Farmhouse, though fully modernised, still retains a traditional character with comfortable lounge, diningroom, and cosy licensed bar. All bedrooms have tea-making facilities, heating and washbasins. Traditional four-course dinner (roast beef, lamb etc) served six nights a week; full English Breakfast every morning. Littletown Farm is featured in Beatrix Potter's "Mrs Tiggy Winkle". Ample parking. Dinner, Bed and Breakfast from £35 to £39 per person; Bed and Breakfast from £24 to £29 per person. SAE please.

Littletown farm

PENRITH. Mrs C. Blundell, Albany House, 5 Portland Place, Penrith CA11 7QN (01768 863072). ETB Listed *COMMENDED.* AA QQQ. Close to town centre, Albany House is a large mid-Victorian terraced house. A high standard of cleanliness, comfort and personal friendly attention is assured at all times. Five spacious nicely decorated bedrooms (one double, three triple all with washbasins, one family en suite). All have central heating, colour/satellite TV and tea/coffee making facilities. Situated close to M6, A6 and A66, ideal base for touring Lake District, Eden Valley, Hadrian's Wall, Scottish Borders and an excellent stopover between England and Scotland. Within easy reach are Lowther Leisure Park, sailing, wind surfing, fell walking, pony trekking, golf and swimming. Bed and Breakfast from £15.50.

PENRITH. Mrs Brenda Preston, Pallet Hill Farm, Penrith CA11 0BY (017684 83247). Pallet Hill Farm is pleasantly situated two miles from Penrith on the Penrith-Greystoke-Keswick road (B5288). It is four miles from Ullswater and has easy access to the Lake District, Scottish Borders and Yorkshire Dales. There are several sports facilities in the area — golf club, swimming pool, pony trekking; places to visit such as Lowther Leisure Park and the Miniature Railway at Ravenglass. Good farmhouse food and hospitality with personal attention. Double, single, family rooms; diningroom and sittingroom. Children welcome — cot, high chair available. Sorry, no pets. Car essential, parking. Open Easter to November. Bed and Breakfast from £9.50 (reduced rates for children and weekly stays).

PENRITH. Mrs Yvonne Dent, Bridge End Farm, Kirkby Thore, Penrith CA10 1UZ (01768 361362).

♚♚ *HIGHLY COMMENDED*. Relax in our 18th century farmhouse on a dairy farm in the Eden Valley. Lovely spacious en suite bedrooms, tastefully furnished with antiques, featuring beautiful handmade patchwork quilts and craft work. All rooms have coffee/tea making facilities, hair dryer, clock radio and TV. Enjoy delicious home made breakfast and dinner served in the dining room. All the food is freshly prepared and you will never forget Yvonne's sticky toffee pudding. Finish the evening in front of the fire in the delightfully furnished guest lounge or take a stroll along the banks of the River Eden. Private fishing available.

PENRITH. Mrs Margaret Taylor, Tymparon Hall, Newbiggin, Stainton, Penrith CA11 0HS (017684 83236).

♚♚ *COMMENDED*. **Working farm.** AA QQQ, RAC Acclaimed, Farm Holiday Bureau Member. Enjoy a relaxing break on the beautiful North Lakes and explore the Eden Valley. A delightful Manor House and colourful summer garden situated on a 150 acre sheep farm in a peaceful rural area close to Lake Ullswater. Enjoy old-fashioned hospitality, home cooked farmhouse breakfasts and three-course dinners. Guests' bedrooms, en suite or standard, offer space and tranquillity with every facility for a memorable time. Evening Dinner, Bed and Breakfast. Brochure on request with SAE.

SHAP. Mr and Mrs D.L. and M. Brunskill, Brookfield, Shap, Penrith CA10 3PZ (01931 716 397).

Situated one mile from M6 motorway (turn off at Shap interchange No.39), first accommodation off motorway. Excellent position for touring Lakeland, or overnight accommodation for travelling north or south. Central heating throughout, renowned for good food, comfort and personal attention. All bedrooms are well appointed and have colour TV and tea/coffee making facilities; en suite available. Diningroom where delicious home cooking is a speciality. Well stocked bar. Residents' lounge. Sorry, no pets. Open from February to December. Terms sent on request. Car essential, ample parking. AA Listed. Fire Certificate granted.

SILLOTH. Mrs M. Greenup, Nook Farm, Beckfoot, Silloth CA5 4LG (01900 881279). Nook Farm is a

family working farm with cattle and sheep. We have views of the Lakeland fells and the Scottish hills over the Solway Firth. Situated half a mile from the sea and equal distance from Silloth and Allonby (four miles) where there is golf, pony rides and stables and leisure centres with indoor swimming pools. Also near Cumbrian cycle way. Guests have their own sitting/dining room where tea facilities are available. A traditional farmhouse breakfast is served with free range eggs.

TROUTBECK. Gwen and Peter Parfitt, Hill Crest, Troutbeck, Penrith CA11 0SH (017684 83935).

Gwen and Peter assure you of a warm and friendly welcome at "Hill Crest" their unique Lakeland home which offers two en suite double/family rooms and one twin room. Home cooking, choice of menu including vegetarian; early morning tea, bedtime drinks, packed lunches. Non-smoking lounge/dining room. Panoramic mountain views, Aira Force waterfalls; Ullswater 10 minutes, Keswick 15 minutes. Good base for walking, boating, touring Lakes, Hadrian's Wall, the Borders. Books, maps and hints from Gwen on what to visit. Walkers, children and dogs welcome. We aim to create a relaxed, informal atmosphere where guests are treated as part of the family. Bed and Breakfast from £14 per person; Dinner from £5 (optional). Weekly rates available.

TROUTBECK. Mrs Anne Ross, Greenah Crag Farm, Troutbeck, Penrith CA11 0SQ (017684 83233).

Ron and Anne welcome you to their lovely 17th century farmhouse. Ideal for touring the Northern Lakes, Ullswater five miles. Accommodation comprises one double en suite, one double and one twin-bedded rooms, all with tea making facilities. Lounge with colour TV. Non-smoking only. Sorry no pets. Bed and Breakfast from £15. Self catering units also available.

ULLSWATER. Mrs S. Hunter, Grove Foot Farm, Watermillock, Penrith CA11 0NA (017684 86416).

Working farm. Grove Foot is a 90 acre dairy farm just off the A66 and two miles from Lake Ullswater. The house, built around 1650, has oak beams and open fires and sleeps six guests. Close by are historic houses and gardens, fishing, swimming pools, golf and pony trekking. Open March to October. Children welcome. Sorry, no pets. Bed and Breakfast from £14.

WIGTON. Mrs Dorothy Studholme, Newlands Grange, Hesket-New-Market, Wigton CA7 8HP

(016974 78676). Newlands Grange Farm is in beautiful open countryside looking onto Caldbeck Fells in renowned John Peel country. Ideally situated for touring Lakes, Roman Wall, the Scottish Borders and is 15 miles from beach at Silloth. We have cows, calves, sheep and poultry and own quarter of a mile fishing rights on the River Caldew. The farm house features oak beams and an open fire in the lounge with good home cooking and some home produce. Two family bedrooms, two doubles and one single. Children and dogs welcome. Bed and Breakfast or Bed, Breakfast and Evening Meal. Terms on application. Six berth caravan on own farm with all modern conveniences also available. A warm welcome awaits all.

See also Colour Display Advertisement **WINDERMERE. The Beaumont Hotel, Holly Road, Windermere LA23 2AF (Tel & Fax: 015394 47075).** 🐾🐾 *HIGHLY COMMENDED.* AA QQQQ Selected, RAC Highly Acclaimed. Elegant Victorian House Hotel displays all the grace and charm of its time skilfully combined with all the comforts of today. Ideally situated for Windermere and Bowness and the perfect location for touring the Lakes. All 12 luxury bedrooms are en suite, each has TV, tea-making facilities and hairdryer; four-poster rooms are available for that special occasion and a "Romantic Presentation" of wine, chocolates, fruit and flowers may be ordered. Private parking. Standards are high, breakfasts are hearty, and the hospitality is warm and sincere. Bed and Breakfast from £23. Full details on request.

See also Colour Display Advertisement **WINDERMERE. Irene and George Eastwood, Sandown, Lake Road, Windermere LA23 2JF (015394 45275).** Superb Bed and Breakfast accommodation. All rooms en suite with colour TV and tea/coffee making facilities. Situated two minutes from Lake Windermere, shops and cafes. Many lovely walks. Open all year. Special out of season rates, also two-day Saturday/Sunday Breaks. From £18 to £29 per person per night. Well-behaved dogs welcome. Each room has own safe private car parking. SAE or telephone for further details.

WINDERMERE. Mrs Sandra Garside, Boston House, 4 The Terrace, Windermere LA23 1AJ (Tel & Fax: 015394 43654). ❦ ❦ ❦ *COMMENDED.* A delightful Victorian Gothic building dating from 1849. Situated in peaceful cul-de-sac on the edge of the village with panoramic views of the lake and surrounding fells, yet close to village centre, train and coach stations (collection by arrangement). Five spacious en suite double/twin/family rooms with tea trays, hairdryers, radio alarms and colour TV; two have four-poster and another has an oak half-tester bed — very romantic! Choose hearty breakfasts from an extensive menu; superb home-cooked dinners are also available. Restaurant/ residential licence. NO SMOKING PLEASE. Private parking. Bed and Breakfast from £19 to £25 per person. Brochure on request. RAC Highly Acclaimed.

Key to Tourist Board Ratings

The Crown Scheme
(England, Scotland & Wales)

Covering hotels, motels, private hotels, guesthouses, inns, bed & breakfast, farmhouses. Every Crown classified place to stay is inspected annually. *The classification:* Listed then 1-5 Crown indicates the range of facilities and services. Higher quality standards are indicated by the terms APPROVED, COMMENDED, HIGHLY COMMENDED and DELUXE.

The Key Scheme
(also operates in Scotland using a Crown symbol)

Covering self-catering in cottages, bungalows, flats, houseboats, houses, chalets, etc. Every Key classified holiday home is inspected annually. *The classification:* 1-5 Key indicates the range of facilities and equipment. Higher quality standards are indicated by the terms APPROVED, COMMENDED, HIGHLY COMMENDED and DELUXE.

The Q Scheme
(England, Scotland & Wales)

Covering holiday, caravan, chalet and camping parks. Every Q rated park is inspected annually for its quality standards. The more √ in the Q – up to 5 – the higher the standard of what is provided.

WINDERMERE. Mrs B.J. Butterworth, Orrest Head House, Windermere LA23 1JG (015394 44315).

This beautiful house is part 17th century, located in three acres of lush garden and woodland. Nestling above Windermere village it enjoys superb views of the Lake and mountains. From February to December guests are assured of comfortable Bed and Breakfast accommodation in five en suite rooms, three double and two twin, all non-smoking and with washbasins, central heating, tea making facilities. Separate dining room. Private parking for up to 10 cars. The ideal choice for a really relaxing holiday. Terms from £19.50 Bed and Breakfast.

WINDERMERE. Mr and Mrs J.N. Fowles, Rockside Guest House, Ambleside Road, Windermere LA23 1AQ (Tel/Fax: 015394 45343). 🌑🌑 Rockside is a family run Guest House, 100 yards from Windermere village, bus stop and railway station. If any help is needed to plan a day's outing the proprietors, Neville and Mavis Fowles, will book trips, loan maps, suggest car routes and plan walks. Single, twin, double and family rooms are all centrally heated and have colour TV, clock radio and telephone; most rooms en-suite with tea/coffee making facilities. A car park at the rear holds 12 cars. Open all year — as every season has its own magic and beauty. RAC Acclaimed. Bed and Breakfast from £14.50 to £22.50 per person. Visa, Mastercard and Access accepted.

HOLLY LODGE · A Lakeland Guest House

Holly Lodge is one of the oldest houses in Windermere and is run by the resident proprietors who give a personal and friendly service. A full English breakfast is provided and an evening meal if required. There is central heating, a comfortable lounge with open fire, and a pleasant dining room. Each bedroom has hot and cold water, tea and coffee making facilities, and colour TV. Some rooms ensuite. No pets except guide dogs. Children welcome; up to 13 years at reduced rates. Open all year.

Bed and Breakfast from £16. Evening Meal £11.

Tony and Lindy Priestley, Holly Lodge, 6 College Road, Windermere LA23 1BX Telephone and Fax: (015394) 43873

AA Listed   Licensed   🌑🌑 Commended   Parking

WINDERMERE. John and Liz Christopherson, Villa Lodge, Cross Street, Windermere LA23 1AE (Tel & Fax: 015394 43318). 🌑🌑 *COMMENDED.* Friendliness and cleanliness guaranteed. Extremely comfortable accommodation in peaceful area overlooking Windermere village, yet only two minutes from station. All seven bedrooms are tastefully decorated, mostly en-suite (some four-posters) with colour TV, tea/coffee making facilities and full central heating, most with magnificent views of Lake and mountains. Access to rooms at all times. Superb English breakfast served in our delightful dining room. Vegetarian and special diets catered for. Open all year. Special offers November to March. Safe, private parking for six cars. An excellent base for exploring the whole of the Lake District. Bed and Breakfast from £16. AA QQQ. Ring John and Liz Christopherson.

See also Colour Display Advertisement **WINDERMERE. Glencree Private Hotel, Lake Road, Windermere LA23 2EQ. (015394 45822).** AA QQQQ Selected, RAC Highly Acclaimed. Warm and friendly hospitality welcomes you to our small hotel which has, over the years, earned an enviable reputation as one of the best in the Lake District. Glencree is beautifully and tastefully furnished and decorated throughout with your comfort in mind; well recommended by major prestigious tourist guides for quality and value for money. Tariff: according to season and duration of stay — from £18.50 per person Low Season (two sharing). Access/Visa accepted. SAE, please for brochure from proprietors Julie and Rip Butler.

DERBYSHIRE

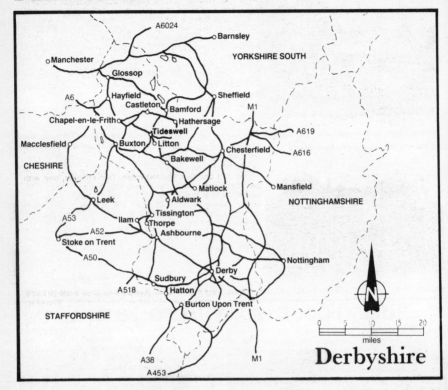

A6024
Barnsley
Manchester
YORKSHIRE SOUTH
Glossop
A6
Hayfield
Sheffield
Castleton
M1
Chapel-en-le-Frith
Bamford
Hathersage
Tideswell
A619
Macclesfield
Buxton
Litton
Chesterfield
A616
Bakewell
CHESHIRE
Matlock
Mansfield
Leek
Aldwark
NOTTINGHAMSHIRE
A53
Tissington
Ilam
Thorpe
A52
Ashbourne
Stoke on Trent
A50
Nottingham
Derby
Sudbury
A518
Hatton
Burton Upon Trent
STAFFORDSHIRE

0   5   10   15   20
miles

Derbyshire

ALDWARK. Mrs D. Forsey, Tithe Farm, Aldwark, Grange Mill, Matlock DE4 4HX (01629 540263).

✿✿ *COMMENDED.* In open countryside, Tithe Farm is a Grade II Listed building, eight miles from Ashbourne, Matlock and Bakewell. Peacefully situated, it is an ideal centre for exploring the Dales and Derbyshire's historic houses. Splendid walking country with much to interest the naturalist. A non-smoking establishment with both the twin-bedded and family rooms having private bathrooms, colour TV and tea/coffee making facilities. Extensive breakfast menu with homemade bread, and preserves. Open April to October. Regret no dogs. Bed and Breakfast £20 with reduced rates for children, also for visits of three nights or longer. Brochure on request.

AMBERGATE. Mrs Carol Oulton, Lawn Farm, Whitewells Lane (off Holly Lane), Ambergate DE56 2DN (01773 852352). ✿ Working farm, join in. Enjoy comfortable Bed and Breakfast accommodation on a working beef and sheep farm, one mile from the A6 at Ambergate. Ambergate has many woodland walks and a picturesque canal which leads to nearby Cromford, home of the Arkwright Mill. Matlock Bath is 10 miles away and offers many attractions including cable cars. Within easy travelling distance of Haddon Hall, Chatsworth House and Gardens, The Peak District National Park and The National Tramway Museum at Crich. Accommodation comprises double en suite room and family room with handbasin. Children welcome at reduced rates. Pets welcome by arrangement. Terms on request from £15 per night. Non-smokers preferred.

ASHBOURNE near. Mr and Mrs P.J. Watson, Weaver Farm, Waterhouses, Near Ashbourne ST10 3HE (01538 702271). Working farm. Situated off A52 on the Weaver Hills close to Ashbourne, Dovedale and Alton Towers. Stone farmhouse with central heating and open fires offering family, twin and double bedrooms with washbasins. Cot. Bathroom with shower and WC. Guest diningroom and lounge with TV. Children welcome. Home produced fresh farmhouse cooking is served. The 320 acre farm with dairy cows, calves, sheep and lambs provides many activities which guests are welcome to watch and they can also enjoy extensive walks and views. Car essential; ample parking. No pets. SAE or ring for terms. A warm welcome awaits you.

ASHBOURNE. Mrs Catherine Brandrick, Sidesmill Farm, Snelston, Ashbourne DE6 2GQ (01335 342710). Tourist Board Listed *COMMENDED.* Peaceful dairy farm located on the banks of the River Dove. A rippling mill stream flows quietly past the 18th century stone-built farmhouse. Delicious English breakfast and the warmest of welcomes are guaranteed. Comfortable accommodation; guests' own lounge, dining room; bathroom; TV in lounge. Ideal base for touring, within easy reach of Dovedale, Alton Towers, stately homes and many other places of interest. Open Easter to October. Car necessary, parking available. Bed and Breakfast from £15 per person. A non-smoking establishment.

ASHBOURNE. Mrs Julia Brookfield, Green Gables, Thorpe, Near Ashbourne DE6 2AW (01335 350386). 🐾 This old farmhouse has been renovated to offer comfortable accommodation for its guests. Two double rooms and one twin-bedded room. Two en-suite, one with own bathroom. Diningroom with oak beams; lounge with colour TV (log fire in winter). Full central heating. Tea and coffee making facilities. Children and pets welcome. Ample parking space. Open March 1st to November 30th. Bed and Breakfast £18; Singles £20.

ASHBOURNE near. Mrs Mary Hollingsworth, Collycroft Farm, Near Ashbourne DE6 2GN (01335 342187). Tourist Board Listed *COMMENDED.* **Working farm.** AA QQQ Recommended. This is a 260 acre mixed farm located two miles south of Ashbourne on the A515, within easy reach of Alton Towers, Peak District and Carsington Water. Accommodation includes double room en suite, twin-bedded room and a family room; colour TV, tea/coffee making facilities and full central heating. All rooms overlook beautiful country views. A warm welcome awaits you at Collycroft Farm which is open all the year round for Bed and Breakfast from £17 to £19 per person including bedtime drink. Reductions for children.

ASHBOURNE near. Mrs H. Leason, Overdale, Lode Lane, Alstonefield, Near Ashbourne DE6 2FZ (01335 310206). Overdale is a beautiful, spacious house situated in one and a half acres of landscaped gardens, including shaded walks, orchard and lily pond. Alstonefield is a quiet, extremely pretty village adjacent to Dovedale, the spa towns of Buxton and Matlock, Chatsworth House and Haddon Hall. The guest house has full central heating, two family and five double bedrooms, all equipped with wash-basins; three toilets, bathroom. A charming sittingroom and pleasant diningroom complete this perfect holiday home in its exclusive setting. Bed and Breakfast including evening drink from £15. Open all year.

ASHBOURNE near. Mrs Dot Barker, Waterkeepers Cottage, Mappleton, Near Ashbourne DE6 2AB (01335 350444). Tourist Board Listed. Cosy cottage in the Dove Valley village of Mappleton with small patio and garden for visitors. It lies to the right of the "Okeover Arms", the village pub. Visitors have use of car park. Everyone is sure of a friendly welcome. Reduced prices for under 12 years. Dogs welcomed by prior arrangement. Excellent food, nicely presented. Special diets catered for by prior arrangement. Bed and Breakfast from £16 per person per night; four night breaks £60 per person.

ASHFORD. Mrs Ann Lindsay, Gritstone House, Greaves Lane, Ashford in the Water, Bakewell DE45 1QH (Tel & Fax: 01629 813563). 🌸 🌸 🌸 *COMMENDED.* Be assured of a warm welcome at this charming Georgian house located in Peak National Park on B6465 leading to Monsal Dale and set in picturesque village on the Wye, one and a half miles north-west of Bakewell off A6. Lounge with TV; one twin-bedded room en suite, two double bedrooms with washbasins, all with TV, tea/coffee facilities. Luxury bathroom with bath, shower, etc; two toilets. Full central heating. A perfect location for visiting the Stately Homes and Dales of Derbyshire. Bed and Breakfast from £18 to £23; reduced for weekly stays. Sorry, no pets.

BAKEWELL. Mrs Sheila Gilbert, Castle Cliffe Private Hotel, Monsal Head, Bakewell DE45 1NL (01629 640258). ⚘⚘ COMMENDED. Monsal Head is a popular beauty spot in the heart of the Derbyshire Dales. There are superb views from all the bedrooms in Castle Cliffe Hotel, some overlooking Monsal Dale and the famous viaduct. It is an ideal centre for visiting the dales, caverns and historic houses. Some of the hotel's three double, two family and four twin rooms have en-suite shower/WC, all have tea making facilities. Centrally heated plus open fires in the lounge and bar. Food is home cooked with the emphasis on British dishes from old traditional recipes. Children welcome. Sorry, no pets. Christmas and New Year and Special Mini Breaks available. Licensed. Bed and Breakfast from £24 to £27.50. AA Listed QQQ.

BAKEWELL near. Mrs P. Stanley, Wheel Cottage, Fennel Street, Ashford-in-the-Water, Bakewell DE45 1QH (01629 814339). Wheel Cottage is a delightful 18th century cottage in the unspoilt village of Ashford, nestling by the River Wye just one and a half miles from the market town of Bakewell. Ashford is situated in the Peak District and is famous for its Well Dressing and Sheep Wash Bridge. It is surrounded by glorious walking country and is just a few miles from Chatsworth House and Haddon Hall. Accommodation is in two double and one single bedrooms with colour TV and tea making facilities. Children and pets welcome. Bed and Breakfast from £12.50, en suite from £17.50. Special diets catered for. Reductions off season from October to March. Open all year.

BASLOW. Mrs S. Mills, Bubnell Cliff Farm, Wheatlands Lane, Baslow, Bakewell DE45 1RH (01246 582454). Working farm. A 300 acre working farm situated half a mile from the village of Baslow in the beautiful Derbyshire Peak District. Guests can enjoy, from their bedroom window, breathtaking views of Chatsworth Park and surrounding area. Chatsworth House, the majestic home of the Duke of Devonshire, medieval Haddon Hall and the traditional market town of Bakewell (famous for its puddings), are all close by. Accommodation comprises one double and one family room, guests' lounge/dining room with TV and log fires in the winter. NON-SMOKERS ONLY. Bed and Breakfast from £14 per person. Reductions for children. Varied breakfast menu.

BUXTON. Mr Rys Edge, "Lakenham", 11 Burlington Road, Buxton SK17 9AL (01298 79209).

⚘⚘⚘ COMMENDED. AA QQQ. Kathryn and Rys invite you to sample Victorian elegance in Buxton's finest guest house. Set in a superb central yet quiet location, on a broad tree-lined avenue overlooking the picturesque Pavilion Gardens, "Lakenham" offers all modern facilities yet successfully retains its Victorian character, being tastefully furnished with period furniture and antiques. The bedrooms are spacious and tastefully furnished with your comfort in mind featuring en suite facilities, TV/Satellite and hospitality trays. Many have their own refrigerators/mini bars. "Lakenham" is the perfect base for exploring the many attractions of the Peak District. Children welcome. Private parking. We hope to give a personal service in a friendly relaxed atmosphere. Bed and Breakfast from £20. For colour brochure contact Kathryn Edge.

BUXTON. Mrs Ann Oliver, "Westlands", Bishop's Lane, St. John's Road, Buxton SK17 6UN (01298 23242). ETB Listed. Close to Staffordshire and Cheshire borders, this well established Bed and Breakfast is for non-smokers. Situated on country lane one mile from town centre and Opera House, Westlands offers three rooms with central heating, washbasins, TV and drinks making facilities. Full English breakfast provided. Ample off-road parking available. Very convenient for Chatsworth House, the Potteries, etc. An excellent centre for walking in the Peak District. Golf facilities available locally. Rates from £15 per person for Bed and Breakfast. Weekly reductions. Special diets catered for by arrangement.

Fernydale Farm

Fernydale Farm
Earl Sterndale, Buxton
Tel: 01298 83236 Fax: 01298 83605
Proprietors: The Nadin Family
Reg: East Midlands Tourist Board
👑 👑

Our luxury farmhouse is part of our 230 acre dairy/sheep farm and is ideally situated in a quiet rural setting within the Peak District National Park amidst superb scenery. We are a short distance from Buxton, famous for its water, and within twenty minutes of Ashbourne and the market town of Bakewell. The accommodation, which is open from January to November offers our guests dining room, luxury lounge and conservatory for relaxed comfort.
There are two double bedrooms furnished to a very high standard of comfort with shower, toilet, tea/coffee making facilities and colour television. There is full central heating and access to rooms during the day. B&B from £20.

BUXTON. Mrs E.B. Faulkner, Mount Pleasant Farm, Elkstones, Near Buxton SK17 0LU (01538 300380). 👑 👑 *HIGHLY COMMENDED.* FHG Diploma. This BTA Farmhouse is set on a two acre smallholding surrounded by lovely countryside, peaceful and relaxing with beautiful open views. It makes a comfortable centre for touring the Peak District; a car is essential to get the most out of your holiday. Plenty of parking space. One spacious double bedroom with en suite bathroom and one twin bedroom with adjacent private bathroom. Both bedrooms have bath and shower, easy chairs, colour TV and beverage making facilities. Guests' lounge/dining room. Traditional English breakfast using local bacon, free range eggs, locally baked bread and with home made preserves. Full central heating. Children over six years welcome. We prefer people not to smoke in the house. Pets by arrangement only. Open March to November inclusive for Bed and Breakfast. Terms on receipt of SAE please, or telephone for personal attention and full details.

CASTLETON. Mrs P.J. Webster, Hillside House, Pindale Road, Castleton S30 2WU (01433 620312). 👑 A large country house in landscaped gardens with panoramic views located on quiet outskirts of this historic village. Come and relax in a friendly atmosphere, emphasis on quality, comfort and good food. We offer clean, spacious twin and double rooms, also de luxe en suite, all have TV, radio and tea-making facilities. Start your day with hearty English or vegetarian breakfasts. Ample parking. Cycle lock up. Children welcome but no pets please. A central base for outdoor pursuits like walking, touring or cycling. Look at our caves or castle, visit our market towns or sit in the garden. A non-smoking establishment. Closed Christmas. From £17.50 per night. Brochure available. Self catering cottage also available.

CASTLETON. Mrs B. Johnson, Myrtle Cottage, Market Place, Castleton, Near Sheffield S30 2WQ (01433 620787). ETB Listed. Myrtle Cottage is pleasantly situated near the village green in the picturesque village of Castleton, famous for its castle and caverns. It is an ideal base for walking, caving, hang gliding or touring the Peak District and Derbyshire Dales. Buxton, Bakewell, Chatsworth House and the plague village of Eyam are within 20 minutes' drive. The guest accommodation comprises family, twin and double bedrooms all with private shower/toilet, colour TV and tea/coffee making facilities; sittingroom with TV and diningroom. Central heating. Fire Certificate. Parking. Regret no pets. Open all year (except Christmas) for Bed and Breakfast only.

See also Colour Display Advertisement **CHELMORTON. Christine Holland, Shallow Grange, Chelmorton, Near Buxton SK17 9SG (01298 23578; Fax: 01298 78242).** *HIGHLY COMMENDED.* Shallow Grange is situated in the heart of the Peak District set amidst beautiful open views. This working dairy farm has numerous unspoilt breathtaking walks, whilst Chatsworth, Haddon Hall, Bakewell and Buxton are all within a short drive. This 18th century farmhouse has recently been fully modernised without detracting from its original character; oak beams, inglenook fireplace, etc. are all complemented with antique furniture. All bedrooms are en-suite with tea/coffee making facilities and colour TVs. The house is fully centrally heated, double glazed and carpeted throughout. Fully licensed. Also holiday cottage, sleeps four. Deluxe caravan site. Terms and brochure on request.

CHINLEY, Near Buxton. Mrs Barbara Goddard, Mossley House Farm, Maynestone Road, Chinley, Near Buxton SK12 6AH (01663 750240). ETB Listed

COMMENDED. **Working farm, join in.** Enjoy a stay in the Peak District on our family dairy farm situated in peaceful attractive surroundings. Chinley village is only half a mile away off the A624 Glossop to Buxton Road. We offer one spacious family room, one double; both have washbasin, hot drinks facilities; guests' bathroom; sitting/dining room with TV. Central heating. Delicious breakfasts. Children welcome. Ideal for all the Peak District attractions and for many fine walks. Open March to November. Bed and Breakfast from £16. We extend a warm welcome to our family home.

DERBY. Mrs Catherine Dicken, Bonehill Farm, Etwall Road, Mickleover DE3 5DN (01332 513553).

This 120 acre mixed farm with Georgian farmhouse is set in peaceful rural surroundings, yet offers all the convenience of being only three miles west of Derby, on the A516 between Mickleover and Etwall. Within 10 miles there is a choice of historic houses to visit; Calke Abbey, Kedleston Hall, Sudbury Hall. Peak District 20 miles, Alton Towers 25 miles. Accommodation in three bedrooms (one twin, one double, one family room with en suite facilities), all with tea/coffee making facilities. Cot and high chair provided. Open all year. Bed and Breakfast from £16. Tennis, croquet available. A warm and friendly welcome awaits you.

DOVEDALE. Mrs Joan Wain, Air Cottage Farm, Ilam, Ashbourne DE6 2BD (01335 350475). Working farm, join in. Holidaymakers to the Peak District will enjoy staying at Air Cottage Farm situated at the edge of Dovedale with picturesque views of Thorpe Cloud and Dovedale Valley. The famous Stepping Stones are just 10 minutes away and it is an ideal base for touring the Peak District National Park, stately homes and many other places of local historic interest. Unlimited walks in the Manifold Valley and the Tissington Nature Trail and scenic routes for motorists. Within easy reach of Alton Towers and Carsington Reservoir for water sports. Activities available include swimming, squash and horse riding, all within easy reach. Two double bedrooms and one single (sleeping two); bathroom, two toilets; sittingroom; diningroom. Cot and high chair provided for children. Open March to November. A car is essential — parking. Terms and further details on request.

GLOSSOP. Margaret Child, Rock Farm, Glossop SK13 9JZ (01457 861086). Peace and quiet, friendly

service, and even a few farmyard pets. Situated in the hills above Glossop, with beautiful scenery in every direction. Looking out over Kinder Scout, the highest peak in the National Park, we are well placed for touring both Dark and White Peak areas. Walks from the doorstep, and plenty of pubs nearby offering good food. Though remote, our central location provides an attractive stopover, as well as access to all major cities of the North West. We offer a double and twin-bedded room, both with beamed ceilings, colour TV, radio, and tea/coffee facilities. Guest bathroom with shower, and guest lounge. Bed and Breakfast from £15. Please send for colour brochure.

HARTINGTON. Mrs Jane Gibbs, Wolfscote Grange Farm, Hartington, Near Buxton SK17 0AX (01298 84342). Tourist Board COMMENDED. Find an ideal "country hideaway" on our secluded hill farm, set high above Wolfscote Dale overlooking Berrisford Dale, with Dovedale downstream. Just a couple of miles along a stone-walled road from the pretty village of Hartington. Feel at home in our ancient 15th century farmhouse with all its character of original oak beams, spiral stairs, old mullion windows. The spacious guest lounge has a cosy log fire and grandfather clock ticking steadily in the corner. Separate dining room. Three bedrooms (one double, one twin/family, one single), have antique furnishings, tea/coffee facilities, washbasins and central heating. Have breakfast, then explore the beautiful surrounding hills and hidden dales below. Bed and Breakfast from £17.

HATHERSAGE. Mrs Jean Wilcockson, Hillfoot Farm, Castleton Road, Hathersage, Near Sheffield S30 1AH (01433 651673). Tourist Board Listed COMMENDED. Welcome Host. Newly built accommodation onto exisisting farmhouse offering comfortable, well appointed, en suite rooms. All with central heating, colour TV, tea/coffee making, hair dryer and comfortable easy chairs. We have a large car park and public telephone for guests' use. Excellent home cooked food including vegetarian meals. Bed and Breakfast from £17 to £20 per person. We are situated in the heart of the Peak District, ideal for walking or visiting Chatsworth House, Bakewell, Castleton, Edale and many more places of interest. Current Fire Certificate held. Open all year. Non-smoking.

MATLOCK. Mrs Margaret Haynes, Packhorse Farm Bungalow, Tansley, Matlock DE4 5LF (01629 582781). ❦ ❦ Working farm. New bungalow set in lovely gardens for guests to enjoy. Quiet rural location with extensive views over the valley. You can find both beauty and solitude available all year except Christmas. Double or twin en suite rooms with tea/coffee making facilities and colour TV. Children welcome, pets allowed if kept in car. Bed and Breakfast from £16 to £20.

MATLOCK. Mrs S. Elliott, "Glendon", Knowleston Place, Matlock DE4 3BU (01629 584732). ❦
Warm hospitality and comfortable accommodation in this Grade II Listed building. Conveniently situated by the Hall Leys Park and River Derwent, it is only a short level walk to Matlock town centre. Large private car park available. Rooms are centrally heated and have washbasins, colour TV and tea/coffee making facilities. No smoking in the dining room. An ideal base for exploring the beautiful Peak District of Derbyshire with easy access to many places of interest including Chatsworth House, Haddon Hall, National Tramway Museum and Heights of Abraham cable car. Bed and Breakfast from £16.50 per person.

MATLOCK. Mrs D. Wootton, Old School Farm, Uppertown Lane, Uppertown, Ashover, Near Chesterfield S45 0JF (01246 590813). ❦ Working farm, join in. This working farm in a small hamlet on the edge of the Peak District enjoys unspoilt views. Ashover is three miles away and mentioned in the Domesday Book; Chatsworth House, Haddon Hall, Hardwick Hall, Matlock Bath and Bakewell all within seven miles. Accommodation comprises two family rooms with en suite facilities, one double, one single rooms. Guests have their own bathroom; washbasins in three of the large rooms. Plenty of hot water; fitted carpets; large livingroom/diningroom with colour TV. Non-smoking accommodation available. Car essential. NO PETS. Disabled guests welcome. Children welcome. Open from April to October. Bed and Breakfast from £18 or Bed, Breakfast and Evening Meal £24 (reductions for children). Take the B5057 Darley Dale Road off the A632 Chesterfield to Matlock main road. Take second left. Keep on this road for approximately one mile. Old School Farm is on left opposite the stone water trough. AA and RAC Listed.

DERBYSHIRE – PEAK DISTRICT AND DALES!

The undulating dales set against the gritstone edges of the Pennine moors give Derbyshire its scenic wealth. In the tourists' itinerary should be the prehistoric monument at Arbor Low, the canal port of Shardlow, the country parks at Elvaston and Shipley, the limestone caves at Creswell Crags and Castleton and the market towns of Ashbourne and Bakewell. For walkers this area provides many excellent opportunities.

DEVON

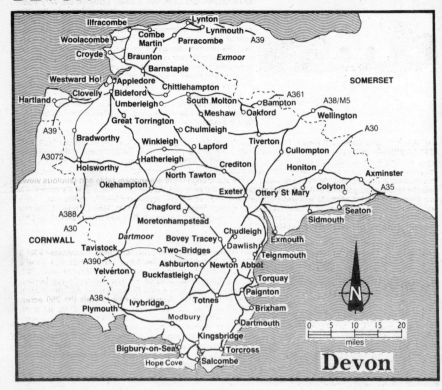

ASHBURTON. **Chris and Annie Moore, Gages Mill, Buckfastleigh Road, Ashburton TQ13 7JW (01364 652391).** 🕷 🕷 🕷 *COMMENDED.* Relax in the warm and friendly atmosphere of our lovely 14th century former wool mill, set in an acre of gardens on the edge of Dartmoor National Park. Eight delightful en suite bedrooms, one on the ground floor, all with tea-making facilities, central heating, hair dryers, radio and alarm clocks. We have a large comfortable lounge with corner bar and granite archways leading to the dining room, and a cosy sittingroom with colour TV. Home cooking of a very high standard. Licensed. Ample car parking. Being one mile from the centre of Ashburton, this is an ideal base for touring South Devon or visiting Exeter, Plymouth, Dartmouth, the many National Trust properties and other places of interest. Children over five years welcome. Sorry no pets. Bed, Breakfast and Evening Meal or Bed and Breakfast only. AA QQQQ Selected, RAC Acclaimed.

ASHBURTON. **Mrs D.M. Dent, Adams Hele Farm, Ashburton TQ13 7NW (01364 652525).** 🕷 🕷 **Working farm.** This 16th century farmhouse nestles on the south facing hill overlooking the Dart Valley and the Moors. The farm consists of 90 acres stocked with cattle, sheep and ponies on pleasant grassland. It is an ideal base for exploring the unspoilt scenery of Dartmoor. The accommodation consists of two double bedrooms each with shower and toilet, one twin room and one family room both with washbasins; two bathrooms, three toilets; sittingroom; two diningrooms. Children are welcome: cot, high chair, babysitting, special mealtimes and reduced rates. Pets by arrangement. Bed and Breakfast from £15. Open March to October. Car essential, parking. The South Devon beaches are only 15 miles; Plymouth and Exeter within half an hour's drive. Excellent fishing, beautiful walks, moorland pony rides and many golf courses within easy reach. A warm welcome to all guests.

ASHBURTON (Dartmoor). Mrs Anne Torr, Middle Leat, Holne, Near Ashburton TQ13 7SJ (01364 631413). Middle Leat, set in three acres, offers very comfortable accommodation with wonderful views, in the picturesque village of Holne, three and a half miles west of Ashburton in the Dartmoor National Park. We have one large ground floor bedroom with private bathroom and full facilities; this has a double bed, bunk beds and a single bed and is available as a double or family room. Full English Breakfast. Vegetarians welcome. Large garden, free-range rare breed chickens and ducks, cows and calves, horse and pets. Visitors are welcome to join in, feeding chicks and ducklings, collecting eggs, etc. A warm welcome and relaxed friendly atmosphere assured in very peaceful surroundings. Sorry, no smoking in the house. Bed and Breakfast from £17. SAE for details or phone for brochure.

AVONWICK. Mrs Sheree Palmer, Hatchlands Farm, Blue Post, Avonwick, Near Totnes TQ9 7LR (01364 72224). Working farm. A very warm welcome awaits you at Hatchlands, a luxury farmhouse set on a working farm amidst Devon's most beautiful scenery, offering tranquillity, magnificent views and unique walks. There are two en suite guest bedrooms with Sky TV, clock/radio, kettle, shaver point, fresh towels, central heating and plenty of hot water. In the sun lounge there is a snooker table and fabulous views over the landscaped gardens and 20ft pond stocked with Koi carp and Golden Orf. Breakfast is a scrumptious four courses served at a time to suit you. Hatchlands is a 275 acre dairy, arable and beef farm. We also have a pony which your children will take delight in riding. Situated in the South Hams, close to many award-winning beaches and near to Dartmoor which must not be missed! Bed and Breakfast £11 to £18; reductions for children and weekly bookings.

AXMINSTER. Christopher and Sandra Holmes, Higher Bruckland Farm, Musbury, Axminster EX13 6SU (01297 552371). Working farm. Chris and Sandie welcome guests to the friendly atmosphere of their 16th century farmhouse situated on the Devon/Dorset border, close to the beach at Lyme Regis, Seaton and the market town of Axminster. Guests are free to walk the 250 acres, with 40 acres of woodland and abundant wildlife, set in an area of outstanding natural beauty. We offer our guests traditional home cooking in the oak-beamed diningroom with comfortable lounge area with colour TV. One family, one double and one twin-bedded rooms, all with washbasins. Children welcome, babysitting available. Open all year. Terms on request.

BAMPTON. Elaine Goodwin, Lodfin Farm, Morebath, Tiverton EX16 9DD (Tel & Fax: 01398 331400). The calming ambience of this beautiful 17th century Devon farmhouse offers everything to relax and unwind. Lodfin Farm is situated on the edge of Exmoor, one mile north of the historic floral town of Bampton and nestles in a secluded valley of which five acres is a natural woodland habitat with a stream and lake for our guests to enjoy. A vast inglenook fireplace forms the heart of the house and original features spread to the guests' lounge with log fire, and all bedrooms which include tea/coffee and TV. We welcome children and pets. Open all year. Bed and Breakfast from £16.50 per person.

BAMPTON. Mrs Lindy Head, Harton Farm, Oakford, Tiverton EX16 9HH (01398 351209). ♛ Working farm, join in. Real farm holidays for country lovers. A unique rural experience for children and the chance to meet the animals on our traditional non-intensive farm near Exmoor. Tranquil 17th century stone farmhouse, secluded but accessible, ideal touring centre. Comfortable accommodation in three double bedrooms with washbasins and tea-making facilities; luxury bathroom with a view; dining room serving real country cooking with farm-produced additive-free meat and organic vegetables; home baking a speciality; guests' lounge with colour TV. Home spun wool. Garden. Children over four welcome. Pets accepted. Car essential — parking. Open for Evening Meal, Bed and Breakfast from £19; Bed and Breakfast from £13. Reductions for children. Farm walks. Fishing, shooting, riding can be arranged. Vegetarian meals available on request.

BAMPTON. Mrs Anne Boldry, Newhouse Farm, Oakford, Tiverton EX16 9JE (01398 351347). 🐦🐦

COMMENDED. Home-baked bread, delicious puddings, home-made pies, pates and preserves . . . the best of country cooking! Newhouse is a 17th century farmhouse tucked down our own stone lane in a peaceful valley. We have prettily and comfortably furnished twin and double rooms, all with private bathrooms and tea trays. We specialise in relaxed, friendly holidays with many guests returning. Newhouse Farm is a perfect base for touring and exploring Exmoor and Devon. We have been awarded QQQQ for Quality by the AA. Sorry, but we do not take children under 10 years or pets. Bed and Breakfast from £16 to £20; Dinner £10. Weekly Dinner, Bed and Breakfast £170 to £180.

BARNSTAPLE. Mrs B. Isaac, Alscott Barton, Alverdiscott, Near Barnstaple EX31 3PT (01271 858336). Our family-run, traditional Devonshire farmhouse offers a delightful holiday base within easy reach of coast and moors. Situated in tiny rural village commanding panoramic views, there are acres of farmland to enjoy incorporating three private lakes for trout and coarse fishing, recreation barn, landscaped gardens and ample parking. Charming accommodation with visitors' lounge, dining room, family and double bedrooms with washbasins also single and twin rooms. Bathroom and shower room facilities. Cots, high chairs provided. Pony available. Pets welcome out of season at our discretion. Bed and Breakfast £15 per person per night; Bed, Breakfast and three-course Evening Meal from £126 weekly. Big reductions for children. Brochure available.

BARNSTAPLE. Mr and Mrs D. Woodman, The Old Rectory, Challacombe, Barnstaple EX31 4TS (01598 763342). Within the Exmoor National Park, easily accessible on a good road, The Old Rectory is tucked away peacefully on the edge of Challacombe. A glance at the map of North Devon will show how excellently the house is placed, either for touring the spectacular coastline or for walking on Exmoor. Superbly furnished bedrooms, with tea/coffee making equipment, washbasins and heating. Ample bathroom, toilet, shower facilities. Comfortable dining room, lounge with colour TV. Bed and Breakfast from £15.50 per night, from £105 per week. No VAT charge. Further particulars on request.

BARNSTAPLE. Mrs Marilyn Purchase, Bridwick Farm, Kentisbury, Barnstaple EX31 4NN (01598 763416). A warm friendly welcome awaits at this working livestock farm beautifully set in quiet Exmoor Valley, where everything possible is done to ensure you enjoy your stay. Situated on A39 half a mile from Blackmoor Gate crossroads towards Barnstaple and midway between Woolacombe and Lynton. Spacious guest rooms equipped with colour TV, washbasins, drinks making facilities; en suite or private bathrooms: Comfortable guest lounge. Ideal location for moors, beaches, fishing or exploring market towns. Children encouraged where possible to meet our pet sheep and cows. Excellent restaurant only half a mile away. Bed and Breakfast from £16 per night. Included in "Which?" Good Bed and Breakfast Guide.

RUSTIC DEVON

Inland from the coastal resorts lies the heart of Devon and the 365 square miles of Dartmoor National Park. Take time to explore the spectacular tors, hills and lakes, and watch out for the famous wild ponies. Picturesque rural villages reflect the unhurried pace of Devon life and there are traces everywhere of the Moor's rich heritage, dating back to the Bronze Age. In the north is Exmoor, one of Britain's smallest National Parks, ideal for rambling, pony trekking and bird watching.

BARNSTAPLE. Mrs L.P.A. Joslin, Stone Farm, Brayford, Barnstaple EX32 7PJ (01271 830473).

Charming 16th century Devon Longhouse on 180 acre working sheep farm and seven acres woodland. Peacefully situated in unspoilt countryside, six miles from the market town of Barnstaple, six miles from Exmoor and 12 miles from North Devon coast with sandy beaches. Spacious, warm and comfortable accommodation in en suite family/double/twin bedrooms with all facilities and colour TV. Oak beams, inglenooks and games room with pool table and darts. Plentiful fresh food of the highest quality offered in four-course Dinner (most nights) and choice of breakfast menu. Vegetarian and special diets catered for. Bed and Breakfast from £18; Dinner £10. Reductions for children and weekly bookings. Brochure with colour photo.

BARNSTAPLE near. Mrs J. Ley, West Barton, Alverdiscott, Near Barnstaple EX31 3PT (01271 858230). Working farm.

West Barton is a mixed family-run farm of 210 acres with a pedigree Friesian herd and sheep. An ideal touring point with Dartington Glass, RHS Rosemoor Gardens, Clovelly, Hartland Point and many other beauty spots and golf courses nearby. Pleasantly situated beside the B3232 Barnstaple to Torrington road with Bideford only five miles away. Sandy beach only six miles. Children welcome. Regret no pets. One twin bedded room with washbasin, one family room and one single room. Lounge with colour TV. Bed and Breakfast from £14. Evening Meal optional.

BEER. Mr and Mrs Les Andrews, The Mullions, New Road, Beer, Seaton EX12 3EB (01297 21377).

The Mullions is situated overlooking the old fishing village of Beer and the sea. Most rooms are large with private facilities. Evening meals are available in the summer months (March to October). The Mullions has a residential licence with a bar situated in the conservatory overlooking the village. Children are welcome at reduced rates. Bed and Breakfast from £18; Evening Meal £8. Special weekly rates from £160 for Bed, Breakfast and Evening Meal.

BIDEFORD. Mrs M. Hillman, Town Farm, Alwington, Bideford EX39 5DA (01237 451254).

Come to Town Farm, a 200 acre dairy farm on the stunning North Devon coast and next to the beautiful 13th century St. Andrews Church. Situated between Bideford and Clovelly it is an ideal base for exploring the coast and the moors. Traditional home cooking is served in the friendly dining room. The lounge has colour TV and video. Orchard and garden have table and chairs for summer evenings. Two doubles and a family room, all with washbasins. Children welcome — slide and swing in garden; cot, high chair and babysitting available. Comfort and friendliness assured. Basic Food Hygiene Certificate and college trained cook.

BIDEFORD. Mrs S. Wade, Collaberie Farm, Welcombe, Bideford EX39 6HF (01288 331391).

Situated on Devon/Cornwall border. Modern farmhouse on 90 acre dairy and beef farm overlooking wooded valley to Atlantic Ocean. Just one and a half miles from Welcombe Mouth, voted cleanest beach in Britain in 1993. Clovelly, Hartland Quay, Bideford, Westward Ho! and Bude all within easy reach. Two bedrooms (one family, one double) both with washbasins and tea/coffee making facilities; bathroom, toilet; lounge with colour TV, video; dining room. Children welcome — high chair, cot; babysitting usually available. Open all year except Christmas. Fire Certificate held. Bed and Breakfast from £14. Evening meal optional. Reductions for children.

BIDEFORD. Mrs C. Colwill, Welsford Farm, Hartland EX39 6EQ (01237 441296). Working farm, join in. Relax, enjoy the peaceful countryside yet be within

easy reach of towns, interesting places and picturesque beaches with miles of scenic cliff walks. This 360-acre dairy farm is situated two miles from Hartland Village; four miles from cobblestoned Clovelly and the rugged Hartland coastline. Comfortably furnished farmhouse with colour TV lounge and washbasins in bedrooms. Children welcome at reduced rates. Wander around the farm and "pets' corner". Babysitting always available. Good country food using home grown produce. Car essential. Bed, Breakfast and four-course Evening Meal from £135 weekly. Warm welcome. Regret no pets. Open April to October.

BIDEFORD. Mrs Joanne Wade, Holloford Farm, Higher Clovelly, Bideford EX39 5SD (01237 441275). ETB Listed *HIGHLY COMMENDED.* We invite you

to stay on our 300 acre dairy farm, the farmhouse dates back to 16th century, with oak beams, open fireplace and pretty bedrooms, all set in peaceful, unspoilt surroundings. Two bedrooms, one twin and one double with single bed. Both have washbasins and drinks trays. Lovely bathroom, sitting room and dining room all beautifully decorated and for guests sole use. Outside enjoy our sheltered garden or take a quiet walk. Come to Holloford to sample a real Devonshire Farmhouse Breakfast and very warm welcome. Two miles from Clovelly and coast. Children welcome. Bed and Breakfast from £18; Evening Meal £10.

BIDEFORD near. Mrs Yvonne Heard, West Titchberry Farm, Hartland, Near Bideford EX39 6AU (01237 441 287). Working farm, join in. Spacious, completely renovated 17th century farmhouse, carpeted and well appointed throughout. One family room with washbasin, one double room with washbasin and one twin room; bathroom and two toilets. Downstairs lounge with colour TV; toilet; diningroom where excellent home cooking is served using fresh farm produce. A games room and sheltered walled garden are available for guests' use. The coastal footpath winds its way around this 150 acre mixed farm situated between Hartland Lighthouse and the National Trust beauty spot of Shipload Bay (sand at low tide). Hartland three miles, Clovelly six miles, Bideford and Westward Ho! 15 miles, Bude 18 miles. Children welcome at reduced rates; cot, high chair and babysitting available. Open all year except Christmas. Sorry no pets. Bed and Breakfast from £15.00 per person per night; Evening Meal (optional) £7.00. Weekly terms: Bed and Breakfast from £91.00 to £94.50; with Evening Meal £125.50 to £130.50. Also self catering cottage available (3 Keys *COMMENDED*).

DEVON – ENDLESS CHOICES!

People never tire of visiting Devon. There's so much to do, like visiting Alscott Farm Museum, Berry Head Country Park, Bickleigh Mill Farm, Farway Countryside Park, Haytor Granite Railway, Kent's Cavern, Dartmoor National Park, Exmoor National Park and of course Plymouth and its Hoe.

BRAUNTON. Mrs Roselyn Bradford, "St. Merryn", Higher Park Road, Braunton EX33 2LG (01271

813805). Set in beautiful, sheltered garden of approximately one acre, with many peaceful sun traps. Ros extends a warm welcome to her guests. Rooms (£15-£17 per person) include single, double and family rooms, with washbasins, central heating, colour TV and tea/coffee making facilities. Two bathrooms plus separate toilets. Evening meal (£8) may be served indoors or out. Guests may bring own wine. Guest lounge with colour TV, patio door access to garden. Swimming pool, fish ponds, hens and thatched summerhouse plus excellent parking. Please send for brochure.

BRIXHAM. Graham and Yvonne Glass, Raddicombe Lodge, 102 Kingswear Road, Brixham TQ5

0EX (01803 882125). The Lodge lies midway between the picturesque coastal harbour towns of Brixham and Dartmouth, overlooking sea and country, with National Trust land between us and the sea. The Lodge is reached by a short drive off the B3205, in a quarter acre garden with the charm and character of pitched ceilings, lattice windows and cosy open log fires for the winter months. Scrumptious traditional English Breakfast with locally baked crusty bread or Continental Breakfast with batons and croissants; light/vegetarian breakfast also available. Colour TV and tea/coffee making facilities in all bedrooms. Come and go as you please, make the Lodge your home from home. Smoking restricted to the lounge area only. Ample parking. Open all year. Children welcome. Sorry no pets. Offering room and breakfast only from £15.40 to £18.70 per night each. En suite rooms £3.20 per night each extra. Popular carvery restaurant just 400 yards away. MasterCard/Access/Visa/ Diners Club cards accepted.

BUCKFASTLEIGH. Suzanne Lewis and Graham Rice, Kilbury Manor Farm, Colston Road, Buckfast-

leigh TQ11 0LN (01364 644079; Fax: 01364 644059). 🐾 This 18th century farmhouse is in a peaceful setting in the Dart Valley, an ideal base for touring Dartmoor and the South Hams Peninsula. Good walking, fishing and golf nearby and many interests for children including wildlife parks, animal sanctuaries, steam trains and good beaches. Bedrooms are attractive and comfortable with TV, tea/coffee facilities; en suite available and a separate bath/shower room. Family suite and self catering loft apartment available. English and Continental breakfast, picnic lunches are provided. Suzanne delights in preparing delicious home cooked food including vegetarian using mostly our own garden produce. Our hospitality will make your stay enjoyable and memorable. Payphone. Brochure on request. Price from £17.50 per night.

CHALLACOMBE. Mrs Christine Johnson, Shorland Old Farm, Challacombe, Bratton Fleming EX31

4TX (01598 763505). Our 16th century farmhouse is beautifully situated in 14 acres overlooking Exmoor, nine miles from the sea. The comfortable farmhouse is centrally heated, and has seven bedrooms, all en suite, guests' lounge with TV and games room. Our visitors can be sure of a homely welcome and enjoy good fresh food. Families are welcome. Reductions for children. Reasonable terms — Bed and Breakfast from £14; optional Evening Meal or young children's early supper. Please send SAE or telephone for full details.

CHUDLEIGH. Jill Shears, Glen Cottage, Rock Road, Chudleigh TQ13 0JJ (01626 852209). 🐾🐾

FHG DIPLOMA AWARDED. Just off the A38 at Chudleigh, Glen Cottage is set in 10 acres of gardens with small lake and waterfall adjoining Chudleigh rocks and caves, providing a natural amphitheatre to this haven of wildlife. Kingfishers, buzzards and herons are a common sight. Swim in the outdoor swimming pool or relax in the tranquil gardens. 20 minutes from Dartmoor and coast. Residents' lounge, TV, tea-making facilities. Bed and Breakfast from £14.

CLAWTON/HOLSWORTHY. Mr T.O.B. Moore, Churchtown House, Clawton, Near Holsworthy EX22 6PS (01409 271467). A warm welcome in centuries-old farmhouse. Delicious home cooking. All rooms tastefully decorated and furnished with antiques. Ideal base for touring nearby Dartmoor and Bodmin Moor. Famous breathtaking local coastline. Idyllic villages and weekly markets. Evening meals if booked in advance. A chance to relax away from the crowds. Set on the edge of small village and off main road. Parking on premises. Bed and Breakfast or Full Board. We have tame sheep, ducks and chickens. See also under Activity Section for painting, craft tuition courses. Golf course, swimming, riding, walking nearby.

CLOVELLY. Mrs J. Johns, Dyke Green Farm, Clovelly EX39 5RU (01237 431699/431279). Situated on the edge of the ancient Roman Dyke at the entrance of famous Clovelly. The tastefully converted barn offers beautiful accommodation furbished to a high standard throughout. All three bedrooms have washbasins (one en suite and one with private WC), colour TV and tea/coffee making facilities. Ideal base for Devon and Cornwall especially lovely Dartmoor and Exmoor. Close to coastal path on South West Way. Amenities close by include golf, tennis, fishing, swimming; perfect for walks and sandy beaches. This lovely home offers you first class Bed and Breakfast from £15 with a warm friendly welcome all year. Evening Meal can be provided from £6. Special rates for children. Please apply for full details.

COLYTON. Mrs Ruth Gould, Bonehayne Farm, Colyton EX13 6SG (01404 871396). Working farm. Bonehayne Farm, situated in beautiful Coly Valley, set amidst 250 acres dairy farmland on banks of the River Coly, where daffodils are a feature in springtime, and Mallard duck and Kingfishers are a common sight. Trout fishing freely available. Woodlands to explore. Visitors welcome to participate in some farm activities and make friends with the animals. One family, one double bedrooms, with washbasins; bathroom, toilet. Spacious, homely lounge with inglenook fireplace, TV. A good English breakfast with our traditional Devonshire farmhouse menu, vegetarian or special diets on request. Play area for children and extended large lawn overlooking surrounding countryside. Reduced rates, cot, high chair, babysitting for children. Small pets accepted. Parking. Farway Country Park, two riding schools, Honiton Golf Course, weekly cattle market, coastal area, all within four and a half miles. Open April to October. Bed and Breakfast; Evening Meal. Terms on request.

COLYTON. Mrs Norma Rich, Sunnyacre, Northleigh, Colyton EX13 6DA (01404 871422). Working farm, join in. Have a relaxing holiday in Bed and Breakfast and Evening Meal accommodation set in an area of outstanding natural beauty with plenty of things to do and see. Accommodation is in a bungalow on a working dairy farm. Join in with farm activities, feeding all the animals, watch cows being milked. Enjoy excellent and varied meals, all home cooked using fresh produce. Full English Breakfast, early morning tea, evening drinks. Three bedrooms with washbasins, separate WC, TV in lounge, games room. Children welcome, cot, high chair and babysitting available. Reasonable rates.

CREDITON. Mr and Mrs R. Barrie-Smith, Great Leigh Farm, Crediton EX17 3QQ (01647 24297).

Working farm, join in. Great Leigh Farm is delightfully set in the mid-Devon hills in a quiet position between Cheriton Bishop and Crediton, two miles off the A30. Ideally situated for a quiet holiday or for touring Devon and Cornwall. Guests are free to wander over the 80 acre sheep farm and may join in farm activities. Outstandingly comfortable accommodation with full central heating. One family room, one double room and two single rooms. Two rooms with bathroom en-suite. Children welcome. Good home cooking. Open all year. Car essential. Babysitting available. Bed, Breakfast and Evening Dinner £21; Bed and Breakfast £15. Children half price.

See also Colour Display Advertisement

CROYDE. Mrs Jean M. Barnes, Denham Farm, North Buckland, Braunton EX33 1HY (Tel and Fax: 01271 890297). ✿✿✿ *COMMENDED.* **Working farm, join in.** 10 beautiful en suite rooms, country views and pretty decor. Here you can relax with the satisfaction of knowing you will be well looked after. Situated in a quiet unspoilt hamlet only two and a half miles from the golden sands of Woolacombe and Croyde. Nowhere is far away. Enjoy the natural beauty that North Devon offers and return to the comfort and charm of Denham. A children's paradise with play area, games room and pets' corner. Taste Jean's delicious home cooking, desserts a speciality. This licensed farmhouse ensures you get a friendly holiday, making Denham a place to return to. Farm Holiday Bureau Member, West Country Tourist Board Member, AA, RAC Acclaimed.

CULLOMPTON. Mr and Mrs T. Coleman, Town Tenement Farm, Clyst Hydon, Cullompton EX15 2NB (01884 277230). A recommended Bed and Breakfast stop in 16th century farmhouse in quiet village, four miles from M5 Junction 28. Guests are accommodated in one double and one family room with bathroom and one double en suite with kitchen (ground floor). All rooms have tea making facilities. The guests' lounge has inglenook fireplace, exposed beams and panelled screen and is comfortably furnished. A farmhouse breakfast is served and a home cooked evening meal can be provided or guests may visit the "Five Bells" in the village. Bed and Breakfast from £14. Reduced rates for children, cots available. Open all year.

CULLOMPTON. Mrs Margaret Chumbley, Fig Tree Farm, Butterleigh, Cullompton EX15 1PQ (01884 855463). Treat yourself to a "special break" and enjoy our welcoming friendly family atmosphere. Set in a magnificent position overlooking the beautiful Burn Valley, Fig Tree Farm is an idyllic rural retreat for that peaceful relaxing holiday. There are many lovely walks in the area, with the coast, Exmoor, Dartmoor and several National Trust properties all within easy reach; Cullompton (M5) four miles. Coarse fishing available. Generous farmhouse hospitality, full menu, delicious four course evening meals using organically grown produce; special diets welcome. Comfortable guest lounge with colour TV, video. Charming double and family rooms, some with verandah, shower, tea/coffee facilities. Bed and Breakfast £14.50; Bed, Breakfast and Evening Meal £132 per week. Phone now, many special offers, "free wine", "free children", "free cycle hire". Open all year.

DARTMOOR. Miss P. Neal, Middle Stoke Farm, Holne, Near Ashburton TQ13 7SS (01364 631444). Working farm, join in. Middle Stoke Farm is a new stone-built barn conversion in an attractive little yard. It stands in 39 acres of beautiful peaceful countryside on Holne Moor, Dartmoor. We have horses, ponies and sheep. The farm is an excellent centre for walking, riding or just relaxing. There are many places of interest to visit including Dart Valley Railway, Butterfly Farm and Otter Sanctuary, the Shire Horse Centre and several rare breed or small animal farms. We have one double/twin room with washbasin, colour TV, tea/coffee making facilities and shaver point; private bathroom. Adults, children, horses and dogs all get a friendly welcome. Bed and Breakfast £16 to £17.50; reductions for children. Reasonably priced evening meals available locally. Dogs £1.50 per night. SAE please, or telephone.

DARTMOUTH. Mr Nigel Peter Jestico, The Captain's House, 18 Clarence Street, Dartmouth TQ6 9NW (01803 832133). ✿✿ *HIGHLY COMMENDED.* The Captain's House is a small Georgian Listed house built about 1730 and is only a few minutes' level walk from the shops and 50 yards or so from the River Dart promenade. Attractions include historic Dartmouth itself, nearby beaches, sailing, fishing and coastal walks. The house is centrally heated and all bedrooms have private facilities, colour TV, radio and alarm clock, fridge, tea and coffee making equipment, and hairdryer, etc. Access to your room at all times. Open January to December. AA QQQQ, RAC Acclaimed. Bed and Breakfast from £20.

DARTMOUTH. Mrs Sue Hutchinson, Sloutts Farmhouse, Slapton, Kingsbridge TQ7 2PR (Tel & Fax: 01548 580872). Sloutts Farmhouse for a relaxing holiday in the country by the sea; a delightful Georgian house tucked down a narrow lane in picturesque Slapton village. Just over half a mile from beach, coastal footpath and Slapton Ley Nature Reserve, midway between Dartmouth and Kingsbridge. En suite bedrooms have lovely open views of village and surrounding South Devon countryside. Wholesome meals prepared with fresh local produce. Log fires, central heating, garden and parking. Open early Spring until late Autumn. Sorry no smoking or pets in the house. Brochure and tariff on request. Self catering family house available nearby.

DAWLISH. Mrs Alison Thomson, Smallacombe Farm, Aller Valley, Dawlish EX7 0PS (01626 862536). 🌺🌺 *COMMENDED.* Off the beaten track yet only two miles from Dawlish and the beach. Enjoy the best of both worlds — country and coast. Children play freely with no fear of busy roads. Meet our three friendly dogs. Relax in the peaceful surroundings and homely atmosphere. Two double rooms, one twin room; family unit available en suite. Bed and Breakfast from £15.00 — £17.00; Evening Meal from £8.50. Reductions for children and weekly discounts. Open all year. Ring or write for brochure.

See also Colour Display Advertisement

DAWLISH. Mr and Mrs T.C. Crump, MHCI, Radfords Country Hotel, Dawlish EX7 0QN (01626 863322). Come and relax at Radfords in one of our lounges, comfortable bar, our lovely garden or alternatively enjoy an action-packed holiday — many activities and sports available here and in the locality. We have family bedrooms or two family suites available, all with private bathroom; accommodation for about 30 families. The children will love their special heated indoor swimming pool, the outdoor playground, the freedom of our large gardens and the assorted ponies and dogs there are to talk to. In the evening they can look forward to a swimming gala, live entertainment, a party and their own cartoon show, etc. Playroom now available. The adults can look forward to superb food lovingly cooked and served and the various entertainments we arrange for them from skittles tournaments to a feature film. We also have a fully equipped launderette and an evening babysitter to help make your holiday as relaxing as possible. Mothers can bring babies and small children here with every confidence. Member West Country Tourist Board. Featured on TV by Judith Chalmers. Farm Holiday Guide Diploma winner. Please telephone or send for illustrated brochure.

EXETER. Mrs Rose Northmore, Marlborough Farm, Clyst Honiton, Exeter EX5 2HN (01392 367500). A warm welcome awaits you at this 300 acre farm. The house stands in its own large garden with lovely views across the Clyst Valley. Coarse fishing is available free to residents in a private pond stocked with carp, roach and perch. We are near many good eating places. Exeter, the Coast, Dartmoor and Exmoor are within easy reach. There are golf courses in various locations. Accommodation comprises two double bedrooms plus cot, one twin-bedded room and single bedroom, private facilities. Bed and Breakfast only. From £77 Low Season to £98 High Season per week; £15 per night. Reductions for children under 10. Open March to November.

EXETER. Mrs Gillian Howard, Ebford Court, Ebford, Exeter EX3 0RA (01392 875353; Fax: 01392 876776). 15th century thatched farmhouse set in quiet surroundings yet only five minutes from Junction 30 M5. The house stands in pleasant gardens and is one mile from the attractive Exe Estuary. The coast and moors are a short drive away and it is an ideal centre for touring and birdwatching. The two double bedrooms have washbasins and tea/coffee facilities, sitting/diningroom with colour TV. Non smoking accommodation. Open all year. Ample parking. Bed and Breakfast from £15 per night, £90 weekly.

EXETER. Mr Derek Sercombe, "Rhona" Guest House, 15 Blackall Road, Exeter EX4 4HE (01392 77791). A small family guest house situated within seven minutes' walk from the centre of historic Exeter, making an ideal base for touring the National Parks of Dartmoor and Exmoor. Luxury en suite accommodation. Colour TV, also tea/coffee making facilities in all rooms. Golf and riding parties catered for. Open all year. Private car park. Single rooms from £11; twin/family rooms from £21 with full English breakfast. Dinner available on request.

EXETER. Mrs Sally Glanvill, Rydon Farm, Woodbury, Exeter EX5 1LB (01395 232341). ❦ ❦ *HIGHLY COMMENDED.* **Working farm.** Come, relax and enjoy yourself in our lovely 16th century Devon longhouse. We offer a warm and friendly family welcome at this peaceful dairy farm. Three miles from M5 Junction 30 on B3179. Ideally situated for exploring the coast, moors and the historic city of Exeter. Only 10 minutes' drive from the coast. Inglenook fireplace and oak beams. All bedrooms have central heating, private or en suite bathrooms, hair dryers and tea/coffee making facilities. One room with romantic four-poster. A traditional farmhouse breakfast is served with our own free range eggs and there are several excellent pubs and restaurants close by. Pets by arrangement. Farm Holiday Bureau member, AA QQQQ Selected. Open all year. Colour brochure available. Bed and Breakfast from £18 to £24.

EXETER. Mr Chris Morris, Clock Tower Hotel, 16 New North Road, Exeter EX4 4HF (01392 424545; Fax: 01392 218445). ❦ ❦ The greatest care and comfort offered by caring resident proprietors of this Grade II Listed historically interesting city centre hotel with its award winning patio/garden and the modern facilities expected of larger hotels at a fraction of their cost. En suite rooms with baths and Satellite TV. Licensed bar. All major credit cards accepted. Bed and Breakfast rates start from £15 per person per night. Send for colour brochure with details of free holiday insurance.

EXMOUTH. Miss T. Webb, Wotton Farm, Lympstone EX8 5AY (01395 264401). Family run pig farm in beautiful countryside just five minutes' drive to the lovely sandy beach of Exmouth. Full farmhouse breakfast served. Comfortable bedrooms with tea/coffee facilities; most have washbasins. Lounge with colour TV. Lovely gardens to sit and relax in. Many pastimes in the area — golf, pony trekking, sailing, surfing and fishing. Bed and Breakfast from £16. Reduced rates for children. Brochure on request.

EXMOUTH. Mrs J. Hallett, Gulliford Farm, Lympstone, Near Exmouth EX8 5AQ (01392 873067). Working farm. You are assured of a warm welcome to our 16th century farmhouse with its spacious rooms and beautiful garden with sun terrace, lawns, tennis court and swimming pool. This working farm stands in the beautiful Exe Valley only a short distance from the many beaches. One family suite, two double or family rooms, one single room, most with washbasin and tea-making facilities. Lounge with colour TV and inglenook fireplace, diningroom with separate tables. Ample parking. There is access to rooms at all times. A full English breakfast is served and there are many delightful inns and restaurants to provide your evening meal. Terms for Bed and Breakfast are from £18 per person per night. We also have TWO comfortable SELF CATERING COTTAGES. From £100 to £300 plus VAT.

HOLSWORTHY. Mrs Linda Cole, The Barton, Pancrasweek, Holsworthy EX22 7JT (01288 381315). 🐾🐾 A peaceful holiday awaits you on our 200 acre working dairy farm situated on the Devon/Cornwall border. Six miles from Cornish coast with quaint fishing villages, beautiful beaches and famous Clovelly. Fishing, sailing, sailboarding at Tamar Lakes, also close to leisure pool and sports centre. Historic Dartmoor and Bodmin Moor within easy reach. The 16th century farmhouse has three bedrooms for guests — two double and one twin, all en suite with tea making facilities. Games room, lounge with TV, separate dining room. Traditional farmhouse cooking with home grown produce when available. Open Easter to end September. Bed and Breakfast from £15; Evening Meal £8. Reductions for children. Brochure on request.

FHG PUBLICATIONS LIMITED publish a large range of well-known accommodation guides. We will be happy to send you details or you can use the order form at the back of this book.

HOLSWORTHY. Mrs Barbara Morris, Chasty House, Chasty, Holsworthy EX22 6NA (01409 253511). Warm welcome assured at Chasty House. We grow our own fruit and vegetables and our free range hens keep us well supplied with eggs. Home cooking for the largest appetite! Tea/coffee making facilities included. Chasty House has lovely views across open country to Bodmin and Dartmoor yet is only three-quarters of a mile from the town of Holsworthy. Just 15 minutes' drive to sandy beaches at Bude and many other unspoilt spots along the rugged coastline of North Devon and Cornwall. Children especially welcome at reduced rates; babysitting available. Sorry, no pets. Bed and Breakfast £13; with Evening Meal £17. Free brochure available.

HONITON. Mrs Elizabeth Tucker, Lower Luxton Farm, Upottery, Honiton EX14 9PB (01823 601269). Working farm. Get away from the toil of everyday life and come to Lower Luxton Farm where a warm welcome awaits you in an area of outstanding natural beauty. Set overlooking peaceful Otter Valley facing south, this olde worlde farmhouse, fully modernised but retaining its charm, is on 140 acres of farmland keeping usual animals and pets to make it a real farm. Carp fishing on site included in terms. Peaceful walks. Ideal base for touring. Several places of interest in area. Coast 14 miles; village inn one mile. Good home cooking assured using fresh farm produce (four-course breakfasts and dinners) — including sweets topped with Devon cream; bedtime beverages with biscuits included. Family, double or twin rooms available with wash-basins and razor points. Tea making facilities. Snooker table and darts available for guests. Pets welcome. Terms from £115 for six Evening Dinners and weekly Bed and Breakfast, £14 Bed and Breakfast nightly. SAE for brochure and terms. Open all year.

HONITON. Pamela Boyland, Barn Park Farm, Near Cotleigh, Stockland Hill, Honiton EX14 9JA (01404 861297). 🏵 COMMENDED. Barn Park Farm is a working dairy farm situated near the A30/A303 junction, set in picturesque countryside within reach of many beauty spots and the coast. The farmhouse is full of character having a homely atmosphere. Children and pets welcome. Traditional English breakfasts using eggs from our free range hens. Bed and Breakfast from £15; Evening meal available. Open all year.

ILFRACOMBE. Michael and Lynda Hunt, Sunnymeade Country House Hotel, Dean Cross, West Down, Ilfracombe EX34 8NT (01271 863668). 🏵🏵🏵 APPROVED. AA QQQ. A charming country house hotel in its own large gardens set in the rolling Devon countryside. Every effort is made to ensure that guests feel welcome and relaxed from the moment they arrive, a feeling which is enhanced by the standard of food and accommodation. Most of the 10 pretty bedrooms are en suite and all have tea-making facilities, phones, colour TV and radios; some of the rooms are on the ground floor. Fresh local ingredients are used in the traditional English cooking which has a regional flavour. There is always a vegetarian choice and any special diets can be accommodated. Clothes drying facilities for walkers and a garage for cycles. Sunnymeade is close to Woolacombe, Exmoor and Ilfracombe. Access and Visa accepted. Bed and Breakfast en suite from £20.50 daily; Dinner, Bed and Breakfast en suite from £179 weekly.

PLEASE SEND A STAMPED ADDRESSED ENVELOPE WITH ENQUIRIES

ILFRACOMBE. Mrs E.A. Barleycorn, Epchris Hotel, Torrs Park, Ilfracombe EX34 8AZ (01271

862751). ✿✿✿ *APPROVED.* A comfortable small hotel with lovely grounds and views in a peaceful setting in Ilfracombe. Perfect for families in high season and for those looking for peaceful walks and touring, all year. Yards from the footpath to the Torrs Walks over National Trust coastline, yet only a short walk to the famous Tunnels Beaches, town centre and seafront. We have a heated swimming pool and paddling pool, putting green, games chalet and a cheerful bar and comfy residents' lounge. All rooms have tea/coffee making facilities, TV and are en suite except one room which has private facilities. Bed and Breakfast from £19. Brochure available, please telephone.

IVYBRIDGE. Mr and Mrs D. Johns, Hillhead Farm, Ugborough, Ivybridge PL21 0HQ (01752

892674). ✿ *COMMENDED.* **Working farm, join in.** Comfortable, welcoming family farmhouse. Guests' sittingroom with TV and woodburner. One twin room, two double rooms both with TV, all with tea/coffee facilities and washbasins. Guests' private bathroom, also separate toilet. Full central heating, open log fire in dining room. Children and pets welcome. Good home cooked and largely home produced food. Open all year except Christmas. Bed and Breakfast from £15 to £17; Evening Meal £10.

IVYBRIDGE. Mrs Paula Salter, Strashleigh Farm, Ivybridge PL21 9JP (01752 892226). ETB Listed

COMMENDED. **Working farm.** Enjoy a relaxing holiday in a friendly atmosphere. Strashleigh is a working farm set between Dartmoor and Bigbury Bay. Easily accessible, it is a perfect base for touring, city entertainment, horse riding, golf and many other attractions. The farm has an interesting history. The house has comfortable, spacious rooms and wide views of the rolling countryside. If you are interested we will be pleased to show you the animals. Children welcome. Two double and one twin rooms, all with washbasins and tea making facilities. Non-smoking accommodation available. Lounge with colour TV. Member of FHB. Self catering accommodation (3 Keys APPROVED) also available. Brochure.

IVYBRIDGE near. Mrs Susan Winzer, "The Bungalow", Higher Coarsewell Farm, Ugborough, Near

Ivybridge PL21 0HP (01548 821560). Working farm. Higher Coarsewell Farm is a traditional family-run dairy farm situated in the heart of the peaceful South Hams countryside, near Dartmoor and local unspoilt sandy beaches. It is a very spacious bungalow with beautiful garden and meadow views. One double room with bathroom en suite and one en suite family room. Guest lounge/dining room. Good home cooked food, full English breakfast served. Children welcome — cot, high chair and babysitting available. Bed and Breakfast from £14 daily; optional Evening Meal extra. Open all year. A379 turnoff from the main A38 Exeter to Plymouth road.

See also Colour Display Advertisement **KINGSBRIDGE near. Mr and Mrs C.M. Davies, Maelcombe House, East Prawle, Near Kingsbridge TQ7 2DA (01548 511300). Working farm.** This small coastal working farm nestles beneath wooded cliffs overlooking Lannacombe Bay. The beach is one minute from the comfortable farmhouse which is nearly the most southerly in Devon. Guests have a choice of family, double or single rooms. Food is excellent, much being produced on the farm, and freshly caught seafood is a speciality. There is a lot to do — fishing, bathing, spectacular walking, exploring, climbing, boating, tennis or just relaxing in the gardens. Prices from £114.50 per week for Bed and Breakfast or £159.50 per week for Bed, Breakfast and Evening Meal, with special reductions for children. Also two self-catering flats to sleep six, and limited camping facilities are provided. Telephone or write for colour brochure.

KINGSBRIDGE. Mrs C. Lloyd, Lower Norton, East Allington, Totnes TQ9 7RL (01548 521246).

Come and enjoy a quiet holiday at Lower Norton, a stone built farmhouse now run as a guest house within a two acre holding providing eggs, milk, etc. The house is surrounded by farmland and is situated approximately five miles from Kingsbridge and eight miles from Dartmouth; the nearest beach is Slapton and Torbay, Plymouth and Dartmoor are all within 20 miles. Four double/family rooms; two bathrooms; separate lounge/dining rooms; utility room and tea making facilities. Children welcome. No smoking. Car essential. Open April to October for Bed and Breakfast only, £105 per week. Reductions for children. Stamp only please for brochure.

BLACKWELL PARK

Loddiswell, Kingsbridge Tel: 01548 821230 ETB ♛♛

Blackwell Park is a 17th century farmhouse situated five miles from Kingsbridge and two miles from Loddiswell. Many beaches within easy reach, also Dartmoor, Plymouth, Torbay and Dartmouth. Seven bedrooms for guests, all with washbasins and tea-making facilities, some en suite. Separate tables in diningroom; lounge with colour TV. Large games room with darts, snooker, skittles etc. Garden with plenty of grass for games adjoining 54 acres of woodland/nature reserve. Large car parking area. Ample food with choice of menu. Help yourself to tea and coffee at any time. Fire Certificate. CHILDREN AND PETS ESPECIALLY WELCOME. Babysitting. Open all year round for Bed, Breakfast and Evening Meal. Reduced rates out of season.

KINGSBRIDGE. Mrs M. Darke, Coleridge Farm, Chillington, Kingsbridge TQ7 2JG (01548 580274).

Coleridge Farm is a 600 acre working farm situated half a mile from Chillington village, midway between Kingsbridge and Dartmouth. Many safe and beautiful beaches are within easy reach, the nearest being Slapton Sands and Slapton Ley just two miles away. Plymouth, Torquay and the Dartmoor National Park are only an hour's drive. Visitors are assured of comfortable accommodation in a choice of one double and one twin-bedded rooms; private shower; toilet; shaver points and tea/coffee making facilities. Spacious lounge with TV. A variety of eating establishments in the locality will ensure a good value evening meal. Children welcome. Terms on request.

KINGSBRIDGE. Beni & Jonathan Robinson, Coombe Farm, Kingsbridge TQ7 4AB (01548 852038).

♛♛ COMMENDED. Come and enjoy the peace and beauty of Devon in our lovely 16th century farmhouse. Wonderful breakfast, large elegant rooms each with own bathroom, colour TV, hot drinks facilities. Artists have use of an art studio and fishermen can enjoy the well known Coombe Water fishery. Open all year except Christmas. Bed and Breakfast from £18.50 to £20.

Terms quoted in this publication may be subject to increase if rises in costs necessitate

KINGSBRIDGE. Anne Rossiter, Burton Farm, Galmpton, Kingsbridge TQ7 3EY (01548 561210).

ww *HIGHLY COMMENDED.* **Working farm, join in.** Working farm in South Huish Valley, one mile from the fishing village of Hope Cove, three miles from famous sailing haunt of Salcombe. Walking, beaches, sailing, windsurfing, bathing, diving, fishing, horse-riding — facilities for all in this area. We have a dairy herd and three flocks of pedigree sheep. Guests are welcome to take part in farm activities when appropriate. Traditional farmhouse cooking and home produce. Four-course Dinner, Bed and Breakfast. Access to rooms at all times. Tea/coffee making and washbasins in rooms, all of which have private facilities, some en-suite. Games room. No smoking. Open all year, except Christmas. Warm welcome assured. Small functions catered for. Self-catering also available. Dogs by arrangement. Details and terms on request.

KINGSBRIDGE. Yvonne Helps, Hillside, Ashford, Kingsbridge TQ7 4NB (01548 550752). Character house set in acre of orchard garden surrounded by lovely countryside, in a quiet hamlet just off the A379 Plymouth to Kingsbridge road. Superb beaches and sandy coves nearby. Dartmoor 20 minutes' drive. Very comfortable accommodation with washbasins, shaver points, tea/coffee making facilities in all bedrooms. Two bathrooms. Colour TV in lounge. Diningroom with separate tables. Car parking. Visitors find a friendly, relaxed atmosphere with own keys. No dogs in the house please. Full central heating. Bed and full English Breakfast from £15; Evening Meal optional. Open all year. Booking any day of the week. Write or phone for brochure.

KINGSBRIDGE near. Mrs M. Newsham, Marsh Mills, Aveton Gifford, Near Kingsbridge TQ7 4JW (01548 550549). Former Mill House, overlooking the River Avon, with gardens, mill leat and duck pond. Small farm with friendly animals. Peaceful and secluded, just off A379. Kingsbridge four miles, Plymouth 17 miles, Bigbury and Bantham with their beautiful beaches nearby, or enjoy a walk along our unspoilt river estuary. Salcombe seven miles, Dartmoor eight miles. A warm welcome awaits our guests, who have access to the house at any time. Bedrooms have washbasins, tea/coffee making and room heaters. Guest bathroom, WC; lounge/dining room with colour TV. Car essential, ample parking. Bed and Breakfast from £15 per person. SAE for brochure, or telephone.

LYNMOUTH. Glenville House, 2 Tors Road, Lynmouth EX35 6ET (01598 752202). Charming licensed Victorian house in sunny position overlooking East Lyn River at the beginning of Watersmeet Valley. Picturesque village and tranquil harbour a short stroll away. Ideally situated for touring/walking this beautiful part of Exmoor with its breathtaking scenery and spectacular coastline. Some bedrooms have private facilities and all have tea/coffee making. Comfortable TV lounge and attractive dining room offering a four-course breakfast. Our guests will be assured of a warm welcome, good food and friendly hospitality for their stay. Non-smoking. Bed and Breakfast from £17 to £20 per person per night. Dinner (optional) £11.50 per person. Open March to November.

See also Colour Display Advertisement **LYNTON. Mr and Mrs B. Peacock, Seawood Hotel, North Walk, Lynton EX35 6HJ (01598 752272).** w w w *HIGHLY COMMENDED.* Seawood Hotel is set in its own grounds overlooking the sea with breathtaking views of Lynmouth Bay and Exmoor. The Peacock family make guests very welcome in their charming old-world house. Five-course dinners with imaginative home cooking, for which great praise is received. Both lounges, diningroom and all bedrooms enjoy sea views. The latter all have en-suite bathroom and/or shower/WC, colour TV and tea/coffee making facilities. Four-posters are also available. Full central heating. Residential licence. Pets welcome. Colour brochure on request. Open March to November. RAC one star. Special award for Hospitality, Service and Comfort. AA one star.

LYNTON. Ben and Jane Bennett, Victoria Lodge, Lee Road, Lynton EX35 6BS (Tel & Fax: 01598 753203; Freephone 0500 303026). ♛♛♛ *HIGHLY*

COMMENDED. Elegant Victorian, family-run, non-smoking hotel, received 1996 RAC Best Small Hotel in South West England award and one of only five in North Devon to be awarded AA Premier Selected for its comfort, hospitality and outstanding cuisine. All our en suite bedrooms are beautifully decorated, with colour TV, radio and tea/coffee making facilities; some are de-luxe four-poster beds or original brass beds with lounge areas. Enjoy a candlelit dinner, which combines an imaginative blend of English and Continental cuisine, complemented by fine wines. We are ideally situated for exploring Exmoor and its spectacular coastline. Full central heating, private car park and secluded gardens. Bed and Breakfast £21 to £32 per person. Dinner £14. Special offers. Children welcome. No pets. Please send or telephone for a free brochure.

LYNTON. Woodlands, Lynbridge Road, Lynton EX35 6AX (01598 752324). ♛ ♛ ♛ *COMMENDED.*

AA QQQ. Peacefully located yet only a few minutes' walk from the centre of Lynton, Woodlands overlooks Summerhouse Hill and the unspoilt wooded valley of the West Lyn River. There is a choice of single, double and twin rooms, all with colour TV, radio and tea/coffee making facilities. Most rooms are very spacious, fully en suite and have glorious views across the valley. Delicious home cooking using fresh produce. Choice of menu including vegetarian option. Private parking, licensed, cosy lounge, log fire and central heating. Non smoking. Ideal base for exploring Exmoor and the stunning coastal scenery. Bed and Breakfast £16 to £22; Evening Meals £12.

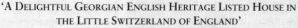

MORETONHAMPSTEAD. Mrs T.M. Merchant, Great Sloncombe Farm, Moretonhampstead TQ13 8QF (01647 440595). 🐾🐾🐾 *HIGHLY COMMENDED.*

Working farm. Share the magic of Dartmoor all year round while staying in our lovely 13th century farmhouse full of interesting historical features. A working dairy farm set amongst peaceful meadows and woodland abundant in wild flowers and animals, including badgers, foxes, deer and buzzards. A welcoming and informal place to relax and explore the moors and Devon countryside. Comfortable double and twin rooms with en suite facilities, TV, central heating and coffee/tea making facilities. Delicious Devonshire suppers and breakfasts with new baked bread. Open all year. No smoking. Farm Holiday Bureau member. AA QQQQ Selected.

NEWTON ABBOT. Mrs Susan Stafford, Newhouse Barton, Ipplepen, Newton Abbot TQ12 5UN (01803 812539). 🐾🐾🐾 A lovely old farmhouse set in 115

acres of Devon's rolling countryside yet only a short drive to the coast or Dartmoor. All bedrooms have private bathroom, tea/coffee making facilities and colour TV. Oak-beamed lounge with stone fireplace. Diningroom with separate tables — plenty of good food. A delightful place in the country with a friendly atmosphere. Bed and Breakfast from £19.00; Evening Meal available from £12.50. Also two newly converted, three-bedroom self catering cottages from £282 per week.

NEWTON ABBOT. Mrs Dawn Cleave, Mill Leat Farm, Holne, Ashburton, Newton Abbot TQ13 7RZ (01364 631283). A friendly welcome awaits you at Mill

Leat, a family-run working farm that's tucked into the foothills of Dartmoor. There is a peaceful atmosphere, where you can relax and unwind and enjoy the birds and wildlife. Plenty of good walks to take in with National Trust woodlands adjoining the farm. The A38 is only three miles and Buckfast Abbey even closer. En-suite is available and tea/coffee making facilities in all bedrooms. Lots of lovely homemade food. Bed and Breakfast from £16 to £17, Evening Meal from £8. Weekly reductions. Open all year except Christmas.

NEWTON ABBOT. Nigel Bell, Sampsons Farm, Preston, Newton Abbot TA12 3PP (01626 54913).

Thatched 14th century longhouse with oak beams, panelling and inglenook fireplaces. Sampsons is a Grade II Listed building featuring low beams, creaky floors and is hidden away in the hamlet of Preston with lovely walks along River Teign. Always a warm welcome and a cheerful atmosphere. All rooms (three double, two family) have tea/coffee making facilities and colour TV. The restaurant has an excellent reputation with only the finest produce being used. There is a licensed bar and cellar containing wines from around the world. Sampsons is well placed to explore Devon and Cornwall. Bed and Breakfast from £15; Dinner from £6.95. Open all year.

OKEHAMPTON. Mrs Jenny King, Higher Cadham Farm, Jacobstowe, Okehampton EX20 3RB (01837 851647). 🐾🐾🐾 *COMMENDED.* **Working farm, join in.** 139 acre beef and sheep farm just off the A3072, five miles from Dartmoor. 16th century farmhouse with barn conversions offering a total of nine rooms — five en suite, the rest have washbasins, shaver points, etc., with bathroom and toilets close by. Two of the four lounges are non-smoking as is the dining room, though smokers are welcome in other rooms. The accommodation is of the highest standard with plenty of hearty Devonshire food, a residential licence and a warm welcome. Babies and dogs are accepted by arrangement only but older children are very welcome. We have farm walks, ducks on the ponds and other animals to amuse all the family. Walkers on the Tarka Trail are fully catered for with drying room, packed lunches, etc. AA QQQQ Selected and DATI Warmest Welcome Award 1992 has helped make Higher Cadham Farm the "place to stay" when in West Devon. Bed and Breakfast from £17; Dinner £8. Weekly from £158; supplement for en suite rooms. Member of Farm Holiday Bureau.

OTTERY ST. MARY. Mrs Susan Hansford, Pitt Farm, Fairmile, Ottery St. Mary EX11 1NL (01404 812439). 🐦🐦 *COMMENDED.* Bed and Breakfast at this most attractive thatched farmhouse, with 190 acres, situated in peaceful village of Fairmile, quarter of a mile off the A30 on the B3176. Enjoying picturesque views of the surrounding countryside it is an ideal base for touring the moors, East Devon, South Devon, Exeter. Double, twin and family rooms, some en suite; three bathrooms; lounge with colour TV; dining room. Regret no pets. Car essential, ample parking. Fire Certificate held. Bed and Breakfast from £17. SAE, or phone, for terms; prompt reply.

PAIGNTON (Torbay). Mrs Mandy Tooze, Elberry Farm, Broadsands, Paignton TQ4 6HJ (01803 842939). Working farm. Elberry Farm is a working farm uniquely situated close to Broadsands Beach, Elberry Cove and a pitch and putt golf course. Close to many of Torbay's tourist attractions. Warm welcome and good hearty meals (using local and home grown produce) are guaranteed. The comfortable rooms (three family and one twin) all have tea/coffee making facilities. Baby listening, cot and high chair available. Pets by arrangement. Restricted smoking. Open January to November. Bed and Breakfast from £12.50 per person; Evening Meals £5.50. Reductions for children.

PLYMOUTH. Mrs Margaret MacBean, Gabber Farm, Down Thomas, Plymouth PL9 0AW (01752 862269). 🐦🐦 *COMMENDED.* **Working farm, join in.** Come and join us on this 120 acre working farm in an area of outstanding natural beauty with lovely walks on the farm and coastline. It is ideally situated for touring and near the historic city of Plymouth. Good food and a warm welcome are assured with Bed and Breakfast or Bed, Breakfast and Evening Meal available. One double and one family room en suite, two twins and family room with washbasins. All have tea/coffee making facilities and clock radios. Iron, ironing board, hair dryer available. Open March to November. TV lounge, dining room. Fire Certificate. Bed and Breakfast from £16. Special rates for Senior Citizens and children. Brochure available on request.

SALCOMBE. Mrs M.E. Lonsdale, Fern Lodge, Hope Cove, Kingsbridge TQ7 3HF (01548 561326). 🐦🐦 "Fern Lodge" is a detached guest house with colourful garden, flanked by palm trees. It is delightfully situated in Hope Cove, an uncommercialised fishing village with safe, sandy beaches, surrounded by National Trust land, offering beautiful cliff and country walks. The scenery is truly magnificent and totally unspoilt. Dartmoor is nearby, Totnes 19 miles, Dartmouth 21, Torbay 25 and Plymouth 23 miles. The eight bedrooms have either a sea or landscape view (sea approximately 250 yards), colour TV and own keys. Full central heating. Two lounges, one with colour TV. Diningroom. Beverage making facilities. Car parking. Children and pets welcome. Bed and Breakfast from £22 to £23.

DEVON – LAND OF DOONE AND DRAKE

Exmoor is the setting of R.D. Blackmore's "Lorna Doone", and visitors today can still soak in the romantic atmosphere of Doone Valley where the outlaws lived, and Oare Church, near Lynmouth, the scene of Lorna's wedding. Devon's most famous son is undoubtedly Sir Francis Drake, born at Crowndale, near Tavistock. It was to Plymouth he returned after sailing round the world in 1580 and on Plymouth Hoe he reputedly finished his game of bowls before tackling the Spanish Armada in 1588.

SALCOMBE. Mrs Madge Bullock, Pine Cottage, Froude Road, South Sands, Salcombe TQ8 8LH (0154 884 2170). A comfortable detached cottage in wooded surroundings with beautiful sea views from all bedrooms; lounge, diningroom and sun terrace. Car preferable, but not essential — parking space provided. Log fires out of season — bedrooms with heaters. Safe, sandy beach within 100 yards for swimming, sailing, windsurfing, diving and fishing. Ideal countryside for walkers and visitors appreciative of wild life, with magnificent views of the estuary and English Channel. Other beaches and coves nearby. Children over three years welcome at reduced rates if sharing parents' room. Substantial cooked breakfast, pot of tea with biscuits early morning and afternoon from £15 inclusive — no extra charge. Bed and Breakfast only. Open from January to December. Reductions for Senior Citizens November to March. SAE, please.

SEATON. Mrs Jenny Webber, Axe Farm, Axmouth, Seaton EX12 4BG (01297 24707). Working farm. 12th century farmhouse situated one mile from Seaton and beach. Accommodation comprises one double and one family room with TV and tea/coffee making facilities; adjoining bathroom; lounge for guests' use. Central heating. Ample car parking. Children and pets welcome. Lovely walks and bird watching on Axe Estuary. Bed and breakfast from £16. Excellent evening meals available at local inns.

SEATON. Three Horseshoes Inn, Branscombe, Seaton EX12 3BR (01297 680251). 🦢🦢 Beautiful 16th century coaching house with log fires and brasses. Jan and John Moore will give you the warmest of welcomes and help plan your days if you wish. Set in an area of outstanding natural beauty. Central for sea or country. Footpaths lead through woodland. Cliff walks. Wonderful wildlife. Honiton's antique shops and lace, historic Exeter, all at hand; Sidmouth is just 10 minutes away. All bedrooms are centrally heated and have tea/coffee making facilities. Traditional jazz every Saturday night in the function room, so if you want a quiet drink in the lounge bar you are not disturbed. Real ales served. Bed and Breakfast from £14.

SIDMOUTH. Mrs Kerstin Farmer, Higher Coombe Farm, Tipton St. John, Sidmouth EX10 0AX (01404 813385). 🦢 *COMMENDED.* **Working farm.** Comfortable farmhouse accommodation, peacefully situated in the beautiful Otter Valley only four miles from Sidmouth seafront and the surrounding National Trust and Devon Heritage Coast. Half a mile off B3176. It is within easy reach of many beaches, ideal for touring all of East Devon, but also Exeter, Dartmoor and Exmoor. Enjoy the full English Breakfast and friendly relaxed atmosphere. Family, double and single bedrooms, all with washbasins, tea-making facilities, electric blankets and TVs. Guests' bathroom, toilet; diningroom and lounge with colour TV. Children very welcome with cot, high chair and babysitting available. Terms from £112 weekly for Bed and Breakfast, £51 for a three-day break.

SIDMOUTH. Mrs Lorna F. Lever, Canterbury House, Salcombe Road, Sidmouth EX10 8PR (01395 513373). 🦢🦢 This charming small Georgian residence overlooking the River Sid offers comfortable accommodation and some free parking. Set in this quaint and interesting town is only a third of a mile from the seafront with level walk to nearby shops, etc. Double, twin and family bedrooms, some ground floor and seven with en-suite facilities. Washbasins, shaver sockets, bedside lamps, colour TV and tea-making facilities in all bedrooms. Partial central heating. Colour TV lounge. Full English breakfast and varied dinner menu. AA and RAC listed, Hotels and Caterers Association. Weekly terms from £180 inclusive. Credit cards accepted.

SIDMOUTH. Mrs Elizabeth Tancock, Lower Pinn Farm, Peak Hill, Sidmouth EX10 0NN (01395 513733). ♛♛ *COMMENDED.* **Working farm.** Lower Pinn

is in an area of outstanding natural beauty, two miles west of the unspoilt coastal resort of Sidmouth and one mile to the east of the pretty village of Otterton. Comfortable spacious rooms, two double/twin en-suite, one double with wash-basin. All rooms have colour TV, hot drink facilities, electric blankets and central heating. Bathroom has bath and shower, separate toilet. Guests have their own keys and may return at all times throughout the day. Ample parking. Substantial breakfast served in dining room. Local inns and restaurants nearby provide excellent evening meals. Children and pets welcome. Open most of the year. Bed and Breakfast from £16 to £20. Full details on request.

Bovett's Farm

Bovett's nestles amid the rolling hills of the truly breathtaking Roncombe Valley. There are many excellent walks nearby. Within easy reach of Exeter and East Devon's Heritage Coast. Guests have use of the garden and are free to come and go as they please. The comfortable lounge has a wood-burning stove, colour TV and a selection of books and games. A full English Breakfast is served in the lovely dining room. We offer a choice of three attractively furnished double/twin bedrooms all with ensuite shower room and shaver point. Bedrooms are heated and have tea/coffee making facilities. Friendly personal service. Ample parking. No smoking. *Call Bridget and Brian Hopkinson for further details.*

Bovett's Farm, Roncombe Lane, Sidbury, Sidmouth, Devon EX10 0QN Telephone: (01395) 597456

SIDMOUTH. Mrs Betty F. Sage, Pinn Barton, Peak Hill, Sidmouth EX10 0NN (Tel & Fax: 01395 514004). ♛♛ *COMMENDED.* **Working farm.** Pinn Barton

is a farm of 330 acres situated on the coast, two miles from Sidmouth, where there is a good choice of eating places. There are many safe bathing beaches nearby and lovely walks along the cliffs and around the farm. It is very peaceful, being just off the coast road, between Sidmouth and the village of Otterton. Pinn Barton has been highly recom-mended and you will be given a friendly welcome in comfort-able surroundings, and a good farmhouse breakfast. All bedrooms have en-suite facilities and all have colour TV, central heating, tea/coffee making facilities, razor plugs and electric blankets for chilly nights. There is a diningroom and separate sittingroom for guests (with colour TV and a fire). Children are very welcome. Bed and Breakfast including bedtime drink from £19. Reductions for children sharing parents' room. Own keys provided. Open all year.

SOUTH MOLTON (6 miles). Tony and Myra Pring, The Gables, On-the-Bridge, Umberleigh EX37 9AB (01769 560461). ♛♛ We offer friendly personal

service here at The Gables, which is situated facing the River Taw, famous for its salmon fishing and "Tarka the Otter". You will find us ideally placed for the beautiful Exmoor National Parks, Dartington Glass, Lynton and Lynmouth and the sandy beaches of Woolacombe. The Barnstaple to Exeter railway line is within easy reach for those who do not wish to drive. The accommodation is in three en suite rooms, one twin and one double and one single, all with central heating and tea/coffee facilities. There is a quiet lounge and a TV lounge. Tea rooms available. Private parking. Sorry, no children. Open all year. Bed and Breakfast from £16.50 to £21.50.

SOUTH MOLTON near. Mrs J.M. Bray, West Bowden Farm, Knowstone, South Molton EX36 4RP

(01398 34224). ✿✿ West Bowden is a working farm, mainly beef and sheep. It is situated just north of the A361, about a mile from Knowstone village which has a thatched pub. The house, which is thatched and has inglenook fireplaces, is thought to date from the 17th century. It is spacious and comfortable, and has a lounge with colour TV and a separate dining room. Accommodation comprises three en suite bedrooms and others with washbasins; all have tea making facilities. Guests receive hospitality in the real Devon tradition, plus good home cooking, fresh vegetables and clotted cream. Pets welcome. Terms from £139 per week for Bed, Breakfast and Evening Dinner.

SOUTH MOLTON near. Mrs Cheryl Woollacott, Capitol Farm, Bishop's Nympton, Near South

Molton EX36 4PH (01769 550435). Welcome to our warm and cosy atmosphere here at Capitol Farm. We are pleasantly situated, within easy reach of Exmoor, the coast and many other attractions. Accommodation provided in two bedrooms — one double and one twin-bedded; bathroom; separate lounge. We serve breakfasts of your choice and three-course dinners (optional). Since we limit the number of guests our visitors are assured of personal attention. Couples can relax and be spoilt or a family with children are most welcome; pony rides available, house cow to milk and eggs to find! Whether a short break or a longer stay we aim to make your holiday a happy one. Further details and terms on request.

SOUTH MOLTON near. Messrs H.J. Milton, Partridge Arms Farm, Yeo Mill, West Anstey, Near

South Molton EX36 3NU (01398 341217; Fax: 01398 341569). ✿✿ *COMMENDED.* **Working farm, join in.** Now a working farm of over 200 acres, four miles west of Dulverton, "Partridge Arms Farm" was once a coaching inn and has been in the same family since 1906. Genuine hospitality and traditional farmhouse fare await you. Comfortable accommodation in double, twin and single rooms, some of which have en suite facilities. There is also an original four-poster bedroom. Children welcome. Animals by arrangement. Residential licence. Open all year. Fishing and riding available nearby. Farm Holiday Guide Diploma Winner. Dinner, Bed and Breakfast from £27.50 per person; Bed and Breakfast from £18.

TAVISTOCK. Mrs B. Anning, Wringworthy Farm, Mary Tavy, Tavistock PL19 9LT (Tel & Fax: 01822

810434). Working farm. This farm is set in a valley with the entrance on the A386. It is mentioned in the Domesday Book and the main part is Elizabethan. It has been modernised for comfort yet retains its old charms such as beams and flagstones. Log fires and a friendly greeting ensure guests of a warm welcome at Wringworthy. The guests have a lounge to themselves with TV; two double bedrooms and one twin with TV and tea/coffee making facilities; two bathrooms; diningroom. Children over two years are welcome and there is a cot and reduced rates. Sorry, no pets. Open from April to October. Car is essential and there is parking. Bed and Breakfast only, from £16. It is near the sea and there is fishing in Tamar and Tavy. Also near the moors; riding, walking and golfing. SAE please for further details. AA QQQ.

TEIGN VALLEY. S. and G. Harrison-Crawford, Silver Birches, Teign Valley, Trusham, Newton

Abbot TQ13 0NJ (01626 852172). A warm welcome awaits you at Silver Birches, a comfortable bungalow at the edge of Dartmoor. A secluded, relaxing spot with two acre garden running down to river. Only two miles from A38 on B3193. Exeter 14 miles, sea 12 miles. Car advisable. Ample parking. Excellent pubs and restaurants nearby. Good centre for fishing, bird watching, forest walks, golf, riding; 70 yards salmon/trout fishing free to residents. Centrally heated guest accommodation with separate entrance. Two double bedded rooms, one twin bedded room, all with own bath/shower, toilet. Guest lounge with colour TV. Diningroom, sun lounge overlooking river. Sorry, no children under eight. Terms including tea on arrival — Bed and full English Breakfast from £23 nightly, £154 weekly. Evening Meal optional. Open all year. Self catering caravans also available.

TORQUAY. Craig Court Hotel, 10 Ash Hill Road, Torquay TQ1 3HZ (01803 294400). 🌑 🌑 RAC

Acclaimed. AA QQQ. The resident proprietors supervise this Grade II Listed building beautifully situated facing south in one of the most convenient positions in Torquay, although away from the main road, within easy walking distance of beaches, amusements and shops. Pleasant TV lounge and separate bar overlook a secluded garden. Dining room has separate tables and there is a choice of menu at all meals. The hotel has six double bedrooms (three en-suite), two family rooms (both en-suite) and two single rooms, all with hand basins; three bathrooms and toilets. Children are welcome. Parking on the premises. Bed and Breakfast from £16.50 per person, Dinner, Bed and Breakfast from £154 per week. Reduced rates for children sharing parents' room. SAE for colour brochure.

TOTNES. Mrs J. Allnutt, The Old Forge at Totnes, Seymour Place, Totnes TQ9 5AY (01803

WINNER SOUTH HAMS
FOR ALL SEASONS AWARD

862174). 🌑 🌑 *HIGHLY COMMENDED.* A charming 600 year old stone building, delightfully converted from blacksmith and wheelwright workshops and coach houses. Traditional forge, complete with blacksmith's prison cell. We have our own bit of "rural England" close to the town centre. Very close to the River Dart steamer quay, shops and station (also steam train rides). Ideally situated for touring most of Devon — including Dartmoor and Torbay coasts. A day trip from Exeter, Plymouth and Cornwall. May to September — Elizabethan costume worn Tuesdays. Double, twin and family rooms, all en suite. Ground floor rooms suitable for most disabled guests. All rooms have colour TV, beverage trays (fresh milk), colour co-ordinated Continental bedding, central heating. Licensed lounge and patio. New conservatory style leisure lounge with whirlpool spa. No smoking indoors. Parking, walled gardens. Excellent choice of breakfast menu including vegetarian and special diets. Children welcome but sorry, no pets. Bed and Breakfast (en suite) from £25 per person. Cottage suite for two or four persons, suitable for disabled visitors. AA Selected (QQQQ) Award.

TOTNES. Mrs Anne Barons, Charford Farm, Avonwick, Totnes TQ9 7LT (01364 73263). 🌑 🌑

Working farm, join in. A warm and friendly welcome awaits you at this lovely old farmhouse on a 340-acre dairy and arable farm where visitors are free to roam. Centrally situated for coast, Dartmoor, Plymouth and Torbay; within easy reach of many tourist attractions. Family and double rooms available with en suite facilities and colour TVs. Tea-making facilities. Dining room and lounge with colour TV. Home from home comfort in a relaxed, informal atmosphere. Children are very welcome at reduced rates. Cot, high chair and babysitting available, also children's ponies. Open Easter to October for Bed and Breakfast from £17; Evening Meal £9. Weekly reductions available. Please telephone or write for terms and brochure.

TOTNES. Mrs Janet Hooper, Great Court Farm, Weston Lane, Totnes TQ9 6LB (01803 862326). 🌑

HIGHLY COMMENDED. A warm welcome awaits you at this lovely Victorian farmhouse overlooking the historic town of Totnes and surrounding countryside. The dairy farm runs down to the River Dart. Ideal centre for touring Dartmoor, beaches, National Trust properties, tourist attractions and the pretty South Devon villages. The spacious double, twin and family rooms are colour co-ordinated and all have washbasins, beverage facilities, TVs and central heating. Guests have their own bathroom plus a second bathroom with a shower and separate WC. Breakfast is served in the dining room overlooking the garden. Choice of menu including Vegetarian. Guest lounge. Garden. Inns and restaurants nearby. Evening meals by arrangement. No smoking in the house. Bed and Breakfast from £14.50; Evening Meal from £9.

If you've found
FARM HOLIDAY GUIDES
of service please tell your friends

TOTNES near. Mrs Miller, Buckyette Farm, Littlehempston, Near Totnes, TQ9 6ND (01803

762638). ✿ ✿ Grassland farm in attractive countryside. From Totnes take A381 towards Newton Abbot follow signpost to Littlehempston, turn right at phone box, farm third to left. Accommodation comprises six bedrooms — one twin with bath/shower, one double with bath and toilet and four family rooms, three with bath and toilet, one with shower and toilet. All rooms have tea/coffee facilities. Central heating. Children are welcome, babysitting available. Open March to October. Table licence. Bed and Breakfast from £17 to £21. Weekly and child rates available. Fire Certificate held. RAC Listed.

UMBERLEIGH. Mrs P. Warne, Emmett Farm, Umberleigh EX37 9AG (01769 540243). Emmett is a

full working farm set in quiet countryside. You will be most welcome to browse around the farm at your own leisure. The traditional farmhouse has a beamed dining room, comfortable lounge with open log fire and colour TV. Relaxing bedrooms are equipped with tea/coffee facilities and radio/ clock/alarms. Fresh home grown produce is used (whenever possible) in the farmhouse cooking, with our farm fresh eggs for breakfast and a different four-course meal each evening if required. We are situated approximately seven miles from Barnstaple, South Molton and Torrington. There are many local places of interest to visit with the sandy beaches of the North Devon coastline within easy reach, as is the scenic Exmoor with its panoramic views. Bed and Breakfast from £15; Evening Meal £8.50. Ample car parking. Sorry no pets.

WOOLACOMBE. Chris and Helen Rook, Seawards, Beach Road, Woolacombe EX34 7AD (01271

870249). Overlooking Woolacombe Bay, with spectacular views, Seawards is a small family-run guest house offering a warm welcome. Our aim is to make you feel at home whether your stay is long or short. We can offer family, double or twin rooms, some en suite, all with tea/coffee making facilities. For those enjoying a winter break the house is fully centrally heated. Children welcome; sorry, no pets. No smoking in the house, please. Ample parking. Licensed. Open all year except Christmas and New Year. Special winter break rates. Bed and Breakfast from £16. Phone or write for further details.

WOOLACOMBE. Dave and Chris Ellis, Crossways Hotel, The Seafront, Woolacombe EX34 7DJ

(01271 870395). ✿ ✿ *COMMENDED.* Cosy, family-run, licensed hotel, situated in one of the finest sea front positions in Woolacombe, overlooking the pretty Combesgate beach and Lundy Island and being surrounded by National Trust land. Bathing and surfing from hotel and ideally situated for golf, horse riding and beautiful walks. Menu choice for breakfast and evening dinner, and children's menu. Varied bar snacks available at lunchtime. All bedrooms individually refurbished to a high standard, many en suite and with fabulous sea views. Colour TV and tea/coffee making facilities in all rooms. Children half price or Free. Pets welcome. Free on-site parking. AA/RAC one star, RAC Merit Award for Hospitality and Service. Why not find out why many of our guests return year after year?

WORLINGTON. Derek and Rosemarie Webber, Hensley Farm, Worlington, Crediton EX17 4TG (Tel

& Fax: 01884 860346). Working farm, join in. Derek, Rosemarie, their son Alan and daughter Paula welcome you to stay on their dairy, sheep and beef farm with farm dogs, cats, hens and rabbits. Their thatched farmhouse is near a picturesque country village overlooking one of the prettiest unspoilt valleys in Devon. Guests are welcome to watch and take part in milking, see the calves and roam around the farm at their leisure. We have superb walks around the village and river, horse riding and golf nearby; fishing on our own stream. Exmoor, Dartmoor and the coast with beautiful sandy beaches nearby. Large lawn; table tennis, toys and board games. Well behaved pets welcome. Large bedrooms with washbasins and colour TV; dining room; lounge with woodburner. Traditional farmhouse breakfast. Brochure available.

DORSET

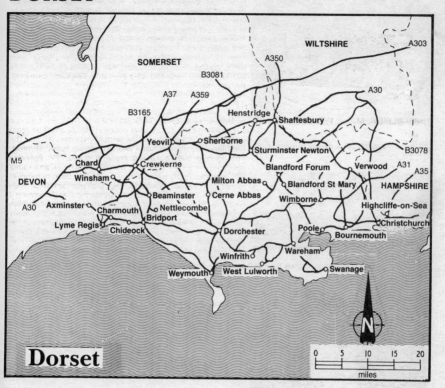

Dorset

BEAMINSTER. **Mrs Jackie Spooncer, Lewesdon Farm, Stoke Abbot, Beaminster DT8 3JZ (01308 868270).** ♥♥ Lewesdon Farm is situated in an area of outstanding natural beauty, five and a half miles from Bridport, close to the Heritage Coast. Free from noise and traffic, off a private road. Warm comfortable double room with en-suite shower. Tea-coffee making facilities and TV. Superb location for walking or just relaxing. NON-SMOKERS PLEASE. See also entry in Self Catering section.

BLANDFORD FORUM. **Mrs C.M. Old, Manor House Farm, Ibberton, Blandford Forum DT11 0EN**

(01258 817349). Working farm, dairy and sheep. Situated nine miles west of Blandford Forum. Small 16th century manor house, now a farmhouse, surrounded by large colourful garden in a quiet unspoilt village which at one time was given to Katherine Howard by Henry VIII. The oak beams and nail studded doors confirm its centuries-old past. Two double bedrooms (one with en suite facilities) and one twin-bedded room, both with tea-making facilities. Bathroom and toilet; lounge with TV, dining room with separate tables. Children welcome, cot and high chair provided. Bed and Breakfast from £12 to £15. Open all year. No evening meal. Good food at Crown Inn nearby. Self catering accommodation also available.

FUN FOR ALL THE FAMILY IN DORSET

Brewers Quay, Weymouth; Deep Sea Adventure, Weymouth; Dinosaur Museum, Dorchester; Dinosaurland, Lyme Regis; Maiden Castle, Dorchester; Natural World, Poole Aquarium; Sea Life Centre, Weymouth; Upton Country Park, Poole; Waterfront Museum, Poole.

BLANDFORD FORUM. Mr and Mrs D.N. Cross, Gold Hill Organic Farm, Childe Okeford, Blandford DT11 8HB (01258 860293). 🌸🌸 Working farm, join in.

60 acres grass and horticulture in beautiful North Dorset countryside. Explore Hardy's country, National Trust houses and the Purbeck coast. Family and twin rooms, both with washbasins, razor points, TV and tea/coffee making facilities; two separate bathrooms; comfortable sittingroom with log fire. Non-smokers only. Breeding Shires, DIY livery, safe good hacking, own ponies welcome for long or short stays; coarse fishing; organic horticulture, harvesting help welcomed. Farmhouse offers Bed and Breakfast for long or short stays in friendly family atmosphere, no Evening Meal (sorry), but good inns within walking distance. Terms from £17 per night. Ample parking. Self catering annexe available, sleeps two/three.

BOURNEMOUTH. Mrs Annie Habgood, Northover Hotel, 10 Earle Road, Alum Chine, Bournemouth BH4 8JQ (01202 767349). 🌸🌸🌸 OLD-FASHIONED

COURTESY AWAITS YOU AT THE NORTHOVER HOTEL situated facing Alum Chine, 400 yards from sea and sandy beaches and only 20 minutes' walk from Bournemouth Pier. Near bus routes for town centre where there is superb shopping and all types of entertainment. The New Forest, Purbeck Hills and lovely Dorset and Hampshire countryside within easy reach. Choice of double, single or family rooms with double or twin beds, tea/coffee making facilities FREE; most rooms with en suite facilities. Attractive lounge, colour TV; spacious diningroom serving varied and excellent food. Residential licence. Central heating. Under personal supervision of proprietor, the hotel is open all year including Christmas. Bed and Breakfast from £17; Dinner, Bed and Breakfast from £24. STAY FOR 7 PAY FOR 6 DAYS. Mid-week bookings accepted. Special rates for Senior Citizens early and late season. Children and pets welcome. Ample parking. Off season bargain breaks. Our aim is to make you want to return. AA/RAC Listed. AWARDED FHG DIPLOMA 1988/89 — ONLY FIVE AWARDED TO HOTELS IN ENGLAND!

BOURNEMOUTH. The Vine Hotel, 22 Southern Road, Southbourne, Bournemouth BH6 3SR (01202 428309). A small family hotel only three minutes' walk from

sea or shops. All rooms bath or shower and toilet en suite; tea-makers and colour TV. Residential licence. Full central heating. Forecourt parking. Pets welcome in lounge and bedrooms. Open all year, including Christmas. For comfort and safety of all our guests, dining room and bedrooms are no smoking. Bed and Breakfast from £15 to £22 per person per night. Please write or telephone for further details.

BRADFORD ABBAS. Wendy and Robin Dann, Heartsease Cottage, North Street, Bradford Abbas DT9 6SA (01935 75480). Wendy and Robin have run a

chalet in the French Alps for a number of years and now own Heartsease, a delightful old stone cottage in a beautiful Dorset village close to Sherborne, Somerset border, A30. They can collect from the local station only two hours from Waterloo — THE PERFECT WEEKEND BREAK, overnight or longer. Three bedrooms with different themes and tea/coffee facilities — Victoria, en suite double, Farmhouse and Napier, each a twin sharing luxury bathroom. Good food is the "heart" in Heartsease — breakfasts, dinners, light suppers, even barbecues and picnics in the idyllic mature garden. Easy motoring to Sherborne, Lyme Regis, Shaftesbury, Longleat, Wells. Marvellous walks. Guests sitting room with log fire. TV/video. Badminton and French boules courts. Prices from £15, May to November.

BRIDPORT. Ann and Dan Walker MHCIMA, Britmead House, West Bay Road, Bridport DT6 4EG (01308 422941). ♛♛♛ *HIGHLY COMMENDED.* AA QQQQ Selected. RAC Acclaimed. Guestaccom Good Room Award 1997. Delightful freshly cooked food, personal service and putting guests' comfort first means visitors return time after time. Situated between Bridport, West Bay harbour with its beaches/golf course/walks, Chesil Beach and the Dorset Coastal Path. Fully en suite rooms (one ground floor), all with colour TV, tea making facilities, hair dryers and mini bar. South facing lounge and dining room overlooking the garden. Optional table d'hôte dinner menu, incorporating local fish and produce. Licensed. Full central heating. Private parking. Dogs by arrangement. Children welcome. Reservations starting any day for any length of stay. Break rates all year. Weekly Bed and Breakfast from £112 to £147; Dinner, Bed and Breakfast from £203 to £238.

MARSHWOOD MANOR

♛♛♛ Commended

Near Bridport, Near Charmouth, Dorset DT6 5NS

Tel. Broadwindsor (01308) 868442

Five tastefully furnished ensuite rooms. Close to Chalmont and Lyme Regis, Bed & Breakfast with Evening Meal on request. Speciality Home Cooking.

AA LISTED

Weekly or Short Breaks available. · *Brochure on request.*

BRIDPORT near. Mrs Sue Norman, Frogmore Farm, Chideock, Bridport DT6 6HT (01308 456159). Working farm, join in. Set in the rolling hills of West Dorset, enjoying splendid sea views, our delightful 17th century farmhouse offers comfortable, friendly and relaxing accommodation. An ideal base from which to ramble the many coastal and country footpaths of the area (nearest beach Seatown one and a half miles) or tour by car the interesting places of Dorset and Devon. Some bedrooms with en-suite shower room. Cosy TV lounge, with wood fire, guests' diningroom and tea making facilities. Children and well behaved dogs welcome. Open all year, car essential. Bed and Breakfast from £14, (Evening Meal optional). Brochure and terms free on request.

CERNE ABBAS. Mrs T. Barraclough, Magiston Farm, Sydling St. Nicholas, Dorchester DT2 9NR (01300 320295). ETB Listed. Magiston is a 400 acre working farm with a comfortable 17th century cob and brick farmhouse set deep in the heart of Dorset. Large garden with river. Situated in an ideal touring centre and just half an hour's drive from coast and five miles north of Dorchester. The farmhouse comprises double, twin and single bedrooms. Delicious evening meals served. Children over 10 years and pets welcome. Central heating. Open January to December. Bed and Breakfast from £16.50 per person per night. Please write or telephone for further details.

FHG PUBLICATIONS LIMITED publish a large range of well-known accommodation guides. We will be happy to send you details or you can use the order form at the back of this book.

CERNE ABBAS. Mrs V.I. Willis, "Lampert's Cottage", Sydling St. Nicholas, Cerne Abbas DT2 9NU

(01300 341659; Fax: 01300 341699). Bed and Breakfast in unique 16th century thatched cottage in unspoilt village. The cottage has fields around and is bounded, front and back, by chalk streams. Accommodation consists of three prettily furnished, double bedrooms with dormer windows, set under the eaves, and breakfast is served in the dining-room which has an enormous inglenook fireplace and original beams. The village, situated in countryside made famous by Thomas Hardy in his novels, is an excellent touring centre and beaches are 30 minutes' drive. West Dorset is ideal walking country with footpaths over chalk hills and through hidden valleys and is perfect for those wishing peace and quiet. Open all year. Terms on request.

CHARMOUTH. Mrs S.M. Johnson, Cardsmill Farm, Whitchurch Canonicorum, Bridport DT6 6RP

(Tel & Fax: 01297 489375). ♛ ♛ Working farm, join in. A Grade II Listed comfortable quiet farmhouse in picturesque Marshwood Vale, three miles from Charmouth. Ideal for beaches, fossil hunting, touring, walking and golf at Lyme Regis. See the animals, pets and crops on this 450 acre family farm. Walk to the village through the fields. Double en suite and family room available with private bathroom, shaver points, tea/coffee trays, cot, hairdryer. Full central heating and double glazed windows throughout. Lounge with log fires, beams and colour TV; dining room with separate tables. Access at all times. English and varied breakfasts. Children and pets welcome. Babysitting. Ample parking. Large garden, picnic table and barbecue. Bed and Breakfast from £15 to £19 per person per night. Senior Citizens' and children's reductions. Open February to end November. Please phone or write for brochure. Also self catering farmhouse (ETB 4 KEYS APPROVED), sleeps up to 12, short or long stays, available all year.

DORCHESTER. Mrs Rita Bown, Lamperts Farmhouse, 11 Dorchester Road, Sydling St. Nicholas, Dorchester DT2 9NU (01300 341790). 🏵🏵 17th century thatched Listed farmhouse nestling in the Sydling valley. Choose either Bed and Breakfast in tastefully decorated en suite bedrooms with Victorian brass beds and antique pine furniture or self catering in our fully restored well-equipped one bedroom farm cottage (3 KEYS). Guests' own sitting room with inglenook fireplace and colour TV. Sheltered garden. Home-cooked evening meal optional. Farm Holiday Bureau member.

Lamperts Farmhouse and Cottage

DORCHESTER. Michael and Jane Deller, Churchview Guest House, Winterbourne Abbas, Near Dorchester DT2 9LS (01305 889296). 🏵🏵 *COMMENDED.* Our 300 year old AA QQQ Guest House is set in a small village five miles west of Dorchester in an area of outstanding natural beauty. Noted for warm, friendly hospitality and delicious home cooked food, it makes an ideal base for exploring Hardy country. Churchview is a non-smoking establishment offering two comfortable lounges, attractive oak-beamed dining room and bar. Our character rooms have hospitality trays and central heating; most en suite. Your hosts will give every assistance with local information to ensure a memorable stay. Pets welcome. Parking. Terms: Bed, Breakfast and four-course Evening Meal £29.50 to £37; Bed and Breakfast from £18.50 to £25.

HINTON ST. MARY. Sally Sofield, Old Post Office Guest House, Hinton St. Mary, Sturminster Newton DT10 1NG (01258 472366; Fax: 01258 472173). 🏵🏵 *COMMENDED.* Comfortable and homely guest house, convenient for exploring the beautiful varied scenery of unspoilt Dorset. Guests' lounge with games, TV, maps and books. Large garden backing onto fields. Footpaths and River Stour (good fishing) nearby. Village has quaint thatched houses, church, Manor House and a traditional sociable Dorset village pub. No one goes hungry here, with good traditional home cooked fayre using local produce where possible. We do our best to provide a warm welcome, good value and a friendly place to stay. Bed and Breakfast from £16; Evening Meal (optional) £7. Cottage (sleeping 3) also available. Brochure on request.

LYME REGIS. Mrs S.G. Taylor, Buckland Farm, Raymonds Hill, Near Axminster EX13 5SZ (01297 33222). We are situated off the A35 in quiet and unspoilt surroundings with gardens and grounds of five acres which are ideal for guests to relax or stroll in. We are about three miles from the lovely coastal resorts of Lyme Regis and Charmouth. A warm welcome awaits you. Accommodation mainly on the ground floor comprises two family bedrooms, one double en suite shower and one twin-bedded room, all with TV, washbasin, tea/coffee making facilities. No smoking in bedrooms. Bathroom, shower, WC plus separate WC. Lounge with colour TV, video and log fire. Dining area with separate tables. A good full English breakfast served. Bed and Breakfast from £13. Self catering also available. Send SAE for further details.

LYME REGIS. Mrs M.J. Powell, Meadow View, Green Lane, Rousdon, Lyme Regis DT7 3XW (01297 443262). A warm welcome awaits you at this working family farm situated quarter of a mile off the A3052 road at Rousdon just three miles from Lyme Regis, four miles from Seaton. Ideal centre to explore the Devon and Dorset countryside, the sand and shingle beaches, or try your hand at fossil hunting. One family/double bedroom with washbasin and another double room; both have colour TV and tea/coffee making facilities; two guest bathrooms, one with shower over bath; lounge with colour TV. Central heating. Access to rooms at all times. Full English breakfast served at separate tables. Bed and Breakfast from £13 to £15. Reductions for children sharing parents' room. Ample car parking.

PLEASE SEND A STAMPED ADDRESSED ENVELOPE WITH ENQUIRIES

LYME REGIS. Jenny and Ivan Harding, Coverdale Guest House, Woodmead Road, Lyme Regis DT7 3AB (01297 442882). 🐾🐾 *COMMENDED*. AA Recom-

mended QQQ. Friendly, well established Guesthouse situated in a quiet residential area of Lyme Regis, a few minutes' walk from the sea and town centre. Fine views over Woodland Trust's land to the rear and sea to the front. Double, twin, family and single rooms (en suite available). Tea/coffee facilities all rooms. Comfortable TV lounge. Attractive dining room with separate tables. Good home cooking using own garden produce. Access to house all day. Private parking. No smoking please. Ideal base for exploring countryside and unspoilt scenic coastline on foot or by car. Walkers welcome — South Coast path/Liberty Trail close by. Bed and Breakfast from £13 to £20. Dinner optional June to September only. Weekly reductions. Write or phone for brochure.

MIDDLEMARSH. Mr O'Neill, White Horse Farm, Middlemarsh, Near Sherborne DT9 5QN (01963 210222). Comfortable country farmhouse within three acres

of gardens, paddock and lake. Our excellent facilities include pine-furnished rooms with comfortable beds en suite or private bathroom; all with washbasins, colour TV and tea/coffee making equipment. Our breakfasts are renowned! Set in peaceful Hardy countryside near Cerne Abbas, the ancient abbey town of Sherborne and historic Dorchester. Easy travelling distance to lovely coastline, including Lulworth Cove, Weymouth and Lyme Regis. Enjoy walking, fishing, horse riding, golf, etc. 100 yards local inn. Open all year except Christmas. Also four attractive self catering cottages where pets are welcome and ideal for partially disabled guests. Bed and Breakfast from £15 to £20 per person. Brochure available.

POWERSTOCK. Mrs D.P. Read, The Old Station, Powerstock, Bridport DT6 3ST (01308 485301).

Peacefully situated deep in the glorious Dorset countryside, one mile south east of Powerstock, in two and a half acres of garden, this former railway station enjoys beautiful views. Conveniently situated for drives into neighbouring counties; many rural walks; can be reached by public transport. Two double bedrooms, one single, all with washbasins and tea-making facilities; bathroom, second toilet; central heating. Daytime access. Off road parking; tennis, fun golf. Hearty English breakfast prettily served (vegetarian breakfast by previous arrangement). Evening meals available locally. Open March through October, from £13. No pets. Badger watching possible most evenings from house. SAE, please, for details.

SHAFTESBURY. Mrs G. Gosney, Kington Manor Farm, Church Hill, Kington Magna, Near Gillingham SP8 5EG (01747 838371). Working farm. Attractive

farmhouse situated in a quiet, pretty village, with splendid views over the picturesque Blackmore Vale. The village lies one mile off A30 between the historic towns of Shaftesbury and Sherborne; Stourhead National Trust house and gardens and stately home of Longleat and Safari Park nearby. Bath 45 minutes' drive. Spacious and comfortable accommodation comprising one double/family room with adjoining private shower room with WC, one twin-bedded room with/without private bathroom. Tea/coffee making facilities. Visitors' dining room and lounge with TV. Bed and hearty breakfast £16 per person per night. Reductions for children. Excellent pub food nearby or evening meals on request.

SHERBORNE. Mrs Pauline Tizzard, Venn Farm, Milborne Port, Sherborne DT9 5RA (01963

250598). The perfect stop when travelling, easy to find on main A30, three miles east of historic castle and abbey town of Sherborne, 30 minutes' drive to coast. Our 200 acre working dairy farm is situated in beautiful wooded parkland within walking distance of local village inn. Attractively furnished accommodation includes one twin, one double and one family room, all with washbasins, colour TV and tea/coffee making facilities. Bathroom equipped with shower and separate WC. Full central heating plus guests' lounge with log fire. Children welcome. AA QQ Recommended. Bed and Breakfast from £15. Reductions for children. Open all year.

SHERBORNE. Mrs J. Mayo, Almshouse Farm, Hermitage, Sherborne DT9 6HA (Tel & Fax: 01963

210296). ♨ ♨ HIGHLY COMMENDED. Working farm, join in. This charming old farmhouse was a monastery during the 16th century, restored in 1849 and is now a listed building. A family-run working dairy farm surrounded by 140 acres overlooking the Blackmoor Vale, just one mile off A352. Accommodation is in three comfortable en suite rooms with colour TV and tea/coffee making facilities. Diningroom with inglenook fireplace, lounge with colour TV, for guests' use at all times. Also garden and lawn. Plenty of reading material and local information provided for this ideal touring area. Bed and Breakfast from £18. AA QQQQ Selected. Excellent evening meals in all local inns nearby. Situated six miles from Sherborne with its beautiful Abbey and Castle. SAE for further details.

SHILLINGSTONE. Mrs Rosie Watts, Pennhills Farm, Sandy Lane, off Larchards Lane, Shilling-

stone, Blandford DT11 0TF (01258 860491). Pennhills Farmhouse, set in one and a half acres, is situated half a mile from the village of Shillingstone in the heart of the Blackmore Vale, with woodland walks extending through unspoiled countryside with abundance of wild life; an ideal peaceful retreat, or exciting drives for 4x4s. It offers spacious comfortable accommodation for all ages, with downstairs bedroom; all rooms have en suite, TV, tea/coffee making facilities, complemented by traditional English breakfast. From £17 per person. Children of all ages welcome. Pets by arrangement. Good meals available locally. Brochure available. A warm and friendly welcome assured by your host Rosie Watts.

STURMINSTER NEWTON. Mrs Sheila Martin, Moorcourt Farm, Moorside, Marnhull, Sturminster Newton DT10 1HH (01258 820271). Working farm. Marnhull is situated four miles from Sturminster Newton, five from Shaftesbury. Central for touring; Longleat, New Forest, coast within 28 miles. We are a modern dairy farm of 120 acres lying in the Blackmore Vale in the midst of Hardy country. Visitors will enjoy wandering around meeting Sunny the little white donkey and his friend Buster the big horse, watching the milking and farm activities or just lazing in our large gardens. The accommodation comprises one bedroom with twin beds and two with double beds; all are adjacent, colour co-ordinated and have washbasins, tea/coffee making facilities and biscuits, colour TV. Flowers, plants; keys to bedrooms. There is a shower room and toilet next to these bedrooms, and a further toilet and bathroom downstairs. There is a sittingroom with woodburner fire and a dining room. Enormous breakfast menu. Children over 10 years welcome, but sorry no pets. A car is essential to explore our lovely Dorset countryside and coastline. There is ample parking. There are two public houses in the village, which both do excellent evening meals. There is a friendly atmosphere created here "Down on the Farm" and Sheila does her best to make your holiday a happy and enjoyable one. Bed and Breakfast from £13/£14. SAE for brochure.

SWANAGE. Mrs Rosemary Dean, Quarr Farm, Valley Road, Swanage BH19 3DY (01929 480865). Quarr is a working family farm steeped in history dating back to the Domesday Book. Animals kept naturally — cows, calves, horses, poultry. Bring your children to feed ducks, chickens, peacocks and watch steam trains passing through our meadows. Accommodation in family room with en suite bathroom, own sitting room with colour TV, real log fire, tea making facilities. Old Dairy, low beamed ceilings, small windows, double room with en suite shower, sittingroom with colour TV, kitchen. Choice of Bed and Breakfast or self catering. Cot and Z-bed available. Easy reach high class restaurants, pubs; sea three miles. Studland, sandy beach just five miles away. Ideal for walking, cycling, coastal path, RSPB Reserves, golf courses, riding. Please write, or telephone, for further details and terms.

SWANAGE. Mrs Justine Pike, Downshay Farm, Haycrafts Lane, Harmans Cross, Swanage BH19

3EB (01929 480316). A working dairy farm on beautiful Isle of Purbeck, half a mile from A351 and midway between Corfe Castle and Swanage. Sandy beaches, coastal path, steam railway nearby. One family room with TV and one double room, both with washbasins. Shower room and bathroom; sittingroom with TV; diningroom. Tea/coffee facilities. Ample car parking and large garden. Children welcome, cot provided on request and babysitting available. Open March to end October for Bed and Breakfast from £16 to £18.

TOLLER PORCORUM. Mrs Rachael Geddes, Colesmoor Farm, Toller Porcorum, Dorchester DT2

0DU (01300 320812). Working farm, join in. Colesmoor Farm, reached by its own private track, is situated 11 miles west of Dorchester in an elevated position surrounded by peaceful countryside with extensive views. An ideal base for exploring West Dorset and only 10 miles from the seaside. We extend a warm welcome to our guests, whose ground floor accommodation includes one double room with en suite shower, basin and WC and colour TV, and one twin-bedded room with private use of an adjacent bathroom. Wide selection of breakfasts, tea/coffee making facilities. Excellent inns and restaurants nearby for an evening meal. Children welcome, babysitting service. Regret no pets. Non-smokers please. Rates £16 to £18. Reductions for more than two days and for children. Please telephone for brochure and further details.

WEST LULWORTH. Mr and Mrs T.H. Williams, Shirley Hotel, West Lulworth, Wareham BH20 5RL

(Tel & Fax: 01929 400358). ❦ ❦ ❦ *HIGHLY COMMEN-DED.* AA Two Star. The Shirley Hotel, situated in the thatched village of West Lulworth, is half a mile from Lulworth Cove with the magnificent Dorset coastline stretching in both directions. The hotel has been run by the Williams family since 1970 with care and consideration and we would like to welcome you to share the relaxing atmosphere and delicious food. To complete your stay we have a splendid indoor heated pool and spa exclusively for guests' use. For walkers we have a drying room as well as a coin-operated laundry. There is a giant outdoor chess game next to a secluded sun bathing terrace. Car parking on site. Dogs and children welcome. Open February to November. Terms half board £257.75 to £275.75 per person per week; Bed and Breakfast £29 to £31 per person daily. Special breaks/early and late season discounts available. Please call Tony, Jess, Kate or David for a colour brochure.

WEYMOUTH. Mrs S. Lambert, The Wessex Guest House, 128 Dorchester Road, Weymouth DT4

7LG (01305 783406). Quality detached residence close to sea and shops. The accent here is on good food and good service. Ideally situated for Lulworth Cove, Corfe Castle and Abbotsbury Swannery. Safe bathing, fishing and riding. Three family rooms and two double, all with washbasins. Ground floor bedroom available. Free tea/coffee anytime. Children welcome. Enclosed garden, play room available. Access at all times. Open May to September for Bed and Breakfast only from £13. Secure parking in grounds. Reductions for children. In the know for local bird watching and rarities. Also self catering holiday flat to let.

FREE and REDUCED RATE Holiday Visits!
See our READERS' OFFER VOUCHER for details!

WINTERBORNE ZELSTON. Mr and Mrs Kerley, Brook Farm, Winterborne Zelston, Blandford DT11 9EU (01929 459267). A warm welcome awaits you at Brook Farm, a friendly working farm situated in a pretty, peaceful hamlet overlooking the River Winterborne, between Wimborne and Dorchester. Central for coast and exploring the beautiful Dorset countryside, New Forest, etc. Comfortable family and twin rooms with either en suite or private facilities, TV, easy chairs, beverage tray and central heating. No parking problems. Access to rooms at all times. Hearty breakfasts are served with own free range eggs and homemade marmalade! The local country inns provide excellent food. Open all year except Christmas. Terms from £16 per person per night, with favourable rates for longer stays and children sharing.

DURHAM

CORNFORTH. Mrs D. Slack, Ash House, 24 The Green, Cornforth DL17 9JH (01740 654654). Ideally situated on lovely quiet rural conservation village green, in the heart of "The Land of the Prince Bishops". Adjacent A1(M) motorway, 10 minutes historic Durham, 25 minutes Beamish Museum, Metro Centre, Newcastle and Darlington. Ash House is a beautifully appointed Victorian home, lovingly restored. The elegant rooms are spacious and comfortable, equipped with washbasins, colour TV, hospitality tray, shaver point, hair dryer, clock/radio alarms and all with open views; traditional four-poster bed available. Mature trees surround the property. Hearty breakfasts are provided. Private parking. Well placed between York and Edinburgh. Excellent value from £17 (£20 single).

MIDDLETON-IN-TEESDALE. Mrs A.M. Sayer, Grassholme Farm, Lunedale, Middleton-in-Teesdale, Barnard Castle DL12 0PR (01833 640494). Working farm. A warm welcome awaits you at our family-run farm set in Lunedale, three miles from Middleton-in-Teesdale, one mile off the B6276 Brough road, overlooking Grassholme reservoir. Grassholme is part of the Earl of Strathmore's estate and has the Pennine Way route crossing the farmyard, making the farm an ideal base for walking. There is also horse riding nearby. Accommodation is in one twin room with tea making facilities. Good plain farmhouse food is offered in our cosy restaurant with open fire. Full English breakfast with free range eggs. Open Easter to September. Bed and Breakfast from £13; Evening Meal from £8.

STANLEY. Mrs P. Gibson, Bushblades Farm, Harperley, Stanley DH9 9UA (01207 232722). Tourist Board Listed COMMENDED. AA QQ. Ideal base for visiting Beamish Museum (two miles), Durham City (20 minutes), Metro Centre (15 minutes), Hadrian's Wall and Northumberland coast (under an hour). Excellent eating places close by. Comfortable Georgian farmhouse set in large garden. Ground floor twin en suite room plus two double first-floor bedrooms. All rooms have tea/coffee making, colour TV and easy chairs. Ample parking. Children over 12 years welcome. Sorry, no pets. Bed and Breakfast from £16 to £18.50; single £20 to £25.

DURHAM – LAND OF THE PRINCE BISHOPS

From the North Pennine hills and dales in the west to the magnificent Cathedral City at its heart, Durham offers so much to the visitor. Step into the past for a day at the award-winning Beamish Open Air Museum, find out how Victorian lead miners lived and worked at Killhope in Weardale. Castles and ancient churches, market towns and unspoilt villages, England's highest waterfall – there's something for everyone.

ESSEX

BRAINTREE. Mrs Delia Douse, Spicers Farm, Rotten End, Wethersfield, Braintree CM7 4AL (01371 851021). ✹✹ *HIGHLY COMMENDED.* **Working farm.** FHG Diploma Winner. Attractive farmhouse with large garden in peaceful rural area designated of special landscape value. Comfortable centrally heated bedrooms, all with en suite shower or bathrooms, colour TV, tea/coffee making facilities, clock radio and lovely views. Breakfast in our sunny conservatory overlooking the large garden and picturesque countryside. There is a separate lounge for guests. Excellent base for walking or touring and convenient for Stansted, M11, Harwich, Cambridge and Constable country. Plenty of parking. Bed and Breakfast from £15 to £17 per person (double or twin).

COLCHESTER. Mrs Jill Tod, Seven Arches Farm, Chitts Hill, Lexden, Colchester CO3 5SX (01206 574896). Working farm. Georgian farmhouse set in large garden close to the ancient town of Colchester. The farm extends to 100 acres and supports both arable crops and cattle. Private fishing rights on the River Colne, which runs past the farmhouse. This is a good location for visits to North Essex, Dedham and the Stour Valley which have been immortalised in the works of John Constable, the landscape painter. Children and pets welcome. Open all year. Bed and Breakfast from £20; Evening Meal from £5. Twin room £36; family room en-suite. Static caravan on caravan site also available.

SAFFRON WALDEN. Mrs Danielle Forster, Parsonage Farm, Arkesden, Saffron Walden CB11 4HB (01799 550306). ✹ We offer top grade accommodation on our 300 acre arable farm, situated in a delightful north-west Essex village. The house is Victorian and there are three bedrooms for guests — one double with en suite bathroom, one double and a twin with a shared bathroom. All rooms have washbasins, shaving points, TV and hot drinks and are centrally heated. There is a large garden with picnic table and tennis court. Full English or Continental breakfast available. Sorry, we are a smoke-free establishment. The city of Cambridge, Duxford Imperial War Museum, Audley End Mansion are within easy reach and London is only 50 minutes away by rail. Bed and Breakfast from £15 to £20 per person per night.

WIX. Mrs H.P. Mitchell, New Farm House, Spinnel's Lane, Wix, Manningtree CO11 2UJ (01255 870365; Fax: 01255 870837). ✹✹✹ *COMMENDED.* A comfortable, centrally heated modern Guesthouse set in beautiful gardens, ideally situated for touring the famous Constable countryside, historic Colchester, local seaside resorts and other towns. Convenient for Harwich (Parkeston Quay) Car Ferry to Holland, Denmark, Germany and Sweden. All bedrooms with colour TV, radio/alarm clock, tea/coffee making facilities, washbasins; most with en suite facilities. Guests' lounge with colour TV, second quiet lounge with kitchenette available for making snacks. Dinners provided with good home cooking using own produce. Residential licence held. Children welcome at reduced prices, cot, high chair and baby monitor provided. Large play area with swings, etc. Pets welcome. Three Day Winter Breaks. AA QQQ, RAC Acclaimed, Les Routiers and "Which?" Guide.

ESSEX – CHOICES!

Essex offers the choice between rural farmland, a marshy coastline, and industrial towns. Worth a visit are Abberton Reservoir, Blackwater Estuary, the country park at Danbury, Hatfield Forest and the Naze.

GLOUCESTERSHIRE

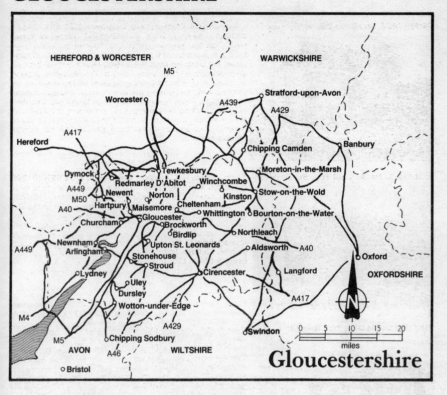

Gloucestershire

ARLINGHAM. Mrs D. Turrell, Horseshoe View, Overton Lane, Arlingham, Gloucester GL2 7JJ (01452 740293). Guests are given a friendly welcome, all year round, in this comfortable private house enjoying beautiful views of River Severn and Forest of Dean. Within easy reach of A38 and M5, and excellent base for touring the Cotswolds, Bath, Slimbridge Wildfowl Trust, Berkeley Castle and many other places of interest. Dry ski slope, Gloucester Leisure Centre and Three Choirs Festival attract many visitors. Accommodation in two double bedrooms (one en suite), one twin-bedded and one single room, with usual amenities; non-smoking accommodation available. Children over five years welcome. Sorry, no pets. Car essential — ample parking. Bed and Breakfast. Reductions for children and Senior Citizens. SAE, please, for terms.

BATH near. Mrs Pam Wilmott, Pool Farm, Wick, Bristol BS15 5RL (0117 937 2284). Working farm, join in.

May we welcome you to our 350 year old farmhouse, a Listed building on a working dairy farm. We are on the A420, only six miles from Bath, nine miles from Bristol, and a few miles from Exit 18 on the M4. This makes us an ideal touring centre for places of interest such as the Cotswolds, Wells, Badminton, etc. Nearby is a shop with newspapers, local pub with good food, Golf and Country Club with squash, tennis, croquet. TV lounge, central heating. Parking. Open all year except Christmas. Terms for Bed and Breakfast on request.

Discounted tickets available using our READERS' OFFER VOUCHER when visiting National Waterways Museum at Gloucester Docks.

BIRDLIP. Mrs P.M. Carter, Beechmount, Birdlip GL4 8JH (01452 862262). 🌸🌸 *COMMENDED.* Good

central base for touring Cotswolds, conveniently situated for many interesting places and picturesque views with lovely walks. "Beechmount" is in centre of Birdlip Village, convenient for post office/village store. Choice of menu for breakfast. Front door key is provided so that guests may come and go freely. All bedrooms with colour TVs, tea/coffee making facilities, washbasins, some with en suite facilities; bathroom, separate shower, shaver points, toilet. Children welcome at reduced rates, cot, high chair provided. Pets allowed by arrangement. Evening Meal by prior arrangement. Home produce when available. Competitive rates. Family-run guest house, highly recommended. Terms on application.

BOURTON-ON-THE-WATER. Mr and Mrs Farley, Rooftrees, Rissington Road, Bourton-on-the-Water

GL54 2EB (01451 821943). 🌸🌸 Warmth, comfort and hospitality are offered in the relaxed atmosphere of this detached Cotswold stone guest house, situated on the edge of the famous village of Bourton-on-the-Water which is eight minutes' level walking distance from the centre of the village. Bourton is central to all the main Cotswold attractions. Rooftrees offers four bedrooms, all en suite, two on the ground floor. Two of the rooms have four-poster beds, TV and tea-making facilities. A payphone is available. Optional traditional English home cooked dinners provided using fresh local produce. An enjoyable stay is assured here while visiting the Cotswolds. No smoking. Double rooms from £39 to £42; four-poster rooms from £42.

BREDON'S NORTON. Michael and Pippa Cluer, Lampitt House, Lampitt Lane, Bredon's Norton, Tewkesbury GL20 7HB (01684 772295). 🌸🌸

COMMENDED. Lampitt House is situated in a large informal garden on the edge of a quiet village at the foot of Bredon Hill. Splendid views across to the Malverns. Ideal for visiting the Cotswolds, Stratford, Worcester, Cheltenham, Gloucester and the Forest of Dean. All rooms are furnished to a high standard and have private bathrooms, central heating, colour TV and tea/coffee making facilities. Ground floor room available. Children are welcome. Ample parking. No smoking. Open all year. Hill and riverside walks. Arrangements can be made for windsurfing and riding. Double room £36, single £26. Bed and Breakfast.

BRISTOL. Mrs Marilyn Collins, Box Hedge Farm, Coalpit Heath, Bristol BS17 2UW (01454 250786).

Box Hedge Farm is set in 200 acres of beautiful rural countryside on the edge of the Cotswolds. Local to M4/M5, central for Bristol and Bath and the many tourist attractions in this area. An ideal stopping point for the south west and Wales. We offer a warm friendly atmosphere with traditional farmhouse cooking. The large spacious bedrooms (one single, one double and one family) have colour TV and tea/coffee making facilities. Adventure days or weekends can also be provided with Clay Pigeon Shooting, Quads and Pilots to name but three events. Bed and Breakfast from £15; Dinner from £7.50.

GLOUCESTERSHIRE – THE IDYLLIC COTSWOLDS COUNTY!

A combination of the Cotswolds and The Vale of Severn, Gloucestershire is a popular tourist destination. Visit Chipping Campden, Cirencester, The Cotswolds Farm Park, The Forest of Dean, Keynes Park and Tewkesbury and you will not be disappointed. If you are around at the right time, the Severn Bore can also be quite a spectacle.

BRISTOL. Mrs Judi Hasell, Woodbarn Farm, Denny Lane, Chew Magna, Bristol BS18 8SZ (01275 332599). ♥ ♥ Woodbarn is a working mixed farm, five minutes from Chew Valley Lake. Chew Magna is a large village with pretty cottages, Georgian houses and is central for touring. There are two en suite bedrooms, one double and one family, both with tea trays. Guests' lounge and dining room. Cream teas Sundays June to September. Open March to December (closed Christmas). Children welcome. Bed and Breakfast from £17 to £20. Non smokers preferred. Brochure available.

BRISTOL. Margaret Hasell, The Model Farm, Norton Hawkfield, Pensford, Bristol BS18 4HA (01275 832144). ♥ ♥ *COMMENDED.* The farmhouse is a Listed building situated two miles off the A37 in a peaceful hamlet nestling under the Dundry Hills. A working arable and beef farm in easy reach of Bristol, Bath, Wells, Cheddar and many interesting places. The accommodation consists of one family room en suite and one double room with washbasin, both with tea/coffee facilities. Guests' lounge with TV and dining room. Open all year except Christmas and New Year. I can assure you of a warm welcome and a peaceful and comfortable stay.

BRISTOL. Mrs Doreen Keel, Valley Farm, Sandy Lane, Stanton Drew, Bristol BS18 4EL (01275 332723). ♥ ♥ *HIGHLY COMMENDED.* 1994 Award-Winning Valley Farm is a modern farmhouse offering Bed and Breakfast accommodation. Pleasantly situated on the edge of an ancient village near the River Chew with Druid Stones and many footpaths to walk. It is located near the Chew Valley Lakes, renowned for trout fishing, and in easy reach of Bath, Bristol, Wells and Cheddar. There are three rooms with double beds; each has washbasin and tea/coffee making facilities; there are also two rooms with en suite and another with private bathroom; all bedrooms have TV. The house is double glazed and centrally heated. We try to create a friendly and relaxed atmosphere in lovely countryside and we are always pleased to give information about the area. Non-smoking. Brochure.

BRISTOL near. Mrs Colin Smart, Leigh Farm, Pensford, Near Bristol BS18 4BA (01761 490281; Fax: 01761 490270). Working farm. Close to Bath, Bristol, Cheddar, Mendip Hills. Large, comfy, stone-built farmhouse with lawns. Twin, single, family, double rooms, some en suite; cot and high chair available. Guests' private lounge with night storage heating and open log fires in cold weather. Traditional farmhouse breakfasts. Tea/coffee facilities, hair dryer available. Carp and tench fishing close to the farmhouse. Floodlit car park with plenty of space. Payphone. Close to Blagdon and Chew Valley reservoirs. Fire Certificate. Sorry, no pets. Bed and Breakfast from £20. Also self catering accommodation available (some units with night storage heating) from £95 to £330 weekly.

CHELTENHAM. Mrs Helen Risborough, Wishmoor Guest House, 147 Hales Road, Cheltenham GL52 6TD (01242 238504; Fax: 01242 226090). ♥ ♥ *COMMENDED.* At Wishmoor Guest House you will find a warm and friendly welcome from your hosts Helen and Robin Risborough whose aim is to provide a relaxed atmosphere so that you may enjoy your stay. Wishmoor is a late Victorian residence, carefully modernised to preserve its charm and character. Situated on the eastern side of Cheltenham at the foot of the Cotswold Hills, it is an ideal base for touring the Cotswold villages, Wye Valley, Malvern Hills and the Royal Forest of Dean. The scenic towns of Hereford, Stratford and Bath are conveniently situated for day visits. Single and double bedrooms available, some en suite. All have colour TV and tea/coffee facilities. Full central heating; adequate hot water; quiet guest lounge. Non-smoking accommodation available. Off road parking. Fire Certificate. Bed and Breakfast from £18; Evening Meal from £12. Reductions for children. AA QQQ. Winner of Cheltenham Spa Award for Hygiene and Healthy Eating.

See also Colour Display Advertisement **CHELTENHAM. Mr and Mrs A.E. Hughes, Ham Hill Farm, Whittington, Cheltenham GL54 4EZ (01242 584415; Fax: 01242 222535).** ✿ ✿ *COMMENDED.* All visitors will be made welcome and everything will be done to make their stay enjoyable at this new farmhouse on a 160-acre farm. Leisure activities nearby include riding, golf, walking on the Cotswold Way. The tastefully decorated and comfortable en suite bedrooms all have colour TV and tea/coffee facilities. Central heating. Open all year. Bed and Breakfast from £20 to £23.50. No smoking. Children over seven years welcome.

CHIPPING CAMPDEN. Lucy Robbins, Manor Farm, Weston Sub-Edge, Chipping Campden GL55 6QH (01386 840390; Mobile: 0589 108812). ✿ ✿

COMMENDED. **Working farm, join in.** Traditional 17th century farmhouse on a 600 acre mixed farm. An excellent base for touring the Cotswolds, Shakespeare country and Hidcote Manor Gardens. Warm, friendly atmosphere. Lovely walled garden. All rooms are en suite with tea/coffee making facilities, TV/radio. Children and dogs most welcome. Only one and a half miles from Chipping Campden which is not only a lovely old market town but also has a good selection of pubs, restaurants and shops. Open all year round. Bed with full English Breakfast from only £20 per person.

CHIPPING CAMPDEN. Mrs Gené Jeffrey, Brymbo, Honeybourne Lane, Mickleton, Chipping Campden GL55 6PU (01386 438890; Fax: 01386 438113). HETB Listed. Brymbo is a warm and spacious farm building conversion with large gardens in beautiful Cotswold countryside. Close to Stratford-upon-Avon, Broadway, Chipping Campden with easy access to Oxford and Cheltenham. Ideal base for walking and touring in the Cotswolds. The comfortable bedrooms all have colour TV and tea/coffee making facilities; two en suite rooms available. Sitting room has extensive views and an open log fire, whilst the breakfast room has the views and sunshine, subject to the English weather, of course! Central heating. Ground floor bedrooms. Parking. There are maps and guides to borrow with quantities of helpful information about the area and sample menus from local hostelries to assist with your choice for meals. FREE Four-Wheel Drive Tour of the area offered to three-night guests. Bed and Breakfast from £15. Children and pets welcome. Brochure on request.

COTSWOLD COUNTRY
BED AND BREAKFAST

CHURCHAM. Penny and Steve Stevens, Edgewood House, Churcham, Gloucester GL2 8AA (01452 750232). ✿ ✿ Family-run country guest house set in two acres of lovely gardens. Ideal for visiting Forest of Dean, Wye Valley, Cotswolds and Malverns. Close to RSPB Reserve and viewpoint for Seven Bore Tidal Wave. Centrally heated double, family and single rooms decorated and furnished to a high standard. Most rooms are en suite and have tea/coffee making facilities. Spacious dining room and lounge with colour TV. Ample parking. Hearty breakfast provided. Several excellent eating places nearby. Bed and Breakfast from £18.50 to £20. Children over five years welcome with reductions if sharing with two adults. Sorry, no smoking or pets. Open all year. Brochure available.

CIRENCESTER. Mrs June Barton, The Coach House, Middle Duntisbourne, Cirencester GL7 7AR (01285 653058). ✿ ✿ *APPROVED.* A warm welcome awaits at the 17th century coach house by the River Dunt. Centrally situated in 400 acre arable and beef farm with lovely views; ideal for visits to Bath, Oxford, Stratford and many pretty villages in and around Cirencester area. Pretty garden with country views. TV, tea/coffee making facilities in bedrooms. Pleasant lounge with colour TV. Always a choice of breakfast including English farmhouse. Children and pets welcome. Open all year except Christmas. Bed and Breakfast from £16 to £22.

DURSLEY. Burrows Court, Nibley Green, North Nibley, Dursley GL11 6AZ (Tel & Fax: 01453 546230).

BURROWS COURT HOTEL

♥♥♥ This 18th century mill is idyllically set in an acre of garden surrounded by open country with beautiful views of the Cotswolds. Decorated and furnished in the country style the house has six bedrooms, all with private bathroom, colour TV, beverage facilities and radio. Other facilities include two lounges, one with residents' bar; central heating. Dinner is available if requested at time of booking. Children over five years welcome. AA Listed, RAC Highly Acclaimed. Bed and Breakfast from £18 to £25 per person.

DURSLEY near. Susan Strain, Cotswold House, 57 The Street, Uley, Dursley GL11 5SL (01453 860305).

Bed and Breakfast is offered in this charming Georgian style house with private parking set in the centre of the pretty village of Uley. We have good access to the Cotswold Way, many local walks and excellent local pubs offering good food. The location is ideal for visits to Tetbury, Berkeley, Badminton, Gatcombe and Slimbridge with easy access to both Cheltenham and Bath. Some bedrooms have en-suite facilities, all have TV, tea/coffee making and double or twin beds. Clothes drying facilities are available. We are open throughout the year and aim to make your visit to our village a relaxing and carefree occasion. Bed and Breakfast from £17.50 per person per night.

DURSLEY near. Gerald and Norma Kent, Hill House, Crawley Hill, Uley, Near Dursley GL11 5BH (01453 860267).

Cotswold stone house situated on top of a hill with beautiful views of the surrounding countryside, near the very pretty village of Uley. Ideal spot for exploring the various walks in the area including the Cotswold Way and there are many places of interest within reasonable driving distance of Uley. Choice of bedrooms with or without en-suite facilities, all with washbasins, central heating, shaver points, tea/coffee making facilities and TV. Your hosts' aim is to make your stay in the Cotswolds an enjoyable and memorable one, with comfort and hospitality of prime importance. Bed and Breakfast from £15 per person; Evening Meals are normally available if required. Please phone or write for brochure.

FALFIELD. Mr and Mrs B.C. Burrell, Green Farm Guest House, Falfield, Gloucestershire GL12 8DL (01454 260319). ETB Listed.

Delightful 16th century stone farmhouse, beautifully converted into a country guest house with style and traditional charm. Open all year. Bath, Cheltenham, Cardiff, Forest of Dean, Cheddar are all approximately 35 minutes away. Easy access M4 and M5 Junction 14, AZTEC Business Park 10 minutes. The ideal touring centre. Bed and Breakfast from £16. Excellent food always available from simple snacks to à la carte dinner. A warm welcome assured at Green Farm. Ample parking. AA QQ.

FOREST OF DEAN. Mrs Joan Thorpe, Brook House Guest House, Bridge Street, Blakeney GL15

4DY (01594 517101). ❦❦ *COMMENDED.* Enjoy a relaxing break in the Forest of Dean and Wye Valley. This area is ideal for walking, mountain biking, canoeing, fishing or simply enjoying the scenery. Brook House is an attractive 17th century building. We offer a warm welcome, personal service and comfortable accommodation. All rooms have central heating, colour TV and tea/coffee making facilities. En suite and four-poster rooms are available. Optional home cooked evening meal; supper licence. Blakeney is midway between Gloucester and Chepstow on A48. Brook House is in the centre of the village behind the Post Office. Car parking. Secure cycle storage. Bed and Breakfast from £16. Colour brochure.

GLOUCESTER. Mrs S. Carter, Severn Bank, Minsterworth GL2 8JH (01452 750357). ❦❦

COMMENDED. Severn Bank is a fine country house standing in its own six-acre grounds on the bank of the River Severn, four miles west of Gloucester. Ideally situated for touring Cotswolds, Forest of Dean and Wye Valley, and at the recommended viewpoint for the Severn Bore tidal wave. Severn Bank has a friendly atmosphere and comfortable accommodation in spacious rooms with superb view over river and countryside. Full central heating, en-suite rooms, tea/coffee making facilities and colour TV in non-smoking bedrooms. Ample parking, with several excellent restaurants and pubs nearby. Terms: Bed and Full English Breakfast from £18 to £20, with rates reduced for children.

GLOUCESTER near. S.J. Barnfield, ''Kilmorie Guest House'', Gloucester Road, Corse, Staunton, Near Gloucester GL19 3RQ (01452 840224). Built in 1848 by the Chartists, Kilmorie is Grade II Listed in a conservation area, and is a smallholding keeping farm livestock and fruit in a lovely part of Gloucestershire. Good home cooking with own produce and eggs when available. Large garden.

Children are welcome to ''help'' with the animals if they wish, and a child's pony is also kept. There are many places of both historic and natural interest to visit, and river trips can be enjoyed from Tewkesbury and Upton-on-Severn. Kilmorie is situated close to the borders of Herefordshire and Worcestershire and the Forest of Dean, the Cotswolds, Malvern Hills, the Wye Valley and four castles are all within easy reach. Four double, one twin, one single and one family bedrooms, all with washbasins and TVs; some with private facilities; two bathrooms and two additional toilets, shower. Lounge with colour TV; diningroom. Central heating. Fire Certificate. Children over five years welcome. Pets accepted; kennels available if required. Ample parking. Three course Dinner, Bed and Breakfast from £20.50; Bed and Breakfast from £14. Reduced rates for children. Open all year.

LECHLADE near. Mrs Elizabeth Reay, Apple Tree House, Buscot, Near Faringdon, Oxfordshire SN7

8DA (01367 252592). ❦❦ 17th century Listed house situated in small interesting National Trust village, two miles Lechlade, four miles Faringdon on A417. River Thames five minutes' walk through village to Buscot lock and weirs. Ideal touring centre for Cotswolds, Upper Thames, Oxford, etc. Good fishing, walking and cycling area. Access at all times to the three guest bedrooms all of which have washbasins, razor points, tea/coffee facilities and central heating when necessary. En-suite room available. Residents' TV lounge with log fire in winter. Bed and Breakfast from £17 per person per night; choice of many restaurants, etc within five mile radius of Buscot. I look forward to welcoming you to Apple Tree House.

LYDNEY. Marion Allen, "Woodcroft", Lower Meend, St. Briavels, Lydney GL15 6RW (01594 530083). Woodcroft is a secluded house set in a five acre smallholding on the side of the Wye Valley near Tintern. A peaceful spot surrounded by woods and lovely walking country, including the Offa's Dyke Path half a mile away. We have two en suite family rooms with tea and coffee making facilities and a guest lounge with colour TV, books, games, maps, etc. To help you enjoy your stay breakfast is served at a time of your choice and includes our own free range eggs; home made bread and home made jams and marmalade. Bed and Breakfast £16. Brochure available.

Aston House is a chalet bungalow overlooking fields in the peaceful village of Broadwell, 1.5 miles from Stow-on-the-Wold. It is centrally situated for all the Cotswold villages, while blenheim Palace, Warwick Castle, Oxford, Stratford-upon-Avon, Cheltenham, Cirencester and Gloucester are within easy reach. Accommodation comprises a twin-bedded and double/twin room, both en suite on the first floor, and a double room with private bathroom on the ground floor. All rooms have tea/coffee making facilities, colour TV and electric blankets. Bedtime drinks and biscuits are provided. Guests, and children over 10 years, are welcomed to our home February to November. No smoking. Car essential, parking. Sorry, no pets. Pub within walking distance. Bed and good English breakfast from £18.50–£20 per person daily; weekly from £129.50 per person. English Tourist Board Listed Commended.

ASTON HOUSE

Broadwell,
Moreton-in-Marsh GL56 0TJ
Tel: 01451 830475

NAILSWORTH. Mrs Lesley Williams-Allen, The Laurels at Inchbrook, Nailsworth GL5 5HA (01453 834021; Fax: 01453 834004). ♛ ♛ ♛ A lovely rambling house, part cottage-style and part Georgian. The emphasis is on relaxation and friendly hospitality. All rooms are en suite and include family, twin and double rooms, each with colour TV and tea making facilities. We have a panelled study/reading room with piano, and a beamed lounge with snooker table and board games. In our licensed dining room we serve excellent breakfasts and home cooked dinners. The secluded garden backs onto fields and offers a swimnming pool and the opportunity to observe wildlife. We are ideally situated for touring all parts of the Cotswolds and West Country, surrounded by a wealth of beautiful countryside and all kinds of activities. Children and pets welcome. Brochure on request.

NORTHLEACH. Market House, Northleach, Cheltenham GL54 3EJ (01451 860557). A 400 year old house of olde worlde charm characterised by exposed beams and inglenook fireplace, yet with modern facilities. Pretty bedrooms, each with washbasin, central heating, tea/coffee making and helpful touring guides. Located in an unspoilt little town in the heart of the Cotswolds near the intersection of the A40 with A429, amidst a selection of inns and restaurants, surrounded by a variety of attractions and beautiful countryside. A delicious breakfast is cooked to order, before you tour to nearby Bath, Stratford-upon-Avon or Oxford. Children over 12 years accepted. No pets. No smoking. Packed lunches available. Bed and Breakfast from £17. One double room en suite, one double/twin, two singles. "Which?" Recommended.

Terms quoted in this publication may be subject to increase if rises in costs necessitate

STOW-ON-THE-WOLD. Mrs S. Davis, Fairview Farmhouse, Bledington Road, Stow-on-the-Wold, Cheltenham GL54 1AN (01451 830279). 🛇🛇 *HIGHLY*

COMMENDED. You are assured of a warm welcome at Fairview Farmhouse, situated one mile from Stow-on-the-Wold on a quiet B road with outstanding panoramic views of the surrounding Cotswold Hills. Ideal base for touring the pretty villages of Bourton-on-the-Water, The Slaughters, Broadway, Chipping Campden, also famous Stratford etc. The cosy bedrooms are furnished to a high standard with a king-size four-poster deluxe for that special occasion, all are en suite with colour TV and tea/coffee making equipment. Lounge and additional lounge area with books, maps, etc. Central heating. Ample parking. Open all year.

Fairview FARMHOUSE

STOW-ON-THE-WOLD. Robert and Dawn Smith, Corsham Field Farmhouse, Bledington Road, Stow-on-the-Wold GL54 1JH (01451 831750). 🛇🛇 Homely farmhouse with traditional features and breathtaking views, one mile from Stow-on-the-Wold. Ideally situated for exploring all the picturesque Cotswold villages such as Broadway, Bourton-on-the-Water, Upper and Lower Slaughter, Chipping Campden, Snowshill, etc. Also central point for places of interest such as Blenheim Palace, Cotswold Wildlife Park, Stratford and many stately homes and castles in the area. Twin, double and family rooms, most with en suite facilities, other with washbasins, TV and tea/coffee making facilities. Pets and children welcome. Good pub food five minutes' walk away. AA Listed. Bed and Full English Breakfast from £13.50 to £18.50 per person.

STOW-ON-THE-WOLD. Graham and Helen Keyte, The Limes, Evesham Road, Stow-on-the-Wold GL54 1EN (01451 830034/831056). 🛇🛇 Over the last 22 years this RAC and AA Listed guesthouse has established a reputation for its homely and friendly atmosphere. It is just four minutes' walk from the town centre; central for visiting Stratford-upon-Avon, Burford, Bourton-on-the-Water, Cirencester, Cheltenham, etc. The Limes overlooks fields and has an attractive large garden with ornamental pool and waterfall. Single, double, twin and family rooms with washbasins. Two rooms en suite, one four poster and one twin bedroom; two public showers, two toilets. All rooms have tea/coffee making facilities and colour TV. Central heating. TV lounge. Diningroom. Children welcome, cot. Pets welcome. Car park. Fire Certificate held. Bed and full English Breakfast from £16 to £19.50 per person. Reductions for children. Vegetarians catered for. Open all year except Christmas.

STROUD. Mrs Salt, Beechcroft, Brownshill, Stroud GL6 8AG (01453 883422). 🛇 *COMMENDED.* Our

Edwardian house is quietly situated in a beautiful rural area with open views, about four miles from Stroud. The house is set in an attractive garden with mature trees, shrubs and herbaceous borders. We are in the midst of good walking country, for which we can lend maps and guides. We provide a full cooked breakfast or fruit salad and rolls with home-made bread and preserves. We welcome the elderly and small children. We are within easy reach of Cheltenham, Gloucester, Cirencester and Bath, also Berkeley Castle, Slimbridge and the North Cotswolds. We are a non-smoking establishment. Evening meal by prior arrangement. Bed and Breakfast from £16 to £20.

TEWKESBURY. Mick and Anne Meadows, Home Farm, Bredons Norton, Tewkesbury GL20 7HA (01684 72322). 🛇🛇 *COMMENDED.* Mixed 150 acre

family-run farm with sheep, cattle and poultry. Situated in an extremely quiet, unspoilt little village nestling under Bredon Hill. Superb position for walking, an excellent base for touring or relaxing. The 18th century farmhouse is very comfortably furnished. All bedrooms have en suite bathrooms. Gas central heating. Good home cooking. Evening meals by arrangement. Lounge, TV. Children and pets welcome. Open mid January to mid December. Bed and Breakfast from £18 to £20; Evening Meal from £12.

TEWKESBURY. Mrs Bernadette Williams, Abbots Court, Church End, Twyning, Tewkesbury GL20 6DA (Tel and Fax: 01684 292515). ♥ ♥ **Working farm.**

A large, quiet farmhouse set in 350 acres, built on the site of monastery between the Malverns and Cotswolds, half a mile M5-M50 junction. Large bedrooms, six en-suite, fully carpeted, with washbasins, tea making facilities and colour TV. Centrally heated. Open all year. Large lounge with open fire and colour TV. Spacious diningroom. Licensed bar. Good home cooked food in large quantities, home produced where possible. Children's own TV room, games room and playroom. Tennis lawn. Play area and lawn. Cot, high chair and babysitting available. Laundry facilities. Ideally situated for touring with numerous places to visit. Swimming, tennis, sauna, golf within three miles. Coarse fishing available on the farm. Bed and Breakfast from £14.50 to £16.50. Reduced rates for children and Senior Citizens.

TIRLEY. Sue Warner, Town Street Farm, Tirley GL19 4HG (01452 780442). ♥ ♥ *COMMENDED.*

Town Street Farm is a typical working farm close to the River Severn, within easy reach of M5 and M50. The farmhouse offers a high standard of accommodation with en suite facilities in bedrooms and a warm and friendly welcome. Breakfast is served overlooking the lawns, flowerbeds and tennis court which is available for use by guests. Children and pets welcome. Open all year except Christmas. Bed and Breakfast from £16 to £21.

WOTTON-UNDER-EDGE. Mrs S. Mayo, Coombe Lodge, Wotton-under-Edge GL12 7NB (01453 845057). Situated in the scenic southern Cotswolds between Cheltenham and Bath. Overlooking the Coombe Valley and standing only one mile from the town centre of Wotton-under-Edge, Coombe Lodge is a family-run Georgian Country House that extends a warm welcome to all its guests.

There are three centrally heated and spacious bedrooms, one with four-poster bed. All rooms have washbasin, TV and beverage facilities. Experience the welcome change of the copious vegetarian breakfast, served in the elegant Victorian dining room. The guests' sitting room provides an extensive range of local guides and maps. To round off a satisfying day why not relax in the sauna. No smoking please. Bed and Breakfast from £20 per person.

HAMPSHIRE

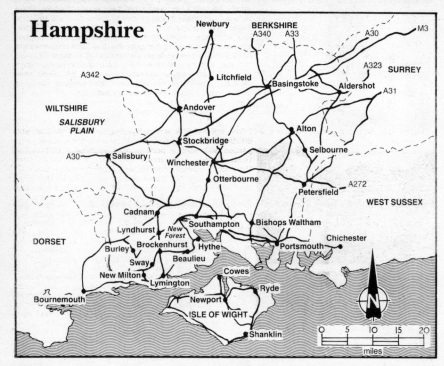

Hampshire

BARTON-ON-SEA. Mrs J. Copeland, Laurel Lodge, 48 Western Avenue, Barton-on-Sea BH25 7PZ

(01425 618309). ♛♛♛ AA QQQ Selected, RAC Acclaimed. A superb area in all seasons for that special break. Scenic clifftop walks, beaches, golf, sailing, riding and the delights of the nearby historic New Forest. Laurel Lodge offers every possible comfort in a cosy atmosphere, friendly personal service, great home-cooked food. Bed and four-course Breakfast from £17 (single occupancy from £21). The centrally heated en suite double, twin and family rooms all have remote-control colour TV, tea/coffee facilities and more; ground floor bedrooms available. An ideal touring base for a holiday to remember. We are open all year.

FRITHAM (New Forest). John and Penny Hankinson, Fritham Farm, Fritham, Lyndhurst SO43 7HH

(Tel & Fax: 01703 812333). ♛♛ COMMENDED. AA QQQQ Selected. Lovely farmhouse on working farm in the heart of the New Forest. Dating from the 18th century, all bedrooms have en suite facilities and provision for tea/coffee making. There is a large comfortable lounge with TV and log fire. Fritham is in a particularly beautiful part of the New Forest, still largely undiscovered and with a wealth of wildlife. It is a wonderful base for walking, riding, cycling and touring. No smoking. Children 10 years and over welcome. Come and enjoy peace and quiet in this lovely corner of England. Bed and Breakfast £17 to £19.

**WHEN MAKING ENQUIRIES PLEASE MENTION
THIS *FHG* PUBLICATION**

LYMINGTON. Our Bench, Lodge Road, Lymington SO41 8HH (Tel & Fax: 01590 673141). ✿ ✿ ✿

COMMENDED. Welcome Host, FHG Diploma Winner. A warm and friendly welcome awaits you in our large bungalow situated in a quiet area between the beautiful New Forest and the Coast. In the large garden stands a chalet which houses an indoor heated swimming/exercise pool, jacuzzi and sauna. We have double, twin and single rooms, all en suite. There is a separate lounge with colour TV and a four-course breakfast is served in our dining room, where evening meals are also available if required. RAC Acclaimed, AA QQQQ Selected. For non-smokers only and sorry, no children. Tariff from £20 per person per night.

LYMINGTON. Mrs R. Sque, Harts Lane, 242 Everton Road, Everton, Lymington SO41 0HE (01590 645902).

Bungalow (non-smoking) set in three acres; large garden with wildlife pond and an abundance of bird life. Quiet location, convenient for A337, three miles from Lymington. Friendly comfortable accommodation comprising three double bedrooms, two en suite, all with tea/coffee making facilities and colour TV. The sea and forest are five minutes away by car. Horse riding, golf, fishing and a real ale pub serving homemade meals are all nearby. Children and pets welcome. Bed and Breakfast from £17.50 per person per night.

See also Colour Display Advertisement **LYNDHURST. Mr P.T. Ames, Ormonde House, Southampton Road, Lyndhurst SO43 7BT (Freephone 0500 240140).** Ormonde House, in the heart of the New Forest, offers elegant luxury accommodation at affordable prices. All rooms en suite, colour TV, phone, beverage facilities. Luxury rooms are spacious with bath and shower, sofas and remote-control colour TV. Comfort extends throughout the lounge and conservatory overlooking the flower filled gardens. Your host, Paul, who has been a leading restaurateur, offers freshly prepared traditional English dinners. Bordering the south coast and famous for its ponies, the New Forest can be reached in under one and a half hours from London. Close to Beaulieu Motor Museum and Exbury Gardens. Special break details on request. Rover welcome! Bed and Breakfast £20 to £35 per person per night.

NEW FOREST. The Woodlands Lodge Hotel, Bartley Road, Woodlands, New Forest SO40 2GN (01703 292257). ✿ ✿ ✿ ✿ HIGHLY COMMENDED.

Luxury hotel set in four acres of grounds opening onto the beautiful New Forest, offers peace and tranquillity. All 18 bedrooms are individually designed and enjoy full en suite facilities with jacuzzi and shower. Sumptuous king-size beds are extremely comfortable; other amenities include Fast Text TV, Teasmaid, telephone, hair dryer and trouser press. Friendly and informal service enables guests to relax and feel at home. Delicious dinner menu and modestly priced wine list. AA Three Star. See also Inside Front Cover.

NEW FOREST. Mrs Sandra Hocking, Southernwood, Plaitford Common, Salisbury Road, Near Romsey (01794 323255 or 322577). Modern country family home, surrounded by farmland, on the edge of the New Forest. Two double, one family and one twin bedrooms; lounge. Full English breakfast. Cots and high chairs available for babies. Four miles from M27 off A36. Salisbury, Southampton 11 miles, Stonehenge 17 miles, Portsmouth half an hour, Winchester 14 miles, Romsey five miles and within easy reach of Continental ferries. Large garden. Ample parking. TV. Tea/coffee always available. Horse riding, golf, fishing, swimming, walking in New Forest 10 minutes. Local inns for good food. Terms from £14. Open all year.

NEW FOREST. Mr and Mrs Michael and Judith Pearce, St. Ursula, 30 Hobart Road, New Milton BH25 6EG (01425 613515). Large, detached family home between New Forest and sea offering every comfort in a friendly, relaxed atmosphere. Quiet, but central for town, station and leisure centre (with pool). Sea one mile, four miles to New Forest with ponies and beautiful walks. Ideal touring base for Bournemouth, Salisbury, etc. Twin, family, double and singles, most en suite, with washbasins and tea making facilities. Excellent beds. Beautiful ground floor twin en suite bedroom suitable for wheelchair/disabled guests. Children and pets welcome. Two bathrooms, one shower, four toilets. Lounge with colour TV, two dining rooms. Pretty "cottage" garden with barbecue. Smoke detectors installed. Full central heating. Open all year. Bed and Breakfast from £17. AA QQQ Recommended.

PETERSFIELD. Mrs Mary Bray, Nursted Farm, Buriton, Petersfield GU31 5RW (01730 264278).

Working farm. This late 17th century farmhouse, with its large garden, is open to guests throughout most of the year. Located quarter of a mile west of the B2146 Petersfield to Chichester road, one and a half miles south of Petersfield, the house makes an ideal base for touring the scenic Hampshire and West Sussex countryside. Queen Elizabeth Country Park two miles adjoining the picturesque village of Buriton at the western end of South Downs Way. Accommodation consists of three twin bedded rooms (one with washbasin), two bathrooms/toilets; sittingroom/breakfast room. Children welcome, cot provided. Sorry, no pets. Car essential — ample parking adjoining the house. Bed and Breakfast from £16 per adult. Reductions for children under 12 years except March and April.

RINGWOOD (New Forest). Mrs Yvonne Nixon, "The Nest", 10 Middle Lane, Ringwood BH24 1LE (Tel & Fax: 01425 476724; Mobile 0589 854505). This

lovely Victorian house is situated in a quiet residential lane within five minutes' walk of Ringwood town centre. The ancient riverside market town has many good restaurants and inns. Ample parking is provided. Beautifully decorated, very clean and well maintained. Breakfast times are flexible and the meal is served in the delightful sunny conservatory overlooking the gardens. Pretty colour co-ordinated "Laura Ashley" style bedrooms with pine furnishings, washbasins, colour TV and tea/coffee making facilities. Local activities include fishing, golf, riding, swimming, visiting historic houses and forest walks. This is an excellent base to explore the New Forest, with Bournemouth, Poole, Salisbury, Southampton and Portsmouth nearby. AA QQQQ Selected. Highly recommended. Bed and Breakfast from £15. No smoking in bedrooms.

RINGWOOD, New Forest. Mrs M.E. Burt, Fraser House, Salisbury Road, Blashford, Ringwood BH24 3PB (01425 473958). Fraser House is situated one mile

from the market town of Ringwood, overlooking the Avon Valley. This comfortable family house is on the edge of the New Forest, famous for its ponies, deer and pleasant walks. It is ten miles from Bournemouth and the south coast, and is convenient for visiting Southampton, Stonehenge and the Cathedral city of Salisbury. All rooms have central heating, hot and cold water, shaver points, comfortable beds, colour TV, tea/coffee making facilities. Some en-suite rooms available at extra charge. Fishing and water sports available nearby. Non-smokers preferred. Ample parking space. Open all year. Bed and Breakfast from £17 — £20 per night.

ROMSEY (New Forest). Mrs J. Hayter, "Woodlands", Bunny Lane, Sherfield English, Romsey SO51 6FT (01794 884840). ❦ ❦ ❦ Woodlands is situated on the edge of the New Forest near the Hampshire/Wiltshire border with the historic city of Salisbury and the ancient town of Romsey only a matter of minutes away in opposite directions. Southampton is also an easy journey away, Isle of Wight ferry at Beaulieu close by. Located in a quiet country lane with bedrooms overlooking dairy fields. All rooms have washbasins and tea making facilities; en suite facilities available. Comfortable lounge with colour TV. Children welcome. Our aim is to provide a personal, friendly service, home cooked food and a comfortable stay in pleasant surroundings — home from home. Bed and Breakfast from £15 single, £30 double, £45 family. Bed and Breakfast from £95 per week; Dinner, Bed and Breakfast from £115 per week. Reductions for Senior Citizens.

PUBLISHER'S NOTE

While every effort is made to ensure accuracy, we regret that FHG Publications cannot accept responsibility for errors, omissions or misrepresentation in our entries or any consequences thereof. Prices in particular should be checked because we go to press early. We will follow up complaints but cannot act as arbiters or agents for either party.

HEREFORD & WORCESTER

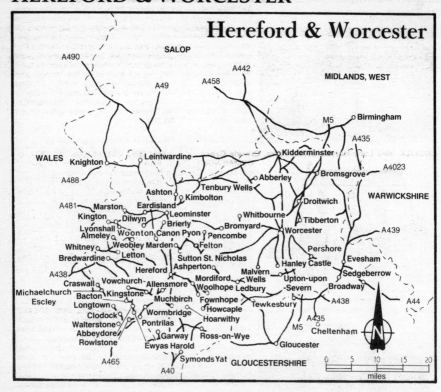

Hereford & Worcester

BREDENBURY. Mrs G. Evans, Red Hill Farm, Bredenbury, Bromyard HR7 4SY (01885 483255 or 01885 483535). ETB Listed. 17th century farmhouse situated in the beautiful peaceful countryside, within easy driving distance of Worcester, Hereford, Malvern, Ledbury and Ludlow. Guest accommodation includes one family room, two double bedrooms, one twin-bedded room all with washbasins and TV; bathroom and shower; lounge with colour TV; central heating throughout. Good food at local pub (one mile) at reasonable prices (small hot evening meals available on premises also — optional). Home from home. Children and pets welcome. Equestrian Centre (all weather gallop half a mile). Bed and Breakfast from £15 to £16 per person. Situated on A44. From Worcester take A44 to Bromyard, proceed towards Leominster for one and a half miles; farm on right with Tourist Board sign at farm entrance. You will receive a very warm welcome on arrival.

BROADWAY. Mark and Wendy Riley, "Olive Branch" Guest House, 78 High Street, Broadway WR12 7AJ (01386 853440). ♣ ♣ ♣ The attractive village

of Broadway is one of the loveliest places in the Cotswolds and has remained completely unspoiled. This guest house, dating back to the 16th century, is conveniently situated, close to the centre of the village which is well provided with places to eat out, ranging from tea rooms to a four star hotel. Combining modern amenities with old world charm, the house has six double/twin/family en suite bedrooms and two single bedrooms; dining room, separate lounge; satellite TV. Parking for eight cars. Cot available. Fire Certificate held. Six miles to Evesham, 10 miles to Bourton-on-the-Water, 15 to Stratford-upon-Avon, 16 to Cheltenham. Open all year. Terms from £20 per person Bed and Breakfast. AA QQQ, RAC Recommended.

BROMSGROVE. Mrs C. Gibbs, Lower Bentley Farm, Lower Bentley, Bromsgrove B60 4JB (01527 821286). ❦ An attractive Victorian farmhouse with modern comforts on a dairy and beef farm is an ideal base for a holiday, Short Break or business stay. Overlooking peaceful countryside, we are situated five miles away from M5 and M42 between Redditch, Bromsgrove and Droitwich. The accommodation comprises spacious double, twin and family rooms with en suite or private bathroom, colour TV and tea/coffee making facilities. The comfortable lounge and separate dining room overlook the large garden. Young children are welcome. We are ideally situated for visits to Stratford-upon-Avon, Warwick, Worcester, Stourbridge, Birmingham, the Black Country, the NEC and International Convention Centre. AA QQQ.

CROWLE. Mrs Lucy Harris, Green Farm, Crowle Green, Worcester WR7 4AB (01905 381807). ❦ *COMMENDED.* Green Farm is a peaceful and substantial oak-beamed Georgian farmhouse set in a large garden and 25 acres of farmland. Architecturally Grade II Listed. Accommodation consists of twin-bedded/double or single room with own basin and a private bathroom, tea/coffee making facilities and central heating. Cosy lounge with wood burning stove and colour TV. Full English breakfast is included in the tariff. Evening Meal available on request or our local country pub within easy walking distance offers good food. Open all year. Bed and Breakfast from £18. Just off the M5 Junction 6, well situated for Worcester, Malverns, Stratford and Cotswolds.

HEREFORD. Mrs Diana Sinclair, Holly House Farm, Allensmore, Hereford HR2 9BH (01432 277294; mobile 0589 830223). ❦❦ *COMMENDED.* Spacious luxury farmhouse and over 10 acres of land with horses, situated in beautiful and peaceful open countryside. Bedrooms en suite or with private bathroom, central heating, TV and tea/coffee making facilities. We are only five miles south west of Hereford city centre. Ideal base for Welsh Borders, market towns, Black Mountains, Brecon and Malvern Hills and the Wye Valley. We have a happy family atmosphere and pets are welcome. Brochure on request. From £16 per person per night and with your delicious English breakfast you will be fit for the whole day!

HEREFORD. Mrs R.T. Andrews, Webton Court, Kingstone, Hereford HR2 9NF (01981 250220). ❦ **Working farm.** Black and white Georgian farm house in the Wye Valley on a working farm. Situated midway between Hay-on-Wye and Ross-on-Wye just off the B4348, ideally situated for touring the places of local interest. We offer a selection of bedrooms including en suite with TV, tea/coffee making facilities and washbasins. Large parties catered for. Rates £16 single, £15 per person double and £20 per person en suite. Evening Meal £8 per person by prior arrangement. Children at reduced rates.

HEREFORD. Mr David Jones, Sink Green Farm, Rotherwas, Hereford HR2 6LE (01432 870223). ❦❦ **Working farm, join in.** Warm and friendly atmosphere awaits your arrival at this 16th century farmhouse, on the banks of the River Wye. Three miles south of the cathedral city of Hereford, with Ross-on-Wye, Leominster, Ledbury, Malvern and the Black Mountains within easy reach. All rooms en-suite, tea/coffee making facilities and colour TV. One room with four-poster, family room by arrangement. Guests' own lounge. Pets by arrangement. Bed and Breakfast from £18 per person. AA QQQQ.

HEREFORD. Ashgrove House, Wellington Marsh, Hereford HR4 8DU (01432 830608). ♛♛

COMMENDED. Mike and Sandra Fletcher welcome you to luxurious accommodation with high standard furnishings and lovely gardens. Situated in a quiet rural location, over-looking cider apple orchards, three miles north of the historic Cathedral City of Hereford. Lovely walks nearby, golf and salmon fishing 10 minutes by car. Double, twin-bedded or single rooms, all en suite with TV and tea-making facilities. Good pub food in old inns nearby. Bed and full English Breakfast £17 to £20 per person.

Ashgrove

APPLE TREE COTTAGE – NEAR HEREFORD

Enquiries to MONICA BARKER,
Apple Tree Cottage, Mansel Lacy,
Near Hereford HR4 7HH
Tel: 01981 590688 – 24 hrs.

15th-century Cruck-construction cottage (full central heating) set in beautiful Hereford countryside – quiet, peaceful and friendly. Ideal for walkers and birdwatchers. Within easy reach of Cotswolds, North and South Wales, Black Mountains and many historic sites. One twin-bedded room with en-suite facilities, one double (single) and one twin-bedded room with shared bathroom; hot drinks tray; extra WC; lounge with TV. No smoking. BED and BREAKFAST from £17 (en-suite) and £14, reductions for 2 & 7 nights. We are open throughout the Winter. Car essential. Situated in the small hamlet of Mansel Lacy, seven miles N.W. of HEREFORD CITY, off the A480.

HEREFORD. Mrs D. Windham, Shobdon Farm, St Margaret's, Hereford HR2 0QW (01981 510310).

Overlooking the Golden Valley close to the Welsh Borders, this beautiful Herefordshire farm offers spacious, comfort-able rooms with spectacular views. One en suite twin room and one twin room with separate shower and WC. Breakfast in our large family farmhouse kitchen with stunning country-side outlook. The farm is midway between Hereford and Hay-on-Wye in an area of outstanding natural beauty, perfect for walkers and lovers of totally unspoilt surroundings. Easy access to Black Mountains and Wye Valley. Please phone for more information. Brochure on request.

FELTON HOUSE
Felton, Near Hereford HR1 3PH
Telephone: 01432 820366

Marjorie and Brian Roby extend a warm welcome to their home, a romantic old country house in beautiful tranquil gardens in the heart of unspoilt rural England. The house combines the very best of modern centrally heated facilities with period furnishings throughout, including four-poster, half-tester and brass beds, superb diningroom, drawingroom, library and garden room. Ensuite and private bathrooms. Wide choice of traditional English and vegetarian breakfasts. Local inns serve excellent evening meals. Off A417 between A49 and A465 just eight miles north of Hereford. Children and pets welcome. B&B from £18.50. Open all year.

ETB ♛♛ **Highly Commended. AA QQQQ Selected. Self-catering cottage in grounds.**

PLEASE ENCLOSE A STAMPED ADDRESSED ENVELOPE WITH ENQUIRIES

KINGTON. Mrs E.E. Protheroe, Bucks Head House, School Farm, Hergest, Kington HR5 3EW (01544 231063). Working farm. Newly modernised farmhouse on 290-acre mixed farm which has been worked by the Protheroe family since 1940 and carries cattle, sheep and crops. Wye Valley, Black Mountains, Elan Valley, Ludlow, Hereford Cathedral, Black and White villages all within easy reach. Two double, two single, two family bedrooms, with washbasins; two bathrooms, two showers, four toilets; two sitting rooms; tea/coffee making facilities in all rooms; diningroom. Snooker room with full size table. Cot, high chair and reduced rates for children; babysitting by arrangement. Pets free of charge, by arrangement only. Car essential, parking. Central heating. Peaceful walks around the farm and its sheep walk "Hergest Ridge". Evening Dinner/Meal, Bed and Breakfast or Bed and Breakfast only. Two six-berth mobile homes also available.

LEDBURY. Mrs Jane West, Church Farm, Coddington, Ledbury HR8 1JJ (01531 640271). Tourist Board Listed. Working farm. A Black and White 16th century listed farmhouse on a working farm, close to the Malvern Hills. Ideal for touring and walking. Warm hospitality assured in happy, relaxed atmosphere. There is accommodation in three double bedrooms, two with washbasins. Bathroom, toilet; sittingroom; diningroom. Plenty of good English fare, everything home made wherever possible. Log fires, TV, pets allowed. Open all year. Bed and Breakfast from £19; Evening Meal if required. Car essential — parking. Situated midway between Ross-on-Wye, Hereford, Gloucester and Worcester. SAE, please, for further details. Excellent self catering cottage (4 KEYS HIGHLY COMMENDED) also available.

LEDBURY. Mrs Blandford, Underhill Farm, Putley, Ledbury HR8 2QR (01531 670695). ✿✿ *COMMENDED.* A warm homely welcome awaits you at Underhill Farm, a 16th century Listed farmhouse, with oak beams and hop kilns, surrounded by large mature gardens and 140 acres of arable land and orchards nestling at the foot of "The Woolhope Dome", a site of natural beauty, with breathtaking views of the Malvern Hills and the Cotswolds to the Black Mountains. Ideally situated for touring, walking, riding and relaxing. Two large double bedrooms, one with private bathroom, one with en suite shower room, tea/coffee facilities. Guests' own sitting room and dining room. Wholesome breakfasts with homemade preserves, free-range eggs. Two award-winning inns nearby serving excellent evening meals. Bed and Breakfast from £16 per person per night.

LEDBURY near. Mrs Elizabeth Godsall, Moor Court Farm, Stretton Grandison, Near Ledbury HR8 2TR (01531 670408). ✿✿✿ *COMMENDED.* Relax and enjoy our attractive 15th century timber-framed farmhouse with its adjoining oast-houses, whose picturesque location will ensure a peaceful stay. We are a traditional hop and livestock farm situated in the beautiful countryside of Herefordshire being central to the local market towns, with easy access to the Malverns, Wye Valley and Welsh Borders. Guests will enjoy spacious bedrooms, all with en suite facilities, their own oak-beamed lounge, dining room and the peaceful setting of the garden or walks through surrounding woods and farmland with their rural views. Fishing is available in our own pool and there are stables on the farm. Bed and Breakfast from £17.50; Evening Meal £12.50. Residential licence.

HEREFORD & WORCESTERSHIRE – THE HEART OF ENGLAND!

A beautiful county which includes The Vale of Evesham and the rugged – if petite – Malvern Hills. It has been designated an "Area of Outstanding Beauty". Places of interest include The Avoncroft Museum of Buildings, Brockhampton, Ross-on-Wye, The Teme Valley and The Hereford & Worcester County Museum.

MALVERN. Jean and John Mobbs, Rock House, 144 West Malvern Road, Malvern WR14 4NJ (01684 574536). *APPROVED.* Attractive, family-run early Victorian guest house situated high on hills in peaceful atmosphere with superb views of over 40 miles. Ideal for rambling on hills or open country. 11 comfortable bedrooms, most overlooking our splendid view, some with showers/bathrooms; TV lounge, separate quiet room. Licensed to enhance excellent home cooked dinners. Groups welcome. Parking on premises. Open all year. Special Christmas package. Bed and Breakfast from £18. Stamp only, please, for brochure. Also pretty self catering cottage available.

MALVERN near. Ann and Brian Porter, Croft Guest House, Bransford, Worcester WR6 5JD (01886 832227). AA QQ Listed. 16th-18th century part black and white cottage-style country house situated in the River Teme Valley, four miles from Worcester and Malvern. Croft House is central for visiting numerous attractions in Worcester, Hereford, Severn Valley and surrounding countryside. There is fishing close by and an 18 hole golf course opposite. Facilities include three en suite rooms (two double, one family) and two double rooms with washbasins, hospitality trays. Double glazing, central heating, residential licence and home cooked dinners. There is a TV lounge, sauna and large jacuzzi for guests' use. A cot and baby listening service are provided. Bed and Breakfast from £18 to £25. Festive Christmas and New Year Breaks available.

MALVERN WELLS. Mrs J.L. Morris, Brickbarns Farm, Hanley Road, Malvern Wells WR14 4HY (016845 61775). Working farm. Brickbarns, a 200-acre mixed farm, is situated two miles from Great Malvern at the foot of the Malvern Hills, 300 yards from the bus service and one-and-a half miles from the train. The house, which is 300 years old, commands excellent views of the Malvern Hills and guests are accommodated in one double, one single and one family bedrooms with washbasins; two bathrooms, shower room, two toilets; sittingroom and diningroom. Children welcome and cot and babysitting offered. Central heating. Car essential, parking. Open Easter to October for Bed and Breakfast from £15 nightly per person. Reductions for children and Senior Citizens. Birmingham 40 miles, Hereford 20, Gloucester 17, Stratford 35 and the Wye Valley is just 30 miles.

OMBERSLEY. Mrs M. Peters, Tytchney, Boreley, Ombersley WR9 0HZ (01905 620185). 16th century medieval Hall House cottage in peaceful country lane, two and a half miles from Ombersley. Ideal for walking and touring the Heart of England. Fishing in the River Severn available nearby and just half a mile to Ombersley Golf Course. Double, family and single rooms; cot available. Bed and Breakfast from £13.50.

ROSS-ON-WYE. Mrs M.E. Drzymalska, Thatch Close, Llangrove, Ross-on-Wye HR9 6EL (01989 770300). *COMMENDED.* **Working farm, join in.** Secluded Georgian farmhouse set in large colourful gardens in 13 acres of pasture situated in the beautiful Wye Valley between Ross and Monmouth. Thatch Close offers a comfortable, homely atmosphere where guests are welcome to help feed the sheep, cows, calves, or just relax and enjoy this traditionally run farm. Places of scenic beauty and historic attractions nearby include Forest of Dean, Black Mountains, Cathedral Cities, old castles and buildings. Guests have their own lounge and diningroom with colour TV. Twin bedroom and one double room, both with bathrooms en-suite, one double room with private bathroom; all bathrooms have showers. Central heating. Non-smokers please. Breakfast and optional Evening Meal are prepared using mainly home grown produce. Vegetarian and diabetic meals arranged. Bed and Breakfast from £15 to £19 with reductions for longer stays. Reduced rates for children. SAE for further details.

ROSS-ON-WYE. Jean and James Jones, The Arches Hotel, Walford Road, Ross-on-Wye HR9 5PT (01989 563348). ♛♛♛ Small family-run hotel, set in half an acre of lawned garden, ideally situated only 10 minutes' walk from town centre. All rooms are furnished and decorated to a high standard and have views of the garden. Tea/coffee making facilities and colour TV are available in bedrooms; some en suite rooms, also one ground floor en suite bedroom available. Full central heating. There is a delightful Victorian-style conservatory to relax in and the garden to enjoy in the summer months. Licensed. Ample parking in grounds. A warm and friendly atmosphere with personal service. Generous weekly reductions. Bed and Breakfast £17, en suite rooms £22. Dinner by arrangement. AA Listed, RAC Acclaimed, Les Routiers Award. Please telephone or send SAE for colour brochure.

ROSS-ON-WYE. The Skakes, Glewstone, Ross-on-Wye HR9 6AZ (01989 770456). ♛♛ 18th century former farmhouse, set in an acre of gardens and Herefordshire's rolling unspoilt countryside at the heart of the Wye Valley. Monmouth, Hereford and the Forest of Dean are all close, with a wealth of places to visit, charming villages, and pubs/restaurants serving excellent food. Our bedrooms are mostly en suite, and all contain colour TV, clock radios and beverage trays. Downstairs are the cosy lounges (log fires when cold), and if the day's exploring leaves you too tired to sample the local hostelries, we can, given warning, usually feed you! Children aged 10 years and over welcome and also dogs by arrangement. Bed and Breakfast from £17.

ROSS-ON-WYE. Mrs Susan Dick, Merrivale Place, The Avenue, Ross-on-Wye HR9 5AW (01989 564929). ♛ *COMMENDED.* Merrivale Place is a lovely big Victorian house set in half an acre of gardens in a splendid tree-lined avenue. Peaceful surroundings overlooking trees and hills, yet close to the old market place centre of Ross, and near the River Wye. Guest accommodation in three spacious, comfortable bedrooms (double, twin and family) with wash-basins and shaver points. Three bathrooms, three toilets. TV lounge and separate diningroom. Full central heating. A very warm welcome extended to all guests. Sorry, no pets. Ample parking space inside grounds. Open April to October. Bed and Breakfast £17. Weekly terms. Come and see the lovely Wye Valley, Malverns, Brecon Beacons and the Golden Valley.

TENBURY WELLS. Mrs Margaret Jane Yarnold, Court Farm, Hanley Childe, Tenbury Wells WR15 8QY (01885 410265). ETB Listed. Working farm, join in. Court Farm is a charming 15th century renovated farmhouse with adjoining listed buildings, on a 200 acre mixed farm located in a quiet village with beautiful church nearby. From April to October, accommodation available in one double room with en suite facilities, one twin-bedded room with adjoining bathroom; visitors' lounge and dining room. Large garden. Home cooking and a comfortable, friendly atmosphere assured. Children welcome. Cot and high chair available. Special diets can be catered for. Regret no pets. Extensive, delightful views within short walking distance across Teme Valley. Market town of Tenbury Wells six miles. Close by are the historic towns of Ludlow, Worcester, Bewdley and Bromyard. Further afield is Stratford, the Cotswolds and Welsh Borders. Several gardens and National Trust properties locally. Car essential. Local shop/post office in village. Terms from £15. Telephone or SAE for further details please.

WINFORTON. Mrs Jackie Kingdon, Winforton Court, Winforton HR3 6EA (01544 328498). A warm welcome and country hospitality awaits you at historic 16th century Winforton Court — former home of Roger De Mortimer, Earl of March. Unwind and enjoy spacious and elegant surroundings in the beautiful Wye Valley. Set in old world gardens with rural views, Winforton Court offers delightfully furnished bedrooms all with private bathrooms, one with four poster; luxurious drawing room, library with wealth of local guide books, etc. Enjoy a hearty breakfast (vegetarian available) in historic former Court Room with its magnificent early 17th century oak staircase. The house abounds in oak beams, open fires, early stencilling, interesting collections of old china, samplers and antiques. Bed and Breakfast from £20 per person per night. 10% discount for five or more nights.

WOONTON. Mrs Tessa Plummer, Rose Cottage, Woonton HR3 6QW (01544 340459). Situated in a peaceful location 13 miles north west of Hereford, within easy reach of the Black Mountains, Hay-on-Wye, the Cotswolds, Worcester and the famous "black and white" villages. Set in two acres of old world gardens and orchard, Rose Cottage offers all modern amenities. One twin-bedded room with en suite bathroom and one double room with private bathroom, each room having tea/coffee making facilities. Cosy beamed sitting room with colour TV. Log fires in winter. Generous breakfasts, vegetarian choice available. Open all year. Reductions for stays of five nights or more. Bed and Breakfast £20 to £22.50 per person (£18 per person per night January, February, November and December). No smoking. Brochure available on request.

WORCESTER near. Mrs J. Webb, Knowle Farm, Suckley, Near Worcester WR6 5DJ (01886 884347). Part-timbered 17th century farmhouse with 25 acres grassland, used mainly for horses. Adjacent to a small, quiet country inn, the house is in an elevated position with unrivalled views of the Malvern Hills and offers accommodation all year round. Large colourful garden. The quaint market towns of Bromyard, Ledbury and Hereford are nearby, and Knowle Farm is in the heart of a fruit-growing area where visitors enjoy the magnificent spring blossom. Superb walking country. One double and one single bedrooms (one with washbasin); bathroom, toilet. Sittingroom with woodburner fire, diningroom. Central heating keeps the house comfortable throughout the year. Car essential — parking. Traditional hearty English Breakfast. Fresh farm eggs. Bed and Breakfast £15 (bedtime drink). Special mid-week "Bargain Breaks" Monday to Thursday, £12.50 per person per night; no single supplement. This is a non-smoking establishment.

WORCESTER near. Sylvia and Brian Wynn, The Old Smithy, Pirton, Worcester WR8 9EJ (01905 820482). HETB Listed *HIGHLY COMMENDED.* A 17th century half-timbered country house set in peaceful countryside with many interesting walks. Centrally situated, within easy reach of Stratford-upon-Avon, Cotswolds, Warwick Castle, Malvern Hills, Worcester Cathedral and Royal Worcester Porcelain. Four and a half miles from junction 7 of the M5 motorway. Private guests facilities include lounge with inglenook log fireplace, colour TV and video, bathroom/dressing room and toilet, laundry, tea/coffee, central heating, gardens. One double bedroom and one twin bedroom. Ample parking. Bed and English Breakfast from £16; Evening Meal optional extra £8.50. Fresh local produce and home cooking. Sorry, no pets or children under 12 years. Craft Workshop (Harris Tweed and knitwear).

HERTFORDSHIRE

BUNTINGFORD. Sally Smyth, Middle Farm, Throcking, Buntingford SG9 9RN (01763 281204).

Victorian farmhouse with wonderful views over the open countryside. Ideally sited for Knebworth Park, Wimpole Hall, Duxford or Cambridge. One beamed double bedroom with en suite and small lobby for child's bed and one twin bedroom. All rooms have tea/coffee facilities and remote controlled colour TV. Lovely walks and good restaurants nearby. No pets. Open all year. Bed and Breakfast from £20 to £25. Holiday cottages also available.

KENT

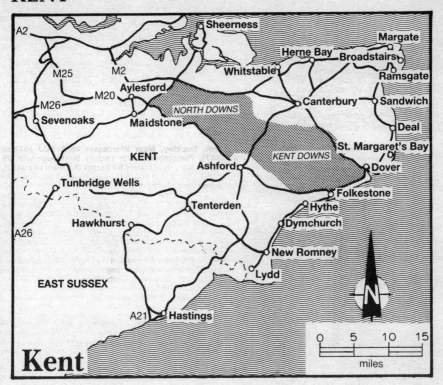

Kent

ASHFORD. Mrs Lilly Wilton, Bulltown Farmhouse, West Brabourne, Ashford TN25 5NQ (01233 813505). An attractively restored 15th century timber-framed Kentish Farmhouse situated on the southwestern side of the North Downs and Pilgrim's Way offering unspoilt countryside and superb walks. The Cathedral City of Canterbury is only 12 miles, Ashford seven miles and the Channel Ports of Folkestone and Dover are 10 and 18 miles respectively. The M20 Junction 10 is only five miles away giving access to other motorways and Gatwick and Heathrow airports. There is an excellent award-winning country inn close by. Accommodation offered in two double and one twin bedded rooms, all en suite and with tea/coffee facilities. Children welcome, cot and reduced terms available. Terms from £19 per person, £18 for three nights or more.

ASHFORD. Ros and John Martin, Hogben Farm, Church Lane, Aldington, Ashford TN25 7EH (01233 720219). Tourist Board Listed. This farmhouse, dating from the sixteenth century, lies in a very quiet location, down its own drive, set among extensive gardens and lawns. It is an ideal centre for visits to Canterbury, Rye, Tenterden etc, and handy for the ferries and the Channel Tunnel. Accommodation comprises one double room and two twin rooms; en suite available. A sitting room with inglenook fireplace and colour TV is available for guests. Not only tea and coffee in your room but also good home cooking for your Evening Meal (available by arrangement). Open all year. Bed and Breakfast from £19.50.

ASHFORD near. Elvey Farm Country Hotel, Pluckley, Near Ashford TN27 0SU (01233 840442; Fax: 01233 840726). Completely secluded, this working farm offers luxury accommodation in converted oak-beamed farm buildings. Five one or two bedroomed ground floor Stables adjoin the old Kent Barn which has two large family rooms. Oast House has a family room and two twin-bedded rooms. Each bedroom has colour TV, central heating and en-suite facilities. Pluckley is ideally situated for visiting the coast, Channel Ports and local attractions, with all outdoor activities being available nearby, especially golf. Excellent farmhouse meals offered for a minimum of 10 people with home made produce to make your stay a holiday to remember. Guided tours arranged. Fully licensed. AA QQQQ.

BIRCHINGTON near. Mrs Liz Goodwin, Woodchurch Farmhouse, Woodchurch, Near Birchington CT7 0HE (01843 832468). This attractive Elizabethan/Georgian farmhouse is situated in a quiet rural area yet only two miles from long stretches of sandy beach. Within easy reach of Canterbury, Sandwich, Rye, Chilham and the cross-Channel ferries. There is ample parking, a car is essential. Very comfortable bedrooms with tea/coffee making facilities. Sittingroom with TV. Bathroom and shower for guests' use only. Separate beamed diningroom. A warm welcome and a comfortable stay assured at Woodchurch. Bed and Breakfast from £16. Please write or telephone for further details.

CANTERBURY. Mrs Joan Hill, Renville Oast, Bridge, Canterbury CT4 5AD (01227 830215). Renville Oast is situated amongst apple orchards in beautiful Kentish countryside, only two miles from the Cathedral City of Canterbury, 10 miles from the coast and two hours' drive from London. Many interesting castles and historic houses within easy reach. Nature reserves, golf courses and Howletts Zoo nearby. A day trip to France is a possibility. All rooms are comfortable and attractively furnished, with tea making facilities. One family room en-suite, a twin-bedded room and double room with washbasins; separate bathroom; lounge/TV room. Bed and Breakfast from £21 per person includes good farmhouse breakfast. Excellent pub food nearby.

CANTERBURY. Mrs Lewana Castle, Great Field Farm, Misling Lane, Stelling Minnis, Canterbury CT4 6DE (01227 709223). ETB Listed *HIGHLY COMMENDED.* In own pastures with friendly ponies, on a quiet country lane, adjacent B2068, comfortable farmhouse with Aga and full central heating. One double bedroom with own stairs, lounge, colour TV, kitchen and bathroom (also available for self catering); double bedroom, en-suite bathroom; twin-bedded room with en suite bathroom and own lounge. Guests welcome in elegant lounge with colour TV, dining room and farmhouse kitchen. Babysitting, refreshments and laundry available. Local restaurants. Bed and farmhouse Breakfast from £18 to £20. Reductions for children. Pets by arrangement. Non-smoking establishment. SAE or telephone.

CANTERBURY. N.J. Ellen, Crockshard Farmhouse, Wingham, Canterbury CT3 1NY (01227 720464; Fax: 01227 721125). Exceptionally attractive farmhouse in beautiful gardens and farmland. Ideally situated for visiting any part of Kent — Canterbury 15 minutes, Dover 20 minutes, Folkestone 30 minutes. Prices from £17.50.

CANTERBURY. Mr and Mrs R. Linch, Upper Ansdore, Duckpit Lane, Petham, Canterbury CT4 5QB (01227 700672). ETB Listed. Beautiful secluded Listed Tudor farmhouse with various livestock, situated in an elevated position with far-reaching views of the wooded countryside of the North Downs. The property overlooks a Kent Trust Nature Reserve, it is five miles south of the cathedral city of Canterbury and only 30 minutes' drive to the ports of Dover and Folkestone. The accommodation comprises three double and one twin bedded rooms and family room. All have shower, WC en-suite and tea making facilities. Dining/sitting room, heavily beamed and with large inglenook. Car essential. Bed and Full English Breakfast from £19 per person. AA QQQ.

English Tourist Board
Listed

CANTERBURY. Mrs A. Hunt, Bower Farmhouse, Stelling Minnis, Near Canterbury CT4 6BB (01227 709430). 🐾🐾 *HIGHLY COMMENDED.* Anne & Nick Hunt welcome you to Bower Farm House, a traditional 17th-century Kentish farmhouse situated in the midst of Stelling Minnis, a medieval common of 125 acres of unspoilt trees, shrubs and open grassland; seven miles south of the cathedral city of Canterbury and nine miles from the coast; the countryside abounds in beauty spots and nature reserves. The house is heavily beamed and maintains its original charm. The accommodation comprises a double room and a twin-bedded room, both with private facilities. Full traditional English breakfast is served with home-made bread, marmalade and fresh free-range eggs. Children welcome; pets by prior arrangement. Open all year (except Christmas). Car essential. Excellent pub food five minutes away. Bed and Breakfast from £18 per person.

FAVERSHAM. N.J. and C.I. Scutt, Leaveland Court, Leaveland, Faversham ME13 0NP (01233 740596). 🐾🐾 *HIGHLY COMMENDED.* Guests are warmly welcomed to our enchanting timbered 15th century farmhouse which nestles between Leaveland Church and woodlands in rural tranquillity. Offering high standards of accommodation whilst retaining their original character, all bedrooms are en suite with colour TV and hot drinks trays. Traditional breakfasts, cooked on the Aga, are available with a choice of alternatives. There is a large attractive garden with heated outdoor swimming pool for guests' use and ample car parking. Ideally situated for visiting Kent's historic cities, castles, houses and gardens with Canterbury only 20 minutes by car and also easy access to Channel ports, 30 minutes. Good walking country, being close to both the Pilgrim's Way and the coast. Terms from £20 for Bed and Breakfast.

FAVERSHAM. Mrs Elizabeth Higgs, Owens Court Farm, Selling, Faversham ME13 9QN (Tel & Fax: 01227 752247). ☙ *COMMENDED.* Owens Court is a gracious Georgian farmhouse set in its own hop and fruit farm. The location is very quiet yet only one and a half miles from the A2 and within easy reach of Canterbury, Faversham and the Channel ports. The house has large, comfortable rooms with a guests' sitting room and tea/coffee making facilities. Each of the three bedrooms has colour TV and washbasins. There is a guests' bathroom and two toilets. The garden is large and well kept. Visitors are welcome to use it and walk on the farm. Children welcome. Nice pubs and restaurants nearby. Bed and Breakfast £17.

MAIDSTONE. Mrs Merrilyn Boorman, The White Lodge, Loddington Lane, Linton, Maidstone ME17 4AG (01622 743129). Guests return again and again to this elegant house beautifully situated in parkland overlooking the Weald of Kent. Just 15 minutes from Leeds Castle, four miles from Central Maidstone and within easy reach of Sissinghurst Castle and many other interesting places. Well established with a friendly relaxed atmosphere, guests are encouraged to enjoy the two and a half acre garden with two ponds. Ample parking. Quiet location. Terms from £20 per person per night with full English breakfast. En suite double/family room with sitting room and kitchen available. Directions: south on A229, onto B2163, first right Loddington Lane, near to the bottom of hill, on right.

Key to Tourist Board Ratings

The Crown Scheme
(England, Scotland & Wales)

Covering hotels, motels, private hotels, guesthouses, inns, bed & breakfast, farmhouses. Every Crown classified place to stay is inspected annually. *The classification:* Listed then 1-5 Crown indicates the range of facilities and services. Higher quality standards are indicated by the terms APPROVED, COMMENDED, HIGHLY COMMENDED and DELUXE.

The Key Scheme
(also operates in Scotland using a Crown symbol)

Covering self-catering in cottages, bungalows, flats, houseboats, houses, chalets, etc. Every Key classified holiday home is inspected annually. *The classification:* 1-5 Key indicates the range of facilities and equipment. Higher quality standards are indicated by the terms APPROVED, COMMENDED, HIGHLY COMMENDED and DELUXE.

The Q Scheme
(England, Scotland & Wales)

Covering holiday, caravan, chalet and camping parks. Every Q rated park is inspected annually for its quality standards. The more √ in the Q – up to 5 – the higher the standard of what is provided.

ROLVENDEN. Mrs B.J. Hilder, Little Halden Farm, Rolvenden, Cranbrook TN17 4JL (01580 241254). Working farm. The farmhouse on a working hop and livestock farm is situated in an area of outstanding natural beauty. The picturesque town of Tenterden with its steam railway and leisure centre is only two miles away. Guests are welcome to walk round the farm and garden. There are two double rooms and one twin, each furnished to a high standard and having washbasins, colour TV and tea/coffee making facilities. Separate shower and bathrooms for guests' use. All rooms are centrally heated. Bed and Breakfast from £15 per person. Non-smoking. Unfortunately we are not able to accept children or pets.

SUTTON VALENCE. Mrs Stephanie Clout, Sparks Oast Farm, Forsham Lane, Sutton Valence, Maidstone ME17 3EW (01622 842213). Sparks Oast is a characteristic converted Kentish Oasthouse, on a small sheep farm in quiet country lane overlooking the Weald of Kent. Ideally situated for visiting the many attractive castles, famous gardens such as Sissinghurst, Scotney Castle, etc and other places of interest in the Garden of England, or just rambling amid orchards and hop gardens. There is a wealth of excellent pubs offering good food. A warm welcome by the family including the animals, waterfowl, barn owls, etc. Bed and Breakfast from £16.50 per person. One double room, one twin and one en suite. TV. Guests' bathroom and beverage facilities. ALSO SELF CATERING SUITE.

TENTERDEN. Mrs M.R. O'Connor, The Old Post House, Stone-in-Oxney, Tenterden TN30 7JN (01233 758258). Experience the peace and tranquillity of rural England at its best. This guest house overlooks the historic expanse of Romney Marsh and nestles against the hill of the Isle-in-Oxney in the heart of Kentish farmland. Only about ten minutes' drive to the delightful market towns of Rye and Tenterden, where excellent meals can be enjoyed. All rooms are equipped with central heating, washbasins, razor points, tea/coffee making facilities. One room with en suite facilities. Bathroom and shower room. Open all year round. Children over eight years welcome. Pets must be left in car. Bed and traditional English Breakfast from £20 to £23 per person; delicious food can also be had in the village. Car essential, ample parking.

WEST HYTHE. Mrs Emma Catt, Harveyland Farm, West Hythe CT21 4NR (01303 873738). Peaceful, friendly farmhouse set in 25 acres of countryside and situated three and a half miles from the Cinque Port of Hythe. Ideal for visiting France, Canterbury, Rye and the beautiful Weald of Kent. Rooms have TV and own bathroom. Amenities are on one level and rooms open onto a patio with lovely views. Mrs Emma Catt provides a delicious English breakfast; in winter tea is served in front of log fires. Supper is served on request and special diets catered for. Ideal area for fishing, walking, cycling. Bed and Breakfast from £15. All welcome.

KENT – THE GARDEN OF ENGLAND!

The pleasant landscape of Kent, including The North Downs and The Weald, is the venue of many engaging places to visit. These include Chiddingstone – the half-timbered village, the sophisticated spa town of Tunbridge Wells and Swanton Mill. There are also day trips to the continent and for railway enthusiasts, The Sittingbourne & Kensley Light Railway, The Kent & East-Sussex Railway and the 'World's Smallest Public Railway' from Hythe to Dungeness.

LANCASHIRE

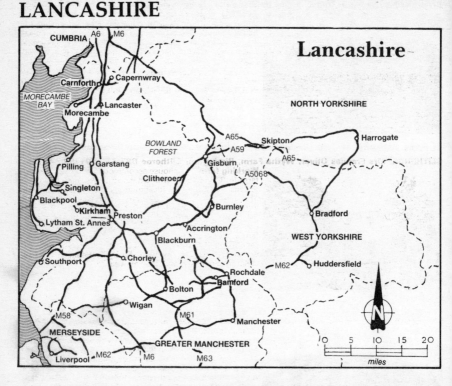

CARNFORTH. Mrs Gillian Close, Cotestones Farm, Sand Lane, Warton, Carnforth LA5 9NH (01524 732418). Tourist Board Listed. Situated on the North Lancashire coast near the M6 (Junction 35) on the Carnforth to Silverdale road, this is a 150-acre family-run dairy farm which adjoins Leighton Moss RSPB Reserve; also very near Steamtown Railway Museum. Lying between Lancaster, Morecambe and the Lake District, it is an ideal base for touring the area. Tea/coffee facilities and washbasins in all rooms. Bed and Breakfast from £14 per person. Reductions for children. Pets welcome. Open all year (closed Christmas).

CARNFORTH. Mrs Vera Carson, Galley Hall Farm, Shore Road, Carnforth LA5 9HZ (01524 732544). Tourist Board Listed. A 17th century farmhouse on a stock rearing farm on the North Lancashire coast, near Junction 35 M6, close to Leighton Moss RSPB, Railway Museum, historic Lancaster; ideal base for touring the Lake District or the coastal resorts. Double, twin and single rooms; tea/coffee and radio in rooms; TV available. Sorry, no pets or smoking. Central heating, log fires. Lounge with TV. Evening meals on request. Good golf courses and fishing in the area. We offer a homely and friendly atmosphere. Open all year except Christmas. Bed and Breakfast from £15 per person.

PLEASE SEND A STAMPED ADDRESSED ENVELOPE WITH ENQUIRIES

CLITHEROE. Mrs M.A. Berry, Lower Standen Farm, Whalley Road, Clitheroe BB7 1PP (01200 424176).

♥ ♥ This farmhouse is situated 20 minutes' walk from town centre, one mile from A59 road. Convenient for M6, 20 minutes drive from Junction 31. There are two double rooms en suite, one twin-bedded room with washbasin only and an additional single room if required. TV and tea/coffee making facilities; cot also available. Own lounge with electric fire and TV; dining room. Full central heating. Pets and children are welcome, reduced rates for children under 12 years. Open all year except Christmas and New Year. Golf club nearby. Bed and Breakfast from £15 per person, £17 in en suite room.

CLITHEROE. Mrs Frances Oliver, Wytha Farm, Rimington, Clitheroe BB7 4EQ (01200 445295).

Working farm. Farmhouse accommodation on stockrearing farm in Ribble Valley with extensive views. Within walking distance of Pendle Hill. Ideal touring centre for Lake District, Yorkshire Dales, Bronte Country, interesting and historic Clitheroe. Children welcome. Babysitting service. Beautiful picnic area. Packed lunches available. Farm produce when possible, and home cooking. Accommodation comprises family and double rooms; TV lounge; central heating. Ample car parking. Pets by prior arrangement (£1 per day). Bed and Breakfast from £14; Evening Meal £8. Reduced rates for children under 11 years. Open all year.

LANCASTER. Roy and Helen Domville, Three Gables, Chapel Lane, Galgate, Lancaster LA2 0PN (01524 752222).

A large detached bungalow, three miles south of Lancaster and 400 yards from Lancaster University. Access from M6 Junction 33 and A6 in Galgate village. Two double bedrooms each with shower, toilet, colour TV and tea/coffee facilities. One bedroom also has a private TV lounge. Open all year with full central heating. A cot and high chair are available. Spacious parking. A good location for visiting Blackpool, Morecambe, the Lake District and Yorkshire Dales. You will be sure of a friendly welcome and a homely atmosphere. Sorry, no pets. Non-smokers only please. Bed and Breakfast £15 per person.

MANCHESTER. Margaret and Bernard Satterthwaite, The Albany Hotel, 21 Albany Road, Chorlton-cum-Hardy, Manchester M21 0AY (0161-881 6774; Fax: 0161-862 9405). ♥ ♥ ♥ COMMENDED. The Albany Hotel, having recently undergone a major refurbishment, offers luxurious and elegant period accommodation with all the comforts of a modern deluxe hotel, plus the personal attention of the owners. Facilities include Erica's Restaurant, licensed bar, games room and full conference facilities. A choice of single, double or family rooms, all with shower or en suite bathroom, direct plan telephone, colour TV, hair dryer, radio and tea/coffee. Conveniently located being only 10 minutes from the city and Airport, five minutes Manchester United, L.C.C.C., Salford Quays, Trafford Park and Universities. Directions: just off the A6010 (Wilbraham Road), approximately one mile from Metrolink, one mile from Junction 7 M63 for M62, M61 and M6 north, two miles M56 and M6 south. AA/RAC two stars. Brochure and tariff on request.

MIDDLETON. Mrs Pauline Bainbridge, Tossbeck Farm, Middleton, Kirkby Lonsdale, Via Carnforth, Lancs LA6 2LZ (015242 76214).

Tossbeck Farm is a 110 acre dairy and sheep farm situated in the beautiful unspoilt countryside of the Lune Valley midway between the market towns of Kirkby Lonsdale and Sedbergh. The farmhouse is a 16th century listed building featuring oak panelling. Ideally situated for visiting both the Lake District and the Yorkshire Dales. One family room and one double room, both spacious with washbasins and tea/coffee making facilities. Lounge with TV, dining room, visitors' bathroom and central heating. Bed and full English Breakfast from £12.50 with reductions for children and weekly stays. No smoking please.

SILVERDALE. Mrs Helen Rushworth, Havendale, 58 Emesgate Lane, Silverdale, Carnforth LA5

0RN (01524 701833). Havendale is a family home on the outskirts of Silverdale with extensive views in beautiful limestone countryside. The house is a fine centre for touring the Lakes, Dales and Blackpool, for bird watching at Leighton Moss, walking, cycling and visiting stately homes, yet is only 10 minutes from the M6. Havendale features en suite rooms with beverage trays, TV and a clock radio. Children are particularly welcome and we provide a play area, books, toys, games, cot and a high chair. Baby sitting by arrangement. Children sharing parents' rooms free. We regret we cannot accommodate smokers or guests with pets. Brochure available.

SOUTHPORT. Mrs Wendy E. Core, Sandy Brook Farm, 52 Wyke Cop Road, Scarisbrick, Southport

PR8 5LR (01704 880337). ✿ ✿ Bill and Wendy Core offer a homely, friendly atmosphere at Sandy Brook, a small working farm situated three and a half miles from the seaside resort of Southport and five miles from the historic town of Ormskirk. Motorways are easily accessible, and the Lake District, Trough of Bowland, Blackpool and North Wales are within easy reach. Six en suite bedrooms with colour TV and tea/coffee making facilities. Central heating throughout. Sittingroom with colour TV; diningroom. High chair, cots and babysitting available. Open all year round. Bed and Breakfast from £15.50; reductions for children. Weekly terms on request. NWTB Silver Award Winner "Place to Stay" Farmhouse Category.

LEICESTERSHIRE

BELTON-IN-RUTLAND, Near Oakham. The Old Rectory, Belton-in-Rutland, Oakham LE15 9LE

(01572 717279; Fax: 01572 717343). Large Victorian house overlooking the Eye Brook Valley and rolling Rutland countryside. A small farm with horses and sheep 10 minutes from Rutland Water. Launde Abbey, stately homes, castles, woodland, farm and country parks locally — lots to see and do. Full traditional English or Continental breakfast (evening meals by arrangement). Eat out at some of the best pubs and restaurants in the country (lots within 10 minutes). Rooms have private bath or shower, TV, tea/coffee. A fully furnished self catering flat also available. New 20 × 40 Manège and stabling, grazing. Phone for brochure.

EARL SHILTON. The Townhouse, 32 Wood Street, Earl Shilton LE9 7ND (01455 847011; Fax: 01455 851490). The Townhouse is a highly rated Two Star hotel which has 26 comfortable bedrooms sleeping a total of 42 guests. All rooms are en suite with either bath or shower and are complete with colour TV, radio alarm and beverage facilities. The Townhouse Restaurant offers à la carte menu and light meals are available in our elegant cafe bar. Free parking for up to 150 cars with a further 300 spaces opposite. The Townhouse is located in the village of Earl Shilton just minutes away from the historic city of Leicester, with easy access to the M69, M1, M6, Coventry, Birmingham and is ideal for sales meetings, seminars or full conferences and weddings. Please send for our brochure.

AMBERLEY

4 Church Lane, Asfordby, Melton Mowbray, Leicestershire
LE14 3RU Tel: 01664 812314 Fax: 01664 813740

Large modern ranch-style bungalow with river frontage set in one acre of floodlit lawns and gardens in the conservation area of the village. Comfortable en suite bedrooms available all with colour TV & tea making facilities. Centrally heated throughout. Ample parking. Enjoy breakfast in the garden room with the interest of swans and birdlife on the riverbank – and in the evenings watch for foxes & fox cubs on the floodlit lawns. Registered with the EMTB. Shop in the bustling street markets of Melton Mowbray on Tuesdays and Saturdays. Within half an hour car ride of Leicester Nottingham and Rutland Water. Excellent meals at the local inns. Bed & Breakfast from £15.00. Self-catering holiday annexe also available. *Full details on request from* Mrs D. Brotherhood.

MELTON MOWBRAY. Mrs Linda Lomas, Shoby Lodge Farm, Shoby, Melton Mowbray LE14 3PF (01664 812156). Set in attractive gardens, Shoby Lodge is a spacious, comfortable, tastefully furnished farmhouse. Enjoy an Aga-cooked breakfast and beautiful views of the surrounding countryside. Accommodation comprises one double en suite room, and two double rooms with private bathroom. All rooms have tea and coffee making facilities and TV. Close to the market town of Melton Mowbray and ideally situated for Leicester and Nottingham. Coarse fishing available on the farm.

RUTLAND BORDERS. Margaret Locke, The Old Forge, Main Street, Medbourne, Market Harborough LE16 8DT (01858 565859). Open all year round for Bed and Breakfast, situated in the centre of the village opposite the church and post office, within easy walking distance of a pub with good food and real ale. Medbourne is a picturesque village in the heart of the Welland Valley famed for its Packhorse Bridge. Accommodation consists of one twin-bedded room with private bath, one twin and one double with washbasin which share shower room; sitting room with colour TV. Central heating throughout. Large garden and ample parking space. Terms from £36 to £38 double, £19 to £22 single.

LINCOLNSHIRE

HORNCASTLE. Mrs J. Bankes Price, Greenfield Farm, Minting, Near Horncastle LN9 5RX (01507 578457).

HIGHLY COMMENDED. Judy and Hugh welcome you to their comfortable farmhouse set in a tranquil location, surrounded by open countryside and spacious gardens with a large pond. It is centrally placed for the main Lincolnshire attractions and borders the Chambers Wood Forest Nature Reserve. Guests have their own sittingroom with colour TV and woodburning stove; modern en suite shower rooms, heated towel rails; radios, tea/coffee making facilities, central heating. One double and one twin with en suite facilities, one double with private bathroom. Excellent pub with traditional country cooking within one mile. Non-smoking household. AA QQQQ Selected. Farm Holiday Bureau member. Bed and Breakfast from £19.

LANGTON-BY-WRAGBY. Miss Jessie Skellern, Lea Holme, Langton-by-Wragby, Lincoln LN3 5PZ (01673 858339). Tourist Board Listed.

Ground floor accommodation in comfortable, chalet-type house set in own half-acre peaceful garden. All amenities. Central for touring Wolds, coast, fens, historic Lincoln etc. So much to discover in this county with wonderful skies and room to breathe. Attractive market towns, Louth, Horncastle (famed for antiques), Boston, Spilsby, Alford, Woodhall Spa (noted for golf). Accommodation offered in two double bedrooms (can be let as single), with washbasins; bathroom, toilet adjoining; lounge with colour TV always available to guests, separate dining room. Drinks provided. Children welcome at reduced rates. Pets welcome (no charge). Car almost essential, parking. Basically room and breakfast, but limited number of evening meals may be available. Numerous eating places nearby. Bed and Breakfast from £16 per person. Open all year.

LINCOLN near. Mrs Brenda Williams, Gallow Dale Farm, Marton Road, Sturton by Stow, Lincoln LN1 2AH (01427 788387). Situated eight miles north west of Lincoln on the A1500 road between the villages of Sturton by Stow and Marton (one mile west of Sturton by Stow village centre). Tastefully refurbished, centrally heated, Grade II Listed Georgian farmhouse set in 33 acres of grass paddocks. TV lounge with beamed ceiling, pretty bedrooms including en suite room with four poster bed. Tea/coffee making facilities in all bedrooms. Full English farmhouse breakfast provided. Lunch and evening meals available at three local public houses. Sorry, no smoking. Bed and breakfast from £14 to £20. AA QQQQ Selected.

LOUTH. Mr and Mrs Brumpton, Glebe Farm, Church Lane, Conisholne, Louth LN11 7LX (01507 358189).

Detached farmhouse with grassland mainly for horses, situated in the peaceful hamlet of Conisholne, off the A1031 road. Convenient for the Lincolnshire coast, city of Lincoln and Market Rasen. Amenities include RSPB Bird Nature Reserve, fishing, horse racing and is ideal countryside for cycling. Family accommodation comprises own entrance, TV lounge, two double bedrooms (cot if required); bathroom and garden. Tea/coffee making facilities. Full English breakfast. Sorry no smoking or pets. Price £15 per adult, reductions for children under 12 years.

NORFOLK

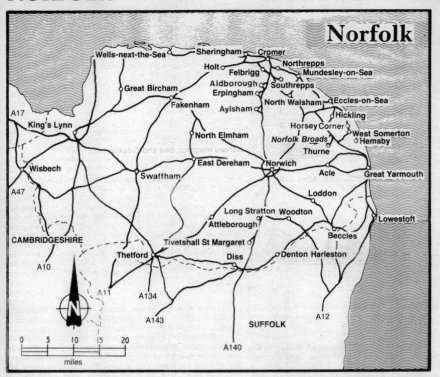

BARTON TURF. Mr Geraint Morgan, The White House, Pennygate, Barton Turf NR12 8BG (01692 536057). Charming 17th century cottage in pretty hamlet of Pennygate, close to Barton Broad. The cottage is quietly situated but close to all of the attractions of the Norfolk Broads, historic Norwich and the coast. Enjoy the pretty cottage gardens, inglenook log fire, beamed sitting room and comfortable conservatory. The tasteful, individually furnished double, twin/king size and family rooms are all en suite and have remote control colour TV, radio and tea/coffee making facilities. Fresh local produce, home made preserves, etc are a speciality. Pets welcome. Dinghy available. Bed and Breakfast from £19 per person; Dinner by arrangement from £10.50. Reduced rates for longer stays. Parking. Self catering cottage (sleeps 2) also available £130 to £200 per week.

BARTON TURF. Gill Law, Broadfields, Staithe Road, Barton Turf NR12 8AZ (01692 536442). A large family house in village location set in lovely gardens where cream teas and light snacks are served during the season. 200 yards away is Barton Staithe, giving access to one of the largest Broads in Norfolk and surrounded by a beautiful nature reserve. Ideal base for touring, boating, cycling etc. Accommodation consists of one twin-bedded room and one double/family room, both en suite with colour TV and tea making facilities. A rowing dinghy is moored at the Staithe for guests' use. Rates from £18 per person per night.

BECCLES. Mrs E. Lord, Maypole Barn, Maypole Green, Toftmonks NR34 0EY (01502 678235).

Tranquil setting just off the village green in the hamlet of Maypole Green but only four miles from Beccles and within easy reach of the market town of Bungay and the Norfolk Broads, 12 miles Yarmouth, 14 miles Lowestoft making an ideal centre for touring both Norfolk and Suffolk. Maypole Barn offers excellent accommodation recently converted to a very high standard and set in three acres of grounds. Family room en suite with TV, double room en suite with TV. Lounge, table tennis room. Full central heating, tea/coffee facilities in all rooms. Terms from £16. Child reductions.

BECCLES near. Mrs Rachel Clarke, Shrublands Farm, Burgh St. Peter, Near Beccles, Suffolk NR34 0BB (01502 677241; mobile 0468 313527). ♥♥

COMMENDED. This attractive homely farmhouse offers a warm and friendly welcome, is peacefully situated in the Waveney Valley on the Norfolk/Suffolk border, and is surrounded by one acre of garden and lawns. The River Waveney flows through the 550 acres of mixed working farmland; opportunities for bird watching. Ideal base for touring Norfolk and Suffolk; Beccles, Lowestoft, Great Yarmouth and Norwich are all within easy reach. The house has one double room and one family room with en suite facilities and one twin-bedded room with private bathroom, shower room and toilet. All have satellite colour TV and tea/coffee making facilities; dining room, separate lounge with colour satellite TV. Non-smoking rooms available. Games room for snooker and darts. Tennis court available; swimming pool and food at River Centre nearby. Children over five years welcome at reduced rates. No pets. Car essential, ample parking. Open all year. Bed and Breakfast from £16.50 to £18.50 per person. SAE please.

BUNGAY. Mrs Bobbie Watchorn, Earsham Park Farm, Harleston Road, Earsham, Bungay, Suffolk NR35 2AQ (Tel & Fax: 01986 892180). ♥♥ *HIGHLY COMMENDED.* Stay with every comfort in our outstanding

Victorian farmhouse with beautiful views, set in the middle of a 600 acre farm. The rooms are warm and elegantly furnished, all having beverage facilities, colour TVs, radios and en suite bathrooms; four-poster bed available. Enjoy our large gardens and collection of unusual farm animals. Lots of lovely home produced food. Evening Meal available by arrangement. Many local attractions including the Otter Trust. Easy access Norwich and the coast. This is a real "home from home". Open all year. FHB Member. Bed and Breakfast from £37 double/twin. Sorry no pets or smoking.

DEREHAM. David and Annie Bartlett, Bartles Lodge, Church Street, Elsing, Dereham NR20 3EA (01362 637177). ♥♥ *COMMENDED.* If you would like a

peaceful tranquil stay in the heart of Norfolk's most beautiful countryside yet only a short drive to some of England's finest sandy beaches, then Bartles Lodge could be the place for you, with all rooms tastefully decorated in country style, with full en suite facilities, TVs, tea/coffee making facilities, etc. Overlooking 12 acres of landscaped meadows with its own private fishing lakes. The local village inn is within 100 metres and has a restaurant which serves "pub grub". Bed and Breakfast from £20. Why not telephone David and Annie so that we can tell you about our lovely home.

DISS near. Strenneth, Airfield Road, Fersfield, Diss IP22 2BP (01379 688182; Fax: 01379 688260). ♥♥ *COMMENDED.* Quality Accommodation.

This family run 17th century farmhouse standing in a lovely garden close to the market town of Diss has been fully renovated to a very high standard while retaining the period features of the building: oak beams, log fires in winter, window seats. All bedrooms are decorated and furnished with taste and style and all are en suite and have colour TVs, tea/coffee making, radio alarms; most of them are on the ground floor. For that special break both the Executive and the Four Poster rooms have "Pharaoh" baths en suite. There is an especially attractive residents' lounge. Open all year. No smoking in certain bedrooms, lounge and part of the dining room. Licensed. Pets welcome. Credit cards accepted. Bed and Breakfast from £18. Two night "Summer Breaks" Bed and Breakfast from £39. Ladies and gents HAIRDRESSING SALON now open. ·

NORFOLK – NOT JUST THE BROADS!

There's more to do in Norfolk than messing about in boats – pleasurable though that may be. Other places of interest include the gardens and steam museum at Bressingham, the Broadland Conservation Centre, the flint mines at Grimes Graves, The Norfolk Rural Life Museum, Sandringham – which is often open to the public – and of course Norwich itself.

EAST DEREHAM. Old Hall Farm, Scarning, Dereham NR19 2LG (01362 691754).

A large 16th century Grade II Listed timber frame farmhouse with one acre garden and lawns, set amongst open countryside, two miles from Dereham town centre, one mile off A47 bypass. Norfolk offers sandy beaches, golf, sailing, riding, swimming and the Norfolk Broads. Also stately homes, museums, bird sanctuary and wildlife parks. Accommodation comprises one double room with en suite facilities, one double and one twin with separate bath/WC. Central heating, TV and tea/coffee facilities in all rooms. Guest lounge with TV and log fire. Open all year for weekly or short stays. Bed and Breakfast from £17.50 per person per day. Car essential, ample parking. Sorry no pets.

FAKENHAM. Mrs Maureen Walpole, "Hardlands", East Raynham, Fakenham NR21 7EQ (01328 862567). ETB Listed *HIGHLY COMMENDED.*

A friendly welcome and relaxing atmosphere await you at "Hardlands". Peaceful countryside surrounds the house and its pleasant one-acre gardens. Furnished to high standards the comfortable five-bedroomed house is four miles from Fakenham on A1065, ideally situated for visiting Royal Sandringham, historic King's Lynn, North Norfolk coast, bird sanctuaries, Pensthorpe Waterfowl Trust, National Trust properties, Norwich and the Broads. Top quality three course Evening Dinner sometimes available by arrangement from £10. Double and twin-bedded rooms with tea/coffee making facilities. Guests' TV lounge/dining room. Log fires and central heating. Bed and full English Breakfast from £16. Seasonal Short Breaks and weekly terms on request.

FAKENHAM. Mrs Elizabeth Savory, Highfield Farm, Great Ryburgh, Fakenham NR21 7AL (01328 829249). Escape to our 19th century farmhouse, set deep in the countryside amidst 500 acres of peaceful rolling farmland. Spacious and comfortable working farmhouse, large garden with cedar trees and sweeping lawns, 10 miles coast, centrally situated for all Norfolk's historic houses, close Pensthorpe Waterfowl Park. Ideal for birdwatchers. Sleeps six including twin room with en suite bathroom, guest sitting room, dining room, log fires in winter to complement central heating. Evening meals available by arrangement (bellringing practice Thursdays!). Closed Christmas and New Year. Children over 12 years welcome, sorry no pets. Grass tennis court and croquet lawn, riding locally.

GILLINGHAM. Mrs Craggs, Windle Hill House, Gillingham, Beccles, Suffolk NR34 0EF (01502 677392; Fax: 01502 678293). Attractive Listed 18th century country house set in extensive gardens and paddocks. Three miles from Beccles and River Waveney, it makes an ideal base for exploring this fascinating part of Broadland. Large bedrooms, one twin, one double; en suite bathrooms. Breakfast served in elegant dining room; use of drawing room with log fire in winter. All rooms centrally heated. No smoking in bedrooms. Children over 10 years welcome. Dogs by arrangement. Open January to December (not Christmas). Prices from £18.50 per person; reduction for longer stays.

HAPPISBURGH. Mrs Jill Morris and Miss Diana Wrightson, Cliff House Guest House, Restaurant and Teashop, Beach Road, Happisburgh, Norwich NR12 0PP (01692 650775).

Commanding views of sea and lighthouse, Cliff House is situated in an attractive, unspoilt and friendly village, six miles east of North Walsham. Happisburgh's wide sandy beach — safe for bathing — is rated as one of the cleanest Norfolk beaches so it is a favourite family resort. Visitors can enjoy the Broads, craft centres, windmills, stately homes and interesting small market towns. Accommodation comprises one twin room, one double and one single room — all with washbasins, TV and tea/coffee making facilities; two bathrooms and a residents' lounge with TV. We offer a warm welcome, excellent home cooking, fresh vegetables and home-made bread. Diets catered for. Bed and Breakfast from £14.50; other meals available. Special prices for children and Senior Citizens. Budget Breaks. Holiday flats also available.

HARLESTON. Mrs June E. Holden, Weston House Farm, Mendham, Harleston IP20 0PB (01986 782206).

17th century Grade II Listed farmhouse set in one acre garden overlooking pastureland on a mixed farm. Close to Norfolk/Suffolk border, it is within easy reach of the Suffolk Heritage Coast, Norfolk Broads, Wild Life Parks and many stately homes. Accommodation comprises one family/double and two twin rooms, all en suite with shaver points and beverage facilities. Comfortable lounge with colour TV for guests' use; dining room with separate tables. Adequate parking space. Bed and Breakfast from £18.00. Discount for longer stays. AA Recommended QQQ.

HOLT. Mrs Lynda-Lee Mack, Hempstead Hall, Holt NR25 6TN (01263 712224). 👒👒 *COMMENDED.*

Working farm. Enjoy a relaxing holiday with a friendly atmosphere in our 19th century flint farmhouse, beautifully set on a 300 acre arable farm with ducks, donkeys and large gardens. Close to the North Norfolk Coast and its many attractions. Take a ride on the steam train or a boat trip to Blakeney Point Seal Sanctuary. There is a five mile circular walk through our conservation award winning farm to Holt Country Park. Large en suite family room, double with private bathroom. Colour TV, tea/coffee facilities. Large lounge with log burning stove. Non smoking. Sorry, no pets indoors. Bed and Breakfast from £18 per person. Children's reductions. Member of Farm Holiday Bureau.

KING'S LYNN, Central Norfolk. Mrs G. Davidson, Holmdene Farm, Beeston, King's Lynn PE32 2NJ (01328 701284). Working farm, join in. Holmdene Farm is a mixed farm with rare breeds situated in central Norfolk within easy reach of the coast and Broads. Sporting activities are available locally, and the village pub is nearby. The 17th century farmhouse is comfortable and welcoming with log fires and beams. Two double rooms, one en-suite, both with beverage trays. Pets welcome. Bed and Breakfast from £14 per person; Evening Meal from £10. Weekly terms available and child reductions. Two self catering cottages, one sleeping four, the other sleeping up to eight persons. Terms on request. Please telephone for further details.

LONG STRATTON, near Norwich. Mrs Joanna Douglas, Greenacres Farm, Woodgreen, Long Stratton, Norwich NR15 2RR (01508 530261). 👒👒

COMMENDED. Period 17th century farmhouse on 30 acre common with ponds and natural wildlife, 10 miles south of Norwich (A140). The beamed sitting room with inglenook fireplace invites you to relax. A large sunny dining room encourages you to enjoy a traditional leisurely breakfast. All en suite bedrooms (two double/twin) are tastefully furnished to compliment the oak beams and period furniture, with tea/coffee facilities and TV. Full size snooker table and all weather tennis court for guests' use. Families welcome, reductions for three nights or more. Come and enjoy the peace and tranquillity of our home. When sunny, you can sit in the garden; when cold, warm yourself by the fire. Bed and Breakfast from £18; Evening Meal £10.

MUNDESLEY near. Mr and Mrs J.A. Harris, Bridge Farm Riding Stables, Windmill Road, Gimingham, Near Mundesley NR11 8HL (01263 720028). We are a working stables situated on the outskirts of Gimingham village just off the coast road between Mundesley and Trimingham near sandy beaches. We offer a friendly atmosphere, good food, special diets, rural views. Central heating, tea/coffee making facilities, TV and clock radios in two of our three bedrooms catering for up to six people. Access to rooms all day. Dogs welcome. An ideal base for touring North Norfolk, The Broads and National Trust properties; horse riding, fishing and golf nearby. Non-riders also welcome.

NORFOLK BROADS/NEATISHEAD. Alan and Sue Wrigley, Regency Guest House, The Street, Neatishead, Near Norwich NR12 8AD (01692 630233).

👒👒 *COMMENDED.* An 18th century guest house in picturesque, unspoilt village in heart of Broadlands. Personal service top priority. Long established name for very generous English Breakfasts. 20 minutes from medieval city of Norwich and six miles from coast. Ideal base for touring East Anglia — a haven for wildlife, birdwatching, cycling and walking holidays. Number 1 centre for Broads sailing, fishing and boating. Guesthouse, holder of "Good Care" Award for high quality services, has five bedrooms individually Laura Ashley style decorated and tastefully furnished. Rooms, including two king-size doubles, and family room have TV and tea/coffee making facilities and most have en suite bathrooms. Two main bathrooms. Separate tables in beamed ceiling breakfast room. Guests' sitting room. Cot, babysitting, reduced rates for children and all stays of more than one night. Pets welcome. Parking. Open all year. Fire Certificate held. AA QQQ. Also self catering cottage, sleeps six, available next to guest house. Bed and Breakfast from £19.50.

FREE and REDUCED RATE Holiday Visits!
See our READERS' OFFER VOUCHER for details!

NORTH WALSHAM. Mr Lindsay Spalding, Beechwood Hotel, 20 Cromer Road, North Walsham NR28 0HD (01692 403231). ✿✿✿ COMMENDED. The Beechwood is a Georgian hotel with a warm and friendly atmosphere, situated in the attractive market town of North Walsham. Set in an acre of mature gardens and yet only three minutes' walk from the town square, the hotel has ten well appointed en-suite bedrooms. There is a small intimate Bar, an attractive Dining Room and a cosy Residents' Lounge in which to relax. The hotel makes an ideal touring base for North Norfolk, the Broads and Norwich. Johansens Recommended. Fully Licensed. Please write or telephone for a brochure. We look forward to welcoming you. See Outside Back Cover for our display advertisement.

NORWICH. Mrs M.A. Hemmant, Poplar Farm, Sisland, Loddon, Norwich NR14 6EF (01508 520706). Working farm. This 400-acre mixed farm is situated one mile off the A146, approximately nine miles south east of Norwich. An ideal spot for the Broads and the delightful and varied Norfolk coast. Close to Beccles, Bungay, Diss and Wymondham. We have a Charolais X herd of cows, with calves born March-June. The River Chet runs through the farm. Accommodation comprises double, twin and family rooms; bathroom; TV sittingroom/diningroom. Central heating. Tennis court. Children welcome. A peaceful, rural setting. Car essential. Open all year for Bed and Breakfast. Terms from £15 per person per night.

SHERINGHAM. Mrs Pat Pearce, The Birches, 27 Holway Road, Sheringham NR26 8HW (01263 823550). Small guest house conveniently situated for town and sea front. Ideal centre for touring North Norfolk. Accommodation comprises one double and one twin-bedded rooms, both with luxury bathrooms, tea/coffee making equipment and colour TV. Full central heating. Open March to November. Bed and Breakfast for two nights £37 per person; Evening Meal available on request. Special diets catered for. No children under 12 years. No pets. NON-SMOKING ESTABLISHMENT. Member of the North Norfolk Hotel and Guest House Association. Heartbeat Award for 1994/95 and 1996/97.

SLOLEY (Norfolk Broads). Mrs Ann Jones, Sloley Farm, Sloley, Norwich NR12 8HJ (01692 536281; Fax: 01692 535162). ✿✿ COMMENDED. Working farm. Sloley Farm is a working mixed farm set in peaceful countryside approximately four miles from the Broadland village of Wroxham, ideally situated for seaside resorts and Norwich, where one can visit the Cathedral, Castle Museum and theatre. Accommodation comprises one double/twin with en suite, one double/family and one single sharing guests' bathroom. TV and tea/coffee making facilities; separate dining room and lounge with TV. Central heating. Open all year (closed Christmas and New Year). Sorry, no pets and no smoking. Bed and Breakfast from £17.50 to £19 per person. Campers and caravanners welcome.

NORFOLK – THE BROADS!

Formed by the flooding of medieval peat diggings, the Broads have a unique quality which attracts thousands of visitors each year. Slow moving waterways are bounded by reed and sedge, and despite the pressures of the modern world are home to rare birds, butterflies and plants. Motor boats and sailing boats can be hired in most towns and villages and there are lots of lively riverbank pubs to round off a day afloat.

STALHAM GREEN. Mrs A. Adams, The Yews, Moor Lane, Stalham Green NR12 9QD (01692 581880). Idyllically situated in a quiet leafy lane just minutes' walk from the nearby Broads. Half an hour's drive from Norwich, Great Yarmouth and the North Norfolk Coast. Beautifully appointed kingsize double/twin bedded suites, both with luxury bathrooms. Complimentary beverage trays, plus a host of extras. Elegant lounge with deep chintzy settees. Separate dining room with choice of hearty English breakfasts. Tranquil and pretty gardens. All day access. Regretfully no children or pets. Open April to October. Illustrated details sent with pleasure.

THETFORD. Mrs Cynthia Huggins, Malting Farm, Blo Norton Road, South Lopham, Diss IP22 2HT (01379 687201). ** *COMMENDED.* **Working farm. Malting Farm is situated on the Norfolk/Suffolk border amid open countryside. It is a working dairy farm where it is possible to see the cows being milked and there are farmyard pets. The farmhouse is Elizabethan timber-framed (inside) with inglenook fireplaces. Central heating. Some four-poster beds. Easy reach of Norfolk Broads, Norwich, Cambridge, Bressingham Steam Museum and Gardens. Cynthia is a keen craftswoman in quilting, embroidery, spinning and weaving. Bed and Breakfast from £17.

WELNEY. Mrs C.H. Bennett, Stockyard Farm, Wisbech Road, Welney, Wisbech, Cambridgeshire PE14 9RQ (01354 610433). A warm welcome awaits you at this cosy former farmhouse in the heart of the Fens. Equidistant from Ely and Wisbech it makes an ideal base from which to explore the numerous historic sites, watch wildlife at the nearby nature reserves or fish the famous Fenland waters. Whatever your interests Cindy and Tim can offer advice and information. Both the double bedroom and the twin have washbasins and hot drinks facilities. Breakfast is served in the conservatory adjoining the guests' TV lounge. Full central heating. Private parking. Non-smokers only. Pets by arrangement. Prices range from £13 to £20 per person depending on length of stay and choice of breakfast (full English or Continental).

FOR THE MUTUAL GUIDANCE OF GUEST AND HOST

Every year literally thousands of holidays, short-breaks and overnight stops are arranged through our guides, the vast majority without any problems at all. In a handful of cases, however, difficulties do arise about bookings, which often could have been prevented from the outset.

It is important to remember that when accommodation has been booked, both parties — guests and hosts — have entered into a form of contract. We hope that the following points will provide helpful guidance.

GUESTS: When enquiring about accommodation, be as precise as possible. Give exact dates, numbers in your party and the ages of any children. State the number and type of rooms wanted and also what catering you require — bed and breakfast, full board, etc. Make sure that the position about evening meals is clear — and about pets, reductions for children or any other special points.

Read our reviews carefully to ensure that the proprietors you are going to contact can supply what you want. Ask for a letter confirming all arrangements, if possible.

If you have to cancel, do so as soon as possible. Proprietors do have the right to retain deposits and under certain circumstances to charge for cancelled holidays if adequate notice is not given and they cannot re-let the accommodation.

HOSTS: Give details about your facilities and about any special conditions. Explain your deposit system clearly and arrangements for cancellations, charges, etc. and whether or not your terms include VAT.

If for any reason you are unable to fulfil an agreed booking without adequate notice, you may be under an obligation to arrange alternative suitable accommodation or to make some form of compensation.

While every effort is made to ensure accuracy, we regret that FHG Publications cannot accept responsibility for errors, omissions or misrepresentation in our entries or any consequences thereof. Prices in particular should be checked because we go to press early. We will follow up complaints but cannot act as arbiters or agents for either party.

NORTHAMPTONSHIRE

KETTERING. Mrs A. Clarke, Dairy Farm, Cranford St. Andrew, Kettering NN14 4AQ (01536 330273). ✿✿✿ *COMMENDED.* Enjoy a holiday in a comfortable 17th century farmhouse with oak beams and inglenook fireplaces. Four-poster bed now available. Peaceful surroundings, large garden containing ancient circular dovecote. Dairy Farm is a working farm situated in a beautiful Northamptonshire village just off the A14 within easy reach of many places of interest or ideal for a restful holiday. Good farmhouse food and friendly atmosphere. Open all year. Pets by arrangement. Bed and Breakfast £20-£30 (Children under 10 half price); Evening Meal £12. Closed Christmas.

PETERBOROUGH. Trudy Dijksterhuis, Lilford Lodge Farm, Barnwell, Oundle, Peterborough PE8 5SA (01832 272230). ✿✿ *COMMENDED.* Mixed farm set in the attractive Nene Valley, situated on the A605 three miles south of Oundle and five miles north of the A14. Peterborough and Stamford are within easy reach. Guests stay in the recently converted original 19th century farmhouse. All bedrooms have en suite bathrooms, central heating, radio and tea/coffee making facilities. Comfortable lounge with satellite TV and separate dining room. Open all year except Christmas and New Year. Children welcome. Coarse fishing available. Bed and Breakfast from £18. Reductions for children.

QUINTON. Mrs Margaret Turney, Quinton Green Farm, Quinton NN7 2EG (01604 863685; Fax: 01604 862230). ✿✿ The Turney family look forward to welcoming you to their comfortable, rambling 17th century farmhouse only 10 minutes from Northampton, yet overlooking lovely rolling countryside. We are close to Salcey Forest with its wonderful facilities for walking. M1 Junction 15 is just five minutes away; central Milton Keynes 20 minutes. Children and pets welcome. Open all year. Bed and Breakfast from £20.

WELFORD. Mrs Susie Bevin, West End Farm, 5 West End, Welford NN6 6HJ (01858 575226). ✿ *COMMENDED.* This comfortable 1848 farmhouse is set in beautiful countryside. Twin and double rooms both have washbasins and tea making facilities, double with en suite WC. Guests' sitting room with woodburner and TV. In a quiet village street with four local pubs. Near A50/A14 access, M1 Junction 20. Convenient for Stanford, Lamport, Althorp and Cottesbrook, Naseby Battlefield, Cold Ashby and South Kilworth Golf. On the Jurassic Way. Children welcome. Good holiday or business base. Open all year. Bed and Breakfast from £16.

NORTHAMPTONSHIRE – WHAT TO DO AND SEE!

Rolling farmland and woods contrasted against industrial towns such as Corby and Kettering, this is what makes up Northamptonshire. The canal centre at Stoke Bruerne, the coloured stone church at Stanford-on-Avon and the country parks at Barnwell and Irchester all make for interesting visits.

NORTHUMBERLAND

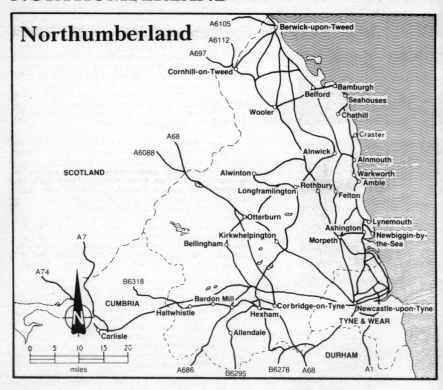

Northumberland

(map showing locations including: A6105, A6112, A697, Berwick-upon-Tweed, Cornhill-on-Tweed, Bamburgh, Belford, Seahouses, Wooler, Chathill, A68, Craster, A6088, SCOTLAND, Alwinton, Alnwick, Alnmouth, Warkworth, Rothbury, Amble, Longframlington, Felton, A7, Otterburn, Lynemouth, Kirkwhelpington, Ashington, Newbiggin-by-the-Sea, Bellingham, Morpeth, A74, B6318, CUMBRIA, Bardon Mill, Corbridge-on-Tyne, Newcastle-upon-Tyne, Haltwhistle, Hexham, TYNE & WEAR, Carlisle, Allendale, DURHAM, A686, B6295, B6278, A68, A1, miles 0 5 10 15 20, N)

ALNMOUTH. Mrs A. Stanton, Mount Pleasant Farm, Alnmouth, Alnwick NE66 3BY (01665 830215). Mount Pleasant is situated on top of a hill on the outskirts of the seaside village of Alnmouth, with spectacular views of the surrounding countryside. We offer fresh air, sea breezes, green fields, beautiful beaches, country roads and peace and quiet. There are two golf courses and a river meanders around the farm with all its bird life. There are also historic castles, Holy Island, the Farnes and the Cheviots to explore. Farmhouse has large rooms, with washbasins, TV, tea-making and en suite facilities. Guest bathroom with shower. Ample parking. Prices from £17.50.

ALNMOUTH. Janice and Norman Edwards, Westlea, 29 Riverside Road, Alnmouth NE66 2SD (01665 830730). ♛♛♛ COMMENDED. We invite you to relax in the warm friendly atmosphere of Westlea situated at the side of the Aln Estuary. We have an established reputation for providing a high standard of care and hospitality. Guests start the day with a hearty breakfast of numerous choices and in the evening a varied and appetising four-course traditional meal is prepared using local produce. All bedrooms are bright and comfortable with colour TVs, hot drinks facilities, central heating, electric blankets; all en suite. Two bedrooms on the ground floor. Large visitors' lounge and diningroom overlooking the estuary. Ideal for exploring castles, Farne Islands, Holy Island, Hadrian's Wall. Fishing, golf, pony trekking, etc within easy reach. Bed and Breakfast from £20.00; Bed, Breakfast and Evening Meal from £32.00. Alnwick District Council Hospitality Award 1989. Alnwick District Council Most Popular Hotel/Guesthouse Award 1991/1992, 1994 Award for Overall Contribution to Tourism.

ALNWICK. The Hotspur Hotel, Bondgate Without, Alnwick NE66 1PR (01665 510101; Fax: 01665 605033).

605033). 🐦 🐦 🐦 AA and RAC Two Star. Originally a coaching inn, The Hotspur is located in the town centre within walking distance of Alnwick Castle, the seat of the Duke of Northumberland. Set between sandy beaches and rolling moorland, surrounded by numerous places of interest, The Hotspur offers a friendly welcome, 23 comfortable en suite bedrooms, a high standard of food and fine ales. Children welcome. Non-smoking accommodation available. Bed and Breakfast from £35 per person, reductions for longer stays, half board rates available, excellent rates for children sharing with adults. Telephone for brochure.

ALNWICK. Charlton House, 2 Aydon Gardens, South Road, Alnwick NE66 2NT (01665 605185).

🐦 🐦 🐦 *HIGHLY COMMENDED.* Beautiful Victorian town house where guests are always welcomed in a friendly, relaxed, informal atmosphere and where there is a real flair for decor with antiques, home-made patchwork quilts and excellent home cooking. Two double, one twin, one family and one single bedrooms have en suite facilities and are complete with colour TV and hospitality trays. Comfortable guests' lounge with satellite TV. We offer a choice of breakfast — full English, Continental, vegetarian, "healthy option", local Craster kippers (when in season), various crepes. We also serve evening meals if required. Alnwick District Council "Lionheart Award" Winners (past three years). Bed and Breakfast from £18 per person. Information leaflet available.

ALNWICK. Mrs B. Gaines, Crosshills House, 40 Blakelaw Road, Alnwick NE66 1BA (01665 602518).

602518). 🐦 🐦 *HIGHLY COMMENDED.* Come and join us at Crosshills for your stay in historic Northumberland. A friendly family-run house situated in a quiet area near golf course and only a short walk into town. We have two double rooms and one twin room, all en suite and having colour TV and tea/coffee making facilities. Twin room has balcony with a beautiful view of coast and countryside. Sorry, no dogs. Bed and Breakfast from £19 per person. Parking available.

ALNWICK near. Mrs Celia Curry, Howick Scar Farm, Craster, Alnwick NE66 3SU (01665 576665).

Tourist Board Listed *COMMENDED.* Comfortable farmhouse accommodation on working mixed farm situated on the Heritage Coast between the villages of Craster and Howick. Ideal base for walking, birdwatching or exploring the coast, moors and historic castles. The Farne Islands, famous for their colonies of seals and seabirds, and Lindisfarne (Holy Island) are within easy driving distance. Accommodation is in two double rooms. Guests have their own TV lounge/dining room with coal fire and full central heating. Bed and Breakfast from £15. Reductions for three nights or more. Open May to November. Also member of Farm Holiday Bureau.

NORTHUMBERLAND – BORDER COUNTRY!

You cannot go any further north and remain in England! There is much outstanding scenery, both inland and on the coast, and a host of interesting places to visit. Border Forest Park has everything you would expect, plus many interesting Roman remains. There are also remains at Housesteads and other places of interest include Lindisfarne, the "conserved" village of Blanchland, Hexham, Heatherslaw Mill and Craster.

AMBLE near. Mrs L.A. Marshall, Togston Hall Farm House, North Togston, Near Amble NE65 0HR (01665 712699). ✿ ✿ ✿ Tranquil farmhouse atmosphere and personal service in country setting. En suite bedrooms plus adjacent cottage for four or more. Colour TV. Varied breakfast menu using our own eggs, Craster kippers, etc and traditional home cooked food served for our ever popular five course evening meal at 7pm. Private parking. Bed and Breakfast from £19 per person per night; Dinner, Bed and Breakfast from £29 per person per night. Weekly rates available.

CORBRIDGE. Mr and Mrs F.J. Matthews, The Hayes, Newcastle Road, Corbridge NE45 5PL (01434 632010). ✿ Spacious, attractive stone-built guesthouse. Set in seven acres of grounds. Single, double, twin, family bedrooms, all with tea making facilities, two with showers; lounge and dining rooms. Open 11 months of the year. Bed and Breakfast from £16. Children's reductions. Stair lift for disabled visitors. Also self catering properties — three cottages, flat and caravan. Two Keys Commended. Awarded two Farm Holiday Diplomas. Car parking. For brochure/booking SAE/phone.

CORNHILL-ON-TWEED. Mrs V. Watson, Flodden Edge Farm, Mindrum, Cornhill-on-Tweed TD12 4QG (01668 216287). Large country house set in own grounds in quiet rural area, one-and-a-half miles from A697 Newcastle to Edinburgh road. Central for hills and coast. Within half an hour's drive of Lindisfarne and Bamburgh Castle, also Border Abbeys. Edinburgh one and a quarter hours' drive. Four miles from Scottish border and one and a half miles from Flodden Field. Ideal for children. Dogs welcome. Homely atmosphere and no restrictions. Bedrooms have washbasins, tea/coffee facilities and TV. Bathroom with shower. Residents' lounge with TV. Separate diningroom. Ideal for fishing, walking and exploring the National Park. Gliding and horse riding nearby, also miniature steam railway. Open all year. Reduced rates for children and for Senior Citizens early and late season.

HEXHAM. Mrs Ruby Keenleyside, Struthers Farm, Catton, Allendale, Hexham NE47 9LP (01434 683580). ✿ ✿ *COMMENDED.* Struthers Farm offers a warm welcome in the heart of England, with many splendid local walks from the farm itself. Panoramic views. Double/twin rooms, en suite, central heating. Good farmhouse cooking. Ample safe parking. Come and share our home and enjoy beautiful countryside. Children welcome, pets by prior arrangement. Open all year. Bed and Breakfast from £16.50; Evening Meal from £8.50. Farm Holiday Bureau Member.

HEXHAM. Mrs Elizabeth Courage, Rye Hill Farm, Slaley, Near Hexham NE47 0AH (01434 673259; Fax: 01434 673608). ✿ ✿ ✿ *COMMENDED.* Rye Hill Farm is a 300 year old Northumbrian stone farmhouse, set in its own 30 acres of rural Tynedale. Guests have the unique opportunity to see life on a small working farm, while the self-contained accommodation in the converted farm buildings offers all the comforts of good farm hospitality. We provide full English Breakfast and optional three course Evening Meal. Table licence held. All bedrooms are centrally heated with colour TV and tea/coffee making facilities and have bathrooms en-suite. Northumberland Moors, Kielder Forest, Kielder Water nearby. Visit the historic city of Durham, or the market town of Hexham which is only five miles away. Bed and Breakfast from £20; Evening Meal £10.

HEXHAM. Mrs Ailsa A. Dixon, Anick Grange Farm, Hexham NE46 4LP (01434 603807). ♛♛

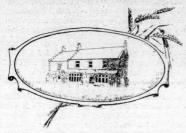

COMMENDED. This is a mixed farm of 363 acres in the Tyne Valley, and the south-facing farmhouse which dates back to the 1600's is warm, welcoming and comfortable. One mile from the market town of Hexham and two miles from Corbridge, a lovely old village to browse around, we are 20 minutes' drive from Hadrian's Wall and the same from the beautiful North Pennines. The Northumbrian coastline is only one and a half hours away — perhaps you could take in one or two National Trust properties en route. One twin-bedded en suite room, one family and one single rooms, all with washbasins, TV and tea/coffee and biscuits. Terms from £15 to £17 per person. Brochure available.

HEXHAM. Mrs Doreen Cole, Hillcrest House, Barrasford, Hexham NE48 4BY (01434 681426). ♛♛♛ HIGHLY COMMENDED. Hillcrest House has been

specifically extended to provide a high standard of accommodation, with a homely, comfortable atmosphere. One family, one double, one twin, one single rooms, all with ensuite shower rooms, colour TV, tea/coffee facilities. Evening meal optional; packed lunches on request. Comfortable lounge, separate tables in diningroom. Residential licence. Accommodation suitable for disabled visitors. Situated seven miles from historic Hexham in beautiful North Tyne Valley. Ideal for touring Hadrian's Wall and within easy distance of Kielder, the Borders, Newcastle and Gateshead Metro Centre. Car essential. Bed and Breakfast £17 single, £30 double.

NEWTON BY THE SEA. Mrs J.I. Patterson, Newton Hall, Newton by the Sea, Alnwick NE66 3DZ (Tel & Fax: 01665 576239). Built in 1750, Newton Hall

provides guests with a taste of luxury in large, spacious, light and airy rooms. Two acres of lawns and gardens in a peaceful country setting approximately three-quarters of a mile from magnificent sandy beaches and cliff walks. Bedrooms have tea and coffee trays; two bathrooms, two showers, three WCs; sauna room; drawing room with colour TV. Bed (white cotton sheets) and full traditional English Breakfast £16.00 per person.

ROTHBURY. Mrs Helen Farr, Lorbottle West Steads, Thropton, Morpeth NE65 7JT (01665 574672). ETB Listed COMMENDED. Situated in the quite

beautiful Whittingham Vale, five miles from Rothbury on a 320 acre farm. Stone-built spacious farmhouse with panoramic views of Thrunton Craggs, Simonside and Cheviot Hills, a perfect base for exploring Northumberland's natural beauty and heritage. Many facilities within four miles — e.g. golf, pony trekking, mountain bikes, fishing and woodland walks. The farmhouse offers spacious TV lounge/diningroom with open fires in colder weather. Bedrooms have tea/coffee making and TV facilities. Guests' bathroom and use of garden. Bed and Breakfast from £14.50. Evening Meal negotiable. Self catering cottage, sleeps five, also available. Further details on request.

WARKWORTH. John and Edith Howliston, North Cottage, Birling, Warkworth NE65 0XS (01665 711263). ♛♛ HIGHLY COMMENDED. Situated on the

outskirts of the historic coastal village of Warkworth, we are an ideal base from which to explore Northumberland with its superb beaches and castles. We have four comfortable, well furnished no-smoking rooms — two double and one twin-bedded rooms en suite and one single with washbasin; all have colour TV. All bedrooms have hospitality trays, central heating and electric overblankets and all are on the ground floor. There is of course a bathroom with shower, and a sitting room with cheery gas fire and colour TV. A full breakfast is served in the dining room and afternoon tea is served (free of charge) with home-made cakes/biscuits. Large well kept garden and water garden. Warkworth has its own castle, river, golf course and beautiful sandy beaches. Bed and Breakfast from £18. Weekly rates from £118. AA QQQ Recommended, RAC Acclaimed.

NOTTINGHAMSHIRE

BLYTH. Mrs Vera Hambleton, Priory Farm Guesthouse, Hodsock Priory Estate, Blyth S81 0TY (01909 591515; Fax: 01427 890611). The Guesthouse is located on Hodsock Priory Estate with its beautiful five acre garden which is open to the public and famous for its display of snowdrops which carpet the ground in February/March. The guesthouse is located within one mile of the A1 and within 10 miles of the M1 giving easy access to the East Midlands and Northern England. Businessmen, tourists, children and dogs are all welcome. All rooms have tea/coffee making facilities and there are en suite facilities in two of the four bedrooms. The lounge with its log fire and TV is the ideal place to relax after a traditional home-cooked evening meal. Bed and Breakfast £16.50 to £20.

MANSFIELD. Mrs L. Palmer, Boon Hills Farm, Nether Langwith, Mansfield NG20 9JQ (01623 743862). Working farm. Farmhouse accommodation in stone-built farmhouse standing in 155 acres of mixed farmland, 300 yards back from A632 on edge of the village. Comfortably furnished with fitted carpets throughout, the house has electric heating and open fire. Large sitting/diningroom with colour TV. One family room, one double room and another room with twin beds. Children welcome and there are many pets for them on the farm. Babysitting arranged. Pets accepted. Situated on edge of Sherwood Forest, six miles from Visitors' Centre; eight miles M1; 10 miles A1. Places of interest include Hardwick Hall, Thoresby Hall, Chatsworth House, Newstead Abbey. Pleasant half-mile walk to picturesque village inn serving evening meals. Car essential, ample parking. Bed and Breakfast only from £15 per night. Non-smokers only. Reductions for children. Open March to October inclusive.

NORTON (Sherwood Forest). Mr F. Palmer, Norton Grange Farm, Norton, Cuckney, Near Mans-

field NG20 9LP (01623 842666). ✿✿ **COMMENDED.**
Working farm, join in. Norton Grange Farm is a listed Georgian-type farmhouse and is situated on the edge of Sherwood Forest overlooking peaceful open countryside, away from the traffic. The 172-acre mixed farm carries poultry and arable crops, also many domestic farm animals. A car is advantageous for visiting the many places of local interest — ample parking. Accommodation comprises family room, double and twin-bedded rooms with washbasins. All rooms have tea/coffee making facilities. Fitted bathroom with shower, separate toilet. Sitting room, dining room. Bed and full English Breakfast from £16 is provided all year except Christmas. Flasks filled on request. Reductions for children sharing family room.

NORTON GRANGE FARM
Tel: 0623 842666

REDMILE (Vale of Belvoir). Redmile House Hotel and Country Restaurant, Main Street, Redmile

NG13 0GA (01949 843086/843706). Circa 1740 non-working farmhouse. Full of character and old world charm, open fires and antique furniture giving a homely atmosphere. Enjoy a freshly cooked meal in our licensed restaurant. All rooms are en suite and have TVs. Situated on the borders of Nottinghamshire, Lincolnshire and Leicestershire and just a stone's throw away from Belvoir Castle. The Grantham to Nottingham Canal runs through Redmile. Many interesting walks and an activity filled area. Please telephone for further details.

STANTON-ON-THE-WOLDS. Mrs V. Moffat, Laurel Farm, Browns Lane, Stanton-on-the-Wolds,

Nottingham NG12 5BL (0115 9373488). Laurel Farm is an old house standing in four acres of garden and paddocks. There are pet sheep, horses, dogs, cats, chickens and ducks. The garden may be used by guests. All rooms have shower and washbasin, three rooms have full private facilities, all have colour TV and tea/coffee; very large family room with cot and high chair also available. Babysitting free by prior arrangement. Bed and Breakfast from £16.50 to £20 per person per night. Many reasonably priced eating places locally. Laurel Farm is on a quiet lane with easy access to main roads, many old towns and castles, Sherwood Forest. Smoking is not allowed. Fully registered.

OXFORDSHIRE

ABINGDON near. Mrs E. Auckland, Home Farm House, Longworth, Near Abingdon OX13 5EB (01865 821151). Perfectly located for visiting the Dreaming Spires of Oxford with its colleges, theatres, restaurants, etc (10 miles), the Cotswolds, Stratford-upon-Avon, Blenheim Palace, Woodstock and lovely walks on the Berkshire Downs close to the Thames. Home Farm House is a fully modernised Victorian family farmhouse with comfortable spacious bedrooms and own bathroom. Set close to the centre of a very pretty Oxford village in its own grounds. Excellent village pub nearby.

BANBURY near. Mrs E.J. Lee, The Mill Barn, Lower Tadmarton, Near Banbury OX15 5SU (01295 780349). ♛♛ Tadmarton is a small village, three miles south-west of Banbury. The Mill, no longer working, was originally water powered and the stream lies adjacent to the house. The Mill Barn has been tastefully converted, retaining many traditional features such as beams and exposed stone walls, yet it still has all the amenities a modern house offers. Two spacious en-suite bedrooms, one downstairs, are available to guests in this comfortable family home. Base yourself here and visit Stratford, historic Oxford, Woodstock and the beautiful Cotswolds, knowing you are never further than an hour's drive away. Open all year for Bed and Breakfast from £17.50, reductions for children. Weekly terms available.

BLETCHINGDON. Mrs P.M. Hedges, Stonehouse Farm, Bletchingdon, Oxford OX5 3EA (01869

350585). Tourist Board Listed. Working farm. 17th century Cotswold farmhouse set in 560 acres. For those who want to get off the beaten track! Situated between A34 Oxford to Bicester and A4260 Oxford to Banbury. 10 minutes from Blenheim Palace and 15 minutes from Oxford; one hour to Heathrow Airport off Junction 9 or 10 M40. Accommodation comprises one double, one twin, one family and one single bedrooms, all with washbasins, TV, tea/coffee facilities. Non-smoking accommodation. Lovely walks in beautiful countryside. Children welcome. Bed and Breakfast from £17.50 to £20 per person per night.

Stonehouse Farm
Bletchington

DEDDINGTON. Mrs Audrey Fuller, Earls Farm, Deddington, Oxford OX15 0TH (01869 338243). ♛♛ **Working farm.** Delightfully situated on edge of village 200 yards from main Banbury to Oxford road, this farm covers 230 acres of cropping fields. Open all year, it has two double, one family bedrooms, all with washbasins; two bathrooms, two toilets; sittingroom, diningroom. Central heating. Children very welcome and facilities for them include cot, high chair, babysitting and reduced rates; also swing and slide. Fishing available on River Swere. Trout fishing on local lake by arrangement. Golf five miles away, tennis two miles, Banbury six miles. This is an ideal touring base. Pets accepted. Car essential, parking. Bed and Breakfast £17 per person per night sharing.

FARINGDON. Mr D. Barnard, Bowling Green Farm, Stanford Road, Faringdon, Oxfordshire SN7

8EZ (01367 240229; Fax: 01367 242568). ♛♛ Attractive 18th century farmhouse offering 20th century comfort. Situated in the Vale of White Horse, just one mile south of Faringdon on the A417. Easy access to M4 Exit 13 for Heathrow Airport. An ideal place to stay for a day or longer. A working farm of cattle, horse breeding, poultry and ducks. Large twin-bedded/family room on ground floor, en suite. All bedrooms have colour TV, tea/coffee making facilities and full central heating throughout. Perfect area for riding, golf, fishing and walking the Ridgeway. Interesting places to visit include Oxford, Bath, Windsor, Burford, Henley, Blenheim Palace and the Cotswolds. Open all year. Member of the Farm Holiday Bureau.

FARINGDON. Mrs Pat Hoddinott, Ashen Copse Farm, Coleshill, Faringdon SN6 7PU (Tel & Fax:

01367 240175). ♛♛ *COMMENDED.* **Working farm.** Perfect place to tour or relax. Our 580 acre National Trust farm is set in wonderful, peaceful countryside, teeming with wildlife. The quiet, comfortable accommodation is a great centre for walking or visiting Cotswolds, Vale of the White Horse, Oxford, Bath, Stratford and all little places in between! So much to see and do. Facilities locally for fishing, golfing, riding, boating and swimming. Many places to eat out nearby. Open all year. One family en suite, one twin and one single bedroom. Bed and Breakfast from £18 to £21. Reduction for children sharing. No smoking please.

FREE and REDUCED RATE Holiday Visits!
See our READERS' OFFER VOUCHER for details!

FREELAND. Mrs B.B. Taphouse, "Wrestler's Mead", 35 Wroslyn Road, Freeland, Oxford OX7 2HJ (01993 882003). A warm welcome awaits you at the home of the Taphouses. We are conveniently located for Blenheim Palace (10 minutes), Oxford (20 minutes) and the Cotswolds (25 minutes). Accommodation comprises one double and one single room both with washbasins and at ground level. Our first floor family room has its own en-suite shower room with washbasin and toilet. The double and the family room each have a colour TV. Cot, high chair and babysitting service available. Pets by arrangement. No hidden extras. Bed and Breakfast from £17.

HENLEY-ON-THAMES. Mrs Liz Roach, The Old Bakery, Skirmett, Near Henley-on-Thames RG9 6TD (01491 638309). This welcoming family house is situated on the site of an old bakery, seven miles from Henley-on-Thames and Marlow; half an hour from Heathrow and Oxford; one hour from London. It is in the Hambleden Valley in the beautiful Chilterns with many excellent pubs selling good food. Riding school nearby; beautiful walking country. Two double rooms with TV, one twin-bedded and two single rooms; two bathrooms. Open all year. Parking for five cars (car essential). Children and pets welcome. Bed and Breakfast from £18 to £21 single, £38 to £42 double.

OXFORD. Mrs E. Hall, Ascot Guest House, 283 Iffley Road, Oxford OX4 4AQ (01865 240259/ 727669; Fax: 01865 727669). RAC Highly Acclaimed. Ascot House is a pretty Victorian house offering six beautifully refurbished en suite rooms affording every comfort to couples, families, business people and tourists. The River Thames and the University boathouses are within a five minute walk and a gentle 15 minute stroll along the towpath takes you into the centre of the City, via Christchurch Meadows and the Cathedral. En suite rooms with colour television, radio alarm, hairdryer, tea/coffee making facilities, fridge and direct-dial telephone. Single from £30.00, double from £40.00.

OXFORD. Mr and Mrs L.S. Price, Arden Lodge, 34 Sunderland Avenue (off Banbury Road), Oxford OX2 8DX (01865 552076 or 04020 68697). Modern detached house in select area of North Oxford off Banbury Road. Within easy reach of Oxford centre, riverside inns, country walks, river, meadows, etc. Excellent position for touring; Cotswolds, Blenheim Palace, Stratford and visits to London. Colour TV, tea/coffee making equipment and private facilities in all rooms. Parking available. Bed and Breakfast from £20 per person per night.

STANTON HARCOURT. Mrs Margaret Clifton, Staddle Stones, Linch Hill, Stanton Harcourt OX8 1BB (01865 882256). A chalet bungalow situated in a peaceful location on the outskirts of the village with four acres of attractive surroundings, including a carp pond; visitors are allowed to fish. A full breakfast is offered to satisfy the keenest of appetites. Disabled persons, children and dogs are welcome. In easy reach of the Cotswolds and Oxford. One double or family room en suite, two twin bedrooms with private bathrooms; also a comfortable TV lounge with tea/coffee available. Bed and Breakfast from £16.50.

TETSWORTH. Julia Tanner, Little Acre, Tetsworth, Near Thame OX9 7AT (01844 281423). A

charming secluded country house retreat, offering every comfort, set in 18 acres of private grounds, nestling under the Chilterns escarpment. Single, twin and double rooms, all with central heating, colour TV, tea/coffee making facilities; some en suite. One ground floor room suitable for disabled guests. Full English or Continental breakfast. A perfect place to relax and enjoy the local countryside in a quiet location but only three minutes from Junction 6 on the M40. Children and well behaved family dog welcome. Pets allowed in bedrooms and there are also outside kennels. Lovely walking area (Oxfordshire Way and Ridgeway Path). Riding, fishing and excellent golf course nearby; within easy reach of many places of interest. Little Acre offers a warm welcome and REAL VALUE FOR MONEY from just £13 per night. Reductions for weekly bookings and children. Highly recommended by previous guests. Plenty of good restaurants nearby. Open all year.

WOODSTOCK. Mrs Kay Bradford, Hamilton House, 43 Hill Rise, Old Woodstock OX20 1AB (01993 812206). High quality Bed and Breakfast establishment with parking, overlooking Blenheim Park, Blenheim Palace and the town centre, with good selection of restaurants, pubs and shops within walking distance. Accommodation offered in one twin-bedded room and two double rooms, all en suite with colour TV and tea/coffee making facilities. Pleasant dining room; excellent selection of Continental and full English breakfast. Comfortable and relaxed atmosphere with informative and very hospitable hostess. Ideal base for Blenheim Palace, Bladon, the Cotswolds, Stratford-upon-Avon, Oxford and major airports. Access off A44 northern end of Woodstock, 200 yards from Rose and Crown pub. Children and pets welcome. Bed and Breakfast from £20.

WOODSTOCK near. Mrs B. Jones, Gorselands Farmhouse Auberge, Near Long Hanborough, Near Woodstock OX8 6PU (01993 881895; Fax: 01993 882799). ♥♥ Situated in an idyllic location in the Oxfordshire countryside, Gorselands has its own grounds of one acre. This Cotswold stone farmhouse has exposed beams, flagstone floors, billiards room (full size table), guest lounge, dining conservatory and tennis court. En-suite rooms, family room, double/twin rooms available. Near to Oxford, Blenheim Palace, East End Roman Villa, Cotswold villages. Children welcome. Bed and Breakfast from £17.50 per person; Evening Meal from £10.95. Licensed. RAC Listed. Elizabeth Gundrey Recommended.

SHROPSHIRE

DINNEY FARM

The Dinney is a small working farm deep in Shropshire's rolling countryside with views across the Severn Valley and nearby lake. There are safe play areas and farm walks from the door, and fishing nearby. The Severn Valley Railway runs through the owners' land. Historic Bridgnorth is five minutes away, with Ironbridge Gorge Museum and the hills of the Long Mynd and Wenlock Edge around seven miles. All bedrooms are centrally heated with en-suite bathrooms. Tea/coffee making facilities are available.
You are assured of a warm welcome at Dinney Farm. Dogs welcome. Brochure available.
Double/twin £32. Single £20.

Mr & Mrs Roberts, Dinney Farm,
Chelmarsh, Bridgnorth WV16 6AU.
Telephone: 01746 861070

BUCKNELL. Mrs Christine E. Price, The Hall, Bucknell SY7 0AA (01547 530249). ♥♥ *COMMENDED.* You are assured of a warm welcome at The Hall, which is a Georgian farmhouse with spacious accommodation. The house and gardens are set in a secluded part of a small South Shropshire village, an ideal area for touring the Welsh Borderland. Offa's Dyke is on the doorstep and the historic towns of Shrewsbury, Hereford, Ludlow and Ironbridge are within easy reach as are the Church Stretton Hills and Wenlock Edge. Three bedrooms — one twin en suite, two doubles with washbasins. All have tea-making facilities and TV. Guest lounge. Ample parking. Bed and Breakfast from £17; Dinner £9. SAE, please, for details.

Terms quoted in this publication may be subject to increase if rises in costs necessitate

CHURCH STRETTON. Mrs Mary Jones, Acton Scott Farm, Acton Scott, Church Stretton SY6 6QN (01694 781260). 👑 *COMMENDED.* **Working farm.**

Lovely 17th century farmhouse in peaceful village amidst the beautiful hills of South Shropshire, an area of outstanding natural beauty. The house is full of character; the rooms, which are all heated, are comfortable and spacious. Bedrooms have washbasins and tea/coffee making facilities; en suite available. Colour TV lounge. Children welcome, pets accepted by arrangement. We are a working farm, centrally situated for visiting Ironbridge, Shrewsbury and Ludlow, each easily reached within half an hour. Visitors' touring and walking information available. Bed and full English Breakfast from £15 per person. No smoking. Farm Holiday Bureau member. Open all year excluding December and January.

𝕸𝖆𝖑𝖙 𝕳𝖔𝖚𝖘𝖊 𝕱𝖆𝖗𝖒

**Lower Wood, Church Stretton,
Shropshire SY6 6LF
Prop. Mrs Lyn Bloor
Tel: Leebotwood (01694) 751379
TOURIST BOARD LISTED**

Comfortable accommodation in our olde worlde farmhouse situated amidst stunning scenery on the lower slopes of the Long Mynd Hills. We are a working farm producing beef cattle and sheep. There is one double bedroom ensuite and one twin bedded room with private bathroom. Sittingroom with colour TV. Breakfast is served in the diningroom which has a lovely Inglenook fireplace. Sorry, no children or pets.
BED AND BREAKFAST FROM £15.00 PER PERSON. EVENING MEAL £10.00.

CHURCH STRETTON. Mrs Barbara Norris, Court Farm, Gretton, Church Stretton SY6 7HU (01694 771219). 👑👑 *HIGHLY COMMENDED.* **Working farm.**

Stone Tudor farmhouse in a very quiet and peaceful area of outstanding natural beauty, ideally situated for visiting Ironbridge, Bridgnorth, Ludlow and Shrewsbury. This is excellent walking country and, round about, there is much to interest the visitor — or simply enjoy relaxing at Court Farm. Riding and trout fishing can be arranged. Three double rooms, one en suite and two with private bathrooms, all en suite and with colour TV and tea/coffee making facilities; also luxurious barn conversion consisting of double en suite and twin en suite rooms. Central heating. High quality cuisine served, and the house is open from February to the beginning of November. Car preferable, ample parking. Sorry, no pets. Non-smoking household. Bed and Breakfast from £21.50; Evening Meal from £13. Further details may be obtained from Mrs Norris. Farm Bureau Member. RAC Acclaimed. RAC comment: "A place worth seeking".

CHURCH STRETTON. Mrs C.J. Hotchkiss, Gilberries Hall Farm, Wall-under-Heywood, Church Stretton SY6 7HZ (01694 771253). Working farm. A warm welcome awaits you from the Hotchkiss family to this modern 275 acre dairy farm, set in a quiet location with superb views and easy road access. Tastefully furnished bedrooms are all en suite (one ground floor) with central heating, colour TV, hair dryers and tea/coffee making facilities. A comfortably furnished guest lounge is available at all times, plus a separate dining room, where a good home cooked English breakfast is provided, or alternatives to suit your requirements. An indoor heated swimming pool is available on a limited basis. The surrounding area is lovely for walking and within easy reach of Ironbridge Gorge, Ludlow, Bridgnorth, Shrewsbury and many National Trust locations. No pets. Car essential, ample parking. Bed and Breakfast from £20.

SHROPSHIRE – HISTORIC BORDER COUNTY!

The lonely Shropshire Hills – an "Area of Outstanding Natural Beauty" – are much favoured by walkers. Those seeking more traditional tourist activities would do well to visit the Acton Scott Working Museum, Ironbridge, Offa's Dyke, the black and white Tudor town of Shrewsbury or the market town of Bridgnorth.

CHURCH STRETTON. Mrs Josie Griffiths, Gilberries Farm Cottage, Wall-under-Heywood, Church Stretton SY6 7HZ (01694 771400; Fax: 01694 771663).

🐾 *COMMENDED.* Country cottage adjoining family farm within easy reach of many places of interest. Ideal walking country. One double, one twin bedrooms, both with washbasins, tea making facilities and radios. Also one bathroom and separate toilet. Guests' lounge with colour TV and separate diningroom are available to guests at all times. Log fires, central heating. Spacious parking. A friendly homely atmosphere. Bed and Breakfast from £16 per person. Excellent evening meals available within five minutes' drive.

CHURCH STRETTON near. Mrs Margaret Robinson, Blakemoor, Marshbrook, Church Stretton SY6 6QA (01694 781345).

Charming beamed farmhouse with rare breed poultry, ornamental waterfowl and panoramic views. A warm welcome, home cooking and personal service await you. Excellent touring/walking centre in peaceful location with a wealth of wildlife just two and a half miles from A49. Close to Long Mynd and Welsh border towns. Historic town of Ludlow approximately 10 miles, Church Stretton four miles. Shrewsbury, Ironbridge and many tourist attractions within easy reach. Two comfortable double rooms; guests' bathroom and separate WC with washbasin. No smoking. Full English Breakfast with free range eggs and homemade preserves. Terms from £15 per person daily. SAE please for details.

CLUN. Bob and Margaret Wall, The Old Farmhouse, Woodside, Clun SY7 0JB (01588 640695). 🐾

Featured in Elizabeth Gundrey's "Staying off the Beaten Track". A warm welcome is extended to all guests seeking peace and quiet in idyllic surroundings, at this 300-year-old farmhouse situated about one mile from Clun, on the sheltered side of Soudley Hill. Offa's Dyke is only three miles away and the surrounding countryside, for many miles, affords delight to ramblers — combined with the historic interest of the many castles and towns of the Border Country making this an ideal holiday location for people of all ages. Accommodation comprises one double and one (twin) family bedrooms, with washbasins; bathroom, toilet; sittingroom; diningroom. Non-smoking accommodation available. Central heating. Car not essential, but an advantage to make the most of touring this picturesque and historic part of England. Parking. Cot, high chair, babysitting, reduced rates for children. Pets welcome. Open March to October for Bed and Breakfast from £16. Evening Meal by arrangement from £8.50. SAE for brochure, please.

CLUN. Mrs Miriam Ellison, New House Farm, Clun SY7 8NJ (01588 638314). 🐾🐾 *HIGHLY COMMENDED.* AA QQQQ Selected. Isolated peaceful 18th century farmhouse set high in the Clun Hills near Welsh border. Hill farm in the Environmentally Sensitive Area of South Shropshire. Additional sheep hill farm which includes an Iron Age Hill Fort. Three major walking routes from the doorstep: Offa's Dyke, Shropshire Way and Kerry Ridgeway.

Scenic views from large comfortable bedrooms, furnished to high standard with TV and tea and coffee making facilities. Twin room en-suite, family room with adjacent bathroom, and double room with shower room nearby. Packed lunches. Comprehensive selection of books. Our aim is to offer clean, comfortable accommodation with a friendly atmosphere in quiet peaceful surroundings. Bed and Breakfast from £20.

CLUN. Mrs M. Jones, Llanhedric, Clun, Craven Arms SY7 8NG (01588 640203). HETB Listed *COMMENDED.* **Working farm.** A mixed farm just two miles off the A488 road, overlooking the picturesque Clun Valley, near the Welsh border and Offa's Dyke. Ideal for walking or exploring the many places of historic interest including Ludlow and Shrewsbury. Attractive beamed farmhouse with

lawns and garden, spacious accommodation, friendly atmosphere and good food. One twin bedroom and two doubles, one ensuite, with washbasins and tea/coffee facilities; visitors' lounge with inglenook fireplace and separate diningroom. Sorry no dogs. Open Easter to October. Non-smoking household. Bed and Breakfast from £15; Bed, Breakfast and Evening Meal from £23. Reductions for children.

CRAVEN ARMS. Mrs S.J. Williams, Hurst Mill Farm, Clun, Craven Arms SY7 0JA (01588 640224).

☙☙ *COMMENDED.* **Working farm.** "Hurst Mill Farm" is situated in the prettiest part of the Clun Valley, renowned as a completely unspoilt part of England. One mile from the small town of Clun, which has a Saxon church and a Norman castle. Legend says one is wiser after crossing Clun Bridge. Within easy reach are Ludlow, Newtown, Elan Valley, Ironbridge and Long-Mynd Hills. Through the fields runs the River Clun where one can bathe. Woods and hills provide wonderful walks, which can be organised. Fishing and pony trekking locally. The farm has cattle, sheep, two quiet riding ponies. Three double, one single bedrooms, all with washbasins and tea/coffee making facilities; guests' lounge, diningroom. Parking. Children and pets welcome; cot and babysitting. Good food, pretty garden. Dinner, Bed and Breakfast from £24; Bed and Breakfast from £17. Lunches. Open all year. AA Recommended. Mrs Williams is the Winner of "Shropshire's Great Farm Breakfast Challenge". Also two holiday cottages available.

CRAVEN ARMS near. Mrs Sheila Davies, Hesterworth, Hopesay, Craven Arms SY7 8EX (01588 660487). Visitors accommodated in cottage or country house apartments surrounded by 12 acres of gardens and grounds, providing comfortable accommodation in a beautiful setting. Central heating, payphone, tea/coffee facilities, private bathroom. Large communal room ideal for families or groups. Evening meals and packed lunches available. Licensed. Well behaved pets welcome. Village half a mile, Ludlow 10 miles. In the heart of Shropshire hill country. Ideal for walking or visiting Shropshire's many attractions. Open all year. Bed and Breakfast from £17 per night. Self catering from £95 to £306 per week.

ELLESMERE. Rodney and Nicky Stokes, Mereside Farm, Ellesmere SY12 0PA (01691 622404). An 18th century farmhouse with a warm, friendly atmosphere, situated betwen the Llangollen Canal and The Mere, part of the Shropshire Lake District. Ideal for walking holidays or for touring North Wales, Shropshire and Cheshire. Ellesmere's shops and restaurants and the new Blackwater Meadow Marina are a few minutes' walk. All bedrooms have tea/coffee making facilities and are non smoking. Guests' sitting room with colour TV and open fire. All rooms recently refurbished and centrally heated. Full farmhouse breakfast with home-made sausages. Packed lunches and special diets on request. Stabling for guests' horses (by prior arrangement). Open all year. Bed and Breakfast from £16.00 per person.

IRONBRIDGE. Mrs Virginia I. Evans, Church Farm, Rowton, Wellington, Near Telford TF6 6QY (01952 770381). ☙☙ **Working farm, join in.** Come and enjoy a large country breakfast in our 300 year old farmhouse where guests are welcome to join in the farming way of life. A real working farm with dairy cows, sheep and free range hens. Guests' TV lounge, dining room, bathroom. Family and four-poster bedrooms en suite, also twin bedded rooms, all with washbasins and tea/coffee facilities; towels provided. Peacefully situated in a quiet village yet near Ironbridge, Shrewsbury, Chester, Ludlow, Potteries, Alton Towers, Cosford Aerospace, etc. Pets and children welcome. Bed and Breakfast from £15 per person. Reductions for children. Also self catering cottages and caravans available.

LUDLOW. Clare and David Currant, Corndene, Coreley, Ludlow SY8 3AW (Ludlow 01584 890324). ☙☙ *COMMENDED.* B&B "PLUS". Relax in the peaceful setting of this former old rectory and farmhouse and enjoy a country holiday in the beautiful South Shropshire Hills close to Ludlow and Tenbury Wells. Convenient for Ironbridge Gorge Museum, Severn Valley Railway, Worcester, Hereford and the Welsh Border. Comfortable and spacious accommodation, all en suite/private, mostly ground floor (single, twin and family bookings welcomed) with friendly and caring service plus use of visitors' own kitchen for preparation of snacks and light meals to give you extra freedom and flexibility. Ideally suited for wheelchair users and the less mobile. Sitting room with books, maps, games, TV and open fire. Central heating throughout. Packed lunches. Dogs by arrangement. B&B £21 per night; discounts for children under 12 and stays of four days or longer. A "no smoking" house. Please write or phone for brochure.

LUDLOW. Mrs Valerie Humphreys, Seifton Court Farm, Culmington, Ludlow SY8 2DG (01584 861214). ♛♛ *COMMENDED.* We invite you to relax in the warm, friendly atmosphere of Seifton Court, a period stone farmhouse situated in the Corvedale near Ironbridge. Excellent centre for touring South Shropshire and the Welsh Borders. Nearby amenities include Ludlow golf course and racecourse, fishing, cycling and walking. All rooms en suite. Residents' lounge, licensed. Open all year. Bed and Breakfast from £18; Evening Meal from £12.

LYDBURY NORTH. Mr and Mrs R. Evans, "Brunslow", Lydbury North SY7 8AD (01588 68244). Working farm, join in. "Brunslow" is a beautiful Georgian style farmhouse, centrally heated throughout, ideal for walking and those who enjoy the peace and quiet of unspoiled countryside. The house is set in large gardens with lovely views in all directions and the farm mainly produces milk; pigs, poultry and calves are reared and "feeding time" is very popular with younger guests. One double, one single and two family rooms, all having washbasins. Bathroom, toilets; separate sittingroom and diningroom; colour TV, high chair and babysitting available. Open all year, except Christmas, for Bed and Breakfast from £16; Evening Dinner £8 if required. SAE, please, for terms. Packed lunches available. Car essential, parking.

NEWPORT. Mrs Janice Park, Lane End Farm, Chetwynd, Newport TF10 8BN (01952 550337). ♛♛ *COMMENDED.* Be sure of a warm welcome at our interesting period farmhouse set amidst lovely countryside. Bedrooms with en suite facilities. Good woodland walks nearby. Located on A41 just two miles north of Newport, ideal touring location for visiting Ironbridge, Weston Park, Cosford, The Wrekin, Potteries, Chester, etc. We keep pedigree Suffolk and Rouge sheep — see the lambs in spring! Open all year. Children and pets welcome. Bed and Breakfast from £18; Evening Meal from £11.00.

OSWESTRY near. Mrs Jill Plunkett, Rhosweil Lodge, Weston Rhyn, Near Oswestry SY10 7TG (01691 777609). ♛♛ Victorian country house in delightful gardens beside the Shropshire Union/Llangollen Canal. We are easy to find, just 400 yards from the A5. A convenient place to stop overnight or better still as a centre to explore the Welsh hills, forests, lakes and castles to the west, or the verdant rural quietness of North Shropshire to the east. We enjoy where we live and would be disappointed should you not enjoy our area and our home — at a price of course! Bed and Breakfast from £17.00 to £20.00 per person. Double room is en suite and twin room has its own separate facilities.

PONTESBURY. "Pinehurst", Shrewsbury Road, Pontesbury SY5 0QD (01743 790737). John and Kath Farmer welcome you to their home in the heart of Mary Webb country, with the South Shropshire hills, the Stiperstones and the Welsh Border near. On the bus route between Shrewsbury and Bishop's Castle. Accommodation comprises one single room, one double and one double with en suite shower, etc and TV. Tea/coffee trays in all rooms. Large lounge with open fire. Parking. Sorry, no smoking and no pets. Bed and Breakfast from £14 to £18 per person per night. Children welcome at a reduced rate. At least 10 local establishments serve evening meals.

SHREWSBURY. Mrs Janet Jones, Grove Farm, Preston Brockhurst, Shrewsbury SY4 5QA (01939 220223). ❀ *COMMENDED.* AA QQQ, RAC Acclaimed.

This lovely 17th century farmhouse with a beautiful view offers warmth and comfort to all guests. It is set in a little village on the A49, seven miles north of Shrewsbury. The house has a large lounge and dining room with fires and colour TV. Four lovely bedrooms (one double/family, one twin, both with showers en suite, one double, one single, both with washbasins) with easy chairs and tea/coffee trays. Guest bathroom. Central heating throughout. Visitors are welcomed with tea and home-made cakes, and there is always a variety of delicious food offered for breakfast. Sorry, no smoking. No pets. Bed and breakfast from £16.50. We look forward to welcoming you into our home. Reduced rates for children in family room. Short breaks, and weekly terms available.

TELFORD. Mrs Mary Jones, Red House Farm, Longdon on Tern, Wellington, Telford TF6 6LE (01952 770245). ❀❀ *COMMENDED.*

Our Victorian farmhouse is on a mixed farm. Two double bedrooms have private facilities within, one family room with separate bathroom, all large and comfortable. Excellent breakfast. Farm easily located — leave M54 Junction 6, follow A442, take B5063. Central for historic Shrewsbury, Ironbridge Gorge Museums or modern Telford. Several local eating places. Open all year. Bed and Breakfast from £17. Families most welcome, reductions for children. Pets also welcome. Brochure on request.

WHITCHURCH. Miss J. Gregory, Ash Hall, Ash Magna, Whitchurch SY13 4DL (01948 663151). ETB Listed. Working farm.

An early 18th century house set in large garden with ample room for children to play, on a medium-sized farm with pedigree Friesians. Situated in the small North Shropshire village of Ash, approximately one and a half miles from A41. Within easy reach of Chester and Shrewsbury (about 20 miles); Crewe 15 miles. Interesting features of this house are two oak-panelled reception rooms and an oak staircase; one of the two guest bedrooms is also panelled. One bedroom has en-suite facilities. Bathroom, toilet; sittingroom; diningroom. Children welcome, cot, high chair and reduced rates available. Open all year for Evening Meal, Bed and Breakfast or Bed and Breakfast.

WHITCHURCH near. Mrs Hibbert, Corner House Farm, The Cadney, Bettisfield, Near Whitchurch SY13 2LD (01948 710572).

A warm welcome awaits at this Welsh smallholding. Accommodation comprises twin room with private bathroom. Visitors can enjoy gentle walks by the Llangollen Canal, and there is easy access to Chester, Shrewsbury, Whitchurch and the Welsh seaside resorts. Very peaceful. Bed and Breakfast from £15.60 per person; Evening Meal on request.

SOMERSET

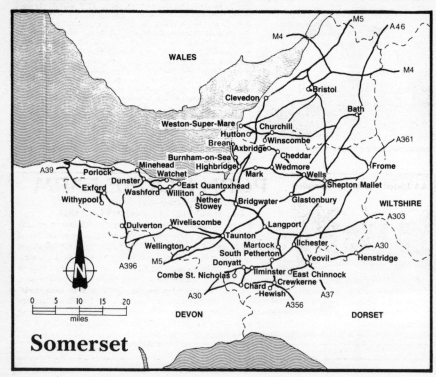

Somerset

ASHBRITTLE. Mrs Ann Heard, Lower Westcott Farm, Ashbrittle, Wellington TA21 0HZ (01398 361296). 🖤🖤 *COMMENDED.* On Devon/Somerset borders, 230 acre family-run farm with Friesian herd, sheep, poultry and horses. Ideal for walking, touring Exmoor, Quantocks, both coasts and many National Trust properties. Pleasant farmhouse, tastefully modernised but with olde worlde charm, inglenook fireplaces and antique furniture, set in large gardens with lawns and flower beds in peaceful, scenic countryside. Two family bedrooms with private facilities and tea/coffee making. Large lounge, separate dining room offering guests every comfort. Noted for relaxed, friendly atmosphere and good home cooking. Brochure by request. Bed and Breakfast from £15; Dinner £8 per person. Reductions for children.

BATH near. Mr and Mrs S.G. Morris, "Midstfields", Frome Road, Radstock, Near Bath BA3 5UD (01761 434440). A large house standing in two acres of charming gardens. Play tennis or relax in the 40ft long indoor heated swimming pool or sauna. Comfortable rooms include washbasins, TV and tea making facilities; one room now en suite. Good walking trails in the beautiful Somerset countryside. Bath and Wells 10 miles away. Full English breakfast. Pets and children welcome. Ample off road parking. Rates from £17 to £22 per person.

BATH near. Mrs B.M. Martin, The Old Inn Farmhouse, Farmborough, Near Bath BA3 1BY (01761

470250). The Old Inn Farmhouse is very attractive, built 1684, and was at one time a Coaching Inn. It has been extensively modernised to offer every comfort, though retaining its charm and character. It stands on the side of a hill overlooking the valley on the edge of Farmborough Village. Attractive landscaped garden. It is highly recommended and maintains a high standard of home cooked food; a family atmosphere prevails, with personal attention. All bedrooms (doubles, twins, and family size) have washbasins. Lounge with TV. Ample parking space. Very central for touring Bath, Wells, Cheddar, Wookey Hole, Longleat, Chew Lake, Wye Valley. Open all the year. Bed and full English Breakfast. Fire Certificate held. SAE or telephone for terms.

AA Listed ✿✿ Commended

PURN HOUSE FARM
Bleadon, Weston-Super-Mare BS24 0QE
Tel: 01943 812324   Fax: 01934 811029

Seventeenth-century creeper-clad house standing on a 700-acre mixed farm at the foot of Purn Hill where there are panoramic views of the Bristol Channel, Glastonbury Tor in the east to Exmoor and the Welsh Mountains in the west. The house contains some period furniture in day rooms. Tastefully decorated bedrooms – three double, one single, four family en suite rooms (one ground floor); modern conveniences; sitting-room, diningroom and games room for use of visitors. Excellent home cooking with traditional menus using home produce when possible. Special diets by arrangement. No pets. Open February to December. A car not essential, though parking provided. Bed and Breakfast. Three day Special Breaks available. Fire Certificate held. Miles of sandy beaches a short distance at Uphill, Weston, Berrow and Brean. Fishing, golf, sailing available; also pony riding locally. En route for the West Mendip Way walk. Milking may be seen in the very modern milking parlour. SAE for brochure, please.

Key to
Tourist Board Ratings

The Crown Scheme
(England, Scotland & Wales)

Covering hotels, motels, private hotels, guesthouses, inns, bed & breakfast, farmhouses. Every Crown classified place to stay is inspected annually. *The classification:* Listed then 1-5 Crown indicates the range of facilities and services. Higher quality standards are indicated by the terms APPROVED, COMMENDED, HIGHLY COMMENDED and DELUXE.

The Key Scheme
(also operates in Scotland using a Crown symbol)

Covering self-catering in cottages, bungalows, flats, houseboats, houses, chalets, etc. Every Key classified holiday home is inspected annually. *The classification:* 1-5 Key indicates the range of facilities and equipment. Higher quality standards are indicated by the terms APPROVED, COMMENDED, HIGHLY COMMENDED and DELUXE.

The Q Scheme
(England, Scotland & Wales)

Covering holiday, caravan, chalet and camping parks. Every Q rated park is inspected annually for its quality standards. The more ✓ in the Q – up to 5 – the higher the standard of what is provided.

BRIDGWATER near. Mrs Helen Fouracre, Oggshole Farmhouse, Broomfield, Bridgwater TA5 2EJ

(01823 451689 or 0850 469220). All the fun of the farm! Paradise for children and animal lovers at this charming 18th century farmhouse nestling in the Quantock Hills. The emphasis is on friendly personal attention in a relaxing family atmosphere. Meet all the hand-tame animals, join in with feeding; pony rides for the children. We have two spacious, tastefully furnished rooms, both double/family with washbasins and tea/coffee trays. TV lounge. Good home-cooked meals optional. Easy access to M5 motorway. Convenient for walking, riding or fishing. Well behaved pets welcome. Stabling available. Please phone for brochure.

THE COTTAGE

A charming country cottage set in 2 acres of garden in an area of outstanding natural beauty and special interest close to rivers and canal where bird and wildlife flourish. A centre not only for the famous Somerset Levels but all of this historic County. We offer you privacy, comfort and tranquillity staying in antique four poster or twin bedded en suite rooms with TV and heating. Easy access with all rooms at ground level opening directly onto the gardens. Ample secure parking. Evening meals available by arrangement. English country cooking at its best using our own fresh vegetables, fruits, honey and free range eggs. Bed & Breakfast from £15 per person per night. Easy access junction 24 M5. Phone or write for brochure and map. No smoking in house please. Open all year.

Beverley and Victor Jenkins, The Cottage, Fordgate, Bridgwater TA7 0AP
Telephone: 01278 691908

BRIDGWATER near. Mrs F.S. Filsell, The Cedars, High Street, Othery, Near Bridgwater TA7 0QA

(01823 698310). A warm welcome awaits guests at this small Grade III Listed Georgian house in the centre of Othery village, well placed for touring and coarse fishing. Two twin and one double bedrooms with washbasins and tea/coffee making facilities; shower, bath, two toilets; diningroom; TV lounge; large garden, parking for six cars. Cot, high chair and babysitting available. Central heating. Car essential. Pets by arrangement. Glastonbury, Taunton only 10 miles away. Brendon, Quantock Hills 30 minutes; Dorset coast half an hour's drive away. Tourist Board registered. Bed and Breakfast from £30 per double/twin room. Reductions for children when sharing.

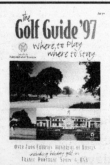

Available from most bookshops, the 1997 edition of THE GOLF GUIDE covers details of every UK golf course – well over 2000 entries – for holiday or business golf. Hundreds of hotel entries offer convenient accommodation, accompanying details of the courses – the 'pro', par score, length etc.

Endorsed by The Professional Golfers' Association (PGA) and including Holiday Golf in Ireland, France, Portugal, Spain and the USA.

£8.99 from bookshops or £9.80 including postage (UK only) from FHG Publications, Abbey Mill Business Centre, Paisley PA1 1TJ.

Brinsea Green Farm

Comfortable 18th century farmhouse on a 500 acre dairy, beef and sheep farm situated one and a half miles from village with views of the Mendip Hills. The farmhouse is located at the end of a quiet country lane surrounded by open fields. Easy access from M5 (approximately 12 to 15 minutes, Exit 21), and centrally situated between Bath, Bristol, Weston-super-Mare, Wells, Cheddar Caves and Blagdon Lake – fishing, dry ski slope, equestrian centre, golf course. The village has nine inns, many serving food. Bed and Breakfast with home-made marmalade and jams, offered to guests all year round. In keeping with their character, both sittingroom and diningroom have inglenook fireplaces. Three double bedrooms, two with en-suite hot drinks facilities. Bathroom with shower and separate toilet. Car essential – ample parking.

Mrs Delia Edwards,
Brinsea Green Farm,
Brinsea Lane, Congresbury,
Near Bristol BS19 5JN
Tel: Churchill (01934) 852278.

BURNHAM-ON-SEA. Mrs F. Alexander, Priors Mead, 23 Rectory Road, Burnham-on-Sea TA8 2BZ (01278 782116; Fax: 01278 782517; Mobile 0860 573018). ❦ ❦ *APPROVED.* "Which?" Recommended. Peter and Fizz welcome guests to enjoy their enchanting Edwardian home set in half an acre of beautiful gardens with croquet and swimming pool. All three rooms have either twin or king-size beds, en suite/private facilities, washbasins, hospitality tray, colour TV, etc. Peaceful location, walk to the sea, town, golf and tennis clubs. Ideal touring base for Bristol, Bath, Wells, Glastonbury, Wookey Hole, Cheddar and Dunster. Parking. Easy access to Junction 22 M5 for Wales, Devon and Cornwall. A no smoking home. Bed and Breakfast from £15 to £17. Reductions for three nights.

CHARD. Mrs Sue Eames, Wambrook Farm, Wambrook, Chard TA20 3DF (01460 62371). Our farm is in a pretty rural village two miles from Chard in the Blackdown Hills. It has an attractive farmhouse and buildings which are listed. On our 300 acre farm we have cattle, breeding sheep, corn. We are half an hour from the Devon/Dorset coast. One double en-suite, one double/family with washbasin, single bed and cot. Bed and Breakfast from £15.50. Children welcome, reduced rates, cot and babysitting available. Good pub food in village.

CHARD. Mrs J. Wright, Yew Tree Cottage, Hornsbury Hill, Chard TA20 3DB (01460 64735; Fax: 01460 68029). ❦ *COMMENDED.* Attractive cottage situated in lovely countryside with an acre garden. One mile from Chard on A358 between Chard and Ilminster, 15 miles from the coast, it makes an ideal base for touring Devon, Dorset and Somerset. Nearby are many historic houses, beautiful gardens, and golf and squash facilities. Comfortable, friendly accommodation — twin and double rooms, all with central heating. En suite rooms; tea-making. Lounge/dining room; colour TV. Parking. Good home cooking. Bed and Breakfast from £18 to £20 per person per night; Evening Meal £10 by arrangement. Ground floor apartment available (3 KEYS COMMENDED). Brochure on request. A NON-SMOKING ESTABLISHMENT.

CHEDDAR. Mrs Sue Barker, Gordon's Hotel, Cliff Street, Cheddar BS27 3PT (01934 742497; Fax: 01934 744965). 🐾🐾 RAC One Star. Gordon's Hotel is set at the foot of the beautiful Cheddar Gorge in glorious Somerset. The Caves and Rural Life Village are within easy walking distance and other large attractions are a short drive away. The hotel has been in the same family for some 25 years and is family-run, which helps to ensure a relaxed and friendly atmosphere. Most of the rooms are en suite, all with TV and tea making facilities; there is a small licensed bar and TV lounge. The Restaurant offers home cooked dishes served with fresh local vegetables. Other facilities include an outdoor swimming pool, car park and garden. Children welcome. Special two/three night breaks available all year round except Christmas week. Bed and full English Breakfast from £19.

TOR FARM

Nyland, Cheddar,
Somerset BS27 3UD
Tel: 01934 743710

High quality farmhouse accommodation on the beautiful Somerset Levels which has open views from every window. The farmhouse is licensed and is fully centrally heated, with tea/coffee making facilities in all rooms. Some rooms have full en suite bathrooms and private patios. One four-poster room. From Cheddar, take A371 towards Wells. After 2 miles, turn right, signposted Nyland. Tor Farm is on the right after 1½ miles.

Open all year (closed Christmas).
Terms from £19 to £25 B&B.

🏅 **Highly Commended**   **AA QQQQ** Selected

CHURCHILL. Lyncombe Lodge, Churchill, Near Bristol BS19 5PQ (01934 852335; Fax: 01934 853314). Family-run licensed farmhouse hotel set in an area of outstanding natural beauty. Well away from the road, our 160 acre farm is tucked away in the Mendip Hills yet is only five miles from the M5. A warm welcome assured, fabulous food (special diets catered for), residents' lounge with log fires, most rooms en suite. Open throughout the year for breaks of any length. Unaccompanied children very welcome. On site BHS Approved riding stables, dry ski slope, snowboarding, quad biking, mountain biking, archery, swimming and more. No previous experience necessary in any activity. Ideal centre for touring.

CREWKERNE. Mrs Sally Gregory, Dryclose, Newbery Lane, Misterton, Crewkerne TA18 8NE (01460 73161). 🐾 *HIGHLY COMMENDED.* Recommended by WHICH. Dryclose is a 16th century former farmhouse set in two acres of garden with swimming pool in a quiet area of the village of Misterton. Close by are historic buildings, beautiful gardens and, within half an hour, the Devon and Dorset coast. Explore Thomas Hardy's countryside, with wonderful walks. We offer Bed and Breakfast with optional Evening Meals or light suppers. Three bedrooms — one twin en suite, one twin and one single. Two separate guest sittingrooms with TV. All bedrooms have hot drinks facilities. Children over eight years welcome. Non-smokers please. Bed and Breakfast from £16.50. Reductions for weekly bookings. Write or phone for further details.

SOMERSET – THE CREAM AND CIDER COUNTY!

Wookey Hole, the great cave near Wells, is the first known home of man in Great Britain. Other places of interest in this green and hilly county include The Mendips, Exmoor National Park, Cheddar Gorge, Meare Lake Village and The Somerset Rural Life Museum. The villages and wildlife of the Quantocks, Poldens and Brendons should not be missed.

BROADVIEW GARDENS

ETB 🌑🌑🌑 De Luxe &
AA QQQQQ Premier Selected
BOTH TOP QUALITY AWARDS

Unusual Colonial bungalow built in an era of quality. Carefully furnished with antiques. En suite rooms overlooking our beautiful 'NGS' acre of secluded, elevated gardens. Achieving top quality awards for comfort, cooking & friendliness. Quality traditional English home cooking. Rooms with easy chairs, col. T.V., Tea/Fac.C/H. Perfect touring base for country & garden lovers, antique enthusiasts, NT houses, moors & quaint old villages. Dorset coast 20 min. List of 50 places provided. A no smoking house. Open all year. B&B £23–£27. Dinner £12.50.

East Crewkerne, Nr Yeovil, Somerset
TA18 7AG (Dorset Border)
Mrs G. Swann   Tel: 01460 73424

DULVERTON. Mrs Carole Nurcombe, Marsh Bridge Cottage, Dulverton TA22 9QG (01398 323197). This superb accommodation has been made possible by the refurbishment of this Victorian former ex-gamekeeper's cottage on the banks of the River Barle. The friendly welcome, lovely rooms, delicious (optional) evening meals using local produce, and clotted cream sweets are hard to resist! Open all year, and in autumn the trees that line the river either side of Marsh Bridge turn to a beautiful golden backdrop. Just off the B3223 Dulverton to Exford road, it is easy to find and, once discovered, rarely forgotten. From outside the front door footpaths lead in both directions alongside the river. Fishing available. Terms from £16.00 per person Bed and Breakfast or £26.00 per person Dinner, Bed and Breakfast.

DULVERTON. Mrs A.M. Spencer, Dassels, Dulverton TA22 9RZ (01398 341203). Superb Georgian-style country guest house magnificently situated on the edge of Exmoor, three miles west of Dulverton on the outskirts of East Anstey. Set in nine and a half acres of tranquil grounds with panoramic views. A spacious house, large dining room, separate lounge, TV and log fires. 10 bedrooms, all en suite and with colour TV and tea/coffee making facilities. A high standard of comfort is maintained and Dassels is noted for its excellent home cooked food, farm produce, delicious sweets served with clotted cream, fresh baked rolls. A beautiful area near the Exmoor National Park where guests may enjoy horse riding, walking, fishing and nature study. Many beauty spots within easy reach, also places of archaeological and historic interest, with easy access to North Devon and West Somerset coastal resorts. Residential licence. Ample parking. Fire Certificate. Stabling. Open all year. Children welcome. Dinner, Bed and Breakfast from £30.

DULVERTON. Mrs P.J. Vellacott, Springfield Farm, Ashwick Lane, Dulverton TA22 9QD (01398 323722). 🌑🌑 COMMENDED. At Springfield we offer you wonderful hospitality and delicious food. We farm 270 acres within the Exmoor National Park, rearing sheep and cattle. Peacefully situated a one and a half mile walk from Tarr Steps, four miles from Dulverton. Much wildlife including red deer can be seen on the farm. An ideal base for walking or touring Exmoor and North Devon coastal resorts. Riding and fishing nearby. One double with private WC and shower, one twin en suite and one double en suite. Drinks making facilities in dining room. Guests' lounge with colour TV. Access to rooms at all times. Ample parking (garage by request). Children welcome. Pets by arrangement. No smoking in the house please. Bed and Breakfast from £17; Evening Meal £11.50. Reductions for children under 10 years and weekly bookings. FHB Member, West Country Tourist Board Member: Welcome Host.

PLEASE ENCLOSE A STAMPED ADDRESSED ENVELOPE WITH ENQUIRIES

DULVERTON — EXMOOR. Mrs Brenda Coates, Chapple Farm, Bury, Dulverton TA4 2DP (01398 331364).

 ₩ Chapple Farm is situated on the slopes of Haddon Hill overlooking a wooded valley rich in wildlife. The farm is an Exmoor working beef and sheep hill farm of 220 acres; chickens, ducks, pheasant and sometimes partridge roam the farmyard. The farmhouse is 16th century and retains its oak beams and original character. It comprises three bedrooms, each with washbasin and tea/coffee making facilities; bathroom with separate toilet; dining room; comfortable lounge with TV and pleasant views across the valley. We serve traditional farmhouse breakfasts and evening meals using farm and dairy produce when available and fresh vegetables from the garden. Children (reduced rates) and dogs welcome. Open March to October.

DUNSTER. Mr & Mrs W.A. Greenfield, Burnells Farm, Knowle Lane, Dunster TA24 6UU (01643 821841). Working farm. Comfortable and friendly farmhouse accommodation, one mile from Dunster, two miles from sea, with glorious views of Exmoor. Ideal walking or touring centre for the National Park. Accommodation comprises one double, one family and one single bedroom, all with washbasins; one public bathroom and one shower room, toilet upstairs and down; lounge with TV and diningroom. Guests are requested to refrain from smoking indoors. Ample parking. Packed lunches on request. Open all year. Bed and Breakfast £16. Evening Meal, Bed and Breakfast £22. Weekly £143.50.

EXMOOR. Abigail Humphrey, Highercombe Farm, Dulverton TA22 9PT (01398 323616). ₩

HighercombE fArm

COMMENDED. Relax and enjoy our special hospitality on a 450 acre working farm (including 100 acres of woodland) in an outstanding peaceful situation on Exmoor. Off the beaten track, yet only four miles from Dulverton, we are an ideal base to explore coast and moor. There is an abundance of wildlife on the farm, including wild red deer. We are happy to take you on a farm tour. The farmhouse enjoys spectacular views, central heating, large visitors' lounge and log fires. Pretty rooms with generous en suite bathrooms. Delicious farmhouse cooking, fresh produce, homemade marmalade, etc. Bed and Breakfast from £18; Dinner, Bed and Breakfast from £29. Private, well equipped self catering wing of farmhouse also available (4 KEYS COMMENDED).

See also Colour Display Advertisement **EXMOOR NATIONAL PARK. Diana Brewer, Wood Advent Farm, Roadwater, Watchet TA23 0PR (Tel & Fax: 01984 640920).** ₩ ₩ *COMMENDED.* Superbly situated in the Exmoor National Park. A Listed spacious farmhouse set in 340 acres of glorious working farmland. Relaxing en suite bedrooms with TV, radio and hospitality trays; full central heating; two reception rooms with log fires on cooler days; dining room with woodburner, delicious dishes prepared here using local produce. Enjoy the gardens with grass tennis court and heated swimming pool, lots of well marked footpaths on the farm. An ideal base for Dunster, Selworthy and the many places of interest in and around Exmoor. Recommended by "Which?" Holiday Guide, AA QQQQ Selected. Accommodation and Breakfast £19.50 to £23.50 per person; Dinner £12 to £15. Please call for brochure.

GLASTONBURY. Mrs Elizabeth Ruddle, Laverley House, West Pennard, Glastonbury BA8 8NE (01749 890696). ₩ ₩

 Tony and Liz look forward to welcoming you to their attractive and spacious Listed Georgian farmhouse with superb views, paddock and gardens, all set in a rural area. There are two double bedrooms with en suite bathrooms and a family bedroom with private bathroom. Colour TV and hospitality trays in all bedrooms. We have a comfortable guests' lounge and dining room and are happy to provide a cot and high chair for children. Fresh produce is served, traditionally cooked. A good area for touring; Wells six miles, Bath 20 miles. Many National Trust houses and gardens. Bed and Breakfast from £18.50. Please telephone for brochure.

GLASTONBURY. Mrs Mary Dodds, Twelve Hides, Quarry Lane, Butleigh, Glastonbury BA6 8TE (01458 50380). A six acre smallholding with small pedigree

 Wensleydale flock (participation welcome), own handspinning. Four miles to Glastonbury and within easy reach of Bath, Cheddar Gorge, Wookey Caves, site of legendary Camelot, Wetlands, etc; yet peaceful and away from it all. Exceptional view across Vale of Avalon to Glastonbury Tor, Wells Cathedral and Mendip Hills. Overlooking picturesque Butleigh village, good pub food within walking distance. Accommodation comprises one double-bedded room, two twin-bedded rooms (one with washbasin), all with tea/coffee making facilities. Guest bathroom with bath, WC and washbasin. Separate guest shower room with WC/washbasin. Traditional English Breakfast. Terms from £15.

GLASTONBURY. Mrs D.P. Atkinson, Court Lodge, Butleigh, Glastonbury BA6 8SA (01458 850575). A warm welcome awaits at attractive, modernised

1850 Lodge with homely atmosphere. Set in picturesque garden on the edge of Butleigh, three miles from historic Glastonbury. Only a five minute walk to pub in village which serves lovely meals. Accommodation in one double, one twin and one single bedrooms; constant hot water, central heating. Bathroom adjacent to bedrooms. TV lounge. Tea/coffee served. Bed and Breakfast from £13.50; Evening Meal by arrangement. Children welcome at reduced rates.

GURNEY SLADE. Mrs Jacqueline Hawkins, Cockhill Farm, Marchants Hill, Gurney Slade, Near Bath BA3 4TY (01749 840125). Farmhouse accommo-

dation on a working farm keeping a small beef suckler herd in the heart of the Mendips. A friendly atmosphere is assured in this Victorian farmhouse. Excellent home cooking using local produce. Bed and Breakfast, optional Evening Meal. Spacious rooms with period furnishings, TV, tea/coffee making facilities. Ideally situated for the Cathedral City of Wells, Glastonbury, Cheddar, Georgian Bath and historic Bristol. Royal Bath and West Showground 10 minutes. Magnificent Chew Valley Lake for bird watching, fly fishing and picnicking 20 minutes. Good local pubs and peaceful country walks. Children welcome, baby facilities available. One twin, one double bedroom and one single bedroom. Open all year. Bed and Breakfast from £14.

HIGHBRIDGE. Mrs V.M. Loud, Alstone Court Farm, Alstone Lane, Highbridge TA9 3DS (01278 789417). Working farm. Tourist Board Listed. 17th cen-

tury farmhouse, situated on outskirts of town, two miles from M5 Edithmead inter-change, on a mixed farm of 200 acres. The land adjoins Bridgwater Bay, ideal as touring centre for Somerset. Within easy reach of Burnham-on-Sea, Weston-super-Mare, Wells, Cheddar Gorge, Wookey Hole and the Mendips. Ideal for sea and coarse fishing. Horse-riding on the farm — qualified instructor. Spacious comfortable bedrooms — two family and one twin-bedded rooms. Lounge with colour TV, large diningroom. Central heating. Home produce when available. Children welcome. Ample parking space. Evening Meal, Bed and Breakfast. Terms on request with SAE, please.

HIGHBRIDGE near. Mrs B.M. Puddy, ''Laurel Farm'', Mark Causeway, Near Highbridge TA9 4PZ (01278 641216). ❤ RAC Commended. Laurel Farm is over 200 years old with 120 acres and 70 milking cows, Friesian and Holstein. We are about two miles from Mark Church and village on the Wells to Burnham-on-Sea B3139 road, two miles from M5 Junction 22. Ideal touring centre or halfway house. There is a large sittingroom with a colour TV, log fires September to May. Central heating, electric blankets. Washbasins in all bedrooms. Nicely decorated with fitted carpets throughout. Separate tables in diningroom. Doubles, singles and family rooms; shower, two baths, three toilets. En suite available. Car essential/or bike. Undercover garages. Open all year.

MARTOCK. Mr and Mrs S.R. Peach, Falconers Farm, Milton, Ash, Martock TA12 6AL (01935 823363). Working farm. A Georgian farmhouse set in 320 acres of mixed farmland on a Duchy of Cornwall farm belonging to the Prince of Wales Estates. Visitors welcome to tour farm and watch. Nearest town Yeovil seven miles. A family farm ideal for walking on the Somerset Levels or Polden Hills, horse riding and coarse fishing or convenient for shopping in Taunton. Local attractions include Montacute House and Cricket St. Thomas Wildlife Park. The coast is three-quarters of an hour's drive. Accommodation in three guest rooms (one family), own bathroom. All children welcome, cot, high chair and babysitting available. Car essential. Bed and Breakfast from £14 to £19 per person per night. Telephone or write for further details.

MARTOCK. Mrs H. Turton, "Wychwood", 7 Bearley Road, Martock TA12 6PG (01935 825601).

🐾🐾 *HIGHLY COMMENDED.* AA QQQQ Selected, RAC Acclaimed, FHG Diploma Award. Quality, comfortable accommodation. Excellent home cooking. In quiet position just off A303. Ideal touring location. Close to Montacute House, Fleet Air Arm Museum, Tintinhull Gardens and eight other "classic" gardens. Walk the "Leland Trail" through Camelot Country and the Legend of King Arthur. Yeovil 10 minutes, Sherborne 15 minutes; Glastonbury, Wells, Taunton, M5 Junction 25 under 30 minutes. TV, radio and tea/coffee making facilities in all bedrooms. Double rooms with en suite, twin with private bathroom. Comfortable residents' lounge, separate dining room. Garden. Full central heating. Parking. No smoking. Bed and full English Breakfast from £18; Dinner £15. Open all year. Credit cards accepted.

NORTH PETHERTON. Mrs Sue Milverton, Lower Clavelshay Farm, North Petherton, Near Bridgwater TA6 6PJ (01278 662347). Working farm.

Buzzards, badgers and beautiful countryside surround our traditional 17th century farmhouse on a 250-acre dairy farm. Peaceful, with a relaxed "home from home" atmosphere. Two doubles and one family room, all with tea making facilities; small kitchen with cooker and fridge — useful for snacks, picnic lunches etc. Sitting/dining room with beams, TV and log fire. Games, books, maps and guide books all freely available. Central heating. Ideally situated for exploring the Quantock Hills, Exmoor, Somerset Levels and coast. Perfect for walking, riding, fishing or just relaxing. Children welcome; cot and high chair available; babysitting. Generous helpings of delicious home cooking using our own produce when possible. Discover why our guests keep returning!

PORLOCK. Bossington Farm and Birds of Prey Centre, Allerford, Near Porlock TA24 8HJ (01643 862816). West Country Tourist Board Listed. Welcome

Host. A unique opportunity to stay at family-run Exmoor bird of prey and farm park, situated just outside the delightful National Trust village of Allerford at the foot of wooded coombes and moors, five miles west of Minehead, with views to North Hill, Dunkery Beacon and the sea. Idyllic character 15th century "open-hall manor house" retaining many original features. Spacious centrally heated family and double bedrooms with tea making facilities, lounge/dining room with inglenook fireplace and woodburning stove provide a warm and friendly family atmosphere. Full farmhouse breakfast with lunch and tea also available. Variety of evening meals in nearby villages of Allerford and Porlock. Riding, cycling and falconry arranged. Dogs and horses welcome. Reduced rates for children.

SHEPTON MALLET. Mrs M. White, Barrow Farm, North Wootton, Shepton Mallet BA4 4HL (01749 890245). Working farm. This farm accommodation is AA

QQQ Listed. Barrow is a dairy farm of 146 acres. The house is 15th century and of much character, situated quietly between Wells, Glastonbury and Shepton Mallet. It makes an excellent touring centre for visiting Somerset's beauty spots and historic places, for example, Cheddar, Bath, Wookey Hole and Longleat. Guest accommodation consists of two double rooms, one family room, one single and one twin bedded room, each with washbasin, TV and tea/coffee making facilities. Bathroom, two toilets; two lounges, one with colour TV; diningroom with separate tables. Guests can enjoy farmhouse fare in generous variety, home baking a speciality. Bed and Breakfast from £15 to £16; Evening Meal from £8. Dinner, Bed and Breakfast from £140 weekly. Car essential; ample parking. Children welcome; cot and babysitting available. Open all year except Christmas. Sorry no pets.

SHERBORNE near. Mrs Sue Stretton, Beech Farm, Sigwells, Charlton Horethorne, Near Sherborne, Dorset DT9 4LN (01963 220524).

A warm welcome awaits you on our 130 acre dairy farm carrying beef and horses in an area with wonderful views and excellent for walking, cycling and horse riding (guests' horses welcome). Located on the Somerset/Dorset border, six miles from Wincanton, four miles from Sherborne and just two miles off the A303. A comfortable, centrally heated farmhouse with a double room en suite and a twin room with guest bathroom, both with tea/coffee making facilities. Laundry facilities and packed lunches available. Bed and Breakfast £15 per person. Less 10% for three or more nights. Evening meals at village inn or by prior arrangement. Open all year.

SHERBORNE near (Dorset). Patricia and Brian Thompson, Quiet Corner Farm, Henstridge, Templecombe BA8 0RA (01963 363045). ✿✿ COMMENDED.

Lovely old stone farmhouse and barns, some converted to self catering cottages sleeping two/four, set in five acres beautiful garden and orchards with sheep and Miniature Shetland ponies. The village, 'twixt Shaftesbury and Sherborne, has super pubs, restaurant, shops and post office. Marvellous centre for touring Somerset, Dorset and Wiltshire with host of National Trust and other properties. Golf and fishing nearby. The spacious farmhouse is centrally heated throughout, log fires; bedrooms with washbasins and tea making facilities. Beautiful garden; orchard and paddocks to walk through. Ample car parking. Payphone. Bed and Breakfast from £19. Reductions for children. SPECIAL OFFER: three days for the price of two (subject to availability) October 1st to end May except Public Holidays. SAE, or telephone, for brochure.

SOMERTON. Mrs J. Ruddle, Mathias House, High Street, Keinton Mandeville, Near Somerton TA11 6DZ (Tel & Fax: 01458 223921).

Luxury accommodation and a warm welcome await you at this village property on the outskirts of a small Somerset village. Ideally situated for touring historic Glastonbury and Wells, four miles from Clarks Village, famous Montacute House a mere 10 minutes' drive. Two double rooms with full bathroom, TV and welcome tray, all with the intent of making your stay as comfortable as possible. Good home cooking, evening meal optional. Guests' own sitting room. £18.00 per person per night. Strictly non smokers.

Hall Farm Guest House

Stogumber, Taunton TA4 3TQ Tel: (01984) 656321

Hall Farm is situated on a working farm in the centre of Stogumber Village, surrounded by the Quantocks and Exmoor. Within easy reach of the sea, Minehead, Blue Anchor, Watchet and St. Audries Bay. Accommodation for 12 to 14 guests. The bedrooms are comfortable and have ensuite facilities. The catering is under the personal supervision of the proprietress, whose concern it is to make your holiday a happy one. Dogs are welcome if kept well under control. Good parking. Breakfast at 9am with Evening Dinner at 6.30pm. Traditional Sunday lunches at 1pm. **Proprietress: Christine M. Hayes.**

See also Colour Display Advertisement **TAUNTON. Mrs Maureen Fewings, Higher Dipford Farm, Trull, Taunton TA3 7NU (01823 275770).** ✿✿✿ COMMENDED. AA QQQQ. This dairy farm is situated two and a half miles from Taunton. The accommodation is in the 600 year old farmhouse where there are many exposed elm beams and inglenook fireplaces. All bedrooms have en suite showers/bathrooms. Children welcome. Central heating. Home cooking is our speciality with fresh produce from the farm and garden, all helped down by a jug of local cider. Please write or telephone for further details and tariff.

WATCHET. Mrs H. North, Swansea Farm, Brendon Hill, Watchet TA23 0LH (01398 371202). Historic 17th century spacious farmhouse on Brendon Hills. Working farm of 300 acres carrying sheep and beef. Stabling available; riding school nearby. Pets and children welcome; cot, high chair and babysitting available. Excellent area for walking, Wimbleball Lake nearby for fishing and sailing. Ideal base for exploring Exmoor, excellent pubs nearby for meals. Four miles from Brompton Regis with its post office/stores and pub. Situated in hamlet of Withiel Florey which boasts charming Norman Church. Bed and Breakfast £15, reductions for children. Two bedrooms — one twin en suite, one family; two bathrooms, two toilets. Central heating. A warm welcome awaits.

WEDMORE. Mrs Sarah Willcox, Townsend Farm, Sand, Near Wedmore BS28 4XH (01934 712342).

Townsend Farm is delightfully situated in peaceful countryside with extensive views of the Mendip Hills. Set on the outskirts of the picturesque Georgian village of Wedmore with easy access to many places of natural and historic interest, such as the famous Cheddar Gorge, Wells Cathedral, Glastonbury Tor and Abbey ruins and only six miles from the M5 motorway, Junction 22 (one night stops welcome). All bedrooms have tea/coffee making facilities and some have portable TVs. Guests can be assured of a warm and pleasant atmosphere. We offer Bed and Breakfast from £15.50 per person, en-suite from £18. Phone for availability. Farm Holiday Bureau member.

WELLS. Mrs Janet Gould, Milton Manor Farm, Old Bristol Road, Upper Milton, Wells BA5 3AH (01749 673394). Working farm. Manor Farm is a Grade II star Listed Elizabethan Manor House superbly situated on southern slopes of Mendip Hills one mile from Wells. It is a beef farm of 130 acres. Three large rooms for visitors with hot and cold water, central heating and tea/coffee facilities. Full English Breakfast with choice of menu served at separate tables in panelled diningroom. Colour TV. Large peaceful garden with lovely view towards the sea. Ideal for walking on the Mendip Hills and exploring local places of historic interest. Access to house at all times. Fire Certificate held. AA Listed QQQ. No smoking. Open January to December for Bed and Breakfast from £14.50 per person. Reductions for children and week-long stays. Brochure on request.

WELLS near. Mrs H.J. Millard, Double-Gate Farm, Godney, Near Wells BA5 1RZ (01458 832217; Fax: 01458 835612). Working farm. Located in the heart of beautiful Somerset, Double-Gate nestles on the banks of the River Sheppey. This beautiful Listed Georgian farmhouse offers comfortable guest lounge with colour TV and fully equipped games room; spacious bedrooms with complimentary tea/coffee, all en suite with remote control TVs. Lovely flower garden; breakfast served outside, weather permitting. Family pets include two golden retrievers and a loving moggy. No restrictions on access. Home from home! Fire Certificate. Food Hygiene Certificate. No smoking in the house. Ideal for touring — Wells Cathedral six miles, Glastonbury Abbey three miles, Wookey Hole Caves, Cheddar Gorge, Bath, Weston-super-Mare all easily accessible. Bed and Breakfast from £18; Evening Meals available at village inn next door. Reduced terms for children and weekly stays. Guide dogs accepted. Excellent cycling, bird watching area.

WELLS near. Mrs Pamela Keen, Crapnell Farm, Dinder, Near Wells (01749 342683). A 300 acre mixed farm of arable, dairy, situated on the Mendip Hills in beautiful surroundings. Listed 16th century house with much character within easy reach of Wells, Cheddar, Wookey Hole, Glastonbury, Bath and many more interesting places. Only a mile from lovely Mendip Golf Club, four miles from Bath and West Showground at Shepton Mallet. All rooms are large and comfortably furnished with washbasins, TV and tea/coffee facilities. TV lounge available; snooker and games room. Small swimming pool. Children welcome. Open all year. Parking. Bed and Breakfast; Dinner available.

See also Colour Display Advertisement **WESTON-SUPER-MARE. Margaret and David Holt, Moorlands, Hutton, Near Weston-Super-Mare BS24 9QH (01934 812283).** ♛♛♛ *COMMENDED*. Enjoy fine food and warm hospitality at this impressive late Georgian house set in landscaped gardens below the slopes of the Western Mendips. A wonderful touring centre, perfectly placed for visits to beaches, sites of special interest and historic buildings. Families with children particularly welcome, reduced terms and pony rides in our paddock. Good wholesome meals with the emphasis on our own home-grown produce. Full central heating, open fire in comfortable lounge. Licensed. Open January to early November.

WESTON-SUPER-MARE. Mr and Mrs H. Wallington, Braeside Hotel, 2 Victoria Park, Weston-super-Mare BS23 2HZ (Tel/Fax: 01934 626642). ♛♛♛ *COMMENDED*. AA QQQQ Selected, RAC Highly Acclaimed. Our delightful family-run Hotel is superbly situated close to the sea front, yet sufficiently far back from the hustle and bustle to enjoy a peaceful and relaxed holiday. Set in a cul-de-sac (with unrestricted parking) we are in a slightly elevated position with magnificent views over Weston Bay. All our nine bedrooms have bath/shower and toilet en suite, colour TV, coffee/tea making and are tastefully decorated, creating just the right atmosphere in which to relax after a busy day. Although we are a fairly small hotel guests can expect quality and service.

WESTON-SUPER-MARE near. Mrs F. Young, Lower Wick Farm, Wick Lane, Lympsham BS24 0HG (01278 751333). ♛♛ A warm welcome awaits you at our delightful old farmhouse, pleasantly situated in peaceful countryside within easy reach of Somerset attractions such as Cheddar Gorge, Wells and Glastonbury. All bedrooms have toilet, shower and washbasin en-suite and views over surrounding countryside. In addition to the diningroom, the large inglenook guests' lounge with colour TV offers quiet relaxation. Lovely garden and spacious lawns for just sitting or sunbathing. Regret unable to accommodate young children. Restricted smoking. Bed and Breakfast £18 daily. Weekly reductions. Brochure available.

EXMOOR Ann & Philip Durbin, Cutthorne Farm, Luckwell Bridge, Wheddon Cross TA24 7EW Tel: 01643 831255 ETB ♛♛♛ Highly Commended

Set in the heart of Exmoor, one of the last truly unspoilt areas of the country, Cutthorne is beautifully secluded and dates from the 14th century. It is an ideal base for exploring the coast and countryside – good touring, walking and riding. Fly-fishing is also available in our well-stocked trout pond. The house is spacious and comfortable with log fires and central heating. The three bedrooms have en-suite bathrooms and the master bedroom has a four-poster bed. Candlelit dinners with traditional and vegetarian cooking and an excellent choice of breakfasts. Bed and Breakfast from £19.50. Dogs welcome. No smoking.

WHEDDON CROSS. Shelagh and Larry Maxwell, Little Brendon Hill, Wheddon Cross TA24 7BG (Tel & Fax: 01643 841556). ♛♛ *HIGHLY COMMENDED*. AA QQQQ. Beautifully appointed farmhouse in the centre of the Exmoor National Park. Three lovely en suite bedrooms with colour TV and hospitality trays. Fully centrally heated, non smoking. Cosy, candlelit dinners, log fires and excellent food. A warm and friendly welcome awaits. Accommodation with full English Breakfast from £17.50; Four-course Dinner £12.50. Please ring for a brochure.

PLEASE ENCLOSE A STAMPED ADDRESSED ENVELOPE WITH ENQUIRIES

YEOVIL. Mrs Jane Pearse, Hill Ash Farm, Woolston, North Cadbury, Yeovil BA22 7BL (01963 440332). ✤ COMMENDED. This lovely thatched house, a Listed building constructed in 1766, is set in a beautiful hamlet of south Somerset, one and a half miles from A303. It is an ideal centre for visiting the many tourist attractions and National Trust gardens in Somerset and Dorset. Two double en suite and two single rooms, all with tea/coffee making facilities and full central heating. Children welcome. Open March to November. Bed and Breakfast from £18 to £22.

YEOVILTON near. Mrs Susie Crang, Cary Fitzpaine Farmhouse, Cary Fitzpaine, Near Yeovilton, Yeovil BA22 8JB (01458 223250). A gracious Georgian Manor Farmhouse set in two acres of gardens on a 600 acre working farm — arable, sheep, beef and horses. Peaceful and friendly atmosphere. Close to a wealth of historic buildings, gardens, towns and an aircraft museum. Plenty to suit all tastes. Bedrooms are beautifully furnished and luxurious; one has four-poster bed, all have en suite bathrooms, TV and tea/coffee making facilities. Packed lunches available. Pets at our discretion. Open all year. Terms from £17.50 to £20 per person.

STAFFORDSHIRE

LEEK. Mrs P. Simpson, Summerhill Farm, Grindon, Leek ST13 7TT (01538 304264). ✤✤ COMMENDED. Traditional dairy farm set in the Peak District amid rolling countryside with panoramic views. Wonderful for walkers. All three rooms are en suite and have tea and coffee making facilities, colour TV, clock radios. Children welcome. Alton Towers only 15 minutes away, 35 minutes to Potteries. Open all year for Bed and Breakfast from £16.50 to £19; Dinner from £10. Directions — Leek to Ashbourne Road A523 through Onecote, first right for Grindon, three-quarters of a mile up no through road. AA QQQ.

STOKE-ON-TRENT. Mrs Anne Hodgson, The Hollies, Clay Lake, Endon, Stoke-on-Trent ST9 9DD (01782 503252). ✤✤ COMMENDED. Beautiful Victorian house in a quiet country setting off the B5051 convenient for the M6, Alton Towers, Staffordshire Moorlands and the Potteries. Five spacious comfortable bedrooms (including four en suite) all with central heating, tea/coffee facilities and TV. Children welcome sharing family room. Dogs by prior arrangement. Secluded garden with ample parking. Choice of breakfast with own preserves. No smoking, please. Bed and Breakfast from £18 with reductions for longer stays. Guests are assured of a warm friendly welcome. AA QQQ.

STAFFORDSHIRE'S
Farm & Country Holidays
BED & BREAKFAST

SLINDON HOUSE FARM, Slindon, Eccleshall, Staffs. (Mrs H. Bonsall) 01782 791 237. Comfortable accommodation situated on the A519 in the tiny village of Slindon. Ideal for M6 Junctions 14 & 15. **1T ensuite. 1D. From £15. pp ETB**

OFFLEY GROVE FARM, Adbaston, Staffs. (Mrs M. Hiscoe-James) 01785 280 205. You'll consider this a good find! Quality accommodation. Excellent breakfasts. Attractive traditional farm. Ideal for Potteries, Ironbridge, Alton Towers etc. Reductions for children. Many guests return. **1D 2T from £15. ETB Commended. AA QQ. RAC Listed.**

BROADFIELDS FARM, Pessall Lane, Edingale, Tamworth, Staffs. B79 9JW (Mrs K. Cliffe) 01827 383 225. Traditional beamed farmhouse situated in peaceful countryside. Five minutes M42 and A38 Tastefully furnished rooms. H & C, tea making, own bathroom and lounge, colour TV. **From £15.**

MARSH FARM, Abbots Bromley, Rugeley, Staffs. (Mrs M. Hollins) 01283 840 323. You will be made welcome at this spacious farmhouse; tastefully furnished bedrooms and good home cooking. Close to Lichfield, Alton Towers and Cannock Chase. **1F 1T. From £15 each ETB.**

WINCOTE FARM, Eccleshall, Staffs (Mrs S. Norbury) 01785 850 337. Wonderful welcome in spacious comfortable working farmhouse, with open fireplaces. Close to Potteries, Ironbridge, Shugborough & Weston Park. Special stress free breaks & reflexology available. **1T 1D 1S from £15.**

LITTLE BROOKHOUSE FARM, Cheddleton, Leek, Staffs. (Mrs N. Sherratt) 01538 360 350. A warm welcome, good food and high level of comfort ensures guests have a memorable stay in this delightfully peaceful rural location. All rooms ensuite. **From £17.50 pp. ETB Highly Commended.**

TAMHORN PARK FARM HOUSE, Fisherwick, Lichfield (Mrs. A. Adams) 01543 432 241. Luxurious welcoming Georgian farm house beside canal. 2 twins, one ensuite. 1 King size double. H & C. Tea/Coffee facilities. TV lounge. Aga cooking, snooker, no smoking. **From £26.**

NORTON FARM, Stone, Staffs. (Mrs M. Brown) 01785 760 224. A beautiful Georgian farmhouse on a working dairy and stock farm overlooking a golf course. Ideally situated for the Potteries (Wedgwood 4 miles), Alton Towers and stately homes of the area. **2D 1T from £15.**

WEAVERS DOWN, Hollington Stoke-on-Trent (Mrs J. Robbins) 01889 507 321. Luxury house in 6 acres of beautiful countryside. Footpaths, free-range chickens etc. Indoor pool usually available, extra cost. Ensuite. Tea/Coffee. 10 mins from Alton Towers. Close Peak District & Potteries. **From £19 pp, £35 Double.**

PARK FARM, Weston Road, Stafford (Mrs J. Williams) 01785 240257. Period farmhouse situated by the County Showground, with lovely views. Private bathroom, TV and tea trays in rooms. Fire Certificate held. **1F 1T from £15. Highly Commended.**

SEE ALSO HALF PAGE SELF CATERING ADVERTISEMENT UNDER STAFFORDSHIRE.
Phone or send a 9 × 4" SAE to any member of our group for their own individual or the group brochure.

STOKE-ON-TRENT. Mrs Diana Edwards, Balterley Hall Farm, Balterley, Crewe CW2 5QG (01270 820206). *HIGHLY COMMENDED.* **Working farm.** AA QQQQ Selected. Balterley Hall is a 17th century farmhouse situated on the Cheshire/Staffordshire border three miles from the M6 motorway, Exit 16. Take A500 towards Stoke-on-Trent, first exit to Audley, take A52/B5500 towards Balterley, keep going over motorway, past pub, then after three-quarters of a mile turn left, 500 yards on left. Many places of interest within easy reach, Wedgwood and Doulton Potteries, Alton Towers, Bridgemere Garden World and also historic towns of Nantwich and Chester. One family en suite, one double en suite (both with draped beds) and one single with washbasin. All are tastefully decorated and have colour TV and tea/coffee making facilities; fully fitted bathroom with bath and shower. Open all year. Bed and Breakfast from £15.50 per night with reductions for children under 12 years.

BALTERLEY HALL.

STOKE-ON-TRENT. Mrs Barbara White, Micklea Farm, Micklea Lane, Longsdon, Near Leek, Stoke-on-Trent ST9 9QA (01538 385006; Fax: 01538 382882). Tourist Board Listed *APPROVED.* Quietly situated off A53 yet ideally located for touring the area, this delightful old stone house, boasting a warm friendly atmosphere and comfortable accommodation, is the perfect base for a family holiday. Open all year; two twin or double rooms and two single rooms; guest lounge with TV; large garden; ample parking. Children welcome. Visitors will enjoy pleasant canal and country park walks, fishing, golf, gliding and hang gliding. Alton Towers and the beautiful Peak District and Potteries are near at hand. Bed and Breakfast £16; Bed, Breakfast and Evening Meal £27. Further details on request.

FREE and REDUCED RATE Holiday Visits!
See our READERS' OFFER VOUCHER for details!

SUFFOLK

BUNGAY/BECCLES. Mrs Sarah Cook, Butterley House, Leet Hill Farm, Yarmouth Road, Kirby Cane, Bungay NR35 2HJ (01508 518301). Working

farm. A warm welcome awaits at this dairy/arable farm set in the heart of the Waveney Valley, with excellent rural views, situated between the historic towns of Beccles and Bungay, 15 miles from Norwich, 20 minutes' drive from Norfolk/ Suffolk coasts, and nearby the famous Otter Trust. Accommodation comprises one double/family room with en-suite facilities, one double room with washbasin and one twin room; bathroom, two toilets. Guests have their own sitting-room with TV, separate diningroom. Full English Breakfast. Evening Meal by arrangement. Farm produce used whenever possible. Car essential. No pets please. Reductions for children. Terms on request. Tourist Board registered.

BURY ST. EDMUNDS. Jenny Pearson, Hay Green Farm, Whepstead, Bury St. Edmunds IP29 4UD

(01284 850567). Tourist Board Listed *APPROVED.* Hay Green Farm, a typical Listed Suffolk farmhouse is quietly situated off the A143 five miles south of Bury St. Edmunds, close to the National Trust property of Ickworth Park. Ideal base for exploring East Anglia, being close to the picturesque villages of Clare, Kersey, Long Melford and Lavenham to the south; Newmarket and Cambridge to the west. Accommodation comprises a family room, double room and single room, all with TV and tea making facilities. Open all year. As there are horses, sheep and other livestock on the farm, sorry, no pets. Paddock and stabling available for horses. Bed and Breakfast from £20.00. Good evening meals in local pubs.

BURY ST. EDMUNDS. Mrs Rachel White, Pear Tree Farm, Hartest, Bury St. Edmunds (01284

830217). ♛♛ *COMMENDED.* A warm welcome awaits you in our spacious bungalow. Every comfort for a relaxing holiday, attractive double and twin en suite rooms with TV, tea/coffee making facilities. Guests' lounge with TV. Our dining room has wonderful views of corn fields and over-looks our conservatory. We are ideally situated for touring many places: Lavenham, Long Melford for antiques, Constable Country, Bury St. Edmunds, Abbey Gardens and many historic places. Take dinner in our super country pub and restaurant. Bed and Breakfast £20 per person.

BURY ST. EDMUNDS. Mrs Sarah Rush, Rymer Farm, Barnham, Thetford, Norfolk IP24 2PP (01842

890233; Fax: 01842 890653). ♛♛ *COMMENDED.* 17th century farmhouse situated eight miles north of the historic town of Bury St. Edmunds in Central East Anglia within easy reach of Newmarket, Norwich and Cambridge. A wonderful welcome awaits guests with tea in the garden room or by the log fire in the elegant sittingroom. Fruit from the garden and full English breakfast offered. Double and single en suite rooms and a twin-bedded room with private bathroom. All centrally heated. Farm walks with wild life everywhere! Open all year except Christmas. Bed and Breakfast from £18 to £21 nightly.

CHEDISTON. Mrs Eileen Webb, "Saskiavill", Chediston, Halesworth IP19 0AR (01986 873067). ♛♛♛ "Saskiavill" is set back from the road and stands in one-and-a-half acres of garden. The spacious bungalow offers holidaymakers an ideal touring base for the fine City of Norwich, the coast and nearby Minsmere Bird Sanctuary. The village has many thatched cottages and an old church and is only two miles from the market town of Halesworth. Convenient for golf courses, nature reserves, museums, National Trust houses, gardens, etc. One double, one family, one twin room adapted for disabled guests, all en-suite; two bathrooms, two toilets; TV lounge, sittingroom, diningroom. Children welcome at reduced rates, babysitting available. Sorry, no pets. Car essential — parking. Open all year for Evening Dinner/Meal, Bed and Breakfast or Bed and Breakfast. Varied menus with good home cooking including home made pastries, bread and preserves. Telephone or SAE for terms. Reductions for Senior Citizens out of season.

COLCHESTER. Mrs C.A. Somerville, Rosebank, Lower Street, Stratford St. Mary, Colchester, Essex CO7 6JS (01206 322259). Attractive 14th-century part Manor House, with river frontage and fishing rights, in peaceful village in the Dedham Vale, which is renowned for its period architecture and old inns. Our boathouse is reputed to have featured in Constable's paintings. Guests are accommodated in two double and two twin bedrooms, all with washbasins, some en suite including a family room; two bathrooms and three toilets. Diningroom. Central heating; woodburner on chilly nights. Rooms are comfortable and attractive with television and tea/coffee making facilities. Delightful chalet set in the grounds, double-bedded with bathroom en-suite. English Breakfast of your choice — good cooking. Tourist Board registered. Terms from £17 for Bed and Breakfast. Winter Breaks with Evening Meal available. Open all year except Christmas week.

EYE. Shelia Webster, Elm Lodge Farm, Chippenhall Green, Fressingfield, Eye IP21 5SL (01379 586249). ♛ ♛ *COMMENDED.* This 112 acre working farm with early Victorian farmhouse overlooks a large common (SSSI) where animals graze in summer — the perfect spot for an after-dinner stroll. Spacious bedrooms — one double en suite, one double, one twin and one single sharing guests' bathroom; separate dining and sitting rooms, log fires and excellent food ensure that a comfortable, relaxing holiday is enjoyed by all those we warmly welcome to this attractive and peaceful corner of Suffolk. Open March to November. Children 10 years and over and pets welcome. Bed and Breakfast from £16; Dinner by arrangement. Non-smokers preferred. AA QQQ, FHB Member.

EYE. Ms. Jenny Grover, Hall Farm, Yaxley, Eye IP23 8BY (01379 783423). Geoff and Jenny Grover extend a warm welcome to all their guests. The farmhouse is set in one acre of gardens along a private lane just off the A140. Two double bedrooms, one with verandah, colour TV and tea/coffee making facilities. Comfortable lounge. We farm 250 acres, mainly arable, 10 acres meadow. Two Jersey house cows and numerous chickens are kept. Guests are welcome to take a pleasant walk around the farm. Bury St. Edmunds, Norwich and Ipswich 20 miles; East Coast and Constable country 25 miles. Places of interest include Bressingham Steam Museum, Otter Trust, Kilverstone Wild Life Park, all within easy reach. RSPB member. Bed and Breakfast from £12.50.

FRAMLINGHAM. Mr and Mrs D. Strachan, Rendham Hall, Rendham, Saxmundham IP17 2AW (Tel & Fax: 01728 663440). Tourist Board Listed. A warm red brick Suffolk farmhouse with guests' rooms overlooking the dairy herd's grazing pasture and beyond over tranquil countryside. The bedrooms, one double en suite and one family, both with washbasins, are delightfully furnished and very peaceful. The guests' lounge and dining room have been carefully renovated and are traditionally furnished. Just two miles from the A12, it is an ideal setting for touring the Heritage coastline from Southwold to Aldeburgh; also convenient for Norfolk Broads. We offer comfort and warm hospitality, as well as excellent food. Non-smokers preferred. Bed and Breakfast from £17 to £24.

SUFFOLK

Bird watchers and nature lovers will find much of interest along the unspoiled stretch of Suffolk's Heritage Coast between Lowestoft and Southwold. The RSPB reserve at Minsmere offers an opportunity to see a large variety of breeding birds and waders, plus other wildlife. Other attractions include Aldeburgh, home of the music festival established by Benjamin Britten; Museum of East Anglian Life at Stowmarket; and the cathedral town of Bury St Edmunds.

FRAMLINGHAM. Brian and Phyllis Collett, Shimmens Pightle, Dennington Road, Framlingham, Woodbridge IP13 9JT (01728 724036). ETB Listed

COMMENDED. Shimmens Pightle is situated in an acre of landscaped garden, surrounded by farmland, within a mile of the centre of Framlingham, with its famous castle and church. Ideally situated for the Heritage Coast, Snape Maltings, local vineyards, riding, etc. Cycles can be hired locally. Many good eating places in the area. Double and twin-bedded rooms with washbasins, on ground floor. Comfortable lounge with TV overlooking garden; central heating and log fires in winter. Morning tea and evening drinks offered. Sorry, no pets or smoking indoors. Bed and traditional English Breakfast, using local cured bacon and home made preserves. Vegetarians also happily catered for. Open all year. SAE please. Self catering flats also available in Southwold.

FRAMLINGHAM. Mrs Jennie Mann, Fiddlers Hall, Cransford, Near Framlingham, Woodbridge IP13 9PQ (01728 663729). Working farm, join in. Signposted

on B1119, Fiddlers Hall is a 14th century, moated, oak-beamed farmhouse set in a beautiful and secluded position. It is two miles from Framlingham Castle, 20 minutes' drive from Aldeburgh, Snape Maltings, Woodbridge and Southwold. A Grade II Listed building, it has lots of history and character. The bedrooms are spacious; one has en-suite shower room, the other has a private bathroom. Use of lounge and colour TV. Plenty of parking space. Lots of farm animals kept. Traditional farmhouse cooking. Bed and Breakfast terms from £19. Tourist Board registered.

FRAMLINGHAM. Mrs Ann Proctor, Grove Farm, Laxfield, Framlingham, Woodbridge IP13 8EY (01986 798235). This is a Georgian farmhouse standing in

a 30 acre mixed farm with pigs and sheep, ponies and pedigree breeding dogs. Beautiful view of village and only 12 miles from the coast. Within easy reach of Norwich, Norfolk Broads, historic houses and quaint unspoilt villages. The accommodation is in two double and two family bedrooms (with washbasins); diningroom; lounge with colour television; bathroom, three toilets; full central heating. Children welcome, cot, high chair and babysitting. Sorry, no pets. Open March to November. The emphasis is on a friendly atmosphere with good home cooking — meat, vegetables, honey, etc., mainly produced on farm. Car essential, ample parking. Bed and Breakfast or Bed, Breakfast and Evening Meal; children under 12 years reduced rates. Please phone or send SAE for terms.

FRAMLINGHAM. Mrs C. Jones, Bantry, Chapel Road, Saxtead, Woodbridge IP13 9RB (01728 685578). ✿ ✿ ✿ Bantry is set in half an acre of gardens

overlooking open countryside in the picturesque village of Saxtead, which is close to the historic castle town of Framlingham. Best known for its working windmill beside the village green, Saxtead is a good central base from which to discover East Anglia. Accommodation is offered in self-contained apartments (one ground floor), each comprising its own private diningroom/TV lounge and bathroom for secluded comfort. Good home cooking from home grown produce. Terms: Bed and Breakfast from £18 per night. Non smoking.

FRAMLINGHAM. Mrs J.R. Graham, Woodlands Farm, Brundish, Near Woodbridge, Framlingham IP13 8BP (01379 384444). ✿ ✿ HIGHLY COMMENDED.

Woodlands Farm has a cottage-type farmhouse set in quiet Suffolk countryside. Near historic town of Framlingham with its castle and within easy reach of coast, wildlife parks, Otter Trust, Easton Farm Park and Snape Maltings for music lovers. Open all year. Twin room wih private shower, washbasin and WC; two double bedrooms with bathroom en-suite. Diningroom and sittingroom with inglenook fireplaces for guests' use. Good home cooked food assured. Full central heating. Car essential, good parking. Sorry, no pets. Bed and Breakfast from £16.50; Evening Meal £12 (six nights). SAE or telephone. FHB Member.

HITCHAM. Mrs Philippa McLardy, Hill Farmhouse, Bury Road, Hitcham IP7 7PT (01449 740651).

Hill Farmhouse has lovely views and is set in its own grounds of three acres. It is an ideal touring centre, close to Lavenham, Constable and Gainsborough country. The coast, Cambridge, Norwich, Ipswich and Colchester are within an hour's drive. Restaurant and three pubs serving food all within two miles. The "Which?" recommended accommodation is in the main farmhouse and adjoining oak timbered Tudor cottage. Twin and double suites all have private or en-suite bathrooms, colour TVs, tea/coffee making facilities. Pets by arrangement. Special diets catered for. Bed and Breakfast £17.50 (one to four nights), £15.50 (five or more nights); Dinner £11. Reductions for children. Tuesdays and Thursdays supper only (set menu) £6. Closed November to beginning of March.

HOLTON, Near Halesworth. Mrs Susan Hart, Gavelcroft, Holton, Near Halesworth IP19 8LY (01986 873117). Enjoy the relaxed atmosphere of Gavel-

croft, a Grade II Listed 16th century farmhouse, set in two and a half acres of garden and apple orchard. We offer comfortable, self-contained, en suite accommodation all year round. Dining room with separate tables, cosy sitting room with wood burner. Ample off street parking. Evening meal available. Bed and Breakfast from £18 per person. Gavelcroft is six miles from the unspoilt Suffolk Heritage coast, the nearest coastal town being Southwold. These unhurried, tranquil surroundings are typical of this agricultural community, and Gavelcroft is in an ideal position from which to explore the attractions that lie further inland or the picturesque coastal towns and villages.

SAXMUNDHAM. Mrs Margaret Gray, Park Farm, Sibton, Saxmundham IP17 2LZ (01728 668324; Fax: 01728 668564). ❀❀ *COMMENDED.* A friendly wel-

come, good food and comfortable accommodation await you at Park Farm. One double and one twin room for guests, each with washbasins, one twin with shower en suite. English breakfast and three course dinner are prepared from our own, or very local, produce and all tastes and special diets gladly catered for. Ideally situated for enjoying the unspoiled Suffolk countryside. Open all year except Christmas and New Year. Children and pets welcome. Bed and Breakfast from £15; Evening Meal from £11.50.

SOUTHWOLD. Mrs S. Jupp, Church Farmhouse, Uggeshall, Southwold NR34 8BD (01502 578532; Fax: 01953 888306). ETB Listed. This lovely 17th century

farmhouse has been sympathetically restored over the last few years and is set in an acre of garden and orchard on the edge of a very quiet hamlet. Near Southwold and within easy reach of Walberswick, Dunwich and Snape, this lovely home offers a very comfortable and peaceful base from which to visit this part of Suffolk. One double room, one twin-bedded room and one single, all with tea and coffee making facilities. The owner is a cook and is happy to prepare a delicious supper for you by arrangement.

STOKE-BY-NAYLAND. Ryegate House, Stoke-by-Nayland, Colchester CO6 4RA (01206 263679).

❀❀ *HIGHLY COMMENDED.* Situated on the B1068 within the Dedham Vale, in a quiet Suffolk village, Ryegate House is a modern property built in the style of a Suffolk farmhouse. It is only a few minutes' walk from the local shops, post office, pubs, restaurants and church and an ideal base for exploring Constable country. A warm welcome, good food and comfortable accommodation in a peaceful setting with easy access to local historic market towns, golf courses and the East Coast. Comfortable en suite bedrooms with colour TV, radio alarms, tea/coffee making facilities, shaver points and central heating. Children welcome. Parking for six cars. Open all year except Christmas. Bed and Breakfast from £23 to £26 per night single, £34 to £39 double.

STOWMARKET. Mrs Mary Noy, Red House Farm, Station Road, Haughley, Stowmarket IP14 3QP (01449 673323). 🐦🐦 *COMMENDED.* **Working farm.**

Attractive farmhouse situated in the peaceful surroundings of mid Suffolk. Warm welcome and homely atmosphere. One and a half miles from A14 which makes it an ideal base for exploring Suffolk, Norfolk, Cambridge, Constable Country and the coast. Central heating. Guests' lounge with TV and dining room. Tea/coffee making facilities in bedrooms. One twin, one double and one single, all en suite, from £17.50. Good local pubs and restaurants. Children over eight years old welcome. No pets or smoking. Open January to November.

TUNSTALL. Mrs J. Pegrum, The Old Rectory, Tunstall, Woodbridge IP12 2JP (01728 688534).

Relax at our home set in two and a half acres of wooded grounds in Area of Outstanding Natural Beauty. Explore Heritage Coast and nearby towns of Woodbridge, Orford, Framlingham and Aldeburgh with delightful ancient houses and shops, castles, quays, etc. Only three miles from Snape Maltings Concert Hall. Many leisure activities can be enjoyed within immediate area — birdwatching at Minsmere and Havergate Island, river trips, swimming, golf, walking on nearby heaths and forests. Washbasins in all bedrooms. Lounge with colour TV. Non-smoking. Bed and Breakfast from £17 including early morning tea and bedtime drink. Evening Meal (tasty vegetarian) £8. Weekly terms available.

YOXFORD. Mrs S. Bloomfield, Priory Farm, Darsham, Near Saxmundham IP17 3QD (01728 668459). Comfortable 17th century farmhouse situated in peaceful Suffolk countryside and an ideal base from which to explore the coast and heathlands and numerous other local attractions. Excellent local pubs and restaurants nearby. Cycle hire is available from the farm. One double and one twin bedrooms, each with private bathroom. Tea/coffee making facilities. Separate guests' dining and sitting rooms. Sorry, regret no pets or smokers. Prices from £18.50 per person per night.

SURREY

LINGFIELD. Mrs Vivienne Bundy, Oaklands, Felcourt Road, Lingfield RH7 6NF (01342 834705).

Oaklands is a spacious country house of considerable charm dating from the 17th century. It is set in its own grounds of one acre and is about one mile from the small town of Lingfield and three miles from East Grinstead, both with rail connections to London. It is convenient to Gatwick Airport and is ideal as a "stop-over" or as a base to visit many places of interest in south east England. Dover and the Channel Ports are two hours' drive away whilst the major towns of London and Brighton are about one hour distant. One family room en-suite, one double and one single bedrooms with washbasins; three bathrooms, two toilets; sittingroom, diningroom. Cot, high chair, babysitting and reduced rates for children. Gas central heating. Open all year. Parking. Bed and Breakfast from £17. Evening Meal by arrangement.

LINGFIELD. Mrs Vanessa Manwill, Stantons Hall Farm, Eastbourne Road, Blindley Heath, Lingfield RG7 6LG (01342 832401).

Stantons Hall Farm is an 18th century farmhouse set amidst 18 acres of farmland and adjacent to Blindley Heath Common. Family, double and single rooms, most with toilet, shower and washbasin en suite. Separate bathroom. All rooms have colour TV, tea/coffee facilities and are centrally heated. There are plenty of parking spaces. We are conveniently situated within easy reach of M25 (London Orbital), Gatwick Airport (car parking facilities for travellers) and Lingfield Park Racecourse. Enjoy a traditional English Breakfast in our large farmhouse kitchen. Bed and Breakfast from £18 per person, reductions for children sharing. Cot and high chair available. Well behaved dogs welcome by prior arrangement.

SUSSEX

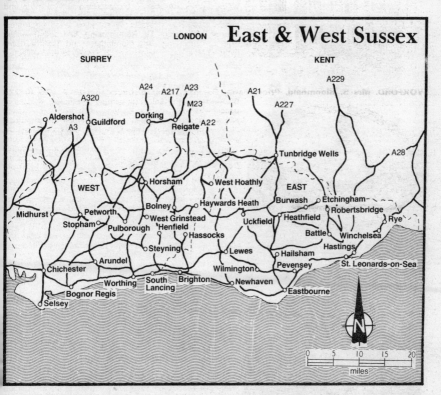

East & West Sussex

EAST SUSSEX

BATTLE. Brian and Sue Leadbetter, Ostlers Cottage Farm, The Stream, Catsfield, Battle TN33 9BB (01424 892406). We offer you a warm welcome to our homely farm, situated in the picturesque village of Catsfield, on the B2204, in the heart of 1066 country. An ideal base for walking, fishing and exploring the many local historic sites and seaside resorts, or simply enjoy feeding our many farm animals. Bed and Breakfast is offered between March and October. There are two bedrooms, one with twin beds, the other has bunks; a high chair is available. Wholesome food, TV lounge, tea/coffee making facilities and off road parking. £14 per person, children under 12 years half price.

BRAKES COPPICE FARM

Telham Lane, Battle, E. Sussex TN33 0SJ

Tel & Fax: 01424 830347

Brakes Coppice Farmhouse is set in the midst of 70 acres of pasture and woodland with panoramic views to the sea five miles away. The house is modernised to a high standard and all bedrooms have en suite bath or shower rooms. A warm welcome and a hearty breakfast are provided by Michael and Fay Ramsden. The large towns of Hastings and Eastbourne are nearby and the surrounding area is famous as '1066 Country' with the Battle of Hastings actually having been fought within a mile of the farm. One double, one twin and one single bedrooms, all en suite with colour TV and tea/coffee making facilities; separate guests' lounge and dining room. No smoking or pets. Bed and Breakfast from £30 single; from £45 double.

RAC Highly Acclaimed   *Proprietors: Michael & Fay Ramsden*   AA **QQQQQ**.

BRIGHTON. Amblecliff Hotel, 35 Upper Rock Gardens, Brighton BN2 1QF (01273 681161; Fax: 01273 676945). 🐛🐛🐛 A NON-SMOKING HOTEL. AA QQQQ Selected, RAC Highly Acclaimed. This stylish hotel, highly recommended as the place to stay when in Brighton by a national newspaper and two television programmes, has been awarded the AA's coveted Select QQQQ, only given to two or three hotels in Brighton and also holds the RAC's Highly Acclaimed endorsement for quality and customer satisfaction. Excellent location, close to the seafront, with historic Brighton, the Conference Centre, Royal Pavilion and the Marina only a short stroll away. All double, twin and family rooms are en suite. Individually designed rooms with four poster and king size beds. Best in its price range, we believe you deserve an excellent service, comfortable accommodation and value for money. Bed and Breakfast from £19 to £28. Special offer — seven nights for the price of six!

BURWASH. Mrs E. Sirrell, Woodlands Farm, Burwash, Etchingham TN19 7LA (01435 882794). Working farm, join in. Woodlands Farm stands one third of a mile off the road surrounded by fields and woods. This peaceful and beautifully modernised 16th century farmhouse offers comfortable and friendly accommodation. Sitting/dining room; two bathrooms, one en suite, double or twin bedded rooms (one has four poster bed) together with excellent farm fresh food. This is a farm of 55 acres with mixed animals, and is situated within easy reach of 20 or more places of interest to visit and half an hour from the coast. Open Easter to December. Central heating. Literature provided to help guests. Children welcome. Dogs allowed if sleeping in owner's car. Parking. Evening Meal optional. Bed and Breakfast from £17. AA QQ. Telephone or SAE, please.

HASTINGS. Mr and Mrs S. York, Westwood Farm, Stonestile Lane, Hastings TN35 4PG (01424 751038). Working farm. Farm with pet sheep, chickens, etc. Quiet rural location off country lane half a mile from B2093 approximately two miles from seafront and town centre. Golf course nearby. Central position for visiting places of interest to suit all ages. Elevated situation with outstanding views over Brede Valley. All bedrooms have washbasins, tea making facilities and TV; some en suite and two bedrooms on ground floor. Full English breakfast. Off-road parking. Bed and Breakfast from £15 to £25 per person for two persons sharing. Reduced rates for weekly booking. Also available six-berth self catering caravan — details on request.

HERSTMONCEUX. Mr and Mrs R.E. Gentry, The Stud Farm, Bodle Street Green, Near Hailsham

BN27 4RJ (Tel & Fax: 01323 833201). ❦❦ COMMENDED. Working farm. The Stud Farm keeps mainly cattle and sheep. It is peacefully situated between A271 and B2096 amidst beautiful undulating countryside. Ideal for walking and touring lovely East Sussex, being within easy reach of Eastbourne (12 miles), Bexhill (10 miles) and Hastings (15 miles). There are many places of historic interest in the vicinity and the coast is only eight miles away at Pevensey. Upstairs there is a family unit (only let to one set of guests — either two, three or four persons — at a time), consisting of one twin-bedded room and one double-bedded room, both with TVs, handbasins and shaver points and their own bathroom with toilet. There is also downstairs one twin-bedded room with TV, shower, handbasin, tea/coffee making facilities and toilet en-suite. Guests have their own sitting-room with TV and diningroom and sunroom. Sorry, no pets. Open all year. Central heating in winter. Car essential — parking available. Bed and Breakfast from £17; Evening Meals from £8.50 by arrangement. SAE, please. AA Recommended QQ.

POLEGATE. Mrs B. Drake, The Braes, 3 Filching Close, Wannock, Polegate BN26 5NU (01323 487181). Welcome to a relaxing holiday at The Braes, situated in a valley in the Sussex Downs where one can ramble for miles. Five miles from the seaside town of Eastbourne, plenty of interest within the area; Rudyard Kipling's home, Hertmonceaux Castle and Science Museum, Michelham Priory etc. Two double and one single bedrooms; two bathrooms; lounge, dining room; kitchen where drinks can be made or sandwiches prepared. Garden and hard standing for cars. No smoking. No pets. Adults only. Terms from £15 per night. Discount for three nights or more. Open Easter to September 30th.

RYE. Mrs Heather Coote, "Busti", Barnetts Hill, Peasmarsh, Rye TN31 6YJ (01797 230408).

Comfortable and clean accommodation in detached house on the edge of the rural village of Peasmarsh. Ideally located for touring both East Sussex and Kent and for visiting Bodiam Castle, the historic town of Rye, Great Dixter, Sissinghurst, Battle Abbey and many other seasonal attractions; lake fishing locally. Guest lounge/dining room with TV. Guests' shower/toilet. Bedrooms have tea/coffee making facilities. Central heating throughout. Hairdryer available. Friendy service and tourist advice provided. Full English breakfast or alternative. Ample off road parking. Bed and Breakfast from £15. No smoking in the house. Member of Rye and District Hotels and Caterers Association.

RYE. Pat and Jeff Sullivin, Cliff Farm, Iden Lock, Rye TN31 7QE (Tel & Fax: 01797 280331 long

ring please). Working farm. Our farmhouse is peacefully set in a quiet elevated position with extensive views over Romney Marsh. The ancient seaport town of Rye with its narrow cobbled street is two miles away. We are an ideal touring base although the town and immediate district have much to offer — golden beaches, quaint villages, castles, gardens etc. Comfortable guest bedrooms with washbasins and tea/coffee making facilities; two toilets; own shower; diningroom and sittingroom. Home produce. Open March to October for Bed and Breakfast from £14.50 to £15. Reduced weekly rates. AA and RAC Recommended.

RYE near. John and Jean Masters, Little Monkings, Rocks Hill, Northiam, Near Rye TN31 6FJ (01424 883027). John and Jean would like to welcome you for a peaceful stay in an idyllic setting with lovely views. Little Monkings is a small farm in rural Sussex close to Rye, Battle and Hastings, ideal for touring. The Bed and Breakfast accommodation comprises one double bedroom with washbasin, one twin and one single bedrooms, all have TV; guests bathroom. Terms £18 per person per night. Please write or telephone for further details and bookings.

EAST SUSSEX – 1066 AND ALL THAT!

The story of the famous battle can be traced from Pevensey, where William the Conqueror first landed; to Hastings, where the Norman and Saxon armies met and King Harold was slain; to Battle, where the victorious William founded an abbey. Visit too the Cinque Port of Rye (now a hilltop town), Michelham Priory and the magnificent moated Bodiam Castle.

RYE. Rita Cox, Four Seasons, 96 Udimore Road, Rye TN31 7DY (01797 224305). Four Seasons is

situated on Cadborough Cliff with spectacular views across the south-facing garden to the Brede Valley, Rye and the sea. We offer excellent B&B in our attractive house which is decorated to reflect the changing seasons. Centrally heated rooms are en suite or have private facilities and have TV and hot drinks tray. Breakfasts are full English or vegetarian with home made preserves and local produce. Four Seasons is a short walk from the town centre, has private parking, is an excellent centre for touring East Sussex and Kent, and is convenient for the Channel Ports and Tunnel. Rates are £15 to £18 per person with special winter bargain breaks mid-November to February. Brochure on request.

CADBOROUGH FARM

Udimore Road, Rye, East Sussex TN31 6AA
Tel: 01797 225426 Fax: 01797 224097
Jane Apperly

A lovely country house set in 24 acres with outstanding views towards the sea overlooking Camber Castle and the medieval towns of Rye and Winchelsea. Spacious sunny bedrooms with ensuite facilities and sea views. Self contained suite with inner hall, bedroom, sitting room and bathroom. Colour TV's, radio/alarms, hairdryers and hot drinks tray. Drawing room with log fire. Superb English, continental and vegetarian breakfast. Ample parking. Short walk from town centre. B&B £20-£25 pppn.

RYE near. Joy and James Ramus, Barons Grange, Readers Lane, Iden, Near Rye TN31 7UU (01797 280478). A charming Georgian farmhouse combining

elegance with home comforts, just two and a half miles from the beautiful medieval town of Rye. Set in an acre of lovely gardens with hard tennis court and swimming pool. The bedrooms are all en suite with colour TV and tea/coffee making facilities. Full English breakfast with home made preserves is served in the attractive dining room or sun lounge. The farm is about 400 acres with sheep, orchards and corn and is an ideal base for visiting the many castles, gardens and other places of interest. No children under seven years. Minimum stay two nights. Reduced rate for three or more nights. Prices from £17.50 to £25 per person. Brochure available.

RYE near. David and Eliane Griffin, Kimblee, Main Street, Peasmarsh, Near Rye TN31 6UL (01797 230514 or 0831 841004 mobile). ♥ ♥ *COMMENDED.* Friendly country house. Views from all aspects. Rye five minutes' drive, beaches 15 minutes. Ample off road parking. Ideal base for visiting Kent and Sussex. Two large rooms with shower, toilet, washbasin en suite. Smaller room with en suite bathroom. Single room possible. All rooms have colour TV, radio alarm, tea/coffee facilities, hair dryers. Locally renowned pub/restaurant 250 metres. Generous English breakfast, vegetarian on request. Reduction for substantial Continental breakfast. French spoken. On A268 three miles from Rye in the direction of London. £18 to £19 per person. Reductions for three nights or more. Mid-week breaks March to May — three nights for the price of two. Brochure on request.

WEST SUSSEX

BOGNOR REGIS. Deborah S. Collinson, The Old Priory, 80 North Bersted Street, Bognor Regis PO22 9AQ (01243 863580; Fax: 01243 826597). A charming 17th century Priory restored to its former glory with a blend of historic charm. Situated in a picturesque rural village close to Bognor Regis, Chichester, Arundel, Goodwood, Fontwell and within easy access of Portsmouth, Brighton, Continental ferry port and all major commuting routes. Facilities include superb en suite rooms equipped to 4 star standard, four-poster water bed with jacuzzi bath, secluded outdoor swimming pool, Cordon Bleu cuisine, residential licence. Open all year. Tariff from £20.

BOGNOR REGIS. Mrs M. Hashfield, Taplow Cottage, 81 Nyewood Lane, Bognor Regis PO21 2UE (01243 821398). The Cottage lies in a residential part, west of the town centre, 600 yards from the sea and shops. Proximity to many beaches and contrasting towns and countryside make for an ideal touring centre. Chichester, Goodwood Racecourse, Arundel Castle, Brighton, Portsmouth and Southsea are but a few of the places of interest within easy reach. Accommodation comprises one double, one twin-bedded and one family bedroom, all with vanity units, tea/coffee making facilities and colour TV. Lounge, diningroom. The cottage is well appointed and the area is served by public transport. Parking space available. Bed and Breakfast from £14. Dogs by prior arrangement. SAE, please.

"TAPLOW COTTAGE"

BOGNOR REGIS. Mr and Mrs G. Soothill, Black Mill House Hotel, Princess Avenue, Bognor Regis PO21 2QU (01243 821945). ⚜⚜⚜ *COMMENDED.* Family-run hotel in Aldwick, the quieter west side of Bognor Regis, only 300 yards from the sea and Marine Park Gardens. The hotel faces south and has all the characteristics of a large private house, surrounded by enclosed gardens. 27 bedrooms, 21 with either private bath or shower and toilet, all with colour TV, telephone and tea/coffee making facilities. Lift; restaurant; attractive bar and two other lounges (one non-smoking), also large games room with table tennis, darts and small snooker table. Bed and Breakfast, Dinner, Bed and Breakfast and Full Board terms on request. Picnic lunches and afternoon teas available and special diets catered for. Children welcome and accommodated FREE if sharing with two adults. Listening service; washing and drying facilities; cots and high chairs available. Two to six night breaks all year; special four-night Christmas Holiday. Dogs welcome. Own car park with level access. An excellent centre for touring the South.

CHICHESTER. Mrs Julie Newman and Mrs Jane Ashby, Abelands House, Merston, Chichester PO20 6DY (01243 532675). Abelands House, a former Victorian rectory, is set in two acres with views towards South Downs and open farmland. Conveniently situated some three miles from Chichester, within easy reach of local unspoilt beaches and Goodwood. Light, spacious, centrally heated family, double and twin rooms with en suite or private bathroom. Tea/coffee making facilities, colour TV. Children welcome, cot and high chair available. Evening meals. Offering a friendly and relaxed atmosphere. For the romantic — a four-poster bed. Strictly no smoking. Member of ETB. Brochure on request.

Terms quoted in this publication may be subject to increase if rises in costs necessitate

GATWICK. Waterhall Country House, Prestwood Lane, Ifield Wood, Near Crawley RH11 0LA (01293 520002). ♛♛ *COMMENDED*. RAC Acclaimed.

Surrounded by open countryside and yet only five minutes from Gatwick Airport, Waterhall Country House is an ideal place for an overnight stay. The house is attractively decorated and furnished, and we offer a warm and friendly welcome to all our guests. We have a variety of rooms, all with en suite bath or shower, remote-control colour TV and tea-making facilities. There is an attractive guests' lounge, and breakfast is served in the luxury dining room. Children are welcome. Holiday parking is available. Double/twin £40.00, single £25.00, family £50.00. Prices include full English or Continental breakfast.

HENFIELD. Mrs J. Forbes, Little Oreham Farm, off Horne Lane, Near Woodsmill, Henfield BN5 9SB (01273 492931). Delightful old Sussex farmhouse situated in rural position down lane, adjacent to footpaths and nature reserve. One mile from Henfield village, eight miles from Brighton, convenient for Gatwick and Hickstead. Excellent base for visiting many gardens and places of interest in the area. The farmhouse is a listed building of great character; oak-beamed sittingroom with inglenook fireplace (log fires), and a pretty diningroom. Three comfortable attractive bedrooms with en-suite shower/bath; WC; colour TV; tea-making facilities. Central heating throughout. Lovely garden with views of the Downs. Situated off Horne Lane, one minute from Woodsmill Countryside Centre. Winner of Kellogg's award: "Best Bed and Breakfast" in the South East. You will enjoy a friendly welcome and pleasant holiday. Sorry, no children under 10. Bed and Breakfast from £17.50 per person. Evening Meals by arrangement. No smoking. Open all year.

HENFIELD. Mrs M. Wilkin, Great Wapses Farm, Henfield BN5 9BJ (01273 492544). Working farm.
The Tudor/Georgian farmhouse is set in rural surroundings, ten miles north of Brighton, off the B2116 Albourne/Henfield road. Hickstead is nearby. There are horses etc. The three comfortable rooms (one with four-poster bed) all have their own bathroom, shower en-suite, TV and tea/coffee making facilities. Children and well behaved dogs are welcome. Hard tennis court. Open all year round for Bed and Breakfast from £18 per person. Snacks usually available by arrangement. There is also an attractive self-contained comfortable cottage, sleeps two/three. Let on weekly basis £110 including electricity, TV etc.

HORSHAM. Mrs Carol Liverton, Goffsland Farm, Shipley, Horsham RH13 7BQ (Tel & Fax: 01403 730434). ♛♛ *COMMENDED*. Listed 17th century farmhouse on a 260 acre working farm with sheep, cattle and dairy herd. Situated in the Sussex Weald central to Gatwick and the South Coast. Family room has double bed and bunk beds with washbasin and tea/coffee making facilities. Own bathroom with WC, own sitting room with TV. Open all year. Children and pets welcome. Bed and Breakfast from £15.

WEST SUSSEX – COASTAL RESORTS AND DOWNS!
Although dominated perhaps by Chichester and Bognor Regis, West Sussex does have much to offer. Places like Arundel, Marden-Stoughton Forest, Midhurst, and its historic inn, the open-air museum at Singleton and the National Butterfly Museum at Bramber are worth a visit.

LITTLEHAMPTON. Mrs Mo Skelton, Bracken Lodge Guest House, 43 Church Street, Littlehampton

BN17 5PU (01903 723174). ♣ ♣ ♣ *HIGHLY COMMEN-DED.* Disabled Category II Accessibility. Friendly atmosphere, first class service. Comfortable, character, detached non-smoking house near town centre, indoor swimming centre, sand dunes, promenade, amusements, golf course and River Arun. All bedrooms en suite, colour TV, drink making facilities, trouser press, iron and board, hair dryer, clock/alarm radio. Ideal touring base. Explore coast and countryside steeped in history. Private parking. Purpose built ground floor twin disabled suite. Spacious comprehensive facilities ensuring accessibility and quality. Leads onto private patio overlooking garden. Open all year. Bed and Breakfast from £23 per person per night. Short Breaks available. Staying for business or pleasure, a warm welcome all year.

PETWORTH. Mr and Mrs Nick Moss, River Park Farm, Lodsworth, Petworth GU28 9DS (01798

861362). Working farm. Situated at the end of a mile long private drive the farm is a perfect spot for nature lovers and walkers. In our 17th century farmhouse we offer full English Breakfast and optional light evening meals using home made produce. The farm comprises 340 acres of corn and grassland which guests are encouraged to walk. Behind the house is a four and a half acre lake attracting an abundance of wildlife. Coarse fishing is available. Most bedrooms have washbasins, all have electric blankets and tea/coffee making facilities. Our Channel Island house cow provides milk and cream for us. Bed and Breakfast from £18.

STEYNING. Mrs A. Shapland, Wappingthorn Farm, Horsham Road, Steyning BN44 3AA (01903

813236). Working farm. Delightful traditional farmhouse with oak-beamed lounge, open log fire and pretty dining room. Situated in rural position viewing "South Downs", four miles from seaside, seven miles Worthing, 12 miles Brighton, Gatwick and Hickstead convenient. Comfortable attractive, spacious bedrooms with en suite shower/bath, WC, colour TV and tea/coffee making facilities. Lovely garden with heated swimming pool. Many footpaths surround the farm and old market town. Bed and Breakfast from £15. Evening meal and picnic baskets available. Children welcome, babysitting possible. There is also a converted barn with two self contained cottages, fully equipped, sleeping two/four from £110 per week. Short Breaks available. Open all year.

WARWICKSHIRE

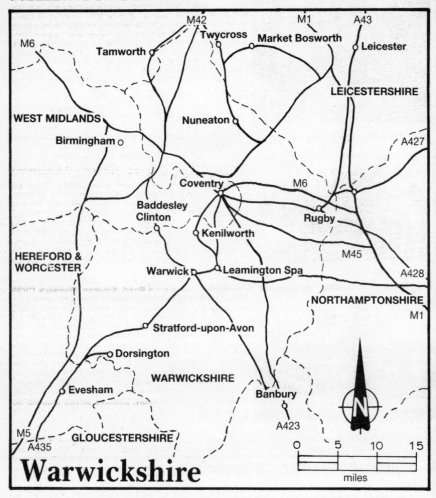

Warwickshire

BRAILES. Mrs M. Cripps, Agdon Farm, Brailes, Banbury OX15 5JJ (Tel & Fax: 01608 685226).

Working farm. A warm welcome awaits all our guests. Our comfortable Cotswold stone farmhouse is set in 500 acres of mixed farming, in an unspoilt part of the countryside. Two miles from B4035, five miles from A422. Within walking distance of Compton Wynyates, in close driving range of the Cotswolds, Warwick, 10 miles Stratford-upon-Avon and Banbury Cross. Many local village pubs. Accommodation with TV room, separate diningroom, guests' bathroom, pleasant bedrooms with tea/coffee facilities. Central heating. Evening Meals available.

COVENTRY. Mrs Barbara Chamberlain, Mill Farmhouse Country Residence, Mill Lane, Fillongley, Near Coventry CV7 8EE (01676 541898). ✿✿✿

Experience the peace and tranquillity of our beautiful country home offering exceptional standards of comfort in idyllic surroundings. All rooms are centrally heated, immaculately furnished with comfortable new beds and hostess tray. Ample private car parking and gardens. No smoking. Tariff: Luxury double/twin en suite room with colour TV, etc £40 to £45; single occupancy £25 including full English breakfast. 15 minutes NEC/Coventry, 30 minutes Birmingham, Stratford, convenient for the Forest of Arden and Belfry Golf Courses. Special rates for lodgings — single and twin rooms.

COVENTRY near. Mrs Sandra Evans, Camp Farm, Hob Lane, Balsall Common, Near Coventry CV7 7GX (01676 533804). Camp Farm is a farmhouse 150 to

200 years old. It is modernised but still retains its old world character. Nestling in the heart of England in Shakespeare country, within easy reach of Stratford-upon-Avon, Warwick, Kenilworth, Coventry with its famous Cathedral, and the National Exhibition Centre, Camp Farm offers a warm, homely atmosphere and good English food, service and comfortable beds. The house is carpeted throughout. Dining-room and sun lounge with colour TV. Bedrooms — five double, three family rooms and five single, all with wash-basins. Part of the house is suitable for disabled guests. Children welcome. Cot and high chair, babysitting on request. Fire Certificate granted 1974. All terms quoted by letter or telephone.

KINETON. Mrs C. Howard, Willowbrook Farm House, Lighthorne Road, Kineton, Warwick CV35 0JL (01926 640475; Fax: 01926 641747). ✿✿ Very

comfortable and interesting house and small farm in rolling countryside, half a mile from Kineton Village, handy for Warwick, Stratford, the Cotswolds, the NEC and NAC. En suite facilities available; all rooms with washbasins, tea trays, colour TV and beautiful views. Guests' own large sittingroom and dining room with antiques and interesting collections. The house is surrounded by gardens and paddocks with terrace and pond. Old breeds of free-ranging poultry supply your breakfast eggs. There is central heating, and winter log fires. Plenty of local eating places. Bed and Breakfast from £16. Friendly, attentive service assured. No smoking in the house. We are three miles from Junction 12, M40.

LEAMINGTON SPA. Mrs R. Gibbs, Hill Farm, Lewis Road, Radford Semele, Leamington Spa CV31 1UX (01926 337571). ✿✿ *COMMENDED.* **Working farm.** Guests are welcome all year at this friendly, comfort-

able farmhouse on 350 acre mixed farm, ideally situated for Warwick, Stratford-upon-Avon, Leamington, Coventry, Royal Showground, Birmingham and N.E.C. and the Cotswolds. Children welcome; reductions for under 12's. Cot and high chair. Large garden. Babysitting. Central heating. Log fires in chilly weather. Four double bedrooms and two twin rooms, some with en suite facilities, all with colour TV. Guests' sitting room, colour TV and dining room. Car preferable; ample parking. Supper drinks available. Spacious five van site available. AA Recommended. Farm Holiday Bureau member. FHG Diploma. Bed and Breakfast from approximately £16 to £20.

WARWICKSHIRE – SHAKESPEARE'S COUNTY

Stratford-upon-Avon is the county's, and indeed one of the country's biggest attractions. Make time however to explore Northern Warwickshire and George Eliot Country around Nuneaton and "England's Historic Heartland" – the three very individual towns of Warwick, Royal Leamington Spa and Kenilworth, together with their surrounding villages.

LEAMINGTON SPA. Miss Deborah Lea, Crandon House, Avon Dassett, Leamington Spa CV33 0AA (Tel & Fax: 01295 770652). ✤✤ *HIGHLY COMMENDED.* **Working farm.** Guests receive a specially warm welcome at our comfortable farmhouse offering an exceptionally high standard of accommodation. Set in 20 acres, with beautiful views over unspoilt countryside, this small working farm has rare breeds of cattle, sheep and poultry. Three attractive bedrooms with private facilities, tea/coffee making equipment and colour TV. Guests' dining room and sitting rooms, one with colour TV. Full central heating and log fire in chilly weather. Electric blankets available. Car essential. Ample parking. Pets by arrangement. Peaceful and quiet yet offers easy access for touring the Heart of England, Warwick, Stratford-upon-Avon, the Cotswolds. Open all year. Bed and Breakfast from £18.50. Winter Breaks. Farm Holiday Bureau member. Write or ring for further details.

Warwickshire Farm Holidays

Warwickshire farming families welcome guests into their homes to enjoy the comforts of a traditional English farmhouse and discover the peace of the English countryside. Each home listed has it own unique character and differs in size, style, and price, but all offer a high standard of accommodation, good food, a warm welcome and excellent value for money to holidaymakers and business travellers. All owners are members of the Farm Holiday Bureau, all properties are inspected, classified and graded by the English Tourist Board. Warwickshire, in the heart of England, provides the perfect setting for the perfect holiday. Mile upon mile of rolling countryside, picturesque villages and meandering waterways. There are castles, stately homes, theatres, country gardens and some of the prettiest villages to be found.

FARM HOLIDAY BUREAU

Places to visit within easy reach include Stratford-upon-Avon, Warwick, Royal Leamington Spa, The Cotswolds, Oxford, Coventry. National Exhibition Centre and National Agricultural Centre.

For further details about Bed & Breakfast or Self-catering cottages, please write, telephone or fax for a free brochure to: Warwickshire Farm Holidays (FHG), Crandon House, Avon Dassett, Leamington Spa CV33 0AA. Tel/Fax: 01295 770652.

LONG COMPTON. Mrs J.R. Haines, Ascott House Farm, Ascott, Whichford, Near Long Compton, Shipston-on-Stour CV36 5PP (Tel & Fax: 01608 684655). ✤✤ **Working farm.** Cotswold stone farmhouse with peaceful surroundings in designated area of natural beauty on edge of the Cotswolds. 500 acre arable/sheep farm, lovely views, attractive garden, outdoor swimming pool, snooker room and interesting walks. Ascott House Farm is ideal for relaxing, as well as being very well situated for exploring Cotswolds, Oxford, Stratford-upon-Avon and Warwick. One mile north of Long Compton on A3400. M40 Banbury 10 miles. One double room en-suite, one family room en-suite and one twin room with vanity unit; all rooms have TV, tea/coffee making facilities, central heating; TV lounge; traditional diningroom. Riding two miles, golf three miles with reduced green fees for guests. Children welcome, dogs by arrangement.Bed and Breakfast from £16 per person. Closed Christmas.

RUGBY. Don and Susan Moses, Lawford Hill Farm, Lawford Heath Lane, Rugby CV23 9HG (01788 542001). ✤ *COMMENDED.* A warm welcome awaits you at our Georgian farmhouse set in a large picturesque garden on our family farm. Attractive bedrooms with tea/coffee making facilities. Fully centrally heated. Guests' own lounge with colour TV. Conveniently situated two miles from Rugby and for visiting Cotswolds, Stratford, Warwick, Royal Showground and National Exhibition Centre. Open all year except Christmas and New Year. No smoking. Bed and Breakfast from £18. FHB Member. Please write or ring us if you require more details.

Cadeby Steam and Brass Rubbing Centre, Warwickshire offers free train ride for two, and two cream teas or similar when using our READERS' OFFER VOUCHER.

SHIPSTON-ON-STOUR. Mrs Fox, Kirby Farm, Whatcote, Shipston-on-Stour CV36 5EQ (01295 680525).

Kirby Farm is situated in beautiful countryside within easy reach of Cotswolds, Stratford-upon-Avon, Banbury, Warwick Castle and many other places of interest. Our spacious, stone built farmhouse is set in 450 arable acres and a long driveway gives it an "off the beaten track" feel. Visitors will receive a warm welcome. Bedrooms have tea/coffee making facilities and en suite accommodation is available. Breakfast is served in separate dining room and guests have access to their own drawing room with TV and log fire on cold evenings. Bed and Breakfast from £11.

STRATFORD-UPON-AVON. Mrs M. Turney, Cadle Pool Farm, The Ridgway, Stratford-upon-Avon CV37 9RE (01789 292494). ☎ ☎ ☎ Working farm.

Situated in picturesque grounds, this charming oak-panelled and beamed family house is part of a 450-acre mixed farm. It is conveniently situated two miles from Stratford-upon-Avon town, between Anne Hathaway's Cottage and Mary Arden's House, also only eight minutes from The Royal Shakespeare Theatre. Ideal touring centre for Warwick, Kenilworth, Oxford, the Cotswolds and Malvern Hills. Accommodation comprises family, double and twin bedrooms, one en suite and one with private bathroom, all with central heating and tea/coffee making facilities. There is an antique oak dining room, and lounge with colour TV. The gardens and ornamental pool are particularly attractive, with peacocks and ducks roaming freely. Children over 10 years welcome at reduced rates. Sorry, no pets. Non-smoking accommodation available. Bed and Breakfast from £20 to £25 per person. Open all year.

STRATFORD-UPON-AVON. John and Julia Downie, Holly Tree Cottage, Birmingham Road, Pathlow, Stratford-upon-Avon CV37 0ES (Tel & Fax: 01789 204461).

Period cottage dating back to 17th century with beams, antiques, tasteful furnishings and friendly atmosphere. Gardens with views over the countryside. Situated three miles north of Stratford towards Henley-in-Arden on A3400 (was A34), convenient for overnight stops or longer stays, and ideal for theatre visits. Excellent base for touring Shakespeare country, Heart of England, Cotswolds, Warwick Castle and Blenheim Palace. Well situated for National Exhibition Centre. Double, twin and family accommodation with en suite and private facilities; colour TV and tea/coffee in all rooms. Full English Breakfast. Restaurant and pub meals nearby. Bed and Breakfast from £19; reductions for children sharing. Telephone for information.

STRATFORD-UPON-AVON. Prim and John Finnemore, Walcote Farm, Walcote, Haselor, Alcester B49 6LY (Tel & Fax: 01789 488264). 👒👒 *COMMEN-DED.* En suite comfortable accommodation in one double and one twin room, both with lovely views. Our easy to find, attractive, 16th century oak-beamed farmhouse which has many antiques, is situated one and a quarter miles from the A46, in a tranquil picturesque hamlet near Stratford-upon-Avon. Full central heating with log fires in winter. Ideal area for walking and a base for Shakespeare's birthplace and theatre, Warwick Castle, The Cotswolds, NEC and National Trust properties. Open all year. Bed and Breakfast £18 to £19. No smoking in the house.

STRATFORD-UPON-AVON. Mrs R.M. Meadows, Monk's Barn Farm, Shipston Road, Stratford-upon-Avon CV37 8NA (01789 293714). Working farm. One and a half miles south of Stratford-upon-Avon on the A3400 (formerly A34) is Monk's Barn, a 75 acre mixed farm welcoming visitors all year. Monk's Barn dates back to the 16th century and succeeds in combining real traditional character with first class amenities. One double room with washbasin, three twin/double rooms with en suite facilities (two on ground floor suitable for some disabled guests) and one single room. Visitors' lounge. Beautiful riverside walk to village. Bed and Breakfast from £15. Tea/coffee facilities and colour TV in rooms. Sorry, no pets. Non-smokers preferred. AA QQ. Details on request.

STRATFORD-UPON-AVON. Judith Spencer, The Poplars, Mansell Farm, Newbold on Stour, Stratford-upon-Avon CV37 8BZ (01789 450540). Tourist Board Listed *COMMENDED.* A warm welcome awaits you on our working dairy farm. Enjoy the views of the Cotswolds from our modern farmhouse which is in easy reach of Stratford, Warwick, Oxford and NEC. One family and one twin bedrooms, both en suite with TV; one single room with washbasin. All have tea trays and central heating. Good food, or walk to local hostelry. Children and pets welcome. Open all year except Christmas and New Year. Bed and Breakfast from £16 to £17.50. Brochure available on request.

STRATFORD-UPON-AVON. Mrs Marion J. Walters, Church Farm, Dorsington, Stratford-upon-Avon CV37 8AX (01789 720471; Fax: 01789 720830; Mobile: 0831 504194). 👒👒 *COMMENDED.* **Working farm.** A warm and friendly welcome awaits you all year at our 127-acre mixed farm with woodlands and stream which you may explore. Our Georgian Farmhouse is situated on the edge of an extremely pretty village. Stratford-upon-Avon, Warwick, NEC, Royal Showground, Cotswolds, Evesham and Worcester all within easy driving distance. Family, twin and double bedrooms, all with tea/coffee facilities; most en suite with TVs, some in converted stable block. Cot and high chair available. Central heating. Gliding, fishing, boating and horse riding nearby. Full Fire Certificate held. Bed and Breakfast from £16. Write or phone for further details.

STRATFORD-UPON-AVON. Mrs J. Wakeham, Whitfield Farm, Ettington, Stratford-upon-Avon CV37 7PN (01789 740260). Working farm. Situated down its own private drive, off the A429, this 220-acre mixed farm (wheat, cows, sheep, geese, horses, hens) is ideal for a quiet and relaxing holiday. Convenient for visiting the Cotswolds, Warwick, Coventry, Stratford, Worcester, near M40. Fully modernised centrally heated house with separate lounge and colour TV; one double with washbasin, one double and one twin en-suite, all with tea/coffee making facilities. Car essential, parking. Open all year (except Christmas) for Bed and Breakfast from £14.50 per night. Home produced food served. Full English Breakfast. AA registered. SAE, please.

Moonraker House

You'll feel at home at the Moonraker!©

English Tourist Board
COMMENDED

- ALL rooms are elegantly decorated and designed with your comfort in mind.
- CAR PARK (open and garage).
- Ideal centre for exploring the Cotswolds, Shakespeare's Countryside, Warwick Castle and Shakespeare Theatres.
- ALL rooms have ensuite bathrooms, tea and coffee making facilities, colour TV, clock radios and fitted hairdryers.
- There are also extra special rooms with FOUR-POSTER BEDS, lounge area and garden patio (non-smoking).
- Enjoy an excellent English Breakfast prepared with care by the resident proprietors, **Mauveen and Mike Spencer**.

AA QQQ
Michelin

40 Alcester Road, Stratford-upon-Avon CV37 9DB
Tel: (01789) 267115/299346 Fax: (01789) 295504

MinOtels
Les Routiers

STRATFORD-UPON-AVON near. Mrs Joan James, Whitchurch Farm, Wimpstone, Near Stratford-upon-Avon CV37 8NS (01789 450275). ♛♛ Working farm. This large Georgian farmhouse is set in parklike surroundings, four-and-a-half miles from Stratford-upon-Avon, on the edge of the Cotswolds and ideal for a touring holiday. It is open to guests all year with central heating. The accommodation is in one twin room and two double rooms, all en-suite with tea/coffee making facilities; bathroom, toilet, shower room; sittingroom, dining room. Children are welcome; there is a cot and babysitting is offered. Sorry, no pets. A car is essential and there is parking space. Good farmhouse English Breakfast served. Evening Meal. Reduced rates for children. Bed and Breakfast from £18 per person nightly; optional Evening Meal £10.

NEWBOLD NURSERIES

Newbold-on-Stour, Stratford-upon-Avon Warwickshire CV37 8DP

You can be sure of personal attention and a friendly welcome here. The modern farmhouse has country views on all sides, but is easy to find, standing just off the A3400. There are 20 acres of arable crops and half an acre of hydroponically-grown tomatoes. Stratford is seven miles, Warwick Castle, the Cotswold area and Blenheim Palace within very easy reach. Accommodation comprises family and double rooms, en suite available. TVs and tea/coffee facilities in all rooms. Dogs accepted. Bed and Breakfast from £15, children half-price. Local pub serves excellent meals at budget prices.

Telephone 01789 450285 Mr R. F. Everett

STRATFORD-UPON-AVON. Ms Diana Tallis, Linhill, 35 Evesham Place, Stratford-upon-Avon CV37 6HT (01789 292879; Fax: 01789 414478). HETB Listed.

Linhill is a comfortable Victorian Guest House run by a friendly young family. It is situated only five minutes' walk from Stratford's town centre with its wide choice of fine restaurants and world famous Royal Shakespeare Theatres. Every bedroom at Linhill has central heating, colour TV, tea/coffee making facilities and washbasin. En suite facilities are also available, as are packed lunches and evening meals. Bicycle hire and babysitting facilities if desired. Leave the children with us and re-discover the delight of a candlelit dinner in one of Stratford's inviting restaurants. Bed and Breakfast from £13 to £18; Evening Meal from £5 to £7.50. Reduced rates for Senior Citizens.

WARWICK. Mrs J. Stanton, Redlands Farm, Banbury Road, Lighthorne, Near Warwick CV35 0AH (01926 651241).

A beautifully restored 15th century farmhouse built of local stone, the "Old Farm House" is set in two acres of garden with its own swimming pool, well away from the main road yet within easy travelling distance of Stratford and Warwick, and handy for the Cotswolds. Guest accommodation is one double (with bathroom), one single and one family bedrooms, all with tea making facilities; bathroom; beamed lounge with TV; diningroom. Rooms are centrally heated and the farmhouse also has open fires. Bed and Breakfast from £17.50. Children welcome — facilities available. No pets. A car is recommended to make the most of your stay. AA QQQ.

WARWICK. Mrs Louise Smith, Oaktree Farm, Buttermilk Lane, Yarningale Common, Claverdon CV35 8HW (01926 842413).

OAKTREE FARM

An idyllic location in the heart of picturesque countryside

Based in 34 acres of traditional meadow and woodland, Oaktree Farm offers country accommodation of the highest standard. Bedrooms are attractive, comfortable and cosy, all with en suite bathrooms, colour TV and tea/coffee making facilities. In winter months our log fires give that special warmth. The farm is also home to a small herd of rare breed cattle and is ideal for nature lovers. We serve excellent home cooked food, with vegetarian food being our speciality. We are ideally situated for Warwick (six miles), Stratford-upon-Avon (eight miles), NEC and NAC. Bed and Breakfast from £20 per night. AA QQQ.

WARWICK. Carolyn Howard, Docker's Barn Farm, Pillerton Hersey, Warwick CV35 0RL (01926 640475; Fax: 01926 641747). Idyllically situated 18th century stone barn conversion surrounded by its own land, handy for Warwick, Stratford-upon-Avon, Cotswolds, NAC, NEC, Heritage Motor Centre and six miles from Junction 12 M40. The house is full of character with antiques and interesting collections. The warm attractive en suite bedrooms have tea/coffee trays and colour TV. The four-poster suite has its own front door. Wildlife abounds and lovely walks lead from the barn, and we keep a few sheep, horses and poultry. If you are looking for total peace with friendly attentive service from £19.00 per person, Docker's Barn is for you. No smoking establishment.

WEST MIDLANDS

SOLIHULL near. Mrs Kathleen Connolly, Holland Park Farm, Buckley Green, Henley in Arden, Near Solihull B95 5QF (01564 792625). ♛ ♛ A Georgian style farmhouse set in 300 acres of peaceful farmland, including the historic grounds of "The Mount" and other interesting walks. Large garden with pond. Livestock includes cattle and sheep. Ideally situated in Shakespeare country within easy reach of Birmingham International Airport, NEC, NAC, Stratford-upon-Avon, Warwick and the Cotswolds. Two large en suite rooms, one with bath/shower and one with shower. Children and pets welcome. Open all year. Bed and Breakfast from £18.

WILTSHIRE

BATH. Mrs Carol Pope, Hatt Farm, Old Jockey, Box SN13 8DJ (Tel & Fax: 01225 742989). ♛ ♛ *COMMENDED.* AA QQQ. Extremely comfortable Georgian farmhouse in peaceful surroundings, far from the madding crowd. A scrumptious breakfast is served overlooking beautiful views of the rolling Wiltshire countryside. What can be nicer than sitting by a log fire in winter or enjoying the spacious garden in summer? Lovely walks and good golfing nearby. Ideally situated for touring the Cotswolds or visiting the endless delights of the relatively undiscovered county of Wiltshire with its ancient monuments and quaint villages. All this, yet only a short distance away is the city of Bath. One twin room with en suite shower, one double/family room with private bathroom. TV lounge. Children welcome, Sorry, no pets. Central heating. Open all year except Christmas and New Year. Bed and Breakfast from £17.50 per person.

BIDDESTONE. Mrs R.E. Sexton, Elm Farmhouse, The Green, Biddestone, Chippenham SN14 7DG (01249 713354). ♛ ♛ *COMMENDED.* A peaceful 17th century Grade II Listed farmhouse now run as a Bed and Breakfast establishment located in the heart of North Wiltshire. Situated opposite the pond and two minutes from the village pub, Elm Farmhouse is traditionally decorated and retains many striking features such as original fireplaces and mullioned windows. Accommodation is offered in three double bedrooms, all en suite with colour TV, tea/coffee making facilities and good views. Biddestone is only four miles from the M4 and is between the famous villages of Lacock and Castle Combe, just nine miles from Bath and close to many National Trust properties and beautiful countryside. Bed and Breakfast from £17.50 per person. Children and pets welcome.

CHIPPENHAM near. Suzanne Candy, Olivemead Farm, Dauntsey, Near Chippenham SN15 4JQ (01666 510205). ♛ *COMMENDED.* **Working farm.** Relax and enjoy the warm informal hospitality at our delightful 18th century farmhouse on a working dairy farm in the Dauntsey Vale. Twin, double and family rooms with washbasins, colour TVs. Tea/coffee making facilities. Generous breakfasts. Oak beamed dining room/lounge for guests' exclusive use. Large garden, children's play area, cot, high chair, baby listening. Excellent food available locally. Convenient for Bath, Cotswolds, Salisbury, M4, South West and Wales. Bed and Breakfast from £15 to £17 per person per night. Reductions for children and long stay guests.

DEVIZES. Mr and Mrs C. Fletcher, Lower Foxhangers Farm, Rowde, Devizes SN10 1SS (01380 828254). ♛ ♛ *COMMENDED*. **Working farm.** Tranquillity awaits you on our 18th century canalside working farm. Situated alongside the Kennet and Avon Canal, at the base of the staircase of 29 locks; assist boats through the locks; scenic walks to pubs. Fish and boat to your heart's desire. Ideal for cycling. Bed and Breakfast in family/double and twin rooms with washbasins, twin room en suite; two bathrooms, three toilets; lounge with TV for visitors' use. Children and pets welcome. Cot, high chair available. Open Easter to end of October. Bed and Breakfast from £34, £37 en suite. Reductions for two or more nights. Weekly rates available. FHB Member. Also available, self catering units and small campsite with electricity and toilets/shower. Brochure on request.

DEVIZES near. Rob and Jacqui Mattingly, The Old Coach House, 21 Church Street, Market Lavington, Devizes SN10 4DU (Tel & Fax: 01380 812879). ♛ ♛ *COMMENDED*. A warm welcome awaits you at this delightful 18th century coaching house. Attractive rooms with en suite facilities and colour TV ensure your stay will be relaxed and comfortable. Whether you enjoy a traditional English breakfast or choose a speciality from the menu you can be sure it will be freshly prepared using the finest local ingredients. Situated a few miles south of Devizes it is a perfect location from which to explore the surrounding area. Bath, Salisbury, Stonehenge and many other places of interest are all within easy reach. Excellent for walking and cycling and ideal for Short Breaks. Children welcome but sorry no pets. Bed and Breakfast from £21 to £25. No smoking. AA QQQ.

MALMESBURY. John and Edna Edwards, Stonehill Farm, Charlton, Malmesbury SN16 9DY (01666 823310). ETB Listed *COMMENDED*. **Working farm.** Superbly located on the edge of the Cotswolds in lush rolling countryside and only 15 minutes from the M4 Junction 16 or 17. John and Edna invite you to stay with them on their dairy farm in a relaxed friendly atmosphere where pets and children are welcome. The charming old farmhouse originally built in 1483, now modernised, offers an ideal centre from which to visit Bath, Avebury, Castle Combe and the beautiful Cotswold Hills and Villages. Three pretty rooms (one en suite) with comfortable beds and a delicious breakfast to start your day. AA QQ.

MALMESBURY. Mrs R. Eavis, Manor Farm, Corston, Malmesbury SN16 0HF (Tel & Fax: 01666 822148; 0374 675783 mobile). ♛ ♛ *COMMENDED*. Within easy reach of Lacock, historic Bath, Tetbury, Badminton and the beautiful Cotswolds, Manor Farm is the ideal location for touring. Two miles from Junction 17 of the M4, the farm nestles in the small village of Corston. The accommodation is comfortable, comprising single, twin, double and family rooms, all with washbasins, colour TV and tea/coffee making facilities. Three rooms have en suite bathrooms. Sittingroom with colour TV, and guests also have use of lovely gardens. Children welcome. Sufficient parking. Bed and Breakfast from £16 to £22. Pub food available within walking distance. Full Fire Certificate. A winner in the 1995 West Country Farm Holiday Awards and AA QQQ. Farm Holiday Bureau member.

FHG PUBLICATIONS LIMITED publish a large range of well-known accommodation guides. We will be happy to send you details or you can use the order form at the back of this book.

MALMESBURY near. Mrs Barnes, Lovett Farm, Little Somerford, Near Malmesbury SN15 5BP

(01666 823268). ❧ ❧ COMMENDED. Enjoy traditional hospitality at our delightful farmhouse on a small working farm with beautiful views from both the double and twin en suite bedrooms, each having tea/coffee making facilities, radio and colour TV. Full central heating. Sample a scrumptious farmhouse breakfast in our cosy dining room/lounge with a log fire for those cold winter days. Situated three miles from Malmesbury on B4042 and within easy reach of Bath, Cotswolds and Stonehenge. Excellent food pubs locally. Horse stabling by arrangement. Bed and Breakfast from £17. Reductions for children. Open all year. Farm Holiday Bureau Member.

SALISBURY. Mrs Suzi Lanham, Newton Farmhouse, Southampton Road, Whiteparish, Salisbury

SP5 2QL (01794 884416). ❧ ❧ COMMENDED. Bordering the New Forest and no longer a working farm, the property was originally part of the Trafalgar Estate gifted to Lord Nelson. All rooms (two with four-poster bed) are fully en suite and have colour TV and tea/coffee making facilities. The dining room has original flagstone floors, oak beams and huge open fireplace. The garden covers two acres and includes a swimming pool. Ideal location for Stonehenge, Salisbury, Wilton House, Broadlands, Beaulieu, Paultons Park, Winchester, Southampton and Bournemouth area, plus golfing, walking, cycling and horse riding nearby. Central heating. Children welcome. No pets. Evening Meals by arrangement. AA QQQ Recommended.

WARMINSTER. Mrs M. Hoskins, Spinney Farmhouse, Chapmanslade, Westbury BA13 4AQ (01373 832412). ❧ ❧ ❧ Working farm. Off A36, three miles west of Warminster; 16 miles from historic city of Bath. Close to Longleat, Cheddar and Stourhead. Reasonable driving distance to Bristol, Stonehenge, Glastonbury and the cathedral cities of Wells and Salisbury. Pony trekking and fishing available locally and an 18 hole golf course within walking distance. Washbasins, tea/coffee-making facilities and shaver points in all rooms. Family room available. Guests' lounge with colour TV. Central heating. Children and pets welcome. Ample parking. Open all year. Bed and Breakfast from £16 per night, £95 per week. Reduction after two nights. Evening Meal £11. Farm fresh food in a warm, friendly, family atmosphere.

WARMINSTER. Mrs Sarah Coward, Manor Farm Bed and Breakfast, Mere, Warminster BA12 6HR

(01747 860242). Manor Farm is a working arable/beef farm run by the Coward family for three generations. Built in 1840 the imposing Victorian farmhouse is set in its own grounds providing tranquillity and privacy for guests. The bedrooms and guest areas are spacious, well furnished and maintained to a high standard. Two double rooms and one family room, all with washbasins, tea/coffee making facilities and colour TV. Totally non-smoking. Within the farm there are excellent walks (170 acres of conserved downland), mountain bike tracks, clay pigeon shooting and ideal hang gliding conditions. Sorry no pets. Bed and Breakfast from £18 to £20.

YORKSHIRE

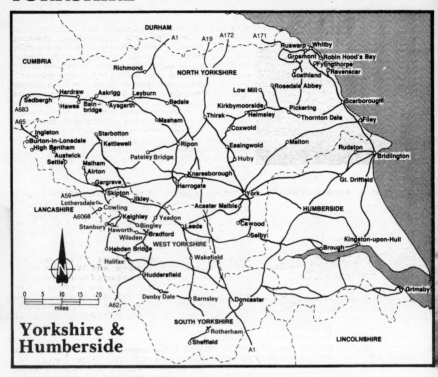

Yorkshire & Humberside

EAST YORKSHIRE (Humberside)

BRIDLINGTON. Mrs Pat Cowton, The Grange, Bempton Lane, Flamborough, Bridlington YO15 1AS (01262 850207). For a relaxing holiday come and stay in our Georgian farmhouse situated in 450 acres of stock and arable land on the outskirts of Flamborough village. Ideally situated for bird watching at RSPB Sanctuary at Bempton, sandy beaches, cliffs and coves on our Heritage Coast. Golf and sea fishing nearby. Children and pets welcome. Open all year except Christmas and New Year. Bed and Breakfast from £15.

GREAT DRIFFIELD. Mrs Tiffy Hopper, Kelleythorpe, Great Driffield YO25 9DW (01377 252297). Tourist Board Listed COMMENDED. **Working farm.** Imagine peacocks strutting, ducks swimming and trout rising. Enjoy a cup of tea on the sun terrace overlooking a crystal clear shallow river. The friendly atmosphere of our lovely Georgian farmhouse with its mellow antique furniture, pretty chintzes and new bathrooms, one en-suite, is sure to captivate you. Delicious country cooking. Children are very welcome, they enjoy playing in our large garden with swings and playcastle. Ideally placed for touring. Bed and Breakfast from £15; optional Evening Meal from £10 by prior arrangement. 10% discount for seven nights or more. Reductions for children under 12 years.

NORTH YORKSHIRE

AMPLEFORTH. Annabel Lupton, Carr House Farm, Shallowdale, Ampleforth, Near Helmsley YO6 4ED (01347 868526). ❦❦ *COMMENDED.* **Working farm.** Carr House — 16th century farmhouse in peaceful, beautiful 'Herriot' countryside, half an hour from York. Recommended by Sunday Observer — "a fresh-air fiend's dream — good food, good walking and a warm welcome". Tour the Moors, Dales, National Parks, York coast, nearby famous Abbeys, Castles and Stately Homes. Carr House provides a comfortable, relaxing homely base. Romantics will love the four-poster double bedrooms, both en-suite. Central heating, log fires. Enjoy a full Yorkshire farmhouse Breakfast with home-made preserves, free-range eggs, own produce used whenever possible. Bed and Breakfast from £15, Evening Meal £10. Sorry, no pets or children under seven. No smoking indoors. Open all year; closed Christmas and New Year. SAE, please, for brochure. Farm Holiday Bureau Member.

ASKRIGG. Mrs B. Percival, Milton House, Askrigg, Leyburn DL8 3HJ (01969 650217). ❦❦ *COMMENDED.* Askrigg is situated in the heart of Wensleydale and is within easy reach of many interesting places — Aysgarth Falls, Hardraw Falls, Bolton Castle. Askrigg is one of the loveliest villages in the dale. This is an ideal area for touring or walking. Milton House is a lovely spacious house with all the comforts of home. There are three pretty double bedrooms, all with private facilities, TV and tea/coffee making facilities. Visitors lounge with TV, dining room. Central heating. Children are welcome. Private parking. Milton House is open all year for Bed and Breakfast or Bed, Breakfast and Evening Meal. You are sure of lovely home cooking, a friendly welcome and a homely atmosphere. Please write or phone Mrs Beryl Percival for details and brochure.

BAINBRIDGE. Mrs A. Harrison, Riverdale House Country Hotel, Bainbridge, Leyburn DL8 3EW (01969 650205). ❦❦❦ Riverdale House overlooks village green and stocks in centre of a lovely village in Upper Wensleydale, the famous "James Herriot Country". Good touring centre for the Dales and other places of interest — Aysgarth Falls, Hardraw Scar, Richmond and Bolton Castles, Ingleton Falls and Caves are but a few. Excellent walking over hills and moors. Good food a speciality, all fresh produce, traditional roasts, home made soups, delicious puddings, plus a carefully chosen wine list. Most bedrooms with private facilities and all expected comforts, colour TV. Fire Certificate granted. Leyburn 11 miles. Bargain Breaks November to March excluding Bank Holidays. SAE for brochure or telephone from November to 31st March **(01969 663381)** — thereafter as above.

BEDALE. Mrs D. Hodgson, Little Holtby, Leeming Bar, Northallerton DL7 9LH (01609 748762). ❦❦ *HIGHLY COMMENDED.* A period farmhouse with beautiful views at the gateway to the Yorkshire Dales, within easy distance of many places of great interest, just 100 yards off the A1 between Bedale and Richmond. Little Holtby has been restored and furnished to a very high standard whilst still retaining its original character; polished wood floors, open fires and original beams in many of the rooms. All bedrooms have colour TV, tea/coffee making facilities and are centrally heated. One double bedroom (en-suite), two twin-bedded rooms with washbasins and one family room (en-suite). Bed and Breakfast from £17.50; Evening Meal available.

BEDALE. Mrs M. Keighley, Southfield, 96 South End, Bedale DL8 2DS (01677 423510). Only five minutes from A1, ideal for breaking a journey to/from Scotland. Good base for touring; attractions in the area include Fountains Abbey, Harewood House, Bolton Castle and Lightwater Valley. Golf and swimming. Marjorie will supply supper and babysitting free. One single, one double, twin and family bedrooms, all with washbasins. Open all year. Bed and Breakfast from £15 to £16.

BEDALE. Mrs Sheila Dean, Hyperion House, 88 South End, Bedale DL8 2DS (01677 422334).

✿✿ *HIGHLY COMMENDED.* An attractive large detached house in the delightful market town of Bedale in lovely North Yorkshire. One large double bedroom with en suite bathroom, one double with adjacent private bathroom or can be shared with twin. Excellent well cooked varied breakfast of your choice (separate tables). Colour TV and tea/coffee in all rooms. Off street parking for four cars. Bar meals and restaurants in Bedale or surrounding villages. Ideal for holidays and north/south stopover. Enquire for Bargain Breaks. Bed and Breakfast £17 to £21, single in double £25. £20 deposit secures room. Completely non smoking and no pets.

BEDALE. Mrs Patricia Knox, Mill Close Farm, Patrick Brompton, Bedale DL8 1JY (01677 450257).

✿✿ *COMMENDED.* Mill Close is a working farm surrounded by beautiful rolling countryside at the foothills of the Yorkshire Dales and Herriot country. Rooms are spacious and furnished to a very high standard. One double or family room, one twin-bedded room, both with tea/coffee making facilities. Guests' own sittingroom with colour TV; diningroom; private bathrooms. Relaxing, peaceful atmosphere with large walled garden, summerhouse and pond. Open fires and central heating. Children welcome, cot available. Pets housed by arrangement. Enjoy wholesome farmhouse cooking using local produce, freshly prepared. Open Easter to October. Bed and Breakfast from £15 to £18; Evening Meal from £10. Please send for full colour brochure.

BENTHAM. Mrs Shirley Metcalfe, Fowgill Park Farm, High Bentham, Near Lancaster LA2 7AH (015242 61630). ✿✿ *COMMENDED.* **Working farm.**

Fowgill is a 200 acre stock rearing farm, situated in an elevated position and having magnificent views of the Dales and Fells. Only 20 minutes from M6 Junction 34. A good centre for touring the Dales, Lakes, coast and Forest of Bowland. Visit Ingleton with its waterfalls and caves only three miles away. Golf, fishing and horse riding nearby. Bedrooms have washbasins, shaver points and tea-making facilities, two bedrooms en-suite. Comfortable beamed visitors' lounge to relax in with colour TV. Separate diningroom. Bed and Breakfast from £14; Evening Meal optional £8.50. Reductions for children. Bedtime drink included in price. Brochure available.

BENTHAM. Betty Clapham, Lane House Farm, Bentham, Near Lancaster LA2 7DJ (015242 61479).

✿✿ *COMMENDED.* **Working farm.** Enjoy a relaxing break at our 17th century beamed farmhouse, within half a mile of the Forest of Bowland, with beautiful views of the Yorkshire Dales. One mile from the market town of High Bentham, half a hour from M6. Ideal for caves, waterfalls, touring the Lakes. Bedrooms have washbasins and tea-making trays. En suite facilities. Guests' lounge with colour TV. Separate dining room. Children and pets welcome. Open February to November. Self catering static caravan also available. Bed and Breakfast from £15.50; Evening Meal from £8.50.

DANBY. Mrs B. Tindall, Rowan Tree Farm, Danby, Whitby YO21 2LE (01287 660396). Tourist Board Listed. Working farm, join in. Rowan Tree Farm is situated in the heart of the North Yorkshire Moors and has panoramic moorland views. Ideal walking area and quiet location just outside the village of Danby. Accommodation comprises one single room, one twin-bedded room and one family room all with full oil-fired central heating. Residents' lounge with colour TV. Children welcome — cot provided if required. Babysitting available. Pets accepted. Good home cooking. Bed and Breakfast from £14; Evening Meals provided on request £7 each. Ample car parking space.

NORTH YORKSHIRE – SCENIC COASTLINE!
Three of England's most popular East Coast resorts sparkle along the dramatic cliffs and bays of the North Yorkshire coast. Filey, Scarborough and Whitby remain popular touring and holiday centres.

EASINGWOLD. Mrs Rachel Ritchie, The Old Rectory, Thormanby, Easingwold, York YO6 3NN (01845 501417). 🌸🌸 A warm welcome awaits you at this interesting Georgian rectory built in 1737 and furnished with many antiques including a four-poster bed. Three comfortable and very spacious bedrooms with tea/coffee making facilities, two en suite; charming lounge with colour TV and open fire. Separate diningroom. Large mature garden. An excellent base for touring the Moors, Dales and York. This is the centre of "James Herriot" country with many historic houses and abbeys to visit in the area. Thormanby is a small village between Easingwold and Thirsk. York is 17 miles. Many delightful inns and restaurants serving good food locally. Bed and Breakfast from £16 — reductions for children under 12 years and reduced weekly rates. Ample parking. Open all year. SAE for brochure or telephone.

GLAISDALE. Mrs H. Kelly, The Grange, Glaisdale, Whitby YO21 2QW (01947 897241). Beautiful stone manor house with magnificent hilltop view. It lies amidst our sheep/arable farm bordering the Esk River which boasts the best salmon fishing in the country. Home grown produce used in our generous meals. Excellent position for walks, steam railway and Whitby. Bathroom en-suite or shared between two rooms. Fishing by arrangement. Open all year except December. Children over 10 years welcome, and pets welcome by arrangement. Bed and Breakfast from £15; Evening Meal from £8. Eden Farm, Eden Camp, Flamingoland, etc all within easy reach.

GOATHLAND. Mrs V.A. MacCaig, Prudom House, Goathland, Whitby YO22 5AN (01947 896368). 🌸🌸 Situated nine miles from the coast, Goathland offers some of the finest walking countryside and is an ideal touring centre. An added attraction is the North Yorkshire Moors Historic Railway Trust running through the village. Delightful scenery. Prudom House is situated in attractive well-maintained gardens in the centre of the village. Careful restoration of the farmhouse has provided guests with modern amenities whilst retaining its character. Open beams a feature and cosy log fires. Razor points and washbasins. Comfortable accommodation and good food. Children are welcome; cot, high chair, babysitting and reduced rates. Dogs allowed. Tea room with crafts on display. Bed and Breakfast from £18.50 per person; Dinner from £9 per person. Open all year except Christmas and New Year. Please phone or send SAE for brochure.

Prudom House

GOATHLAND, WHITBY, NORTH YORKSHIRE.

Guest House Accommodation and Tea Rooms

GOATHLAND. Mrs Christine Chippindale, Barnet House Guest House, Goathland, Whitby YO22 5NG (01947 896201). Situated in large garden on edge of the delightful village of Goathland, an ideal centre for walking and touring the North Yorkshire Moors, Dales and coast. Warm, comfortable accommodation, friendly atmosphere, excellent food. Lounge with colour TV; three double, three twin-bedded, one family room all with washbasins, razor points, heating, tea/coffee making facilities, magnificent views over surrounding moorland. Bathroom, shower room, three toilets. Reductions for children 11 years and under (minimum six years) sharing parents' room. Sorry no pets. Parking. Open from March to November for Bed and Breakfast from £18.50; Evening Meal, Bed and Breakfast from £26. Brochure on request.

GROSMONT. Mrs S. Counsell, Eskdale, Grosmont, Whitby YO22 5PT (01947 895385). Tourist Board Listed. Eskdale is a Georgian detached house set in large attractive gardens. The house overlooks the Esk Valley with views to the North Yorkshire Moors. Good walking area and convenient for coast and steam railway. Two double rooms and two single. Families can also be catered for. Separate lounge for guests' use. Ample parking is available. Children welcome with babysitting offered. Pets also welcome. Bed and Breakfast from £16. Full English Breakfast. SAE, please, or telephone.

HARROGATE. Mrs Christine Ryder, Scaife Hall Farm, Blubberhouses, Otley, West Yorkshire LS21

2PL (01943 880354). 🐦🐦 *HIGHLY COMMENDED.* Farm Holiday Bureau member. Scaife Hall is a working farm set in picturesque countryside on the edge of the Yorkshire Dales. Ideal location for visiting the Dales, Harrogate, Fountains Abbey, York, Skipton and Emmerdale country. Sheep and beef cattle are kept and guests are free to roam and even take part in some seasonal activities such as lambing, etc. One twin-bedded and two double rooms, each tastefully decorated and having en suite facilities, central heating and beverage tray. Guests' private sittingroom with colour TV and log fires on chilly nights. Open all year. Local inns provide excellent evening meals. Bed and Breakfast from £20.

HARROGATE. Anne and Bob Joyner, Anro Guest House, 90 King's Road, Harrogate HG1 5JX (01423 503087). 🐦🐦 *COMMENDED.* AA QQQ, RAC Listed. "Excellent!", "Exceptional value!", "Good food!", "Quiet!", "Never had it so good!" — just a few testimonials visitors have written in our book on leaving. Situated in a tree-lined avenue in a central position close to all amenities. Conference and Exhibition Centre two minutes' walk. Valley Gardens, town and local swimming baths close by. Our house is centrally heated, with tea/coffee making facilities and colour TV in all rooms, hot and cold throughout. Some rooms en suite. Home cooking. Bed and Breakfast from £20; four-course Dinner, plus tea or coffee on request, £12. Ideal centre for touring Dales/Herriot country. Well recommended. FHG Diploma Winners.

HARROGATE. Mrs A. Wood, Field House, Clint, Near Harrogate HG3 3DS (01423 770638). Field House is situated five miles from Harrogate and a mile above the attractive village of Hampsthwaite, commanding beautiful views over the Nidd Valley. Ideal for exploring the Dales and Moors with ancient abbeys, castles and country houses. The market towns of Skipton, Ripon and Knaresborough and the historic city of York are all within easy reach. Accommodation is in one twin and one double room with private bathroom. Private sittingroom with TV, etc. Open all year. Car essential — private parking. Bed and Breakfast from £12.50 with Evening Meals readily available. A warm welcome guaranteed in a peaceful friendly atmosphere. Telephone or SAE, please, for further details.

HARROGATE. Mrs Judy Barker, Brimham Guest House, Silverdale Close, Darley, Harrogate HG3

2PQ (01423 780948). The family-run guest house is situated in the centre of Darley, a quiet village in unspoilt Nidderdale. All rooms en suite and centrally heated with tea/coffee making facilities and views across the Dales. Full English breakfast served between 7am and 9.30am in the dining room; a TV lounge/conservatory is available for your relaxation. Off street parking. Central for visits to Harrogate, York, Skipton and Ripon, or just enjoying drives through the Dales and Moors where you will take in dramatic hillsides, green hills, picturesque villages, castles and abbeys. Children welcome. Bed and Breakfast from £15 (double room) to £20 (single room).

HARROGATE near. Mrs Audrey Crabtree, Crag Lane House, Crag Lane, Kettlesing, Near Harrogate

HG3 2JY (01423 770888). Country residence with scenic surroundings, situated five miles from Harrogate just off A59. Convenient for the Yorkshire Dales and numerous market towns. Accommodation comprises one family/double room, one twin-bedded room and one single. Vanity units with washbasins in each room and central heating. TV lounge with open fire. Children welcome but sorry no pets. Bed and Breakfast from £15. Evening meal optional. Open all year. Non-smoking household. Tea/coffee and home made scones on arrival.

NORTH YORKSHIRE – RICH IN TOURIST ATTRACTIONS!

Dales, moors, castles, abbeys, cathedrals – you name it and you're almost sure to find it in North Yorkshire. Leading attractions include Castle Howard, the moorlands walks at Goathland, the Waterfalls at Falling Foss, Skipton, Richmond, Wensleydale, Bridestones Moor, Ripon Cathedral, Whitby, Settle and, of course, York itself.

HAWES. Mrs M.A. Iveson, The Homestead, Hardraw, Hawes DL8 3LZ (01969 667003).

A 17th century house situated two miles out of Hawes in Hardraw village. Lovely big house with very large rooms — one bedroom with shower and washbasin, one family room with full bathroom. Central heating. Pub in village. Beautiful garden for relaxing in. Ideal for walkers on Pennine Way, also good fishing country. Children welcome, but sorry, no pets. Open all year. Bed and Breakfast from £16.00 per person.

HELMSLEY. Mrs Elizabeth Easton, Lockton House Farm, Bilsdale, Helmsley YO6 5NE (01439 798303). Working farm, join in.

16th century farmhouse on mixed family-run farm of 400 acres with sheep, cattle and ponies. Ideally situated for touring North Yorkshire Moors and the many other attractions of this area. There are peaceful panoramic views from the farm. Guest accommodation is in two double and one family rooms all with washbasins; lounge with colour TV. Good home cooking in abundance. One dog per family welcome. Open March to October. Bed and Breakfast from £14.50; Bed, Breakfast and Evening Meal (optional) from £24. Reduced rates for children.

HELMSLEY. Mrs Sally Robinson, Valley View Farm, Old Byland, Helmsley, York YO6 5LG (01439 798221). ♛♛ HIGHLY COMMENDED. Working farm.

Stylish, well appointed farmhouse accommodation twixt Moors and Dales in the North Yorks Moors National Park with outstanding views across beautiful countryside. Relax in rural peace and tranquillity. Excellent walking country. Warm, spacious en suite rooms, each with tea/coffee making facilities, colour TV and central heating. Residents' lounge furnished traditionally with open fire and your comfort always in mind. Dining room where substantial breakfasts and old fashioned leisurely farmhouse dinners are served. Licensed. Vegetarian meals on request. Open all year. Bed and Breakfast from £25; Dinner, Bed and Breakfast from £37. Self catering cottages also available. Please phone for brochure.

HELMSLEY. Mrs J. Milburn, Barn Close Farm, Rievaulx, Helmsley YO6 5LN (01439 798321). ♛♛♛ COMMENDED. Working farm.

Farm Holiday Bureau member. Farming family offer homely accommodation on mixed farm in beautiful surroundings near Rievaulx Abbey. Ideal for touring, pony trekking, walking. Home-made bread, own home produced meat, poultry, free range eggs — in fact Mrs Milburn's excellent cooking was praised in the "Daily Telegraph". Modern home — two double bedrooms with washbasins, one family room (one room en-suite); all with tea/coffee making facilities. TV lounge; diningroom. Children welcome, babysitting. Sorry, no pets. Open all year round. Open log fires. Storage heaters in bedrooms. Car essential — parking. Bed and Breakfast from £20 to £22; Dinner £10. Reduced rates for children under 10 sharing parents' room.

WHEN MAKING ENQUIRIES PLEASE MENTION
THIS *FHG* PUBLICATION

HELMSLEY. Mrs Margaret Wainwright, Sproxton Hall, Sproxton, Helmsley YO6 5QE (01439 770225; Fax: 01439 771373). 👑 👑 *HIGHLY COMMEN-*

DED. **Working farm.** Enjoy the peaceful atmosphere, magnificent views and comfort of Sproxton Hall, a 17th century Grade II listed farmhouse on a 300 acre family farm. A haven of peace and tranquillity, lovingly and tastefully furbished with antiques and co-ordinating fabrics to give the warm and cosy elegance of a country home. Set amidst idyllic countryside, one and a half miles from Helmsley. Excellent base for touring North Yorkshire Moors, Dales, Coast, National Trust properties and York. One double room en suite, one twin with private bathroom, double and twin with shared luxury shower room. Colour TV, central heating, drinks facilities, washbasins and razor points in all rooms. Laundry facilities. No children under 10 years. A "Non-Smoking" household. Bed and Breakfast from £18.50. Five self catering award-winning cottages also available. See our separate entry in the Self Catering Section of this guide. Brochures available.

HELMSLEY near. Sue Smith, Laskill Farm, Hawnby, Near Helmsley YO6 5NB (01439 798268).

👑 👑 👑 Amidst beautiful North Yorkshire Moors, in heart of James Herriot Country. Attractive farmhouse with own lake and large walled garden. Own natural spring water. High standard of food and comfort. Two double rooms en suite, two twins en suite, one double and one twin each with shower and washbasins, one single; all with colour TV and beverage tray. Ideal for nearby places of interest and scenic beauty, or simply enjoy peaceful and tranquil surroundings. Open all year except Christmas Day. Children and pets welcome. Bed and Breakfast from £18. Self catering accommodation also available. Brochure on request.

HORTON-IN-RIBBLESDALE. Marilyn Pilkington, Middle Studfold Farm, Horton-in-Ribblesdale, Settle BD24 0ER (01729 860236). 👑 *HIGHLY COMMEN-*

DED. 18th century Dales farmhouse superbly situated on the lower slopes of Pen-y-ghent (one of the famed "Three Peaks") and overlooking the lovely valley of Upper Ribblesdale, Middle Studfold provides an ideal base for exploring the Yorkshire Dales National Park. A homely lounge with real log fire, makes for the cosiest of evenings whilst hearty dinners, with fine wines if desired, are enjoyed in the oak beamed dining room to round off another perfect day. The visitors' book is testimony to the excellence of the cuisine — breakfast especially! Facilities include a free "taxi" service to Horton and the scenic Settle to Carlisle railway and early breakfast for "Three Peakers". Our quiet location, with private approach road offers ample parking. Bed and Breakfast from £15; Dinner from £7. Child reductions. Residential licence. Pets by arrangement.

INGLETON. Carol Brennand, Nutstile Farm, Ingleton, Via Carnforth LA6 3DT (015242 41752). **Tourist Board Listed** *COMMENDED.* Surrounded by the

outstanding beauty of the Yorkshire Dales, Nutstile is a typical working farm providing first class accommodation. The mountains, caves and waterfalls of Ingleton are immediately accessible, the Lake District also close by. Try a leisurely ride on the scenic Settle-Carlisle railway. Three bedrooms (all with views) with washbasin and tea/coffee facilities, en suite available. Guests' lounge with TV. Children welcome. Open all year. Bed and Breakfast from £15 to £17.

INGLETON. Mrs Nancy Lund, Gatehouse Farm, Far Westhouse, Ingleton, Carnforth LA6 3NR (015242 41458/41307). 👑 👑 *COMMENDED.* Bryan and

FARM HOLIDAY BUREAU

Nancy invite you to their farm which they run with their son who lives at Lund Holme (next door). You are welcome to wander round and look at the cows, calves and sheep or stroll in the quiet country lanes and enjoy the wild flowers. Gatehouse, situated in the Yorkshire Dales National Park, is in an elevated position with beautiful views over open countryside; it was built in 1740 and retains the original oak beams. Double or twin rooms (families welcome), all with private facilities and tea/coffee trays; guests' diningroom and lounge with colour TV. M6 turnoff 34, 15 miles, one and a half miles west of Ingleton, just off A65. Bed and Breakfast from £16; Evening Meal from £9.

See also Colour Display Advertisement INGLETON. **Mrs Mollie Bell, "Langber Country Guest House", Ingleton (Via Carnforth) LA6 3DT (015242 41587).** ♥ ♥ Ingleton, "Beauty Spot of the North", in the National Parks area. Renowned for waterfalls, glens, underground caves, magnificent scenery and Ingleboro' mountain — 2,373 ft. An excellent centre for touring Dales, Lakes and coast. Golf, fishing, tennis, swimming and bowls in vicinity. Pony-trekking a few miles distant. Guests are warmly welcomed to "Langber", a detached country house, having beautiful views with 82 acres of gardens, terrace and fields. Sheep and lambs kept. There are three family, three double/twin and one single bedrooms — all with washbasins and razor points; some en-suite. Friendly personal service. Sunny, comfortable lounge and separate dining room. Central heating. Fire precautions. Babysitting offered. Open all year except Christmas. Fire Certificate granted. AA and RAC Listed. SAE for terms for Evening Dinner, Bed and Breakfast or Bed and Breakfast only. Reductions for children under 13 sharing parents' room.

INGLETON (via Carnforth). **J.A. and M. Charlton, Stacksteads Farm, Ingleton, Via Carnforth, Lancashire LA6 3HS (015242 41386).** Stacksteads Farm,

a smallholding, situated in the beautiful Yorkshire Dales, dates back to the 1600s. We are approximately one mile from the village centre and half a mile from the main A65 Settle to Kendal road with panoramic views of Ingleborough. Our location is 10 miles from Settle, five miles from Kirkby Lonsdale and 17 miles from Hawes. We are surrounded by some of the most beautiful limestone countryside in England, ideal for walking, with prime historical and geological features in the nearby surrounding area. We offer Bed and Breakfast, together with Evening Meal if required. We have two double en-suite rooms and one twin-bedded room with its own separate bathroom. Residents' diningroom and lounge with TV. All are centrally heated. Open all year round. Bed and Breakfast £16 per person per night. AA QQ.

KEIGHLEY. **Joe and Joyce Sawley, The Hawthorns, Ickornshaw, Cowling, Keighley BD22 0DH (01535 633299 or 0831 720796). Tourist Board Listed.**

"HILTON"! But have you stayed at the "HAWTHORNS", set in its own grounds just off the beaten track in the lovely hamlet of Ickornshaw. Ample parking, heated outdoor swimming pool (weather permitting). Ideally situated for Skipton, Yorkshire Dales, Haworth and the Bronte country. Marvellous centre for touring or walking. Colour TV and tea/coffee facilities in all bedrooms; en suite rooms. Recommended for home cooking and a "BIG" farmhouse breakfast. Guests are assured of a warm, friendly "at home" atmosphere. Situated three miles from Crosshills just off the A6068 road at Cowling. Bed and Breakfast from £15. SAE for further details.

KIRKBYMOORSIDE. **Mrs M.P. Featherstone, Keysbeck Farm, Farndale, Kirkbymoorside YO6 6UZ (01751 433221). Working farm, join in.** Friendly accommodation on a 200 acre farm. There are one double, one single or twin bedrooms; diningroom with open log fire where good home cooking is served. Car essential, parking. Children and pets welcome; babysitting available. Open all year round. Evening Meal, Bed and Breakfast £17; Bed and Breakfast £12. Reduced rates for children and weekly terms.

MALTON. **Mrs Marion Shaw, Abbotts Farm, Ryton, Malton YO17 0SA (01653 694970).** A

comfortable family farmhouse surrounded by fields and trees, ideal for country lovers wishing to relax in natural surroundings. Near old market town of Malton and central for North Yorkshire. Within easy reach of the coast, Moors, Castle Howard and "Heartbeat" country as well as towns and villages such as Pickering, Whitby, Scarborough, Kirkbymoorside, Helmsley and the beautiful historic city of York. Abbotts Farm has lovely open views and a large, sheltered garden giving a delightful aspect from the house yet allowing guests to make the most of the sun in the more secluded parts. Accommodation is in two large double bedded rooms with single and bunk beds for children; pleasant dining/sitting room with central heating and open fires in cooler weather. Hearty Yorkshire breakfast served; tea/coffee and biscuits served anytime (small charge). Special facilities for families. Bed and Breakfast from £16. Lunches and evening meals available at many good local inns and hotels. No smoking. Sorry no pets. Self catering accommodation also available. Stamp please for brochure. Yorkshire Tourist Board member.

PLEASE SEND A STAMPED ADDRESSED ENVELOPE WITH ENQUIRIES

MASHAM. Mrs Rosemary Robinson, Lamb Hill Farm, Lamb Hill, Masham, Ripon HG4 4DJ (01765 689274). 🖤🖤 *COMMENDED.* **Working farm.** A warm welcome awaits you in our genuine old farmhouse on a working farm situated off the A6108 between West Tanfield and Masham. Accommodation comprises large, comfortable bedrooms with private bathrooms. We are centrally situated for exploring "Herriot" and "Heartbeat" country. Many National Trust properties within easy reach. Excellent opportunities for eating out wihin a two-mile radius. York 45 minutes, Durham one hour. Children over 8 years welcome. Open all year. Bed and Breakfast from £16.00.

NORTH YORKSHIRE MOORS NATIONAL PARK. Mrs Marion N. Cockrem, Dale End Farm, Green End, Goathland, Whitby YO22 5LJ (01947 895371). Working farm. 140 acre working farm, 500 year old stone-built farmhouse in North Yorkshire Moors National Park. Generous portions of home cooked food. Rare breeds of animals kept including llama and Vietnamese pot-bellied pigs. Children and pets welcomed. Guests' lounge with TV and log fire. Homely olde worlde interior, oak beams and panelling. Many repeat bookings. Sensible prices. SAE for brochure.

NORTHALLERTON. John and Freda Coppin, Richmond House, 6 Beech Close, Scruton, Northallerton DL7 0TU (01609 748369). Stay awhile at our detached house in a lovely rural village between Bedale and Northallerton. "Welcome Host" establishment. Only three miles off A1. Ideal stopover for north/south travellers. One double room with colour TV, radio/alarm, tea/coffee making facilities, central heating and double glazing. Luxury bathroom with shower, shaver point. Home cooked full English breakfast is served in our dining room/lounge. Private parking. Centrally located for touring Yorkshire Dales and Moors. York, Durham and coast all within one hour's drive. Bed and Breakfast from £14. Special reduced rates during July and August. Open April to October. Brochure available.

OTLEY. Mrs C. Beaumont, Paddock Hill, Norwood, Otley LS21 2QU (01943 465977). 🖤 Converted farmhouse on B6451 south of Bland Hill. Open fires, lovely views, in the heart of the countryside. Within easy reach of Herriot, Bronte and Emmerdale country and with attractive market towns around — Skipton, Knaresborough, Otley and Ripon. Walking, bird watching and fishing on the nearby reservoirs. Residents' lounge with TV. Comfortable bedrooms. Non-smoking accommodation available. Children welcome. Pets by arrangement. Bed and Breakfast £14, en suite £18.

PATELEY BRIDGE near. Mrs Margaret Watson, High Winsley Farm, Burnt-Yates, Ripley, Near Harrogate HG3 3EP (01423 770376). ETB Listed. A warm welcome is assured on this 120 acre stock rearing farm situated in peaceful scenic countryside just seven miles from and central to Harrogate, Ripon and Pateley Bridge areas. Brimham Rocks and Ripley Castle just three miles away. Accommodation is in two double and one twin-bedded rooms, all en suite, comfortable and spacious with tea/coffee facilities. TV lounge with open fire. Bed and Breakfast from £13 to £16.50; Evening Meal optional, or eat at one of the nearby country inns. Ideal base for touring the Yorkshire Dales.

PICKERING. Mrs Ella Bowes, Banavie, Roxby Road, Thornton-le-Dale, Pickering YO18 7SX (01751 474616). 🖤🖤 *COMMENDED.* A warm welcome awaits all guests at Banavie, a large stone-built semi-detached house situated in a very nice part of Thornton-le-Dale which, with the stream flowing through the centre, is one of the prettiest villages in Yorkshire. Nearby are two restaurants and three pubs which provide meals. Ideal centre for touring coast, moors, forest, Scarborough, Castle Howard, Flamingo Park and Eden Camp. Three double bedrooms, one en suite, all with washbasins, shaver points, colour TV and tea making facilities. Bathroom, toilet. Dining room and lounge with colour TV. Central heating. Own door keys. A real Yorkshire breakfast is served by Mrs Bowes. Visitors' book reads "Excellent", "Real Yorkshire Hospitality", "Wonderful holiday; will come again". Large car park. Children made very welcome; cot, high chair, babysitting provided. Dogs welcome. Open all year. Bed and Breakfast from £14 (including tea and biscuits at bedtime). SAE, please, for early reply.

PICKERING. Mrs Livesey, Sands Farm Country Hotel, Wilton, Pickering YO18 7JY (01751 474405). Enjoy a relaxing holiday in a friendly atmosphere where food, rooms and service are of the highest standard. Laura Ashley style bedrooms, with flowers, colour TV and tea-making facilities, all en-suite; some with four-poster beds. Full English Breakfasts; tea-trays in front of a log fire. Evening Meals on request. Many sporting facilities and places of interest nearby — we are happy to suggest many places to visit. NO SMOKING. No dogs. No children under 10 years. Private parking. Terms from £17.50 per person per night. Special Low Season breaks. Special low fat diets on request. Self-catering Cottages also available set in 15 acres. SAE for brochure.

PICKERING. Stan and Hilary Langton, Vivers Mill, Mill Lane, Pickering YO18 8DJ (01751 473640). Vivers Mill is an ancient watermill situated in peaceful surroundings, quarter mile south of Pickering Market Place on Pickering Beck. The Mill is a Listed building constructed of stone, brick and pantiles, part of which possibly dates back to the 13th century. The property with its characteristic beamed ceilings has been renovated, whilst most of the machinery, including the water wheel and millstones, is being retained. Pickering is an excellent centre from which to explore the North Yorkshire Moors National Park, Ryedale and the spectacular Heritage Coast. It is the terminal station for the preserved North Yorkshire Moors Railway and is only 26 miles from historic York. Visitors are assured of a friendly welcome with nourishing, traditional breakfast. Large lounge and six comfortable en suite bedrooms with tea/coffee making facilities. Bed and Breakfast £23 per day; £145 per week. Reductions for family room. Pets welcome.

PICKERING. Judy and Keith Russell, Heathcote House, 100 Eastgate, Pickering YO18 7DW (01751 476991). ♛ ♛ COMMENDED. Judy and Keith look forward to welcoming you to their lovely stone-built Victorian house on the outskirts of the charming market town of Pickering, which is centrally placed for York, Castle Howard (Brideshead Revisited), Heartbeat country, North York Moors National Park and Heritage Coast. We have five comfortably furnished bedrooms (double or twin), all with en suite facilities, hostess tray, colour TV, hair dryer, radio alarm and toiletries. Optional dinner (£12). Table licence. TOTALLY NON SMOKING. Secluded parking. Bed and Breakfast from £19.50 per person per night. Reductions for seven nights or more. Off-season breaks available. Colour brochure on request.

RICHMOND. Colin and Helen Lowes, Wilson House, Barningham, Richmond DL11 7EB (01833 621218). ♛ ♛ COMMENDED. Situated on the North Yorkshire/Co. Durham border, one mile from the A66, this working family farm is ideally situated for a family holiday. The historic towns of Richmond and Barnard Castle are less than 10 miles away and the Lake District, Durham City, York, Beamish Museum and the Metro Centre are within one hour's drive. There is ample walking amidst beautiful scenery plus farm walks and children's play area. Pony trekking at Barnard Castle. The newly renovated accommodation comprises two family apartments with two or three bedrooms, en-suite facilities, colour TV and a kitchenette. Non-smoking accommodation available. Bed and Breakfast or Bed, Breakfast and Evening Meal. Babysitting available. Write or phone for brochure.

RICHMOND. Mrs Dorothy Wardle, Greenbank Farm, Ravensworth, Richmond DL11 7HB (01325 718334). This 170 acre farm, both arable and carrying livestock, is four miles west of Scotch Corner on the A66, midway between the historic towns of Richmond and Barnard Castle, and within easy reach of Teesdale, Swaledale and Wensleydale, only an hour from the Lake District. The farm is one mile outside the village of Ravensworth with plenty of good eating places within easy reach. Guests' own lounge; dining room; two double bedrooms, one en suite and one family room. All have washbasins, tea/coffee facilities, heating and electric blankets. Children welcome. Sorry, no pets. Car essential. Bed and Breakfast from £12.50 includes light supper/bedtime drink. Evening Meal on request. Reductions for children and Senior Citizens. Open all year. Luxury mobile home also available.

RIPON near. Peter and Irene Foster, Lime Tree Farm, Hutts Lane, Grewelthorpe, Near Ripon HG4 3DA (01765 658450). ꕔ ꕔꕔ Working farm, join in.

Secluded Dales farm near Ripon where horses are bred; ideal for touring and visiting Yorkshire's many attractions. The farmhouse is almost 200 years old with exposed beams, oak panelling and open fires, clipped rugs, grandfather clocks, etc., plus central heating throughout. All bedrooms are en suite and have colour TV and tea/coffee making facilities. The dining room has separate tables and guests have their own lounge with access to books and games. Full English breakfast, good traditional home cooking with four course Evening Meal. Open all year. Bed and Breakfast from £17.50; Evening Meal £12.50. Brochure on request.

ROBIN HOOD'S BAY. David and Angela Pattinson, Hogarth Hall, Boggle Hole Road, Robin Hood's Bay, Whitby YO22 4QQ (01947 880547). Hogarth Hall is a newly built farmhouse set in 145 acres of habitat, situated

at the top of the valley with wonderful views of sea, farmland, moors and sky. Experience the wonder of glorious sunrises and sunsets, June being the loveliest month for these. Bring your binoculars to view the wildlife all around. All rooms are en suite with jacuzzi baths, showers and TV; tea/coffee making facilities are available. There is a large lounge for relaxing and enjoying these views and we also have a sauna. Scarborough is 15 miles, Whitby nine miles, York 40 miles, Durham 60 miles, Hornsea 50 miles. Bed and Breakfast from £30 per room.

ROBIN HOOD'S BAY. Mrs B. Reynolds, Gilders Green, Raw, Robin Hood's Bay YO22 4PP (01947 880025). Comfortable accommodation in 17th century farm cottage on a sheep rearing and stock farm. Pleasantly situated in the hamlet of Raw, overlooking Robin Hood's Bay and close to the Moors, it is ideal for walking and touring. One mile from A171, it is within easy reach of Whitby, Scarborough and many more places of interest. There is one family room, with children welcome. Bed and Breakfast from £15, with bedtime drink included. Open Easter to October. Also available, self catering house in village.

ROSEDALE. Mrs B. Brayshaw, Low Bell End Farm, Rosedale, Pickering YO18 8RE (01751 417451). Working farm. The farm is situated in the North Yorkshire Moors National Park about 15 miles from the nearest seaside resort of Whitby. Scarborough and Bridlington are within easy reach, also York, Pickering and Helmsley, all places of historic interest. The farm, a 173 acre beef and sheep farm, is one mile from the village of Rosedale Abbey and there are many lovely walks to be taken in the area. A car is essential with ample parking space. Sorry, no pets. One double, one bunk-bedded, one family rooms; bathroom and toilet; combined sitting/diningroom with colour TV. Children welcome at reduced rates. Cot, high chair, babysitting available. Central heating and open fires. Open all year. Evening Dinner, Bed and Breakfast or Bed and Breakfast. Terms on request.

Terms quoted in this publication may be subject to increase if rises in costs necessitate

ROSEDALE ABBEY. Mrs Alison Dale, Five Acre View, Rosedale, Near Pickering YO18 8RE (01751 417213). Working farm. This 150-acre dairy farm is within easy driving distance from Scarborough, Whitby, York and various leisure parks. Nearer to home there is a wide range of walks set in the North Yorkshire Moors National Park. A small golf course within walking distance is a challenge for any enthusiast. Three-quarters-of-a-mile of trout fishing is also nearby. The "Olde Worlde" farmhouse has all modern-day comforts and offers one family and two double rooms, all with washbasins, tea/coffee making facilities and colour TV. The open-beamed lounge, complete with log fire, has colour TV and satellite. Bed and Breakfast from £13.50; Evening Meal from £6.50. Reductions for children. Pets welcome.

ROSEDALE EAST. Maureen and John Harrison, Moordale House, Dale Head, Pickering YO18 8RH (01751 417219). ❦❦ *COMMENDED.* Dating back to the mid 17th century Moordale House once served the local iron ore mining community as a granary and general stores. Today after extensive refurbishment and modernisation Maureen and John offer you a visit they hope will remain in your heart and memory for years to come. Accommodation is available in one family, two double, two twin bedded rooms, all with en-suite facilities, one double bedded room with washbasin. Tea/coffee making facilities. Full central heating. Separate shower room, bathroom and toilets. Guests are offered Bed and full English Breakfast, five course Evening Dinner optional in the spacious diningroom which benefits from magnificent views over the valley. Comfortable, relaxing lounge with open fire and colour TV, also quiet lounge. A family-run licensed guest house offering good home cooking, every comfort and a happy, friendly atmosphere. Members of the Yorkshire and Humberside Tourist Board. Full Fire Certificate. Brochure and terms on request.

SCARBOROUGH. Mrs M. Edmondson, Plane Tree Cottage Farm, Staintondale, Scarborough YO13 0EY (01723 870796). This small mixed farm is situated off the beaten track, with open views of beautiful countryside and the sea. We have rare breed sheep, spotted pigs, hens, two ginger cats and special sheep dog "Bess". This very old beamed cottage, small but homely, has one twin and one double rooms with washbasins and tea makers. Meals of very high standard served with own fresh eggs and garden produce as available. Staintondale is about half way between Scarborough and Whitby and near the North York Moors. Pretty woodland walks nearby. Car essential. Also six-berth caravan available. SAE please for details, or telephone.

SCARBOROUGH. Mrs Andrea Wood, Wrea Head House, Wrea Head Farm, Barmoor Lane, Scalby, Scarborough YO13 0PG (01723 375844; Fax: 01723 500274). ❦❦ *HIGHLY COMMENDED.* A lovely country house where you are always assured of a warm welcome. A beautiful location with outstanding sea and country views on the edge of the North York Moors National Park, only three miles from Scarborough. All bedrooms en suite with colour TV and tea/coffee trays. Ample parking, telephone, lawns and garden furniture. No smoking in the house please. Sorry, no pets. Bed and Breakfast from £25 to £27. Self catering luxury cottages also available (ETB 4 Keys HIGHLY COMMENDED). HEATED SWIMMING POOL, JACUZZI AND SAUNA.

SCARBOROUGH. Mrs D.M. Medd, Hilford House, Crossgates, Scarborough YO12 4JU (01723 862262). Detached country guest house, quietly situated in own grounds adjoining Scarborough — Seamer road just off A64. Near Scarborough, but handy for touring all coast and countryside of North Yorkshire. Three double, one single and one family bedrooms all with washbasins and central heating. Bathroom, two toilets; diningroom with separate tables and guests' lounge with colour TV. Cot, high chair and babysitting available. Full Fire Certificate held. Open all year round. Personal supervision ensures complete satisfaction of guests. Non-smoking accommodation available. Own home grown fruit and vegetables served in season, also fresh Scarborough cod and local meats. Private car parking. Bed and Breakfast from £15 to £18. Reductions for children sharing.

SCARBOROUGH. Sue and Tony Hewitt, Harmony Country Lodge, Limestone Road, Burniston, Scarborough YO13 0DG (01723 870276). DISTINC-

TIVELY DIFFERENT, HARMONY COUNTRY LODGE is a peaceful and relaxing retreat, octagonal in design and set in two acres of private grounds overlooking the National Park and sea. An ideal centre for walking or touring. Three miles from Scarborough and within easy reach of Whitby, York and the beautiful North Yorkshire countryside. Comfortable standard or en suite centrally heated rooms with colour TV and all with superb views. Attractive dining room, guest lounge and relaxing conservatory. Traditional English breakfast, optional evening meal, including vegetarian. Fragrant massage available. Bed and Breakfast from £18.50. Non smoking, licensed, private parking facilities. Personal service and warm, friendly Yorkshire hospitality. Spacious six berth caravan also available for self-catering holidays. Open all year. Please telephone or write for brochure.

New Inn Hotel

Clapham, Near Settle, North Yorkshire LA2 8HH

Tel: 015242 51203 Fax: 015242 51496
ETB ♥♥♥ Commended
Member of Wayfarer Inns

Keith and Barbara Mannion invite you to their friendly 18th century residential coaching inn in the picturesque Dales village of Clapham. Ideal centre for walking the three peaks of Ingleborough, Pen-y-ghent and Whernside. Kendal and Skipton 21 miles. All rooms have full ensuite facilities, colour TV and tea/coffee facilities. Enjoy good wholesome Yorkshire food in our restaurant or bar meals in either of our two bars. Dogs welcome. Ring for details of special mid-week breaks.

Ring Barbara for full details on 015242 51203.

SKIPTON. Rosie Lister, Bushey Lodge Farm, Starbotton, Skipton BD23 5HY (01756 760424). ♥♥

HIGHLY COMMENDED. Traditional Dales farmhouse in quiet position in Upper Wharfedale village, with extensive views along the valley, much of which is owned and protected by the National Trust. Superb walking and sightseeing in the area. Local inns provide excellent evening meals. Each bedroom has en suite bathroom, hair dryer, TV and tea/coffee making facilities. Open all year except Christmas. Bed and Breakfast from £20 per person per night. Welcome Host 1995.

SKIPTON. Mrs Heather Simpson, Low Skibeden Farmhouse, Skibeden Road, Skipton BD23 6AB (01756 793849; mobile 0831 126473). ♥♥ *COMMEN-*

DED. "Where quality and value for money are guaranteed". Detached 16th century farmhouse set in private grounds with panoramic views, situated one mile east of Skipton off A59/A65. Open all year. Smallholding keeping Charolais cattle and breeding sheep. A warm, friendly welcome awaits all guests (Welcome Host Award) who are served cakes and tea or coffee on arrival and again at 9.30pm. Washbasins and tea/coffee making facilities in all rooms and electric overblankets and heating (October to April). Farmhouse Bed and Breakfast with two en suite rooms and one with two piece toilet en suite; separate WC on first floor; visitors lounge with TV; dining room. Parking. No smoking. No pets. No children under 12 years. Bed and Breakfast from £16/£17.50 per person per night. Single occupancy from £25/£30. New arrivals before 10pm. "Which?" Guide recommended, Welcome Host.

THIRSK. Mrs Tess Williamson, Thornborough House Farm, South Kilvington, Thirsk YO7 2NP (Tel & Fax: 01845 522103). 💐💐 *COMMENDED.* **Working**

farm. This is "James Herriot's" town! Situated one and a half miles north of Thirsk, a warm welcome awaits you in this 200 year old farmhouse set in lovely countryside. Ideal location for a walking or touring holiday. The bedrooms are warm and comfortable: one family room, one double room en suite and one twin room with washbasin and private bathroom. Guests' own sitting and dining rooms with colour TV and open fire. Non-smoking accommodation available. Children most welcome. Babysitting available. Pets accepted. Good home cooking is a speciality; special diets catered for. Guests can choose to have Bed and Breakfast or Bed, Breakfast and Evening Meal. The North Yorks Moors, Pennine Dales, York, the East Coast, Scarborough, Whitby, Ripon, Fountains Abbey, Harrogate are all very near. Golf courses, fishing, horse riding available locally. Bed and Breakfast from £14 per person.

THIRSK. Mrs Barbara Ramshay, Garth House, Dalton, Near Thirsk YO7 3HY (01845 577310). Tourist Board Listed. Working farm, join in. Garth House

is situated in Herriot country amidst beautiful scenery. Near to York, Harrogate and many historic buildings this area with its many attractions is ideal for touring. Guest accommodation is in one family room and one twin room, both with washbasins and tea/coffee making facilities; TV in lounge; central heating. Large gardens and lawns, children's pets and toys. Access to badminton court and other sporting facilities. Bed and Breakfast from £12 to £14. Easy access — from A1 turn off onto A168 and follow signposts for Dalton. Brochure on request.

THIRSK. Joyce Ashbridge, Mount Grace Farm, Cold Kirby, Thirsk YO7 2HL (01845 597389). 💐💐

COMMENDED. A warm welcome awaits you on working farm surrounded by beautiful open countryside with magnificent views. Ideal location for touring or exploring the many walks in the area. Luxury en suite bedrooms with tea/coffee facilities. Spacious guests' lounge with colour TV. Garden. Enjoy delicious, generous helpings of farmhouse fayre cooked in our Aga. Bed and Breakfast from £18; Evening Meal from £9.50. Weekly rates. Open all year except Christmas.

THIRSK. Mrs Helen G. Proudley, Doxford House, 73 Front Street, Sowerby, Thirsk YO7 1JP (01845 523238). 💐💐 *APPROVED.* A warm welcome awaits guests at this handsome Georgian house which overlooks the greens in Sowerby, a delightful village one mile south of Thirsk (James Herriot's Darrowby). Centrally situated for touring the North York Moors and the Dales National Park; within easy reach of York, Harrogate and the East Coast; places of interest include Coxwold, Shandy Hall, Newbrough Priory with beautiful lake and gardens. Ideal walking and riding countryside. Golf at Thirsk. Accommodation has full central heating, all bedrooms (no smoking in bedrooms please) have private bath and/or shower, WC, colour TV and tea/coffee making facilities; one ground floor bedroom suitable for the disabled. Residents' lounge, diningroom. Large garden with a paddock. Children and pets welcome. Cot, high chair, babysitting available. Open all year. Bed and Breakfast from £16; Evening Meal £8. Single occupancy £22 in high season. Reductions for children and weekly bookings.

DOXFORD HOUSE

THORNTON LE DALE. Mrs Sandra M. Pickering, Nabgate, Wilton Road, Thornton le Dale, Pickering YO18 7QP (01751 474279). ❧ *APPROVED.*

Situated at the eastern end of this beautiful village "Nabgate" was built at the turn of the century. Accommodation comprises three double rooms, one being en suite, all with washbasins, shaver points, TV, tea making facilities. Bathroom, toilet. Central heating. Dining room/lounge with Sky TV. Keys provided for access at all times. Car park. Children and pets welcome. Thornton le Dale has three pubs all providing meals, also cafes and fish and chip shop. Situated in the North Yorkshire Moors National Park it is an ideal base for East Coast resorts, Steam Railway, Flamingoland, Castle Howard, York and "Heartbeat" village. Open all year. Bed and Breakfast from £14. Welcome Host and Hygiene Certificate held.

WHITBY. Jim and Mu Wilkinson, High Whins, Tranmire, Whitby YO21 2BW (01947 840546). ❧ Situated on the side of a peaceful pastoral valley in the heart of the North Yorkshire National Park. Apart from the moorland and woodland that decorate our area we have the sea just down the road with good beaches at Sandsend and Runswick Bay. Staithes and Whitby are within easy reach. Good walking country with numerous public footpaths and bridle paths. Real food (home-made bread a speciality), real hospitality from real people. All bedrooms have washbasins, tea/coffee facilities and central heating. Guests' sitting room with TV and separate dining room. Flexible meal times. Unrestricted access. Bed and Breakfast; optional Evening Meal. Brochure available.

See also Colour Display Advertisement **WHITBY near. Mrs Pat Beale, Ryedale House, Coach Road, Sleights, Near Whitby YO22 5EQ (01947 810534).** Welcoming non-smoking Yorkshire house of charm and character at the foot of the moors, National Park and "Heartbeat" country, three and a half miles from Whitby. Rich in history, magnificent scenery, picturesque harbours, cliffs, beaches, scenic railways, superb walking. Three double/twin beautifully appointed bedrooms with private facilities. Guests' lounge and dining room (separate tables) with breathtaking views over Eskdale. Enjoy our large sun terrace and gardens, relax, we're ready to pamper you! Long established; delicious Yorkshire fare; extensive breakfast and snacks menu, picnics (traditional and vegetarian). Recommended local inns and restaurants. Parking, and near public transport. Regret no pets. Bed and Breakfast £16.50 to £18 per person, minimum two nights. Weekly reductions, special breaks spring and October. Tourist Board Member since 1985.

YORK. Mrs K.R. Daniel, Ivy House Farm, Kexby, York YO4 5LQ (01904 489368). Working farm. Bed

and Breakfast on a mixed dairy farm six miles from the ancient city of York on the A1079. Central for the east coast, Herriot country and dales. We offer a friendly service with comfortable accommodation consisting of double or family rooms, all with colour TV and tea/coffee making facilities. We provide a full farmhouse English Breakfast served in separate diningroom; colour TV lounge. Ample car parking with play area for children, who are most welcome. Bed and Breakfast from £15 per person. We are within easy reach of local restaurants and public houses serving excellent evening meals. AA and RAC Listed.

YORK. Mr Bill Frost, Old Farmhouse Country Hotel, Raskelf, York YO6 3LF (01347 821971; Fax: 01347 822392). ❧ ❧ ❧ *HIGHLY COMMENDED.* Old Farm-

house, the small, award-winning comfortable hotel, is ideally situated for exploring the Moors, Dales and York, being some 15 miles north of the City. Huge Yorkshire breakfasts, home baked bread, splendid dinners, with a famous English cheese board, fine wines, malt whiskies, open fires and a warm welcome from the resident chef/proprietors ensure a memorable Short Break or longer holiday. All rooms en suite with central heating, colour TV, phone and hospitality tray. Car parking. Dinner, Bed and Breakfast from £39. Short Breaks at reduced rates available in the winter. Why not ring us for a brochure and sample menu? AA QQQQ Selected.

YORK. Gordon and Trudi Smith, Rosedale Guest House, Wetherby Road, Rufforth, York YO2 3QB (01904 738297). ❧ ❧ *COMMENDED.* Rufforth is a delight-

ful village situated three and a half miles west from the historic city of York, ideally situated for touring Yorkshire Moors and Dales. Rosedale offers you the comfort of a family guest house; all our rooms are furnished to a high standard, some with en-suite facilities, and for the comfort of our guests we provide tea/coffee making facilities and TV in all bedrooms. Guest lounge. Full central heating. Private parking. Children welcome, reduced rates available. Low season rates. Open all year. Bed and full English Breakfast from £16.

YORK. Mrs Cynthia Fell, The Hall Country Guest House, Slingsby, York YO6 7AL (01653 628375).

♛♛♛ *COMMENDED.* The Hall is a Regency house of character set in five acres of delightful grounds, with croquet lawn and stream, situated in a 'real' English village with a ruined castle. A genuine Yorkshire welcome awaits every guest, many of whom return year after year. Excellent varied cuisine with fresh produce. Ideally situated for visiting York, the North Yorkshire Moors, coast and stately homes such as Castle Howard (three miles). We also have bicycles for hire. Double rooms, twin and family rooms, all en suite. A car is essential. Ample parking. Pets welcome. Brochure available. Open Easter to October. Table Licence. Bed and Breakfast from approximately £19; Dinner, Bed and Breakfast from £28.50 (£165 weekly).

Key to Tourist Board Ratings

The Crown Scheme
(England, Scotland & Wales)

Covering hotels, motels, private hotels, guesthouses, inns, bed & breakfast, farmhouses. Every Crown classified place to stay is inspected annually. *The classification:* Listed then 1-5 Crown indicates the range of facilities and services. Higher quality standards are indicated by the terms APPROVED, COMMENDED, HIGHLY COMMENDED and DELUXE.

The Key Scheme
(also operates in Scotland using a Crown symbol)

Covering self-catering in cottages, bungalows, flats, houseboats, houses, chalets, etc. Every Key classified holiday home is inspected annually. *The classification:* 1-5 Key indicates the range of facilities and equipment. Higher quality standards are indicated by the terms APPROVED, COMMENDED, HIGHLY COMMENDED and DELUXE.

The Q Scheme
(England, Scotland & Wales)

Covering holiday, caravan, chalet and camping parks. Every Q rated park is inspected annually for its quality standards. The more ✓ in the Q – up to 5 – the higher the standard of what is provided.

YORK. Mrs Diana Susan Tindall, Newton Guest House, Neville Street, Haxby Road, York YO3 7NP (01904 635627). 🐝 Diana and John offer all their guests a friendly and warm welcome to their Victorian End Town House, a few minutes' walk from City centre, York's beautiful Minster, the City Walls and museums. Situated near an attractive park with good bowling greens. York is an ideal base for touring Yorkshire Moors, Dales and coastline. One bedroom (private facilities outside), all other rooms en suite, colour TV, tea/coffee making tray. Full central heating. Fire Certificate. Private car park. Personal attention. We are a non-smoking house.

YORK. Pauleda House Hotel, 123 Clifton, York YO3 6BL (01904 634745; Fax: 01904 621327). Enjoy superb accommodation centrally situated only minutes away from all the historic attractions. A warm and friendly welcome awaits you at Pauleda, a small family-run hotel offering excellent value for money. All rooms are en suite and tastefully equipped, some with four-poster, colour TV with satellite, tea/coffee tray, etc. Car park. Reduced rates for weekly bookings. Bed and Breakfast from £20 to £35.

YORK. Mr Mike Cundall, Orillia House, 89 The Village, Stockton on Forest, York YO3 9UP (01904 400600). 🐝🐝 A warm welcome awaits you at Orillia House, conveniently situated in the centre of the village three miles north east of York, one mile from A64. The house dates back to the 17th century and has been restored to offer a high standard of comfort with modern facilities yet retaining its original charm and character. All rooms have private facilities, colour TV and tea/coffee making facilities. Our local pub provides excellent evening meals. We also have our own private car park. Bed and Breakfast from £17. Telephone for our brochure.

YORK. Mrs Jackie Cundall, Wellgarth House, Wetherby Road, Rufforth, York YO2 3QB (01904 738592 or 738595). 🐝🐝 AA Listed. FHG Diploma. A warm welcome awaits you at Wellgarth House, ideally situated in Rufforth (B1224) three miles from York and one mile from the ring road (A1237). Also convenient for "Park and Ride" into York City. This country guest house offers a high standard of accommodation with en suite Bed and Breakfast from £16. All rooms have complimentary tea/coffee making, colour TV with Satellite. Rooms with four-poster or king-size beds also available. Excellent local pub two minutes' walk away serves lunches and dinners. Large private car park. Telephone or write for brochure. Access/Visa accepted.

YORK. Keith Jackman, Dairy Guesthouse, 3 Scarcroft Road, York YO2 1ND (01904 639367). Beautifully appointed Victorian town house that was once the local dairy. Well equipped cottage-style rooms that include colour TVs, CD players, hairdryers and hot drinks facilities. Some en suite, one four-poster bedroom. Informal and relaxed, non-smoking environment. Traditional or vegetarian; Bed and Breakfast from £17 per person. Write or phone for reservations or colour borchure.

DAIRY
GUESTHOUSE
Traditional and Wholefood

YORK. Mont-Clare Guest House, 32 Claremont Terrace, Gillygate, York YO3 7EJ (01904 627054;

Fax: 01904 651011). ✿ ✿✿ *COMMENDED.* Take advantage and enjoy the convenience of City Centre accommodation in a quiet location close to the magnificent York Minster. A warm and friendly welcome awaits you at the Mont-Clare. All rooms are en suite, tastefully decorated and have colour TV (Satellite), radio alarm, direct-dial telephone, hairdryer, tea/coffee tray, shoe cleaning, etc. All of York's attractions are within walking distance and we are ideally situated for the Yorkshire Dales, Moors and numerous stately homes. Fire and Hygiene Certificates. Cleanliness, good food, pleasant surroundings and friendliness are our priorities. Private car park. Open all year. Reduced rates for weekly stays. Bed and Breakfast from £17.50 per person per night.

YORK. Mrs Susan Viscovich, The Manor Country House, Acaster Malbis, York YO2 1YL (Tel & Fax:

01904 706723). ✿ ✿✿ *HIGHLY COMMENDED.* Atmospheric Manor in rural tranquillity with our own private lake set in five and a half acres of beautiful mature grounds. Close to Racecourse and only 10 minutes' car journey from the city or take the leisurely river bus (Easter to October). Conveniently situated for trips to Dales, Moors, Wolds and splendid coastline. Find us via A64 exiting for Copmanthorpe-York, Thirsk, Harrogate or Bishopthorpe (Sim Balk Lane). Centrally heated. 10 en suite bedrooms with full facilities. Cosy lounge and lounge bar; licensed, open fire. Conservatory dining room with Aga-cooked food. Four-poster. Stair lift. Bed and Breakfast from £22.50 to £30.00 per person per night. For full details SAE or telephone. Also see our advertisement on the Inside Back Cover of this guide.

YORK near. Meg Abu Hamdan, High Belthorpe, Bishop Wilton, Near York YO4 1SB (01759

368238; mobile 0973 938528). ✿ National Tourist Board Approved. Set on an ancient moated site in the Yorkshire Wolds, this large Victorian farmhouse has spacious bedrooms with uninterrupted panoramic views. The centre of a working livery yard, the house has its own private fishing lake and access to fabulous country walks. Croquet, lawn badminton, small snooker table available. York 12 miles, coast 20 miles. Open all year. Children and pets welcome. Bed and Breakfast from £15.

YORKSHIRE DALES (Horton-in-Ribblesdale). Mr and Mrs Colin and Joan Horsfall, Studfold House, Horton-in-Ribblesdale, Near Settle BD24 0ER (01729

860200). This Georgian house, standing in one acre of beautiful gardens, has panoramic views and is near the Three Peaks in the Dales National Park. The house is an ideal centre for visiting the Dales, Lake District and Bronte country. There are oak beams in most rooms and a log fire in the lounge, with colour TV. Bedrooms have central heating, hot and cold water, colour TV and tea/coffee making facilities. Open all year, except Christmas. Vegetarians, children and pets very welcome. Reduced rates for children sharing rooms. Mountain bikes for hire. Pub half a mile away. Bed and Breakfast £16; four course Evening Meal £8. Also available, self catering unit. SAE for brochure.

WEST YORKSHIRE

KEIGHLEY (Bronte Country). Currer Laithe Farm, Moss Carr Road, Long Lee, Keighley BD21 4SL

(01535 604387). An extensive 180 acre Pennine hill farm rearing and pasturing 140 cattle, some pigs, goats and donkeys. It and the 16th century farmhouse, beamed, mullioned and with inglenook fireplace, offer panoramic views of Airedale and are covenanted to The National Trust. Satisfied guests, still returning after 15 years, create a warm, friendly atmosphere. Food is traditional Yorkshire fare. Pets and children welcome. Ground floor accommodation is frequently used by guests in wheelchairs. Bed and Breakfast £12; Bed, Breakfast and Evening Meal £15.50. We also have two self-catering cottage flats from £50 to £150 per week. Group accommodation can be arranged, serviced or self catering.

NORMANTON. Mrs V. Sharpe, Station Lodge Guest House, 21/27 Lower Station Road, Normanton

WF6 2BE (01924 223741). Attractive guest house and tea shop recently converted and refurbished to a high standard in Normanton town centre. 10 bedrooms, excellent en suite accommodation. TV and tea/coffee facilities in each room. Satellite TV. Licensed. Fire Certificate. Good parking. Very good rates from as little as £15 per person per night. Open all year. Dogs by arrangement. Children welcome. Ideally situated near M62/M1 network.

Eureka The Museum for Children, West Yorkshire offers FREE child entry with two adults paying full price when using our READERS' OFFER VOUCHER.

ISLE OF WIGHT

SHANKLIN. Denise and Martin Nickless, Keats Cottage Hotel and Tea Rooms, 76 High Street,

Shanklin Old Village PO37 6NJ (01983 866351). Keats Cottage is situated next to the old village in the High Street of Shanklin. A small family-run licensed hotel, centrally heated. TV lounge with log fire. Tea making facilities and washbasins in all rooms; en suite rooms available. Children welcome. Open all year. A five minute walk through tree-lined Chine Avenue to the sandy beach. Bed and Breakfast from £13.50; Bed, Breakfast and Evening Meal from £18.50. 1992 PRICES HELD. Mini Breaks welcome. "One night or more — that's what we're here for." Credit cards accepted. Holiday insurance available.

PLEASE ENCLOSE A STAMPED ADDRESSED ENVELOPE WITH ENQUIRIES

COUNTRY INNS

CAMBRIDGESHIRE, CAMBRIDGE. Crown and Punchbowl Inn, Horningsea, Cambridge CB5 9TG (01223 860643; Fax: 01223 441814). This charming, recently restored 17th century inn, situated in the centre of the unspoilt riverside village of Horningsea which lies four miles north-east of Cambridge, is an ideal stop-over, not only for visitors to the city but also those touring East Anglia. The bedrooms all offer the highest standards of comfort with private bathrooms, tea/coffee making facilities, telephones, and colour TV. The inn has an enviable reputation for its food. A speciality of the house is a five-course dinner included in the daily and weekend rates. Further details and brochure on request.

CUMBRIA, BRAITHWAITE. Coledale Inn, Braithwaite, Near Keswick CA12 5TN (017687 78272). ♛♛♛ A friendly family-run Victorian Inn in a peaceful hillside position above Braithwaite, and ideally situated for touring and walking, with paths to the mountains immediately outside our gardens. All bedrooms are warm and spacious, with en suite shower room and colour television. Children are welcome, as are pets. Home-cooked meals are served every lunchtime and evening, with a fine selection of inexpensive wines, beers and Coledale XXPS and Yates real cask ale. Open all year except midweek lunches in winter. Tariff and menu sent on request.

DEVON, SEATON. Three Horseshoes Inn, Branscombe, Seaton EX12 3BR (01297 680251). The Sea Mist Bungalow adjoins the famous Three Horseshoes Inn. Accommodation in two bedrooms (one has twin beds and the other a double), bathroom, large sitting room with bed settee, kitchen with fridge. Central heating if required. Colour TV. Set in its own little garden, but many guests like to use the full facilities of the inn. 10 minutes from Sidmouth, Seaton and Beer. Glorious countryside yet close to the sea. Terms range from £100 (low season) to £235 (high season). Open all year.

HEREFORD & WORCESTER, KINGTON. The Burton Hotel, Mill Street, Kington HR5 3BQ (01544 230323). HETB ♛♛♛♛ The list of sporting and leisure activities available around this charming little town is truly amazing, ranging from golf and walking to paragliding. Of course, there is always the option of doing nothing in particular, a most inviting prospect when one's base is the warmly welcoming Burton Hotel, an attractive former coaching inn which has been tastefully modernised. The en suite bedrooms are comfortable and spacious with colour TV, direct-dial telephone and tea/coffee making facilities. There are three large family rooms. Sunny lounge bar overlooks the garden and offers real ales or a tasty snack from the varied menu while the highly recommended restaurant features the finest ingredients prepared with flair and imagination. Ask for details of Getaway Breaks/Golfing Escapes.

Matlock Bath, a spa with medicinal springs and wells on the River Derwent, Derbyshire.

SHROPSHIRE, KNIGHTON near. Chris and Judy Stevenson, Red Lion Inn, Llanfair Waterdine, Near Knighton LD7 1TV (01547 528214). "Simple and comfortable" is how hosts Chris and Judy Stevenson sum up what is on offer at this centuries-old inn, and it is just these qualities which endear the Red Lion to both locals and visitors alike. Set in a pretty garden below which the River Teme draws a silvery border between England and Wales, accommodation is limited to one double en suite guest room and two twin-bedded rooms, all freshly decorated, well furnished and spotlessly clean. The hearty breakfast included in the room rate is served in a dining room overlooking the Teme Valley and good, home-cooked bar food is served lunchtime and evenings to the accompaniment of fine traditional ales. Tariff: double room with en suite facilities £40, twin-bedded room £33. Please write or telephone for our brochure.

SOMERSET, EXMOOR. The Rest and Be Thankful Inn, Wheddon Cross, Exmoor TA24 7DR (01643 841222). ♛♛♛ *HIGHLY COMMENDED.* RAC Acclaimed, AA QQQQ. After an exhilarating day exploring the wild and picturesque moorland, one's first thought on catching sight of this neat cream-painted inn must surely be "what an appropriate name!" Rest is assured in the comfortable, well-appointed bedrooms, each with en suite shower and enjoying sweeping views of Dunkery Beacon, the highest point in Somerset. The hungry or thirsty traveller will be thankful too for the traditional home-cooked meals and snacks served in the restaurant and bar, accompanied perhaps by a glass of well-kept ale or a selection from the carefully chosen wine list. In finer weather patrons can relax in the charming garden patio, while the more actively inclined can make use of the games room and skittle alley. Credit cards accepted.

Monsal Dale, one of the beautiful valleys in Derbyshire.

SELF-CATERING HOLIDAYS

BEDFORDSHIRE

BEDFORD. Mrs Sheila Mousley, Lea Cottage, Old Harrowden Road, Bedford MK42 0TB (01234 740182). Members of the Bedfordshire Farm and Country Accommodation Group can offer a selection of Bed and Breakfast and Self Catering accommodation in rural areas. Thirteen properties offering Bed and Breakfast with prices from £15 per person per night; nine self catering units with prices from £90 to £310 per week. Easily accessible by road or rail and offer a variety of country pursuits such as walking, cycling, fishing, golfing and water sports. Only 50 miles north of London. All accommodation in our brochure is inspected annually by the Tourist Board. Further information and a colour brochure on application.

BERKSHIRE

MAIDENHEAD near. Mrs G. Reynolds, Moor Farm, Holyport, Near Maidenhead SL6 2HY (Tel & Fax: 01628 33761). ♀♀♀♀ *HIGHLY COMMENDED.* **Sleep 2/4.** In the pretty village of Holyport, Courtyard Cottages are on the 700 year old Listed manor of Moor Farm and are conversions from a Georgian stable block and two small barns. They retain the charm of their original features and are furnished with antique pine. The four cottages are well placed for touring the Thames Valley and are four miles from Windsor and convenient for visiting London. Sheep and horses are on the farm. Weekly terms from £200 to £395.

BUCKINGHAMSHIRE

See also Colour Display Advertisement **WOOBURN GREEN. Thames Valley Holiday Homes. Properties sleep 1/6.** Two holiday homes situated in a picturesque village a short distance from the famous Cliveden Estate, and within easy reach of London (25 miles) and Windsor (10 miles). OVERLEIGH sleeps two to six people and UNDERLEIGH sleeps one to four people. Both properties are fully equipped with central heating, colour TV, telephone, pretty gardens/orchard and plenty of parking. For further details send for free colour brochure to **Mrs Griffin, Myosotis, Widmoor, Wooburn Green HP10 0JG (01628 521594; Fax: 01628 850471).**

CAMBRIDGESHIRE

ELY. Quaint Cottage, 10 Nutholt Lane, Ely. ♀♀♀ *COMMENDED.* **Sleeps 2/6.** Period terrace cottage, comfortable and cosy, with stunning views to Ely Cathedral which is floodlit at night. Three minutes' walk to shops, cathedral and leisure centre with swimming pool, British Rail (we will collect you from station), near marina on River Great Ouse.

Accommodation in one double (downstairs), one twin and one double bedrooms; sitting/dining room with colour TV and sofa bed. Kitchen with cooker, refrigerator, washing machine and microwave. Two bathrooms. Gas central heating by £1 coin meter. Linen provided. Garden with furniture. No smoking, no pets, suitable for disabled visitors. Weekly terms from £130 for two in self contained flat, £260 for six. Minimum stay two nights, £60 for two persons. Contact: **Peter Sicard, The Laurels, 104 Victoria Street, Littleport, Ely CB6 1LZ (01353 861972).**

ELY. La Hogue Cottage, La Hogue Farm, Chippenham, Ely. **♀♀♀♀♀** *DE LUXE.* **Working farm. Sleeps 6.** The farm cottage has been completely refurbished to the highest standard and provides accommodation that is both luxurious and comfortable for up to six persons.

Comprising one double and two twin bedrooms; drawing room with open log fire and colour TV; dining room; modern kitchen with dishwasher, microwave, etc; utility room with washing machine and tumble dryer; bathroom, shower/ cloakroom. Full central heating throughout, payphone and large garage with deep freeze. Situated half a mile off the A11 and one mile from the A14 giving excellent access to all of East Anglia and only one and a half hours from London and East Coast. Carp fishing is available on farm pond for all tenants, day fishing and excellent riding are available locally, plus numerous golf courses in the area. Children welcome, sorry no pets. Terms from £360 to £460 per week. Brochure available, contact: **R. & J. Tilbrook, The Grange, Barton Mills, Bury St. Edmunds, Suffolk IP28 6BG (01638 750433; Fax: 01638 712833).**

CORNWALL

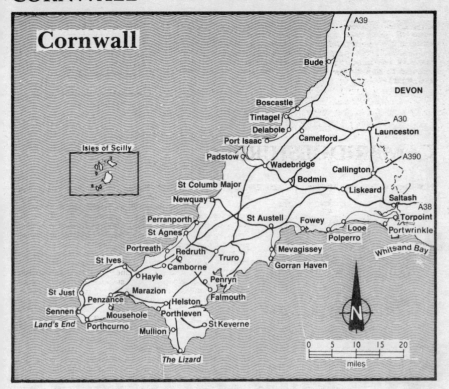

Cornwall

BODINNICK-BY-FOWEY. **Penmariam Quay Cottage, Yeate Farm, Bodinnick-by-Fowey. Sleeps 6.**

The cottage, carefully converted from a 14th century barn, is situated in an enviable position, overlooking Mixtow Pill and the Fowey Estuary. With its own quay, slip and mooring, it is ideally placed for sailing, boating and fishing. Nearby footpath leads across our fields to the Old Ferry Inn at Bodinnick, and many other walks are available in surrounding countryside which is mainly National Trust land. Cottage stands in own grounds, 120 yards above the river. Open plan living and dining area contains a feature fireplace of Cornish stone; fuel supplied in winter; colour TV; three double bedrooms; shower room with toilet. Electric cooker. Night storage heater. Well behaved pets welcome. Ample parking. Available all year. Please send SAE (22cm by 11cm) for brochure. **Mrs Angela M. Oliver, Yeate Farm, Bodinnick-by-Fowey PL23 1LZ (01726 870256).**

BODMIN. **Mr T. Chadwick, Skisdon, St. Kew, Bodmin PL30 3HB (01208 841372).** Charming flats in lovely old country manor house, Grade II Listed. Beautiful spacious gardens, lawns, streams and woodlands in sheltered peaceful valley only four miles from spectacular North Coast. Outstanding local coastline and countryside; many unspoiled stretches maintained by the National Trust. Bathing, surfing, sailing, sailboarding, golf, hill walking, fishing, pony trekking, cycleways, tennis, squash and modern sports centre all within six miles — Camel Estuary, Polzeath, Daymer, Rock, Port Isaac and Bodmin Moor. Spacious self contained flats sleep from one to seven (for large parties interior communicating doors can be opened). Fully equipped kitchens, colour TVs, night storage heaters, communal laundry facilities. Very attractive village pub serving excellent food only 200 yards away, shops one mile, market town (Wadebridge) five miles. Prices from £115 to £345. Brochure available on request.

BODMIN MOOR. Furswain Farmhouse, Near famous Jamaica Inn, A30.

Romantically set on the edge of Bodmin Moor, bounded by River Fowey, between two lakes, 900ft above sea level, one mile nearest neighbour, down its own lane, only seven miles Jamaica Inn A30 and A38, half an hour Looe and Polperro, two and a half miles beauty spot with ancient bridge, waterfalls and woodland walks amidst breathtaking countryside, convenient North and South Cornish coasts. A very cosy four bedroomed 17th century detached farmhouse, sleeps two/eight with climbing ivy to front, surrounded by farmyard with doves and pigeons, old stone barns, walled gardens, gravelled parking and interspersed with trees. This special little property up and away from it all, has Aga in modern kitchen, woodburner in massive granite fireplace to beamed lounge, beamed dining room. Tastefully furnished including colour TV. Contact: **Graham Wrights, Guardian House, Barras Street, Liskeard PL14 6AD (01579 344080).**

BOSCASTLE. Mrs Ann Harding, Ringford Farm, St. Juliot, Boscastle PL35 0BX (01840 250306). Working farm, join in.

A two bedroomed converted barn sleeping up to six persons comfortably. Fully equipped and has magnificent sea views. Pure spring water. Set on a 25 acre stock farm with cows, sheep, goats, pigs, ducks and chickens — you are welcome to look around and help with feeding if you so wish. Ideally situated for touring Devon and Cornwall, many footpaths to explore. Children and pets welcome. Weekly terms from £80 to £310.

See also Colour Display Advertisement **BOSCASTLE near. Mr D. Clough, Courtyard Farm, Lesnewth, Near Boscastle PL35 0HR (01840 261256). ETB ♀♀/♀♀♀ COMMENDED. Sleep 2-8.** Picturesque group of 17th century luxury stone cottages overlooking beautiful National Trust valley, some with sea views. All the cottages are individually designed and furnished, and equipped to a high standard with colour TV etc. They are warm and comfortable and are open all year round. Virtually all the coastline around Boscastle is National Trust owned and provides fabulous walks and beaches. Our cottages offer you quality and comfort at reasonable rates. Home cooked food available. Activity Breaks. Colour brochure available.

BUDE. Sharland House, Marhamchurch, Bude. Sleeps 10.

From A39 take unclassified turning to Marhamchurch. Pleasantly situated, Sharland House overlooks its own lawned garden adjacent to the square of this attractive village and, in a favoured position, is surrounded by white-painted cottages with thatched or slated roofs. The spacious house dates from Victorian and even earlier times with an interesting interior created by thick walls, low beamed ceilings and window seats. Comfortable accommodation for up to 10 persons is provided by two sittingrooms, diningroom and well-equipped kitchen, five bedrooms and a playroom for young children. Ideally placed for exploring with easy access to many good beaches and cliff walks along the beautiful Cornish Coast. Pets welcome. One and a half miles from Bude. Children welcome. Terms from £220 to £467. SAE for further details to **Mrs P. Gilhespy, 2 Church Cottages, Marhamchurch, Bude EX23 0EN (01288 361570).**

BUDE near. Mr and Mrs F.H.G. Cummins, Mineshop, Crackington Haven, Bude EX23 0NR (01840 230338).

Within 100 yards of unspoilt beach abounding with prawning pools and lobster hides. Cottages at Millook featured in GOOD HOLIDAY COTTAGE GUIDE. Area of Outstanding Natural Beauty, unspoilt and uncommercialised. Coastal footpath and wooded valley walks. Open all year. All rooms with electric heaters. Night store heating free early and late season. Wood burning stoves. Sands at Widemouth Bay one and a half miles. Crackington Haven five miles, Bude five miles (fishing, golf, heated swimming pool, tennis, etc). Pets and children welcome. Colour brochure and terms on request.

CALLINGTON. Brenda Crago, Cadson Manor Farm, Callington PL17 7HW (01579 383969). ♀♀♀

HIGHLY COMMENDED. **Sleeps 4 plus cot.** Cadson Manor lies just off the A390 close to Newbridge which spans the River Lynher three miles west of Callington; Liskeard seven miles. Situated in secluded position yet close to all main towns, riding, golf, beaches. Farm and river walks. The apartment has two large bedrooms (one double, one with two single beds); shower room; spacious lounge/kitchen/diner with colour TV, all necessary kitchen fittings, automatic washing machine and tumble dryer. Night storage heating. Electricity and bed linen included in the tariff. Sorry, no pets. Bed and Breakfast accommodation also available. Please do not hesitate to phone or write for further assistance and our brochure. We are Farm Holiday Bureau and Cream of Cornwall Farm Holiday Group members.

COVERACK. Harbour Cottage, Coverack. Sleeps 6. Cosy 18th century cottage in the beautiful village of Coverack.

A most comfortable little cottage with three bedrooms, all with washbasins; small bathroom, separate toilet. Washing machine, TV and telephone. For the past 24 years guests have returned year after year. Fishing, safe bathing and wonderful walks all nearby, 10 minutes from market town of Helston. For further details contact **Mrs E. Parr, Beach House, Coverack TR12 6TE (01326 280621) if no reply try (01243 841485).**

CRACKINGTON HAVEN. Mr and Mrs O.H.F. Tippett, Trelay, St. Gennys, Bude EX23 0NJ (01840 230378). Sleep 2/8.

Lovely stone cottages converted from traditional barns and period farmhouse (accommodate two, four, six or eight). Idyllic setting on small working sheep farm at the head of a deep wooded valley. Area of Outstanding Natural Beauty. Five minutes to sandy beach at Crackington Haven and coast path along spectacular National Trust cliffs. Ideal area for surfing, walking, bird-watching etc. All cottages furnished in character — much pine and oak, comfortable suites and beds. Log fires, dishwashers, linen, fenced gardens, patios, laundry room and payphone. Pets welcome. Low season from £90 per week, also short breaks. Main season £155 to £650 per week. Colour brochure sent on request. Cornwall Tourist Board inspected.

CUSGARNE. Joyce and George Clench, Saffron Meadow, Cusgarne, Truro TR4 8RW (01872 863171). Sleeps 3 plus baby. A cosy single storey, detached dwelling with garden, within the grounds of Saffron Meadow, set in quiet hamlet, safe parking in drive. Secluded and surrounded by wooded pastureland. Double bedroom with double vanity unit. Single bedroom. Fully tiled shower, WC and L.B. suite. Well equipped kitchen/diner. Compact TV room. Hot water and gas included. Metered electricity. Ample external lighting. Post, shop, inn a short walk. Central to Truro, North and South coasts. Dogs welcome. For two: June £130, July £180, August £190.

FALMOUTH. Nantrissack, Constantine, Falmouth. NANTRISSACK is an impressive farmhouse standing in a delightful garden. It is ideally situated for touring this lovely southern coast of Cornwall. Being two miles from Gweek — the little creek of the Helford River — it is also ideal for visiting Falmouth and the Lizard Peninsula. The farm and small woodland with a freshwater stream is available for those who wish to walk.

The furnishings are nice, and beds are new divans. Bathroom; hot and cold water in all bedrooms. Partial central heating. New 30ft sun lounge. Colour TV. Fully equipped with all linen except towels; iron provided. Kiddies welcome also well-behaved dog. Premises thoroughly cleaned and checked by owners between each let. Sea about four-and-a-half miles. Illustrated brochure available. SAE please. Terms from £180 including VAT per week. **Mr T.P. Tremayne, "The Home", Penjerrick, Falmouth TR11 5EE (01326 250427; Fax: 01326 250143).**

Terms quoted in this publication may be subject to increase if rises in costs necessitate

FALMOUTH. Mrs B. Newing, Glengarth, Burnthouse, St. Gluvias, Penryn TR10 9AS (01872 863209). Ideally situated, four miles from Falmouth, for touring Cornwall and furnished to a high standard. Centrally heated first-floor apartment in a delightful detached house. Two double bedrooms and one with full-size bunk beds; comfortable lounge with colour TV; fully equipped kitchen/diner; bathroom; shower room with toilet. Hot water, electricity, bed linen and towels included in tariff. Garden and ample parking. Children and pets welcome. Open all year. Member of Cornwall Tourist Board.

FALMOUTH (near Helford River). Mrs R. Matthews, Boskensoe Farm, Mawnan Smith, Falmouth TR11 5JP (Tel & Fax: 01326 250257). Sleeps 6/8. BOSKENSOE FARM HOLIDAY BUNGALOW. Situated in picturesque village of Mawnan Smith, Falmouth five miles, one and a half miles from lovely Helford River famous for beautiful coastal walks, gardens and scenery. Several quiet, safe beaches for bathing, also excellent sailing and fishing facilities. Bungalow has three bedrooms, colour TV, electric cooker, fridge/freezer, washing machine and microwave. Fitted with storage heaters and electric fires. Spacious garden and ample parking for cars and boats. Terms from £130 to £375. Brochure on request.

FLUSHING. Quayside Cottage, Flushing, Near Falmouth. This comfortable, furnished cottage, sleeping up to six in three bedrooms is situated on beautiful Falmouth Harbour. The village pubs, restaurants and shops are all close by, as is the ferry to Falmouth. The sandy beach is about 10 minutes' walk. Colour TV, cooker and microwave, bath with shower, separate utility room. Storage heaters, double glazing and high insulation for holidays at any time of the year. Views across the harbour. Children and pets welcome. Terms from £100 to £335 per week; electricity by slot meter. Full details available from **Mr A. Bromley, 22 Gravel Lane, Ringwood, Hampshire BH24 1LN (01425 476660).**

GORRAN HAVEN, Near Mevagissey. Ken and Sally Pike, Tregillan, Trewollock Lane, Gorran Haven PL26 6NT (01726 842452). Beautiful rural area, 600 yards from safe, clean, sandy beach. Ideal for children. Harbour with boat launching facilities, temporary boat moorings. Swimming, fishing. Children and pets very welcome. Ground floor flat sleeping two/seven, bedroom with double bed, double bedroom with twin beds or fullsize bunk beds, plus folding bed available; double bed settee in lounge. Kitchen, shower, toilet. First floor flat sleeping two/six in double en suite bedroom, bunk bedroom, double bed settee in lounge. Kitchen, dining area, shower, toilet. Each flat has colour TV, radio, fridge/freezer, full size electric cooker, microwave, electric heaters (night storage heating out of season). Use of washing machine. Private parking, secluded garden, sea views. Cleanliness assured. Pets welcome. Open all year. Weekly terms from £95 to £360. Member of both English and Cornwall Tourist Boards.

HELFORD ESTUARY. Mrs S. Trewhella, Mudgeon Vean Farm, St. Martin, Helston TR12 6DB (01326 231341). Leave the hustle and bustle of town life. Come and enjoy the peace and tranquillity of the Helford Estuary. Three homely cottages sleep four/six, equipped to a high standard. Open all year for cosy winter breaks. Open fires/heating. Set amidst a small 18th century working farm with magnificent views across an extensive valley area, surrounded by fields and woodland — a walk through the woods takes you to the Helford River. A superb location in an area of outstanding natural beauty with the rugged coastline of the Lizard Peninsula and beaches only a short drive away. Children and pets welcome. From £100 to £325 per week.

HELFORD RIVER near. Mrs Pam Royall, Glebe Hall, Mawgan, Near Helston TR12 6AD (01326 221257).

Enchanting creekside cottages, luxuriously appointed, Central heating, log fires, sleeping two to 10. Ideal for sailing, walking or a peaceful retreat. Also attractive old stone coach house cottages, two/three bedrooms, fully equipped to a high standard in a sheltered two acre garden with splendid heating swimming pool and games room. Long weekends early and late season.

HELSTON. Fuchsia Cottage, Tregarne, Manaccan, Helston.

Secluded country bungalow (owner's home) in large, mature garden, one mile from fishing cove of Porthallow. Lovely area for walking, touring, boating and fishing. Shop, pub and beach one mile. Ideal for a relaxing holiday. The well carpeted, fully equipped accommodation comprises three double bedrooms, two with double beds, one with bunks/twin beds, all with Continental quilts; large dining room/kitchen with electric cooker, twin tub washing machine, fridge/freezer, electric water heater and toaster. The large lounge has an inglenook with stone fireplace, TV and radio. Ideal for children, cots available on request. Electricity by meter. Car essential, access by private lane; ample parking. Pets by arrangement. Available April to October. Special rates for Senior Citizens except June, July and August. For dates telephone after 4pm. **Mrs P.M. Jones, "Avisford", Chase Road, Brocton, Stafford ST17 0TL (01785 662470).**

HELSTON. Mrs A.G. Farquhar, Porthpradnack, Mullion, Helston TR12 7EX (01326 240226).

At Mullion Cove on the Lizard Peninsula is Porthpradnack, a well built house with two flats, each accommodating four/six persons. A 10 minute walk from house to Mullion Cove and three other beaches. Both flats have fully equipped kitchens with all modern facilities. Colour TV. Each flat has separate front door. Pets permitted by arrangement. Car essential, large car park. Panoramic rural views from all rooms. One acre gardens at tenants' disposal. Weekly terms from £100 to £275. Other holiday accommodation also available, please enquire.

HELSTON near. Troon Cottage, Breage, Near Helston. Sleeps 2/5.

Take an early or late break in this charming old cottage, attractively furnished to a high standard, situated in a quiet country lane near the sea. Modern kitchen, microwave, tumble dryer, colour TV, oil-fired central heating, beds made up ready. Secluded garden, patio, garage. Children welcome, cot provided. Breage is an ideal centre for exploring the numerous beaches and National Trust coastal walks in the area and within easy motoring distance of Land's End, The Lizard, Helford, Falmouth, Penzance, St. Ives and many other well known beauty spots. Sorry, no pets. Telephone or write to **Mrs A.M. Graham, Long View, Maple Avenue, Bexhill-on-Sea, East Sussex TN39 4ST (01424 843182).**

See also Colour Display Advertisement **HELSTON. Sharon Darling, "Halwyn", Manaccan, Near Helston TR12 6ER (01326 280359). Properties sleep 2/12.** "Halwyn" is an ancient Cornish farmstead converted into a family home and four self-catering holiday cottages, all fully equipped. Situated in two acres of delightful secluded gardens including a small lake, badminton court, children's play area and a putting green. "Halwyn" also boasts an indoor heated swimming pool, sauna and solarium. The perfect holiday retreat. Heating available for out of season bookings and well behaved pets welcome. Please write or phone for brochure.

HELSTON. Mrs Julie Bray, Tregevis Farm, St. Martin, Helston TR12 6DN (01326 231265). ♀♀♀♀

Tregevis Farm · St Martin

COMMENDED. **Sleeps 7 + cot.** Come and relax at Tregevis, a working dairy farm in the picturesque Helford River area, just half a mile from the little village of St. Martin and five miles from sandy beaches. The accommodation is a self contained, spacious part of the farmhouse, very comfortable, well equipped and with a games room. The large lawn area with swings will prove popular with children, as will our farm animals. Open Easter to October. Terms from £170 to £400 per week.

LAUNCESTON near. Mrs A.E. Moore, Hollyvag, Lewannick, Near Launceston PL15 7QH (01566 782309; Fax: 01566 782956). Working farm, join in. Sleeps 5.

Part of 17th century farmhouse, self contained and full of old world charm with own lawns, front and back. Set in secluded position in wooded countryside with views of the moors. Central for North and South coasts. Family farm with ducks on the pond, horses, sheep and poultry. Sleeps up to five, fully furnished with all modern conveniences, folding bed and cot available. Colour TV, fridge, electric cooker, solid fuel heater if needed. Babysitting available free. Linen not provided. Within five miles of market town; golf, fishing and riding nearby. Terms from £120 to £180. Brochure on request.

ENJOY A HOLIDAY ON OUR TRADITIONAL WORKING FARM

A warm welcome awaits you at our 17th century farmhouse, centrally situated for touring Devon and Cornwall. Wander across fields to the River Tamar or carp lake (good fishing available). Well furnished accommodation including fully fitted kitchen with automatic washing machine, tumble dryer, standard electric cooker, microwave and toaster. Sitting room with colour TV, video. Storage heaters, bed linen inclusive in price; towels can be hired. Three bedrooms (sleeps 2/6) plus cot; tastefully decorated with matching duvets and curtains. Bathroom; shower in separate room. Children very welcome. ♀♀♀♀ Commended.

TERMS £100-£350 PER WEEK. BED & BREAKFAST ALSO AVAILABLE FROM £15.00 PER NIGHT 🌼🌼 Commended

Mrs K. W. Broad, Lower Dutson Farm, Launceston, Cornwall PL15 9SP   Tel: 01566 776456

LAUNCESTON. Mrs E.M. Budge, Meadow Croft, East Kitcham Farm, St. Giles, Launceston PL15 9SL (01566 784829). Working farm, join in. Enjoy a country holiday in a luxury six-berth caravan, all amenities, equipped and maintained to a high standard, includes two bedrooms, one double, one twin (not bunks). Lounge with colour TV, kitchen with full-size cooker and fridge, shower room with shower, basin and toilet. Linen supplied. The caravan is sited in its own garden (with parking) and has lovely views of the surrounding countryside. Central for coast and Dartmoor; Leisure Centre, golf, bowls, etc. at Launceston (five miles); also fishing, sailing, walks and birdwatching, etc at Roadford Lake nearby. Visitors are encouraged to enjoy farming activities. Own lake for TROUT FISHING on farm. Pets welcome by arrangement. SAE for terms.

LAUNCESTON. Mrs H.H. Rowe, Godcott, North Petherwin, Launceston PL15 8NX (01566 785223). Working farm. Sleeps 6. Solid stone farm cottage situated on parish road. The dairy farm is set in beautiful Cornish countryside, with fishing, surfing, golf, squash, tennis and leisure centres at both Launceston and Bude, also in Holsworthy and surrounding districts. Near Devon Border so guests can enjoy the facilities of both Devon and Cornwall. Six people accommodated in one double, one twin and one room with bunk beds and cot. Bathroom and toilet; also immersion heater; mains water and electricity (meter £1); Rayburn in kitchen. Car essential — parking. Pets welcome. Open January to December; terms from £120 weekly. SAE, please.

LISKEARD. Mrs E. Coles, Cutkive Wood Chalets, St. Ive, Liskeard PL14 3ND (01579 362216).

Properties sleep 4 adults; 2 children. Six only detached, self catering cedarwood chalets in 41 acres of private woodland. Personally supervised; the owners take great pride in the cleanliness and condition of these two and three bedroomed chalets which are fully equipped, including bed linen, colour TV, full size cooker, fridge and microwave oven. Terms from £90 to £280 per week. Picturesque resorts of Looe and Polperro a short drive away; Plymouth 30 minutes; St. Mellion Championship Golf Course five miles. On-site shop, milk and papers daily. Pets corner with goats, rabbits, ducks, hens, geese. Children welcome to help feed the animals and milk the goats. Three-hole golf course, tuition available, games room, adventure playground. Dogs welcome.

LOOE. Allen Cottages. A choice of six attractive character cottages situated in the heart of Looe, close to

the beach, harbour and shops. Set in quiet streets, our cottages are clean, comfortably furnished and fully equipped to allow you to enjoy a peaceful, carefree holiday. Open all year. Centrally heated. No pets. Further details in our comprehensive brochure, available on request. **Mr S. Allen, Allen Cottages, The Old Barn, Polperro Road, Looe PL13 2JS (Tel/Fax: 01503 262695; Tel: 01503 264910).**

Key to
Tourist Board Ratings

The Crown Scheme
(England, Scotland & Wales)

Covering hotels, motels, private hotels, guesthouses, inns, bed & breakfast, farmhouses. Every Crown classified place to stay is inspected annually. *The classification:* Listed then 1-5 Crown indicates the range of facilities and services. Higher quality standards are indicated by the terms APPROVED, COMMENDED, HIGHLY COMMENDED and DELUXE.

The Key Scheme
(also operates in Scotland using a Crown symbol)

Covering self-catering in cottages, bungalows, flats, houseboats, houses, chalets, etc. Every Key classified holiday home is inspected annually. *The classification:* 1-5 Key indicates the range of facilities and equipment. Higher quality standards are indicated by the terms APPROVED, COMMENDED, HIGHLY COMMENDED and DELUXE.

The Q Scheme
(England, Scotland & Wales)

Covering holiday, caravan, chalet and camping parks. Every Q rated park is inspected annually for its quality standards. The more √ in the Q – up to 5 – the higher the standard of what is provided.

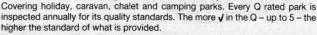

THE COTTAGES at Trefanny Hill Nr. LOOE

GORGEOUS OLD WORLD COUNTRY COTTAGES

Cornish Charm: Enchanting medieval hamlet with cottages dating back to the 15th century. Log fires, antiques and lovely country furnishings, fresh white linen, flowers and the comforts of home – for family, friends, children, or a cosy cottage for two. Nestling on a south-facing hillside, with your own private garden, fabulous views, friendly farm animals, including shires, lakeside and woodland walks and beautiful heated pool, tennis court and play area. Delicious home-cooked cuisine in our own tiny inn (including fresh fish), and meals service. Open all year.

O. Slaughter, Trefanny Hill, Duloe, Nr. Liskeard PL14 4QF
Telephone 01503 220200

A COUNTRY LOVER'S PARADISE – WITH AN ABUNDANCE OF COUNTRY WALKS FROM YOUR GARDEN GATE AND COASTAL WALKS ONLY 4 MILES AWAY.

LOOE. Robert and Jean Henly, Bucklawren Farm, St. Martins, Looe PL13 1NZ (01503 240738; Fax: 01503 240481). ♀ ♀ ♀ ♀ *HIGHLY COMMENDED.*

Bucklawren is situated deep in unspoilt countryside yet only one mile from the beach and three miles from Looe. Delightful cottages recently converted from farm buildings and furnished to a high standard. Large garden with sea views. Ideal position for beach, coastal paths, Woolly Monkey Sanctuary, National Trust properties, fishing trips, golf and water sports. Evening Meal available in the farmhouse. Terms from £100 to £420. Short Breaks available. Open all year.

MARAZION. Trenow Farm Cottage, Perranuthnoe, Marazion, Penzance TR20 9NW. ♀ ♀ ♀ *COMMENDED.* **Sleep 4/5.**

Commanding a superb coastal position with unrivalled views of Mount's Bay and St. Michael's Mount, this barn conversion to two character cottages provides a high standard of accommodation. There are accessible coves along the Coastal Footpath to the picturesque village of Perranuthnoe with pub and lovely sandy beach. The magical St. Michael's Mount can be reached from the old market town of Marazion (one mile) with a safe beach and water sports facilities. St. Ives, Penzance, Land's End and The Lizard Peninsula are all within easy reach of this ideal holiday location. Both cottages have own garden, patio, barbecue, bath, electric shower, lounge diner, fitted kitchen, electric cooker, microwave, fridge/freezer, automatic washing machine, colour TV, video, night store heaters. Linen provided. Cot and high chair available. Open all year. Sorry, no pets. Terms from £110. Contact **David and Frances Phillips (01736 710421).**

MARAZION near. "Sunnyside", Perranuthnoe, Near Marazion. Sleeps 5. This fully modernised furnished cottage has superb views and is situated in the small, unspoilt village of Perranuthnoe, two miles from Marazion. The village has a pub and ancient church. Sunnyside is only five minutes' walk from the sandy family beach. There are good coastal walks and fishing from the rocks. Nearby are St. Michael's Mount and many tourist attractions, within easy reach of St. Ives, Penzance, the Land's End area, Helston and the Lizard Peninsula. The cottage has fine coastal views from livingroom and bedrooms. The livingroom has sliding glass doors on to a sheltered patio and small secluded garden. Upstairs, the bedroom verandah has a panoramic view of Mount's Bay. It sleeps four, but a fifth folding Z-bed can be supplied. Bed linen is provided but please bring your own towels, otherwise the cottage is fully equipped including TV and a modern all-electric kitchen. Also night storage heaters for winter use. "Cornwall Registered Accommodation." SAE please to **Mrs F.S. Roynon, "Treetops", Perran Downs, Goldsithney, Near Penzance TR20 9HJ (01736 710482).**

MEVAGISSEY. Treleaven Farm Cottages. Sleep 2/6 persons. ♀♀♀♀ *HIGHLY COMMENDED.* Three luxury converted barns situated close to village, harbours, shops, safe sandy beaches and coastal walks. Each cottage is equipped to a very high standard with luxury kitchens and bathrooms. Some have en suite bedrooms. Games barn and putting green available. Ample parking. Sorry no pets. Please telephone for brochure **01726 843558.**

MULLION (near Helston). Mr and Mrs R.P. Tyler-Street, Trenance Farm Cottages, Mullion, Near Helston TR12 7HB (01326 240639). ♀♀♀♀ *COMMENDED.* Trenance Farm Cottages are situated halfway between the village and Mullion Cove. Only half a mile to swimming/surfing beach, plus footpath to cliff top and lovely coastal walks mainly over National Trust land. Golf, fishing and riding locally. The old farm outbuildings have been converted into ten comfortable two/three bedroomed cottages, all fully equipped, with colour TV, etc. Bed linen provided. Summer swimming pool, games room, laundry, children's play area, ample parking, metered electricity. Children and pets welcome; field to exercise dogs. Bed and Breakfast available in the farmhouse.

NEWQUAY. Heather Harvey, Shepherds Farm, Newlyn East, Newquay TR8 5NW (01872 540340). Sleeps 6-12. Enjoy a carefree holiday on our 600 acre farm in one of our delightful self-contained cottages, or try our bungalow — four properties in total. Ideal for touring and enjoying our superb sandy beaches; five within a five mile radius. Free horse riding. Children welcome. Bed and Breakfast also available in four en suite bedrooms in our farmhouse.

PADSTOW. The Brewer Family, Carnevas Farm Holiday Park, Carnevas Farm, St. Merryn, Padstow PL28 8PN (01841 520230). Bungalow/Chalets sleep 4/6. √ √ √ √ Rose Award Park 1996. Situated only half a mile from golden sandy beach, fishing, golf, sailing etc. Quaint harbour village of Padstow only four miles. Bungalows/chalets sleep four/six, have two bedrooms, bathroom, kitchen/diner, airing cupboard, colour TV. Caravans six berth or eight, all have showers, toilets, fridge, colour TV (also separate camping and caravan facilities). Newly converted barns now available, sleep four/six persons, furnished to a high standard. AA Three Pennant site. Brochure on request.

WHEN MAKING ENQUIRIES PLEASE MENTION
THIS *FHG* PUBLICATION

PENZANCE. Mrs Catherine Wall, Trenow, Relubbus Lane, St. Hilary, Penzance TR20 9EA (01736 762308). Mini bungalow sleeps two within the grounds of an old country house. Lovely garden, wide views of surrounding rural area. Lounge/diner with cooking area, fridge, cooker, colour TV etc; shower room. Linen not provided. Beaches within easy reach, sporting activities, bird watching. No pets. Parking. Terms from £70 per week. Available March to October and Christmas. Please write or phone for further details.

PENZANCE. Mrs Rosemary J. Warren, Tredinney Farm, Crows-an-Wra, St. Buryan, Penzance TR19 6HX (01736 810352). Cornwall Tourist Board *APPROVED.* **Working farm.** Attractive rural position for farmhouse accommodation on a family-run dairy and beef farm. Situated half way between Penzance and Land's End (five miles to each) and nestled beneath gorse and heather clad hills. Ideal for beaches, sightseeing and scenic walks from our own unspoilt hill offering marvellous views of this peninsula. Peaceful, away from traffic, with pleasant gardens. One double, one family bedroom, both with washbasins, shaver points and tea making facilities; bathroom/toilet, separate shower room; dining/sitting room with colour TV. Car essential, ample parking. Good home cooking, fresh farm produce. Bed and Breakfast with Evening Meal optional. Reduced rates for children.

PENZANCE. Mrs James Curnow, Barlowenath, St. Hilary, Penzance TR20 9DQ (01736 710409). Working farm. Cottages sleep 4/5. These two cottages are on a dairy farm, in a little hamlet right beside St. Hilary Church, with quiet surroundings and a good road approach. A good position for touring Cornish coast and most well-known places. Beaches are two miles away; Marazion two-and-a-half miles; Penzance six miles; St. Ives eight; Land's End 16. Both cottages have fitted carpets, lounge/diner with TV; modern kitchen (fridge, electric cooker, toaster, iron); bathroom with shaver point. Electricity by £1 meter, night storage heaters extra. One cottage sleeps five in three bedrooms (one double, twin divans and one single). The second cottage sleeps four in two bedrooms (twin divans in both). Linen not supplied. Cot by arrangement. Available all year. £95 to £285 weekly, VAT exempt.

PORT ISAAC. Mr and Mrs R.W. Mably, Trentinney Farm, St. Endellion, Port Isaac PL29 3TS (01208 880564). These cottages sleep up to six. They are

approached from St. Endellion down a winding country lane with woods on either side. The traditional Listed buildings have been recently converted and provide very high standard accommodation with outstanding views of the surrounding countryside. Come and enjoy a holiday on our family-run working farm which has ponies and other animals. The cottages are fully equipped with washing machine, microwave, Fastext/Nicam stereo TV, iron, etc. Cot, highchair and barbecue available. Shared dryer in utility room. Fully insulated and double glazed for Autumn and Winter use. Storage heaters, bed linen, electricity and VAT included in price. Terms from £99 to £450 per week.

PORT ISAAC. The Lodge, Treharrock, Port Isaac. Sleeps 6. Pleasant, south facing and convenient

bungalow, set in its own small, natural garden and surrounded by fields and woodland with streams. About two miles inland from Port Isaac, a sheltered, secluded spot at the end of driveway to Treharrock Manor. Rugged North Cornish cliffs with National Trust footpaths and lovely sandy coves in the vicinity. Excellent sandy beach at Polzeath (five miles), also pony trekking, golf etc. in the area. South facing sun room leads on to terrace; TV. Accommodation for six plus baby. Bathroom, toilet; sittingroom; kitchen/diner. Open all year. Linen extra. Sorry, no pets. Car essential — parking. Terms from £150 to £300 per week (heating included). SAE to **Mrs E.A. Hambly, Home Farm House, Little Gaddesden, Berkhamsted, Hertfordshire HP4 1PN (01442 843412; Fax: 01442 842741).**

PORT ISAAC. The Dolphin, Port Isaac. Sleeps 9. This delightful house, originally an inn, is one of the most attractive in Port Isaac. Fifty yards from the sea, shops and pub. Five bedrooms, three with washbasins. Two bathrooms and WCs. Large diningroom. Cosy sittingroom. Spacious and well-equipped kitchen with electric cooker, gas-fired Aga, dishwasher, washing machine. Sun terrace. Port Isaac is a picturesque fishing village with magnificent coastal scenery all round. Nearby attractions include surfing, sailing, fishing, golf, tennis, pony trekking. The Dolphin sleeps nine but reduced rates offered for smaller families and off-peak season. Weekly terms: £370 to £525 inclusive. SAE for details to **Mrs Thomas, 2 Stephenson Terrace, Worcester, Hereford and Worcester WR1 3EA (01905 20518/21967).**

PORT ISAAC. Treharrock, Port Isaac. Sleeps up to 15. Built in 1815 in an elegant and spacious style, it

is set in 14 acres of its own grounds amongst farmland about two miles inland from Port Isaac. There are extensive sandy beaches in the area with intriguing coves and rock pools, and surfing at Polzeath (five miles away). The house is comfortably furnished, has central heating and is fully equipped; it has period atmosphere with appropriate facilities. Games basement with table tennis and billiards; hard tennis court. Adjacent caretaker. Sorry no pets. Rents from £800 per week low season to £1200 per week high season. For further information and bookings contact: **Mrs E.A. Hambly, Home Farm House, Little Gaddesden, Berkhamsted, Herts HP4 1PN (01442 843412; Fax: 01442 842741).**

PORT ISAAC. Salters Cottage and Penny Cottage, Port Gaverne, Port Isaac. Sleep 4/6. On National

Trust Land. Port Gaverne is a hamlet adjoining Port Isaac on an inlet in the magnificent rugged North Coast, and its shingle beach is one of the safest bathing beaches in Cornwall. Salters and Penny Cottages are about 100 yards from the sea, made from the old fishermen's netting lofts and fish "cellars", dating from the days when Port Gaverne had a flourishing herring and pilchard trade. The cottages are fully equipped and most comfortably furnished and Penny Cottage, being all on the ground floor, is most suitable for the elderly or disabled. Salters Cottage has a piano which is tuned each Spring. I will be most happy to send you full details of rents and all vacant dates on receipt of SAE. **Mrs M.M. Cook, The Beach House, Port Gaverne, Port Isaac PL29 3SQ (01208 880296).**

PRAA SANDS near. Lower Kenneggy Farm, Rosudgeon, Near Praa Sands. Working farm. Sleeps 6. A comfortable, modernised cottage near the farm, with its own garden and ample parking space. The cottage accommodates six persons, has three bedrooms, fully fitted kitchen, diningroom and lounge with TV; bathroom and toilet; airing cupboard with immersion heater. Metered electricity; linen not supplied. Children are welcome, cot provided. Sorry, no pets. Lower Kenneggy is in a country area with sea views, but close to Marazion (three miles) and Praa Sands (one mile) beaches; seven miles from Penzance and Helston. SAE, please, for terms to **Mrs P. Laity, Lower Kenneggy Farm, Rosudgeon, Penzance TR20 9AR (01736 762403).**

See also Colour Display Advertisement **ST. AUSTELL. Mrs J. King, St. Margaret's Holiday Park, Polgooth, St. Austell PL26 7AX (01726 74283; Fax; 01726 71680). √ √ √ √ √ BHP Approved.** Family owned and run Holiday Park set in six acres of beautiful parkland and offering good quality accommodation of varying sizes from detached bungalows (sleep up to eight) to self contained chalets (sleep two to five people). Two bungalows suitable for disabled visitors. All the properties are well equipped with the usual facilities. Colour TV and fitted carpets. Launderette and pay phone on park. Golf course is 400 yards away and the Polgooth shops and inn are conveniently near. Well controlled pets allowed. Special rates available. Open March to December. Terms and colour brochure available.

ST. AUSTELL BAY. Mrs A. Buckingham, 16 Haddon Way, Carlyon Bay, St. Austell PL25 3QG (01726 815566). Tourist Board APPROVED. **Sleep 1/5.**

Two charming 18th century cottages, one harbourside only yards from the sea and one in the delightful countryside village of Charlestown. Both superb locations in beautiful settings. Sleep one/four. Two detached seaside bungalows, one at Carlyon Bay with its award-winning beach, coastal walks and cliff top golf course and the other only five minutes' walk from Par Sands and the wildlife pond. All at good coastal locations with parking. Quality assured and cleanliness guaranteed. Prices from £110 to £350. Telephone for colour brochure.

ST. MARGARET'S HOLIDAY PARK
Tel: (01726) 74283 Fax (01726) 71680

Family owned and run holiday park, set in six acres of beautiful parkland and offering good quality accommodation of varying sizes, from detached bungalows sleeping up to eight persons to self contained chalets nestling amongst the trees and sleeping from two to five people. Two of the bungalows are suitable for disabled persons. All property is well equipped including colour TV and microwave ovens. Launderette and pay phone on park. St. Austell golf course is 400 yards away and the Polgooth shops and inn are conveniently near. Well controlled pets allowed. Special rates early/late season or for two persons. Open March to December. Terms and colour brochure from: **Mrs M. King, St. Margaret's Holiday Park, Polgooth, St. Austell, Cornwall PL26 7AX.**

ST. COLUMB. Mrs J.V. Thomas, Lower Trenowth Farm, St. Columb TR9 6EW (01637 880308).

Sleeps 6. This accommodation is part of a large farmhouse, all rooms facing south. Situated in the beautiful Vale of Lanherne, four miles from the sea, eight miles from the holiday resort of Newquay. Golf, horse riding, etc all within easy reach. One double room, one twin-bedded room and one single room with bunk beds, all with washbasins. Bed linen provided. Bathroom. Large lounge with colour TV. Fully equipped kitchen/diner. Electricity included in tariff. Large lawn. Ample parking. Dogs accepted if kept under control. SAE for further details please.

ST. IVES. Myrtwedhen, Hellesveor, St. Ives. Tourist Board Category 3. A country cottage and garden

surrounded by farmland, one mile from St. Ives town, harbour and beaches and a short walk to the cliffs via the footpaths which pass the cottage — close to lovely countryside with plenty to see and do as well as being just a short distance from the town. A lovely house in a superb setting, comfortably equipped for four to six people, clean, warm and well maintained with every need provided for. Colour TV, central heating, automatic washing machine (a cot and high chair can be provided on request). Available all year round for full weeks in the summer or off-peak breaks of any length. We are very happy to have children and dogs stay and personal supervision assures you of a very warm welcome at any time of the year. Prices from £210 to £410 (including linen and heating) dependent on season. Details from **Mrs F.H. Seabrook, 30 Newcombe Street, Market Harborough, Leicestershire LE16 9PB (01858 463723).**

"HALWYN"
MANACCAN
Nr. HELSTON
TR12 6ER

Tel: 01326 280359

"HALWYN" is a family-run ancient Cornish farmstead situated in beautifully natural surroundings.

The former farm buildings have been converted into delightful self-catering holiday cottages, all fully equipped, and only 1 mile from the sea at Porthallow and 2 miles from Helford River.

"HALWYN" is set in 2 acres of beautiful gardens which include a small lake, children's play area, putting green and barbecue area. "Halwyn" also has an indoor swimming pool, sauna and solarium.

All cottages include TV, electricity (no meters) mircowave and fridge. There are laundry facilities on sight and a pay-phone.

For a tranquil, relaxing holiday, come to "HALWYN". Heating available for out of season bookings. Well behaved pets welcome. For brochure contact **Sharon Darling.**

SEE OUR COLOUR DISPLAY ADVERTISEMENT

ST. IVES. Mrs E.J. Jefferies, "Chy-an-Veor", Hellesvoer, St. Ives TR26 3AD (01736 795372). Country cottage situated one mile from St. Ives on the Land's End coast road. Three bedrooms: two double bedrooms and one room fitted with adult-sized bunk beds. Fully equipped kitchen including microwave, fridge, cooker, etc. Lounge with colour TV. Victorian bathroom, open beams, slate floor. Large garden and garage. Horse riding, golf, walking, beaches, fishing are all within easy reach. Available June to September.

ST. KEVERNE. Mrs Rosemary Peters, Trenoweth Valley Farm Cottages, St. Keverne, Helston TR12 6QQ (01326 280910). ETB ♀♀♀ APPROVED. Spacious, comfortable rural cottages, fully furnished and carpeted with well equipped kitchen, colour TV and laundry facilities. Kitchen/diner, lounge/sittingroom, shower room/toilet. Sleeping six persons, each cottage has two bedrooms with duvets and covers for each bed. Surrounded by trees and fields, there is a safe play area for young children and a barbecue. Quiet, relaxing environment, midway between St. Keverne and Porthallow. Pleasant walks; beach, village shops and inns one and a half miles. Open Easter to end October. Sorry, no pets. Attractive early and late prices. Terms from £60 to £300 per week.

TRABOE. Mrs Jan Oates, Rosuick Farm, St. Martin, Helston TR12 6DZ (01326 231302). CTB

APPROVED. Sleep 6-10. Offering atmosphere, tradition and quality, our cottages are on or near our family-run 200 acre beef and sheep farm, nestling in a picturesque valley. We are within easy reach of sandy beaches, Helford River. Children welcome. Secluded gardens, log fires, four-poster beds, bed linen supplied, dishwasher. Rosuick Cottage: spacious and comfortable, has snooker table and is set in one acre of enclosed gardens; sleeps six. Trewoon Farmhouse: traditional feel with open beams and slate floors; sleeps seven. Rosuick Farmhouse — with its history in the Domesday Book — and Newinn Farmhouse — a large 17th century cottage — both sleep 10, each with five spacious bedrooms. Brochure available. Terms from £90 to £510 per week.

WADEBRIDGE. Down Below. Sleeps 6 + cot. Luxury converted barn with large garden, ample parking

space. Situated in its own grounds on 140 acre dairy farm in the centre of beautiful peaceful hamlet of Trewethern. Only four miles from the lovely beaches at Rock, Polzeath, Daymer Bay and Port Isaac, ideal for surfing, fishing, safe bathing and golf. Two local pubs one mile either side with excellent food. Also village stores and Post Office, lovely walk to both and 15th century church of St. Kew. Furnished to a very high standard, accommodation comprises very large lounge featuring open fire with millstone hearth, colour TV and video. Fully equipped kitchen/diner including fridge, electric cooker, toaster and microwave. Three large bedrooms; two twin-bedded, one double. All bedding supplied. Electric heaters in all rooms. Shower room, separate toilet. Suitable for six people plus baby. Cot and high chair available. 50p slot meter. Laundry room available with automatic washing machine and tumble dryer. Linen on request. Pets by arrangement only; please enquire. Friday to Friday bookings. Available all year. SAE for prompt reply. Details from **Mrs V. Davey, Carns Farm, Trewethern, Amble, Wadebridge PL27 6EB (01208 880398).**

WADEBRIDGE/BODIEVE. Sleeps 6 plus cot. 300 year old farmhouse, converted in 1990, surrounded by

sunny gardens, ample parking space in front of house in quiet country crescent. Only three miles from the sandy beaches at Rock and Daymer Bay, the surfing beach at Polzeath, close to the ancient fishing harbour of Padstow. Ideal for surfing, safe bathing, walking, fishing, sailing, golf, cycling (cycle hire in Wadebridge). The excellent shops, pubs, markets at Wadebridge are half a mile away. Wadebridge Leisure Centre with its brand new indoor swimming pool is only a five minute walk. The house comprises lounge with wood/coal burner in fireplace, colour TV, comfortable sofa bed (double). Large, cosy, well equipped kitchen/diner with fridge, electric cooker, microwave, double aspect windows; laundry room with automatic washing machine, tumble dryer, fridge/freezer. Three bedrooms — large master bedroom (double aspect windows) with king size bed, one twin bedroom and a bedroom with bunk beds (brand new beds, mattresses and bedding). Linen and towels on request at extra charge. Bathroom, shower, toilet. Night storage heaters. Pets by arrangement. Available all year. Terms from £120 to £380 per week (including electricity and cleaning). Saturday to Saturday bookings. Ring or write for further details. **Mr and Mrs Peter Simpson, 32 Wolsey Road, East Molesey, Surrey KT8 9EN (0181-979 2433; Fax: 0181-224 6806) or Angela Holder (01208 813204).**

HELP IMPROVE BRITISH TOURIST STANDARDS

You are choosing holiday accommodation from our very popular FHG Publications. Whether it be a hotel, guest house, farmhouse or self-catering accommodation, we think you will find it hospitable, comfortable and clean, and your host and hostess friendly and helpful. Why not write and tell us about it?

As a recognition of the generally well-run and excellent holiday accommodation reviewed in our publications, we at FHG Publications Ltd. present a diploma to proprietors who receive the highest recommendation from their guests who are also readers of our Guides. If you care to write to us praising the holiday you have booked through FHG Publications Ltd. – whether this be board, self-catering accommodation, a sporting or a caravan holiday, what you say will be evaluated and the proprietors who reach our final list will be contacted.

The winning proprietor will receive an attractive framed diploma to display on his premises as recognition of a high standard of comfort, amenity and hospitality. FHG Publications Ltd. offer this diploma as a contribution towards the improvement of standards in tourist accommodation in Britain. Help your excellent host or hostess to win it!

FHG DIPLOMA

We nominate ....

....

Because ....

Name ....

Address ....

.... Telephone No. ....

CUMBRIA — including "The Lakes"

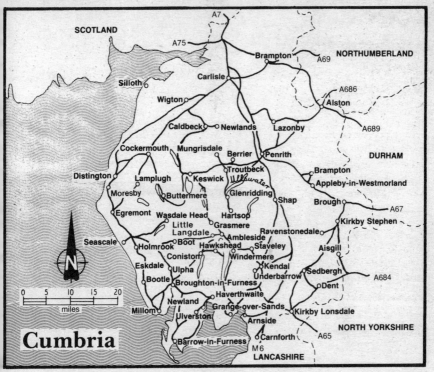

Cumbria

ALSTON. Lorne House, Alston. ♀♀♀ *COMMENDED.* **Sleeps 6.** Lovely old stone house in large garden 200 yards from centre of England's highest market town. Set in magnificent North Pennines, ideally situated for touring North Yorkshire Dales, Hadrian's Wall, Northumbrian Coast, the Lakes. Walking, cycling, fishing, golf, swimming all available nearby. Accommodation sleeps six in three bedrooms and has two bathrooms; excellent, well equipped kitchen; living room with wood stove, sitting room with open fire, colour TV. Washing machine. Gas central heating. Open all year. Prices from £150 to £320 per week inclusive of bed linen. Short breaks available. Children very welcome. Contact: **J.H. Kendall, "Marsh End", 28 Woolsington Park South, Woolsington, Newcastle-upon-Tyne NE13 8BJ (0191 2869771).**

AMBLESIDE. Hole House, High Wray, Ambleside. A charming detached 17th century Lakeland cottage set in idyllic surroundings overlooking Blelham Tarn with magnificent panoramic views of the Langdale Pikes, Coniston Old Man, the Troutbeck Fells and Lake Windermere. High Wray is a quiet unspoilt hamlet set between Ambleside and Hawkshead making this an ideal base for walking or touring. This charming cottage which once belonged to Beatrix Potter has original oak beams and feature stone staircase, and has been recently restored to provide very comfortable accommodation without losing its olde worlde charm. One double and two twin bedrooms (all linen and towels provided); bathroom with shower; large spacious lounge with Sky TV and video; fitted kitchen with microwave oven, fridge freezer, tumble dryer, automatic washing machine and electric cooker. Storage heating included in the cost. Ample parking. Play area. For terms and further details please contact: **Mrs P. Benson, Tock How Farm, High Wray, Ambleside (015394 36481).**

AMBLESIDE. Peter and Anne Hart, Bracken Fell Cottage, Outgate, Ambleside LA22 0NH (015394 36289). Sleeps 2/4. Bracken Fell Cottage is situated in beautiful open countryside between Ambleside and Hawkshead in the picturesque hamlet of Outgate. The two bedroomed accommodation has central heating and is immaculately furnished. Fully equipped kitchen. Linen and electricity included. Ideally positioned for exploring the Lake District. All major outdoor activities catered for nearby. Ample parking. Patio area and two acres of gardens. Open all year. Terms from £140 per week. Sorry, no pets or children under eight years. Bed and Breakfast accommodation also available (two Crowns Commended). Non smoking. Write or phone for brochure and tariff.

Bracken Fell

AMBLESIDE. "Chestnuts" and "Beeches". This tasteful conversion offers excellent accommodation in a former Bank Barn and Coach House, with external balconies giving superb views towards Lake Windermere and the fells to the north. Each apartment has its own private entrance, with large, well appointed lounge/dining area, electric fire, colour TV and double glazed French windows to the balcony. Both have fully fitted kitchens with electric cooker, microwave, fridge, washing machine and tumble dryer. Both sleep up to six persons in one double bedroom and two twin rooms, and have bathrooms with bath, shower and WC. Night storage heating and lighting included; other power by £1 coin meter. Ample parking. For more details phone or write to **J.R. Benson, Tock How Farm, High Wray, Ambleside LA22 0JF (015394 36481).**

AMBLESIDE. 2 Lowfield, Old Lake Road, Ambleside LA22 0DN. Sleep 4/5. Ground floor garden flat situated half a mile from town centre. The accommodation comprises lounge/dining room, kitchen, bathroom/WC, two bedrooms with twin beds. Linen supplied. Children and pets welcome. Ample private parking. Bookings run from Saturday to Saturday. Terms from £80 to £170 per week. Contact: **Mr P.F. Quarmby, 3 Lowfield, Old Lake Road, Ambleside LA22 0DH (015394 32326).**

AMBLESIDE. Betty Fold, Hawkshead Hill, Ambleside LA22 0PS (015394 36611). ♀♀♀ *APPROVED.*

Properties comfortably sleep 4. Betty Fold is a large country house in its own spacious grounds with magnificent views and set in the heart of the Lake District National Park. The quaint village of Hawkshead is nearby and Coniston and Ambleside are within four miles; the beauty spot of Tarn Hows is 20 minutes' walk away. As well as being a Guest House, Betty Fold offers self catering accommodation for up to four persons; there is "Garden Cottage" in the grounds and a flat which is part of the main house. All accommodation is centrally heated and facilities such as linen, colour TV and cots are provided, also heating, power and lighting. Pets welcome. Terms approximately £260 to £360 per week, in main season, reductions for reduced occupancy. Special Packages from November to Easter. Dinner available in Guest House. See also advertisement in BOARD SECTION of this guide.

AMBLESIDE. West Vale Cottage, Far Sawrey, Hawkshead, Ambleside LA22 0LQ (015394 42817). Sleeps 2. The cottage is superbly situated on the edge of the picturesque village of Far Sawrey in the heart of Beatrix Potter country; within the grounds of the owners' guest house. The accommodation is all on one level and has lovely open views over the patio and garden from the lounge French windows. The cottage is centrally heated throughout. Lounge/dining room, kitchen, double bedroom and bathroom. Sorry no pets and non-smokers only. Duvet and linen provided and all gas and electricity is included in the rental. Terms from £170 to £290. Contact: **Mrs Gee.**

AMBLESIDE. Mr Evans, Ramsteads Coppice, Outgate, Ambleside LA22 0NH (015394 36583). Six timber lodges of varied size and design set in 15 acres of mixed woodland with wild flowers, birds and native wild animals. There are also 11 acres of rough hill pasture. Three miles south west of Ambleside, it is an ideal centre for walkers, naturalists and country lovers. No pets. Children welcome. Open March to November.

APPLEBY near. "The Yews", Long Marton, Appleby. Sleeps 5. This is a comfortable old cottage, fully modernised, well furnished with fitted carpets throughout. Situated in a small village three miles from Appleby where swimming, golf and riding are available. Ideal for walkers with Fells nearby, also within easy reach of Lakes and Dales. Accommodation comprises double bed, twin beds and single bed in three bedrooms. Cot also available. Well equipped kitchen — cooker, microwave, fridge and spindryer. Sitting-room, diningroom, coal or electric fire, colour TV. Linen provided. Attractive garden. Children especially welcome. One dog only. Available all year. Terms from £120 to £185 weekly. Weekend/Short Breaks available. Contact: **Mrs B.M. Sowerby, Hawthorn Cottage, Long Marton, Appleby CA16 6BT (017683 61392).**

APPLEBY-IN-WESTMORLAND. Mrs Edith Stockdale, Croft House, Bolton, Appleby-in-Westmorland CA16 6AW (017683 61264). Sleeps 2/4. THE HAYLOFT: Recently converted form the original hayloft this cottage is situated between the barn and the owners' house with an abundance of open stonework and oak beams. The cottage still retain lots of character and is an excellent base for fell and country walking, horse riding or as a touring base for the Lake District, beautiful Eden Valley, Scottish Borders, Hadrian's Wall and the North Yorkshire Dales. One double bedroom; shower room with electric shower, washbasin and WC; well equipped kitchen/dining/sitting room. Facilities include electric cooker, microwave, fridge, double bed settee for extra guests, colour TV, etc. All linen supplied. Storage heaters. Electricity included in the rent. Use of owners' garden. Ample parking. Well behaved pets welcome. Terms from £145 to £215 per week. Brochure available.

APPLEBY-IN-WESTMORLAND near.Mrs M.J. Burke, Milburn Grange, Knock, Appleby-in-Westmorland CA16 6DR (Tel & Fax: 017683 61867; Vodaphone 0836 547130). ♀♀♀/♀♀♀♀ *COMMENDED.* **Sleeps 2/7.** Milburn Grange is a tiny hamlet nestling at the foot of the Pennines enjoying extensive views over Lakeland Hills and Pennines. Six quality cottages (three beamed) equipped to highest standards set within two acres. All cottages have either their own washing machine or use of utility room with washing machine, drying and ironing facilities. Linen included free of charge and cots and high chairs; babysitting available. Children's safe play area, picnic tables, guests' garden and barbecue. Shop, Post Office, garage close by, selection of public houses in the vicinity. Well behaved pets welcome at a charge of £10.00 per week each pet. Two other cottages available in nearby idyllic villages. Nearest lake 11 miles (Ullswater), children's fun park 11 miles, Appleby five miles (castle, golf, swimming, fishing, tennis). Open all year. OFF SEASON BARGAIN BREAKS FROM NOVEMBER TO MARCH (excluding Christmas and New Year). TERMS from £80 to £350. SAE please for brochure. ALSO FEATURED IN GOOD HOLIDAY COTTAGE GUIDE.

APPLEBY-IN-WESTMORLAND near. "Jubilee Cottage". Sleeps 6/7. 18th century cottage, fully equipped except linen. Two bedrooms (sleeps six plus small child). Bathroom, lounge with colour TV and kitchen/diner with electric cooker, automatic washing machine, fridge, iron, etc. Economy 7 storage heater. Carpeted throughout. Situated between North Lakes and the Pennines. Car essential, off road parking for two cars in front of cottage. Open all year. Well behaved pets welcome. Terms £140 to £220 inclusive of all electricity. **Miss L.I. Basten, Daymer Cottage, Lee, Near Ilfracombe, Devon (01271 863769).**

BASSENTHWAITE. Mrs V. Trafford, Peter House Farm, Bassenthwaite, Keswick CA12 4QX (017687 76278). Working farm. Tastefully furnished barn conversion holiday cottage sleeping two to five people. The cottage has spectacular views, oak beams, colour TV; storage heating provided in rent, also open fire. Ideal centre for touring the Lakes or fell walking from the cottage door. 10 minutes' drive to Keswick and a short walk gives a lake view. Children and pets are welcome. Accommodation is suitable for disabled visitors. Terms from £150 per week. Short Breaks available out of high season. SAE, please, or telephone.

BOWNESS-ON-WINDERMERE. Fernville, 6 Queens Drive, Bowness-on-Windermere. Sleeps 5 adults; 1 child. Fernville is in the centre of a terrace built in Lakeland stone and in a quiet residential road off the main Windermere-Bowness bus route. Two minutes away a delightful path leads to the lake in about 20 minutes' walk. There is a hall, living and dining rooms, with sliding doors between; kitchen; one double and two single bedrooms; attic bedroom with twin beds; cot also available. Comfortably furnished, electric heating, TV, modern kitchen with fridge, dishwasher and electric cooker. Fully equipped except linen. Well behaved pets allowed. Shops half a mile. Small paved garden at front, parking at rear. Swimming, golf, fishing, water ski-ing, riding, etc available nearby. Bowness is a very pleasant resort on Lake Windermere. Terms approximately £180 per week according to season, etc. SAE, please, or phone **Mrs Christine Walmsley, Godferhead, Loweswater, Cockermouth CA13 0RT (01900 85013).**

BOWNESS-ON-WINDERMERE. Mrs P.M. Fanstone, Deloraine, (Dept F), Helm Road, Bowness-on-Windermere LA23 2HS (015394 45557). ♥♥♥/

♥♥♥♥ COMMENDED and Disabled Scheme Category 2 (first in Cumbria). Deloraine spells seclusion, space, convenience and comfort for all seasons, while exploring Lakeland heritage. Parties of two/six have choice of five apartments within an Edwardian mansion, and a detached cottage with four-poster bed. Set in one and a half acres of private gardens, yet only a few minutes' walk from Bowness centre and water sports. Each unit has distinctive qualities and character. Two command dramatic views of the Langdale Pikes and Lake at 300 foot elevation. Ground floor flat and cottage include disabled facilities. All properties have free parking, private entrances, full equipment, colour TV, electric heaters and central heating. Double glazing. Fire prevention systems. Payphone. Washing machine. Barbecue. Sun room. Cot hire. Linen included. Free swim tickets. No pets. Brochure on request. Terms from £100 to £355 per week. Winter breaks available. Resident owners. Inspected by Lakeland Self Caterers Association.

CALDBECK near. Croft House, Brocklebank, Wigton, Near Caldbeck. This beautiful farmhouse is in quiet country setting with large garden. Easy reach of Lake District, Scottish Borders and the Solway Firth, half a mile from open fells. Caldbeck is the nearest village with shops and pub. Lounge, dining room, kitchen, three bedrooms — two double, one twin; bathroom with toilet and shower. Night storage heaters, electric fire, coal, logs, cooker, fridge, colour TV, duvets all included. Bed linen and towels can be hired. Weekly terms from £130 to £250. Sorry no pets. Brochure from **Mrs Joan Todd, Wyndham Farm, Brocklebank, Wigton CA7 8DH (016974 78272).**

See also Colour Display Advertisement **CARLISLE. Mrs Ivinson (FHG), Green View, Welton, Near Dalston, Carlisle CA5 7ES (016974 76230; Fax: 016974 76523).** ♥♥♥♥ & ♥♥♥♥♥ up to HIGHLY COMMENDED. **Properties sleep 2/7.** Three superb Scandinavian pine lodges, surprisingly spacious, two 17th century oak beamed cottages, one with wood burning stove, also delightful pine panelled converted chapel for two. Tiny picturesque rural hamlet, unspoilt open views to Caldbeck Fells three miles away. Every home comfort provided for a relaxing country holiday in peaceful surroundings. Own gardens. All properties have shower/bath, colour TV, microwave, telephone, laundry, central heating, linen and towels. Second WC in three-bedroomed properties. Within half an hour's drive of Keswick, Lake Ullswater or Gretna Green. Golf five miles. Dogs permitted. Open all year. Ideal for an off season break, warm for your arrival. Resident owners. Weekly terms £145 to £480. Winter Breaks £95. Car essential. Accommodation is suitable for accompanied disabled visitors.

CARLISLE. Mrs J.T. James, Midtodhills Farm, Roadhead, Carlisle CA6 6PF (016977 48213). Up to ♥♥♥♥ HIGHLY COMMENDED. **Working farm.** Situated overlooking beautiful Lyne Valley on the Cumbria/Scottish border. On a traditional working farm guests are welcome to join in and learn about life on a farm, and may also enjoy guided walks. We are ideally situated for touring Hadrian's Wall, Kielder, Carlisle, Gretna and Lakes. Good fishing and walking area. ARCH VIEW sleeps eight, new sandstone barn conversion comprising kitchen/diner, shower room, lounge, twin bedroom; first floor two double rooms with vanity units, two single bedrooms and bathroom. RIGGFOOT sleeps four/five, detached cottage, open plan kitchen/lounge, log fire; one double room with four-poster bed, one twin bedroom; bathroom. Properties have dishwasher, microwave, fridge/freezer, cooker, washer/dryer, radio, colour TV, video, telephone. Storage heaters. Garden with barbecue and furniture.

Prices from £120 per week. £415 for eight people/five bedrooms. Use of swimming pool May to September.

CARLISLE. Mrs S. Chandley, Dovecote, Cleughside Farm, Kirklinton, Carlisle CA6 6BE (01228 75650). ♥♥♥ COMMENDED. The cottage is tucked away amongst green fields, with sheep, goats and ducks. It sleeps four and has a double and a twin bedroom upstairs, with an open plan living area on the ground floor. Every admirable blend of 'mod cons' and traditional charm are mixed perfectly for your assured comfort. Why not relax by the pond or enjoy our local country pursuits? Walk Hadrian's Wall, tour Cumbria's Borderlands, visit Carlisle Castle or even the famous Gretna Green, just five miles away. It's a home from home with a peaceful atmosphere, where you will be made most welcome. Phone for a colour brochure.

CARLISLE. Mrs Georgina Elwen, New Pallyards, Hethersgill, Carlisle CA6 6HZ (01228 577308).

♀♀♀♀ *COMMENDED.* **Working farm, join in.** GOLD AWARD WINNER. Filmed for BBC TV. Relax and see beautiful North Cumbria and the Borders. A warm welcome awaits you on our 65 acre livestock farm tucked away in the Cumbrian countryside, yet easily accessible from M6 Junction 44. In addition to the surrounding attractions there is plenty to enjoy, including hillside walking, peaceful forests, ponies and sea trout/salmon fishing — or just nestle down and relax with nature. One comfortable well-equipped bungalow, three/four bedrooms. Two lovely, pleasant cottages on a working farm, one/two bedrooms. Terms from £80 to £370 weekly. Also Award Winning Bed and Breakfast and Half Board. HWFH, ETB, FHB.

CARLISLE. Mrs D. Carruthers, University of Northumbria, Old Brewery Residencies, Bridge Lane, Caldewgate, Carlisle CA2 5SW (01228 597352). The

University of Northumbria's self catering holiday flats are set in the attractive surroundings of the restored Theakston's Old Brewery on the banks of the River Caldew and adjacent to Carlisle Castle. The recently built self-contained flats are ideal for holiday accommodation with a choice of four, five or six bedrooms and comprise shower room, bathroom with WC, separate WC, a well fitted kitchen/dining room with microwave, electric cooker and fridge/freezer. Bed linen and tea towels are provided but not personal towels. Disabled visitors accommodated. Children welcome but sorry no pets. The pedestrianised city centre is only a few minutes' walk away and features high quality shopping centres and a Victorian covered market. Weekly terms from £200 to £290.

COCKERMOUTH. Mrs B. M. Chester, Bouch House Farm, Embleton, Cockermouth CA13 9XH

(01900 823367). Cosy centrally heated cottage with picturesque views of Skiddaw and Buttermere fells. Walled in garden play area with garden furniture and barbecue. One and a half miles from Cockermouth, a pleasant historic market town with good bus service. Recreation facilities including fishing, golf, sports centre and horse riding. Well situated for touring lakes and coastline, nearby lakes include Bassenthwaite, Buttermere, Crummock and Loweswater. Accommodates six with cot available, bathroom, shower unit, drying room, lounge, colour TV, dining room, fully equipped kitchen, carpets throughout. Linen supplied. Car advisable, ample parking. Open all year. Special winter rates. Terms on application.

COCKERMOUTH. Mrs M.E. Teasdale, Jenkin Farm, Embleton, Cockermouth CA13 9TN (017687

76387). ♀♀♀♀ *COMMENDED.* **Sleeps 6.** Come and enjoy a peaceful away from it all holiday at our family-run working hill farm three miles from Cockermouth. Jenkin Cottage has a spectacular outlook over open countryside with views extending to the Solway Firth and the Scottish Lowlands. We are in an ideal situation for fell walking on the Buttermere and surrounding fells or for touring the Lakes by car. The cottage is personally supervised and has a homely atmosphere. We are open all year with long weekends and midweek breaks in the winter months. All linen provided. Lounge with an open log fire. Fully equipped modern kitchen. Full central heating. Sorry, no pets. Children welcome. We also extend a welcome to business people. Brochure available.

COCKERMOUTH. Mrs J. Hope, Cornhow Farm, Loweswater, Cockermouth CA13 9UX (01900 85200). Working farm. Sleeps 8. Ideal for a family holiday, spacious, fully modernised house adjoining an 18th-century farmhouse on a 250-acre stock-rearing farm. Situated in the beautiful Loweswater Valley it is well-placed for all country activities and central for the coast and lakes (Crummock half-a-mile). Fully equipped for eight people, the house is quiet and comfortable and accommodation comprises four double bedrooms; two bathrooms, two toilets; sittingroom. Electric cooking facilities and solid fuel heating. Everything supplied for the ease and enjoyment of your holiday. Private fishing. Children welcome and they may bring their pets. Open all year, a car is essential and there is parking. Three miles from shops. Weekly terms £200 to £300 (inclusive of electricity). No linen supplied. Further details on request with SAE, please.

CONISTON. Mrs J. Meredith, High Arnside Farm, Coniston LA21 8DW (01539 432261). Working

farm. In a unique position — being one of the highest situated farm houses in the Lakes, High Arnside offers spectacular views in peaceful and tranquil surroundings. Two cottages are available (accommodating nine and six people) dating from the 16th century and both have many interesting and beautiful features including oak panelling, beamed ceilings and open fires. Fully equipped. Fishing available on farm. Short breaks available. Pets only by arrangement. Ample parking space is available. Colour brochure on request.

CONISTON. Mr E. Usher, Dixon House, Coniston LA21 8HQ (015394 41217). ♀♀♀ *COMMENDED.* "Graythorne" is a stone-built detached bungalow, set in its own garden, in the centre of Coniston village. It is ideally situated with only two minutes' level walk to the shops, whilst enjoying magnificent views of the Coniston fells. The lake is only a 15 minute walk away for sailing, rowing and the beautiful steam yacht Gondola. The accommodation comprises one double bedroom, one twin bedroom (all beds have continental quilts); lounge with stone fireplace, colour TV, video and radio; fully fitted kitchen; bathroom with shower; private parking. Linen provided; owner maintained. For terms/further details telephone or write for brochure.

CONISTON. Mrs D.A. Hall (FHG), Dow Crag House, Coniston LA21 8AT (015394 41558). Two chalet

bungalows to let, sleeping two/six. One mile from Coniston village on A593. Resident owner. Cleanliness assured. First bungalow has sittingroom, kitchen/diningroom, three bedrooms sleeping six; bathroom, separate toilet. Electric cooker, fridge/freezer. Night store heaters. Second bungalow comprises livingroom/kitchen, three bedrooms sleeping five, shower room. All equipped with continental quilts. Please bring own linen. Parking space. These holiday chalets are set in private garden with direct access to the Fells and Hills. Superb views overlooking Lake towards Grizedale Forest. Freedom, yet safe for children. Pets welcome by arrangement. Mountain walks, boating, fishing, tennis and bowls in village. Available March till November. Terms on application with SAE, please.

CONISTON. Hanson Ground, Coniston. Sleeps 4. Hanson Ground is situated at the northern end of the road running along the eastern shore of Coniston Lake, two miles from Coniston Village. Set high up amidst the fields with Grizedale Forest behind, it occupies the first floor of a barn on the small agricultural holding of Knipe Ground, standing adjacent to the 16th century farmhouse. Though secluded it is ideal for exploring Lakeland. Two bedrooms, one with twin beds, one with bunk beds, cot; bathroom with toilet; sitting/diningroom with balcony overlooking lake; electric kitchen. No linen supplied. Sorry, not suitable for disabled guests. Terms from £100 to £160. Pets £20 (one only). SAE to **Mrs Mary Dutton, Knipe Ground, Coniston LA21 8AE (015394 41221).**

CONISTON near. Mrs J. Halton, "Brookfield", Torver, Near Coniston LA21 8AY (015394 41328).

♀♀♀ *APPROVED/COMMENDED.* **Sleeps 2/4.** This attractive, modern Bungalow property in quiet picturesque surroundings has a lovely outlook and extensive views of the Coniston mountains. It is completely detached and stands in its own half acre of level garden and grounds. The accommodation inside is in two entirely separate self-contained units. The holiday bungalow is spacious but compact, and is suitable for two/four persons (special rate for two persons). It contains large sitting/diningroom, kitchen, utility room, two double bedrooms, bathroom and toilet. Fully equipped except linen. Good parking space. Village inns are handy (300 yards). Coniston three miles. Available all year. Small dogs only, by arrangement. From £145 to £235 weekly. SAE for further details and terms stating number of persons and dates required.

ENNERDALE. Mrs E.J. Vickers, Mireside Farm, Ennerdale, Cleator CA23 3AU (01946 861276). ♀♀♀ *APPROVED.* **Sleeps 6.** Comfortable country cottage near beautiful Ennerdale Lake (one field away) surrounded by mountains with spectacular views and many interesting walks. The cottage adjoins the farmhouse at Mireside Farm and is completely self contained. Open all year. Car essential, parking. Accommodation for six in three double bedrooms; bathroom/toilet; sitting/dining room; kitchen with electric cooker and all kitchen equipment provided (fridge, etc). Central heating throughout. Electric fire, colour TV. Children welcome, cot available. Linen supplied. Weekly rates from £120 (low season) to £220 (high season). SAE for brochure please.

PLEASE SEND A STAMPED ADDRESSED ENVELOPE WITH ENQUIRIES

ELTERWATER. Lane Ends Cottages, Elterwater. ♀♀♀ *COMMENDED.* Three cottages are situated next to "Fellside" on the edge of Elterwater Common. Two cottages accommodate a maximum of four to six persons: double bedroom, twin bedded room; fully equipped kitchen/dining room; bathroom. Third cottage sleeps five: as above plus single bedroom and separate dining room. Electricity by meters. The cottages provide an ideal base for walking/touring holidays with Ambleside, Grasmere, Hawkshead and Coniston within a few miles. Parking for one car per cottage, additional parking opposite. Open all year; out of season long weekends available. Rates from £150 per week. Brochure on request (SAE please). **Mrs M.E. Rice, "Fellside", Elterwater, Ambleside LA22 9HN (015394 37678).**

TEL. MRS J. HALL   (019467) 23319

SELF-CATERING IN STYLE

Get away from it all on our lovely Lakeland farm. Traditionalists love the stone cottages, – or how about a beautiful modern pine lodge? All fully fitted and equipped of course, – even including dishwashers. Couples will love the peace and tranquillity, and walking the dog couldn't be easier, for Eskdale is walking country – riverside, valley or high fell, you choose! Children too love Fisherground, spending hours up at the Adventure playground, or taking Dad on at table tennis or badminton in the Sports Hall, or playing on the rafts on the shallow pond. We even have our own station on the Ravenglass and Eskdale miniature railway. Pets Welcome.

Colour brochure on request. E.T.B. ♀♀♀♀ commended.

FISHERGROUND   FARM   ESKDALE   CUMBRIA   CA19 1TF

GRASMERE. 3,4 & 5 Field Foot, Broadgate, Grasmere. ♀♀♀ *APPROVED.* **Properties sleep 4,7 & 8.** Three terraced cottages situated down a private lane in the heart of Grasmere village bordering the River Rothay. Literally one minute from bus route and shops, they are convenient for those without their own transport. Built of traditional Lakeland stone, our fully equipped cottages stay cool in summer but are very cosy in winter. No. 3 sleeps eight, No. 4 sleeps four, No. 5 sleeps seven and has its own riverside patio. Cots, high chairs and extra camp beds available. Come to Grasmere, "the jewel of the Lakes", and enjoy a wonderful holiday. Contact **Mrs S.H. Brown, High Dale Park Farm, Satterthwaite, Ulverston LA12 8LJ (01229 860226).**

GRIZEDALE FOREST. High Dale Park Barn, High Dale Park, Satterthwaite, Ulverston LA12 8LJ. ♀♀♀♀ *HIGHLY COMMENDED.* Delightfully situated south-facing barn, newly converted, attached to owners' 17th century farmhouse, with wonderful views down secluded, quiet valley, surrounded by beautiful broadleaf woodland. Oak beams, log fires, full central heating, patio. Grizedale Visitor Centre (three miles) includes the indoor Theatre-in-the-Forest, award-winning sculpture trails, gallery and unique sculptured playground. Grizedale Forest is one of the Lake District's richest areas of wildlife. Accommodation in two self contained units, one sleeping eight, the other two plus baby; available separately or as one unit at a reduced rate. Hawkshead three miles, Beatrix Potter's home three miles. Contact: **Mrs S.H. Brown, High Dale Park Farm, High Dale Park, Satterthwaite, Ulverston LA12 8LJ (01229 860226).**

HAWESWATER. Goosemire Cottages. Lovely Lakeland self catering cottages for two to eight people. Furnished and equipped to a high standard, set in one of the Lake District's loveliest corners, the tranquil Lowther Valley lies between Haweswater and Ullswater. An ideal base for walking, fishing, bird watching, visiting historic sites or just relaxing in a beautiful and peaceful setting. Local pubs and post office/shop nearby. Log fires and central heating. Heating, electricity and bed linen included in the tariff. Open all year. Short Breaks available. Details and brochure from **Anne Frith, "Goosemire", The Mews, Bampton, Penrith CA10 2RE (Tel/Fax: 01931 713245).**

HAWKSHEAD. Peter and Anne Hart, Bracken Fell Cottage, Outgate, Ambleside LA22 0NH (015394 36289). Sleeps 2/4. Bracken Fell Cottage is situated in beautiful open countryside between Ambleside and Hawkshead in the picturesque hamlet of Outgate. The two bedroomed accommodation has central heating and is immaculately furnished. Fully equipped kitchen. Linen and electricity included. Ideally equipped for exploring the Lake District. All major outdoor activities catered for nearby. Ample parking. Patio area, two acres of gardens. Open all year. Terms from £140 per week. Sorry, no pets or children under eight years. Bed and Breakfast accommodation also available (two Crowns Commended). Non smoking. Write or phone for brochure and tariff.

Bracken Fell

HOLMROOK. G. and H.W. Cook, Hall Flatt, Santon, Holmrook CA19 1UU (019467 26270). Working farm. Sleeps 7. This comfortably furnished house is set in own grounds with beautiful views. The approach road is a short but good lane off Gosforth/Santon Bridge road. Ideal centre for climbers and walkers. Within easy reach of Muncaster Castle and Narrow Gauge Railway from Ravenglass to Eskdale, about three miles from the sea and Wastwater. Accommodation comprises two double bedrooms, two single and child's bed; cot; bathroom, two toilets; sittingroom; diningroom; all electric kitchen with cooker, fridge, kettle, immersion heater, stainless steel sink unit. Fully equipped except for linen. Open Easter to Christmas. Pets by arrangement. Shopping about two miles and car essential. Electricity by 50p meter. SAE, please, for weekly terms.

KENDAL. The Barns, Field End, Patton, Kendal. ♛ ♛ ♛ ♛ *COMMENDED.* Two detached barns converted

into five spacious architect-designed houses. The Barns are situated on 200 acres of farmland, four miles north of Kendal. A quiet country area with River Mint passing through farmland and lovely views of Cumbrian Hills, many interesting local walks with the Dales Way Walk passing nearby. Fishing is available on the River. The Barns consist of four houses with four double bedrooms and one house with three double bedrooms. Each house fully centrally heated for early/late holidays; lounge with open fire, diningroom; kitchen with cooker, fridge, microwave and washer; bathroom, downstairs shower room and toilet. Many interesting features include oak beams, pine floors and patio doors. Central to Lakes and Yorkshire Dales, National Parks. Terms from £120 to £320. Electricity at cost. Pets welcome. For brochure of The Barns apply to **Mr and Mrs E.D. Robinson, 1 Field End, Patton, Kendal (01539 824220 or 0378 596863).**

KENDAL. Mrs E. Barnes, Brackenfold, Whinfell, Kendal LA8 9EF (01539 824238). Working farm, join in. Sleeps 5. Brackenfold is a 217-acre dairy/sheep farm set in a quiet country area. There are beautiful scenic views from the farm and also a river running through the middle of the farm which is suitable for paddling and picnicking. Brackenfold is situated centrally for touring the Lake District and the Yorkshire Dales. All children are welcome and babysitting is available. Milk can be obtained from the farm. The accommodation is part of the farmhouse and has two double bedrooms, cot; bathroom, toilet; sitting/ diningroom; fully equipped kitchen with electric cooker, fridge, etc. Shops four miles, sea 20. Sorry, no pets. Open March to November. SAE, please, for terms.

KENDAL. Mrs E. Bateman, High Underbrow Farm, Burneside, Kendal LA8 9AY (01539 721927). Working farm. Sleeps 4. The cottage, converted in 1985, adjoins the 17th century farmhouse in a sunny position with wonderful views. Ideal spot for touring the Lake District and Yorkshire Dales, with many pleasant walks around. There are two bedrooms (one with double bed, the other with two singles). Children are welcome and a cot is available. Bathroom with bath, shower, toilet and washbasin. Large livingroom/ kitchen with colour TV, fitted units, fridge and cooker. Electricity by £1 coin meter. Storage heaters 50p meter. Understairs store. Fitted carpets throughout. Own entrance porch. Sorry, no pets. Shops at Burneside two miles away, Kendal four miles, Windermere eight miles. Linen provided. Car essential — parking. Terms from £120 weekly. There is also a new six-berth holiday caravan to let from £120 per week.

KENDAL. Dora's Cottage, Natland, Kendal. ♀ ♀ ♀ *COMMENDED.* **Sleeps 2/4.** Adjoining farmhouse in a tranquil village south of Kendal, this delightful cottage overlooks the garden amid the Lakeland Fells. Ground floor bedrooms, TV, fridge, ironing facilities, electric cooker, microwave, central heating and linen provided to help make the most of a country holiday with the hills and Dales nearby. Golf, riding, inns, restaurants, leisure centre, historic visits within easy distance. Pets and children welcome. Car parking. Terms from £180 to £285 per week. Short Breaks can be arranged. Farmhouse Bed and Breakfast also available. For further details apply to **Mrs Val Sunter, Higher House Farm, Oxenholme Lane, Natland, Kendal LA9 7QH (015395 61177; Fax: 015395 61520).**

KESWICK. Barn Croft, Applethwaite, Keswick. Sleeps 5/6 This former 18th century barn has been

converted into a lovely two-storey detached cottage and still retains a number of original features. Set in an enclosed garden amid farmland, it lies directly off the Bassenthwaite to Latrigg road with easy access to Keswick and is centrally located for the whole of the Lake District. One double and one twin bedroom; bathroom, WC and shower; modern kitchen with electric cooker, washing machine and microwave; two lounges (one with studio couch). Beds have duvets; please supply own bed linen and kitchen linen. All lighting and heating costs included in rental. Pets allowed under strict control. Bookings from Sunday to Sunday. Terms £175 — £395 per week according to season. **Mrs M.J. Matthews, The Vicarage, Braithwaite, Keswick CA12 5RY (017687 78243; Fax: 017687 78037).**

KESWICK. 9 St Herbert Street, Keswick. This comfortable terraced house is an ideal base for your

holiday or short break in Northern Lakeland, only a few minutes' walk from Keswick's shops, leisure facilities and the fells. The house has full central heating, a pine kitchen with cooker, fridge/freezer, microwave and washing machine; dining room with maps, books and games; sitting room with colour TV; bathroom and three bedrooms — one double, one twin and one with 2'6" bunk beds. Families welcome (cot available). Sorry, no pets or smokers please. Car not essential. Weekly terms from £165 including electricity and gas (weekend or short breaks also available). Further details from **Mr and Mrs H. Marriott, Kirkland House, 9 Lower Church Street, Ashby-de-la-Zouch, Leicestershire LE65 1AB (01530 414553).**

KESWICK. Stoney Gill, Newlands, Keswick. Situated three miles from Keswick on the Braithwaite to Buttermere Road, with the most magnificent views across Newlands Valley to Catbells, Stoney Gill flat makes an excellent base for walking directly onto the fells. Also convenient for touring in the Lake District, fishing, sailing, pony trekking and golf. Stoney Gill consists of one single and two double bedrooms, all with washbasins; bathroom; open plan lounge with dining and kitchen area. Electric meter. Central heating included in rent. Weekly terms from £140 to £220. Parking for two cars. One dog only please. Further details apply to: **Mrs L. Edmondson, Stoney Acre, Newlands, Keswick CA12 5TS (017687 78200).**

KESWICK. Mr and Mrs J. Pepper, Beckstone Farms, Thornthwaite, Keswick CA12 5SQ (017687

78510). BARF COTTAGE: Near the village of Thornthwaite set in peaceful surroundings is this pretty two bedroomed cottage with superb panoramic views over the mountains and valley. This cottage is ideal for a relaxing holiday, walking or touring. Also a few minutes' walk away from Bassenthwaite Lake which is a bird reserve. Owner maintained. Please write or telephone for further details and tariff.

CUMBRIA – LAKELAND SPLENDOUR!

The Lake District has for long been a popular tourist destination; however, the Fells and Pennine areas are also worth exploring. The many attractions of Cumbria include the Ennerdale Forest, St. Bees Head, Langdale Pikes, Bowness-on-Solway, the market town of Alston, Lanercost Priory, Scafell Pike – England's highest mountain – and the Wordsworth country around Ambleside, Grasmere and Cockermouth.

KESWICK near. Mrs A.M. Trafford, Bassenthwaite Hall Farm, Bassenthwaite Village, Near Keswick CA12 4QP (017687 76393). Working farm. By a

stream with ducks and a white wooden bridge we have delightful cottages of charm and character, in this tranquil and pretty hamlet, six miles north of Keswick. Children spend many happy hours nearby playing on the swings in the wood whilst the ducks and hens roam freely. Lovely walks to the Lake, Skiddaw Dash Falls and surrounding hills. Excellent inn nearby serving good food. All cottages are situated around the farmyard. We have small properties for two and family properties sleeping four to 10. Large groups of up to 20 can also be catered for. Pets welcome. Terms from £90 to £550. Reduction off peak. Long weekends, cheap mid-week breaks from November to March. Also farmhouse Bed and Breakfast. Colour brochure available.

KIRKBY LONSDALE near. Mrs M. Dixon, Harrison Farm, Whittington, Kirkby Lonsdale, Carnforth, Lancashire LA6 2NX (015242 71415). Properties sleep 2/8. Near Hutton Roof, three miles from Kirkby Lonsdale and central for touring Lake District and Yorkshire Dales. Coast walks on Hutton Roof Crag, famous lime stone pavings. Sleeps eight people, one room with double and single bed and one room with double and cot, while third bedroom has three single beds. Bathroom. Sittingroom, diningroom and kitchen. Everything supplied but linen. Parking space. Pets permitted. Other cottages available for two to eight people. Electric cooker, fridge, kettle, iron, immersion heaters and TV. Electricity and coal extra. Terms on request. SAE brings quick reply.

See also Colour Display Advertisement **KIRKOSWALD. Mike and Toni Parsons, Howscales, Kirkoswald, Penrith CA10 1JG (01768 898666; Fax: 01768 898710).** ♀♀♀ **and** ♀♀♀♀ *HIGHLY COMMENDED.* **Sleep 2/4.** COTTAGES FOR NON-SMOKERS. Howscales is a former farm built in local red sandstone with the buildings grouped around a central courtyard. Located in a rural setting one and a half miles from Kirkoswald. Three cottages are two storey, with the lounge, kitchen and dining areas on the first floor; the bedrooms and bathroom are on the ground floor. One is single storey at ground level, suitable for accompanied disabled guests, with two en suite double bedrooms. All cottages have full central heating, are equipped with colour TV and have a fully equipped kitchen/dining area with microwave, electric cooker, gas hob and fridge. Shower room and WC. Everything supplied including linen. Gas and electricity paid by meter reading at end of stay. Sorry, but no pets or children under six. Please ring or write for our colour brochure.

KIRKOSWALD. Crossfield Cottages with Leisure Fishing. ♀♀♀♀ *COMMENDED.* Tranquil quality cottages overlooking modest lakes amid Lakeland's beautiful Eden Valley countryside. Only 30 minutes' drive from Ullswater, North Pennines, Hadrian's Wall and Scottish Borders. You will find beds freshly made up for your arrival, tranquillity and freedom in your surroundings, and good coarse and game fishing at hand. Accommodation is guaranteed clean, well equipped and maintained; laundry area; pets welcome. Centrally located, good fishing and walking. Relax and escape to YOUR home in the country — why settle for less? No silly rules. Telephone or SAE for terms and full details: **Crossfield Cottages, Kirkoswald, Penrith CA10 1EU (24 hour Brochure Line 01768 898711 (manned most Saturdays). Bookings 8am to 10pm 01768 896275 (Fax available)).**

LEVENS. Mrs H. Bland, Ninezergh Farm, Levens, Kendal LA8 0PA (015395 63274). Luxury static caravan set on a single working farm site. Carpeted lounge area with colour TV and gas fire. Two bedrooms with bed linen provided, kitchen with fridge and gas cooker. Hot and cold water. Bathroom with flush toilet and shower. Children and pets welcome. Ideal centre for touring and walking Lake District and Fells. Fishing, horse riding, swimming and shops all within easy reach. Four miles from Junction 36 off M6 motorway. Available March to October from £100 to £150 weekly.

LOWESWATER. Latterhead Cottage, Loweswater, Cockermouth. Sleeps 4. Charming country cottage, recently modernised, yet retaining many of its original features and charm. Seven miles from Cockermouth, 10 miles from Keswick. Self catering cottage comprising lounge with feature fireplace and colour TV; fully fitted kitchen/dining area including electric cooker, microwave, fridge and kettle. Shower room/WC. Two bedrooms. Cot and high chair available. All very comfortably furnished. Everything supplied except linen. Electricity payable by 50p coin meter. Children and pets welcome. Available all year. Weekly terms from £150 to £170. Booking forms, etc from: **R.F. Bell, Oakbank, Loweswater, Cockermouth CA13 0RR (01900 85227).**

PENRITH. Mrs S. Grave, West View Farm, Winskill, Penrith CA10 1PD (01768 881356). ♀♀♀♀

COMMENDED. Situated on a working farm in the beautiful village of Winskill in the Eden Valley, with panoramic views to the Pennines and Lake District peaks. The well equipped cottages have everything you need — central heating, TV, washing facilities, linen, children's play area and games room. They are ideally placed for touring in the Lakes, the Borders and Roman Wall area, but there are also many walks nearby. Open all year. Short breaks available in Low Season from £175 to £320. Brochure available on request.

See also Colour Display Advertisement **ULLSWATER. The Estate Office, Patterdale Hall Estate, Glenridding, Penrith CA11 0PJ (Tel & Fax: 017684 82308 24 hours). Apartments** ♀♀♀♀ *COMMENDED;* **Cottages** ♀♀♀ *APPROVED;* **Pine Lodges** ♀♀♀ *COMMENDED;* **Chalets** ♀ *COMMENDED;* **The Dairy and Bothies** ♀ *COMMENDED.* Our range includes three very comfortable,

large apartments, two stone-built cottages with open fires, two three-bedroomed pine lodges, six two-bedroomed cedar chalets, a unique, detached, converted dairy, and two converted gardeners' bothies which make ideal, low cost accommodation for two people. All set in a private 300 acre Estate between Lake Ullswater and Helvellyn and containing a working hill farm, a Victorian Waterfall Wood, private lake foreshore for guests to use for boating and fishing, and 100 acres of designated ancient woodland for you to explore. Children welcome. Dogs by appointment in some of the accommodation. Colour TV, central heating, launderette. Day time electricity metered. Linen hire available. Please phone for full brochure.

ULLSWATER. South View, Dacre, Ullswater. Working farm. Sleeps 6. The farmhouse is situated in

the small village of Dacre just four miles from M6 and Penrith. There is a large walled garden and plenty of parking space. Car essential. The house is comfortable, clean and well equipped for six people including bed linen. Children welcome. Cot available on request. Well controlled pets only. One double-bedded room, two twin-bedded rooms; bathroom with toilet and shower; diningroom, sittingroom with electric fire and colour TV. Kitchen with electric cooker, microwave and fridge. Storage heaters downstairs and in bathroom, included in rent. Other electricity on £1 meter. Weekly terms from £175. **Mrs N. Bennett, Hollins Farm, Dockray, Penrith CA11 0JY (017684 82374).**

WASTWATER LAKE. Mrs J. Burnett, Greendale, Wasdale CA20 1EU (019467 26243). ♀♀♀

COMMENDED. Lakeland cottage-style apartments to sleep four/five people half a mile from Wastwater Lake. All apartments have one double and one twin bedded room and some have a third bedroom with a small single bed. Bathroom with shower. Colour TV. Economy 7 electric heating and hot water. Linen supplied. Electricity included in the weekly price of £180 — £275. Fell walkers and mountaineers alike will be attracted to the impressive peaks within easy reach — Great Gable, Scafell etc. Other interests include Ravenglass Miniature Railway, Muncaster Castle. Golf, fishing and pony trekking may be enjoyed in this area. Sandy beaches eight miles away. Full details on request.

CUMBRIA – THE GREAT OUTDOORS

Lakes, rivers, mountains and moors (and a mild climate) make Cumbria a paradise for the outdoor enthusiast — with something to suit every age group and every level of ability. Practically every kind of watersport can be enjoyed — if you haven't tried water ski-ing, canoeing, windsurfing or yachting, then now's your chance! Climbing, abseiling, walking, cycling, mountain biking, pony trekking, fishing, orienteering . . . the list is endless!

WINDERMERE. Mr and Mrs F. Legge, Pinethwaite, Lickbarrow Road, Windermere LA23 2NQ (Tel & Fax: 015394 44558). ♀♀♀ & ♀♀♀♀ *COMMENDED.* **Properties sleep 2/7.** Pinethwaite offers more than just somewhere to stay for your Lake District holiday. Our unique cottages and apartments nestle in the heart of our private woodland, the haunt of roe deer, red squirrels and extensive bird life. A tranquil location, yet only one mile from Windermere and Bowness villages. Superb viewpoints close by. Lovely walks in our grounds and local footpaths (Cumbrian Way) through surrounding farmland and fell. Well equipped accommodation (colour TVs, microwaves, electric heating, log fires). Central washing machine/dryer. Private parking. Children welcome, but sorry no pets. Open all year. Short Breaks available in the Low Season. Tariffs from £150 to £420 per week. Full details in our brochure, sent on request.

See also Colour Display Advertisement **WINDERMERE. Birthwaite Edge Apartments, Windermere. ♀♀♀** *COMMENDED.* Situated in extensive grounds in one of the most exclusive areas of Windermere, 10 minutes' walk from village and Lake. This is the perfect all year round holiday base. 10 self catering apartments for two to six people. Resident proprietors personally ensure the highest standards of cleanliness and comfort. Swimming pool open May to September. Colour TV. Well equipped kitchens. Hot water included. Coin metered electricity for lighting, cooking and electric fires. Background central heating during winter. Duvets and linen provided. High chairs and cots extra. Ample car parking. Regret no pets. Terms from £110 to £410. Brochure from **Bruce and Marsha Dodsworth, Birthwaite Edge, Birthwaite Road, Windermere LA23 1BS (Tel & Fax: 015394 42861).**

Key to Tourist Board Ratings

The Crown Scheme
(England, Scotland & Wales)
Covering hotels, motels, private hotels, guesthouses, inns, bed & breakfast, farmhouses. Every Crown classified place to stay is inspected annually. *The classification:* Listed then 1-5 Crown indicates the range of facilities and services. Higher quality standards are indicated by the terms APPROVED, COMMENDED, HIGHLY COMMENDED and DELUXE.

The Key Scheme
(also operates in Scotland using a Crown symbol)
Covering self-catering in cottages, bungalows, flats, houseboats, houses, chalets, etc. Every Key classified holiday home is inspected annually. *The classification:* 1-5 Key indicates the range of facilities and equipment. Higher quality standards are indicated by the terms APPROVED, COMMENDED, HIGHLY COMMENDED and DELUXE.

The Q Scheme
(England, Scotland & Wales)
Covering holiday, caravan, chalet and camping parks. Every Q rated park is inspected annually for its quality standards. The more √ in the Q – up to 5 – the higher the standard of what is provided.

DERBYSHIRE

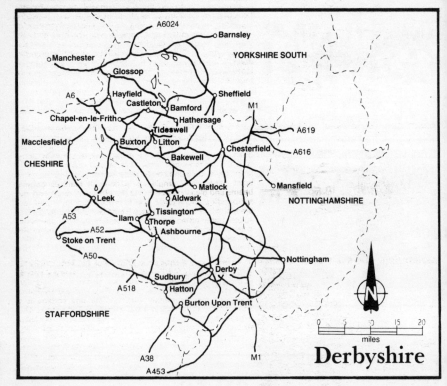

Derbyshire

ASHBOURNE. Dove Cottage, Church Lane, Mayfield, Ashbourne. ♀♀♀ *APPROVED.* **Sleeps 8.** This

modernised 200-year-old cottage in Mayfield village is ideally situated for shops, pubs, busy market towns, sporting facilities, lovely Dove Valley, Alton Towers, Peaks and Staffordshire Moorlands and many other places of interest. The cottage is comfortably furnished and well equipped with TV, fridge, automatic washing machine, gas central heating. The fenced garden overlooks farmland. Garage and parking. Children welcome. Pets by arrangement. Available for long and short lets, also mid-week bookings. Price and brochure on request. Further details from **Arthur Tatlow, Ashview, Ashfield Farm, Calwich, Ashbourne DE6 2EB (01335 324443 or 324279).**

ASHBOURNE. Mrs M. Large, Overtown Farm, Hognaston, Ashbourne DE6 1NR (01629 540365). Self catering holiday cottage sleeps four/six, beautifully converted from an attractive barn. Surrounded by farmland and overlooking Carsington Water. Situated between Ashbourne and Wirksworth. Sailing, sailboarding and canoeing with instruction are available on Carsington Water; horse riding, fishing, bike riding and bird watching are all within five minutes of the cottage. Chatsworth House and Haddon Hall are just two of the historic houses within easy visiting distance. The cottage has full central heating and facilities include microwave, electric cooker, washing machine, TV, video, payphone. Linen and towels supplied. There is a small garden. Available all year. Brochure on request.

ASHBOURNE. Mrs Louie Tatlow, Ashfield Farm, Calwich, Near Ashbourne DE6 2EB (01335 324279 or 324443). ♀♀♀ APPROVED. **Working farm. Sleeps 5.** Ashfield Cottage is a recently renovated oak-beamed cottage on this working farm well situated for the Peak District and many other places of interest with beautiful views of Dove Valley and Weaver Hills. Accommodation is for five persons in two bedrooms (one family room and one with twin beds). Well furnished and equipped with storage heaters, colour TV, automatic washing machine, tumble dryer, fridge/freezer. Coloured bathroom suite and shower. Linen for hire. Parking space. Further details and brochure on request.

ASHBOURNE. Mr Lennard, The Chop House, Windle Hill Farm, Sutton-on-the-Hill, Ashbourne DE6 5JH (01283 732377). The Chop House has been carefully converted from the farm corn shed where animal feeds were once chopped and mixed. Providing accommodation for up to six it has three twin bedrooms, a fully equipped kitchen, large dining area and comfortable lounge. Outside there is a quiet garden and ample car parking. It features original beams and pleasant views over the farmyard, duckpond and surrounding countryside. The farm has traditional and rare breeds of livestock and poultry (some of our hens lay GREEN eggs). Local attractions include stately homes, adventure theme parks, museums and the glorious Derbyshire Countryside.

ASHBOURNE. Mrs Sue Prince, Beechenhill Farm, Ilam, Ashbourne DE6 2BD (01335 310274). ♀♀♀ and ♀♀♀♀ HIGHLY COMMENDED. **Sleep 2 and 6.** At Beechenhill Farm there are two warm and delightful cottages, both look out over rolling hills, a wooded valley and cows or sheep peacefully grazing. One tiny cottage is a secluded haven for two in its own little walled garden. Our large cottage has three bedrooms and two bathrooms, sleeps six and is specially designed to be accessible for all including wheelchair users. Both cottages are beautifully decorated and comfortably furnished and both have real fires for cosy evenings. Beechenhill is in the Peak National Park, beside the charming Dove and Manifold Valleys, many glorious walks lead from our door. Farm Holiday Bureau member.

ASHBOURNE near. Yeldersley Hall. ♀♀♀♀ COMMENDED to ♀♀♀♀♀ DE LUXE. We have two delightful flats (each to sleep two) in the stable block and a fabulous apartment (to sleep four) in the East Wing of our historic Georgian house, two miles from Ashbourne. This is an operational country house with 12 acres of gardens and grounds to explore. Each flat is furnished and equipped to a very high standard with full heating, colour TV, microwave, payphone, etc. Use of washing machine and dryer. All linen and electricity included. Cot available. Regret no pets or children under 12 except baby in cot. Terms from £150 per week. Further details and brochure from **Mrs J. Bailey, Yeldersley Hall, Ashbourne, Derbyshire DE6 1LS (01335 343432).**

ASHBOURNE near. Tony and Linda Stoddart, Cornpark Cottage, Swinscoe, Near Ashbourne DE6 2HR (01335 345041). Adjacent to our old farmhouse, overlooking the hills of Dovedale and with extensive views over three counties, this exciting barn conversion, set beside a pond, affords privacy with easy access to all of the Derbyshire/Staffordshire attractions. Dovedale and Alton Towers 15 minutes. Converted to use all of the ground floor and part of the first, the barn sleeps four/five. All necessary modern conveniences are provided in a beamed setting. Large gardens, tennis court, barbecue all surrounded by open countryside. Well behaved pets welcome. Linen provided, electricity metered. Car essential. Open March to November, Saturday to Saturday booking. Terms from £85 to £190. Also available Bed and Breakfast (at farmhouse) from £15. Phone or write for brochures.

ASHBOURNE near. Throwley Moor Farm and Throwley Cottage, Ilam, Near Ashbourne. ♛♛♛♛

Working farm, join in. Properties sleep 7/12. Self catering farmhouse and cottage on this beef and sheep farm near Dovedale and Manifold Valley. Approached by A52/A53 Ashbourne to Leek road, then via Calton and follow signs for Throwley and Ilam. Within easy reach of Alton Towers, cycle hire and places of historic interest. An ideal touring centre. The cottage accommodates seven people and the farmhouse 12. Sittingrooms and diningroom (kitchen/diner in cottage). Electric cookers; fridges; washing machine and dryer. Pay phone. Pets permitted. Car essential — parking. Available all year; terms according to season. Nearest shops three miles away. SAE, please, for further details to **Mrs M.A. Richardson, Throwley Hall Farm, Ilam, Near Ashbourne DE6 2BB (01538 308 202/243).**

ASHBOURNE near. Very picturesque stone holiday cottage with superb views in delightful setting by river and close to Dovedale. Ideally situated for quiet, peaceful holidays walking/touring in the Peak District with stately homes, cycling, trekking, fishing and Alton Towers close by for those who seek a more active holiday. This property has been sympathetically modernised to a high standard, retaining its old beams and character. It sleeps up to six and has fitted carpets, electric cooking/heating and all modern conveniences, cots, Satellite TV, etc. Available for weekly periods at a charge of between £100 and £280 per week. Leaflet giving full information from **Mrs Y. Bailey, 4 Woodland Close, Thorpe, Ashbourne DE6 2AP (01335 350447).**

ASHFORD IN THE WATER. Mrs Ann Lindsay, Gritstone House, Greaves Lane, Ashford in the Water, Bakewell DE45 1QH (Tel & Fax: 01629 813563). ♛♛♛ *COMMENDED.* **Sleeps 2.** Gritstone Cottage, adjacent to owner's home (see B&B entry), is a charming holiday house in a quiet street forming the middle part of a group of three 18th century cottages and stable. The interior has been completely renovated, furnished and equipped to a high standard for two people (sorry, no pets or children except babies in arms — cot available). Ashford in the Water (jewel of the Peak) is an ideal centre for all Derbyshire attractions and activities. Village shop, post office and dining facilities within a few minutes' walk. Non-smoking. Weekly terms from £126 to £210 inclusive of linen and energy. Brochure available.

BAKEWELL. Jan and Tony Staley, Bolehill Farm, Monyash Road, Bakewell DE45 1QW (Tel & Fax: 01629 812359). ♛♛♛♛ *COMMENDED.* **Sleep 2/8 adults plus 2 children.** AWARD WINNING COTTAGES. Charming collection of eight stone cottages grouped around an attractive courtyard and incorporating high quality furnishings and equipment. Situated in 20 acres of open fields and woodland with magnificent views over Lathkill Dale (Bakewell two miles). Leisure facilities include sauna, solarium, table tennis, pool table, children's play area and barbecue. From £180 to £450 weekly. Winner of East Midlands Tourist Board Self Catering Holiday of the Year Award.

BARLOW. Mr & Mrs R. Ward, Barlow Trout, Mill Farm, Barlow, Sheffield S18 5TJ (0114 289 0543). ♛♛♛♛ *COMMENDED.* Mill Farm Holiday Cottages are situated in a conservation area with post office and pub/bar meals just 300 yards away; bus stop at gate. Horse riding can be arranged and coarse and fly fishing is available locally. Children and pets welcome. Central heating. Four-poster bed in three of the five units. Weekly terms from £90 to £195. Linen provided free of charge. Short break bookings accepted any time of year. Please write or phone for full details.

Terms quoted in this publication may be subject to increase if rises in costs necessitate

---

BELPER. Mr and Mrs C. Postles, Chevin Green Farm, Chevin Road, Belper DE56 2UN (01773 822328). One property ♀♀♀ COMMENDED, four properties ♀♀♀♀ COMMENDED.

Enjoy a holiday in one of our five attractive bungalows overlooking rolling Derbyshire countryside. The bungalows, with original beams and are fully equipped to a high standard accommodating four/six people with lounge, fully fitted kitchen, bathroom; two or three bedrooms, one has wheelchair access throughout. Ideally situated for all places of interest, Alton Towers, American Adventure, Chatsworth, Dovedale, Peak District. Terms £80 to £295. Also farmhouse Bed and Breakfast accommodation (all rooms en suite) available.

BUXTON. Mrs Gill Taylor, Priory Lea Holiday Flats, 50 White Knowle Road, Buxton SK17 9NH (01298 23737). ♀♀/♀♀♀ APPROVED.

Priory Lea

We would be pleased to welcome you to the Roman town of Buxton, nestling in a unique situation amongst the Pennine Hills, boasting many fine buildings including the Opera House and with shops to suit all tastes. Priory Lea is one mile from the town centre, walks start from our car park. Poole's Cavern Country Park adjoins our own farmland. Each flat is equipped to Tourist Board standard. Colour TV. Children and pets especially welcome. Central for Alton Towers and Chatsworth House. Established for 30 years. Terms from £80 to £175. Short breaks available.

BUXTON near. Mrs V. Lawrenson, Grove House, Elkstones, Near Warslow, Buxton SK17 0LU (01538 300487). ♀♀♀ COMMENDED. Sleeps 2/3 plus cot.

Welcome Host. A character stone country cottage, sympathetically modernised to retain original oak beams with attractive galleried landing. In quiet Peak District village near Manifold Valley with Dovedale six miles away. Comfortable and very well equipped including bed linen and towels. Patio garden with sunny aspect and parking close to cottage. Good walking and cycling area with five Country Parks within a 12 mile radius. Convenient for Alton Towers, Staffordshire Potteries factory shops, and the National Trust properties in Derbyshire and Staffordshire and RSPB Reserve. Pub/restaurant nearby. Dogs by arrangement. The perfect location for the true country lover. Weekly terms from £125 to £195.

CASTLETON (Peak National Park). Sleeps 5. Seventeenth century farm cottage restored and maintained to a high standard. Central heating and double glazing. Fitted carpet in living areas, colour TV, radio. Fully equipped, including linen, for up to five persons. One double and one twin bedded room, two bathrooms, kitchen/diner, lounge. Pets by arrangement. Children welcome. Ample parking. Private terrace with view to Mam Tor — the "Shivering Mountain". Ideal for walking. Terms £150 to £290 (heating and electricity supplied extra through meters). The farm lies half a mile from A625 in the beautiful Hope Valley. **Mrs C. Bell, Spring House Farm, Castleton S30 2WB (01433 620962).**

CUTTHORPE. Mr and Mrs D. Sutton, Cow Close Farm, Overgreen, Cutthorpe, Chesterfield S42 7BA (01246 232055). ♀♀♀ Working farm. Sleep 4.

A small farm dating from the 17th century, situated in the tiny hamlet of Overgreen. It lies on the B6050, four miles from Chatsworth, on the edge of the Peak. A country inn across the road serves good food and traditional ales. The two fully equipped cottages are renovations of single storey farm buildings, which surround a central courtyard and accommodate four persons. Fitted carpets, exposed timbers, central heating, separate kitchen, colour TV, garden sitting areas and ample car parking. Beds made up for your arrival; children, pets welcome. Terms from £90 to £170 per week includes heating and hot water. Brochure on request.

WHEN MAKING ENQUIRIES PLEASE MENTION
FARM HOLIDAY GUIDES

DOVEDALE. Mrs Beryl Howson, Hallfields Farm, Wetton, Ashbourne DE6 2AF (01335 310282).

ΨΨΨΨ *COMMENDED.* Recently renovated from stables, the self-catering holiday cottage sleeps four/five. Situated in the country with panoramic views overlooking the Manifold Valley and Thor's Cave. A quarter mile from the next residence and the village of Wetton. Central heating is by storage radiators (included in the price). TV supplied. There is unlimited parking, an excellent choice of country pubs and inns for your evening meals, some within walking distance. Dovedale is two miles, Ashbourne, Leek and Buxton 10 miles. Alton Towers and Chatsworth House are close by. Open all year. Terms from £100 — £250 per week. Short stay holidays available off season. Pets and children welcome.

DOVEDALE/PEAK DISTRICT. Alstonefield Holiday Homes, Post Office House, Alstonefield, Ashbourne DE6 2FX (01335 310201). ΨΨΨ/ΨΨΨΨ A choice of five properties sleeping two/six people, all situated in the quiet picturesque limestone village of Alstonefield, five times winner of the Best Kept Village award. Complete with a 13th century church, an old coaching inn and village shop. An ideal base to explore the Peak National Park situated between Dovedale and Manifold Valleys, also near the attractions of Alton Towers, Chatsworth House, etc. All accommodation recently modernised and tastefully furnished in country style to a high standard. Ideal for those Short Winter Breaks. Children and pets welcome. Terms from £95 (three nights) to £450.

HARDSTOFT. Pear Tree Cottage, Locke Lane, Hardstoft, Near Chesterfield. A delightful fully modernised cottage on a smallholding. Ideal base for Peak District and Derbyshire's many attractions. There is a pleasant conservatory overlooking fields. The dining kitchen is large and well equipped including automatic washer. The lounge is comfortably furnished and has a colour TV. There are two bedrooms (one with double bed, one with three single beds); fully equipped bathroom. Attractive garden. Ample parking. Bed linen, central heating and electricity are included in the rental. Well behaved dogs allowed. Open all year. Terms from £140 to £225 per week. Weekend Breaks also available. Contact: **Mrs C. Beckett, Laburnum Cottage, 46 Hardstoft Road, Pilsley, Chesterfield S45 8BL (01773 872767).**

HARTINGTON. P. Skemp, Cotterhill Farm, Biggin-by-Hartington, Buxton SK17 0DJ (01298 84447; Fax: 01298 84664).

ΨΨΨΨ *HIGHLY COMMENDED.* Two recently converted cottages, one sleeping four, the other two. Exposed beams, two-person cottage has galleried bedroom, log burner, five piece suite in bathroom and more. High and tasteful specification. Patio, substantial garden area, croquet lawn and barbecue. Laundry room. Glorious location in rolling countryside. Excellent views with privacy. Half a mile from village and pub. Tissington Trail three-quarters of a mile, two other cycle/footpath trails within three miles, nature reserve on our land leading after one and a half miles to River Dove, four miles down river is Dovedale. Footpaths/bridleways surround our farm. Highly praised, personalised information pack in each cottage giving loads of advice on attractions, walks, etc. Terms from £150 to £320 per week.

HOPE. Crabtree Cottages, Crabtree Meadow, Aston Lane, Hope, Via Sheffield S30 2RA (Tel & Fax: 01433 620291).

ΨΨΨΨ *HIGHLY COMMENDED.* **Four cottages sleep 2/6.** Four beautifully converted, well-equipped cottages in the grounds of a country house in Peak District National Park, sleeping two to six persons. Beautifully fitted kitchens with microwave ovens. Colour TV's. Laundry. Payphone. Central heating, fuel and linen included in rental. Ample off road parking but car not essential. Superb walking country and facilities in the area for golf, tennis, climbing, gliding, fishing, pony trekking and caving. Convenient for shops and pubs, visiting historic houses. Weekly all year £140 to £330. Short breaks in winter from £55. Contact: **Mrs P.M. Mason.**

SHEFFIELD. Mrs J.S. Hill, Oxton Rakes Hall Farm, Barlow, Sheffield S18 5SE (0114 289 0268).

Luxurious 18th century barn conversion set in 30 acres of beautiful Derbyshire countryside; Chatsworth House five miles, "Pheasant Croft" opened 1994 by His Grace The Duke of Devonshire. Outdoor heated swimming pool, indoor games room with table tennis, pool table and tiny tots corner. To the rear of the farm house a small lake with private fishing. Many animals including Ebb and Flo the wallabies, and barn owls. Full facilities for wheelchair users. Everything has been done to make your holiday as comfortable and enjoyable as possible. Brochures, photographs available.

PLEASE SEND A STAMPED ADDRESSED ENVELOPE WITH ENQUIRIES

DEVON

Devon

APPLEDORE. Sea Birds Cottage, Appledore. Sea edge, pretty Georgian cottage facing directly out to the open sea. Sea Birds is a spacious cottage with large lounge, colour TV; dining room with french windows onto garden; modern fitted kitchen; three double bedrooms; bathroom, second WC downstairs; washing machine. Lawned garden at back overlooking the sea with garden furniture. Own parking. Sea views from most rooms and the garden is magnificent; views of the open sea, boats entering the estuary, sunset, sea birds. Appledore is still a fishing village — fishing trips from the quay, restaurants by the water. Area has good cliff and coastal walks, stately homes, riding, swimming, golf, surfing, excellent beaches. Off peak heating. From £95. Other cottages available. Send SAE for colour brochure to **F.S. Barnes, Boat Hyde, Northam, Bideford EX39 1NX (01237 473801).**

APPLEDORE. Mariner's Cottage, Irsha Street, Appledore. Sleeps 6. Elizabethan fisherman's cottage right at the sea edge — the high tide laps against the garden wall. Extensive open sea and estuary views of ships, lighthouses, fishing and sailing boats. The quayside, beach, ships, restaurants and fishing trips are close by. Riding, sailing, tennis, golf, sandy beaches, historic houses, beautiful coastal walks, and the Country Park are all near. Mariner's Cottage (an historic Listed building), has three bedrooms, modern bathroom, fitted kitchen with washing machine, diningroom and large lounge with colour TV. Children's play house. Gas central heating makes Mariner's good for winter holidays. Dog welcome. Own parking. Picture shows view from back garden. From £95 per week. SAE, please, for brochure of this and other cottages to **Mrs F.A. Barnes, Boat Hyde, Northam, Bideford or telephone (01237 473801)** for prices and vacancies only.

The view from
Mariners' Cottage Garden

HELPFUL HOLIDAYS
for West Country self-catering

We have a wonderful variety of cottages, houses, apartments all over the West Country - seaside, moorland, farmland or villages. All and their surroundings, are very fully described and star rated by us in our free colour brochure.

HELPFUL HOLIDAYS
Coombe 2, Chagford, Devon TQ13 8DF
Tel: **01647 433593** (24 hours)
Brochure line: **01647 433535**

---

classic
cottages

Choose your cottage from 300 of the finest coastal and country cottages throughout the West Country

Owls Barn
Beaworthy, Devon

Classic Cottages (25) Helston Cornwall TR13 8NA
24 hour dial a brochure 01326 565555

ASHBURTON. Mrs P.D. Coulter, 30 East Street, Ashburton, Newton Abbot TQ13 7AZ (01364 652589). Ashburton is a small charming town, full of historic interest, situated on edge of Dartmoor, within the bounds of Dartmoor National Park. The Parish of Ashburton is surrounded on three sides by moorland, woods and rolling hills and, to the west, some of the most beautiful reaches of the River Dart. It is near Widecombe-in-the-Moor, Haytor Rock, Becky Falls and many other beauty spots and within easy reach of Torbay, Teignmouth and other seaside resorts. Flat is fully furnished and carpeted; lounge with colour TV; kitchen/diner; all essentials; two bedrooms (one double and one twin-bedded). Constant hot water to kitchen and bathroom. Completely self-contained. No linen supplied. Pets allowed. Car desirable — parking. Open all year. Shops nearby. SAE, please, for terms.

ASHBURTON. Mrs Angela Bell, Wooder Manor, Widecombe-in-the-Moor, Near Ashburton TQ13 7TR (01364 621391). ♀♀♀♀ COMMENDED. Modernised granite cottages and converted coach house, on 108 acre working family farm nestled in the picturesque valley of Widecombe, surrounded by unspoilt woodland, moors and granite tors. Half a mile from village with post office, general stores, inn with dining room, church and National Trust Information Centre. Excellent centre for touring Devon with a variety of places to visit and exploring Dartmoor by foot or on horseback. Accommodation is clean and well equipped with colour TV, central heating, laundry room. Children welcome. Large gardens and courtyard for easy parking. Open all year, so take advantage of off-season reduced rates. Short Breaks also available. Two properties suitable for disabled visitors. Brochure available.

See also Colour Display Advertisement **BARNSTAPLE. North Devon Holiday Homes, 19 Cross Street, Barnstaple EX31 1BD (01271 76322 24-hour brochure service; Fax: 01271 46544).** With our Free Colour Guide and unbiased recommendation and booking service, we can spoil you for choice in the beautiful unspoilt region around Exmoor and the wide sandy beaches and coves of Devon's Golden National Trust Coast. Over 500 selected properties including thatched cottages, working farms, beachside bungalows with swimming pools, luxury manor houses, etc. From only £69 to £690 per week. First class value assured.

**FREE ENTRY offers on visits to THE BIG SHEEP, Bideford –
see our READERS' OFFER VOUCHER for details.**

BARNSTAPLE. Huish Farm, Kings Heaton, Marwood, Barnstaple. Working farm. Sleeps 10. This

17th century farmhouse, in a quiet, yet not secluded position is three-and-a-half miles from market town of Barnstaple and five miles from Saunton. A ten-minute walk takes you to Marwood Hill Gardens with lakes (open to public from March to October). Four spacious double bedrooms (one room contains four beds). Bathroom, separate toilet; sittingroom; large kitchen with all essentials. Colour TV. Cot and high chair provided. Plenty of room for children to play. Ten people accommodated. Electricity included in price. No linen supplied. Pets permitted. Car essential, parking. Open all year. Terms from £160 to £350 weekly. Out of season from £20. Fresh milk available daily. Apply to **Mrs. V.M. Chugg, Valley View, Marwood, Barnstaple EX31 4EA (01271 43458).**

BARNSTAPLE. Mr and Mrs C.L. Hartnoll, Little Bray House, Brayford, Barnstaple EX32 7QG

(01598 710295). ♀ ♀ Properties sleep 2/6. Situated nine miles east of Barnstaple, Little Bray House is ideally placed for day trips to East Devon, Somerset and Cornwall, the lovely sandy surfing beaches at Saunton Sands and Woolacombe, and many places of interest both coastal and inland. Exmoor has much charm. Lovely walks abound, and there is a large garden with lawn and woodland, ducks and hens, fun for children. Indoor badminton and ping-pong rooms. The accommodation is in three cottages sleeping from four to six people and a flatlet which sleeps two, all self-contained and fully furnished with well-equipped kitchens and colour TV. Cot and high chair available on request. Bring own linen and towels. Linen hire on request. Well behaved dogs allowed, on lead. Terms range from £100 to £275 per week, depending on season. Telephone or write for brochure.

BARNSTAPLE near. Mrs Veronica Ley, "Stock Farm", Brayford, Barnstaple EX32 7QQ (01598

710498). Working farm, join in. Sleeps 7. This completely self-contained part of the farmhouse is beautifully situated on 280-acre beef and sheep farm in beautiful countryside with lovely views over the moors and along the Bray Valley. Ideal for touring and walking; two miles from Exmoor and 10 miles from the sea. Visitors are welcome to join in the working life of the farm. The house has two bedrooms, sleeping seven, with sofa bed. All fully carpeted. Fitted electric kitchen/diner with microwave and washer/dryer. The oak beamed lounge is full of character. Colour TV. Own garden, lawn and drying area. Adjacent patio and barbecue area. Personally cleaned; linen/bedding and towels provided. Cot and babysitting. Separate play area where children can play safely with our own family. Pets under supervision. Terms from £100 to £240. Excellent sporting facilities in the area including windsurfing, fishing, riding and golf. SAE please.

BIDEFORD. Jenny and Barry Jones, The Pines at Eastleigh, Near Bideford EX39 4PA (01271

860561; e-mail Barry@barpines.demon.co.uk). Jenny and Barry Jones invite you to try one of their luxury cottages sleeping 2 to 5 people. Open all year, full central heating, colour TV, laundry facilities, etc. Quiet locations yet convenient for North Devon beaches, gardens and other attractions. Furnished and equipped to a high standard. Two cottages in grounds of hotel (offering benefits of restaurant and baby listening service) and third about 15 minutes' drive. Pets and children welcome. Weekend breaks available off-peak. Credit Cards. No Smoking. Telephone for colour brochure.

BIDEFORD. Webbery Cottages, Webbery, Alverdiscott, Bideford. Once the home farm and stables of

the old Manor of Webbery, our architect-designed conversions of farm buildings offer a high degree of modern comfort and luxury. Set in a peaceful walled garden at centre of private five acre grounds with views extending to Exmoor, Bideford Bay and Lundy Isle. Two all-electric, two-bedroomed cottages. One centrally heated three bedroomed cottage. All tastefully furnished. Colour TV, fitted carpets. Fridge, toaster, coffee maker, etc. Separate laundry room. Ample parking. Quietly situated between market towns of Bideford and Barnstaple. Beaches, birdwatching, fishing, golf, riding, sailing, surfing and walks nearby. Brochure with pleasure. **Mrs B.M. Wilson, Webbery Garden Cottage, Webbery, Alverdiscott, Bideford EX39 4PU (01271 858430).**

PANORAMA
Millards Hill, Instow, Bideford

Photo shows superb view across garden to the estuary and Lundy Island. This spacious bungalow – less than 500 yards from safe sandy beach – has double bedroom and lounge/diner, both with fabulous sea views; single and twin-bedded rooms; fully fitted kitchen (electric cooker, fridge/freezer, microwave, dishwasher), bathroom, separate WC. Gas fired c.h., basement with washing machine and table tennis; free parking. Pets & children welcome. Sleeps 7 + cot. Terms from £150. SAE please for brochure of this and two other cottages to: **Mr F.H. Baxter, Huish Moor Farm, Instow, Bideford, N. Devon EX39 4LT or phone 01271 861146.**

Enjoy the
FREEDOM
of a self catering or farmhouse holiday

Farm & Cottage
HOLIDAYS

Discover the delights of self catering and farmhouse holidays in Cornwall, Devon and Somerset. Many are farm based and offer fun for the children and space and freedom for you.

Or consider a half board holiday where English breakfast and a three course evening meal is provided each day.

Whatever your preference Farm and Cottage Holidays offers a large selection of properties to choose from. Please call us (24 hrs a day) for a free colour brochure on:

(01237) 479698
or write to
Dept FHG, 12 Fore Street, Northam, Bideford, Devon EX39 1AW

BIDEFORD near. West Titchberry Farm Cottage, Hartland, Near Bideford. Sleeps 5 adults, 1 child.

♀♀♀ *COMMENDED.* Situated on the coast near Hartland Point (follow signs to Hartland Point Lighthouse), this recently renovated farm cottage comprises (upstairs) double and family rooms (plus cot); bathroom, toilet. Downstairs is a fully fitted kitchen with dining area. Electricity for the cooker, fridge/freezer, microwave oven and washing machine is on a 50p meter. In the lounge the settee converts into a double bed; colour TV, video, wood-burning stove (logs provided free), central heating downstairs (no charge), portable heaters upstairs. The lounge door opens onto a small enclosed garden. The cottage is carpeted throughout and well appointed. Open all year. Guests have freedom of this 150-acre mixed farm. A nearby cliff path leads to the National Trust beauty spot of Shipland Bay, a sandy cove at low tide. Clovelly six miles, Hartland three miles. Sorry, no pets. Terms approximately £90 to £310 weekly according to season. SAE please **Mrs Yvonne Heard, West Titchberry Farm, Hartland, Near Bideford EX39 6AU (01237 441287).**

BIGBURY near. Bennicke Farm, Modbury, Ivybridge and The Bungalow, Buckleys Harraton. Properties sleep 6/8. Main part of Bennicke Farmhouse (self contained) in peaceful situation reached by lane, quarter of a mile from road. Large garden. Three bedrooms sleeping eight. Sunday bookings. Also small bungalow with garden situated on Plymouth/Kingsbridge main road near Modbury. Sleeps six. Saturday bookings. Both properties five miles from sandy beaches of Bigbury Bay. Within easy reach of Cornwall (15 miles) and Dartmoor (10 miles). Both have mains water, electricity and colour TV. Linen is not provided. SAE for details. Terms from £170 to £235 weekly. No VAT. **C.M. Hodder, Bennicke Farm, Modbury, Ivybridge PL21 0SU (01548 830265).**

See also Colour Display Advertisement BRAUNTON. Marsdens Cottage Holidays, Dept 13, The Square, Braunton EX33 2JB (01271 813777; Fax: 01271 813664). ♀♀♀/♀♀♀♀ There is no better way to experience the charm of North Devon than from the comfort and luxury of a Marsdens Cottage Holiday. Romantic white-washed cottages nestling in the heart of the countryside; secluded beach houses just a stone's throw away from some of Britain's most spectacular coastlines — whatever your idea of a perfect holiday we can help make it reality. And, as an extra bonus, our prices will come as a pleasant surprise too. Call or write today for your free brochure. Choose from a one-bed cottage with swimming pool from £70 for four nights up to a beach house for 17 from £295 for four nights.

BRAUNTON. Mrs J.M. Barnes, Denham Farm Holidays, North Buckland, Braunton EX33 1HY (Tel & Fax: 01271 890297). ♀♀♀♀ *COMMENDED.* Friendly folk required to fill our cottages with fun and laughter. Beautifully furnished accommodation just right for your holiday. Only two and a half miles from golden sandy beaches of Croyde and Woolacombe. One cottage will sleep eight with four bedrooms and the other sleeping four in one bedroom. Spacious lounges and kitchens with all you require for an easy holiday. Have home cooked meals in farmhouse or in your cottage, be spoilt. Large garden and play area. Small pets for children to enjoy. Prices from £160 to £595 all inclusive. You can't afford to miss the hospitality at Denham. Farm Holiday Bureau member.

BRAYFORD. Mrs Shirley Barrow, Lower Hall Farm, Brayford, Barnstaple EX32 7QN (01598 710569). Working farm, join in. A peaceful scenic setting on Exmoor boundary of a 200 acre mainly dairy farm, some beef cattle and sheep. Guests are welcome to watch activities and walk on the farm. Ideal for walks — the "Tarka Trail" goes through the farm. Small river for fishing. Beaches half-hour drive. Ideal for touring local beauty spots — Tarr Steps, Dunkery, Doone Valley, etc. Market town of South Molton seven miles, Barnstaple nine miles. End of farmhouse cottage sleeps four/six in double bedroom plus cot and bunk-bedded room leading to second double, all with superb views. Comfortable lounge with stone fireplace, woodburner and colour TV. Fitted kitchen/diner. Bathroom/WC. Baby-sitting by arrangement. Walled garden used by family, ideal for the children; tennis court, also suitable for other games. No pets. Electricity, bed linen and wood inclusive. Terms from £100 to £300 weekly. Reduced rates for two persons out of season.

CHALLACOMBE. Mrs Christine Johnson, Shorland Old Farm, Challacombe, Bratton Fleming EX31 4TX (01598 763505). Our 16th century farmhouse and adjoining barn is beautifully and peacefully situated in 14 acres overlooking Exmoor, nine miles from the sea. The farmhouse provides Bed and Breakfast accommodation while the barn is tastefully converted, retaining much character, to provide self catering accommodation for six people. It has two bedrooms, comfortable lounge and well equipped kitchen, all with beautiful views across the Moors. Bed linen is provided, cot and high chair available, babysitting by arrangement. Terms from £130. Please telephone for brochure.

CHALLACOMBE. Mrs Rosemarie E. Kingdon, Whitefield Barton, Barnstaple EX31 4TU (01598 763271). ♀♀♀ *COMMENDED.* **Working farm, join in.** We are a 200 acre working Exmoor farm surrounded by glorious countryside. There are animals to see and freedom for children to play. Spacious characteristic accommodation in half of 16th century farmhouse with modern luxuries. Tastefully furnished to high standard. Warm, cosy lounge with colour TV, video recorder; large kitchen; family and twin bedrooms; bathroom with shower. Babysitting and equipment available. Ample parking. Private patio/barbecue. Garden with stream. Inclusive of all linen and electricity. Peaceful surroundings with scenic walks and footpath direct to Exmoor. The best sandy beaches of North Devon are within easy reach and we are central for touring around Lynton and Lynmouth.

DEVON – ENDLESS CHOICES!

People never tire of visiting Devon. There's so much to do, like visiting Alscott Farm Museum, Berry Head Country Park, Bickleigh Mill Farm, Farway Countryside Park, Haytor Granite Railway, Kent's Cavern, Dartmoor National Park, Exmoor National Park and of course Plymouth and its Hoe.

CHULMLEIGH. Joyce Middleton, Beech Grove, East Westacott, Riddlecombe, Chulmleigh EX18 7PF (01769 520210). ♀♀♀♀ *COMMENDED.* **Working farm, join in. Sleeps 5/7 plus cot.** A peaceful place, where there is time to pause and enjoy the beauty of an unspoilt countryside. Situated midway between Dartmoor and Exmoor and set in pretty gardens, our spacious bungalow with glorious views is warm and comfortable. Superbly equipped, even a dishwasher! Central heating, log fires; linen provided. Large games room provides entertainment for all ages. Friendly folks and animals on family-run mixed farm. Children love Rosie and Lassie our sheep dogs, and enjoy feeding lambs. Spend lazy days exploring local markets and delightful villages, where charming old pubs offer tempting meals. Fishing, riding and golf nearby. Beach 30 minutes. Open all year. Terms from £150 to £375 per week.

CHULMLEIGH near. Sandra Gay, Northcott Barton Farm, Ashreigney, Near Chulmleigh EX18 7PR (01769 520259). ♀♀♀ *COMMENDED.* Northcott Barton is a working farm set amidst green fields, wooded valleys and quiet country lanes where you can explore the farm and see the animals. The holiday wing of our lovely old farmhouse sleeps seven/nine people plus cot and offers well equipped "home from home" comfort with oak beams, heating throughout and a log fire to welcome early and late season guests. Bed linen provided. Large south-facing garden. Golf, riding, fishing close by. Handy for sea/moors. Terms from £140 weekly. Farm Holiday Bureau Member.

CHULMLEIGH near. Mrs M.E. Gay, Manor Farm, Riddlecombe, Chulmleigh EX18 7NX (01769 520335). ♀♀♀♀ *COMMENDED.* Working dairy and sheep Farm. Three bedrooms sleeping seven/eight plus baby. You are assured of a friendly welcome at our lovely farmhouse which has a self catering wing with glorious views and large garden. Children can bottlefeed baby lambs, watch the milking, see baby calves, make friends with "Nibbles" our tame sheep, collect eggs, etc. Superb adjoining games room with endless range of toys, games, etc for all ages including ride-on-toys, snooker, table tennis, piano, Fisher Price kitchen, play cottage, swing, etc. Bed linen provided, washer/dryer, fridge freezer, microwave. Woodland walks nearby. Central heating and lovely stone fireplace with gas woodburner. Handy for sea and Moors. Terms from £160 per week.

COLYTON. Mrs R. Gould and Mrs S. Gould, Bonehayne Farm, Colyton EX13 6SG (01404 871396 or 871416). Working farm. Bonehayne Farm is situated in the beautiful Coly Valley amidst 250 acres working farmland on the banks of the River Coly. Daffodils are quite a feature in Springtime. Mallard Duck and Kingfishers too are a common sight. Trout fishing freely available and woodlands to explore. This is an annexe of the farmhouse, completely modernised and tastefully furnished, with fitted carpets, to accommodate up to six people. Master bedroom with double and bunk beds, also a twin-bedded room. Lounge with oak beams, inglenook fireplace, TV; fully centrally heated making it ideal for out of season holidays. Kitchen and diningroom with electric cooker, fridge/freezer; electricity by meter; bathroom and toilet; cot and babysitting available. Fully equipped except linen. Parking space. The sea four miles. Weekly terms on application. Caravan also available.

RUSTIC DEVON

Inland from the coastal resorts lies the heart of Devon and the 365 square miles of Dartmoor National Park. Take time to explore the spectacular tors, hills and lakes, and watch out for the famous wild ponies. Picturesque rural villages reflect the unhurried pace of Devon life and there are traces everywhere of the Moor's rich heritage, dating back to the Bronze Age. In the north is Exmoor, one of Britain's smallest National Parks, ideal for rambling, pony trekking and bird watching.

COMBE MARTIN. Mr and Mrs T. Massey, Wheel Farm Country Cottages, Berrydown 12, Combe Martin EX34 0NT (01271 882100). ♀♀♀♀ *HIGHLY COMMENDED.* Enjoy the freedom of self catering with friendly five star service. A little bit of heaven, beautiful gardens surround watermill and pretty cottages, nestling in a valley, a wildlife haven, lovely Exmoor views, near superb beaches. Spoil yourself, inclusive indoor pool, fitness room, maid service, linen, flowers, four-poster beds, beams, log fires. Plus central heating, dishwashers, home made meals, sauna, tennis with tuition, garden visitors. Families welcome, walking, riding, cycling nearby. Prices from £180 to £840 per week. Off peak Short Break holidays available.

Compton Pool Farm, South Devon

★ *Heated indoor swimming pool* ★ *Children's play area* ★ *Fishing lakes*
★ *Tennis court* ★ *Games barn* ★ *Sauna* ★ *Family holidays*
★ *Farm animals* ★ *Lots to do*

Nestling in a sheltered sunny valley, surrounded by red Devon hills, the nine tastefully converted, comfortably furnished stone cottages are grouped around a central courtyard and fish pond. All cottages are attractively decorated and fully equipped. The farm is kept tidy and the gardens colourful. Torquay and the sea are nearby and Dartmoor is close at hand.

JOHN & MARGARET PHIPPS, COMPTON POOL FARM, COMPTON, DEVON TQ3 1TA.
Tel: 01803 872241 Fax: 01803 874012

SEE ALSO OUR COLOUR ADVERTISEMENT

CROYDE BAY. "Sandyholme". Sleeps 6. Chalet bungalow, comfortably furnished and carpeted. Lounge/diner, colour TV, good selection of books, maps and games. Bathroom with separate shower. Well equipped all electric kitchen including microwave, fridge, cooker, spin dryer. Situated on quiet private road, safe for children with enclosed garden, ample parking. Just five minutes through sand dunes leads to the superb sheltered bay with golden sands and rock pools. The old world village with quaint cottages, pubs and restaurants five minutes' amble away. Set amidst National Trust protected countryside offering wonderful walks. Excellent base for touring beautiful North Devon. Sorry, no pets. Brochure on request from **Mrs J. Pearce, 59 Avonmead, Greenmeadow, Swindon, Wiltshire SN2 3NY (01793 723521).**

DARTMOOR NATIONAL PARK. Susan Booty, Rogues Roost, Poundsgate, Newton Abbot TQ13 7PS (01364 631223). Properties sleep 4/7. Two self catering properties, off the beaten track, they are surrounded by open moorland and ideal for dogs, riding, walking and fishing. Within easy reach of many interesting places and the sea at Torbay — 22 miles. The first property, part of a large house, sleeps seven and consists of four bedrooms, bathroom with shower and toilet, second toilet, large sitting room and dining room/kitchen. The second property — a bungalow for four — comprises two bedrooms, sittingroom, dining room, bathroom, toilet, kitchen (electric cooker). Open from May to early September. Car essential. Terms include bed linen.

Rogues Roost

DARTMOOR NATIONAL PARK. L.A. Astley, Summersbridge Cottage, Higher Coombe, Buckfastleigh (01364 642388). Self-catering old world, picturesque, detached country cottage situated in an idyllic spot, surrounded by woodlands, moorland, valleys and rivers. Ideal for walking, horse riding, fishing and sightseeing. Within easy reach of Torbay and Plymouth for sea and shops. The cottage sleeps four/five, is well equipped, fully modernised, comfortable and has a "fairy-like magic". Pets allowed. Parking. Children over seven years welcome.

A warm family **WELCOME** *is here for you!*

* Stylish **DOLPHIN CLUB** & Entertainment Centre
* Super Indoor Heated **NEPTUNE TROPICANA** Water Leisure Complex – four Feature-packed Pools, Solarium, Sauna, spectator viewing.
* **CRUISERS** adult Cocktail bar
* Children's **JOLLY ROGER** Club with Disco, Cinema & large Games arcade
* Short, level walk to safe sandy beach
* Great *Value - for - money* prices

See our MAIN AD in the colour section!

* **FREE** Electricity, Linen, Colour TV
* Welcome T.V. – great films, local attractions, and more
* 2 Shops ● Cafe
* 2 Takeaways
* Crazy Golf
* Adventure Playground
* Laundrette
* Hire Service with computer games
* Pets *Welcome* (at small charge)
* Choose from economy 4-berth to luxury 8-berth caravans.

WELCOME FAMILY HOLIDAY PARK DAWLISH WARREN SOUTH DEVON EX7 0PH

DARTMOUTH. The Mates House, 17 Higher Street, Dartmouth. Sleeps 4/6. The Mates House is a small cottage situated in the centre of town and originally built in 1628 in the reign of King Charles I. It is about 100 yards from the River Dart frontage. There is one double and one twin-bedded room and a double bed-settee in the lounge. Cot is also available. Colour television. Electric heating, cooking, microwave and fridge. Linen provided, towels on request. There are no extra charges except for electricity from October to May. Open all year from £130 per week. **Mr N.P. Jestico, The Captain's House, 18 Clarence Street, Dartmouth TQ6 9NW (01803 832133).**

EXMOOR. Mrs C.M. Wright, Friendship Farm, Bratton Fleming, Barnstaple EX31 4SQ (01598 763291 evenings). Working farm, join in. Friendship Bungalow is quietly situated down a short drive from the farmhouse, in its own garden, and surrounded by fields. There is ample parking space. The farm is situated 12 miles from Barnstaple and Ilfracombe, at the junction of roads A399 and B3358, within easy reach of the beaches of Woolacombe and Combe Martin. Exmoor is literally on the doorstep. The accommodation comprises three bedrooms (sleep six), plus cot. Linen supplied. Lounge with colour TV. Well equipped kitchen/diningroom. Bathroom, laundry room, spin dryer. Metered electricity. Weekly terms, low season from £100, high season £220.

BEACH & BRACKEN EXMOOR HOLIDAYS

ALL E.T.B. INSPECTED

- Quality Cottages at Sensible prices
- Farmhouse Accommodation with Food
- Short notice all season breaks
- Riding, Cycling, Shooting & Fishing

Beach & Bracken Holidays, Bratton Fleming,
Barnstaple, Devon EX32 7JL
Telephone anytime (01598) 710702

HOLSWORTHY. Pauline and Tony Blight, Blagdon Farm Country Holidays, Ashwater, Beaworthy EX21 5DF (01409 211509; Fax: 01409 211510). ♀♀♀

HIGHLY COMMENDED. Superb south-facing holiday bungalows which overlook our own lake and are set within 38 acres of glorious countryside. Each one has been designed to be fully wheelchair accessible, as have all of the facilities which include a nature trail, adventure playground, pets corner, picnic areas, large games room and tea room/shop. A take away service and equipment loan are also available. We can assure you of the warmest of welcomes. Free colour brochure available.

HONITON. Francis Wigram, Riggles Farm, Upottery, Honiton EX14 0SP (01404 891229). Working farm. Caravans sleep 6. Two beautifully situated caravans on 400 acre beef/arable farm, six miles from Honiton, with easy access to many lovely beaches, moors and local attractions. Visitors welcome on farm, well behaved pets accepted. Children's play area, table tennis, darts. Linen hire, washing machine and dryer. Caravans set in two peaceful acres near farmhouse. Each is fully equipped for two/six people. Two separate bedrooms and spacious living areas. Own bathroom with shower, flush toilet, washbasin. Gas cooker, heater, colour TV, fridge. Terms from £95 to £195 per week (10% reduction for couples, not school holidays). For brochure please write or telephone.

See also Colour Display Advertisement **ILFRACOMBE. J. Elstone, Smythen Farm Coastal Holiday Cottages, Sterridge Valley, Berrynarbor, Ilfracombe EX34 9TB (01271 882875).** ♀♀♀
COMMENDED and HIGHLY COMMENDED. The cottages are set in an area of natural beauty, with unspoilt views over the beautiful Sterridge Valley to the sea and the coast of Wales beyond. Heated swimming pool in a suntrap enclosure, spacious lawns and gardens. Children's play area with treehouse, swings and slide; garden funiture, barbecues. 14 acre recreation field. Games room, laundry room and payphone. All cottages are well equipped and cleanliness guaranteed. Central for sandy beaches and for touring Exmoor; the village of Berrynarbor is just two miles away with stores, an inn and many good quality eating places. The area is well blessed with tourist attractions, also surfing, golf and pony trekking. Please telephone for brochure and terms.

ILFRACOMBE near. Mrs M. Cowell, Lower Campscott Farm, Lee, Near Ilfracombe EX34 8LS

(01271 863479). Four excellent holiday cottages on a 90 acre dairy farm with a delightful one mile walk down to the beach at Lee Bay. The cottages have been newly converted from the original farm buildings to a high standard. Two of the cottages will accommodate four people, one will accommodate up to six people and the large one will take eight/ten people; laundry room; linen included in the price. We also have a large, self-contained six-berth caravan to let, with Bed and Breakfast in the farmhouse. Children welcome but regret no pets. Terms from £129 weekly. Spring Mini Breaks (three nights) from £70.

PLEASE ENCLOSE A STAMPED ADDRESSED ENVELOPE WITH ENQUIRIES

INSTOW. Beach Haven Cottage. Sleeps 5. Seafront cottage overlooking the sandy beach. Instow is a

quiet yachting village with soft yellow sands and a pretty promenade of shops, old houses, pubs and cafes serving drinks and meals. Beach Haven has extensive beach and sea views from the house and garden, own garage and parking, gas fired central heating, colour TV, washing machine. Lawned garden overlooking sea with terrace and garden furniture. Coastal walks and cycle trails, boat to Lundy Island. Dog welcome. Please send SAE for colour brochure of this and other cottages to: **F.I. Barnes, Boat Hyde, Northam, Bideford EX39 1NX (01237 473801).**

KING'S NYMPTON. Venn Farm Cottages. ♀♀♀♀ *COMMENDED.* **Sleep 2/6 adults; 2/4 children.**

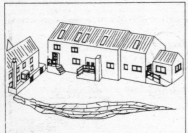

Delightful holiday cottages converted from old stone barn on small working farm set in beautiful Devon countryside. The children will love to feed the lambs and goat kids. Nearly 50 acres of rolling fields to wander over with views to Exmoor and Dartmoor. The cottages are furnished and equipped to a high standard and have patios with a picnic table and barbecue. Cottages have two or three bedrooms sleeping up to six persons plus cot. One cottage is suitable for disabled visitors. Bed linen provided. Laundry room and children's play area. Pets welcome. Weekly terms from £120 to £420. For brochure apply to: **Mrs Martin, Venn Farm, King's Nympton, Umberleigh EX37 9TR (01769 572448).**

KINGSBRIDGE. Allan and Marcia Green, Gara Mill, Slapton, Kingsbridge TQ7 2RE (01803

770295). Sleep 1-7. We offer eight comfortable cedar lodges in idyllic setting on a sunny slope above the River Gara. Two bedrooms, fully equipped including colour TV. There are also two cosy self-contained flats within the 16th century mill building. Four acre site off quiet lane, sheltered and peaceful, yet convenient for Dartmouth and Kingsbridge. Children's play area, outdoor badminton court, games room, launderette. Cots available. Dogs welcome. Woodland walks on your doorstep. Two miles to beaches and spectacular coastline. Daily rates for Short Breaks out of season. From £130 to £280 per week. Free brochure on request.

KINGSBRIDGE. Mr and Mrs A.R. Wotton, "Andryl", Lower Farm, Beeson, Kingsbridge TQ7 2HW (01548 580527). Working farm. Sleeps 4 adults; 2 children. "Andryl" is situated in a sheltered sunny position with wonderful countryside views. The flat is part of "Andryl", with bathroom, separate toilet, kitchen/diner/lounge with TV. Linen is optional. The garden has a swing, and there are other attractions for the children including chicks, ducks and ponies. The countryside around is very picturesque, and there are numerous walks including the very pleasant coastal paths. Beesands is half a mile away, and other beaches are very near; Kingsbridge is the nearest town, while Dartmouth and Salcombe are within easy reach. Babysitting can be arranged. Pets are not allowed. Car essential. Terms from £100 to £220 per week including domestic hot water. Reductions for two people in out of season weeks. SAE, please, for brochure.

KINGSBRIDGE. "Savernake," Thurlestone Sands, Kingsbridge. Sleeps 10. This substantial house, with a beautiful and unobstructed view of the sea and Thurlestone Rock, stands in its own grounds, adjoining the dunes and beach. The area is of outstanding beauty with wonderful cliff walks. Golf, tennis, quarter mile. Sailing and riding in area. Accommodation for 10 in three twin-bedded double rooms with washbasins; three single rooms (one with washbasin); cot; bathroom, three toilets; lounge and diningroom. Kitchen fully equipped with electric cooker, fridge, kettle and toaster. Linen not supplied. Regret no pets. SAE to **Mrs M.D. Horsfall, Century Cottage, Foxdon Hill, Wadeford, Chard, Somerset TA20 3AN (01460 62475).**

KINGSBRIDGE. Mrs M. Goodman, Mattiscombe Farm, Stokenham, Near Kingsbridge TQ7 2SR (01548 581058). Working farm. Sleeps 8. Mattiscombe is a 150 acre mixed farm between the coastal towns of Kingsbridge and Dartmouth, close to the three mile stretch of Slapton Sands and the conservation area of Slapton Ley. Within easy reach are spectacular coastal footpaths, beautiful beaches and good fishing. The flat at Mattiscombe Farm offers comfortable accommodation for eight people. There are four bedrooms (two double, two twin) and a large lounge/diner with colour TV. The kitchen has electric cooker, microwave, fridge/freezer and washing machine and the bathroom has bath and shower. Children welcome, cot and high chair available. Sorry no pets. Open April to October. SAE please for details.

KINGSBRIDGE. Mr and Mrs M.B. Turner, Cross Farm, East Allington, Kingsbridge TQ9 7RW (01548

521327). Working farm, join in. Sleeps 11 plus 2 cots. Get away from the hustle and bustle of everyday life and enjoy the peace and tranquillity of Cross Farm, surrounded by South Hams countryside of outstanding natural beauty. Children love to help feed the animals while you take a leisurely farm walk or relax in the garden. Lovely 17th century part farmhouse and delightfully converted barn; both sleep 11 in four bedrooms; equipped to very high standard including colour TV, dishwasher, microwave, washing machine, dryer, fridge freezer, showers, duvets and linen. Cleanliness guaranteed. Play area and recreation barn. Heating included for early/late holidays. Only four miles to Kingsbridge (one mile to village pub!) and close to many lovely coves and beaches. Central for Dartmoor, Salcombe, Dartmouth, Torbay; riding, fishing, golf, etc. Ideal touring area. Rough shooting on farm in season. Brochure available.

Toad Hall Cottages

100 outstanding waterside & rural properties from cosy cottages - large farmhouses, in truly beautiful locations in Devon. Call for our highly acclaimed brochure. Video also available.

Tel: **01548 853089**

WEST COUNTRY TOURIST BOARD MEMBER

KINGSBRIDGE near. Mrs J. Tucker, Mount Folly Farm, Bigbury-on-Sea, Near Kingsbridge TQ7 4AR (01548 810267). Working farm. Sleeps 6. A delightful family farm, situated on the coast, overlooking the sea and sandy beaches of Bigbury Bay. Farm adjoins golf course and River Avon. Lovely coastal walks. Ideal centre for South Hams and Dartmoor. The spacious wing comprises half of a farmhouse, self-contained with separate entrance. Large, comfortable lounge with sea views; colour TV. Well equipped kitchen/diner — all electric; metered. Sleeps six persons in three bedrooms — one family, one double and one single; two have washbasins and sea views; bathroom and toilet. All rooms attractively furnished. Visitors made most welcome. Nice garden, ideal for children. Cot and babysitting available. Car essential, ample parking. Available all year. Large SAE for terms please.

LYNTON/LYNMOUTH. Mr H.D. King-Fretts, West Lyn Farm, Barbrook, Lynton EX35 6LD (01598

753618). Working farm. Farmhouse sleeping 8/9; one Cottage sleeping 4 on traditional 134 acre working sheep farm. Adjoining coastal footpath and National Trust woodland with breathtaking views across the Bristol Channel. Farmhouse has four bedrooms, one double, one family, one twin and one bunk bedded. Two bathrooms. Cottage has one double and one twin bedrooms, colour TV and all amenities. Ample gardens and parking. Shop/launderette within walking distance. Long SAE for brochure and tariff for friendly farm holidays.

NEWTON ABBOT. Averil Corrick, Shippen and Dairy Cottages, c/o Lookweep Farm, Liverton, Newton Abbot TQ12 6HT (01626 833277). Sleep 1/5.

Come and relax in the peace and tranquillity of these two delightful barn conversion cottages. Set within the Dartmoor National Park with easy access to the coast, golf, riding, walking and fishing locally. Sleep four/five, fully equipped and well furbished throughout. Own garden with beautiful views. Ample parking. Use of outdoor heated swimming pool. Children welcome, high chairs, cots and linen available. Pets also welcome. Terms from £135 to £394.

NEWTON ABBOT near. Mrs Y. Tully, Dunscombe Farm, Chudleigh, Near Newton Abbot TQ13 0BS (01626 853149). Working farm. A 150 acre mixed farm situated in a valley just under Haldon Moor, midway between Exeter and Newton Abbot. Chudleigh one and three-quarter miles away; main road A380. Ideal position for touring moors and also within easy reach of the sea, riding, climbing and golf. The accommodation comprises kitchen, large living/diningroom which has a bed settee, bathroom with washbasin, bedroom (large) with double bed and bunk beds. Separate toilet. TV in livingroom. Calor gas cooking. Electricity metered. Linen available by arrangement. Children and pets welcome. Prices from £120 weekly. SAE or telephone for further details.

NEWTON FERRERS. Mrs Sandy Cherrington, Slade Barn, Netton Farm Self Catering Holiday Cottages, Noss Mayo, Near Plymouth PL8 1HA (Tel & Fax: 01752 872235). ♀ ♀ COMMENDED. Nestled into one

of the most beautiful stretches of the South Devon coastline, bordering the picturesque Yealm Estuary, Netton Farm Cottages are uniquely situated to cater for all tastes. Easy access to fabulous National Trust cliff walks. Nearby sandy beaches, golf, fishing and riding. An area with many attractions and an ideal base for day trips to Cornwall or exploring the Moors. Open fires, exposed beams and galleried area are some of the features that have transformed these traditional barns into comfortable, cosy, fully equipped cottages (one large property sleeps 12). We also have a lovely indoor swimming pool, games room and tennis court. For the ultimate in relaxation, appointments may be made for professional Reflexology or Aromatherapy. SAE for colour brochure. Bed and Breakfast accommodation also available.

NORTH MOLTON. Mrs Gladys Ayre, Pitt Farm, North Molton EX36 3JR (01598 740285). ♀ ♀ ♀ ♀ COMMENDED. Sleeps 5/6. Enjoy peaceful surroundings at

our charming cottage set in lovely Exmoor countryside. One mile from village of North Molton with local pubs, shops, garage. Accommodation has recently been converted and is equipped to high standard throughout with night storage heating. Three bedrooms, bath/shower room, beamed lounge with colour TV, woodburner, oak fitted kitchen/diner with automatic washing machine, fridge, microwave, etc. Your own patio overlooking the valley with garden furniture and barbecue. There is a small pond nearby with ducks and geese. Our guests are welcome to explore our sheep farm and to observe seasonal activities. Cot and high chair available and babysitting by arrangement. Dog by arrangement. Linen available. Electricity by coin meter. Terms from £140 to £340 per week. Short Breaks available end October to Easter. Ilustrated brochure on request.

OKEHAMPTON. East Hook Cottages, Okehampton. Cottages sleep 2/6. In the heart of Devon on the fringe of Dartmoor, with woodland surroundings, two comfortably furnished holiday cottages. One mile north of the A30 at Okehampton, quiet and peaceful, 50 yards from a country road. Ample car parking space. The accommodation comprises a pleasant sitting room with a TV set; kitchen with electric cooker and refrigerator; modern bathroom with shaver point; three bedrooms. Visitors are requested to supply their own bed linen. Electricity by 50p meter. Children and pets welcome. Terms from £90 to £165 per week. Open all year. Midweek/weekend breaks possible. **Mrs M.E. Stevens, West Hook Farm, Okehampton EX20 1RL (01837 52305).**

PAIGNTON. Mrs J. Smerdon, Glenside, Moles Cross, Marldon, Paignton TQ3 1SY (01803 873222).

Working farm. Large, self-contained and completely on its own (nearest neighbour 200 yards), THE MAISONETTE — Glenside, having been the residence of the former owner of the property is modern and maintained to a high standard. Comprising three bedrooms, one with balcony; lounge/diningroom with colour TV. Beautifully fitted kitchen with breakfast bar, fridge freezer, washing machine, microwave. Bathroom, fully tiled and with shower. Open all year. 100 yards up the lane stands the FARM BUNGALOW, Glenside. Self-contained (owners' living accommodation to one side), well maintained — being the owners' winter residence. Comprises three bedrooms, large lounge/diningroom with colour TV. Kitchen with fridge, electric cooker, microwave and washing machine. Bathroom with separate shower. Both properties ideally located for Torbay, three miles, Dartmoor, 12 miles. Many interesting local walks. Farm shop for eggs, fruit, vegetables. Both properties sleep and are fully equipped for up to seven people. Large lawn and field for children. Central heating available. Terms £120 low season to £260 high season — inclusive of electricity.

PLYMOUTH. Mrs Suzanne MacBean, Coombe Farm, Wembury Road, Plymstock, Plymouth PL9 0DE (01752 401730). ♀ ♀ ♀ *APPROVED.* **Sleeps 6.**

Coombe Farm dates back to the 14th century and is situated in a peaceful valley on the outskirts of Plymouth. An ideal centre for touring and within easy reach of moors and coast. The cottage is well equipped with two bedrooms, lounge, kitchen/diner, bathroom. Linen and electricity included. Safe parking. Children and pets welcome. Open all year. Terms from £100 to £340 per week.

SEATON. Mrs E.P. Fox, West Ridge, Harepath Hill, Seaton EX12 2TA (Tel & Fax: 01297 22398). ♀ ♀ ♀ *COMMENDED.* West Ridge bungalow stands on elevated ground above the small coastal town of Seaton. It

has one and a half acres of lawns and gardens and enjoys wide panoramic views of the beautiful Axe Estuary and the sea. Close by are Axmouth, Beer and Branscombe. The Lyme Bay area is an excellent centre for touring, walking, sailing, fishing, golf, etc. This comfortably furnished accommodation (including the spacious kitchen/living room on the right of the picture) is ideally suited for three to five people. Cot can be provided. Available March to October. £125 to £315 weekly (fuel charges included). Full gas central heating; colour TV. SAE for brochure.

SEATON.Mrs Elsie Pady, Higher Cownhayne Farm, Cownhayne Lane, Colyton, Near Seaton EX13 6HD (01297 552267). Working farm. Properties sleep

4/8. Higher Cownhayne is a family working farm. Accommodation consists of three self catering farmhouse holiday apartments which are open all year round. Each apartment has all modern conveniences, with its own dining room, kitchen, bathroom and WC (no linen is provided). Caravan site on farm — four-berth caravan, fully equipped. Farm produce available, including milk from a brucellosis-free herd, eggs, etc. Babysitting can be arranged. Fishing Holidays from the 1st March to end of October — trout fly fishing on the River Coly on farm. Leisure facilities available to visitors include badminton, squash, gymnasium, sauna, solarium, swimming pool and licensed restaurant. Air strip on farm for small plane enthusiasts. No pets. Terms on application, at a price families can afford to pay. Open all year.

SEATON near. Mr and Mrs H.J. Pountney, Little Trill, Musbury, Near Axminster EX13 6AR (01297 34731). Little Trill Cottages are set around cobbled courtyard with spectacular views overlooking rolling Devon countryside, five miles from the sea at Seaton or Lyme Regis. Cared for by resident owners, the cottages, converted from stone barns, are furnished to a high standard providing two or three bedrooms and fitted kitchens which include automatic washing machine. Children welcome, cot, high chair, stair gate provided free. Colour TV and gas central heating make these properties ideal for winter breaks. Each cottage has a private patio, use of four acres of beautiful gardens and grounds including garden games. Bed linen can be hired and pets accepted at extra cost. Ample safe parking. Terms from £100 to £270 per week.

SOUTH DEVON. Lower Coombe Farm and Studio. Working farm. Cottage sleeps 5. Twixt moor and sea. Cottage, split level, courtyard with small garden. TV, central heating, wood burner, microwave. From £110 to £170 per week. Mobile Home (only two on site) sleeping two adults and two children, toilet, shower, TV, small garden. From £65 to £90 per week including electricity. Working farm (sheep and horses) in secluded valley one mile from Bovey Tracey. Professional artist gives personal tuition £50 per week. Riding instruction available. Dogs by arrangement £7 per week. Quiet and peaceful. Details **Mrs S.D. Ansell, Lower Coombe, Bovey Tracey TQ13 9PH (Tel & Fax: 01626 832914).**

SOUTH MOLTON. Ruth Ley, Drewstone Farm, South Molton EX36 3EF (01769 572337). ♀♀♀♀ & ♀♀♀♀♀ *COMMENDED.* Our 300 acre family run farm is set in the foothills of Exmoor surrounded by a wooded valley with breathtaking views and full of wildlife. We offer a superb farmhouse and barn conversion with beams, three bedrooms, oak fitted kitchens, electric cooker, autowasher, dryer, freezer, microwave and phone. Heating throughout and log fires and woodburner. Furnished and equipped to the highest standards with real country cottage charm. Guests may wander amongst the farm animals, enjoy country walks, small games room, clay shooting, own trout fishing or just relax in the garden. South Molton two miles, beaches 25 minutes' drive. From £150.

SOUTH MOLTON. Mike and Rose Courtney, West Millbrook, Twitchen, South Molton EX36 3LP (01598 740382). ♀♀♀ up to *COMMENDED.* **Properties sleep 2/9.** Adjoining Exmoor. Three fully equipped bungalows and one farmhouse annexe in lovely surroundings bordering Exmoor National Park. Ideal for touring North Devon and West Somerset including moor and coast with beautiful walks, lovely scenery and many other attractions. North Molton village is only one mile away. All units carpeted, have electric cookers, fridge-freezers, colour TVs; some units have a washing machine and microwave. Children welcome, cots and high chairs available free. Linen hire available. Games room. Car parking. Central heating if required. Electricity metered. Out of season short breaks. Weekly prices from £60 to £270. Colour brochure available.

SOUTH MOLTON near. Court Green, Bishop's Nympton, Near South Molton. Sleeps 5. A most attractive well-equipped, south facing cottage with large garden, on edge of the village of Bishop's Nympton, three miles from South Molton. Ideal holiday centre, within easy reach of Exmoor, the coast, sporting activities and places of interest. Three bedrooms — one double, one twin-bedded, one single with washbasins. Two bathrooms with toilet. Sitting and dining rooms, large kitchen. Central heating, wood-burning stove, TV. One mile sea trout/trout fishing on River Mole. Well behaved pets welcome. Terms April to October £100 to £200. **Mrs J. Greenwell, Tregeiriog, Near Llangollen, Clwyd LL20 7HU (01691 600672).**

PLEASE SEND A STAMPED ADDRESSED ENVELOPE WITH ENQUIRIES

TAVISTOCK. Mrs P.G.C. Quinton, Higher Quither, Milton Abbot, Tavistock PL19 0PZ (01822

860284). A modern self contained, open-plan barn conversion on the edge of Dartmoor, four miles from the ancient stannary town of Tavistock. The cottage is an ideal base for a whole variety of enjoyable holiday activities and both coasts are within easy reach. The cottage has its own private garden. Amenities include colour TV, electric cooker, microwave, washing machine, refrigerator, electric fires; coal and logs for the open fires and duvets and linen all provided. The village of Chillaton is three-quarters of a mile away with pub, village shop and post office. Children and pets welcome. Terms from £195.

See also Colour Display Advertisement **TORRINGTON. Mrs M. Bealey, Week Farm, Torrington EX38 7HU (01805 623354). ♀♀♀♀** *COMMENDED.* Excellent accommodation (enjoyed by many) in a farmhouse flat, enjoying scenic views and beautiful surroundings. The farm is situated one mile from Great Torrington which has a heated swimming pool, tennis, golf, Dartington Glass Factory, RHS Rosemoor Gardens and Tarka Trail. Within easy reach of beaches and the beauty of Exmoor and Dartmoor. Accommodation comprises well equipped kitchen/diner, lounge with colour TV. One room with double bed, one with twin beds; convertible bed and cot if required. Bathroom with WC. Electric cooker, heaters, automatic washing machine and tumble dryer. Electric meter. Linen for hire. Children welcome. No pets please. Advance booking. Terms from £95 to £195 weekly. SAE please, or phone.

See also Colour Display Advertisement **TOTNES. Hemsford Country Holidays, Hemsford, Littlehempston, Totnes TQ9 6NE (01803 762637). ETB ♀♀♀ & ♀♀♀♀** *COMMENDED.* HEMSFORD — A COUNTRY HOLIDAY FOR ALL SEASONS. Hemsford is ideally situated in the heart of South Devon with Torbay, Dartmoor and the excellent beaches of the South Hams only a short drive away. Our 16 comfortable and well appointed cottages (one suitable for disabled guests) accommodate two to 10 people. All have night store heating and are available throughout the year. Facilities include our own riding stables, heated indoor pool, sauna, solarium, games room, licensed bar, two all-weather tennis courts, 9 hole approach golf and children's play area. Terms from £110 to £920 per week. Full colour brochure on request. Regret no pets.

TOTNES. Mr and Mrs D. Christie-Mutch, Lower Well, Broadhempston, Totnes TQ9 6BD (01803 813417). Not a working farm. Charming, comfortable, well equipped self contained one and two bedroomed cottages, formerly part of Georgian farm. Colour TV; laundry facilities; cot and high chair available. Orchard garden. Linen not provided. Lovely unspoiled Devon village with two pubs, church and shop, situated between Dartmoor and the Torbay coast with easy access to the beautiful South Hams, historic Totnes, Dartington and Exeter, etc. Telephone or write for details.

PUBLISHER'S NOTE

While every effort is made to ensure accuracy, we regret that FHG Publications cannot accept responsibility for errors, omissions or misrepresentation in our entries or any consequences thereof. Prices in particular should be checked because we go to press early. We will follow up complaints but cannot act as arbiters or agents for either party.

WELLINGTON. Mr and Mrs L.J. Tristram, West End, Holcombe Rogus, Wellington, Somerset TA21 0QD (01823 672384). Working farm, join in. Sleeps 6.

This 16th century olde worlde farm cottage in Devon has an inglenook fireplace and bread oven. It is approached by a private tarmac road and surrounded by a large garden. Situated on 180-acre family farm, over which guests are free to wander. Half-a-mile from the small village of Holcombe Rogus which has general store with post office, garage, public house, church. Within easy reach of Exmoor, Taunton, Exeter and the coast. Excellent walks in unspoilt countryside; extensive views. Six people accommodated in three double rooms, cot; bathroom, toilet; sitting/diningroom. Kitchen with electric cooker, fridge, kettle, iron, etc.; glass conservatory at front of house. Linen by arrangement. Pets allowed. Car an advantage, ample parking. Open all year. TV provided. SAE, please, for terms.

See also Colour Display Advertisement WESTWARD HO!. John and Gill Violet, West Pusehill Farm, Westward Ho! EX39 5AH (01237 475638 or 474622). Cottages sleep 2/8. A PERFECT HOLIDAY FOR ALL. A small group of picturesque stone-built country cottages accommodating two to eight. Set in an area of outstanding natural beauty, only one mile from the coast. Prices from £108 to £590. Swimming pool, sauna, games room plus family run country Inn/Restaurant all set in 20 acres of tranquil gardens and farmland. Please write or telephone for full colour brochure.

WOOLACOMBE. Resthaven Holiday Flats. Situated in own grounds on the sea front with magnificent views of the glorious North Devon coast including the headlands of Morte and Baggy Point with Lundy Island on the horizon. Two self-contained flats, one ground floor which sleeps five and one first floor sleeping nine. Family, double and single bedrooms. Lounges furnished to high standard with colour TV and videos; fully equipped kitchens; bathrooms have bath, shower and toilet (first floor flat has extra toilet). Electricity by 50p meter, lighting, hot water and parking free. Laundry and payphone. Award-winning beach. Write or telephone **Mr B.A. Watts, Resthaven Holiday Flats, The Esplanade, Woolacombe EX34 7DJ (01271 870298 or 870248).**

YELVERTON. Mrs M. Sherrell, Hole Farm, Bere Alston, Yelverton PL20 7JE (01822 840241). Working farm. Sleeps 4 adults; 1 child. Hole Farm is situated in the beautiful Tamar Valley and near the edge of Dartmoor. This working farm enjoys beautiful estuary views with lovely walks and good bird watching. Riding, fishing and golf nearby. It is within easy reach of both the North and South coasts of Devon and Cornwall. Accommodation comprises a self contained wing of this attractive and tastefully modernised 350 year old farmhouse. One twin-bedded room and one double with washbasin; shower room and WC, extra folding bed or cot available. Large lounge/kitchen equipped with electric cooker, fridge, spin dryer and microwave. Colour TV and electric heating. Personally cleaned. Terms from £80.

FOR THE MUTUAL GUIDANCE OF GUEST AND HOST

Every year literally thousands of holidays, short-breaks and overnight stops are arranged through our guides, the vast majority without any problems at all. In a handful of cases, however, difficulties do arise about bookings, which often could have been prevented from the outset.

It is important to remember that when accommodation has been booked, both parties — guests and hosts — have entered into a form of contract. We hope that the following points will provide helpful guidance.

GUESTS: When enquiring about accommodation, be as precise as possible. Give exact dates, numbers in your party and the ages of any children. State the number and type of rooms wanted and also what catering you require — bed and breakfast, full board, etc. Make sure that the position about evening meals is clear — and about pets, reductions for children or any other special points.

Read our reviews carefully to ensure that the proprietors you are going to contact can supply what you want. Ask for a letter confirming all arrangements, if possible.

If you have to cancel, do so as soon as possible. Proprietors do have the right to retain deposits and under certain circumstances to charge for cancelled holidays if adequate notice is not given and they cannot re-let the accommodation.

HOSTS: Give details about your facilities and about any special conditions. Explain your deposit system clearly and arrangements for cancellations, charges, etc, and whether or not your terms include VAT.

If for any reason you are unable to fulfil an agreed booking without adequate notice, you may be under an obligation to arrange alternative suitable accommodation or to make some form of compensation.

While every effort is made to ensure accuracy, we regret that FHG Publications cannot accept responsibility for errors, omissions or misrepresentation in our entries or any consequences thereof. Prices in particular should be checked because we go to press early. We will follow up complaints but cannot act as arbiters or agents for either party.

DORSET

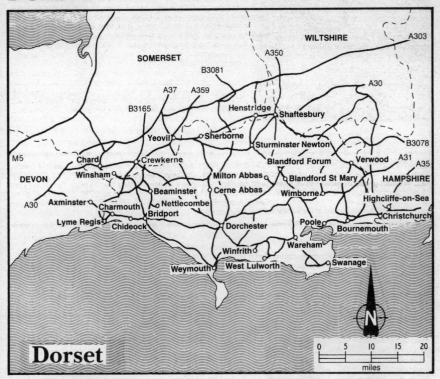

Dorset

BEAMINSTER. 33A St. Mary Well Street, Beaminster. Sleeps 5. Lovely two bedroomed bungalow in heart of "Hardy's Wessex". Peaceful position yet only 200 metres from market square with shops, restaurants, pubs, etc. Each bedroom has washbasin; one contains a double bed and the other two singles; Z-bed and cot available. Separate WC and bathroom. Colour TV in lounge. Gas cooker, microwave, fridge/freezer in well furbished kitchen/dining room. Utility room has WC, shower and automatic washing machine. Patio garden and large car park. Hardy's Cottage, Parnham House, Forde Abbey, Cricket St. Thomas and many other places of interest nearby. The beautiful unspoilt coast is eight miles away. Terms from £90 to £240. For brochure, SAE to **Mrs L. Watts, 53 Hogsmill Street, Beaminster DT8 3AG (01308 863088).**

BEAMINSTER. Mrs Jackie Spooncer, Lewesdon Farm, Stoke Abbot, Beaminster DT8 3JZ (01308 868270). ♛ ♛ ♛ ♛ *COMMENDED.* **Sleep 5/6.** Lewesdon Farm nestles in the soft rolling hills of Dorset. Beneath magnificent hill forts, in an area of outstanding natural beauty. Blissfully peaceful. An abundance of wildlife, ideal for walking. Stable and Barn Cottages offer superior accommodation, equipped to a high standard, sleeping five/six, all bedrooms en-suite. Warm and cosy, log fires if you wish. Electric blankets. Safe play area, cot, high chair and babysitting service. Bed linen available. Washer/dryer. Special Winter Breaks. Our barn conversion is designed with disabled visitors in mind. Non-smokers please. Weekly terms from £160 to £435.

BEXINGTON. Mrs Josephine Pearse, Tamarisk Farm, West Bexington, Dorchester DT2 9DF (01308 897784). ♛ ♛ ♛ On slope overlooking Chesil Beach between Abbotsbury and Burton Bradstock. One large and two smaller bungalows (ETB 3 Key Classification) and two chalets; properties sleep four/eight. Terms from £105 to £450. Each one stands in own garden. Glorious views along West Dorset and Devon coasts. Lovely walks by sea and inland. Mixed organic farm with arable, sheep, cattle, horses and market garden — vegetables available. Sea fishing, riding in Abbotsbury, lots of tourist attractions and good markets in Bridport (six miles), Dorchester, Weymouth and Portland, all 13 miles. Good centre for touring Thomas Hardy's Wessex. Safe for children and pets can be quite free.

FREE and REDUCED RATE Holiday Visits!
See our READERS' OFFER VOUCHER for details!

BLANDFORD. Mrs M.J. Waldie, The Old Rectory, Lower Blandford St. Mary, Near Blandford Forum DT11 9ND (01258 453220). Sleeps 6. Completely self-contained wing of Georgian Old Rectory, one mile from the market town of Blandford Forum, within easy reach of the south coast, Poole, Bournemouth, Salisbury and Thomas Hardy country around Dorchester. Local fishing and many places of historical interest. Accommodation for six in three rooms, one double bedded, one twin bedded and smaller room with bunk beds, cot. Large well equipped kitchen, spacious sitting/diningroom with colour TV; cloakroom downstairs; bathroom and separate toilet upstairs. Pets allowed by prior arrangement. Children welcome. Parking spaces. Use of secluded garden. Everything provided except linen and towels. Terms from £160 to £215 per week. May to September. SAE, please, for further details.

GOLD HILL

Organic Farm Annexe

Childe Okeford, Blandford Forum, Dorset DT11 8HB

Telephone: 01258 860293

Self-catering ground floor flat suitable for 2 adults and child over 5 years. Light and airy, tastefully furnished and set in peaceful surroundings. Well equipped kitchen. Sitting room with colour TV. Central heating. Toilet with basin and separate shower. Prices include own linen. Gold Hill is a 60 acre working farm specialising in vegetable and salad crops, and raising rare breed British White Cattle. We also breed and work Shire Horses. Childe Okeford is in Dorset's beautiful Blackmore Vale, with its associations with Thomas Hardy and Lawrence of Arabia. Only 20 miles from the nearest coast at Poole. Ideal for walking, riding (own horses taken), National Trust Properties and places of historical interest. Short breaks available during winter. Prices from £115 to £235 per week. Contact D. N. & A. D. Cross for further details. ETB ♀♀♀ Commended.

BOURNEMOUTH. Bournemouth Holiday Bureau, Henbury View, Dullar Lane, Sturminster Marshall BH21 4AD (01258 858580). For more than a quarter of a century, Bournemouth's oldest self catering holiday accommodation agency has been providing a letting service for scores of privately owned houses, cottages, bungalows, flats, caravans and chalets in Bournemouth, Poole, Ringwood, Christchurch and about 20 miles around. All inspected before acceptance and accurately described. Prices to suit every pocket. Most properties welcome children and many accept pets. Colour brochure on request.

BOURNEMOUTH HOLIDAY BUREAU

BRIDPORT. Mrs Sandra Huxter, Strongate Farm, Strongate Lane, Salwayash, Bridport DT6 5JD (01308 488295). A picturesque thatched cottage off the beaten track in peaceful surroundings. Situated on a small working family farm with cows, sheep, geese, ducks, pond, etc. Seaside five miles, within easy reach of charming Dorset villages, beautiful walking areas. Ideal for recharging batteries in relaxing unspoilt countryside. Families especially welcome, children can play freely. Secluded garden and space for cars. Cottage has two bedrooms, one with double bed, the other with two single beds, cot available; bathroom; fitted carpets. Price includes electricity and bedding. Dogs by arrangement. Non smokers only please. Further details on request.

BRIDPORT. Mrs Carol Mansfield, Lancombes House, West Milton, Bridport DT6 3TN (01308 485375). ♀♀♀♀ APPROVED. Lancombes House is a 200 year old stone barn built 300 feet above sea level set in 10 acres; there are tame animals for children to play and help with including horses, ponies, goats and ducks. Farm has panoramic views to the sea only four miles away. There are four superbly converted cottages, each with its own sitting out area, barbecue and garden furniture. They have spacious open plan living areas, most with wood burning stoves. Modern fitted kitchens, double and twin-bedded rooms. Electric central heating, shared laundry. Deep in the heart of Hardy country, this is a delightful area to explore whether on foot or horseback. There are many things to do and pets and children are very welcome. Prices start at £120 for mini breaks and we are open all the year round.

BRIDPORT near. Mrs S. Norman, Frogmore Farm, Chideock, Bridport DT6 6HT (01308 456159).

Working farm, join in. Sleeps 5 adults, 1 child. Delightful farm cottage on ninety acre grazing farm set in the rolling hills of West Dorset. Superb views over Lyme Bay, ideal base for touring Dorset and Devon or rambling the many coastal and country footpaths of the area. This fully equipped self-catering cottage sleeps six, plus cot. Bed linen supplied. Cosy lounge with woodburner and colour TV, French doors to a splendid columned sun verandah. Children and well behaved dogs welcome. Car essential. Open all year. Short breaks available, also Bed and Breakfast in the 17th century farmhouse. Brochure and terms free on request.

MANOR FARM HOLIDAY CENTRE
Charmouth, Bridport, Dorset
Situated in a rural valley, ten minutes' level walk from the beach.
1983 Built Two-Bedroomed Houses: *Sleep 4-6 *Lounge with colour T.V. *Fully fitted kitchen/diner *Fitted carpets *Double glazing *Central heating *Parking space.
Three-Bedroomed House and Bungalow: *Sleep 4/6 each *Lounge with colour T.V. *Central heating available *Parking within grounds *Enclosed garden.
Luxury six-berth Caravans: *One or two bedrooms *Toilet *Shower *Refrigerator *Full cooker *Television *Gas fire.

FULL CENTRE FACILITIES AVAILABLE INCLUDING SWIMMING POOL, SHOP, FISH AND CHIP TAKEAWAY, BAR, LAUNDERETTE, ETC.
Send SAE for colour brochure to **Mr R. B. Loosmore** *or Tel.* **01297 560226**
See also Colour Display Advertisement in this Guide.

CHARMOUTH. Taphouse Farmhouse, Whitchurch Canonicorum. ♥♥♥♥ *APPROVED.* **Sleeps 12.**

Stay on a working, family farm. Large comfortable farmhouse with five bedrooms, two bathrooms, kitchen/dining room (22'6" x 15') and lounge (16' x 13') with colour TV and log fireplace. Additional features include fully equipped kitchen, oil-fired Rayburn, part central heating, payphone, sun lounge/greenhouse; half an acre of lawns, garden table and chairs, barbecue, automatic washing machine, tumble dryer, smoke alarms, shower, linen hire, cot, safety chair, fire guard. Ample parking. Dogs by arrangement only. Ideal for beaches, fossil hunting, fishing and golf at Lyme Regis; countryside walking and touring Dorset, Devon and Somerset. Available all year for weekly bookings; weekends, short breaks, early or late season for family and friends. For large parties Bed and Breakfast available at nearby farmhouse. For details please phone or write to **Mrs S.M. Johnson, Cardsmill Farm, Whitchurch Canonicorum, Bridport DT6 6RP (01297 489375).**

BERE FARM

Winsham, Chard, Somerset TA20 4JQ
Telephone 01460 30207

Peaceful quality cottages
in a quiet valley.

Surrounded by lawns,
trees, the stream,
meadows and the lake.

Children and pets
welcome.

A place for 'Adventures'.

A place to sit and dream.

NEAR FORDE ABBEY

Mr & Mrs John Jeffery

DORCHESTER. Mrs J.M. Morris, Huish Farm, Sydling St. Nicholas, Dorchester DT2 9NS (01300 341265). Working farm. Sleeps 2. The perfect place for a peaceful holiday for two people only, this self contained flat in thatched farmhouse is set amidst beautiful countryside, within easy reach of the coast, and near Cerne Abbas village abounding with historic interest dating back to the 14th century, including remains of the Abbey. The Cerne Giant, 180 feet high, is a curious figure cut in the chalk hillside to the north east of the village. Upstairs, one very large sunny room with twin beds, private bathroom, toilet; downstairs, large kitchen equipped with electric cooker, fridge and all utensils. Linen not supplied. No TV. Car essential, ample parking. Own entrance and sunny corner of garden. Pets are permitted. Weekly terms from £90 including fuel. SAE, please, for further details.

DORCHESTER near. Old Dairy Cottage, sleeps 6; Clyffe Dairy Cottage, sleeps 3. ♀♀♀

COMMENDED. Two attractively furnished, comfortable character cottages with beams and inglenook fireplaces; central heating. Garden. On mixed farm with cows, calves, horses and beautiful woodland walks; ducks and wildlife on the pond and streams nearby. Easy reach of coast, golf, trekking, fishing and leisure centre; ideal cycling location. Children welcome. Excellent value low season breaks/winter breaks. Senior Citizens' reductions in low season. Open all year. Terms from £140 to £350 per week. Contact: **Rosemary Coleman, Clyffe Farm, Tincleton, Dorchester DT2 8QR (01305 848252).**

DORCHESTER near. Pitt Cottage, Ringstead Bay, Near Dorchester. Sleeps 6. An attractive thatched

stone-built cottage, surrounded by farmland and situated on the edge of a small wood about quarter of a mile from the sea, commanding outstanding views of Ringstead Bay on the Dorset Heritage Coast. The cottage has been renovated and is equipped to sleep six; three bedrooms (two beds in each), two bathrooms, sitting room with open fire and large kitchen/dining area. Cot/high chair; washing machine; TV; electric radiators in all rooms. Car essential. Available from £125 per week. For details please send SAE (reference FHG) to: **Mrs S.H. Russell, 14 Brodrick Road, London SW17 7DZ or telephone 0181-672 2022.**

PITT COTTAGE

**GILLINGHAM. Mrs J. Wallis, Meads Farm, Stour Provost, Gillingham SP8 5RX (01747 838265). ETB ♀♀♀♀ COMMENDED. Working farm, join in.

Sleeps 6.** Mead Bungalow is a superior property enjoying outstanding views over Blackmore Vale. Situated one mile from A30 at the end of the lovely village of Stour Provost. Shaftesbury with its famous Gold Hill is nearby and within easy reach are Bournemouth, Weymouth and Bath. Many attractive and interesting places lie a short car ride away. Over one mile of private coarse fishing 160 yards from bungalow. Spacious accommodation sleeps six plus cot. Large lounge with colour TV, diningroom, three double bedrooms, bathroom, luxury oak kitchen with automatic washing machine etc; all electric (no meters), full central heating; linen supplied. Quarter acre lawns. Sorry no pets.

HOLDITCH. Old Forge Cottage, Holditch, Chard. Sleeps 4. Ideal for peace and seclusion in glorious

unspoilt countryside within easy reach of the sea. This delightful old world cottage with oak beams stands just outside Holditch on the Devon/Dorset/Somerset borders, affording splendid views over beautiful countryside. Charmouth and its sandy beaches seven miles distant. Lyme Regis, with safe bathing and recreational facilities eight miles. The cottage is completely modernised and tastefully furnished with fitted carpets throughout, for up to four people. One twin-bedded room and two single rooms; sittingroom with colour TV; kitchen with dining area; modern bathroom; second toilet; electric cooker, fridge, vacuum cleaner, modern sink unit, immersion heater, night storage heaters throughout (included in terms). Everything supplied except linen. Electricity charged by meter reading. Phone; walled garden; garage. Chard four and a half miles. Terms £105 to £150 weekly. Open all year. Regret no children under 12 years. No pets. All enquiries to **Mrs P.A. Spice, Orchard Cottage, Duke Street, Micheldever, Near Winchester, Hants SO21 3DF (01962 774563).**

LYME REGIS. Mrs S. Denning, Higher Holcombe Farm, Uplyme, Lyme Regis DT7 3SN (01297 443223). Working farm, join in. Sleeps 6 plus cot.

Completely separate part of farmhouse on the working dairy farm, which was once a Roman settlement. Surrounded by pleasant country walks; golf, fishing, horse riding and safe sandy beaches are all nearby. There are three bedrooms — one double and two twin; two bathrooms; lounge with inglenook fireplace, colour TV; kitchen/diningroom with electric cooker, microwave, fridge, etc; use of washing machine and tumble dryer. Central heating (50p slot meter). Plenty of parking. One mile from village shops and pub, two miles coast of Lyme Regis. Winter Breaks. Linen provided. One pet by arrangement.

MILTON ABBAS. Primrose Cottage, 29 Milton Abbas, Blandford Forum. ♀♀♀ *HIGHLY COMMEN-DED.* **Sleeps 6.** Primrose Cottage is one of the semi-detached cob and thatched houses that make up a unique village created around 1770 by Lord Milton and landscaped by Capability Brown. The model village itself is said by many to be one of the prettiest in England. Certainly each house has individual charm whilst the winding valley setting with its lake at the bottom is the ideal base for walking through the Dorset countryside. The cottage, which sleeps four to six, has everything you would expect from a Grade II Listed building. The beamed sitting room, of course, has an inglenook fireplace with wood stove. Low doors remind you of the building's age but the 20th century has taken over everywhere else, from modern kitchen and bathroom to the two bedrooms. Non-smoking accommodation available. Really it's a cottage in which romantics can relax. Weekly rates from

£175 to £375. Contact: **Mr R.A. Garvey, 16 Mole Road, Hersham, Surrey KT12 4LU (01932 220395).**

PIDDLETRENTHIDE. Mr & Mrs R.C. Drewe, Lackington Farmhouse, Piddletrenthide, Dorchester DT2 7QU (01300 348253). ETB ♀♀♀ *COMMENDED.* **Sleeps 4.** Beautifully converted former coach house in the attractive Piddle Valley. Built in traditional brick and flint, the accommodation comprises one double and one twin bedroom, a bathroom with shower, a very well-equipped kitchen and a spacious living room (with colour TV) which commands superb views over local farmland. Secluded walled patio to the rear. Parking for two cars. Children and well-behaved dogs welcome. Peacefully located away from the main road but within easy reach of village shops, places to eat and beaches on the south coast. Ideal walking country. Brochure available. £150 to £300 per week.

SHAFTESBURY. Mrs Sue Smart, Hartgrove Farm, Shaftesbury SP7 0JY (01747 811830). ♀♀♀♀ *COMMENDED.* **Working farm. Four cottages sleep 2/5; Farmhouse flat sleeps 2.** Situated in glorious countryside with panoramic views, in an area of outstanding natural beauty four miles south of Shaftesbury, our 145 acre family farm is the ideal place for a relaxing holiday. The character cottages are situated in the centre of the farm and have oak fitted kitchens, close carpeted beamed lounge and private gardens. The delightful farmhouse flat has stunning views and private access from gardens. All are equipped and furnished to a very high standard with central heating and linen; log fires available. Laundry room, cot and high chair also available. Tennis court and games barn. Free swimming at local leisure centre. Glorious walking, pretty thatched villages and good pubs. One cottage graded Category 1 for disabled facilities. Brochure available.

STURMINSTER NEWTON. Mrs Sheila Martin, Moorcourt Farm, Moorside, Marnhull, Sturminster Newton DT10 1HH (01258 820271). Working farm. Sleeps 4. Ground floor flat with own entrance and front door key. It is part of the farmhouse, kept immaculately clean and furnished to the highest order. We are a 117 acre dairy farm in the middle of the Blackmore Vale. Guests are welcome to wander round, watch the farm activities and laze in the large garden — we have some garden loungers for your use. We are very central for touring with easy access to New Forest, Longleat Wildlife Park, Cheddar, Stonehenge and the lovely Dorset coast. Accommodation for four people in two double bedrooms, one with a double bed, the other with twin beds. Bathroom, separate toilet. Sittingroom with colour TV and door leading straight onto the back garden. Well equipped kitchen/diner, with fridge/freezer, microwave and washing machine; all utensils colour co-ordinated, matching crockery,

etc. Beds made up with fresh linen on arrival. Towels, tea towels, etc provided. Electric heaters in all rooms. Electricity payable by meter, units to be read at the start and finish of your holiday. Sheila creates a friendly atmosphere here "down on the farm" and does her best to make your holiday an enjoyable one. Open April to November. Car essential. Sorry, no pets. Weekly terms from £100 to £200. SAE please.

WHEN MAKING ENQUIRIES PLEASE MENTION
FARM HOLIDAY GUIDES

SWANAGE. Mrs Rosemary Dean, Quarr Farm, Valley Road, Swanage BN19 3DY (01929 480865). ♀ ♀ *APPROVED.* **Sleeps 10 plus cot.** Quarr Farmhouse is a 17th century stone building built in Purbeck marble quarried on farm. The farm is family farmed in a close to nature way. Chickens run free and hatch eggs in barns, while peacocks, cows, calves and horses are much in evidence. You will see chicks and ducks on your lawn, watch steam trains passing through our meadows. The house has four bedrooms, two double rooms (plus one single in each) and two twin rooms; bathroom with shower; large sittingroom with stone walls and 1651-built fireplace with log fire, colour TV; well-equipped kitchen including washer/dryer, dishwasher, microwave, fridge/freezer. Three miles from Swanage and five miles from Studland's sandy beach. Further details available on request.

WAREHAM near. Mrs M.J.M. Constantinides, "Woodlands", Hyde, Near Wareham BH20 7NT (01929 471239). THE MAISONETTE, north wing of secluded house, formerly Dower House of Hyde Estate, stands alone on a meadow of the River Piddle in four and a half acres in the midst of "Hardy Country". The Maisonette comprises upstairs lounge with colour TV; one bedroom (two single beds); downstairs large kitchen/diner, small entrance hall, bathroom; electric cooker (in addition to Aga cooker), refrigerator. Independent side entrance. Extra bedroom (two single beds) on request at £24 per week. Visitors are welcome to use house grounds; children can fish or play in the boundary stream. Pleasant walks in woods and heath nearby. Golf course half a mile, pony trekking nearby. All linen included, beds ready made and basic shopping arranged on arrival day. Aga will be lit and maintained on request. Ideal for a quiet holiday far from the madding crowd. Cot and high chair available and children welcome to bring their pets. SAE, please, for terms and further particulars.

PUBLISHER'S NOTE

While every effort is made to ensure accuracy, we regret that FHG Publications cannot accept responsibility for errors, omissions or misrepresentation in our entries or any consequences thereof. Prices in particular should be checked because we go to press early. We will follow up complaints but cannot act as arbiters or agents for either party.

DURHAM

HARWOOD-IN-TEESDALE. Upper Teesdale Estate, Raby Estate Office, Middleton-in-Teesdale,

Barnard Castle DL12 0QH (01833 640209; Fax: 01833 640963). ♀ ♀ *APPROVED.* HONEY POT AND FROG HALL sleeping four and six respectively, are two former farmhouses remotely situated in completely unspoilt countryside in the heart of the North Pennines area of outstanding natural beauty, with the National Nature Reserve, Cauldron Snout and High Force Waterfalls close by, a haven for walkers, naturalists and fishermen. Ideally situated for touring Durham, Cumbria, the Yorkshire Dales and Lake District. Both cottages have background heating, are simply furnished yet fully equipped; fuel for open fires is included in price. Cot and high chair available. Please write for a brochure.

MIDDLETON-IN-TEESDALE. Mrs June Dent, Wythes Hill Farm, Lunedale, Middleton-in-Teesdale

DL12 0NX (01833 640349). ♀ ♀ ♀ ♀ *COMMENDED.* Standing on the Pennine Way, backed by Lune Moor and surrounded by a working farm, this 18th century house has upland views in all directions. Only three miles from Middleton-in-Teesdale and 11 miles from Barnard Castle, this is a peaceful spot, centrally situated for Teesdale, Weardale and the Yorkshire National Park. Lounge with open and electric fires and colour TV; dining kitchen with automatic washing machine, tumble dryer, microwave; bathroom with shaver point, toilet; separate toilet with basin; three bedrooms — one downstairs. Garden with garden chairs. One small pet only please. Full gas central heating. All fuel, power, bed linen and towels included in the rent. Terms from £150 to £300 per week.

Key to
Tourist Board Ratings

The Crown Scheme
(England, Scotland & Wales)

Covering hotels, motels, private hotels, guesthouses, inns, bed & breakfast, farmhouses. Every Crown classified place to stay is inspected annually. *The classification:* Listed then 1-5 Crown indicates the range of facilities and services. Higher quality standards are indicated by the terms APPROVED, COMMENDED, HIGHLY COMMENDED and DELUXE.

The Key Scheme
(also operates in Scotland using a Crown symbol)

Covering self-catering in cottages, bungalows, flats, houseboats, houses, chalets, etc. Every Key classified holiday home is inspected annually. *The classification:* 1-5 Key indicates the range of facilities and equipment. Higher quality standards are indicated by the terms APPROVED, COMMENDED, HIGHLY COMMENDED and DELUXE.

The Q Scheme
(England, Scotland & Wales)

Covering holiday, caravan, chalet and camping parks. Every Q rated park is inspected annually for its quality standards. The more √ in the Q – up to 5 – the higher the standard of what is provided.

GLOUCESTERSHIRE

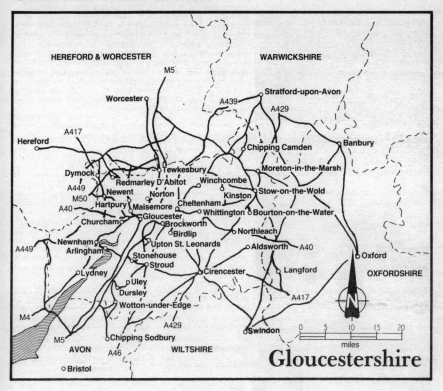

CHELTENHAM. Mr and Mrs J. Close, Coxhorne Farm, London Road, Charlton Kings, Cheltenham GL52 6UY (01242 236599). ♀♀♀ *COMMENDED.* **Sleeps 3.** Eastern outskirts of Cheltenham. Self catering in a well equipped studio apartment of Annexe adjoining farmhouse on working dairy farm. Accommodation consists of large lounge with sleeping for three plus extra bed on request. Gas fire and full central heating. Comfortable chairs and colour TV. Large fully fitted kitchen and en suite bathroom. Steps from kitchen leading to garden and plenty of parking space. Sorry, no smoking or pets. Children welcome. Electricity and linen included in rental. Ideal location for touring and walking Cotswolds. The farm is situated half a mile off the Cotswold Way with lovely views. Terms from £120 to £160 per week.

CHIPPING CAMPDEN. The Honey Pot. ♀♀♀♀ *HIGHLY COMMENDED.* Set in one of the most beautiful

towns in the country. Cotswold stone ground floor apartment in quiet mews. Half a minute from High Street for shops, inns and restaurants. Comfortably furnished with old world charm. Full central heating and carpets throughout. One bedroom with four-poster bed, as seen on BBC Holiday Programme. Superb fully fitted kitchen, washer/dryer, shower, pleasant lounge, stone fireplace, gas fire, colour TV, sofa bed. Includes heating and linen. Parking and small garden. Convenient for touring Cotswolds and Shakespeare country. From £220 per week. Apply: **Mrs D. Brook, Tod Cot, Noel Court, Calf Lane, Chipping Campden GL55 6BS (01386 841127).**

COTSWOLDS/DURSLEY. Mrs Ann Harris, Church Farmhouse, Upper Cam, Dursley GL11 5PB (Tel & Fax: 01453 543165). Sleeps 5/6.

Church Farm Cottage is a converted coach-house adjacent to a listed farmhouse in the village of Upper Cam, lying between the Cotswold Escarpment and the Severn Vale in lovely countryside. The Cotswold Way runs through the village. Nearby are Slimbridge Wild Fowl Trust and Berkeley Castle. Within a wider radius are Gloucester, Bath, Cheltenham, Wye Valley and Forest of Dean. The well equipped cottage sleeps five/six in three bedrooms, with extra bed and cot available. A large comfortable sittingroom has gas fire and colour TV. Washing machine available. Bedroom on ground floor has en-suite basin and toilet. Lawn with picnic table for guests' use. Reasonable rates. Details on request.

DURSLEY near. Gerald and Norma Kent, Hill House, Crawley Hill, Uley, Dursley GL11 5BH (01453 860267). Sleeps 2.

The flat is a separate part of this Cotswold stone house which stands in four and a half acres and is situated on top of a hill with beautiful views of the surrounding countryside. The accommodation consists of double bedroom, kitchen with cooker, microwave, fridge, etc., lounge with TV and video, toilet and shower. Car port and garden area. We supply a comprehensive set of maps and tourist information as well as routes to the many places of interest in the area. Bed linen and towels not supplied. Electricity by meter. Open all year. Sorry, no pets. Terms from £60 per week. Please telephone, or write, for brochure.

TEWKESBURY. Mick and Anne Meadows, Home Farm, Bredons Norton, Tewkesbury GL20 7HA (01684 772322).

STABLE COTTAGE: Delightful Cotswold stone stable/barn conversion on a mixed working family farm in a quiet and picturesque village under Bredon Hill. Very cosy and tastefullly furnished. Full central heating, lots of beams, own paddock. Perfect location for touring the Cotswolds, Severn Valley and Malverns with many wonderful walks. Open all year. Children and pets welcome. Weekly terms from £120.

FOR THE MUTUAL GUIDANCE OF GUEST AND HOST

Every year literally thousands of holidays, short-breaks and overnight stops are arranged through our guides, the vast majority without any problems at all. In a handful of cases, however, difficulties do arise about bookings, which often could have been prevented from the outset.

It is important to remember that when accommodation has been booked, both parties — guests and hosts — have entered into a form of contract. We hope that the following points will provide helpful guidance.

GUESTS: When enquiring about accommodation, be as precise as possible. Give exact dates, numbers in your party and the ages of any children. State the number and type of rooms wanted and also what catering you require — bed and breakfast, full board, etc. Make sure that the position about evening meals is clear — and about pets, reductions for children or any other special points.

Read our reviews carefully to ensure that the proprietors you are going to contact can supply what you want. Ask for a letter confirming all arrangements, if possible.

If you have to cancel, do so as soon as possible. Proprietors do have the right to retain deposits and under certain circumstances to charge for cancelled holidays if adequate notice is not given and they cannot re-let the accommodation.

HOSTS: Give details about your facilities and about any special conditions. Explain your deposit system clearly and arrangements for cancellations, charges, etc, and whether or not your terms include VAT.

If for any reason you are unable to fulfil an agreed booking without adequate notice, you may be under an obligation to arrange alternative suitable accommodation or to make some form of compensation.

While every effort is made to ensure accuracy, we regret that FHG Publications cannot accept responsibility for errors, omissions or misrepresentation in our entries or any consequences thereof. Prices in particular should be checked because we go to press early. We will follow up complaints but cannot act as arbiters or agents for either party.

HAMPSHIRE

LOCKERLEY. No 2 Thatched Cottage, Carter's Clay, Lockerley, Near Romsey. Sleeps 5. Delightful thatched self-catering cottage set in beautiful countryside in rural hamlet four miles from Romsey. Ideally situated for exploring New Forest and within easy reach of many places of interest and tourist attractions. Cottage has modern conveniences — TV, fridge, etc, with linen provided. It is clean, homely and very comfortable with a large garden. A warm welcome awaits all visitors including children and pets. Terms from £125 to £210 weekly. For further details SAE to **Mrs R.J. Crane, 1 Thatched Cottage, Carter's Clay, Lockerley, Romsey SO51 0GN (01794 340460).**

LYMINGTON (New Forest). Greenacre, Woodenhouse Lane, Pilley Bailey, Lymington. Sleeps 6/7.

GREENACRE

Delightful self catering thatched cottage about 150 years old, in peaceful village on lane leading down to shallow stream and open forest. Few miles from the sea and attractive harbour town. Ideal for walking, sailing, boat trips, pony riding, etc. Suits families, set in a garden with living room and dining room with open fireplaces, breakfast room/kitchen downstairs; upstairs bathroom, three bedrooms (one room double and single beds and cot, one twin-bedded, one with bunk beds). Traditional furnishings. Duvets provided but no sheets or towels. Children and pets welcome. Weekly terms from £190 to £390. Details from **Mrs Alison Du Cane, Hanover Lodge, 14 Lansdowne Road, London W11 3LW (0171-727 5463; Fax: 0171-221 3936).**

ROMSEY. Maxine Vine, Owl Cottage, Lye Farm, West Tytherley, Romsey SP5 1LA (01794 341667). ♀♀ to ♀♀♀ COMMENDED. Sleeps 5. Owl Cottage has been skilfully converted from an old barn. It is situated in one of the most beautiful parts of Hampshire with outstanding views and is located close to the New Forest, Salisbury and Winchester, ideal for touring, walking, and riding in Southern England. The excellently equipped cottage has central heating, washer/dryer, TV and cot. Electricity included. Peaceful and relaxing environment. Children and pets welcome. Open all year. Terms from £180.

ROMSEY. Mrs Wendy Graham, Meadow Cottage, c/o Farley Farm, Braishfield, Romsey SO51 0QP (01794 368265; Fax: 01794 367847). ♀♀♀♀ COMMENDED. Sleeps 5 plus cot. This well equipped semi-detached cottage is situated on a 400-acre beef and arable farm, with outstanding views of the beautiful surrounding countryside. Ideal for walking or riding (own horse welcome) or touring the historic centres of Romsey, Winchester, Salisbury, New Forest and the coast. The cottage has central heating, log fire, colour TV, downstairs WC, washer/dryer and cot. Garden with barbecue. Pets welcome. Open Easter to October. Terms from £150. Phone for brochure.

SWAY. Mrs H.J. Beale, Hackney Park, Mount Pleasant Lane, Sway, Lymington SO41 8LS (01590 682049). Properties sleep 4/6. Situated in commanding and tranquil setting two miles from Lymington and Sway village. Delightful residence in own extensive grounds adjoining New Forest Heath with superb walks, rides and drives. Apartment to sleep six (further bedrooms available). Coach House cottage to sleep four. Comfortable and modern, colour TV, bed linen and electricity included. Pets by prior arrangement. First class stables for those wishing to bring own horse and excellent riding facilities within walking distance. Many famous places of interest nearby. Close to Isle of Wight ferry and within six miles of sandy beaches, 15 miles Bournemouth and Southampton. Open all year.

HEREFORD & WORCESTER

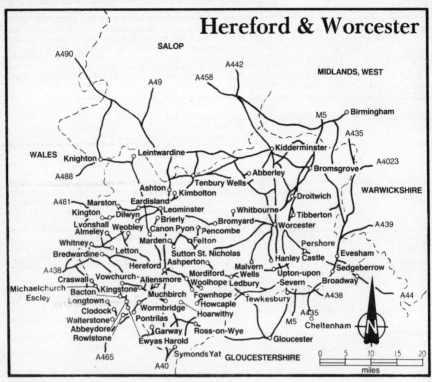

Hereford & Worcester

ABBEYDORE (Golden Valley). Ivy Green Cottage, Abbeydore. Sleeps 4. Traditional two bedroomed cottage painted white in pretty garden setting, sheltered but with lovely views all around. Situated on minor, quiet road two miles from A365, equidistant Hereford and Abergavenny. Close to Welsh border country. Explore North, South, East or West. The Cottage is fully equipped and has electric heaters throughout plus log fires; electric cooker, fridge, microwave and immersion heater. Bathroom with bath, heated towel rail; spin dryer, colour TV. One double bedroom and one twin-bedded room. Children and dogs welcome; fields all around. Price from £100 to £140 per week. Dogs £5 extra. Electricity by meter reading. Please write, or telephone, **Mrs D. Jeffreys, Wellfield, Abbeydore HR2 0AD (01981 570347).**

FELTON. Marjorie and Brian Roby, Felton House, Felton, Herefordshire HR1 3PH (01432 820366).

The Lodge is a spotlessly clean, cosy, restful cottage in the beautiful grounds of Felton House, the former rectory, just off A417 between Hereford, Leominster and Bromyard. The Lodge has been restored to its Victorian character but with the convenience of electric heating, a modern kitchen, two shower rooms, a dining room and a sitting room with TV. Guests are accommodated in one double, one twin and one single bedroom and a cot is available. Linen may be hired. Children and pets with responsible owners are most welcome. Private parking, patio and garden. Weekly terms £150 to £250 exclusive of electricity. Brochure available.

HEREFORD. Rose Cottage, Craswall, Hereford. ♀♀ APPROVED. Sleeps 5. Rose Cottage is a modernised stone-built cottage, retaining its original character situated at the foot of Black Mountains, on a quiet country road. Hay-on-Wye, Hereford, Abergavenny easily accessible and ideal base for walking and touring. Many churches and castles of historic interest; close to River Monnow where trout fishing is available. Pony trekking, hang gliding nearby. A car is essential and there is ample parking. Rose Cottage is comfortably furnished with full central heating and wood fire (heating and hot water included). Linen provided free of charge. Electricity by meter reading. Two bedrooms, one with double bed, one with three single beds. Cot can be provided. Bathroom, toilet. Kitchen fully equipped with electric cooker, kettle, fridge etc. Sittingroom; diningroom. TV. Dogs are allowed. Available all year round. Terms from £120 to £130. **Mrs M. Howard, The Three Horseshoes, Craswall HR2 0PL (01981 510631).**

HEREFORD. Mrs S. Dixon, Swayns Diggins, Harewood End, Hereford HR2 8JU (01989 730358).

This highly recommended first floor flat is completely self-contained at one end of the main house. The bedroom, sitting room and private balcony all face south with panoramic views over farmland towards Ross and Symonds Yat. The fully equipped kitchen overlooks the garden with grand views towards Orcop Hill and the Black Mountains. Open all year, rental from £110 per week includes electricity, linen, heating, colour TV. Ideal base for exploring the beautiful Wye Valley, Herefordshire, Gloucestershire and the historic Welsh Marches. There is much to see and do in the area. Write or phone for further particulars.

KINGTON. Bradnor Farm Cottage, Kington. ♀♀♀ *APPROVED.* Stone Farm cottage on beautiful Welsh Border. Panoramic views over miles of unspoilt countryside.

The cottage is very comfortable with night storage heaters and thoughtfully equipped. One double bedroom, one twin bedroom, double put-u-up in living room, colour TV; bathroom, separate toilet. Fully modernised kitchen, utility room with automatic washing machine. Cot and high chair available. Linen to hire. Pets by arrangement only. Superb walks on National Trust Land. 100 yards from highest golf course in England and Wales. Offa's Dyke path adjacent to cottage. Visit world-famous Hergest Croft Gardens, Black and White Villages, Wye Valley, Mid Wales Coast. Weekly terms from £140 to £205. Contact: **Mrs J.E. Burgoyne, Nash's Oak, Lyonshall, Kington HR5 3LT (01544 340272).**

KINGTON. The Harbour, Upper Hergest, Kington. Properties sleep 5/9. This bungalow is on a good second-class road facing south with beautiful views from its elevated position, across the Hergest Ridge and Offa's Dyke. The Welsh border is a mile away. Shops are two-and-a-half miles away. Kington Golf Club nearby. Accommodation for five/nine in two double rooms (one with extra single bed) downstairs and two double dormer bedrooms; two cots; bathroom, toilet; sittingroom (TV); diningroom; sun porch for relaxing; kitchen with electric cooker, fridge, food store and usual equipment. No linen. Suitable for the disabled. Children and pets welcome. Car essential — parking. Available all year. Also mobile home sleeping two with bathroom and flush toilet. SAE, please, to **Mr A.J. Welson, New House Farm, Upper Hergest, Kington, Herefordshire HR5 3EW (01544 230533).**

LEDBURY near. Mrs G.M. Thomas, White House Farm, Preston Cross, Near Ledbury HR8 2LH (01531 660231). ♀♀♀ *APPROVED.* **Working farm. Properties sleep 6.** High House Farmhouse (part 13th century), is divided into two holiday houses, equipped to very good standard. Superb views towards Ross-on-Wye (eight miles) and Gloucestershire. Fully electric kitchen/diner; sittingroom; bathroom and toilet; three bedrooms, all with fitted carpets; TV; telephone. Garage (car essential). All rooms have either night storage or electric heaters. Each house sleeps six. No linen supplied. Electricity extra. Farm buildings are nearby (this is a working stock and arable farm). Dogs allowed, under strict control. Children welcome, cot provided. Historic market town of Ledbury three miles, Malvern eight miles. Weekly terms from £180 to £250; reductions off season.

LEOMINSTER. Mrs M. Brooke, Nicholson Farm, Leominster HR6 0SL (01568 760269). Self catering cottages in rural area — "a land that time forgot". Three cottages sleep from four to seven persons; also self contained wing of 17th century farmhouse sleeps up to four. Two of the cottages are suitable for wheelchairs. All properties are carpeted and have colour TV; electric blankets on request. Washing machine and tumble dryer available. All have storage heaters (included in rental); two have solid fuel fires (some wood provided). Cleaning help and linen can be hired at modest cost. Dogs allowed at small charge. Trout and carp fishing on farm, also dairy produce. Golf, riding, swimming and tennis 15 minutes. Wide choice of hotel and bar meals in area; Leominster 6 miles.

LEOMINSTER. Mrs E. Thomas, Woonton Court Farm, Leysters, Leominster HR6 0HL (01568 750232). ♀♀♀♀ *COMMENDED.* MILL HOUSE FLAT: We have recently converted the first floor of an old cider house to provide a high standard of comfort comprising one large double room with washbasin, one smaller bedroom with twin beds (extra accommodation available in the farmhouse, also Bed and Breakfast); comfortable sitting room with colour TV, central heating and panel electric fire; kitchenette with electric cooker, microwave, fridge; bathroom. Patio. Ample car parking. Children welcome, cot, high chair and babysitting available. Linen provided, electricity included. Pets welcome by special arrangement. Terms from £160 to £250 per week. Short Breaks available. Brochure on request.

LUCTON. Mrs S.M. Sampson, Puddlecroft, Lucton HR6 9PH (01568 780537). ♀♀ *COMMENDED.* Our self-contained detached first floor "black and white" loft flat is ideally suited for two. It is in the grounds of the main house "Puddlecroft" and a private sitting out area complete with brick built barbecue is provided. Our own fields, where our free range chickens and sheep roam, provide lovely views from the flat and of course there is plenty of private parking. Puddlecroft is set in its own grounds on the edge of Lucton, a small peaceful hamlet which lies in North Herefordshire, close to borders of Wales and Shropshire. The area is ideally suited for walkers and as a central base for trips into Wales, Shropshire and Herefordshire. Terms from £100 to £180 per week. Available for weekly and weekend bookings throughout the year. Brochure available.

MICHEALCHURCH ESKLEY. Mrs P. Goodwin, The Glebe, Michealchurch Eskley, Hereford HR2 0PR (01981 510324). This family-run working hill farm at the foothills of the Black Mountains with Offa's Dyke dividing England and Wales offers two six-berth caravans and part of the farmhouse for self catering; also camping facilities available. Equal distance from Hereford and Abergavenny and eight miles to the largest second-hand book shops in Hay-on-Wye. A wealth of activities at hand, pony trekking, golf, private fishing, mountain climbing, walking and many places of historic interest. Linen provided. Children and pets welcome. Terms £150 per week.

PEMBRIDGE. Mrs N. Owens, The Grove, Pembridge, Leominster HR6 9HP (01544 388268).

♀♀♀♀ *COMMENDED.* **Sleeps 4.** Stone building divided horizontally. Each flat has open plan lounge, fitted kitchen/dining area, bathroom and toilet. Electric storage heating, automatic washing machine, microwave, colour TV, radio. The Granary has a wood burner, the Dairy on the ground floor an open fireplace. All linen and towels included. Ideal base for touring beautiful Border country, black and white villages and for walking in some extremely peaceful surroundings. The farm is mixed arable and stock and there are lovely little woodland and riverside walks on the farm itself. Pets welcome under strict control. Friendly farm atmosphere.

PRESTON WYNNE. Rachel or Julie Rogers, New House Farm, Preston Wynne (Tel & Fax: 01432 820621).

♀♀♀♀ *HIGHLY COMMENDED.* Featured in the Good Holiday Cottage Guide. Deep in the heart of rural countryside you will find our outstanding country cottages, full of character and charm. An ideal haven to relax and unwind. The children can enjoy pets corner, feed the animals, watch the milking or have a pony ride while mums and dads relax in the garden or maybe treat themselves to a sauna, jaccuzi or get fit in the gym. We guarantee you will not be disappointed. We also offer babysitting and Farmhouse Bed and Breakfast.

ROSS-ON-WYE (Welsh Borders). Mrs D. Wilding, Linden House, Vowchurch Common, Hereford HR2 0RL (01981 550360).

LANGSTONE COURT — no longer needed by ourselves we open our lovely old home for families up to 24 people. Local caterers available for dinner parties. Drawing room and dining room each measure approximately 15 x 18 feet. Wings divided and separately self-contained sleep from two to 10 plus cots with no sharing except large garden and car park. We specialise in Hen Parties, Birthdays or any reason to celebrate in this lovely home and beautiful Herefordshire countryside. Ground floor twin en suite room for disabled guests. Central heating, log fires, laundry, payphone, mountain bike store. Christmas and New Year whole building for 24; free tree and hamper. Please send for our colour brochure.

ROSS-ON-WYE. Mainoaks Farm Cottages, Goodrich. ♀♀♀ **and** ♀♀♀♀ *HIGHLY COMMENDED.* **Six units sleeping 2,4,6 & 7.** Set in 80 acres of pasture and woodland beside the River Wye in an area of outstanding natural beauty with an abundance of wildlife, this 15th century listed farm has recently been converted to form six cottages of different size and individual character. All with exposed beams, pine furniture, heating, fully equipped kitchens (four have microwaves), washer/dryers, colour TV. Private gardens and barbecue area. Linen and towels provided. Cot and high chair on request. An ideal base for touring the local area, beautiful walks including Forestry Commission, fishing, canoeing, pony trekking, bird watching or just relaxing in this beautiful tranquil spot. Short Breaks available. **Mrs P. Unwin, Northend Farmhouse, Madresfield, Malvern WR13 5AD (01684 577252).**

WINFORTON. Mrs Jackie Kingdon, Kilverts Cottage, Winforton Court, Winforton HR3 6EA (01544

328498). Relax in the beautiful Wye Valley at delightful Kilverts Cottage — a detached stone and oak "half-timbered" cottage set in the grounds of historic 16th century Winforton Court. Kilverts offer spacious and luxurious accommodation. Fitted kitchen with dishwasher (separate laundry room), elegant dining room, hall with oak staircase to first floor; bathroom; twin bedroom and double bedrooms, both with washbasins; large oak beamed lounge with spectacular views to Black Mountains, colour TV and good books. Delightful gardens. Fishing, riding and canoeing available. Pets welcome. £210 to £280 per week. Short Breaks available. All linen and electricity included plus "welcome hamper".

HERTFORDSHIRE

ROYSTON. Mrs A. Wilson, New England Farm, Tadlow, Royston SG8 0EN (01767 631247; mobile:

0374 273516). ♛ ♛ ♛ ♛ *APPROVED.* "LEYLANDII" is a spacious modern bungalow offering comfortable accommodation for six. Situated 300 yards off the B1042 between Bedford and Cambridge, an excellent location for visiting Wimpole Hall and Farm, RSPB, Shuttleworth Collection, Duxford; London only 50 minutes away by road/rail. Open all year. Terms from £175 to £250.

HELP IMPROVE BRITISH TOURIST STANDARDS

You are choosing holiday accommodation from our very popular FHG Publications. Whether it be a hotel, guest house, farmhouse or self-catering accommodation, we think you will find it hospitable, comfortable and clean, and your host and hostess friendly and helpful. Why not write and tell us about it?

As a recognition of the generally well-run and excellent holiday accommodation reviewed in our publications, we at FHG Publications Ltd. present a diploma to proprietors who receive the highest recommendation from their guests who are also readers of our Guides. If you care to write to us praising the holiday you have booked through FHG Publications Ltd. – whether this be board, self-catering accommodation, a sporting or a caravan holiday, what you say will be evaluated and the proprietors who reach our final list will be contacted.

The winning proprietor will receive an attractive framed diploma to display on his premises as recognition of a high standard of comfort, amenity and hospitality. FHG Publications Ltd. offer this diploma as a contribution towards the improvement of standards in tourist accommodation in Britain. Help your excellent host or hostess to win it!

FHG DIPLOMA

We nominate ....

....

Because

Name ....

Address ....

.... Telephone No. ....

KENT

ASHFORD. Christine Gorell Barnes, Hazel Tree Cottage, Hassell Street, Hastingleigh, Ashford TN25 5JE (01233 750324). ♀ ♀ ♀ COMMENDED. Sleeps 4/5 plus cot. A recently converted barn by a lovely old farmhouse is now an attractive and comfortable cottage for holiday makers. Sleeping four persons plus cot and sofa bed. Children welcome. Surrounded by fields, it has its own garden and terrace, and is ideally situated for sightseeing and exploring coast and countryside and for day trips to France. Canterbury 9 miles, Hythe 10 miles. Open all year. Terms from £160 to £280 per week.

BENENDEN. Miss P.A. Cyster, Spider's Lodge, Iden Green, Benenden, Cranbrook TN17 4HH (01580 240509). Sleeps 4. Self catering accommodation is offered in this charming two-bedroomed Cottage which stands on the edge of an orchard on the outskirts of a small hamlet called Iden Green which has one shop and a pub. A car is essential here to take advantage of the many historic and interesting places to visit in this beautiful area. Children are welcome but sorry, no pets. Weekly terms from £100 to £140. Non-smokers only. SAE or phone for full details.

BENENDEN. Waggon Lodge. Working farm. Sleeps 6. The cottage is situated down a private road. Beautiful and peaceful countryside, much of historic interest in the area. Recently converted to sleep six in three double bedrooms; bathroom, shower and toilet; lounge; dining area; kitchen with electric cooker, fridge, washing machine etc. Linen supplied. Storage heaters and electric fire. Colour TV. Cleaner calls once a week. Shop half a mile. Car essential — plenty of parking space. No pets. Terms from £180 to £250. SAE to **Mrs Anne Cyster, Walkhurst Farm, New Pond Road, Benenden TN17 4EN (01580 240677).**

LANCASHIRE

CLITHEROE near. Mrs S. Parker, Horns Farm, Church Street, Slaidburn, Near Clitheroe BB7 3ER (01200 446288). Sleeps 4. Working farm. Cosy semi-detached, two bedroomed cottage situated in small picturesque village and overlooking farmland, makes an ideal base from which to explore the Forest of Bowland, an area of outstanding natural beauty. Within easy reach of Yorkshire Dales, Lake District and seaside. Fishing at Stocks reservoir two miles away. On North Lancashire Cycle Way. Sorry, no pets. Garden up steps at rear. Linen and electricity included in the rent of £150 per week. Open all year. Short Winter Breaks £26 per night. Our farmhouse and phone box nearby; five miles from the centre of Kingdon.

LINCOLNSHIRE

GREAT STURTON. Mr and Mrs D. Dobson, Beech House, Great Sturton, Horncastle LN9 5NX (01507 578435). OLD BARN COTTAGES. Sympathetic conversion of Georgian barn into luxury two and three bedroomed cottages, each with own patio and garden commanding panoramic views of the beautiful Lincolnshire Wolds. Country-style kitchens (with microwave), central heating, colour TV, linen provided free of charge, clothes washing and drying machine, telephone available for the exclusive use of guests. Children welcome, dogs accepted by prior arrangement. Non smoking establishment. Nature trail through private wood. Croquet lawn. Barbecue area. Fly fishing in private lake. Mountain bikes for guests' use. Golf, riding, etc. Ideally located for touring. Open all year. Prices from £175 to £275.

NORFOLK

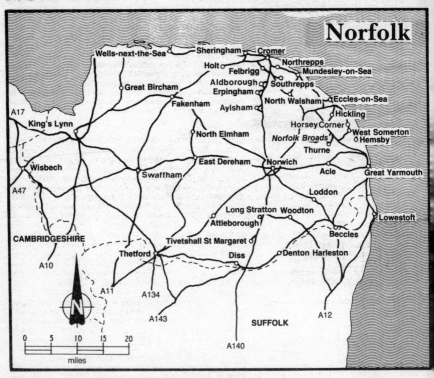

BLAKENEY. 4 Mariners Hill, Blakeney & Starlings, 82 High Street, Blakeney. Properties sleep 8/6.
All year round, house and cottage available to visitors hoping for a holiday that combines true relaxation,
comfortable accommodation and splendid scenery. MARINERS HILL is a flint/brick-built house sleeping
eight, with spectacular views over the quay and marsh. Small, secluded, walled garden. Well furnished and
equipped. Colour TV, washing machine, dishwasher, microwave and fridge/freezer. STARLINGS is a
pink-washed cottage with a part covered courtyard. With accommodation for six, it provides TV and night
storage heaters. Good dinghy sailing and birdwatching at hand, golf courses nearby. For further details
please write to: **Mrs A. Suckling, 8 Home Farm, Letheringsett, Holt, Norfolk NR25 7JL (01263
712636).**

BRISLEY. Church Farm Cottages, Brisley, East Dereham NR20 5LL. ♀♀♀♀ COMMENDED.

Properties sleep 2/4. Situated just off 170 acres of village
green between East Dereham and Fakenham. These cottages
are on a working farm of 230 acres. Kept to a very high
standard of cleanliness and comfort, they have full central
heating, log fires, colour TV, video, washing machine,
freezer, etc. Each has a garden and plenty of parking space.
Open all year. Short Breaks available October to April. Linen,
logs and heating included in price of £150 to £315 per week
for four. For further details contact **Mrs Gillian Howes
(01362 668332).**

CLIPPESBY. Mrs Jean Lindsay, Clippesby Holidays, Clippesby, Near Great Yarmouth NR29 3BJ (01493   369367). 🍷🍷 to 🍷🍷🍷🍷 *APPROVED.*

√ √ √ √ √ **Excellent.** Set in the Broadlands National Park where the tranquil waterways are a traditional haunt of fishermen, naturalists and sailors and where the nearby golden sand beaches stretch for miles. Broadland abounds in nature reserves and tourist attractions and Clippesby is perfectly placed for exploring these. When a change from exploring is called for guests can enjoy the amenities of the park itself — lawn tennis and swimming are just two of the things that families can enjoy together. Clippesby Holidays is a family-run country park with 23 courtyard cottages and an award-winning touring park in its spacious wooded grounds. Send for colour brochure.

CROMER. Northrepps Holiday Properties, Cromer NR27 0JW (01263 578196 and 512236). Sleep 4/7. Our cottages are very comfortably furnished, generously equipped and very carefully maintained. All are fully electric with cooker, water heater, fridge, colour TV and electric fires. Accommodation for four to six persons. Cots available on request. Pets always welcome. Some of the cottages have their own enclosed garden, ideal for children and pets. Ample parking for cars. As well as local wonderful sandy beaches we have golf, sailing, lake fishing, bird watching and miles of good walking in lovely surroundings. Cromer has a cinema and Pier with first rate live shows. Inclusive charges from £200 to £380 per week. Detailed brochure on request.

Holiday
Properties
at
Northrepps

CROMER. Hobby Cottage, Driftway Farm, Felbrigg, Cromer. Sleeps 4/6 plus cot. Completely modernised, comfortable cottage at the end of a quiet farm lane. Two miles from sandy coast and within easy access of North Norfolk bird sanctuaries, stately homes and Norfolk Broads. The cottage sleeps four/six, having a sitting room with TV and bed settee; two double bedrooms (one with double bed, one with twin beds); diningroom, well-equipped kitchen and bathroom. Garden and parking for two cars. Own transport essential. Available March-October. From £115 — £240 per week, including electricity. No linen. Enquiries, with SAE please, to **Mrs E. Raggatt, The Ferns, Berkeley Street, Eynesbury, St. Neots, Cambs PE19 2NE (01480 213884).**

DEREHAM. Mr Paul Davis, Moor Farm, Foxley, Dereham NR20 4QN (01362 688523). 🍷🍷🍷 *APPROVED.* A courtyard of seven two/three bedroomed converted stables plus two cottages, all with central heating and colour TV. Woodland walks. Central for coast, Broads, Sandringham and Norwich. Disabled facilities available. Open all year. Terms from £90 to £330 according to length of break and season.

DILHAM ISLAND. Dairy Farm, Dilham Island. 🍷🍷🍷🍷 *HIGHLY COMMENDED.* **Sleeps 4 plus cot.** Dairy Farm Cottages are the result of an excellent conversion fully equipped offering top quality accommodation, bathrooms en suite. Each with own patio garden, furniture and barbecue. Situated in rural and peaceful surroundings on the edge of the Norfolk Broads and only 15 minutes from coast. Games room, children's play area, laundry facilities. Open March to October; Christmas and New Year Breaks available. Weekly terms from £150 per week. Bookings: **James and Annabel Paterson, Manor Farm, Dilham, North Walsham (01692 535178/536883).**

FAKENHAM. Saddlery Cottage and Hillside Cottage, Colkirk, Fakenham. ♀♀♀ **Sleep 7 and 6**

respectively. Both cottages are situated near the farm on the outskirts of Colkirk village, overlooking farmland. Saddlery Cottage (shown in picture) has large and light sittingroom with beams and woodburner, fully fitted kitchen/dining room with fridge and electric cooker, utility room with automatic washing machine. Garage, parking and fenced garden. Hillside Cottage has sittingroom with colour TV, large airy kitchen/dining room with fitted units and washing machine. Fenced garden, parking. Both have central heating/Calor gas heating. Children and pets welcome. Cots available; linen supplied. Apply **Mrs C. Joice, (FHG), Colkirk Hall, Fakenham NR21 7ND (01328 862261; Fax: 01328 856464).**

GELDESTON. Hillside, 15 Kells Way, Geldeston, Beccles. Sleeps 4/6. This bungalow situated in small

country village, very quiet and near River Waveney, is within easy reach of Great Yarmouth, Norwich, Lowestoft, Southwold and seaside. Accommodates four/six people; one double, one twin bedroom; bed settee in lounge, storage heaters, colour TV, wood burner, beams; diningroom; bathroom/shower, toilet; kitchen, electric cooker, microwave, etc. Carpets throughout. Cot available. Sorry, no pets. Bed linen supplied. Open all year. Car essential — parking. Shops nearby. Terms on request. Special winter rates. **Mrs M. Rolt, "Conifer", 17 Kells Way, Geldeston, Beccles, Suffolk NR34 0LU (01508 518689).**

GREAT YARMOUTH near. Chalet 18G, Sundowner Holiday Park, Newport Road, Hemsby, Near

Great Yarmouth. ♀♀♀ **Sleeps 6.** Chalet accommodation for hire on an excellent holiday park situated near Great Yarmouth with its many attractions. Chalet comprises two bedrooms; lounge with studio couch; kitchen and bathroom. All rooms nicely furnished. Site facilities include indoor heated swimming pool, night club and bar with cabaret, dancing, bingo and children's club; large site shop and laundry. Children and pets welcome. Terms from £75 to £175 per week. Further details and bookings to **Mrs Gloria White, 2 Cherry Tree Lane, North Walsham, NR28 0HR (01692 403461; Fax: 01692 431500).**

HAPPISBURGH. Miss D. Wrightson or Mrs J. Morris, Cliff House, Beach Road, Happisburgh, Norwich NR12 0PP (01692 650775). Sleeps 7 plus. Spacious self-contained flat in large, Edwardian house, overlooking sea and countryside with magnificent views from all rooms. Heating by electric storage heaters. Cot and high chair available. The well equipped kitchen includes a washing machine, there is a large lounge with TV and guests enjoy the use of a small secluded garden. Location is ideal for families as the beach is only two minutes' walk away. The flat is attached to a tea shop and restaurant, where meals and snacks are available all day and evening. One small dog welcome. Three-day off season breaks £85.

HOLT near. 8 Marryat's Loke, Langham, Near Holt. Sleeps 5. A modern red brick house on the edge of a small village. Ideal for bird watching on nearby Cley and Blakeney Marshes, and near beaches such as Cromer, Sheringham and Wells. It is also within easy reach of Norwich and the Norfolk Broads. There are many places of historic interest to visit such as Sandringham and Holkham Hall. The house accommodates five people in three bedrooms. Cot available. Fully equipped except linen. Electricity £1 meter. Heating costs extra in winter. Sorry no pets. Terms from £90 to £230 per week. SAE or telephone for details to **Mrs L Thirtle, Rectory Road, Bodham, Holt NR25 6PR (01263 822274).**

NORFOLK – THE BROADS!

Formed by the flooding of medieval peat diggings, the Broads have a unique quality which attracts thousands of visitors each year. Slow moving waterways are bounded by reed and sedge, and despite the pressures of the modern world are home to rare birds, butterflies and plants. Motor boats and sailing boats can be hired in most towns and villages and there are lots of lively riverbank pubs to round off a day afloat.

HUNSTANTON. Mr & Mrs Reynolds, 4 Victoria Avenue, Hunstanton PE36 6BX (01485 532714).

Large Victorian house with two flats both sleeping four people. One with bathroom and the other with shower room; lounge, colour TV, kitchen. Linen available. Within walking distance of sandy beach and swimming, wind surfing, golf and convenient for visiting Sandringham, village pubs, Norfolk Lavender, bird reserves, historic houses, craft centres; gourmet restaurants nearby. Pets and children welcome. Open all year. Short Breaks available. Please write or telephone for further details.

KING'S LYNN. Mrs Angela Ringer, Sid's Cottage, c/o The Grange, West Rudham, King's Lynn PE31 8SY (Tel & Fax: 01485 528229). ♀♀♀♀ *APPROVED.*

Sleeps 4. Sid's Cottage is semi-detached, surrounded by grass but has no enclosed garden. Overlooks a small orchard, patio at rear. Sleeps four in three bedrooms. Linen provided. Gas central heating, open fire, colour TV, microwave, automatic washing machine, fridge/freezer. Cot and high chair available on request. Electricity 50p meter. Carp fishing on farm. Heated indoor swimming pool. Good base for seeing Norfolk. Sandy beach in easy reach. Children welcome. Sorry, no pets. Open all year. Terms from £120 to £250.

LITTLE WALSINGHAM. Candlemas Cottage, 2 Guild Street, Little Walsingham. Sleeps 6/8.

Intriguing detached 18th century Grade II Listed flint and brick cottage, creatively and comfortably furnished, in unspoilt medieval shrine village amongst beautiful rolling countryside, with pine edged sandy beaches approximately five miles; Norwich, Sandringham not far. Sleeps six in three bedrooms plus one in small attic bedroom with single bed and further divan in small sitting room for eighth person. Kitchen with fridge, freezer, dishwasher, washing machine, microwave, electric cooker and hob. Dining room with large farmhouse table and Rayburn; two sitting rooms and study. Colour TVs, open fires (fuel included). Pubs, butcher's, baker's (candlestick maker's), grocer's, doctor's, horse stables. Terms from £300. Details **Valerie Goodsell, Candlemas Barns, 3 Guild Street, Little Walsingham NR22 6BU (01328 820748).**

MUNDESLEY-ON-SEA. 47 Seaward Crest, Mundesley-on-Sea. Sleeps 4. Mundesley-on-Sea is an

attractive seaside village situated centrally on the Norfolk coast, within 10 miles of the Norfolk Broads, seven miles from Cromer and 20 miles from Norwich. The clean sandy beaches stretch for miles with safe bathing and natural paddling pools. This attractive west-facing brick-built chalet is in a delightful setting with lawns, flower beds, trees and ample parking. Beach 500 yards away and shops 800 yards. There is an excellent golf course nearby and bowls and riding are within easy reach. Large lounge/diningroom tastefully furnished including easy chairs, settee and colour TV. Kitchenette with electric cooker, fridge, sink unit, etc. One double, one twin-bedded rooms. Fully carpeted. Bathroom and toilet. Lighting, hot water, heating and cooking by electricity (50p slot meter). Fully equipped except for linen. Weekly terms from £75. East Anglia Tourist Board registered. Details, SAE, please, **Mrs J. Doar, 4 Denbury Road, Ravenshead, Nottinghamshire NG15 9FQ (01623 798032).**

FREE and REDUCED RATE Holiday Visits!
See our READERS' OFFER VOUCHER for details!

NORWICH. Sunnybank, Blofield, Norwich. Sleeps 4/5 plus baby. Comfortable, well equipped,

detached bungalow in quiet location close to village centre. Excellent road access providing ideal base for exploring Braodland, historic Norwich and Great Yarmouth Coast. Boating and fishing nearby. Comprises sun porch, fitted kitchen with automatic washing machine and microwave; sitting room with colour TV, radio, toys, games. Double-bedded room, twin-bedded room with Z-bed (for child); bathroom. Ample parking. Attractive enclosed lawned garden. One well behaved dog accepted. Railway one and a half miles, bus stop 400 yards. Terms: £120 per week inclusive of central heating, electricity and linen, November to March (excluding Christmas and New Year) to £240 high season. Contact: **Mrs C. Pritchard, 18 Danesbower Lane, Blofield, Norwich NR13 4LP (01603 713986).**

NORWICH. Mrs G.L. Coiley, Pond Farm, Cringleford, Norwich NR4 6UE (01603 454895).

HIGHLY COMMENDED. One mile A11/A47 intersection, excellently situated three miles south Norwich, easy access to city centre and all Norfolk. Imaginative barn conversion into two cottages, courtyard garden set in grounds of owner's picturesque, thatched 16th century farmhouse with duck pond, adjacent village green. The Old Stables (sleeps four) and Horseshoe Cottage (sleeps two), both have twin bedded rooms, cot and high chair available; bathroom; attractive beamed lounge/diner, colour TV; fully fitted kitchen. No stairs, therefore suitable for those with limited mobility. Bed linen (duvets), towels, electricity, gas central heating included in price. Telephone. Regret no smoking, nor pets. Terms: Old Stables £220 to £290, Horseshoe Cottage £160 to £230 per week. Please telephone or send for brochure.

WINTERTON-ON-SEA. Timbers, The Lane, Winterton-on-Sea. Sleeps 5. Comfortable, well furnished

ground floor flat in attractive timber cottage situated in quiet seaside village just eight miles north of Great Yarmouth. Broad sandy beach and sand dunes (nature reserve) for pleasant walks. Three miles from Norfolk Broads (boating and fishing). Flat is carpeted throughout and is fully equipped for self-catering family holidays. Ideal for children, and pets are welcome. One double, one twin-bedded and one single bedroom. Sleeps five plus cot. Bed linen provided and maid service every other day for general cleaning. Beamed sitting-room with colour TV. Secluded garden. Car parking. Available May to September. Terms from £140 to £300 per week. For full details write to **Mr M.J. Isherwood, 79 Oakleigh Avenue, London N20 9JG (0181-445 2192).**

NORTHAMPTONSHIRE

YARDLEY GOBION.The Stable, Old Wharf Farm, The Wharf, Yardley Gobion NN12 7VE (01908

542293). Sleeps 4 plus cot. The Stable is a historic stone building situated in the farmyard adjacent to the Grand Union Canal with views over open countryside. The centrally heated accommodation comprises an open plan first floor with many original features, a galley kitchen, living area and separate double bedroom. Downstairs is the shower room and toilet plus a second twin bedroom. The Wharf is used as a canal service point and a day-boat is available for exploring the canal and for fishing. Old Wharf Farm is situated off the A508 between Northampton and Milton Keynes. Bedding and electricity is included. Gas by meter. Terms from £185 to £285 per week.

NORTHUMBERLAND

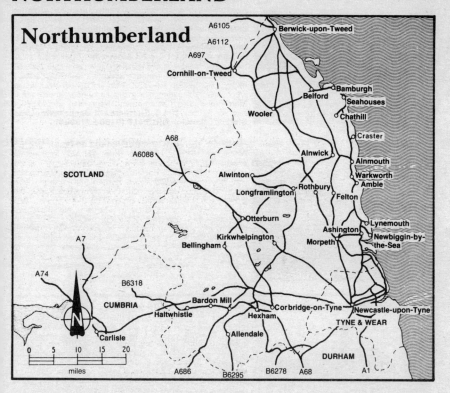

ALNWICK. Birling Vale, Warkworth, Alnwick. Tourist Board *COMMENDED.* Birling Vale is an attractive stone-built, detached house standing in a very pleasant, secluded garden (which can be appreciated from the recently completed garden room). This house is approximately one-third of a mile from picturesque village of Warkworth which is beside the River Coquet and dominated by an ancient Norman Castle. Birling Vale is only half-a-mile from lovely sandy beaches; 15 minutes from trout and salmon rivers, and within a comfortable drive of many places of interest, including Hadrian's Wall, Holy Island and Scottish Borders. The house, which is tastefully furnished and fully equipped including colour TV, has two bedrooms with double beds and a third bedroom with single divans. Cot available. Oil for full central heating is provided free of charge. Well trained dogs welcome. Weekly terms from £120 low season; £230 mid-season; £340 high season. SAE to **Mrs Janet Brewis, Woodhouse Farm, Shilbottle, Near Alnwick NE66 2HR (01665 575222).**

NORTHUMBERLAND – HADRIAN'S WALL

Nearly 2000 years ago Hadrian's Wall defined the northern frontier of Rome's mighty empire. Today large sections still remain, with major sites at Vindolanda, where displays and reconstructions give an idea of life for civilians and soldiers during the Roman occupation, and at Chesters, Corbridge and Housesteads. The Roman Army Museum near Greenhead gives a vivid insight into the Roman soldier's way of life.

ALNWICK. Mrs V. Purvis, Titlington Hall Farm, Alnwick NE66 2EB (01665 578253). ♀♀♀♀

COMMENDED. **Sleeps 2-10.** Two lovely country cottages available for holiday lets all year round. They are situated in a quiet and beautiful area with many interesting places just a short drive away. Facilities include central heating, TV, fridge, microwave, washing machine, tumble dryer and linen. Children welcome, pets by arrangement. Prices from £155 to £295 per week.

BERWICK-UPON-TWEED. Mrs H. Wight, Gainslawhill Farm, Berwick-upon-Tweed TD15 1SZ (01289 386210). Well equipped cottage with own walled garden on mixed farm, three miles from Berwick-upon-Tweed, situated between the Rivers Tweed and Whiteadder (last farm in England). Ideal position for touring north Northumberland and the Border country. Good beaches, golf, riding nearby. Lovely walks along both rivers. Trout fishing. Sleeps six, cot available. Pets welcome. Livingroom with open fire, colour TV, telephone. Three bedrooms (linen provided), kitchen with dining area, fridge freezer, automatic washing machine, microwave oven. Bathroom. Night store heaters. Terms from £170.

CORBRIDGE. Mr F.J. Matthews, The Hayes, Newcastle Road, Corbridge NE45 5LP (01434 632010). ♀♀ *COMMENDED.* Self catering properties — three cottages, flat and caravan. Spacious attractive stone-built guesthouse (One Crown). Set in seven acres of grounds. Single, double, twin, family bedrooms, all with tea making facilities, two with showers; lounge and dining rooms. Open 11 months of the year. Bed and Breakfast from £16. Children's reductions. Stair lift for disabled visitors. Awarded two Farm Holiday Guide Diplomas. Car parking. For brochure or booking SAE/phone.

CORNHILL-ON-TWEED. Springwood, Cornhill-on-Tweed. ♀♀♀ *COMMENDED.* **Sleeps 4.** This charming semi-detached bungalow is situated on the edge of Cornhill village overlooking farmland to the rear. It is well placed for exploring the beautiful Tweed Valley with many stately homes, castles and museums. It is within 30 minutes travelling to the outstanding Northumberland coastline on the peaceful Cheviot Hills. There is a hotel, shop, post office, church, public telephone, petrol station, police station and riding school in the village. This nicely furnished cottage has fitted carpeted throughout, sitting room, dining room, bathroom with shower over bath, modern fitted kitchen with automatic washing machine, one double bedroom, one twin bedroom and sun lounge. Heated by night storage heaters plus an electric fire and portable gas heater. Enclosed garden. Parking. Duvets, towels, linen and electricity included. Terms from £130 to £230 per week. For more information contact **Cathie and Allan Martin, Cookstead, Cornhill-on-Tweed TD12 4SG (01890 820288).**

FHG PUBLICATIONS LIMITED publish a large range of well-known accommodation guides. We will be happy to send you details or you can use the order form at the back of this book.

HEXHAM. Mr Richard Macdonald, Beaumont Cottage, Allenheads, Hexham NE47 9HJ (01434

685026). Beaumont Cottage adjoins Beaumont House, they are Listed buildings surrounded by walled gardens near the centre of an unspoilt village. Available in the village are post office/shop, hotel and coffee shop. The cottage has modern amenities with two large bedrooms, one double and one twin. Central heating, colour TV, fitted carpets throughout apart from traditional stone flagged floor in modern kitchen/diner. Centrally situated in the North Pennines. Northumberland, Durham and Roman Wall are easily accessible, the Lake District 75 minutes' drive away. Ideal peaceful countryside location for walking, with fishing and horse riding available locally. Children welcome, sorry no pets. No smoking.

MORPETH. Mrs G. Graham, The Newton Farm, Newton, Rothbury, Morpeth NE65 7DP (01669

650275; Fax: 01669 650259). ♀ ♀ ♀ *APPROVED.* **Sleeps 6 plus cot.** This mid-terraced cottage, formerly a farm worker's dwelling, is to be found on the working farm of Newton, situated in the heart of rural Northumberland. The farm lies on the edge of the National Park, 10 miles west of Rothbury, midway between the villages of Alnwinton and Netherton. The cottage comprises spacious dining kitchen; sitting room with open fire; double, twin and bunk-bedded rooms; bathroom with WC and feature cast iron bath. Partial night storage heating, included in price, wall mounted electric heaters, immersion heater. Colour TV, gas cooker, fridge/freezer. Electricity by £1 coin meter. Duvets, bed linen and towels provided. Weekly rates from 150 to £190. Brochure available.

MORPETH. Mr & Mrs A.P. Coatsworth, Gallowhill Farm, Whalton, Morpeth NE61 3TX (01661

881241). ♀ ♀ ♀ ♀ ♀ *HIGHLY COMMENDED.* **Working farm. Sleeps 4-6.** Relax in our two spacious stone-built cottages. Recently converted and modernised to give you every facility you require. Electric cooker, fridge, freezer, dishwasher, washer/dryer, microwave, colour TV. Located in the heart of Northumberland on a very tidy farm with private gardens. Bolam Lake two miles, Belsay Castle four miles, coast 20 minutes, Hadrian's Wall 30 minutes, to name only a few attractions. All linen, heating, electricity included in price. Sorry, no pets. All children welcome. Brochure on request. Terms £190 to £385.

NEWTON BY THE SEA. Mrs J.I. Patterson, Newton Hall Cottages, Newton Hall, Embleton, Alnwick

NE66 3DZ (Tel & Fax: 01665 576239). ♀ ♀ ♀ ♀ *COMMENDED.* Converted stone built Georgian Coach House and Stables located in courtyard of Newton Hall. Magnificent sandy beaches — lovely coastal walks. The cottages offer an ideal base for exploring the local unspoilt countryside. Places to visit include Kielder Water, Hadrians Wall, Cheviot Hills, Cragside Rothbury, Farne Islands, Holy Island, Alnwick and Bamburgh Castles and Tyneside Metrocentre. Outdoor activities include tennis court and childrens' play area in the grounds, bird watching, golf — many courses close by, fishing and pony trekking. Clean comfortable cottages — 3 bedroomed sleeps 6; 2 bedroomed sleeps 4/5; 1 bedroomed sleeps 2/3. Pets welcome. All centrally heated. Car parking. Shops, post office, inns and restaurants close by. Colour brochure, please telephone.

NORTHUMBERLAND – BORDER COUNTRY!

You cannot go any further north and remain in England! There is much outstanding scenery, both inland and on the coast, and a host of interesting places to visit. Border Forest Park has everything you would expect, plus many interesting Roman remains. There are also remains at Housesteads and other places of interest include Lindisfarne, the "conserved" village of Blanchland, Hexham, Heatherslaw Mill and Craster.

NORTHUMBERLAND. Northumbria Coast and Country Cottages Ltd., Riverbank Road, Alnmouth NE66 2RH (01665 830783 & 830902 (24 hours); Fax: 01665 830071). We are the longest established Agency in Northumberland and have built up a substantial portfolio of properties, many of which are firm favourites with our holidaymakers who return year after year. Each property has been carefully selected either for its beautiful surroundings and views or for its ideal position in which to explore this magnificent county. A number of properties are added to our brochure each year and we aim to provide the ideal cottage for most tastes at affordable prices. Please send for our full colour brochure giving details on all properties available, prices and general information.

OXFORDSHIRE

COTSWOLDS. Manor Cottages, Village Farm, Little Barrington, Burford OX18 4TE (01451 844643; Fax: 01451 844607). ♀♀♀/♀♀♀♀♀ Set in some of the prettiest villages in England, our properties are all furnished to a high standard whilst retaining their essential character. Their rural location in unrivalled scenery will ensure a relaxing stay, whether driving to nearby places of interest or discovering the countryside on foot. Rolling hills dotted with sheep, villages of natural golden stone, historic houses and local heritage combine to give the Cotswolds their unique charm. Add this to the surrounding towns of Oxford, Stratford-upon-Avon, Cheltenham and Bath — you can see why we think you will like it! We are a small company and can give individual help with the selection of your cottage. Free brochure.

SHROPSHIRE

BISHOP'S CASTLE. Walcot Hall, Lydbury North, Bishop's Castle. Flats sleep 4/9. Spacious flats in Stately Home. Secluded location in own grounds; splendid scenery and ideal area for peaceful holiday for young and old. All flats fully furnished and recently decorated and sleep four/nine. Larger parties by arrangement. Village shop half a mile; local market towns, castles, villages and hill country of the Border Counties provide opportunities for exploration and walking. Coarse fishing in pools and lake. Boats and bicycles available, and riding locally. Terms from £182 to £295 weekly. **Mrs M. Smith, 41 Cheval Place, London SW7 1EW (0171-581 2782).**

CLUN VALLEY (South Shropshire). Mrs Sue Wheeler, Brynmawr, Newcastle-on-Clun, Craven

Arms SY7 8QU (01588 640298). Sleeps 5. Self catering mobile home on busy stock rearing farm overlooking the Clun Valley. On the mid-Wales Border in easy reach of Snowdonia National Park, Brecon Beacons, Ironbridge Gorge Museum, Shrewsbury, etc. Beautiful touring/walking area along "Offa's Dyke". The mobile home stands in its own garden. Lovely views from lounge overlooking valley and hills. Kitchen, double bedroom, single, double bunk room and bathroom. Central heating from Parkray fire. Immersion heater. Babysitting available. Sorry, no pets. Disabled persons welcome if facilities are suitable. 35 miles to Hereford, Shrewsbury and 12 miles to Newtown. Warm welcome assured. Terms from £95 to £130.

CRAVEN ARMS. Mrs B. Freeman, Upper House, Clunbury, Craven Arms SY7 0HG (01588 660629).

Welcome to Horseshoe Cottage which is situated in the beautiful gardens of Upper House (17th century Listed) in Clunbury, a village of archaeological interest in a designated area of outstanding natural beauty — A.E. Housman countryside. This private self catering cottage is completely furnished and equipped; being on one level the accommodation is suitable for elderly and disabled persons. Colour TV. Sleeps four; cot available. Children and pets welcome. Ample parking. This Welsh Border countryside is rich in medieval history, unspoilt villages and natural beauty. Enjoy walking on the Long Mynd and Offa's Dyke, or explore Ludlow and Ironbridge. £130 to £160 per week. Please write or phone for further details.

IRONBRIDGE. Mrs Virginia Evans, Church Farm, Rowton, Wellington, Telford TF6 6QY (01952

770381). ♀♀♀ *COMMENDED.* **Working farm, join in. Sleep 2/5.** Two beautifully converted barn cottages equipped and furnished to a high standard, carpeted and centrally heated throughout, linen included. Lounge/dining area, patio doors leading to enclosed garden with patio furniture and barbecue. Fully fitted kitchen with microwave and washing machine. Double bedroom downstairs with bathroom opposite which includes bath, electric shower and toilet, one twin and one single bedroom on balustraded gallery above lounge. Cot and high chair available. Pets welcome. Guests welcome to join in farming way of life on our dairy/sheep farm where extra Bed and Breakfast accommodation is available. Also for hire two six/eight berth holiday caravans. We are peacefully situated in a quiet hamlet yet near Shrewsbury, Ironbridge, Bridgnorth, Ludlow, Wales. Terms from £140 to £280 per week.

LUDLOW. Hazel Cottage, Duxmoor, Onibury, Craven Arms. ♀♀♀♀ *HIGHLY COMMENDED.* **Sleeps**

4. Beautifully restored, semi-detached, yet private, period cottage, set in its own extensive "cottage" garden with drive and ample parking space. It has panoramic views of the surrounding countryside and is situated five miles north of historic Ludlow. The cottage comprises a comfortable living-room with colour TV, radio and telephone, diningroom; fully equipped kitchen; hall; bathroom; two bedrooms (one double and one with twin beds) with washbasins. Electric central heating throughout. All linen included. No pets. The cottage retains all the original features having been decorated traditionally and furnished with antiques throughout. Tourist information. Winter breaks. Terms from £140 to £315 per week. **Mrs Rachel Sanders, Duxmoor Farm, Onibury, Craven Arms SY7 9BQ (01584 856342).**

LUDLOW. R.E. Meredith, The Avenue, Ashford Carbonell, Ludlow SY8 4DA (01584 831616). ♀ ♀ ♀ ♀ *COMMENDED.* **Sleeps 6.** Spacious self-contained flat in large attractive country residence set in its own quiet grounds on edge of village three miles from historic Ludlow. With easy access by wide outside staircase, the flat affords excellent views and is furnished to a high standard of comfort. Two double, one twin bedrooms; bathroom/WC; fully equipped kitchen/diner, electric cooker, fridge, automatic washing machine, microwave; lounge, colour TV; cot/high chair. Electric fires, immersion heater by meter; full night storage central heating by separate meter. Ample parking and private lawn. Linen and garage on request. Open all year. Terms on request.

NEWCASTLE ON CLUN. Mr and Mrs J.K. Goslin, The Riddings Firs, Crossways, Newcastle-on-Clun, Craven Arms SY7 8QT (01686 670467). Sleeps 2 adults, 3 children.

Ideal holiday location on the Welsh Borders, at 1300 feet, in an area designated as being of Outstanding Natural Beauty. For those seeking complete peace and relaxation, this attractive self-catering family accommodation, for four people, is in a self-contained traditional farmhouse annexe with own private entrance. Fully equipped and attractively furnished including colour TV, wood burning stove. Open plan arrangement comprises one double, two bunk beds and bed settee; electric cooker, fridge etc.; shower, toilet, washbasin. Children especially welcome. Pleasantly situated in excellent walking country; several interesting market towns, hospitable inns with dining facilities, Castle within easy reach. Pony trekking and trout fishing can be arranged; area is suitable for mountain bikes. Grazing available for visitors' ponies. No pets. Self-catering from £100 per week. Linen supplied at extra cost if required. Out of season and week-end visitors welcome.

OSWESTRY. Mrs Glenice Jones, Lloran Ganol Farm, Llansilin, Oswestry SY10 7OX (01691 791287). WTB Four Dragons. Working farm. Sleeps 5.

A luxury self-catering bungalow on mixed farm in quiet valley. Farm and bungalow are situated over the border in the Welsh hills in Clwyd. Five people accommodated in two double and one single bedrooms; bathroom, toilet; sittingroom, diningroom; colour TV; long kitchen with dining area; automatic washing machine, tumble dryer, dishwasher, microwave and fridge. Linen supplied. Extra charge for pets. Two and a half miles from the shops. Car essential — parking. Shooting, horse riding and trout fishing on farm; fishing, golf and trekking in surrounding area. Open all year round, the bungalow is suitable for disabled guests. Storage heaters, fitted carpets and garden furniture provided. Glass conservatory. Weekly terms from £80. Bed and Breakfast also available with family in house adjoining from £12.50 per night, Bed, Breakfast and Evening Meal from £24 per night.

OSWESTRY Near. Mrs E.M. Lloyd, Rhiwlas, Llanwddyn, Near Oswestry SY10 0NN (01691 870222).

Semi-detached farmhouse, peacefully situated on a 320 acre family farm three miles from Lake Vyrnwy, eight miles west of Llanfylhin. On the ground floor is a kitchen with fridge/freezer and the sitting/dining room with TV. The first floor comprises bathroom and two bedrooms, one with children's bunk beds; one with double and single beds. The top floor has a beamed room with double and single beds, and a lovely view. Heating is by a wood burner and electric fire in the lounge, storage heaters in the bedrooms, all of which have washbasins. Enclosed garden with patio furniture. Baby sitting available.

OSWESTRY near. Mr and Mrs Breeze, Lloran Isaf, Llansilin, Near Oswestry SY10 7QX (01691 791376 or 01691 780318). Working farm.

This beautiful bungalow is set on a working farm in its own valley which has wonderful scenery and walks. Accommodation comprises kitchen with microwave, washer/dryer, fridge and cooker; large lounge and dining area with colour TV and woodburning stove; three bedrooms — one twin, one double, one single; separate toilet and bathroom. Fitted carpets and electric heating in bedrooms and lounge; barbecue, garden furniture in enclosed garden. One and a half miles from the village, in a wonderful touring area with lots of attractions. Open all year. Pets welcome. Sorry no children. Newly decorated throughout. Prices from £95. 3 Dragon Grade.

PLEASE SEND A STAMPED ADDRESSED ENVELOPE WITH ENQUIRIES

SOMERSET

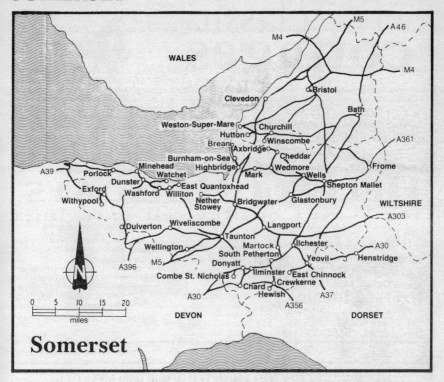

Somerset

BARTON ST. DAVID. Trevor and Brigitte Norton, Watercress Cottage, Jarmany Hill, Barton St. David, Somerton TA11 6DA (01458 850905). **Sleeps 5/6.** Comfortable spacious fully furnished kitchen/lounge. Colour TV, fitted carpets throughout, full gas central heating. Two bedrooms: one with double bed, single bed plus folding bed if necessary, one with full size bunk beds. Bathroom with bath, washbasin and toilet. Quiet rural area with excellent south-facing views. Ideal for touring — Clarks Village, Street, Yeovilton Air Museum, Glastonbury, Wells, Cheddar. Linen provided except towels. Sorry, no pets. Ample car parking. Terms from £135 to £250 per week. Open January to November.

BATH near. Mrs Audrey Rich, Whitnell Farm, Binegar, Emborough, Near Bath BA3 4UF (01749 840277).

Delightful manor house has two self-contained units sleeping two to eight people on a working farm set in peaceful countryside on the edge of this pretty Mendip Village. Very central for touring, lots to do, things to see, garden to relax in, open fields for children to play in or take a stroll in the country lanes. You will find us just off the B3139 Wells to Bath road. Open all year. Children welcome. Farmhouse B&B also available. Telephone for details or SAE for brochure.

HELP IMPROVE BRITISH TOURIST STANDARDS

You are choosing holiday accommodation from our very popular FHG Publications. Whether it be a hotel,
guest house, farmhouse or self-catering accommodation, we think you will find it hospitable, comfortable
and clean, and your host and hostess friendly and helpful. Why not write and tell us about it?

As a recognition of the generally well-run and excellent holiday accommodation reviewed in our
publications, we at FHG Publications Ltd. present a diploma to proprietors who receive the highest
recommendation from their guests who are also readers of our Guides. If you care to write to us praising
the holiday you have booked through FHG Publications Ltd. – whether this be board, self-catering
accommodation, a sporting or a caravan holiday, what you say will be evaluated and the proprietors who
reach our final list will be contacted.

The winning proprietor will receive an attractive framed diploma to display on his premises as
recognition of a high standard of comfort, amenity and hospitality. FHG Publications Ltd. offer this
diploma as a contribution towards the improvement of standards in tourist accommodation in Britain.
Help your excellent host or hostess to win it!

FHG DIPLOMA

We nominate ....

....

Because

Name ....

Address ....

.... Telephone No. ....

TOGHILL HOUSE FARM

Luxury barn conversions on working farm just 3 miles north of the historic city of Bath. Each cottage is equipped to a very high standard with bed linen provided. You are welcome to roam amongst our many animals and enjoy the outstanding country views or relax in the secluded walled garden. We also provide Bed and Breakfast accommodation in our warm and cosy 17th century farmhouse where all rooms are ensuite with TV and tea making facilities.

Brochure – Tel: 01225 891261; Fax: 01225 892128

David and Jackie Bishop, Toghill House Farm, Freezing Hill, Wick BS15 5RT

Stoneycroft House

Stock Lane, Langford, Bristol,
North Somerset BS18 7EX
Tel: 01934 852624   Mobile: 0973 737441
Proprietor: Mrs Griffin

Superb location, surrounded by open countryside, and set in 27 acres of farmland. Close to the Mendip Hills and only 10 minutes from Bristol Airport. Nearby attractions are the Cheddar Gorge, Wells Cathedral and the historic cities of Bath and Bristol. Sporting facilities and seaside nearby.

Two bedrooms, sitting room, fully fitted kitchen (dishwasher, washing machine, tumble dryer and microwave). Private patio with own garden furniture. Sleeps 4/5. All linen supplied. No smoking. No pets. Furnishings are superb. From £295.

Leigh Farm

Pensford, near Bristol BS18 3HA
Tel: Mendip 01761 490281   Fax: 01761 490270

Leigh Farm is situated between Bath and Bristol, close to Cheddar Gorge, Wells, Blagdon Lake and the Mendip Hills. Large 3 bedroomed Cottage with heavily beamed lounge, sleeping 6 plus baby. The terraced bungalows built in natural stone, with beams, are either one or two bedroomed, with shower room, W.C. and basin. TV is included in all self-catering units and linen may be hired. Large lawns with picnic sets, barbecue. Pony, donkey and rabbits for the children to pet. Coarse fishing pools with carp and tench close to the farmhouse. A wildlife haven is being created around the pools with many species of duck, butterflies, dragonflies etc. Ample floodlit car parking. Payphone. Long weekends, split week bookings at short notice. Plenty of good recommended pubs nearby. Unable to accept pets. Open all year. Some units have night store heating. Highchair, cot available.

Enquiries please telephone or SAE – Mrs Josephine Smart.

BRISTOL near. Mrs C.B. Perry, Cleve Hill Farm, Ubley, Near Bristol BS18 6PG (01761 462410). **Working farm.** This is a family-run dairy farm in beautiful countryside, and visitors are free to explore it at their leisure. The Cider House adjoins the main farmhouse and is on a single level and comprises spacious lounge with colour TV, beamed ceiling and stone chimney breast with a log stove for winter use and electric heaters for those who prefer them; large kitchen/diner with modern pine units, electric cooker, refrigerator, automatic washing machine (tumble dryer in porch), etc.; one double bedroom, one twin-bedded room and a double bed settee in the lounge. Blankets and pillows provided but not linen or towels. Car parking. Obedient pets welcome. Cot and high chair available on request. £1 coin meter for electricity. Terms from £95 to £200 per week.

BURNHAM-ON-SEA near. Mrs W. Baker, Withy Grove Farm, **East Huntspill, Near Burnham-on-Sea TA9 3NP (01278 784471). Properties sleep 4/6.** Come and enjoy a relaxing and friendly holiday "Down on the Farm" set in beautiful Somerset countryside. Peaceful rural setting adjoining River Huntspill, famed for its coarse fishing. The farm is ideally situated for visiting the many local attractions including Cheddar Gorge, Glastonbury, Weston-super-Mare and the lovely sandy beach of Burnham-on-Sea. Self catering barns and cottages are tastefully converted and fully equipped including colour TV. Facilities also include heated swimming pool, licensed bar and entertainment in high season, games room, skittle alley. Reasonable rates. Please write or telephone for further details.

CHARD. Mrs Guppy, Hornsbury Hill Farm, Chard TA20 3DB (01460 65516). Situated on the main A358 road, one and a quarter miles from Chard, this detached farmhouse makes an ideal centre for touring Somerset, Devon and Dorset. The accommodation comprises three double bedrooms, lounge with colour TV, dining room, kitchen with fridge, cooker, etc. Bathroom downstairs with hot and cold water. Cot available, babysitting if required. Several lovely coastal resorts approximately 12 miles away; Cricket St. Thomas Wildlife Park three miles; Forde Abbey Gardens four miles; Arts and Crafts Museum quarter of a mile. General store just down the road. Ample parking. Open Easter to October. Children and pets welcome. Terms from £180 to £210 per week.

CHEDDAR. Kay Richardson, South Barn, The Hayes, Cheddar BS27 3AN (01934 743146). Sleep 4.

Comfortable, self-contained converted stone barn. Secluded off the road position in village centre, five minutes' walk to Gorge with own parking and patio, garden, table and chairs. Fully equipped with colour TV, duvets, microwave, gas oven, heating, etc. Short breaks with optional breakfast available all year or Bed and Breakfast in our own family home with facilities. Non-smoking cottage. Special rates for three or more nights. Further details on request.

CHEDDAR. Mrs K. Thompson, Hillside, Venns Gate, Cheddar BS27 3LW (01934 742493). ♀♀♀

COMMENDED. **Sleep 2/4.** Four comfortable, well maintained, holiday cottages in converted barn and farmhouse, on southern slopes of the Mendips. Sleep two/four persons in one/two bedrooms, some en-suite (extra sofa bed and cot available). All fully equipped including linen, central heating, colour TV and garden furniture. Ample car parking. Cheddar with its famous Gorge, caves and many tourist attractions is within walking distance. Ideally situated for touring West Country, with Bath, Wells, Weston-super-Mare, Bristol and coast all within easy travelling distance. Nearby activities include walking, golfing, fishing, swimming, sailing, riding and caving. Prices from £140 per week Low Season to £280 per week High Season.

EAST COKER, Near Yeovil. Mrs C. Williams, Prymleigh, East Coker, Near Yeovil BA22 9HW (01935 863313). ♀♀♀ *HIGHLY COMMENDED.* **Sleeps 2.** This

bright little two-storey house with two bathrooms is ideal for two people. It is very well furnished and set in our two-thirds acre garden with panoramic views of nearby Dorset hills. Completely rural, on edge of lovely village (church, pub, shop) yet only two miles Yeovil. Sherborne seven miles, Dorset coast 20 miles. The surrounding countryside is really beautiful with many places of interest. Hall, sitting room/diner with French window onto roses and lawn. Colour TV and many books. Well equipped compact modern kitchen, double aspect twin-bedded room. Central heating, electricity and linen included. £140 to £260. Open January to November.

EXFORD. The Edwards Family, Westermill Farm, Exford, Minehead TA24 7NJ (01643 831238; Fax: 01643 831660). ♀/♀♀♀ *COMMENDED.* Try the

excitement of staying in one of our six delightful Scandinavian log cottages on our 500 acre working farm in the centre of Exmoor National Park. Two and a half miles of river for fishing or bathing and four waymarked walks. Our farmhouse cottage and Bracken, Molinia, Whortleberry, Ling, Holly and Gorse log cottages have individual colour schemes. All are comfortable and well equipped having electric cookers, fridges and colour TVs. The log cottages are in sheltered grass paddocks. Dogs are welcome and have their own exercise field.

Discounted price at Wookey Hole Caves and Papermill, Somerset for maximum of six people. For further details see our READERS' OFFER VOUCHER.

EXMOOR. Mrs Jones, Higher Town, Dulverton TA22 9RX (01398 341272). Our property is set in 80 acres of National Park, half a mile from open moorland and visitors are welcome to walk over our beef and sheep farm. The bungalow is situated on its own with lovely views, lawn and parking space. It sleeps six with one bunk-bedded room, double bedroom and one bedroom with two single beds. Bedding, linen and electricity are provided. The bathroom and toilet are separate and the bath also has a shower over. The lounge has an open fire and colour TV, the kitchen has electric cooker, fridge freezer and washer dryer. Centrally heated and double glazed. SAE please for further information.

EXMOOR (Dulverton). Mrs Sally Wade, Liscombe Farm, Winsford, Dulverton TA22 9QA (01643 851551). Liscombe is a mixed farm of 385 acres adjoining Exmoor National Park and close to Tarr Steps. Peaceful spacious farmhouse and converted barns furnished to a high standard with every convenience for a relaxing holiday. Perfect for riding, walking and within easy reach of the beach. The farmhouse sleeps nine plus cot and the barns six plus cot. All are heated, with luxury kitchen, one en suite bedroom, dishwasher, fridge, freezer, washing machine, tumble dryer, microwave, TV, video and hi-fi. Play area, garden and barbecues. Electricity, linen included. Babysitting and stabling for your horse available. Open all year. Prices from £100 to £500. Please telephone for brochure.

GLASTONBURY. Mrs M. Moon, West Town Farm, Baltonsborough, Glastonbury BA6 8QX (01458 850217). Spacious, fully furnished flat in wing of 17th century farmhouse, situated in lovely Somerset countryside. Ideal for touring — Glastonbury, Wells, Cheddar, Wookey, Longleat — and midway between south and north coast seaside resorts. Self contained with own bathroom/toilet. Lounge/diner with TV and electric fire; fitted kitchen with electric cooker, fridge and breakfast bar. One bedroom with double and single beds, washbasin; second bedroom with two single beds, washbasin; cot. Central heating. Large walled garden with lawns. Visitors must supply own linen. Children most welcome. Sorry, no pets. Holder of FHG Diploma. SAE for full details, terms and dates available.

ILMINSTER. Mrs J. Durman, Whitehouse Farm, Rapps, Ilminster TA19 9LH (01460 54417). ♀ ♀ ♀ ♀ Detached fully renovated and modernised Victorian farm cottage with large enclosed garden. Many local attractions and excellent pubs. Relaxing at any time of the year, central for touring. Situated on large estate, the cottage has upstairs two bedrooms, one with 5' divan and the other with twin beds, both have excellent views of farmland. Downstairs there is a comfortable lounge with open fire and colour TV, dining room and a small fully fitted kitchen (microwave, dishwasher, washing machine, tumble dryer, etc), bathroom (suite and shower). Electric wall panel heaters. Linen and towels are provided. Cot/camp bed by arrangement. Electricity is metered (£1 coin). Pets by arrangement.

SOMERSET HAS IT ALL!

Peaceful thatched cottages, stately homes, sandy beaches, breathtaking caves, churches and cathedrals, romantic legends, heather-covered moorland — Somerset has something for everyone! Much of West Somerset lies within Exmoor National Park, and the county's many areas of upland make it ideal for a walking or nature-study holiday.

ILMINSTER. Toll House, 12 Bay Hill, Ilminster. Sleeps 6 plus cot. The Toll House (Grade II) was built in

1816 by the Ilminster Turnpike Trust in the local hamstone and is located at the eastern edge of the town. Recently renovated, it is well appointed yet retains many of its old features. Three double bedrooms (one double with wash-basin, two twin-bedded) and a cot and high chair are available. Bathroom with shower and WC, separate WC downstairs. Well equipped kitchen and utility room, separate living and dining rooms, full central heating and colour TV. Large south-facing garden with open views and ample parking. Pets by arrangement. Available all year. £170 to £320 per week — includes all linen, towels, gas and electricity. Contact: **Mr and Mrs K. Crowhurst, 8 Drakes Way, Portishead, Bristol BS20 9LB (01275 847181).**

MINEHEAD. Mrs N.E. Cobb, Burrow Farm, Wootton Courtenay, Minehead TA24 7UD (01643

841361). Burrow Farm is a thatched Grade II Listed house in the glorious country of the Exmoor National Park about one mile from the village and five miles from the coast. We have a large farmyard with lots of animals, a stream and a donkey for children to ride. The two bedroom wing is let for holidays. It has a pine fitted kitchen with electric cooker, fridge, washing machine, microwave and oil fired central heating boiler, use of a freezer and tumble dryer. The sitting room has a wood burner and dining alcove with glass doors to the garden. Games room with snooker and table tennis. Children and pets welcome. Please phone for brochure.

MINEHEAD. Mrs D. Rusher, Higher Burrow Farm, Timberscombe, Minehead TA24 7UD (01643

841427). ♀ ♀ ♀ *COMMENDED.* This delightful cottage with own garden is set in a small hamlet on quiet country lane, 200 yards from farm with lovely views of this spectacular countryside. Croft was originally two cottages, now made into one offering spacious accommodation for seven. One double room, two twin and a single; large bathroom upstairs, second WC downstairs. Kitchen with Rayburn, electric oven, microwave and automatic washing machine; sitting room with small library, colour TV and log fire; separate dining room. Night storage heaters throughout. Ideal for walkers; riding, fishing and golfing locally. Friday changeover, short breaks taken off season, pets welcome.

NORTON-SUB-HAMDON. Byways, Broadmead Lane, Norton-Sub-Hamdon. Sleeps 4. A pretty,

detached stone cottage, quiet attractive garden front and rear, situated on no-through-road in this tranquil hamstone village with pub, shop and post office within 400 yards. Ideal centre to explore the fine historic houses and delightful gardens or walk in the unspoilt countryside of South Somerset. Large sitting-room, dining room, kitchen, bathroom, one double bedroom and one twin. Linen and towels included. Garage and parking. Regret no pets and no smoking. From £145 to £260 per week. For brochure and further details contact: **Dorothy Jennings, Manor House, Muchelney, Langport, Somerset TA10 0DL (01458 250287).**

PORLOCK. Lucott Farm, Porlock, Minehead. Sleeps 2/10. Isolated farmhouse on Exmoor, with wood burning fireplaces and all modern conveniences. It lies at the head of Horner Valley and guests will delight in the wonderful scenery. Plenty of pony trekking in the area. Ten people accommodated in four double and two single bedrooms, cot; bathroom, two toilets; sittingroom; diningroom. Kitchen has oil-fired Aga and water heater. No linen supplied. Shops three miles; sea four miles. Car essential — parking. Open all year. Terms (including fuel) on application with SAE please to **Mrs E.A. Tucker, West Luccombe Cottage, Porlock, Minehead TA24 8MT (01643 862810).**

Terms quoted in this publication may be subject to increase if rises in costs necessitate

SHEPTON MALLET. Mrs J.A. Boyce, Knowle Farm, West Compton, Shepton Mallet BA4 4PD (01749 890482; Fax: 01749 890405). ♕♕♕♕ COMMENDED. **Working farm. Cottages sleep 2/5/8.**

Knowle Farm Cottages are converted from the old cowstall and stables, set around the old farmyard now laid out as a pleasant garden. Quiet location at the end of a private drive. Excellent views and plenty of wildlife. All cottages furnished to a high standard — bathroom (bath, shower, toilet, washbasin); fully fitted kitchen (automatic washing machine, fridge/freezer, full size cooker). Two cottages have kitchen/diner, separate lounge, colour TV, the other two have kitchen, lounge/diner, colour TV. Cot, high chair by prior arrangement. Bed linen supplied, towels by request. Surrounding area full of interesting places to visit. Good golf courses, fishing, selection of pubs and restaurants. Around the farm plenty of walks, play area for children. Sorry no pets. Terms: low season £145 to £230, high season £160 to £360. Car essential, ample parking. Payphone for guests. Open all year.

SIMONSBATH. Jane and Barry Styles, Wintershead Farm, Simonsbath, Exmoor TA24 7LF (01643 831222; Fax: 01643 831628). ♕♕/♕♕♕♕ HIGHLY COMMENDED. Four tastefully furnished and well equipped spacious cottages offering all the comforts of home, situated in the midst of beautiful Exmoor with panoramic views. The area is ideal for enjoying the country pursuits of walking, riding, fishing or just relaxing while taking in the spectacular scenery. A safe place for children and pets, with a recreation room for those not so sunny days. The cottages sleep from two to six people plus cots. There is also a small bedsit flat for one or two people. All are centrally heated, two also have open fires. Situated 10 miles from Lynmouth, Wintershead makes an ideal base to explore North Devon and Exmoor. From £105 weekly. Short Breaks out of season. Please telephone, fax or write for a colour brochure.

TAUNTON. Mrs Joan Greenway, Woodlands Farm, Bathealton, Taunton TA4 2AH (01984 623271).

You can be assured of a warm and friendly welcome on our family-run dairy farm, with a small carp pond. Children are welcome and will enjoy feeding the animals. We are in the heart of beautiful unspoilt countryside within easy reach of the North and South Coasts and Exmoor. Both the cottage and wing of the farmhouse sleep five people and are furnished to a high standard to enjoy a relaxing holiday. Both kitchens have washing machines, microwaves, etc. Bathrooms with baths and showers. Electricity, central heating and bed linen included in the tariff. Terms from £125 to £285 per week. Please write or phone for colour brochure.

TAUNTON. Liz Smith, Holly Cottage, Stoke St. Gregory, Taunton TA3 6HS (01823 490828). ♕♕♕♕ HIGHLY COMMENDED. **Sleeps 4/6.** Converted barn on a small arable farm near the Somerset Levels; the peat moors are an area of special scientific interest — rich in wildlife, especially birds. There are many attractions within easy reach: Glastonbury, the Quantocks, Yeovilton, beaches on the north and south coasts. There are several pubs serving good food within walking distance. Riding, fishing and cycling may be enjoyed locally. The cottages are clean, comfortable and well equipped. Games barn. Heating and linen provided. Pets welcome. Terms from £150 to £350. Please write or phone for a brochure. Three-day breaks at short notice. Reduction for two or more weeks.

TIMBERSCOMBE. Mrs S.M. Derby, Oaktrow Farm, Timberscombe, Minehead TA24 7UF (01643 841373). ♕♕♕/♕♕♕♕ **Working farm, join in.** Two single storey cottages adjoining farmhouse in an "L" shape. The larger sleeps up to six and the smaller sleeps two. Oaktrow Farm is a Welsh Cob Stud and sheep farm set in Exmoor National Park with spectacular views and plenty of walks and rides. Guests can bring their horses and dogs by arrangement. Plenty of wildlife can be seen on the farm and lots of small animals for children. Situated just half a mile from the A396. Weekly terms from £105 to £275.

WEDMORE. Mrs J. Tucker, Court Farm, Mudgley, Wedmore BS28 4TY (01934 712367). ♀♀♀♀ *HIGHLY COMMENDED.* **Cottages sleep 2/5. Working farm.** Wedmore is a charming Georgian village with historic connections, pleasant shops, banks, post office etc. Cheddar, Wells and Glastonbury are a short drive away. Accommodation is situated on dairy farm one and a half miles from the village, in a delightful converted stone-built barn called 'Hayloft Cottage'. It commands superb views over Somerset levels to Polden Hills and consists of spacious superbly equipped fitted kitchen/diner, a large lounge with colour TV. One double room with adjoining bathroom and a twin bedded room with adjoining shower room. Bed linen supplied. Cot, highchair available. Ample parking. Central heating, electricity included. Open March to New Year. Rates from £185 to £400. Regret no pets. First class stamp for brochure.

WELLS near. Mr T.R. Millard, Double Gate Farm, Godney, Near Wells BA5 1RZ (01458 832217; Fax: 01458 835612). THE OLD CART HOUSE: is a first floor barn conversion with lovely views of the Mendip Hills and Glastonbury Tor. Offers excellent well equipped accommodation. Heating, electricity and bed linen included. Ground floor games room, open to all residents with full-size snooker table, table tennis, darts, etc. Ideal base for touring, cycling, birdwatching and fishing. Village inn nearby for those days when you don't want to cook! Open all year. Bed and Breakfast accommodation also available. Please write or telephone for further details.

DOUBLE-GATE FARM.
GODNEY. NR. WELLS. SOMT.

WIVELISCOMBE near. Oddwell and Cridland Cottages, Brompton Ralph, Near Wiveliscombe. ♀♀♀ *COMMENDED.* **ETB and WCTB APPROVED. Cottages each sleep 7.** Charming 300 year old cottages with beamed ceilings and inglenook fireplaces for cosy open fires, standing in peaceful and unspoilt countryside at foot of Brendon Hills. Equipped for seven, plus a cot in each. Two bedrooms, one with three single beds, other with double bed; bed/sitting room with double bed/settee; bathroom, toilet, with extra toilet/washbasin upstairs in Oddwell and downstairs in Cridland; dining/living room; kitchen with oil-fired Rayburn (in Oddwell only), both with electric cooker, fridge, iron, toaster, spin-dryer, etc; separate larder in Oddwell. Available all year, indoor games and books provided. Cot, high chair. Trout fishing, riding, walking, pony trekking. Nine miles to sea and half a mile to shop/post office. Car essential, ample parking; garage in keeping with

character of cottage. Pets by arrangement. Weekly terms from £120 to £260. **Adrian and Pippa Blizzard, Talgarth, Bentley, Near Farnham, Surrey GU10 5LN (01420 23839).**

STAFFORDSHIRE

ABBOTS BROMLEY. John Myatt, Priory Farm Fishing House, Priory Farm, Blithbury, Rugeley WS15 3JA (01889 504269). ♀♀♀ Working farm. Tastefully converted, listed 18th century fishing house overlooking the picturesque River Blithe, offers unique accommodation for up to four persons on secluded dairy farm. Ideal for lovers of the countryside and wildlife. Badger watching can usually be arranged as well as bird watching on the beautiful Blithfield Reservoir. The farm is convenient for visitors to Cannock Chase, Lichfield, Alton Towers and the Peak District. Comfortable accommodation includes large bed-sitting room with colour TV, modern kitchen and shower room. Terms from £70 to £120 per week. Open all year. Well behaved pets welcome. Brochure on request.

LEEK. Edith and Alwyn Mycock, Lower Berkhamsytch Farm, Bottom House, Near Leek ST13 7QP (01538 308213). ♀♀♀ APPROVED. Sleep 6 plus cot. Two tastefully converted flats with their own private entrance, each sleeping six plus cot, on traditional family-run stock rearing and pig farm, within walking distance of two pubs serving meals and a "Little Chef" restaurant. Central to Alton Towers, Potteries and Peak District. One double bedroom, one twin-bedded room and double bed settee in lounge. Colour TV. Shower room and toilet. Sitting area. Children welcome, cot and high chair available; children's play area. Well behaved pets welcome. Visitors can walk in the fields. Guests are offered a warm welcome by the owners who are on hand to help in any way. Terms from £100 to £195 per week, electricity included.

SUFFOLK

BAYLHAM. Ann Storer, Baylham House Farm Annexe & Flat, Mill Lane, Baylham IP6 8LG (01473 830264). ♛ ♛ ♛ ♛ *COMMENDED.* Two self-contained units in old farmhouse, sleeping four plus cot, and two plus cot. Small rare breeds farm on River Gipping with sheep, cattle, poultry, pigs and goats. Peaceful setting, good walks, good touring base. Fishing, garden, barbecue. Both fully equipped to high standard. Children welcome. Sorry no pets. Open all year. Please phone or write for further details.

KESSINGLAND. Kessingland Cottages, Rider Haggard Lane, Kessingland. Sleeps 8. An exciting three-bedroom recently built semi-detached cottage situated on the beach, three miles south of sandy beach at Lowestoft. Fully and attractively furnished with colour TV and delightful sea and lawn views from floor to ceiling windows of lounge. Accommodation for up to eight people. Well-equipped kitchen with electric cooker, fridge, electric immersion heater. Electricity by 50p meter. Luxurious bathroom with coloured suite. No linen or towels provided. Only a few yards to beach and sea fishing. One mile to wildlife country park with mini-train. Buses quarter-of-a-mile and shopping centre half-a-mile. Parking, but car not essential. Children and disabled persons welcome. Available 1st March to 7th January. Weekly terms from £50 in early March and late December to £195 in peak season. SAE to **Mr S. Mahmood, 156 Bromley Road, Beckenham, Kent BR3 6PG (0181-650 0539).**

SAXMUNDHAM. Mrs Mary Kitson, White House Farm, Sibton, Saxmundham IP17 2NE (01728 660260). Working farm. Sleeps 4/6 adults; 2/4 children. The flat is a self-contained part of late Georgian farmhouse standing in 130 acres of quiet farmland with a variety of livestock. Fishing on farm. Accommodation in three double bedrooms (two double/two single beds) plus cot; livingroom with TV; shower/toilet on first floor. Entrance hall, kitchen/diner on ground floor. Full central heating. Situated one-and-a-half miles from village shops, etc. Ten miles from coast at Dunwich, Minsmere Bird Sanctuary, Snape Maltings. Linen optional. Pets permitted. Car essential — parking. Available all year. Terms from £130 to £180 per week. SAE, please, for further details.

STANSFIELD. Plough Hill Bungalow, Stansfield, Sudbury. Sleeps 4. Plough Hill Bungalow, with attractive garden to front, is situated in a small village with pub, within 15 miles of Sudbury, Gainsborough's birthplace, Newmarket Racecourse and historic Bury St. Edmunds, Long Melford and Lavenham. At picturesque Clare, five miles distant, there are good shopping facilities. The Bungalow is well equipped to accommodate four people in two twin-bedded rooms, sittingroom, kitchen/diner with electric cooker, fridge, cutlery and crockery. Colour TV. Bathroom, toilet. Car essential, parking. Children and pets welcome; cot available. Solid fuel heating or electric fires. Linen supplied on request. Open all year round at very reasonable rates. Terms from £57 to £102 per week. For further details send SAE to **Mrs M. Winch, Plough House, Stansfield, Sudbury CO10 8LT (01284 789253).**

WALSHAM-LE-WILLOWS. Bridge Cottage, Walsham-le-Willows, Near Bury St. Edmunds. ♛ ♛ ♛ *APPROVED.* **Sleeps 5.** Bridge Cottage is illustrated in the book "English Cottages", with introduction by John Betjeman. Built in the 17th century it has been attractively modernised. There are fitted carpets and comfortable beds; centrally heated and well furnished. The kitchen is well equipped with electric cooker and fridge. Plenty of hot water. Children and well behaved pets are welcome. Electricity and heating included in rent. Colour TV. Tennis court and swimming pool available in summer by arrangement. Walsham-le-Willows is in the centre of East Anglia (11 miles from Bury St. Edmunds) and has shops and post office. Available all year. Terms from £190 to £250. **Mrs H.M. Russell, The Beeches, Walsham-le-Willows, Near Bury St. Edmunds IP31 3AD (01359 259227; Fax: 01359 258206).**

Terms quoted in this publication may be subject to increase if rises in costs necessitate

SUSSEX

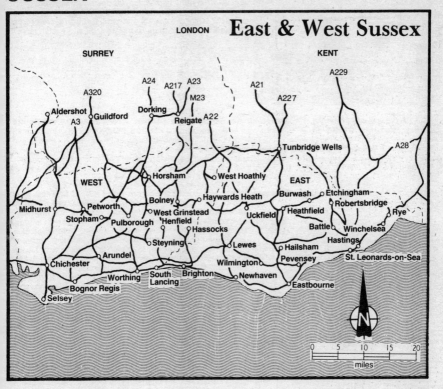

EAST SUSSEX

BATTLE. Mrs Brenda Ware, 2 Loose Farm Barns, Hastings Road, Battle TN33 0TG (Tel & Fax: 01424 773829). Sleeps 5.  Great Barn, a converted stone farm building, is quietly situated at the end of a farm lane, one third of a mile from the main road. There are panoramic views and country walks from the building. The seaside is 15 minutes away.This open plan apartment has been decorated and furnished to a high standard with a well equipped kitchen, bathroom with shower, central heating; access independent of the main building. There is a colour TV, radio, washing machine and a swing from one of the high beams. All linen supplied. Details, maps and photographs on request. From £210 per week.

BEACHY HEAD. Mrs J.A. Higgs, Black Robin Farm, Beachy Head, Eastbourne BN20 7XX (01323 643357). Two self contained farm bungalows, each sleeping six in two twin rooms and one double room. Colour TV in lounge, fully carpeted and full central heating. Cooking, hot water and heating is run on gas which is on a meter and read at end of your holiday. Situated down our farm drive overlooking the Downs. A five minute drive takes you into Eastbourne, close to theatres, cinemas, beach, golf course, etc. Excellent walks over the Downs. You are more than welcome to walk around the farm — lambing times January, March and April. Children welcome, cots and high chairs supplied. Dogs welcome. All bed linen provided free of charge. Open all year. Further details available on request.

DANEHILL. Jean and David Salmon, Sliders Farm, Furners Green, Uckfield TN22 3RT (01825 790258; Fax: 01825 790125). Sliders Farm offers a converted 16th century barn which has been tastefully converted to allow an open plan lounge, dining and kitchen area on the first floor while the double and twin bedrooms are on the ground floor. The cottage is on one level and is still part of the original barn, having two bedrooms, one twin, one double; large lounge with bed settee and sunny kitchen. Both properties have colour TV and central heating; use of swimming pool, tennis court and fishing lakes. Close to Sheffield Park Gardens, Bluebell Railway, Ardingly Show Ground; Brighton, Gatwick 30 minutes by car. Terms from £280 to £450 per week. Bed and Breakfast also available in the main house.

HASTINGS. Mrs D. Beynon, C/o Havelock Accommodation Service, Cross Wing, 72 All Saints Street, Hastings (01424 436779; evenings and weekends 0181-399 9605). This charming small cottage is the southern "cross wing" of a 15th century Hall House. It stands at the heart of Hastings Old Town, just off the sea front and fishing quarter with the new Sea Life Centre. The cottage sleeps three, has a new oak fitted kitchen and a colour TV and stereo. Children and well behaved pets are welcome. Linen is supplied at £5 per week if required. The sandy beach at Camber, the battle site and ancient Cinque Ports are all within easy reach and there are many local walks. From £130 to £220 per week.

NUTLEY. 2 Victoria Cottage, c/o Hole and Alchorne Farm, Bell Lane, Nutley TN22 3PD (Tel & Fax: 01825 712475). ♀ ♀ ♀ ♀ *HIGHLY COMMENDED.* **Sleeps 5 plus baby.** A warm welcome awaits you at our comfortable, well appointed semi-detached cottage, with lovely garden, on our dairy farm, near Ashdown Forest. Accommodation comprises three bedrooms (one double, one twin and one single); bathroom and separate WC; sittingroom with TV and telephone; diningroom; kitchen with electric cooker, microwave, fridge, washing machine and tumble dryer. Beds made up. Ideal base for visiting South Downs, castles and coast. Children welcome. Terms from £160 to £280 per week.

POLEGATE, near Alfriston. Lakeside Farm Holiday Bungalows. Sleeps 4 to 6. Lakeside Farm is situated on the edge of Arlington Reservoir, with views of the South Downs. Eastbourne, Brighton and Lewes within 15 miles, Drusillas Zoo two miles, shopping half a mile. Modern comfortable accommodation, two double rooms, lounge with colour TV, dining area, bathroom, toilet. Well equipped kitchen with electric cooker, microwave, fridge. Duvets on all beds. Open April to October. Car essential, parking. Suitable for disabled guests. Children welcome, cot and high chair available. Well controlled pets accepted. Electric heating. Weekly terms from £160. Electricity included. **Mrs P. Boniface, Lakeside Farm, Arlington, Polegate BN26 6SB (01323 870111).**

ST. LEONARDS-ON-SEA. Rose Marine House, 132 Marina, St. Leonards-on-Sea TN38 0BN (Tel & Fax: 01424 715269 or 01424 438059). For peace of mind, free from every day life's worries, come and have an enjoyable holiday, mini break or on business. We are open all year round including Christmas and New Year. All our flats have a sea view of gardens, plus putting green, bowls, etc. We have our own parking area for guests. Fire escape at rear. Close to town shops and local railway stations; regular bus service. Large lounges/bedrooms, all with showers/shaver. Duvets/covers, sheets etc can be provided. Kitchens have fridge/freezers, microwaves, etc; washing machine and dryer service available at small charge. Many places of interest to visit. Suitable for any age group (children 10 years plus). Pets welcome. Prices: out of season £130; in season £260.

UCKFIELD. John Francis, Whitehouse Farm, Horney Common, Nutley, Ashdown Forest TN22 3EE (01825 712377). ♀♀♀ COMMENDED. Sleep 4.

Whitehouse Farm Holiday Homes are situated on a small working farm overlooking the beautiful Ashdown Forest, home of that fictional bear Winnie the Pooh. An ideal place for a varied holiday. National Trust properties, castles and gardens abound, and London, Brighton and the coast are within easy reach. Sleeping four with full central heating, double glazing and showers. Large lounge/diners leading to individual patios. Newly installed colour TV and cassette recorders. Full pine kitchens with washer/dryers, fridge/freezers, slow cookers and coffeemakers. Personalised parking. Pets welcome. Full linen supplied. Heating and cots free. Weekly terms from £199 to £371. Brochure on request.

WEST SUSSEX

HENFIELD. The Holiday Flat and Cottage, New Hall, Small Dole, Henfield BN5 9YJ (01273 492546). ♀♀♀ COMMENDED. New Hall is the manor house of Henfield, it stands in three and a half acres of mature gardens, surrounded by farmland with abundant footpaths. The holiday cottage is the original 1600 AD farmhouse. It has one en suite bedroom with large living room with a folding bed, dining room and kitchen. A door opens into the walled garden. Holiday flat is the upper part of the dairy wing. Its front door opens from a Georgian courtyard. It has three bedrooms sleeping five, lounge/diner, kitchen and bathroom. Both units are fully equipped and comfortably furnished. Children welcome. Open all year. Terms from £120 to £270 per week. Send SAE for details, or phone **Mrs M.W. Carreck.**

MIDHURST. The Coach House, Bepton, Midhurst GU29 0HZ (01730 812351). In a peaceful rural setting 10 miles north of Chichester, at the foot of the South Downs. Garden Flat and Flatlet, offering weekly or daily terms, repectively. Both are very well furnished and have beautiful views. The double-bedded studio flat has its own entrance and private patio, and includes a fully fitted kitchen (with microwave). The spacious twin-bedded flatlet is at one end of the house and has a sitting/dining room area near the window as well as a side unit incorporating microwave, kettle, toaster and fridge (there is no separate kitchen so servicing of crockery, etc is included). Both the flat and flatlet have their own parking space, colour TV and spacious shower room/WC. Terms from £95 to £150 per week or £20 to £25 per night. Please telephone for further details and photographs.

The Coach House

STORRINGTON. Byre Cottages. Working farm. ETB ♀♀♀♀ Sleep 2/6. Attractive conversion of stables into four self-contained cottages, situated in rural location on working farm. Good walking district with South Downs Way going through farm one and a half miles from Storrington and eight miles from Worthing. Each cottage has central heating and is well equipped; use of outdoor swimming pool. Laundry/drying room and payphone. Gas and electricity charges extra. Prices range from £90 per week in winter for the one bedroomed cottage to £240 per week in July/August for the three bedroomed cottage. No pets but kennels are available for dogs. Contact: **Mr and Mrs Kittle, Sullington Manor Farm, Storrington RH20 4AE (01903 745754).**

WARWICKSHIRE

LEAMINGTON SPA. Mr T.M. Tutton, Post Box Cottage, Avon Dasset, Leamington Spa CV33 0AP

(01295 690224). Sleeps 2. Pretty cottage annexe, part of a 16th century Grade II Listed cottage, close to the Burton Dasset Country Park. Five miles M40 Junction 12 and within easy reach of the Cotswolds, Stratford-upon-Avon, Warwick, Banbury and Leamington Spa. The annexe is completely self contained with its own garden entrance. It has an attic bedroom (double) via tiny stairs, living area with colour TV, kitchenette with hob, microwave and fridge, ground floor full bathroom with shower, separate dressing area. Available throughout the year; weekends and weekly breaks. Terms from £75 to £170 inclusive of linen and towels.

Warwickshire Farm Holidays

Warwickshire farming families welcome guests into their homes to enjoy the comforts of a traditional English farmhouse and discover the peace of the English countryside. Each home listed has it own unique character and differs in size, style, and price, but all offer a high standard of accommodation, good food, a warm welcome and excellent value for money to holidaymakers and business travellers. All owners are members of the Farm Holiday Bureau, all properties are inspected, classified and graded by the English Tourist Board. Warwickshire, in the heart of England, provides the perfect setting for the perfect holiday. Mile upon mile of rolling countryside, picturesque villages and meandering waterways. There are castles, stately homes, theatres, country gardens and some of the prettiest villages to be found.

FARM HOLIDAY BUREAU

Places to visit within easy reach include Stratford-upon-Avon, Warwick, Royal Leamington Spa, The Cotswolds, Oxford, Coventry. National Exhibition Centre and National Agricultural Centre.

For further details about Bed & Breakfast or Self-catering cottages, please write, telephone or fax for a free brochure to: Warwickshire Farm Holidays (FHG), Crandon House, Avon Dassett, Leamington Spa CV33 0AA. Tel/Fax: 01295 770652.

STRATFORD-UPON-AVON. Meadow View Cottage. Sleeps 4. Immaculate detached holiday bungalow,

two and a half miles from Stratford, surrounded by open countryside, near to owner's property. Lounge/diner, colour TV. Fully fitted kitchen with electric cooker and fridge, shower room; all towels provided. Two attractive bedrooms, one with double bed, one with twin beds, matching bed linen and drapes, all bed linen provided. Carpeted, double glazed, heating in all rooms. Patio with garden furniture, overlooking fields, south facing. Ample secure parking. 50p meter for electricity. No smoking. No pets. Convenient for Cotswolds, Stow on the Wold, Broadway, Oxford, Worcester, Malvern Hills, Warwick Castle, Blenheim Palace and much more. Open all year. £140 to £250 per week inclusive of towels and bed linen. Details from **Mrs Sue Cox, Spring Farm House, Warwick Road, Blackhill, Stratford-upon-Avon CV37 0PZ (01789 731046).**

STRATFORD-UPON-AVON. Lilian Court, off Vincent Avenue. Sleeps 4/6. A select development of two-bedroom flats and three-bedroom chalet bungalows, half a mile from Shakespeare's birthplace. Fully equipped kitchens with washing machine, dishwasher, fridge, freezer and microwave oven. Electric shower. Electric central heating to flats, gas to bungalows. Colour TV. Twin or double beds available. En suite bathrooms in bungalows. Fitted carpets throughout. Linen available. Small landscaped garden to bungalows and patio area to flats, each with barbecue facilities. Adequate car parking. No pets. No smoking. £300 to £500 per week. **Mr Fraser, 21 Vincent Avenue, Stratford-Upon-Avon CV37 6SR (01789 269572).**

Two persons admitted for the price of one when visiting HATTON COUNTRY WORLD, near Warwick. Our READERS' OFFER VOUCHER gives full details.

STRATFORD-UPON-AVON. Knightcote Farm Cottages, The Bake House, Knightcote, Near Leamington Spa CV33 0SF (01295 770637; Fax: 01295 770135). Working farm. Three newly converted luxury self-catering farm cottages, each sleeping four to six people. En suite facilities in master bedrooms, well equipped kitchens, fitted carpets, colour TV, phone, gas central heating, separate patio gardens, large car park adjacent to the cottages. The perfect location for a peaceful and relaxing holiday. The cottages stand in 500 acres of working farm land, on the edge of quiet and historic village of Knightcote, nestling in the beautiful countryside of South Warwickshire, in the "Heart of Shakespeare Country". Excellent touring or business base, M40 (Junction 12) two miles, Warwick nine miles, Banbury 10 miles, Stratford 15 miles, easy reach of Birmingham, Oxford and London. One cottage suitable for disabled guests and wheelchair users. Dogs welcome. Non smokers only.

WILTSHIRE

CALNE near. Mrs Janet Tyler, Home Farm Barn and The Derby, Home Farm, Heddington, Near Calne SN11 0PL (Tel & Fax: 01380 850523). ♀♀♀♀ COMMENDED. **Sleep 5/2.** Home Farm is a dairy and arable farm with its own private lake, panoramic views and unbeatable downland walks in small village. Riding school and golf course adjoin farm. The 17th century barn traditionally furnished sleeps five. Also stable conversion, bungalow-style, sleeps 2. Set in paved courtyard with Victorian lamp. Quiet idyllic spot. Children welcome. Terms from £150 to £340 per week. Colour brochure available.

DEVIZES. Miss M.I. Marks, Mulberry Lodge House, Rowde, Devizes SN10 2QQ (01380 723056). ♀♀ APPROVED. **Sleeps 5/6.** Come and relax in "GLORIOUS WILTSHIRE, PEACEFUL COUNTRYSIDE", Devizes two miles. Self contained, warm, cosy, fully equipped furnished flat with panoramic views on first and second floors in wing of Georgian house (own entrance). Children welcome. Large bedroom, double and single beds (first floor), second bedroom (curtain divided, with two windows), three single beds, cot and high chair; bathroom with shower, toilet; sitting/dining room; TV; electric fires; kitchen, electric cooker, fridge, spin dryer; £1 meter. Night storage heating in bedrooms and dining room. This seven acre farm is on the fringe of village. Ideal touring centre for historic places — Avebury, Longleat, Salisbury, Stonehenge. Fishing, shops and village. Canal trips. Ample parking. Sorry, no smoking and no pets. Weekly terms from £80 to £155 April to September. Weekend Breaks. SAE, please, for colour brochure.

MALMESBURY. Mrs Edwards, Stonehill Farm, Charlton, Malmesbury SN16 9DY (01666 823310). ♀♀♀ COMMENDED. **Sleeps 2/3.** Superbly located on the edge of the Cotswolds in lush rolling countryside and only 15 minutes from the M4 (Junction 16 or 17). John and Edna invite you to stay with them on their dairy farm in a relaxed friendly atmosphere, where pets and children are welcome. North of the county on the border with Gloucestershire making it ideal for business or pleasure. Two pretty, well equipped converted farm buildings, warm, cosy and private. Bedroom, bathroom, kitchen and lounge. From £150 to £210 per week.

YORKSHIRE

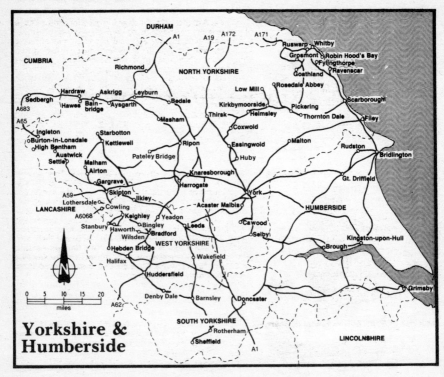

Yorkshire & Humberside

EAST YORKSHIRE

FOXHOLES. Manor Farm Cottage, Foxholes, Near Driffield. ♀♀♀♀ *COMMENDED.* **Working farm. Sleeps 7.** Manor Farm Cottage is a detached brick cottage with garage and enclosed garden in small Wolds village 12 miles from East Coast and within easy drive to Yorkshire Moors and York. Three double bedrooms accommodating seven. Bathroom, toilet, sittingroom with colour TV and open fireplace with electric fire. Diningroom. Fully equipped electric kitchen. Immersion heater in bathroom. Economy 7 heating. Open from May to October. Pets welcome. Terms from £170 to £200 per week. SAE, please, for terms and further details to **Mrs M. Lamplough, Manor Farm, Foxholes, Near Driffield YO25 0QH (01262 470255; Fax: 01262 470555).**

PUBLISHER'S NOTE

While every effort is made to ensure accuracy, we regret that FHG Publications cannot accept responsibility for errors, omissions or misrepresentation in our entries or any consequences thereof. Prices in particular should be checked because we go to press early. We will follow up complaints but cannot act as arbiters or agents for either party.

NORTH YORKSHIRE

ASKRIGG. Fern Croft, 2 Mill Lane, Askrigg. Sleeps 4. A modern cottage enjoying quiet location on edge of village with open fields rising immediately behind. Attractive and compact, this Wensleydale village is an ideal centre for Dales, with facilities for everyday needs, including two shops, post office, restaurant and a couple of pubs. Furnished to a high standard for four, ground floor accommodation comprises large comfortable lounge/diner with colour TV and well equipped kitchen. Upstairs there are two double bedrooms with a double and twin beds respectively, and modern bathroom. Storage heating included, other electricity by meter. Regret no pets. Terms from £95 to £210 weekly. Brochure: **Mr and Mrs K. Dobson (01689 838450).**

ASKRIGG. Mrs Kate Empsall, Whitfield, Helm, Askrigg, Near Leyburn DL8 3JF (Tel & Fax: 01969 650565). ♀ ♀ ♀ *COMMENDED.* Traditional Dales cottage facing southwards in a quiet road, 100m from the Herriot Bar from "All Creatures Great and Small" BBC series, two shops, close to waterfalls, river and fell walks. Lynburn has a cosy sitting room with dining area, beamed ceiling, colour TV; well kept kitchen has electric cooker, microwave oven and fridge. There is a double and twin bedded room. The bathroom contains a cubicle shower and bath. Storage heaters, electric fire, bed linen and towels are included in the rent £130 to £275 per week. Children and well behaved dogs welcome. Strictly non-smoking.

ASKRIGG/WENSLEYDALE. Mrs E. Scarr, Coleby Hall, Askrigg, Leyburn DL8 3DX (01969 650216). Working farm. Sleeps 5 plus cot. Situated in Wensleydale, half a mile from Bainbridge and one mile from Askrigg, Coleby Hall is a 17th century gabled farmhouse with stone mullioned windows, the west end being to let. A stone spiral staircase leads to two bedrooms; linen provided. The kitchen is equipped with electric cooker, fridge, crockery, etc., and coal fire. The lounge has an inglenook coal fire and metered TV. Oil-fired central heating throughout. Coleby has lovely views and is an ideal situation for walking, fishing and driving round the Yorkshire Dales. Children and pets welcome. Terms from £140 to £150 per week.

COVERDALE. Mrs Caroline Harrison, Hill Top Farm and Livery Yard, West Scrafton, Leyburn DL8 4RU (01969 640663). ♀ ♀ ♀ ♀ *HIGHLY COMMENDED.* **Working farm. Properties sleep 4/6.** Relax in our recently converted traditional Dales stone barns with panoramic views of Rova Crag and open moorland. This peaceful hamlet nestles in the heart of the Yorkshire Dales National Park, Herriot country. The properties' fully equipped kitchens and modern en suite bathrooms retain much character with original exposed beams and open fireplaces. Facilities include central heating, log fires, colour TVs, dishwashers, automatic washing machines, fridges, deep freeze facilities, microwaves, electric cookers, fitted carpets throughout. Linen provided. Games room. Pets corner with pony. Ideal for children, walkers or relaxing. Livery yard with qualified registered instructor. BHF book of bridling provided. Fishing, shooting. Comprehensive brochure provided.

FHG PUBLICATIONS LIMITED publish a large range of well-known accommodation guides. We will be happy to send you details or you can use the order form at the back of this book.

EASINGWOLD. Mrs Rachel Ritchie, The Old Rectory, Thormanby, Easingwold, York YO6 3NN (01845 501417). The Old Rectory's Coach House and Stable have been lovingly converted into two holiday cottages and enjoy a delightful setting in a quiet country lane, just out of the small village of Thormanby (three miles north of Easingwold). It is an excellent base for visiting York (17 miles), the North Yorkshire Moors to the east and Dales to the west. There are many country houses, abbeys and castles in the area. Stable Cottage has one double and one twin-bedded rooms plus cot. The Coach House has one double and two twin rooms plus cot. They are fully equipped. All linen and towels provided. Colour TV, open fires (fuel supplied). Night storage heaters when required. Children and well behaved pets welcome. Electricity by meter reading. Open all year. From £130 weekly. SAE for brochure.

GRASSINGTON near. Mrs Judith M. Joy, Jerry and Ben's, Hebden, Skipton BD23 5DL (01756 752369; Fax: 01756 753370). Properties sleep 3/6/8/9. Jerry and Ben's stands in two acres of grounds in one of the most attractive parts of the Yorkshire Dales National Park. Seven properties; Ghyll Cottage (sleeps eight); Mamie's Cottage (sleeps eight); Paradise End (sleeps six); Robin Middle (sleeps six); High Close (sleeps nine); Cruck Rise (sleeps six); Raikes Side (sleeps two/three). All have parking, electric cooker, microwave, toaster, fridge, colour TV, electric heating and immersion heater; lounge, dining area, bathroom with shower; cots if required. Fully equipped, including linen if requested. Washing machine and telephone available. Well behaved pets accepted. Open all year. Fishing and bathing close by. Terms from £80. SAE, please for detailed brochure. Suitable for some disabled guests.

HARDRAW. Cissy's Cottage, Hardraw, Hawes. Sleeps 4. A delightful 18th century cottage of outstanding character. Situated in the village of Hardraw with its spectacular waterfall and Pennine Way. Market town of Hawes one mile. This traditional stone built cottage retains many original features including beamed ceilings and an open fire. Sleeping four in comfort, it has been furnished and equipped to a high standard using antique pine and Laura Ashley prints. Equipped with dishwasher, microwave and tumble dryer. Outside, a south-facing garden, sun patio with garden furniture, and a large enclosed paddock make it ideal for children. Cot and high chair if required. Open all year. Terms £95-£250 include coal, electricity and trout fishing. For brochure, contact **Mrs Belinda Metcalfe, Southolme Farm, Little Smeaton, Northallerton DL6 2HJ (01609 881302).**

HARROGATE. Mrs Janet Hollings, Dougill Hall, Summerbridge, Harrogate HG3 4JR (01423 780277). ♥♥♥/♥♥♥♥ up to *COMMENDED.* **Working farm. Sleeps 4.** Dougill Hall Flat occupies the top floor of the Hall, which is of Georgian design, built in 1722 by the Dougill family who lived on this farm from 1496 to 1803. It is in Nidderdale, half a mile from the village of Summerbridge, just by the River Nidd, where there is fishing available for visitors. There are good facilities for horse riding, tennis, swimming, squash, etc. Well situated for the walking enthusiast and within easy reach of the Dales, the beautiful and ancient city of York, Fountains Abbey, How Stean Gorge and many other places of interest. The flat sleeps up to four people. Well equipped, with electric cooker and fridge, iron, vacuum cleaner. Linen by arrangement. Pets permitted. Car essential, parking. The old Cooling House flat attached to the house is now available and sleeps four. Terms £119 — £200. Bring your own horse — stables, hay and grazing available. SAE, please, for details.

NORTH YORKSHIRE – RICH IN TOURIST ATTRACTIONS!

Dales, moors, castles, abbeys, cathedrals – you name it and you're almost sure to find it in North Yorkshire. Leading attractions include Castle Howard, the moorlands walks at Goathland, the Waterfalls at Falling Foss, Skipton, Richmond, Wensleydale, Bridestones Moor, Ripon Cathedral, Whitby, Settle and, of course, York itself.

Harrogate/Yorkshire Dales ... in peaceful and private woodland setting
Helme Pasture Cottages & Lodges up to 🎗🎗🎗🎗 HIGHLY COMMENDED

*Two charming **cottages** (combine into one big house)
*One delightful and quiet **Private Suite** for two
*Three genuine **Scandinavian lodges**
*Superb **quality**, linen included
***Area of Outstanding Natural Beauty**
*Wealth of attractions, **rural villages, floral town**
*Rich in **abbeys, castles and markets**
*Attractive hill, valley and woodland walks
***Welcome Host** Award; **David Bellamy** Silver Award; **Pets** welcome
***Open all year** with **short breaks** and **special offers**
*Parking, payphone, barbecue. Prices from £115-£415 per week

Brochure from **Rosemary Helme, Helme Pasture, Old Spring Wood, Hartwith Bank,**
Summerbridge, Harrogate, North Yorkshire HG3 4DR. Tel: 01423 780279; Fax 01423 780994.

HAWES. River View, Dyers Garth, Hawes. Sleeps 6. A spacious three-bedroomed terraced cottage, River View is situated in a cul-de-sac overlooking "Duerley Beck", an attractive trout stream which runs through Hawes, a market town in the centre of Yorkshire Dales National Park and on the Pennine Way. The cottage has the benefit of storage heaters and also an open coal fire for out of season lets which is an attraction. An ideal situation for walking, fishing and visits to local scenic attractions which include Hardrow Scar, Aysgarth Falls and National Carriage Museum, Castle Bolton; the Lake District is approximately 30 miles away. The cottage accommodates six plus baby (cot); three double bedrooms, bathroom, lounge with colour TV and fully equipped kitchen/diner. Shops 30 yards. Parking space for one car. SAE, please, for terms to **Mrs Sheila Alderson, "Inverdene," Hawes DL8 2NJ (01969 667408).**

HAWNBY. Mrs Sue Smith, Laskill Farm, Hawnby, Near Helmsley YO6 5BN (01439 798268).

🎗🎗🎗🎗 COMMENDED. Two newly converted upmarket cottages, "The Forge" sleeping six people and "The Smithy" sleeping four people, each with inglenook fireplace, dishwasher, washing machine, microwave, etc. Retaining lots of character situated round the courtyard on a 600 acre farm. Peaceful, rural retreat in glorious countryside, large gardens with own lake and fishing. Also "Ceadda Cottages" offer luxurious yet cosy accommodation in tiny hamlet just off maket town of Kirkby Moorside near Pickering. Three warm spacious cottages sleeping two to five people with beautiful views all round offering peace and tranquillity in North Yorkshire Moors National Park and yet near to the coast and York. All cottages have washing machine, microwaves, etc., and lovely gardens. Please write or phone for further details.

HELMSLEY. Mr and Mrs Wainwright, Sproxton Hall Farm Cottages, Sproxton, Helmsley YO6 5EQ (01439 770225; Fax: 01439 771373). 🎗🎗🎗🎗 HIGHLY

COMMENDED. Award-winning conversions of 17th century stone barns providing five self-contained cottages, accommodating three/eight people. Lovingly and imaginatively restored and furnished to an exceptionally high standard, whilst retaining an atmosphere of character and charm. A haven of peace and tranquillity amidst idyllic countryside with superb views. On family farm, one and a half miles south of Helmsley on edge of North Yorkshire Moors. Central heating, log fires, linen and towels, colour TV, laundry facilities, payphone. South-facing gardens with barbecue area. Regret, no dogs. Cottage suitable for disabled visitors. B&B in farmhouse also available. Brochure on request.

FREE and REDUCED RATE Holiday Visits!
See our READERS' OFFER VOUCHER for details!

HELMSLEY. Mrs Sally Robinson, Valley View Farm, Old Byland, Helmsley, York YO6 5LG (01439

798221). ♀ ♀ ♀ ♀ *HIGHLY COMMENDED.* Three holiday cottages sleeping two, four and six persons respectively. Each with colour TV, video, washer, dishwasher, microwave. Peaceful rural surroundings on a working farm with pigs, sheep and cattle. Winter and Spring Breaks available. Short Breaks from £80 and High Season weeks up to £380. Bed and Breakfast also available. Please telephone for brochure and further details.

HELMSLEY near. Mrs Rickatson, Summerfield Farm, Harome, Near Helmsley, York YO6 5JJ

(01439 748238). Working farm, join in. Sleeps 6. Enjoy walking or touring in North Yorkshire Moors National Park. Lovely area 20 miles north of historic city of York. Modernised, comfortable and well equipped farmhouse wing; sleeps four/six plus cot. Kitchen equipped with electric cooker, fridge and automatic washing machine. Sit beside a log fire in the evenings. Linen supplied to overseas visitors. Weekly terms from £75 to £190. Mid-week and weekend bookings are possible in winter. For further information send SAE, or phone.

NORTHALLERTON. Lady Mary Furness, Stanhow Farm, Langton-on-Swale, Northallerton DL7 0TJ (01609 748614). ♀♀♀♀ *COMMENDED.* Delightful, homely detached bungalow with its own garden, garage and parking. Wonderful views over tranquil countryside on traditional mixed working farm. Cosy, spacious and very well furnished. Economy 7 heating, open fire in living room. Colour TV. Well equipped kitchen/diner, fridge/freezer, microwave, automatic washer, tumble dryer. Three bedrooms (one double, two twin) plus cot. Close to market towns of Richmond and Northallerton and central for the Dales and York Moors, historic cities and country houses. Good local hospitality and recreations. Family and business guests welcome. Open all year. Prices from £150 to £320. Brochure available.

PICKERING. Mrs Livesey, Sands Farm Country Hotel Cottages, Wilton, Pickering YO18 7JY (01751 474405). Quietly secluded in 15 acres of fields, gardens and a wildlife pond, the delightfully renovated four/five/six and eight bedded cottages are grouped round an attractive courtyard amidst shrubs, roses and honeysuckle. They are individually designed, luxuriously decorated in Laura Ashley style, with exposed beams; some four-poster beds; colour TV, gas central heating, log fires and farmhouse style kitchens. Bed linen provided and beds are made up for your arrival. All the cottages have private parking. Also adjacent to the cottages stands Sands Farm Country Hotel with beautifully designed en suite bedrooms, dining room, tea room and gift shop. Bed and Breakfast with Evening Meal is also available from the main hotel. NO SMOKING. No pets. Wilton is an ideal base for visiting the Moors, coast, stately homes, North York Moors Railway and the ancient attractive city of York. Fishing, riding, swimming is less than five miles away. Special low season breaks. SAE for brochure.

PICKERING. Town End Farm Cottage, Pickering. Sleeps 6. A well appointed south-facing Cottage on the outskirts of Pickering, with large garden and secluded paved area with garden furniture. Ample parking space and field at the side of the house for games or exercising the dog. Dining kitchen, sittingroom with colour TV and bedsitting room on the ground floor, three bedrooms and bathroom on first floor. Central heating and automatic washing machine available. Shop and telephone kiosk nearby. The property is thoroughly checked before arrival of visitors as our aim is to cater for those who wish for the best. House trained pets welcome. Pickering is a good centre for touring the North Yorks Moors, Forestry and is 24 miles from York, the ancient capital of the North, dominated by the Minster and steeped in history. Flamingo Park Zoo, riding, fishing and swimming pool in the vicinity. 18 miles to the coast. Another self catering property is available, send SAE, or telephone for enquiries. Terms from £70 to £270. Apply **Mr P.R. Holmes, Town End Farm, Pickering YO18 7HU (01751 472713/473983).**

PICKERING. Mrs Sue Cavill, Badger Cottage, Stape, Pickering YO18 8HR (01751 476108).

Comfortable self catering on small, remote, moorland farm. Seven miles from Pickering on edge of Cropton Forest. Wonderful area for touring, walking, cycling or riding. Accommodation available for guests' horses. Cottage is converted from original stone milking parlours, so all on ground floor. Open plan well equipped kitchen, dining and sitting room with sofa bed and cosy woodburning stove. Spacious bedroom with double and single beds, en suite shower room. Parking space and a garden to sit in. Linen and power included. Also large static caravan available sleeping up to six. Terms £120 to £180 per week.

ROBIN HOOD'S BAY. Working farm. Near Robin Hood's Bay at Boggle Hole. Five minutes' walk to beach. Between Whitby and Scarborough. Super detached stone cottages and bungalow on dairy farm. Two and three bedrooms and cot. Fully equipped with central heating, fitted carpets, colour TV, microwaves, fridge, washbasins in bedrooms. Own garden and car parking. North York Moors all around. Pony trekking nearby. Open all year. Sorry, no pets. Terms from £70 to £300. **Mrs N. Pattinson, South House Farm, Robin Hood's Bay, Whitby YO22 4UQ (01947 880243).**

SCARBOROUGH. Peter and Maggie Martin, Gowland Farm, Gowland Lane, Cloughton, Scarborough YO13 0DU (01723 870924).

HIGHLY COMMENDED. **Sleep 2/7.** Four charming converted stone barns situated within the beautiful North Yorkshire Moors National Park enjoying wonderful views of Harwood Dale and only two miles from the coast. The cottages have been sympathetically converted from traditional farm buildings, furnished and fitted to a very high standard, retaining the old features as well as having modern comforts. They are fully carpeted, warm and cosy with central heating and double glazing. Electric fires and colour TVs in all lounges. Well equipped kitchens. All linen and bedding provided (duvets). Large garden with plenty of car parking space. Garden furniture and laundry facilities. Sorry, no pets. Open all year. From £90 to £390 per week. Bed, Breakfast and Evening Meal also available from April to October. White Rose Award Self Catering Holiday of the Year runner-up 1993.

SKIPTON. Mrs Brenda Jones, New Close Farm, Kirkby Malham, Skipton BD23 4DP (01729 830240; Fax: 01756 797551). Sleeps 5. A supa dupa cottage on New Close Farm in the heart of Craven Dales with panoramic views over the Aire Valley. Excellent area for walking, cycling, fishing, golf and touring. Two double and one single bedrooms; bathroom. Colour TV. Full central heating and double glazing. Bed linen and all amenities included in the price. Low Season £180, High Season £220; deposit required. Sorry, no young children. Non-smokers preferred. The weather can't be guaranteed but your comfort can. Yorkshire and Humberside Tourist Board Member; FHG Diploma Award Winner.

STAITHES. Garth End Cottage, Staithes. Sleep 5/6. Victorian cottage situated on sea wall in this old fishing village in the North Yorkshire Moors National Park. Excellent walking centre. Small sandy beach with numerous rock pools. Cottage has feature fireplace, beamed ceilings, pine panelled room, well equipped kitchen including microwave. Warm, comfortable, well equipped with central heating, electricity and bed linen included in rent. Two lounges, front one with picture window giving uninterrupted panoramic views of sea, harbour and cliffs. Dining kitchen; bathroom with toilet; three bedrooms — one double, one twin, one single (two with sea views); colour TV. Front terrace overlooking the sea. Sorry, no pets. Terms from £190. Apply **Mrs Hobbs (01132 665501).**

SUTTON-ON-FOREST (Near York). Stable and Wren Cottages. ♀♀♀ *COMMENDED.* **Sleeping 2 and 4.** Converted from old working stables these single storey cottages while retaining the old roof beams are spacious, comfortable and fully equipped. Storage heating plus electric fire and bed linen are all included in the price — no extras. Set on a mainly arable farm one mile from Sutton the cottages are in a very peaceful rural location yet are very handy for trips into the old city of York with many stores and shops on the outskirts of town. This is a good central touring base for visits to the North Yorkshire Moors, East Coast and Dales. Well insulated and cosy, these cottages are also ideal for winter holidays/short breaks. Plenty of excellent reasonable eating places all round the area. Children welcome, cot available. Prices from £125 to £260 per week. Brochure from **Mrs H. Knowlson, Thrush House, Sutton-on-Forest, York YO6 1ED.**

THORNTON DALE (near Pickering). Beechwood, Peaslands Lane, Thornton Dale. Sleeps 4. This popular touring and walking centre, on the edge of the North Yorkshire Moors National Park, offers riding stable, ample shops, eating places and bus service. Moors Railway, swimming pool, historic houses and Flamingoland nearby. Beechwood is a detached two-bedroomed bungalow with own parking and gardens; sleeps four plus cot. It offers lounge, diningroom, kitchen, bathroom. Uninterrupted view of the Vale of Pickering. Fully equipped with electric cooker, fridge, fires, colour TV and immersion heater. Storage heaters and linen available. Sorry, no pets. Weekly rates £195 to £278. SAE, please to **Mrs J. Clayton, Low Mill Garth, Maltongate, Thornton Dale YO18 7SE (01751 474365).**

WENSLEYDALE. Moorcote, Ellingstring, Masham. Three delightful cottages around a sunny courtyard. Granary Cottage sleeps four in double and bunk rooms; Hayloft Cottage sleeps four in double and twin rooms; Stable Cottage sleeps six in double and twin rooms. All equipped to very high standard. Central heating, linen and towels provided. Large gardens and private patios. Overlooking Jervaulx Abbey with fabulous views of 40 miles. All the peace and quiet you could wish for, yet only one hour to York and under half an hour to the A1. Children and pets welcome. Open all year. Short Breaks from £80; weekly prices from £155. Details from **Mrs Pat Cooper, Moorcote Farm, Ellingstring, Masham HG4 4PL (01677 460315).**

WHITBY. Mrs K. Wilkinson, Mickleby Moorside Farm, Ugthorpe, Whitby YO21 2BL (01947 840333). Tourist Board *HIGHLY COMMENDED.* **Sleeps 2/3.** This comfortable cottage is a self contained annexe of the main farmhouse. Situated one mile outside Ugthorpe it is in easy reach of Staithes, Runswick Bay, Sandsend, Whitby and the Moors. The cottage comprises a fitted kitchen with electric cooker, fridge/freezer, washing machine and radio; bedroom with double bed and adjoining shower room; comfortable lounge cum dining room with colour TV and open fire, fuel provided. A folding bed and cot are also available. Car space and garden for guests' use. Children welcome. Non-smokers preferred. Terms from £80 to £160 weekly. SAE, or telephone, for brochure.

WHITBY near. Mr and Mrs Geoffrey Hepworth, Land of Nod Farm, Near Whitby YO21 2BL (01947 840325). Sleeps 6 plus cot. Attached sandstone bungalow, situated in the clean air, carefree part of North Yorkshire Moors National Park. All five windows face south across pastures, the sittingroom window also faces east across six miles of widening valley to Whitby Abbey Headland. Runswick Bay is three miles northward. The holiday property is separated from the farm house by a dividing passage. There are three compact bedrooms, one of which has two single beds. Modern toilet facilities and shower. Kitchen/diner fully equipped with electric cooker, microwave, fridge; spin dryer, colour TV. Bed linen, electricity included in hire. Only extra charge is for pets! No telephone bookings. Owner attended. For availability, enquiries, brochure phone (01947 840325). Rates from £78 Low Season to £159 High Season per week.

YORK. Orillia Cottages, Stockton-on-Forest, York. Three converted farmworkers' cottages in a courtyard setting at the rear of the 300 year old farmhouse in Stockton-on-Forest; three miles from York. Golf course nearby, pub 200 yards away serves food. Post office, newsagents and general stores within easy reach. Convenient half-hourly bus service to York and the coast. Fully furnished and equipped for two to eight, the cottages comprise lounge with colour TV, etc; kitchen area with microwave oven, grill and hob. Bedrooms have double bed or twin beds. Gas central heating. Non-smokers preferred. Children and pets welcome. Available Easter to October. Short Breaks may be available. Terms from £150 to £300 weekly includes heating, linen, etc. Contact: **Mike Cundall, Orillia House, 89 The Village, Stockton-on-Forest, York YO3 9UP (01904 400600).**

WHEN MAKING ENQUIRIES PLEASE MENTION
THIS *FHG* PUBLICATION

YORK. Mrs M.S.A. Woodliffe, Mill Farm, Yapham, Pocklington, York YO4 2PH (01759 302172). Three attractive self-catering choices on the farm. 12 miles from York with fine views of the Yorkshire Wolds. WOODLEA, detached house, sleeping five/six people, with fully equipped kitchen, dining area, large lounge with colour TV, bathroom, downstairs cloakroom and three bedrooms. BUNGALOW adjacent to farmhouse sleeps two/four with kitchen, bathroom, lounge/diningroom with colour TV and double bed settee, twin room with cot. Children and pets welcome. STUDIO adjacent to farmhouse, sleeps two. Modern kitchen, lounge/diningroom with colour TV, twin bedroom, bathroom/toilet. Parking for all. Open all year. Shopping and other amenities at Pocklington (two miles). Eating out, stately homes, a variety of activities available locally; coast 28 miles. SAE for details.

WEST YORKSHIRE

HAWORTH. 7 Upper Marsh, Oxenhope. Tourist Board Category 3. A small stone cottage and garden  on the edge of moorland, one mile from Haworth, well maintained and cared for. Sleeps six in two bedrooms and the lounge. The cottage has sunny rooms, lovely views, colour TV, gas central heating, well equipped kitchen including washing machine. Waymarked walks to miles of moorland start near the cottage. Spectacular countryside close by and you are within easy driving distance of the beautiful Yorkshire Dales with Skipton, Bolton Abbey, Burnsall and Malham as well as many other places of interest — not forgetting the historic and popular village of Haworth. We are pleased to have children and dogs to stay and personal supervision assures you of a very warm welcome at any time of year. Prices £210 to £300 including linen and heating. Details from **Mrs F.M. Seabrook, 30 Newcombe Street, Market Harborough, Leicestershire LE16 9PB (01858 463723).**

ISLE OF WIGHT

FRESHWATER. 1 Cliff End, Monks Lane, Freshwater. Sleep 4/6. A small attractive coastal development  of brick-built bungalows on high ground with beautiful views over the sea and rolling countryside. It overlooks Colwell beach. There is a clubhouse with a bar, heated swimming pool, a small shop and family entertainment for which membership is available. There are telephones, reception office and a launderette on site. The Bungalow is well furnished and carpeted throughout and comprises two bedrooms; bathroom with electric shower; kitchen/lounge with put-u-up bed, colour TV, electric cooker, fridge, toaster, etc. Electric heating. Bed linen, high chairs and cots can be hired. Sorry, no pets. Please write or telephone for our brochures which give full accommodation details plus Island information to **Mr and Mrs N. Timmins, "Westward Ho!", 1 Marlborough Close, Fleet, Hampshire GU13 9HY (01252 621700).**

NEWPORT. Mrs P. Chick, Plaish Farm, Carisbrooke, Newport PO30 3HU (01983 520397). ♀♀♀

COMMENDED. THE BAKERY: Self contained wing of 17th century farmhouse sleeping six/eight in spacious bedrooms. Set in the beautiful countryside of Bowcombe Valley in the lea of Carisbrooke Castle. Excellent walking, touring, biking. Well equipped, electricity included. Linen available.

TOTLAND BAY. 3 Seaview Cottages, Broadway, Totland Bay. Sleeps 5. ♀♀ This well-modernised cosy old coastguard cottage holds the Farm Holiday Guide Diploma for the highest standard of accommodation. It is warm and popular throughout the year. Four day winter break — £35; a week in summer £220. Located close to two beaches in beautiful walking country near mainland links. It comprises lounge/dinette/kitchenette; two bedrooms (sleeping five); bathroom/toilet. Well furnished, fully heated, TV, selection of books and other considerations. Another cottage is also available at Cowes, Isle of Wight. Non-smokers only. **Mrs C. Pitts, 11 York Avenue, New Milton, Hampshire BH25 6BT (01425 615215).**

CHANNEL ISLANDS

ST. MARY'S. Mrs Pamela Mumford, Sallakee Farm, St. Mary's TR21 0NZ (01720 22391). ♀♀♀ **Sleeps 5.** Self catering farm cottage available all year round. Children and pets welcome. Please write or telephone for further details.

ST. PETERS PORT. Mr and Mrs J. Woolston, Le Pont Renier, Ruettes Brayes, St. Peters Port GY1 1PL (01481 720370). Sleep 4/6 plus children. Le Douit

Farm Holiday Flats have been converted from an old Guernsey farmhouse and outbuildings. They are situated in two acres of land in lovely countryside on the south west corner of Guernsey about 10 minutes' stroll from the bays of Rocquaine and L'Eree; shops and cafes are handy. They are furnished and equipped to a good standard and each unit is vitually a complete home itself. The flats are open all year. Inclusive in the charge: all bed linen, bath towels, tea towels, colour TV, radio, cutlery, china, glasswear, cots and high chairs. Electric kitchen including fridge, hoover, water heater and iron. Electricity by £1 coin meter. Coin washing machine and dryer. Ample car parking. Cars and cycles may be hired by arrangement. Please write or telephone for our brochure and tariff.

Caravan and Camping Holidays.

CARAVAN AND CAMPING HOLIDAYS

CORNWALL

See also Colour Display Advertisement **HELSTON. Mrs J. Lugg, Tregaddra Farm, Cury, Helston TR12 7BB (0326 240235).** "Hide-a-way" luxury mobile home is tucked away in the grounds of Tregaddra Farmhouse in the centre of the Lizard Peninsula. Furnished to a high standard with one double bedroom and one twin-bedded room. Bathroom with shower and basin, separate toilet. Kitchen, dining area and lounge with colour TV. Linen, gas and electricity included in rental. Open all year. Meals can be provided in nearby guesthouse by arrangement. Terms from £100 per week. Colour brochure available.

CORNWALL
ST IVES BAY
HOLIDAY PARK
BRITISH GRADED HOLIDAY PARKS

CHALETS CARAVANS AND CAMPING
with private access to a huge sandy beach. With a large indoor pool and 2 clubs on the Park. Phone us NOW on the toll free number below for your FREE colour brochure

right on the beach!

Call our 24hr BROCHURE LINE on 0800 317713

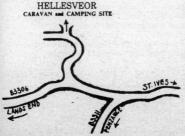

HELLESVEOR
CARAVAN and CAMPING SITE

B3306
LANDS END
ST. IVES →
PENZANCE

ST. IVES. G. & H. Rogers, Hellesveor Caravan and Camping Site, Hellesveor Farm, St. Ives TR26 3AD (01736 795738). Six berth caravans for hire on small secluded approved farm site, one mile from St. Ives town centre and nearest beaches, five minutes from bus route on Land's End Road (B3306). Coastal and countryside walks nearby. Shop and laundry facilities on site. Special terms for early and late season. Campers and touring caravans welcome. Electrical hook-ups available. Dogs allowed under strict control. Nearby horse riding, pony trekking, golf course, bowling greens and leisure centre. Cottage sleeping six persons also available. SAE please for further details.

CUMBRIA — including "The Lakes"

APPLEBY-IN-WESTMORLAND. Mrs L.M. Watson, Whygill Head Farm, Little Asby, Appleby-in-Westmorland CA16 6QD (017683 71531). Two six-berth caravans on their own private site in two and a half acre sheltered copse near the farm. Fully equipped except for bed linen. Electricity and running water in both vans. Heating and cooking by Calor gas (no extra charge). Flush toilet and hot water a few yards away, also shower and telephone. Children welcome and pets if kept under control. An ideal centre for walkers and naturalists — rare plants and wildlife near at hand. Golf, fishing, swimming and pony trekking; interesting market towns, villages, craft workshops and artists' studios in the surrounding area. Price from £70 per week low season, £75 high season; weekend breaks available at short notice £12 per night.

BROUGHTON-IN-FURNESS. Mrs H. Glessal, Whineray Ground, Broughton-in-Furness LA20 6DS (01229 716500). Working farm. Private, sheltered yet within easy reach of a whole host of facilities — miniature railway, castles, gardens, beach, museum, fishing, bird watching, fell walking — attractive six-berth, 30' modern static caravan set in its own half acre on a working fell farm. Marvellous views and absolute seclusion can be guaranteed. Two bedrooms (one with bunks, one with double bed), spacious living area and separate kitchen; shower and toilet. Fridge, gas fire and cooker — no additional charge for electricity and gas. Hot and cold water. River Duddon close by, indoor swimming pool, village, shops, pub, restaurant and golfing within two miles. Ulverston market town about ten miles. Further details on request. Terms from £120 weekly.

CARLISLE. Mrs P.E. Johnston, Yeast Hall, New House Farm, Newby West, Carlisle CA2 6QZ (01228 23545). Two attractive caravans on private farm site — 28 foot Belmont six-berth, 30 foot Willerby six-berth, both with lounge, kitchen, bedroom, bathroom and each completely private in own enclosure. Situated three and a half miles west of Carlisle, a quarter-mile from road down private lane. It is ideally situated for visiting Lake District, Solway Coast, Scottish Borders, Roman Wall, Eden Valley, etc. Vans are very well equipped, with everything supplied except linen, and thoroughly cleaned between visitors. Electric lighting, heating. Calor gas/electric cooker, water heater. Terms from £60. Further details with pleasure. Phone or write (SAE please).

CONISTON. Mrs E. Johnson, Spoon Hall, Coniston LA21 8AW (015394 41391). Caravans sleep 6. Three 33ft caravans situated on a 50 acre working hill farm one mile from Coniston, overlooking Coniston Lake. All have flush toilet, shower, gas cookers, fires and water heaters, electric lighting and fridge plus colour TV. Children are welcome. Pets are allowed free. Available all year round. Pony trekking arranged from farm. Weekly terms on request.

NEWBY BRIDGE. Oak Head Caravan Park, Ayside, Grange-over-Sands LA11 6JA (015395 31475). Family owned and operated. Select, quiet, clean wooded site in the picturesque fells of the Lake District. Easy access from M6 Junction 36, 14 miles A590. On-site facilities include flush toilets, hot showers, hot and cold water, deep sinks for washing clothes, washing machine, tumble dryers and spin dryers, iron and deep freeze; hair dryers. Milk and gas on sale. Tourers (30 pitches) £7 per night (including electricity and VAT); Tents (30 pitches) £5 per night minimum. Open March 31st to October 31st.

THIRLMERE. Mrs Gaskell, Thirlspot Farm Caravan Park, Thirlmere, Keswick CA12 4TW (017687 72551 and 72224). Small caravan park situated between Keswick and Grasmere on a Lakeland hill farm. All caravans sleep six and have full facilities including hot water, showers, toilet, fridge and TV. The site is conveniently placed for hill walking and forest trails and the lake is nearby. There are many local attractions including Wordsworth Museum, Beatrix Potter exhibition and Keswick Leisure Pool. Keswick and Grasmere have interesting shops and galleries and Carlisle with its castle and Roman Wall is not far away. We also have a small camping and mobile caravan site with its own toilet and shower block.

WASDALE. Mrs Elsie Knight, Church Stile Farm, Wasdale CA20 1ET (019467 26388). Church Stile Camp Site is situated on a working family farm in Nether Wasdale village. The picturesque countryside all around is ideal for fell walking, low country walks or sightseeing in the Lake District. Facilities available on site include flush toilet, hot and cold showers, washbasins, razor points, laundry rooms, chemical disposal point, mains electricity and mains water. There are plenty of wooded play areas for children. The Ravenglass and Eskdale Miniature Railway and Muncaster Castle are seven miles away. Pets permitted. All visitors made welcome. Tents, trailer tents and motor caravans only; no touring vans. Open March to November. Terms £5 per night (two persons, car and tent).

DERBYSHIRE

ASHBOURNE. Mrs Louie Tatlow, Ashfield Farm, Calwich, Near Ashbourne DE6 2EB (01335 324279 or 324443). Working farm. Five modern six-berth caravans, fully equipped, each with gas cooker, fridge, TV; shower and flush toilet; mains electricity. Ashfield Farm overlooks the peaceful Dove Valley and is convenient for the Peak District. The old market town of Ashbourne only two miles away with golf course, swimming pool, squash and bowling. Within easy reach of stately homes like Haddon Hall and Chatsworth, with the Potteries and Lichfield 25 miles distant, Uttoxeter 10 miles, while Alton Towers Theme Park is under five miles away. Prices and brochure on request. Write or telephone for further information.

BUXTON near. Mr and Mrs J. Melland, The Pomeroy Caravan Park, Street House Farm, Flagg, Near Buxton SK17 9QG (01298 83259). √ √ √ Working farm. This site for 30 caravans is situated five miles from Buxton, in heart of Peak District National Park. Ideal base for touring by car or walking. Site adjoins northern end of now famous Tissington and High Peak Trail. Only nine miles from Haddon Hall and ten from Chatsworth House. Landscaped to the latest model standards for caravan sites; tourers and campers will find high standards here. New toilet block with showers, washing facilities and laundry; mains electric hook-up points. Back-packers welcome. Large rally field available. Children welcome; dogs on lead. We now have six-berth 28ft x 10ft Holiday Van with separate end bedroom; hot and cold water; WC and shower. Fridge, full size gas cooker and fire, TV. Weekly rates only £85 to £120. Fully equipped except linen. Open Easter to end of October. SAE, please, for further details.

KNIVETON/ASHBOURNE. Mrs Martin, The Alamo, Kniveton Wood, Kniveton, Ashbourne DE6 1JF (01335 345731). Situated two miles from the market town of Ashbourne this pleasant site of one and a half acres overlooks Dovedale. Fairly flat with 15 pitches, mostly hardstandings; all have electric hook-ups and awnings. Tents are also welcome. Site facilities include toilets, hot and cold water, Elsan waste disposal, etc. Two miles Carsington Water, eight miles Alton Towers, American Adventure half an hour's drive. Also close to Matlock and Bakewell. Children and pets welcome. From £4 per night, £1.50 electricity, 50p all awnings. Early booking Bank Holidays. Directions: B5035 Ashbourne to Wirksworth, turn left to Kniveton Wood, past second house take second gate.

DEVON

ASHBURTON. Mrs Rhona Parker, Higher Mead Farm, Ashburton TQ13 7LJ (01364 652598; Fax: 01364 654004). A friendly, family-run farm site, set in 400 acres and surrounded by beautiful countryside. 12 miles to the sea and close to Dartmoor National Park. Ideal for touring Devon/Cornwall. Perfect for children and pets with all farm animals, play area and plenty of space to roam, also large area for dogs. Holiday cottages and caravans fully equipped except for linen. Level touring site with some hard standings. Electric hook-up. Free showers in fully tiled block, laundry room and games room. Small family bar, shop and phone. Prices start from £90 Low Season to £380 High Season. Good discounts for couples. To find us: from Exeter take A38 to Plymouth till you see "26 miles Plymouth" sign; take second left at Alston Cross signposted to Woodland and Denbury.

BIDEFORD. Mrs Sarah Hunt, Greencliff Farm, Abbotsham, Bideford EX39 1JL (01237 424674). Only one caravan, peaceful situation, panoramic sea views, beautiful North Devon coastline. Mixed farm, Tudor farmhouse, easy access cliffs (Coastal Footpath) and rocky shore (prawning and surfing — for the experienced). Sleeps six in one double plus bunks. Gas cooker, fridge, hot and cold water, flush toilet, colour TV and fan heater. Separate building with toilet plus shower. Village amenities one mile, sandy beach at Westward Ho! three miles; water sports on Taw/Torridge estuary. Historic market town of Bideford two miles and convenient for Clovelly, Exmoor, Lundy. Price from £85 to £130 per week.

BIDEFORD. Mrs J.A. Fox, Highstead Farm, Bucks Cross, Bideford EX39 5DX (01237 431201).

Large and attractive modern caravan on a private farm site with fine sea views nearby. Just off the A39 Bideford/Bude road close to the coast of North Devon and convenient for Clovelly, Bideford and Westward Ho! Luxury accommodation for six adults (sleeping accommodation for up to 11 at extra charge) with bath/shower, separate toilet, fully equipped kitchen including microwave, gas fire and colour TV. Babysitting also available. Pets welcome by arrangement. Linen supplied as extra. Shopping, beaches, local attractions and Moors within easy reach. Car essential but good walking country. Open March to October from £90 weekly low season.

COLYTON. Mrs M.A. Virgin, Shortlands Farm, Southleigh, Colyton EX13 6SA (01404 871236).

Working farm, join in. Six-berth caravan on 40 acre farm in small orchard through which a small brook runs. Woodland walks, wildlife park nearby and within easy reach of Seaton Tramways. Beer, the old smugglers village which also has Peco Railway six miles from Seaton, Sidmouth. The caravan has double bedroom, two single bedded rooms, hot and cold water, shower, flush toilet; full gas cooker, electric light, fridge, TV. No linen supplied. Car parking space. Main shops two and a half miles away. Open Whitsun to October. Terms from £90.

COLYTON. Mrs S. Gould and Mrs R. Gould, Bonehayne Farm, Colyton EX13 6SG (01404 871416 or 871396). Working farm.

Six-berth luxury caravan in secluded spot on farmhouse lawn, overlooking the river, fields and woodlands where wildlife is a common sight. Many animals to make friends with on this 250 acre farm. Good trout fishing available. Caravan contains well fitted master bedroom, twin bedded room with cot rail available, and convertible double in lounge. Kitchen with cooker and fridge freezer. Spacious lounge and dining area. Colour TV. Bathroom with toilet, washbasin, shower and bath, heated towel rail. Fully equipped except linen. All rooms with plenty of cupboard space. Built-in radiators, fully insulated, making it ideal for out of season holidays. Laundry facilities and barbecue available. Milk and eggs obtainable from farmhouse. Colyton two miles, sea four and and a half miles. Brochure available.

CREDITON. Yeatheridge Farm (Touring)

Caravan Park, East Worlington, Crediton EX17 4TN (01884 860330). √ √ √ √ AA 3 Pennants, RAC. Why are we different? We are a small central park with panoramic views on a genuine working farm with plenty of animals to see and some to touch! We also offer peace and space with freedom to roam the farm with its woodland walks, coarse fishing lake, indoor heated swimming pools with 200ft water flume, TV lounge, children's play area, hot and cold showers, wash cubicles — ALL FREE. A welcome for dogs. Other amenities include horse riding from the park, electric hook-up points, campers' dish washing, laundry room, shop with frozen food, fresh dairy products, ice pack service. Summer parking in our storage area to save towing. Ideally situated for touring coast, Exmoor and Dartmoor. Golf and tennis locally. Two caravans for letting. Write, or phone, for FREE colour brochure. Proprietors: Geoffrey and Elizabeth Hosegood.

CULLOMPTON. Mrs J. Davey, Pound Farm, Butterleigh, Cullompton EX15 1PH (01884 855 208). Working farm. Sleeps 6. A Pound Farm holiday combines finest English scenery with traditional beauty of village of Butterleigh, half a mile away. Enjoy family break from April to November on this 80-acre sheep and beef farm. Spacious comfortable caravan accommodation for six, in grass paddock with paths and parking for two cars. Enter by road. Well-equipped; linen hire by arrangement. Hot and cold water, shower. Electric cooker, kettle, iron (plus ironing board), toaster, fridge, heater, electric blanket, colour TV, lights, several power points (8). All cutlery, utensils, blankets and pillows. Washroom/Utility room. Adjoining caravan has flush toilet, double drainer stainless steel sink unit in utility room with shaving point, hot/cold water, electric light and two-bar heater. Farmstead within sight of caravans. Visitors free to walk over the farm. South and North coast 45 to 60 minutes' drive. Four miles from M5, Cullompton, North Devon Link road (A361), Tiverton, Silverton, Bickleigh thatched olde worlde village in heart of beautiful Exe Valley. Pets allowed. Free coarse fishing, no closed season — carp, tench, perch, roach, rudd. Terms from £120 to £175. FHG Diploma Winner. Also separate small site suitable for a few tents or caravanettes.

EXETER near. Mr D.L. Salter, Haldon Lodge Farm, Kennford, Near Exeter EX6 7YG (01392 832312). Working farm.  Peace and seclusion are assured on this private residential site. The Salters offer a family holiday for all ages, with a special invitation to younger members to join in pony riding and enjoy a free and easy farm holiday with them. Exeter four and a half miles, Dawlish (short car drive away) ideal centre for touring all South Devon resorts and Dartmoor. The two luxury six-berth residential holiday caravans adjoin a large lawn with a background of fields, pine trees and rhododendrons. Six comfortable beds, blankets, pillows. Fully equipped kitchen, carpeted lounge with TV, bathroom (hot and cold), flush toilet, electricity and mains connected. Horses and ponies nearby are an interest to everyone. Horse lovers and children are invited to explore the beautiful Teign Valley Forest on horseback. Day pony treks are arranged for small parties. The well-known Nobody Inn is one of the attractive country inns where you can have a drink and a meal in a friendly atmosphere. Pets allowed. Riding and Trekking Holidays can be arranged. Three well stocked fishing lakes. Caravans can be hired from March to December from £70 to £195 per week. Tourers and campers at very reasonable daily charge. No extra charge for pets etc.

LYNTON. Mrs Una McCallum, Middle Ranscombe Farm, Lynton EX35 6JR (01598 763 258). Sleeps 6/8. One two bedroomed caravan on a small farm with sheep, Alpacas and cattle. Offering peace and tranquillity in glorious Devon countryside, twixt coast and Exmoor. Ideal for walking and touring. Come and explore the area with dramatic coastline, unique cliff railway and Lorna Doone country. Woolacombe's famous sands are only about 15 miles away; riding stables half a mile, surfing and fishing nearby. The caravan is fully equipped except for linen, with electric lights, fridge, TV, gas cooker and fire. Cars can be parked alongside. Pure spring water to drink. Sorry no pets.

TOTNES. J. and E. Ball, Higher Well Farm and Holiday Park, Stoke Gabriel, Totnes TQ9 6RN (01803 782289). √ √ √ A quiet secluded farm park welcoming tents, motor caravans and touring caravans. It is less than one mile from the riverside village of Stoke Gabriel and within four miles of Torbay beaches. Central for touring South Devon. Facilities include toilets, showers, launderette, shop, payphone and electric hook-ups. There are also static caravans to let. Enjoy a delightful relaxing holiday in the beautiful Devonshire countryside. Static caravans from £115 per week or £17 per night.

WOOLACOMBE. Twitchen House and Mortehoe Caravan Park, Woolacombe. √ √ √ √ LUXURY

CARAVANS AT WOOLACOMBE. Have a carefree and comfortable holiday in one of our Executive, luxury or modern caravans on this attractive, well equipped Rose Award Park. Park facilities include heated pool, licensed club with two bars, snooker, activities room, games and family areas, free entertainment, shop, launderette, putting green, etc. We offer a wide selection of caravans all on concrete bases, with mains water and drainage, flush toilets, hot and cold water to sinks/shower, refrigerators, heating, TV, etc. Fully inclusive terms from £95 per week, with special low rates/Senior Citizen discounts out of season. For colour brochure and tariff, SAE or phone **Woolacombe Caravan Hirers, Dept FHG, Garden Cottage, 27 East Street, Braunton EX33 2EA (01271 816580).**

WOOLACOMBE SANDS. CARAVANS TO LET. Farm site above Rockham Beach (only 500 yards). Delightful

situation in the heart of National Trust land, magnificent sea views. Famous three miles of Woolacombe Sands only one mile away. Marvellous walking, surfing. Magnificent coast for lovers of unspoilt beauty. Wide choice of new king-size caravans (33ft.) with toilet, shower, hot water, fridge, TV etc. Very well equipped, parking beside caravan. On site shop, laundry, showers etc. Rates from £99 to £299. SAE please. **Morte Point Caravans, 23 Brooks Road, Wylde Green, Sutton Coldfield B72 1HP (Tel & Fax: 0121-354 1551; 0831 768358).**

HELP IMPROVE BRITISH TOURIST STANDARDS

You are choosing holiday accommodation from our very popular FHG Publications. Whether it be a hotel, guest house, farmhouse or self-catering accommodation, we think you will find it hospitable, comfortable and clean, and your host and hostess friendly and helpful. Why not write and tell us about it?

As a recognition of the generally well-run and excellent holiday accommodation reviewed in our publications, we at FHG Publications Ltd. present a diploma to proprietors who receive the highest recommendation from their guests who are also readers of our Guides. If you care to write to us praising the holiday you have booked through FHG Publications Ltd. – whether this be board, self-catering accommodation, a sporting or a caravan holiday, what you say will be evaluated and the proprietors who reach our final list will be contacted.

The winning proprietor will receive an attractive framed diploma to display on his premises as recognition of a high standard of comfort, amenity and hospitality. FHG Publications Ltd. offer this diploma as a contribution towards the improvement of standards in tourist accommodation in Britain. Help your excellent host or hostess to win it!

FHG DIPLOMA

We nominate ....

....

Because ....

Name ....

Address ....

.... Telephone No. ....

DORSET

MANOR FARM HOLIDAY CENTRE
Charmouth, Bridport, Dorset
Situated in a rural valley. Charmouth beach a level ten minutes' walk away.
Luxury 6-berth Caravans for Hire with toilet/shower, refrigerator, full cooker, colour TV, gas fire.
30-acre Tourist Park for touring caravans, dormobiles and tents.
Centre facilities include * Toilets; * Hot showers; * Fish and chip takeaway; * Licensed bar with family room; * Amusement room; * Launderette; * Shop and off-licence; * Swimming pool; * Electric hook-up points; * Calor gas and Camping Gaz; * Ice pack service; * Chemical disposal unit; * Disabled facilities.
Send SAE for colour brochure to Mr R. B. Loosmore or Tel: 01297 560226
See also Colour Display Advertisement in this Guide.

LYME REGIS. Mrs J. Tedbury, Little Paddocks, Yawl Hill Lane, Lyme Regis DT7 3RW (01297 443085). Sleeps 6. A six-berth caravan on Devon/Dorset border in a well-kept paddock overlooking Lyme Bay and surrounding countryside. Situated on a smallholding with animals, for perfect peace and quiet. Lyme Regis two-and-a-half miles, Charmouth three-and-a-half miles. Both have safe beaches for children. Easy driving distance to resorts of Seaton, Beer and Sidmouth. The caravan is fully equipped except linen. It has shower room with handbasin and toilet inside as well as flush toilet just outside. Electric light, fridge and TV. Calor gas cooker and fire. Car can be parked alongside. Dogs welcome. Terms from £80. Also fully equipped chalet for two from £65. SAE, please.

LYME REGIS. Mrs C. Grymonprez, Beechfield Cottage, Yawl Hill Lane, Uplyme, Lyme Regis DT7 3RW (01297 443216). Caravans sleep 4/6. Beechfield is a four-acre smallholding situated on Yawl Hill, commanding a truly scenic outlook over Lyme's countryside and the sea. It is conveniently located on the borders of Devon, Somerset and Dorset. To ensure utmost privacy we have a well-kept one acre field, hedge-screened and peaceful, set aside for only two modern caravans. Both are fully equipped (except linen), with fridge, mains electricity and water, inside flush toilet, shower, gas cooker and fire, colour TV. Cleanliness guaranteed. Well behaved pets welcome. Lyme Regis is only two and a half miles away. Organically grown vegetables according to season, home made bread, some herbs and free-range eggs available. SAE appreciated.

WAREHAM. Birchwood Tourist Park, North Trigon, Wareham BH20 7PA (01929 554763). √ √ √ √ One of the newest and probably the finest touring park in Dorset. Situated in Wareham Forest with direct access to forest walks. Large, level, well drained pitches together with facilities comparable with the best in Europe. The ideal base for exploring this beautiful part of Dorset. Facilities include FREE hot showers, electric hook-ups, self service shop, off sales, take away foods, launderette, gas cylinder exchange, motor home waste disposal, games room, children's pool, children's playground plus lots more. Dogs welcome if kept on lead. Open 1st March to 31st October. Please write or telephone for our colour brochure.

PLEASE SEND A STAMPED ADDRESSED ENVELOPE WITH ENQUIRIES

HAMPSHIRE

HAYLING ISLAND. Lower Tye Camp Site, Copse Lane, Hayling Island PO11 0QR (01705 462479), The Oven Camp Site, Manor Road, Hayling Island PO11 0QX (01705 464695) and Fleet Farm Camp Site, Yew Tree Road, Hayling Island PO11 0QB (01705 463684).

Sites from £7 per unit per night. Parking by unit. Safe beaches, windsurfing, golf, horse riding, swimming pool on site at Oven Camp Site, etc. Ideal touring area for Portsmouth, Isle of Wight, New Forest. Follow A3023 from Havant, turn left into Copse Lane where indicated for Fleet and Lower Tye; for Oven Camp Site continue on main A3023 until roundabout, bear right, site 200 yards on left. Caravans permanently sited (£10 per week plus VAT) or stored (£3.50 plus VAT) if required. Rallies catered for. RAC and AA registered.

LANCASHIRE

BLACKPOOL. Mrs Barbara Rawcliffe, Pipers Height Caravan and Camping Park, Peel Road, Peel, Blackpool FY4 5JT (01253 763767). The site is three miles from Blackpool, near A583 and half a mile from M55 — exit Junction 4, turn left, well signed. It accommodates 50 tents, 100 touring caravans and has 16 static vans. New static caravan sales. Cottage hire. Booking is advisable in high season. Hot showers, flush toilets, power points, also caravan hard standings and electric hook-up points. Site shop, licensed bar and family lounge with entertainments mid and high season, snack bar, children's play area, launderette. Dogs welcome. Hourly bus service. Facilities available for disabled visitors. Open March to October. Terms from £9 per night. Strictly families only.

NORTHUMBERLAND

ALNWICK. Mrs J.W. Bowden, "Anvil-Kirk", 8 South Charlton Village, Alnwick NE66 2NA (01665 579324). Tourist Board COMMENDED. One six-berth cara-

van on single private site. Hard standing and lovely spacious surroundings. Three-quarters of a mile from the A1; six miles north of Alnwick and six miles also from the lovely clean beaches of Beadnell, Seahouses, Craster Village; nine miles from the Cheviot Hills. Many castles nearby — Bamburgh and Alnwick being the largest; wild cattle and bird sanctuaries; Ingram Valley for the hill walker, Berwick and Morpeth markets. Holy Island is a must with its tiny castle and harbour with fishing boats. Many places to eat out within a radius of 10 miles. The caravan has mains water and electricity; electric cooker, fridge, microwave, TV. End bedroom (bunk beds); flush toilet in bathroom. Open Easter to October. Children and pets welcome. Milk and bread delivered, papers and greengrocery daily. Terms from £165 to £195 per week. One Rose Award. SAE, please. Also Bed and Breakfast available in house from £16 to £18 per night.

SHROPSHIRE

IRONBRIDGE. Mrs V. Evans, Church Farm, Rowton, Wellington, Telford TF6 6QY (01952 770381). √ √ Working farm, join in. Two six/eight berth caravans in garden setting with unspoilt views of the Wrekin; well spaced on hard standing with parking. Each caravan is fully equipped with double and bunk bedrooms, shower/toilet, spacious lounge, colour TV, dining/kitchen area. Electricity and gas. Barbecue and croquet available. Pets welcome. Central for interesting places to visit including Ironbridge, Bridgnorth, Shrewsbury, Chester, Alton Towers, Cosford Aerospace Museum and the Potteries; Wales also within easy reach. Visitors are welcome to join in the farming way of life. Terms from £60 to £160 per week. Touring caravans and tents welcome. Bed and Breakfast available in farmhouse. Also two cottages for hire.

SOMERSET

DULVERTON. Mrs M.M. Jones, Higher Town, Dulverton TA22 9RX (01398 341272). Working farm.

Caravans sleep 8. Our farm is situated half a mile from
open moorland, one mile from the Devon/Somerset border
and four miles from Dulverton. 80 acres of the farm is in the
Exmoor National Park. We let **two caravans** which are
quarter of a mile apart and do not overlook each other, and
have lovely views, situated in lawns with parking space. Both
are eight berth, with a double end bedroom, bunk bedroom,
shower, flush toilet, hot/cold water and colour TV. The
caravans are modern and fully equipped except linen. Cot
and high chair available. Visitors are welcome to watch the
milking or walk over our beef and sheep farm. Riding and
fishing nearby. Open May to October. Price from £70,
includes gas and electricity.

WARWICKSHIRE

STRATFORD-UPON-AVON. Mrs M.J. Reading, The Elms Camp, Tiddington Road, Stratford-upon-Avon CV37 7AG (01789 292312 or 293356). Stratford-upon-Avon one and a half miles. On B4086 Wellesbourne/Stratford. Terms for caravan and tent pitches from £5.50 per night including VAT. Warwick, NEC, Royal Showground, Cotswolds and the Vale of Evesham are all within easy driving distance; golf course quarter of a mile away, bowling club at site entrance. Gliding, fishing, boating and horse riding are all nearby. Many picturesque pubs and restaurants in the locality for lunches and dinners. Ideal for theatre visits. Limited number of hook-ups available, £2 extra charge.

NORTH YORKSHIRE

WHITBY. Mrs A.G. Shardlow, Beckside Farm, Sneatonthorpe, Whitby YO22 5JG (01947 880550 and 880213). One 25ft two bedroomed static caravan accommodating six persons, plus cot, situated on small livestock farm on edge of North Yorkshire Moors, overlooking small beck and wooded area, five miles from the sea. The beautiful coastline, with sandy beaches and rocky coves, is an ideal location for fishing, riding, boating on river; visiting tea gardens, craft centres, steam railway, zoo and enjoying many lovely walks. The caravan is equipped with cooker, microwave, fridge, colour TV, hot and cold water, mains sanitation, gas heater and all necessary utensils. Shower on site. Everything supplied for your holiday requirements, except linen. Children's play area and parking space. Available April to October. SAE for weekly terms.

WHITBY near. Partridge Nest Farm, Eskdaleside, Sleights, Whitby YO22 5ES (01947 810450). Set

in beautiful Esk Valley, six caravans on secluded site in 45 acres of interesting land reaching up to the moors. Just five minutes from the sea and the ancient fishing town of Whitby. The North Yorkshire Moors Steam Railway starts two miles away at Grosmont. Ideal for children, birdwatchers and all country lovers. Each caravan has mains electricity, gas cooker, fire, colour TV, fridge and shower/WC. Ideal touring centre. Riding lessons available on our own horses/ponies. Terms from £115. Telephone or write with SAE, please.

Riding the range of the Yewdale Fells around Coniston, Cumbria.

ACTIVITY HOLIDAYS

DEVON, ASHBURTON. Mrs Rhona Parker, Higher Mead Farm, Ashburton TQ13 7LJ (01364 652598; Fax: 01364 654004). SELF CATERING:

GENERAL. A friendly, family-run farm site set in 400 acres and surrounded by beautiful countryside. 12 miles from the sea and close to Dartmoor National Park; ideal for touring Devon/Cornwall. Perfect for children and pets with all farm animals, play area and plenty of space to roam, also large area for dogs. Holiday cottages and caravans, fully equipped except for linen. Level touring site with some hard standings. Free showers in fully tiled block, laundry room and games room. Small family bar, shop and phone. Prices start from £90 Low Season to £380 High Season. Good discounts for couples. From Exeter take A38 to Plymouth till you see "26 miles Plymouth" sign; take second left at Alston Cross signposted to Woodland and Denbury.

DEVON, EXETER near. Mr D.L. Salter, Haldon Lodge Farm, Kennford, Near Exeter EX6 7YG (01392 832312). Working farm. SELF CATERING: RIDING &

TREKKING. Peace and seclusion are assured on this private residential site. The Salters offer a family holiday for all ages, with a special invitation to younger members to join in pony riding and enjoy a free and easy farm holiday with them. Exeter four and a half miles. Dawlish (short car drive away) ideal centre for touring all South Devon resorts and Dartmoor. The three six-berth residential holiday caravans adjoin a large lawn with background of fields, pine trees, rhododendrons. Six comfortable beds, blankets, pillows. Fully equipped kitchen, carpeted lounge (TV), bathroom (H/C), flush toilet, electricity and mains connected. Horses and ponies nearby are an interest to everyone. Horse lovers and children we invite to explore the beautiful Teign Valley Forest on horseback. Day pony treks arranged for small parties. The well-known Nobody Inn is one of the many attractive country inns where you can have a drink and a meal in the midst of a friendly atmosphere. Pets allowed. Three well stocked fishing lakes. Riding and Trekking Holidays from £55 per week. Caravans March to December from £70 to £195 per week. Tourers and campers from £4 per day. No extra charge for pets, etc.

DEVON, HOLSWORTHY near. Churchtown House, Clawton, Near Holsworthy EX22 6PS (01409 271467). BOARD: PAINTING COURSES. A warm welcome in centuries old farmhouse. Full board and residential courses in painting. Watercolours, oils, pastels and acrylics; spinning, dying, rug making, baskets; make and decorate paper, etc. Two tutors who also lecture at the local college. A chance to learn and relax away from the crowds. Set on the edge of small village and off main roads, also ideal base for touring famous breathtaking local coastline. Both Bodmin and Dartmoor within easy reach. Idyllic villages, golf, swimming, riding, walking. Non participant partners welcome. Comfortable rooms tastefully decorated and furnished with antiques. Open all year round.

DORSET, DORCHESTER. Mrs Jacobina Langley, The Stables, Hyde Crook (on A37), Frampton, Dorchester DT2 9NW (01300 330075). ♥ ♥ BOARD: RIDING. The Stables is a large equestrian property which sits in a small area of woodland off the A37 which provides easy travelling to Dorchester from a location which enjoys uninterrupted views of open Dorset countryside. We are a registered smallholding of approximately 20 acres, with sheep, ducks and horses and specialise in providing accommodation and livery for cross country riding. Pets, particularly dogs, are always welcome.

DURHAM, WATERHOUSES. Roger and Pauline Booth, Ivesley Equestrian Centre, Waterhouses DH7 9HB (0191 3734324; Fax: 0191 3734757). ♥ ♥ ♥ *HIGHLY COMMENDED.* Elegantly furnished country house set in 220 acres. All bedrooms decorated to high standard — most en suite. Wine cellar. Adjacent to Equestrian Centre with first class facilities. An ideal centre for walking, sightseeing and excellent mountain biking. Collection arranged from Durham Station and Newcastle Airport. Durham seven miles. Dogs welcome. "Good food, good company and beautiful surroundings". Please write or telephone for further information and rates.

NORTHUMBERLAND, NINEBANKS. Mrs Mavis Ostler, Taylor Burn, Ninebanks, Hexham NE47 8DE (01434 345343). BOARD: GENERAL. Warm welcome, good food on quiet working hill farm with spectacular views of Pennine Dales, three miles above Ninebanks. Large, comfortable, centrally heated farmhouse with spacious bedrooms, hospitality trays; guests' bathroom; guests' lounge with log fires and colour TV; beamed dining room with Aga. Excellent for walkers, ornithologists, country lovers — but no smoking. Pets welcome. Guests free to join in farm activities, observe cattle, sheep, free range hens — even learn to work a sheep dog or build a stone wall. Bed and Breakfast from £14 to £16 per adult; Evening Meal £9. Special diets catered for, home produce whenever available. Special weekend breaks and 10% reductions for one week's stay. Write or ring for personal reply.

SOMERSET, CHEDDAR. Broadway House Holiday Touring Caravan and Camping Park, Cheddar (01934 742610; Fax: 01934 744950). SELF CATERING: GENERAL. ✓ ✓ ✓ ✓ Cheddar Gorge — "England's Grand Canyon". A totally unique five star caravan and camping family experience. One of the most interesting inland parks in the West Country. A family business specialising in family holidays. A free cuddle with the llamas a speciality. Prices include the use of the heated outdoor swimming pool and entrance to the Bar/Family room. Activities on the park include archery, abseiling and shooting; mountain bike/tandem hire; table tennis, crazy golf, boules, croquet, skate-board ramps. AA 4 Pennants; RAC Appointed, Rose Award Park.

FOR THE MUTUAL GUIDANCE OF GUEST AND HOST

Every year literally thousands of holidays, short-breaks and overnight stops are arranged through our guides, the vast majority without any problems at all. In a handful of cases, however, difficulties do arise about bookings, which often could have been prevented from the outset.

It is important to remember that when accommodation has been booked, both parties — guests and hosts — have entered into a form of contract. We hope that the following points will provide helpful guidance.

GUESTS: When enquiring about accommodation, be as precise as possible. Give exact dates, numbers in your party and the ages of any children. State the number and type of rooms wanted and also what catering you require — bed and breakfast, full board, etc. Make sure that the position about evening meals is clear — and about pets, reductions for children or any other special points.

Read our reviews carefully to ensure that the proprietors you are going to contact can supply what you want. Ask for a letter confirming all arrangements, if possible.

If you have to cancel, do so as soon as possible. Proprietors do have the right to retain deposits and under certain circumstances to charge for cancelled holidays if adequate notice is not given and they cannot re-let the accommodation.

HOSTS: Give details about your facilities and about any special conditions. Explain your deposit system clearly and arrangements for cancellations, charges, etc, and whether or not your terms include VAT.

If for any reason you are unable to fulfil an agreed booking without adequate notice, you may be under an obligation to arrange alternative suitable accommodation or to make some form of compensation.

While every effort is made to ensure accuracy, we regret that FHG Publications cannot accept responsibility for errors, omissions or misrepresentation in our entries or any consequences thereof. Prices in particular should be checked because we go to press early. We will follow up complaints but cannot act as arbiters or agents for either party.

WALES

BOARD ACCOMMODATION

NORTH WALES (formerly Clwyd and Gwynedd)

Aberconwy & Colwyn, Anglesey, Denbighshire, Flintshire, Gwynedd and Wrexham

ABERDARON. Barbara and David Marshallsay, Carreg Plas, Aberdaron, Pwllheli LL53 8LH (01758 760308).

🌼🌼🌼 17th century manor house of historic interest in sheltered position on west side of Lleyn Peninsula, set in five acres of secluded wooded grounds, surrounded by National Trust land. Only half a mile from the well-known Whistling Sands Beach, and two miles from the picturesque village of Aberdaron. Lovely coastal scenery and sandy beaches nearby. Seven bedrooms available with washbasins and tea-making facilities, five en-suite or with private bath/ shower room. Central heating throughout. Large lounge; separate TV lounge; two diningrooms. Cots, high chairs provided, children especially welcome (reduced rates). Pets by arrangement. Ample car parking. Open all year. Bed and Breakfast from £17.50 to £24.50; Evening Meal, Bed and Breakfast from £27.50. Guests requested not to smoke in house.

ANGLESEY SOUTH. Mrs Naylor, Bryntirion Working Farm, Dwyran, Anglesey LL61 6BQ (01248 430876). 🌼 Bryntirion is situated just off the A4080 midway between Brynsiencyn and picturesque Newborough beach. The farmhouse is pleasant with guests' TV lounge, tea making facilities and dining room. A Fire Certificate is held. Bed and full Breakfast from £14. Children's play area. The farm is open to the public for guided tours from May to September. There is a tea room with home made cakes and scones and an interesting exhibition plus antique farm machinery; wood turning, fishing. Our farm tours are a fascinating experience, which children enjoy particularly. Large car park. Open March to October. Leaflet available.

BALA. Mrs C.A. Morris, Tai'r Felin Farm, Frongoch, Bala LL23 7NS (01678 520763). WTB

COMMENDED. Tai'r Felin Farm is situated three miles north of Bala (A4212 and B4501 roads). Double and twin bedrooms with washbasins, tea/coffee facilities, clock radio; bathroom with shower; lounge with colour TV and log fire when weather is cool. Separate tables in the dining room. Recommended for excellent cooking and friendly atmosphere. Ideal base for walks, sailing (Bala Lake) and for touring Snowdonia Mountains and coast. National White Water Centre is nearby. Relax and enjoy a homely welcome. Please write or telephone for further information.

BALA. Mrs S.E. Edwards, Bryn Melyn, Rhyduchaf, Bala LL23 7PG (01678 520376). ✿ *COMMEN-DED.* **Working farm.** Bryn Melyn, Rhyduchaf is situated in the beautiful countryside of Bala, and offers accommodation all year. The house is stone-built and stands on 56 acres of mixed farmland. Home cooking and home produced food makes this a real home from home. Two double and one twin bedrooms (two with washbasins); two bathrooms, toilet; sittingroom; diningroom; central heating. Children welcome at reduced rates. Sorry, no pets. A car is necessary to ensure that visitors derive all the pleasure that this region offers. Parking space. Sea 28 miles. Good recreation facilities in the area. Evening Dinner, Bed and Breakfast from £148 weekly or Bed and Breakfast £14.50 per person, with Dinner £23. No smoking. Mrs Edwards is a Farm Holiday Guide Diploma winner.

BALA. Mr T. Glyn Jones, Frondderw Private Hotel, Stryd-y-Fron, Bala LL23 7YD (01678 520301).

✿✿ *COMMENDED.* Delightful period mansion on the hillside five minutes from the town of Bala and within the boundaries of Snowdonia National Park. There are lovely walks, boating, swimming, fishing and picnic facilities, golf and magnificent scenery. The accommodation is well maintained and consists of eight bedrooms, four en suite, two with showers, all with washbasins, central heating and tea/coffee making facilities. Guests' lounge, separate TV lounge and diningroom. Non-smoking accommodation available. Residential licence. Free parking. Sorry, no pets in the house. Open March to November inclusive. Bed and Breakfast from £15 to £21 daily, £101.50 to £143.50 per week; Dinner optional £9. Dinner, Bed and Breakfast from £161 to £203 per person per week. AA QQ. WTB Welcome Host.

BALA near. Mrs J. Best, Cwm Hwylfod, Cefn-Ddwysarn, Bala LL23 7LN (01678 530310). ✿

Cwm Hwylfod

COMMENDED. **Working farm.** Remote, peaceful 400 year old farmhouse on working sheep farm. Beautiful countryside and wonderful views. Two double rooms, one large family room, all with washbasins and tea making facilities. Two bathrooms; clothes washing and drying machines. Guest lounge with colour TV. Full central heating. Cot, high chair available. Parking space. All meals are home cooked. Special diets catered for. Ideal centre for touring, walking, fishing, pony trekking and watersports. Bala Lake 10 minutes by car. Snowdon and many beaches can be reached in 40 minutes. Bed and Breakfast from £14 to £16; Evening Meal optional from £10. Reductions for long stays and children under 10 years. Brochure available. Children most welcome.

BARMOUTH. Mrs A. Jones, Byrdir Farm, Dyffryn Ardudwy, Barmouth LL44 2EA (01341 247200).

✿✿ *HIGHLY COMMENDED.* Dragon Award. Welsh stone farmhouse in peaceful setting in Snowdonia National Park with coastline in front, mountains to rear. Woods, streams, beaches, lovely walks, golf, swimming pools, fishing, riding nearby. Double and family bedrooms, three en suite; sitting room with colour TV; dining room. Children welcome at reduced rates. Open March to September. Bed and Breakfast from £17 per person per night.

BEDDGELERT. Joan Williams, Colwyn, Beddgelert, Gwynedd LL55 4UY (01766 890276).

✿✿✿ Welcome to Colwyn. Warm, small and friendly our 18th century cottage guesthouse, with its original stone fireplace in the low beamed lounge, is restful and cosy. Old fashioned (but modernised of course), most rooms en suite with white linen, warm duvets, Welsh tapestry covers and central heating. Colwyn overlooks the river in the centre of picturesque Beddgelert, probably the most popular and unspoilt village in the area, lying in a National Trust valley right at the foot of Snowdon with lakes, streams and forests all around. Spectacular scenery both winter and summer, a perfect central base for the whole National Park. There are small shops, inns, cafes in the village. Walkers, muddy boots and exhausted dogs welcome. Bed and Breakfast from £19. Booking advisable. Also tiny cottage, sleeps two, £165 weekly, self-catering. Low Season Breaks, Monday-Friday (4 nights B&B) £60 p.p.

Terms quoted in this publication may be subject to increase if rises in costs necessitate

BETWS-Y-COED. Mrs E. Jones, Maes-y-Garnedd, Capel Garmon, Llanrwst, Betws-y-Coed (01690 710 428). Tourist Board *APPROVED.* **Working farm.** This

140-acre mixed farm is superbly situated on the Rooftop of Wales as Capel Garmon has been called, and the Snowdonia Range, known to the Welsh as the "Eyri", is visible from the land. Two miles from A5. Surrounding area provides beautiful country scenery and excellent walks. Safe, sandy beaches at Llandudno and Colwyn Bay. Salmon and trout fishing (permit required). Mrs Jones serves excellent home produced meals with generous portions including Welsh Lamb and Roast Beef. Gluten-free diets can be arranged. Packed lunches, with flask of coffee or tea. One double and one family bedrooms with washbasins; bathroom, toilet; sitting-room and diningroom. Children welcome, cot, high chair and babysitting available. Regret, no pets. Car essential, ample parking. Open all year. Bed and Breakfast, Evening Meal optional. SAE brings prompt reply with details and terms. Reductions for children. Bala Lakes, Bodnant Gardens, Ffestiniog Railway, slate quarries, Trefriw Woollen Mills nearby. Member of AA.

BETWS-Y-COED. Mrs Meryl Metcalfe, Tan Yr Eglwys, Llanrhychwyn, Trefriw, Llanrwst LL27 0YJ

(01492 640547). ✿ 'Tan Yr Eglwys' is a modernised farmhouse where some of the walls are a yard thick! Llanrhychwyn is a little hamlet, conveniently situated above the Conwy Valley between the market town of Llanrwst and Trefriw village. A car is essential, unless very energetic! Ideal haven for country lovers and hill walkers. Central for mountains and lakes of Snowdonia and also the coast. The farmhouse is surrounded by fields and woods. The ancient Church at St. Rhychwyn is about 800 yards up a path leading from the farm. Places of interest include Betws-y-Coed (golf) four miles; Trefriw (Woollen Mill) one mile; Llanrwst two miles, Geirionnydd Lake two miles, Llanberis (Snowdon) 17 miles, Llandudno 10 miles. A homely welcome with log fires available on chilly evenings, and good home cooking is assured. All rooms have washbasins. Open Easter to October. Terms on application. Reduction for children in family rooms. SAE for prompt reply and directions from main road. OS Grid Reference 777616. We also have a static caravan in a lawned garden backed by forest.

BETWS-Y-COED. Jim and Lilian Boughton, Bron Celyn Guest House, Llanrwst Road, Betws-y-Coed

LL24 0HD (01690 710333; Fax: 01690 710111). ✿✿✿ *HIGHLY COMMENDED.* A warm welcome awaits you at this delightful guest house overlooking the Gwydyr Forest and Llugwy/Conwy Valleys and village of Betws-y-Coed in Snowdonia National Park. Ideal centre for touring, walking, climbing, fishing and golf. Also excellent overnight stop en-route for Holyhead ferries. Easy walk into village and close to Conwy/Swallow Falls and Fairy Glen. Most rooms en-suite, all with colour TV and beverage makers. Lounge. Full central heating. Garden. Car park. Open all year. Full hearty breakfast, packed meals, snacks, evening meals — special diets catered for. Bed and Breakfast from £16 to £20, reduced rates for children under 12 years.

BETWS-Y-COED. Mrs M. Jones, Tyddyn Gethin Farm, Penmachno, Betws-y-Coed LL24 0PS (01690 760392). Working farm. 80 acre mixed farm situated 200 yards off B4406 quarter of a mile from village, one mile from woollen mill and falls. Very central for touring and within easy reach of the sea, mountains. Pony trekking nearby; walks. Stone farmhouse with lovely views, clean and comfortable and serving good breakfasts. Always a warm welcome. All bedrooms have washbasins and shaving points; bathroom with shower and separate shower room; two lounges, one with colour TV; log fires when needed; dining room with separate tables. Ample parking. Bed and Breakfast from £13.50 to £15. Self catering cottage nearby (sleeps four) also available from £90 to £258 per week.

BETWS-Y-COED. Ann and Arthur Eaton, Crafnant Guest House, Trefriw LL27 0JH (01492 640809). Quality accommodation and service can be enjoyed at Crafnant, an elegant Victorian residence in the charming village of Trefriw, Conwy Valley. The village is known for its Woollen Mill, Roman Spa, fishing, lakes and forest walks. The RSPB Nature Reserve, Snowdon, Bodnant Gardens and other attractions are within easy reach. Five en suite double/twin rooms with drinks tray and TV. Bed and Breakfast from £15 to £16. Children up to 12 years £8. Special Discount — book seven nights pay only for six. Evening Meal (optional) £8.50 plus coffee. Dogs by arrangement £2 per night. Non-smoking. Private parking. Open all year except Christmas and Boxing Day.

BLAENAU FFESTINIOG. Keith and Liz Lethbridge, Cae Du Guest House, Manod, Blaenau Ffestiniog LL41 4BB (01766 830847). ❀ ❀ ❀ Cae Du is a part 16th century farmhouse in the heart of Snowdonia. It is no longer a working farm but is quiet and peaceful whilst central to most of Snowdonia's varied attractions. There are wonderfully scenic walks direct from the house which is set up on a mountain looking down the beautiful Vale of Ffestiniog. Also available in the area: fishing, canoeing, climbing, birdwatching, pony trekking and a dry ski slope, as well as castles, mines and a steam railway. Keith and Liz run Cae Du as their own home to which you are given a warm welcome as guests or friends; they provide home cooking with a vegetarian menu too. Bed and Breakfast from £21.50. Children over 12 welcome. Brochure available.

CAERNARFON. Mrs Lilian Wyn Griffiths, Meifod, Bontnewydd, Caernarfon LL55 2TY (01286 673351). ❀ ❀ ❀ Lilian and Rodney welcome you to Meifod in the Royal town of Caernarfon, set in five acres of mature gardens with own tennis court, plus games room. The en suite bedrooms (two double, one twin and one family) have TV and tea/coffee facilities. Beach, golf, Snowdonia and many more attractions only a few minutes' drive away. We will assure you a comfortable stay with real Welsh hospitality. From £15 per night.

CAERNARFON. Mrs V. Edwards, Chatham Farmhouse, Llandwrog, Caernarfon LL54 5TG (01286 831257). ❀ ❀ HIGHLY COMMENDED. Croeso, welcome to our peaceful 18th century guesthouse situated four miles from Caernarfon, two from Dinas Dingle beach, very near good bird watching area. All Snowdonia's attractions within easy reach. Enjoy lazy breakfasts that include free range eggs from our own hens. Wholesome evening meals include vegetables organically grown in our own garden. Tea-making facilities in all the cosy rooms (two en suite, one with private bathroom). Rooms have central heating, dining room has a wood burning stove. Guests' TV lounge. Children welcome, sorry no pets. Bed and Breakfast £17; Evening Meal £10. Looking forward to meeting you.

CAERNARFON. Mrs B. Cartwright, "Tan Dinas", Llanddeiniolen, Caernarfon LL55 3AR (01248 670098). Tourist Board Listed. A modernised stone farmhouse situated in a picturesque, secluded, yet very central location and surrounded by typical Welsh scenic beauty, with a pleasant garden sloping down to a small stream running alongside the woods. Guests have their own private and centrally-heated lounge and diningroom. The area is ideal for touring, all types of fishing, walking and pony trekking if required. Caernarfon, Bangor, Anglesey and Snowdon itself are all within very easy reach. Take the B4366 out of Caernarvon. One mile through Bethel come to the "Gors Bach Inn". Turn into lane by side of Inn and travel on for half a mile. Children welcome, cot, high chair, babysitting available. Car essential — parking. Open March to October with central heating and open fires. Pets accepted. Bed and Breakfast from £15; Evening Dinner optional. Reductions for children.

TAN Y GAER

Rhosgadfan, Nr. Caernarvon, LL55 7LE · Phone Paula & David Foster 01286 830943

Set in spectcular scenery with views to the top of Snowdon and over the Irish Sea, this farmhouse with beams and open fires offers a restful atmosphere from which to enjoy beautiful North Wales. Riding, climbing, walking and beaches are all close by. The homemade bread and farmhouse cooking are done on the 'Aga' and much of the food is home produced. Guests have their own diningroom and lounge with TV, books, etc. The ensuite bedrooms include family room and a downstairs bedroom. Evening Meal with Bed and Breakfast from £20. Reductions for weekly stays. Telephone/SAE for details, please.

CONWY. Mr and Mrs W. Hansel, Llys Gwilym Guest House, 3 Mountain Road, Cadnant Park, Conwy LL32 8PU (01492 592351). 🌸 *COMMENDED.* Llys Gwilym is just a few minutes' walk to Conwy Castle, the town, quayside and close to the Conwy Valley and all Snowdonia. Quietly located at the foot of Conwy Mountain and adjacent to the Sychnant Pass. Bill and Barbara offer you a warm and friendly welcome. We have seven letting bedrooms comprising singles, double, twin and family; all have washbasins, colour TV and tea/coffee making facilities. There is also a homely residents' lounge with books and games, etc. A hearty breakfast is one of our features with other meals by arrangement. Special off season price Bed, Breakfast and Evening Meal £18 per person.

CONWY. Mrs Sylvia Baxter, Glyn Uchaf, Conwy Old Road, Dwygyfyichi, Penmaenmawr, Conwy LL34 6YS (01492 623737). 🌸🌸 *HIGHLY COMMENDED.* Enjoy a quiet, peaceful holiday at this old mill house set in 11 acres of National Parkland in beautiful mountainous countryside. Ideal touring centre for Snowdonia. Accommodation comprises three bedrooms, all en-suite and having lovely views. Lounge with colour TV; diningroom. Excellent cuisine with varied menus and home produce. Tea/coffee making facilities available. Children welcome. Two-and-a-half miles to Conwy, five to Llandudno and Colwyn Bay — three minutes' walk to village. Pony trekking and fishing locally. Ample parking. Guests have access to house at all times. Bed and Breakfast from £18 to £20, or Bed, Breakfast and Evening Meal. Moderate terms, reductions for children under 12. Highly recommended. SAE or phone please.

CRICCIETH. Mrs S.A. Reynolds, Glyn-y-Coed, Porthmadoc Road, Criccieth LL52 0HL (01766 522870; Fax: 01766 523341). 🌸🌸🌸 *HIGHLY COMMENDED.* Lovely Victorian family Hotel facing sea, mountains and two castles. Full central heating, cosy bar, private parking. Highly recommended home cooking with most diets catered for. All bedrooms en suite (one ground floor bedroom) with colour TV and tea-making facilities. Moderate rates with good reductions for children. Also available self catering accommodation sleeping nine plus cot. In own grounds with parking, just two minutes from beach and four minutes from shop and pub. Terms: Bed and Breakfast from £19 to £22 per person per night; Self Catering accommodation from £120 to £500 per week.

PLEASE SEND A STAMPED ADDRESSED ENVELOPE WITH ENQUIRIES

DOLGELLAU. Mrs Griffiths, Llwyn Tal Cen, Brithdir, Dolgellau LL40 2RY (01341 450276). WTB

Welcome Home Commended. "Taste of Wales" member. Situated in an acre of rhododendron and azalea gardens, Llwyn Tal Cen offers a warm welcome, outstanding views, together with peace and quiet. Our location, about four miles east of Dolgellau, makes an ideal centre for hill walkers and nature lovers. We offer good fresh food, organic whenever possible. Traditional and vegetarian fare are both available. Bed and Breakfast from £15 to £18; Evening Meal £9. En suite rooms available. Reduced rates are available for children. Ample parking. To find us take narrow lane from the centre of the village of Brithdir (telephone box) past the village hall and wooden houses for about half a mile until you reach a crossroads, turn right, Llwyn Tal Cen is on the right in the trees after about 200 yards.

DOLGELLAU. Mrs Olwen Evans, Tyddyn Mawr Farmhouse, Islawrdref, Dolgellau LL40 1TL (01341 422331). WTB ✹ ✹ DE LUXE. Working farm, join in. Welcome Host Award, Farm and Guest House Award. It's paradise! Honestly! Situated in the Snowdonia National Park, a warm Welsh welcome awaits you in this lovingly restored 18th century farmhouse with its beams, log fires and superbly furnished en suite bedrooms with fantastic mountain views creating a heavenly atmosphere. We actually farm 800 acres of the magnificent Cader Idris mountain with its waterfalls, slate mines, caves and fishing in the mountain lake on the farm. We offer peace, tranquillity and seclusion. Bed and Breakfast £20.

DOLGELLAU. Mrs D.M. Rowlands, Tanyfron, Arran Road, Dolgellau LL40 2AA (Tel & Fax: 01341 422638). ✹ ✹ HIGHLY COMMENDED. A warm welcome and hearty breakfast, cooked to your liking, awaits you in this 100 year old former stone farmhouse. Modernised with all amenities. Three good sized bedrooms, all en suite with matching decor, hair dryers, tea/coffee making, colour TV with 10 channels, clock/radio and full central heating. Open February to end of November. There is ample private, safe parking within the grounds with flowers in abundance. The use of laundry facilities and public telephone are at hand, and we are only a 10 minute walk from Dolgellau for your evening meal. There is also a two-bedroomed converted barn for self catering holidays (Grade 4). Non smokers only. Sorry, no pets.

HARLECH. Mrs G.M. Evans, Glanygors, Llandanwg, Harlech LL46 2SD (01341 241410). ✹ HIGHLY

COMMENDED. This detached house with two acres of land is situated 400 yards from sandy beach, and has beautiful views of the mountains. It is one and a half miles from Harlech Castle, golf club and swimming pool, and within a quarter mile of train station. Ideal place for bird watching. Presenting good home cooking in a homely and relaxed atmosphere and run by a Welsh-speaking family. Open all year. Central heating and electric blankets for Winter months. Accommodation comprises two double, one twin and one family bedrooms, all with washbasins, TV and tea-making facilities; bathroom, toilet; TV lounge and diningroom. Reduced rates for children and Senior Citizens. Bed and Breakfast from £14 per night; Evening Meal optional.

LLANBERIS. Dolafon Hotel, High Street, Llanberis LL55 4SU (01286 870993). ✹ ✹ A small

family-run NON SMOKING hotel, all rooms are en suite with colour TV and tea/coffee making facilities. We have a small licensed restaurant and bar which offers a varied menu including home-made Welsh dishes and a good vegetarian selection. Dolafon is situated on the main street of Llanberis and is separated from the road by a large lawned garden bordered by mature trees and a small mountain streams, offering ample secluded private parking. Llanberis has many places of interest, the Slate Museum, Dinorwic Hydro Electric Power Station, Dolbadarn Castle and nearby Caernarfon and Beaumaris Castles. Bed and Breakfast from £16.

PUBLISHER'S NOTE

While every effort is made to ensure accuracy, we regret that FHG Publications cannot accept responsibility for errors, omissions or misrepresentation in our entries or any consequences thereof. Prices in particular should be checked because we go to press early. We will follow up complaints but cannot act as arbiters or agents for either party.

LLANDRINDOD WELLS. Mrs Ruth Jones, Holly Farm, Howey, Llandrindod Wells LD1 5PP (01597

822402). ✿ ✿ ✿ *HIGHLY COMMENDED.* Holly Farm, set in beautiful countryside, offers guests a friendly welcome. Situated one and a half miles south of the spa town of Llandrindod Wells, it is an excellent base for exploring lakes and mountains and for birdwatching. Most rooms are en suite with beverage trays. There is a TV lounge with log fire; in the dining room, which has separate tables, superb meals are served using home produce. Safe car parking. Brochure on request. Bed and Breakfast from £17; Bed, Breakfast and Evening Meals from £25 to £27. Weekly rates from £170 to £180. AA QQQ.

LLANDUDNO. Mrs E. Jones, Gloddaeth Isa Farm, Derwen Lane, Penrhynside, Llandudno LL30 3DP

(01492 549209). A warm welcome awaits you at Gloddaeth Isa Farm, situated close to the village of Penrhynside, two miles from the popular Victorian holiday resort of Llandudno with its many and varied attractions. The Great Orme and Happy Valley are always a source of interest. Ideally located for touring the North Wales coast and Anglesey, within easy reach of the famous Bodnant Gardens and the historic town of Conway. We offer spacious and comfortable bedrooms with tea/coffee making facilities; two bathrooms; TV lounge. Ample car space. Children welcome. Bed and Breakfast; Evening Meal by arrangement. Enquiries to **Mrs Eirwen Jones.**

LLANFAIRFECHAN. Mrs K.M. Coleman, Plas Heulog, Mount Road, Llanfairfechan LL33 0HA (Tel &

Fax: 01248 680019). ✿ ✿ *COMMENDED.* Situated in the Snowdonia region, Plas Heulog gives breathtaking views of both sea and mountains. It offers total seclusion in its nine acres of woodland, yet it is easily accessible from the A55 expressway and main line station. Sailing, windsurfing, jet ski-ing, golf, bowls, riding, sea and freshwater fishing are all within easy reach as well as several nature reserves. Centrally heated double and twin en suite bedrooms are situated in modern chalets above the main house with provision for making tea and coffee. Breakfast is taken in the main house, where a spacious lounge is available for guests' use. Facilities include drying room, secure bicycle storage and ample parking. Wales Tourist Board Approved for walkers and cyclists.

MACHYNLLETH. Mrs Lynwen Edwards, Bryn Sion Farm, Cwm Cywarch, Dinas Mawddwy,

Machynlleth SY20 9JG (01650 531251). A very warm welcome awaits you when you visit Bryn Sion Farm which is situated in the quiet, unspoilt valley of Cywarch at the foot of Arran Fawddwy (3,000ft), within easy reach of the beach. Fishing and shooting available on farm. Bryn Sion is a mixed farm of 700 acres offering a variety of good farmhouse meals and bed-time tea/coffee. Log fire in sittingroom in evening. Two double rooms, both with tea making facilities, shaving points, washbasins; bathroom. Car essential — parking. Open April to November for Bed and Breakfast at £15 per person. SAE, please, with enquiries.

WALES

PENGWERN. Gwyndaf and Jane Lloyd Rowlands, Pengwern, Saron, Llanwnda, Caernarfon LL54 5UH (Tel & Fax: 01286 831500; 0378 411780 mobile).

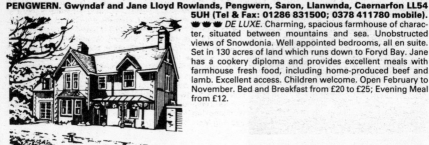

🐾 🐾 *DE LUXE.* Charming, spacious farmhouse of character, situated between mountains and sea. Unobstructed views of Snowdonia. Well appointed bedrooms, all en suite. Set in 130 acres of land which runs down to Foryd Bay. Jane has a cookery diploma and provides excellent meals with farmhouse fresh food, including home-produced beef and lamb. Excellent access. Children welcome. Open February to November. Bed and Breakfast from £20 to £25; Evening Meal from £12.

See also Colour Display Advertisement **PORTHMADOG. Tyddyn Du Farm Holidays, Gellilydan, Near Ffestiniog LL41 4RB (Tel & Fax: 01766 590281).**

🐾 🐾 🐾 *HIGHLY COMMENDED.* Enchanting old world farmhouse, set amidst spectacular scenery in the heart of the Snowdonia National Park, with a friendly, relaxed atmosphere. Excellent central base for North Wales. One superb private ground floor cottage suite (WTB Farmhouse Award). Delicious candle-light dinners with excellent farmhouse cuisine. Working farm — feed the ducks and fuss over Polly the pony. We are easy to find near village of Gellilydan. Open all year. Bed and Breakfast from £17, Dinner £10; weekly Dinner, Bed and Breakfast £165 to £200. Stamp please for brochure to **Mrs P. Williams.**

RHOS-ON-SEA, near Llandudno. Mr and Mrs Mike Willington, Sunnydowns Hotel, 66 Abbey Road, Rhos-on-Sea, Near Llandudno LL28 4NU (01492 544256; Fax: 01492 543223).

🐾 🐾 🐾 A family run hotel. All rooms en suite with colour TV, video and Satellite channels, clock radio, tea/coffee facilities, hair dryer, mini bar refrigerator, direct dial telephone and central heating. Hotel facilities also include bar, pool room, restaurant, sauna and car park. Situated just a five minute walk from Rhos-on-Sea Golf Club and with four more championship courses close by. Telephone, or fax, for brochure and special group terms.

FOR THE MUTUAL GUIDANCE OF GUEST AND HOST

Every year literally thousands of holidays, short-breaks and overnight stops are arranged through our guides, the vast majority without any problems at all. In a handful of cases, however, difficulties do arise about bookings, which often could have been prevented from the outset.

It is important to remember that when accommodation has been booked, both parties — guests and hosts — have entered into a form of contract. We hope that the following points will provide helpful guidance.

GUESTS: When enquiring about accommodation, be as precise as possible. Give exact dates, numbers in your party and the ages of any children. State the number and type of rooms wanted and also what catering you require — bed and breakfast, full board, etc. Make sure that the position about evening meals is clear — and about pets, reductions for children or any other special points.

Read our reviews carefully to ensure that the proprietors you are going to contact can supply what you want. Ask for a letter confirming all arrangements, if possible.

If you have to cancel, do so as soon as possible. Proprietors do have the right to retain deposits and under certain circumstances to charge for cancelled holidays if adequate notice is not given and they cannot re-let the accommodation.

HOSTS: Give details about your facilities and about any special conditions. Explain your deposit system clearly and arrangements for cancellations, charges, etc, and whether or not your terms include VAT.

If for any reason you are unable to fulfil an agreed booking without adequate notice, you may be under an obligation to arrange alternative suitable accommodation or to make some form of compensation.

While every effort is made to ensure accuracy, we regret that FHG Publications cannot accept responsibility for errors, omissions or misrepresentation in our entries or any consequences thereof. Prices in particular should be checked because we go to press early. We will follow up complaints but cannot act as arbiters or agents for either party.

RUTHIN. Mrs S.M. Edwards, Cynet, Llangynhafal, Near Denbigh LL16 4LN (Tel & Fax: 01824 790322). ✿✿✿ *DE LUXE.*

Cygnet is situated below the Clwydian Hills close to 15th century church and inn hosting Welsh singing (Saturday evenings). Magnificent views of the Vale of Clwyd. Ideal for visiting Snowdonia, Llangollen, Chester; Ruthin four miles, Denbigh six miles. All bedrooms have tea/coffee facilities, colour TV, central heating and en suite bathrooms. Children welcome, cots and high chairs available. Dogs by arrangement. Accessible to a wheelchair user with an assistant; ground floor bedrooms available. Discounts for two nights or more. Christmas and New Year Breaks. Telephone or fax for colour brochure. Open all year. Non-smoking. Welcome Host. Bed and Breakfast from £20; Evening Meal by prior arrangement £15 with free wine.

RUTHIN. Mrs E.O. Jones, Llanbenwch Farm, Llanfair D.C., Ruthin LL15 2SH (01824 702340).

Traditional longhouse situated three miles south from Ruthin, on the main (A525) Wrexham road, this is a 40-acre working farm amidst beautiful scenery. The old house, oak-beamed and modernised without spoiling its character, is conveniently situated for travelling throughout North Wales. There is a nice garden and quiet roads for evening walks. Good food is assured, with personal attention. One family, one double and one twin bedrooms, all with washbasins, TV and tea-making facilities; bathroom, two toilets; diningroom with separate tables, sittingroom with TV. Central heating. Sorry, no dogs in house and no children under five years. Ample parking. Open February to November. Bed and Breakfast from £13.50 daily. SAE, please, for reply.

RUTHIN. Mrs B. Quinn, Berllan Bach, Ffordd Las, Llandyrnog, Ruthin LL16 4LR (01824 790732 or 01374 128494). ✿✿✿

This 18th century cottage nestles at the foot of the Clwydian Hills. En suite bedrooms with French windows opening onto individual patios to give our guests freedom and privacy. The "Olde Worlde" sittingroom with inglenook and beamed ceiling and a bright conservatory are available for your pleasure. Situated equidistant between the medieval towns of Ruthin and Denbigh with castles and medieval banquets. While evening meals are available there are country pubs and restaurants within one and a half miles. Ideally situated for touring with Chester and Snowdonia Park less than 25 miles away and Caernarfon and Conwy Castles reached in less than one hour. Children and pets warmly welcomed. Bed and Breakfast from £17.50 to £20. FHG Diploma Winner. Further details on request.

ST. ASAPH. Mrs Eirlys Jones, Rhewl Farm, Waen, St. Asaph LL17 0DT (01745 582287). ✿✿

COMMENDED. Enjoy Welsh hospitality on our 180 acre farm, conveniently situated three-quarters of a mile from A55 expressway in peaceful and beautiful setting. Comfortable bedrooms with radiators and tea/coffee making facilities. Double room has en suite facilities, twin and family rooms have washbasins. Spacious lounge with inglenook fireplace and colour TV. Convenient for Chester, coast and Snowdonia. Free fishing. Reductions for children. Bed and Breakfast from £15 to £16.50. This is a non-smoking household. Welcome Host Certificate. Please send SAE for brochure.

WALES

DYFED

Cardiganshire, Carmarthenshire and Pembrokeshire

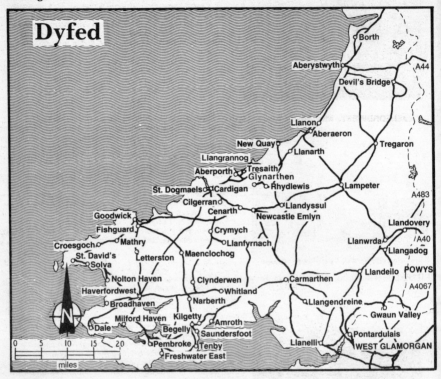

ABERAERON. Mrs Lisa Raw-Rees, Moldavia, 7/8 Bellevue Terrace, Aberaeron SA46 0BB (01545 570107). ♥♥ *HIGHLY COMMENDED.* Aberaeron is described as the prettiest face on the West Wales coast with its Georgian houses painted in vivid colours. Award-winning Moldavia, situated on the quiet side of the pretty harbour, was featured in "Country Living" May 1993. There are four large traditionally furnished rooms; some en suite. Downstairs room suitable for disabled visitors or families. Lovely garden and flower-filled conservatory to relax in. Single guests and children warmly welcomed. Two minutes from beach, shops, bus, restaurants. Good local walks and expert help to plan your days, use of maps and brochures. Fresh coffee, homemade marmalade and breakfast when you want it. Bed and Breakfast from £18.00 to £20 per person; £40 en suite.

BROAD HAVEN near. Sandra Davies, Barley Villa, Walwyn's Castle, Near Broad Haven, Haverfordwest SA62 3EB (01437 781254). ♥♥ *COMMENDED.* Situated in peaceful, attractive countryside, our comfortable modern house overlooks a small nature reserve and is an ideal base for touring Pembrokeshire's beautiful coastline and sandy bays, which are suitable for sailing, surfing and swimming. Visit the bird islands, famous for puffins, Manx shearwaters, kittiwakes and many other species. We have one double room and one twin en suite room with tea/coffee making facilities; spacious lounge/dining room has TV, board games and coal fire on chilly evenings. Comfort, cleanliness and personal attention assured. Substantial breakfasts; packed lunches, special diets catered for. Off road parking. Bed and Breakfast from £14.50 to £16. Six berth caravan also available for hire.

FISHGUARD near. Heathfield Mansion, Letterston, Near Fishguard SA62 5EG (01348 840263).

WTB ❀❀❀ *HIGHLY COMMENDED.* A Grade II Listed Georgian country house in 16 acres of pasture and woodland, Heathfield is the home of former Welsh rugby international, Clive Rees, and his wife Angelica. This is an ideal location for the appreciation of Pembrokeshire's many natural attractions. There is excellent golf, riding and trout fishing in the vicinity and the coast is only a few minutes' drive away. The accommodation is very comfortable, two of the three bedrooms have en suite bathrooms, and the cuisine and wines are well above average. This is a most refreshing venue for a tranquil and wholesome holiday. Children and pets welcome. Bed and Breakfast from £18 per person; Dinner by prior arrangement.

HAVERFORDWEST. Mrs Susan Evans, Spittal Cross Farm, Spittal, Haverfordwest SA62 5DB

(01437 741206). ❀ *HIGHLY COMMENDED.* Come and soak up some of the peaceful atmosphere on our 200 acre dairy farm. We are located in the heart of the beautiful Pembrokeshire countryside, making it an excellent base to visit all parts of the county. From the Preseli Hills to our sandy beaches and colourful cliff tops, all are within easy reach. We offer a hearty Welsh breakfast each morning with optional evening meal. The comfortable guests' lounge has a colour TV, lots of books and board games for guests' use. Bedrooms have washbasins, beverage trays and radio/clock alarms. You can be assured of a real Welsh welcome — Welcome Host Gold Award; Food Hygiene Certificate. Brochure on request. Bed and Breakfast from £15 to £16.

HAVERFORDWEST. Mrs M.E. Davies, Cuckoo Mill Farm, Pelcomb Bridge, St. David's Road, Haverfordwest SA62 6EA (01437 762139). Tourist Board Listed. Working farm. This farm is situated in central Pembrokeshire, two miles out of Haverfordwest on St. David's Road. It is within easy reach of many beaches and coastline walks. There are peaceful country walks on the farm, also a small trout stream. Children are welcome at reduced rates and cot, high chair and babysitting provided. The house is cosy with open fires and welcomes guests from January to December. Car is not essential, but parking available. Home-produced dairy products; poultry and meats all home-cooked. Mealtimes arranged to suit guests. Well appointed, warm, comfortable bedrooms with washbasins and tea-making facilities. Pets permitted. Evening Dinner/Meal, Bed and Breakfast or Bed and Breakfast only. Rates also reduced for Senior Citizens.

HAVERFORDWEST. Joyce Canton, Nolton Haven Farm, Nolton Haven, Haverfordwest SA62 1NH (01437 710263). The farmhouse is beside the beach on a 200 acre mixed farm, with cattle, calves and lots of show ponies. It has a large lounge which is open to guests all day as are all the bedrooms. Single, double and family rooms; two family rooms en suite, four other bathrooms. Pets and children most welcome, babysitting free of charge. 50 yards to the beach, 75 yards to the local inn/restaurant. Pony trekking, surfing, fishing, excellent cliff walks, boating and canoeing are all available nearby. Riding holidays and short breaks all year a speciality. Colour brochure on request.

HAVERFORDWEST. Austalise, Keystone Hill, Camrose, Haverfordwest SA62 6EJ (01437 710303). **❀❀** *HIGHLY COMMENDED.* Newly built guest house surrounded by lawns and flower borders in elevated position with panoramic views of countryside. Within easy reach of many sandy beaches, golf courses, fun park, marvellous coastal walks. 20 minutes from Irish ferry. Free parking within grounds. Children and pets welcome. Open January to December. Bed and Breakfast from £17 to £20.

Key to
Tourist Board Ratings

The Crown Scheme
(England, Scotland & Wales)

Covering hotels, motels, private hotels, guesthouses, inns, bed & breakfast, farmhouses. Every Crown classified place to stay is inspected annually. *The classification:* Listed then 1-5 Crown indicates the range of facilities and services. Higher quality standards are indicated by the terms APPROVED, COMMENDED, HIGHLY COMMENDED and DELUXE.

The Key Scheme
(also operates in Scotland using a Crown symbol)

Covering self-catering in cottages, bungalows, flats, houseboats, houses, chalets, etc. Every Key classified holiday home is inspected annually. *The classification:* 1-5 Key indicates the range of facilities and equipment. Higher quality standards are indicated by the terms APPROVED, COMMENDED, HIGHLY COMMENDED and DELUXE.

The Q Scheme
(England, Scotland & Wales)

Covering holiday, caravan, chalet and camping parks. Every Q rated park is inspected annually for its quality standards. The more √ in the Q – up to 5 – the higher the standard of what is provided.

HAVERFORDWEST. Mrs A.M. Roberts, Haroldston Tongues Farm, Portfield Gate, Haverfordwest SA62 3LE (01437 781287). ☙ Working farm, join in. This comfortable farmhouse on a working dairy farm with lovely views of the Preseli Hills is excellently situated near many sandy beaches — Broad Haven two miles, Newgale three, St. David's 13. Islands of Skomer and Ramsey worth visiting especially during May and June. Riding for novice or expert one mile away. Two double rooms and two single rooms, all with washbasins; room with bath and shower, two toilets; TV lounge and quiet sitting area in large L-shaped dining room. Sorry, no pets and no smoking. Open March to November with central heating. Car essential, parking. Evening Dinner, Bed and Breakfast; Bed and Breakfast. Reduced rates for Senior Citizens in low season. Terms on request. SAE, please.

LLWYNDRAIN. Cwm Bach Guest House, Llwyndrain SA35 0AU (01239 698225). ☙☙ *COMMEN-*

DED. Farmhouse set in idyllic position overlooking panoramic scenery including lake, woodlands and bordered by a stream. Plenty of free parking. Cwm Bach offers comfortable quiet accommodation — double en suite bedrooms with colour TV and tea/coffee making facilities. Ground floor rooms available. Convenient base for touring, walking, beach, golf, fishing, horse riding and visiting Cenarth Waterfalls. Children welcome. Choice of English, Indian or vegetarian food. Bed and Breakfast £13.50 per person per night; optional Evening Meals. Children under 12 years half price if sharing family room. 10% discount if staying three nights or more. Dogs welcome FREE of charge.

MARTINS HAVEN/MARLOES. Mrs Christina Chetwynd, East Hook Farm, Marloes, Haverfordwest SA62 3BJ (01646 636291). Farm on Pembrokeshire Coast Path offering Bed and Breakfast, camping, caravans, horse and pony riding, cycle hire, sea fishing, bird watching and walking. Convenient for boat trips to Skomer and Skokholm Islands and next to Marloes Mere Nature Reserve. 110 acres of natural unspoilt beauty. Bedrooms with washbasins, TVs and tea/coffee making facilities available. Reception room on site. Collection service offered from Haverfordwest. Also transport to Martins Haven for boat trips, diving and Marine Nature Reserve. Bed and Breakfast £15 per person per night. Children welcome.

MYNACHLOG-DDU. Mrs Vivienne Lockton, Dolau Isaf Farm, Mynachlog-Ddu, Clunderwen SA66 7SB (01994 419327). ☙ *HIGHLY COMMENDED.* **Working**

farm, join in. Welcome Host, Taste of Wales. Nestling in the Preseli Hills within the Pembrokeshire National Park we are a 70 acre traditional livestock farm situated in a peaceful setting with a relaxed atmosphere. We have sheep and cattle and also a flock of mohair producing goats and their products for you to see. We have comfortable rooms with tea making facilities and lovely views. There is a guests' lounge with TV and log fire. All meals are home cooked and when possible home or local produce is used. Walking, riding and fishing in vicinity. Centrally situated for touring countryside and coast. Children welcome, sorry no pets. Bed and Breakfast from £16 to £18.

PEMBROKE. Mrs Sheila Lewis, Poyerston Farm, Cosheston, Pembroke SA72 4SJ (01646 651347; mobile 0402 391013). ☙☙ *HIGHLY COMMENDED.*

Working farm. AA QQQQ Selected, Taste of Wales Member, Farm Holiday Bureau Member. Welcome Host. Enjoy a relaxed holiday and warm hospitality at our old farmhouse set in 300 acres of picturesque, unspoilt countryside, two miles east of Pembroke, six miles Tenby. Centrally situated on a dairy farm where home cooking is assured. Ideal base for exploring National Park, beaches and coastal walks, lily ponds, Carew Castle and local inns near by. Relax in our Victorian conservatory; comfortable lounge with colour TV, separate dining room; double and family bedrooms tastefully decorated and having en suite facilities, beverage trays, full central heating. Sorry no pets. Regret no smoking in farmhouse. Ample parking. Bed and Breakfast, or Bed, Breakfast and Evening Meal. Three miles to B&I ferry to Ireland. Brochure on request.

WALES

PEMBROKE. Mrs Ruth Smith, Chapel Farm, Castlemartin, Pembroke SA71 5HW (01646 661312).

WTB *HIGHLY COMMENDED.* Chapel Farm offers comfortable accommodation for a relaxing holiday. The 260 acre dairy farm is a mile from the coast in Pembrokeshire Coast National Park and has splendid views out to sea. The large bedrooms are equipped with radios and tea making facilities. The TV lounge with its inglenook fireplace has a grand piano for guests to enjoy. Good tasty farmhouse food is prepared. Packed lunches on request. The long distance footpath passes the farm and within five miles are wild surfing beaches, quiet bathing coves, riding and fishing. Bed and Breakfast from £16; Dinner, Bed and Breakfast £150 to £160 per week. Reductions for children sharing.

VINE FARM
The Ridgeway, Saundersfoot SA69 9LA
Telephone 01834 813543

Situated half mile from the village centre and beaches, this delightful former farmhouse has been sympathetically modernised whilst retaining its charm. Centrally heated throughout; licensed; ample parking and an exercise paddock for dogs. All five bedrooms are ensuite with colour TV, tea/coffee tray and clock/radio. We take great pride in the quality of our food, with choices on all menus, including a 5 course dinner, using local produce and vegetables from our own garden in season.

| AA Listed QQQ | B&B from £21 pp; Dinner, B&B from £27 pppd. Also one bedroom s/c flat for 2 from £120 per week. | RAC Acclaimed |

SAUNDERSFOOT. Mrs Joy Holgate, Carne Mountain Farm, Reynalton, Kilgetty SA68 0PD (01834 860546). WTB Listed *COMMENDED.* **Working farm.** A warm welcome awaits you at our lovely 200 year old farmhouse set amidst the peace and tranquillity of the beautiful Pembrokeshire countryside. Distant views of Preseli Hills, yet only three and a half miles from Saundersfoot. Pretty, picturesque bedrooms with colour TV, washbasins, tea/coffee tray, central heating. Separate dining room with interesting plate collection, books and maps. Delicious traditional or light farmhouse breakfast; vegetarians very welcome. Let the strain and stress slip away as you enjoy the peaceful atmosphere and friendly farmyard animals. Bed and Breakfast from £14.00. Welcome Host and Farmhouse Award. Quality six-berth caravan also available in pretty, peaceful setting from £90 per week. SAE please.

SOLVA. Mrs Sarah C. Griffiths, Llanddinog Old Farmhouse, Solva, Haverfordwest SA62 6NA (01348 831224). 🐦🐦🐦 Reached by peaceful flowery lanes, this 16th century farmhouse offers warm, friendly accommodation in two family bedrooms, both with private bathing facilities, teatrays, clock radios, etc. The cosy sitting-room with inglenook fireplace and roaring fire on chilly nights has a colour TV, books and games and leads into the diningroom with separate tables overlooking the extensive garden, reached through French windows. Children enjoy the rope swings and variety of small animals. Good country cooking from local foodstuffs is offered, and picnics, laundry services and hairdryer can all be provided. Close to Solva Harbour and St. David's. Bed and Breakfast from £16. Child reductions. Holder of Hygiene Certificate and "Welcome Host" award. SAE please.

POWYS

BRECON. Mrs Pamela Boxhall, The Old Mill, Felinfach, Brecon LD3 0UB (01874 625385). ♛♛

HIGHLY COMMENDED. Peacefully situated in its own grounds in the village of Felinfach on the A470 Brecon to Hereford Road. The Old Mill has a wealth of character with original features being retained. Friendly atmosphere, large garden. One double with bathroom and two en suite twin-bedded rooms; TV lounge, tea/coffee facilities. Within easy reach of Brecon Beacons, Black Mountains, Hay-on-Wye. Pony trekking nearby. Local pubs within walking distance. Packed lunches by arrangement. Children welcome. Terms: Double from £15; twin en suite from £16 per person; single from £16 to £18. Reductions for weekly stays.

BRECON. Mrs Theresa Jones, Trehenry Farm, Felinfach, Brecon LD3 0UN (01874 754312). ♛♛♛

DE LUXE. Trehenry is a 200 acre mixed farm situated east of Brecon, one mile off A470. The impressive 18th century farmhouse with breathtaking views, inglenook fireplaces and exposed beams offers comfortable accommodation, good food and cosy rooms. TV lounge, separate dining tables, central heating, tea-making facilities, all rooms en suite. Brochure on request. Farmhouse Award winner. Open all year except Christmas.

BRECON. Mrs Eileen Williams, Upper Farm, Llechfaen, Brecon LD3 7SP (01874 665269). WTB *COMMENDED.* **Working farm.** A modernised farmhouse offering Bed and Breakfast only, situated just off the A40 Brecon to Abergavenny road, two miles from Brecon town. A 64-acre dairy farm in the heart of the National Park directly facing Brecon Beacons. Ideal for touring, with golf, trekking and fishing nearby and many Welsh craft shops to visit. Two double and one family bedrooms with washbasins and tea/coffee facilities; bathroom, toilet; sittingroom; diningroom. Cot, babysitting, reduced rates for children. Open all year. Car essential — parking. No pets.

BRECON near. Gwyn and Hazel Davies, Caebetran Farm, Felinfach, Brecon LD3 0UL (01874 754460). ♛♛♛ *HIGHLY COMMENDED.* **Working farm, join in.** "Welcome Host". A warm welcome, a cup of tea and home-made cakes await you when you arrive at Caebetran.

Visitors are welcome to see the cattle and sheep on the farm. There are breathtaking views of the Brecon Beacons and the Black Mountains and just across a field is a 400 acre Common, ideal for walking, bird watching or just relaxing. Ponies and sheep graze undisturbed, while buzzards soar above you. The farmhouse dates back to the 17th century and has been recently modernised to give the quality and comfort visitors expect today. There are many extras in the rooms to give that special feel to your holiday. The rooms are all en suite and have colour TV and tea making facilities. Comfortable lounge with colour TV and video. Caebetran is an ideal base for exploring this beautiful, unspoilt part of the country with pony trekking, walking, birdwatching, wildlife, hang gliding and so much more. For more details, a brochure and terms please write or telephone. "Arrive as visitors and leave as our friends".

GLADESTRY. Mrs M.E. Hughes, Stonehouse Farm, Gladestry, Kington, Herefordshire HR5 3NU (01544 370651). Working farm. Large Georgian farmhouse, modernised whilst retaining its character, situated on Welsh border with Offa's Dyke Footpath going through its 380 acres of mixed farming. Beautiful unspoiled area for walking. Many places of interest within driving distance such as Elan Valley Dams, Devil's Bridge, Llangorse Lake, Kington golf course. Guests are accommodated in one double and one twin-bedded rooms, with washbasins; bathroom, two toilets; sitting and diningroom. TV. Homely informal atmosphere with home produced food and home cooking. Vegetarian meals on request. Children welcome. Babysitting available. Bed and Breakfast from £13.00; Evening Meals by arrangement. No pets.

PLEASE ENCLOSE A STAMPED ADDRESSED ENVELOPE WITH ENQUIRIES

LLANDRINDOD WELLS. Mrs Shirley Evans, Highbury Farm, Llanyre, Llandrindod Wells LD1 6EA

(Tel & Fax: 01597 822716). 🌸🌸 *HIGHLY COMMENDED.* Welcome Host. A warm welcome awaits guests at our smallholding on the outskirts of the village of Llanyre, one mile from the spa town of Llandrindod Wells. A spacious farmhouse and large garden. One double bedroom en suite, one family and a double room each with washbasin; beverage trays provided in all rooms. Modern bathroom with shower. Comfortable lounge with colour TV, large dining room with separate tables; snooker table. Enjoy a relaxed holiday touring and exploring the picturesque scenery of Mid Wales; only one hour's drive from the coast. Please write, or phone, for our brochure and terms.

LLANIDLOES. Mrs L. Rees, Esgairmaen, Y Fan, Llanidloes SY18 6NT (01686 430272). 🌸🌸🌸

"Croeso Cynnes" a warm welcome awaits you at Esgairmaen, a working farm one mile from Clywedog reservoir where fishing and sailing can be enjoyed, an ideal base for walking, bird watching and exploring nearby forests. The house commands magnificent views of unspoilt countryside, only twenty-nine miles from the coast. One double and one family room, both en suite with tea/coffee facilities. Central heating. Open April to October. Children and pets welcome. Camping also available from £5 per unit. We offer peace and tranquillity.

LLANWRTHWL. Dyffryn Farm, Llanwrthwl, Llandrindod Wells LD1 6NU (01597 811017). Situated in

the picturesque Upper Wye Valley dating from the 17th century this stone farmhouse with exposed beams offers relaxing accommodation — one double room with en suite shower room, another double and one twin room. Shared bathroom. Large lounge in converted hayloft. Pleasant gardens. Close to the Elan Valley with its magnificent dams and lakes. Wonderful walking country. Kite country; near RSPB reserve. Ideal for quiet retreat. Bed and Breakfast from £16.50; Dinner by prior arrangement. No smoking. One mile off A470 three miles south of Rhayader. Keep to right through village, right at T-junction on hill, quarter of a mile along.

MACHYNLLETH. Jill and Barry Stevens, Yr Hen Felin, Abercegir, Machynlleth SY20 8NR (01650

511868). 🌸🌸 Peace and relaxation can be enjoyed at "The Old Mill" set on the bank of the River Gwydol; watch the trout from your bedroom window! The walking and scenery are some of the finest in Wales and the coast with its fine sandy beaches can be reached in 20 minutes by car. Heavily beamed throughout with original stripped pine floors the character of our converted stone watermill has been enhanced with antique furniture and an interesting collection of china and clocks. Our double and two twin-bedded rooms have en suite facilities. Large comfortable guests' sitting room with TV. The Mill is NOT suitable for smokers. Traditional or vegetarian breakfasts. Bed and Breakfast £19 per person per night. Brochure available.

The CENTRE for ALTERNATIVE TECHNOLOGY, Machynlleth offers free entry for one child when accompanied by a paying adult when using our READERS' OFFER VOUCHER.

MACHYNLLETH. Mrs E.O. Harris, Cefn Coch Uchaf, Cemmaes Road, Machynlleth SY20 8LH (01650 511 552). WTB Merit Award. 16th century farmhouse in the Welsh hills. Excellent country for bird watching, walking, golfing and fishing. Easy access to beaches. Good home cooking — vegetarians catered for. One en-suite bedroom available. Central heating. Bed and Breakfast from £15; Evening Meal £7.50. Open April to October. Children and pets welcome. Babysitting offered.

MACHYNLLETH. Mrs Gwen Hughes, Aberffrydlan, Llanwrin, Machynlleth SY20 8NA (01650 511265). WTB Listed *HIGHLY COMMENDED.* 15th century

Listed farmhouse featuring a relaxing oak-beamed lounge with inglenook fireplace. Spacious bedrooms with private bathroom and beverage making facilities. A 450 acre working family farm situated in the picturesque Dovey Valley. Within easy reach of Machynlleth where you may explore Owain Glyndwr's Parliament House and experience the magical world of the Celts at Celtica. Aberffrydlan is an excellent base for a wide range of activities including bird watching, hill walking and, for the more adventurous, Quad Trekking, or discover a new future at the Centre for Alternative Technology. Please write or telephone for further details and terms.

MONTGOMERY. Mrs G.M. Bright, Little Brompton Farm, Montgomery SY15 6HY (01686 668371).

🌸 🌸 🌸 *HIGHLY COMMENDED.* **Working farm.** Robert and Gaynor warmly welcome you to their charming 17th century farmhouse on a working farm situated on B4385 two miles east of the Georgian town of Montgomery. Many rooms have a wealth of oak beams. Family, double or twin bedrooms, some en suite. Good traditional cooking. An ideal place to explore Mid Wales and the Border country. Offa's Dyke passes through the farm. AA Selected QQQQ. Open all year. Bed and Breakfast from £18; Evening Meal from £8.

WALES

NEWTOWN. M.S. Griffiths, Lower Penygelly Farm, Kerry, Newtown SY16 4LX (01686 670610).

WTB *HIGHLY COMMENDED.* Lower Penygelly Farm is six miles from Newtown which has sports centre, swimming pool and pony trekking nearby. Within easy reach of Powis Castle and the coast. Lower Penygelly offers two miles of fishing in the River Mule, shooting on the farm and 9 hole putting green on the lawn. Mrs Griffiths provides home produced chicken, beef, lamb from the farm and uses fresh vegetables and home cooking. One family room en suite, tea and coffee facilities and Sky TV viewing in lounge and bedrooms. Children and pets welcome. Open February to November. Terms from £16.

PENYBONT-FAWR. Mrs Anne Evans, Glanhafon, Penybont-Fawr, Oswestry SY10 0EW (01691 860377). 🖐 *HIGHLY COMMENDED.* **Working farm, join in.**

Glanhafon is a working sheep farm situated in the heart of the magnificent Tanat Valley. The traditional Welsh farmhouse offers good home cooking with fresh farm produce which makes it attractive to families or those who seek the peace and quiet of the countryside. Bordering the Berwyn Mountains with easy access to Lake Vyrnwy and Bala Lake, both offering water sports. You may wish to spend a day browsing in the old market towns of Oswestry and Welshpool. Accommodation comprises three bedrooms, all en-suite, with own sittingroom. Tea making facilities in bedrooms. Full central heating. Ample parking. Children and pets welcome. Open Easter till October. Bed and Breakfast from £15.

RHAYADER. Mr and Mrs Roger Price, Downfield Farm, Rhayader LD6 5PA (01597 810394). 🖐

COMMENDED. Downfield Farm is a 60-acre farm situated one mile east of Rhayader on A44 Crossgates Road, with ample parking space. Surrounded by hills and lakes, fishing, pony trekking and good walking country nearby. We extend a warm welcome to all our guests. There are three double bedrooms, all with washbasins and tea-making facilities; two bathrooms; comfortable lounge with colour TV. Children are welcomed and pets allowed. Open from February to November. Car is essential. Bed and Breakfast from £15 to £16 daily.

WELSHPOOL. Mr A. and Mrs S. Jones, Lower Trelydan Farm, Guilsfield, Welshpool SY21 9PH (01938 553105). 🖐🖐 *HIGHLY COMMENDED.*

National Award-winning farmhouse. Graham and Sue welcome you to their wonderful black and white home, set on this working farm and Listed for its history and beauty. The bedrooms are tastefully furnished with en suite facilities and colour TV (on request), there is an oak beamed lounge and a dining room where home cooking is a speciality, also a licensed bar. Enjoy Powis Castle, canal rides, steam railway, riding, lakes and scenic waterfalls. Relax in this lovely house and capture the atmosphere of four centuries of history. Large gardens and lawns. Peaceful situation. AA QQQQ Selected.

WELSHPOOL. Mrs Joyce Cornes, Cwmllwynog, Welshpool SY21 0HF (01938 810791). 🐦🐦🐦

HIGHLY COMMENDED. A traditional Welsh farmhouse built in the early 17th century on a working dairy farm, three miles west of Llanfair Caereinion where there is a good range of shops and other facilities including the famous Llanfair Light Railway station. We offer our guests lounge, comfortably furnished with a wealth of oak panels and beams, inglenook fireplace with log fire. Dining room also with oak beams and traditional furniture. Attractive bedrooms have colour TV and drink making facilities. Double with en suite shower. Twin has washbasin and private bathroom. Spacious garden with stream at the bottom and an abundance of wildlife. Bed and Breakfast from £18; Evening Meal £10. Brochure available. AA QQQ, Member of Taste of Wales.

SOUTH WALES (formerly Glamorgan and Gwent)

Blaenau Gwent, Bridgend, Caerphilly, Cardiff, Merthyr Tydfil, Monmouthshire, Neath & Port Talbot, Newport, Rhondda Cynon Taff, Swansea, Torfaen, and Vale of Glamorgan

ABERGAVENNY. Mr and Mrs S. Watkins, Treloyvan Farm, Llantilio, Crossenny, Abergavenny NP7 8UE (01600 780478). 🐦

Friendly family-run 113 acre working farm in beautiful rural setting mid-way between Abergavenny and Monmouth on B4233. Within walking distance of White Castle: Offa's Dyke, the long distance footpath, runs by the castle, also three Castles of Gwent — White, Skenfrith and Grosmont, another nice long walk. Nearby you will find golf, fishing and canoeing. Magnificent views. Children welcome, lots of farm animals and pets to see. Bed and Breakfast from £13 to £16; weekly from £84. Good home cooking with a Swiss cook. Cot and high chair available. Reductions for children. Two bedrooms with shower and washbasin. Family speaks German and a little French. For further details write or phone Mrs S. Watkins.

BLAINA. Malcolm and Betty Hancocks, Chapel Farm, Blaina NP3 3DJ (01495 290888). 🐦🐦

COMMENDED. Guests are assured of a warm welcome when they visit this 15th century renovated farmhouse and many return each year. A good base for touring Big Pit, Blaenavon; Bryn-Bach Park, Brecon Beacons, Abergavenny. Family and double rooms; one bedroom has shower en suite. Packed lunches available; Evening Meal on request. There is a drinks licence. No smoking in bedrooms. Bed and Breakfast from £17. Full details available.

COWBRIDGE near. Mrs Sue Beer, Plas Llanmihangel, Llanmihangel, Near Cowbridge CF7 7LQ

(01446 774610). Plas Llanmihangel is the finest medieval manor house in the beautiful Vale of Glamorgan. We offer a genuine warmth of welcome, delightful accommodation, first class food and service in our wonderful home. The baronial hall, great log fires, the ancient tower and acres of beautiful historic gardens intrigue all who stay in this fascinating house. Its long history and continuous occupation have created a spectacular building in romantic surroundings unchanged since the sixteenth century. A great opportunity to experience the ambience and charm of a past age. Guests are accommodated in three double rooms. Bed and Breakfast £25. High quality home-cooked Evening Meal available on request.

GOWER. Mrs C.W. Ashton, Fairfield Cottage, Knelston, Gower SA3 1AR (01792 391013). Fairfield

Cottage is an 18th century Gower cottage set in attractive gardens in the hamlet of Knelston. Approximately 12 miles west of Swansea with its marina, theatres and excellent shopping and entertainment facilities. The Cottage has comfortable lounge with wood fires set in an inglenook fireplace, pretty double bedrooms with washbasins, tea/coffee making facilities and full central heating. Home cooking is to a high standard with locally produced vegetables and fruit when in season. Elizabeth Gundrey recommended. There is also ample parking. Sorry no dogs unless prepared to leave in cars. No smoking. Bed and Breakfast £16/£17 per person; Dinner £11. Brochure available.

MONMOUTH. Rosemary and Derek Ringer, Church Farm Guest House, Mitchel Troy, Monmouth

NP5 4HZ (01600 712176). 🐾🐾 *COMMENDED.* AA QQQ. A spacious and homely 16th century former farmhouse with oak beams and inglenook fireplaces, set in large attractive garden with stream. An excellent base for visiting the Wye Valley, Forest of Dean and Black Mountains. All bedrooms have washbasins, tea/coffee making facilities and central heating; most are en-suite. Own car park. Colour TV. Non-smoking. Terrace and barbecue area. Bed and Breakfast from £17 to £20 per person. Evening Meal by arrangement. We also offer a programme of guided and self-guided Walking Holidays and Short Breaks. Separate "Wysk Walks" brochure on request.

NEATH. Mr S. Brown, Green Lantern Guest House, Hawdref Ganol Farm, Cimla, Neath SA12 9SL

(01639 631884). 🐾🐾🐾 *HIGHLY COMMENDED.* West Glamorgan's only AA QQQQQ Premier Selected House. Family-run 18th century luxury centrally heated farmhouse with beautiful scenic views over open countryside. Close to Afan Argoed and Margam Parks; 10 minutes from M4; one mile from birthplace of Richard Burton. Ideal for walking, cycling, horse riding from farm; perfect base for touring South Wales Valleys and the beautiful Gower coast. Large guest room with inglenook fireplace and TV; colour TV and tea/coffee facilities in all rooms; en suite available. Pets welcome. Reductions for children. Please telephone for colour brochure.

SWANSEA. Winston Hotel, 11 Church Lane, Bishopston, Swansea SA3 3JT (01792 232074). 🐦🐦

This medium-sized, comfortable hotel is set in quiet wooded surroundings at the entrance to a National Trust Valley. Convenient for the beautiful beaches of Gower, it is just six miles from Swansea and three-and-a-half from Mumbles with its watersports, dancing etc. Most bedrooms have showers, some have en suite facilities and all have wash-basins. Two lounges (one with TV). Indoor heated swimming pool. Billiards room, sauna and solarium. Residential licence. Excellent Welsh cooking. AA Listed, RAC Acclaimed.

TINTERN. Anne and Peter Howe, Valley House, Raglan Road, Tintern, Near Chepstow NP6 6TH (01291 689652). 🐦🐦 *COMMENDED.*

Valley House is a fine Georgian residence situated in the tranquil Angidy Valley 800 yards from the A466 Chepstow to Monmouth road and within a mile of Tintern Abbey. Numerous walks through picturesque woods and valleys right from our doorstep. The accommodation is of a very high standard; all rooms are en-suite, have tea/coffee making facilities and colour TV. The guests' lounge has a wealth of exposed beams and a working range whilst the diningroom has an arched stone ceiling. Numerous places to eat nearby. Bed and Breakfast from £19 per person. Open all year. No smoking. AA QQQ, RAC Acclaimed.

SELF-CATERING HOLIDAYS

NORTH WALES (formerly Clwyd and Gwynedd)
Aberconwy & Colwyn, Anglesey, Denbighshire, Flintshire, Gwynedd and Wrexham

ABERDARON. Mrs J.J. Evans, Bodrydd, Rhoshirwaun, Pwllheli LL53 8HR (01758 780257). Accommodation for six in self-contained farmhouse, Bodrydd Farm, centrally situated near tip of Lleyn Peninsula, standing back from main road, in lovely Welsh countryside and peaceful surroundings with open view of hills and fields. Within easy reach of Whistling Sands, numerous picturesque sandy beaches. Riding stables at nearby farm. Licensed hotels in Aberdaron (two miles). Small river running through farmland for trout fishing. Small working farm with plenty going on to interest all ages. Comfort and cleanliness guaranteed. Three double bedrooms; cot, high chair; bathroom, toilet; sittingroom with colour TV; diningroom with electric fire; kitchen all electric with all utensils, etc. No linen. Shop 10 minutes' walk. Sea one and a half miles. Sorry, no pets. Car essential, ample parking. Available May to September. SAE please for terms and brochure.

Aberdovey Sea Front ... beach 10 seconds!

Guests continually write: "The cleanest, best, most welcoming self catering ever." Very special maisonettes and flats overlooking the sandy beach, sleep 2/7, from £70 to £350 per week. Hillside Bungalow and House – balcony, flower filled terraces, fantastic views, spacious rooms, superbly equipped, even a Jacuzzi – top Tourist Board Grade 5 – £99 to £495 per week. Superb scenery/walking in Snowdonia National Park, beautiful, magical village – watersports, super restaurants, sandy beach, canoe and boat hire, fishing, golf, pony trekking, tennis, bowls – something for every member of the family and return, at end of day to superb comfort.

Please write – Mrs F. H. Bendall, Hafod, Aberdovey LL35 0EB for colour brochure or FREEPHONE 0800 212305, Fax 01654 767078.

ABERSOCH. Quality Cottages. Around the magnificent Welsh coast. Away from the madding crowd. Near safe sandy beaches. A small specialist agency offering privacy, peace and unashamed luxury. Wales Tourist Board 1989 Award Winner. Residential standards — dishwashers, microwaves, washing machines, central heating, log fires, no slot meters. Linen provided. Pets welcome free. All in coastal areas famed for scenery, walks, wild flowers, birds, badgers and foxes. Free colour brochure. **S.C. Rees, Quality Cottages, Cerbid, Solva, Haverfordwest, Pembrokeshire SA62 6YE (01348 837871).**

Llanberis Lake Railway, Gwynedd offers one child FREE travel with two adults paying full price when using our READERS' OFFER VOUCHER.

WALES

ABERSOCH. Mrs Rhian Parry, Crugeran, Sarn Meylltern, Pwllheli LL53 8DT (01758 730375). WTB Grade 4. Sleep 8 and 4. A warm "CROESO" (welcome) awaits you on our working farm set in unspoilt countryside, with a beautiful coastline all around. The 17th century farmhouse for eight has an antique pine kitchen with dishwasher, washing machine, electric or open fire. The Stableloft for four has a Victorian brass and iron double bed, with a wealth of beams. Both are tastefully decorated in keeping with their characters with antique furniture throughout. Both have separate sitting areas in large communal garden with barbecue facilities. Cots, high chairs, bed linen and electricity are included in the rent. Brochure available.

BALA near. Rhyd Fudr, Llanuwchllyn, Near Bala. Sleeps 6. Stone farm cottage set in an isolated position with views of five mountain peaks and Bala Lake. Accommodation comprises three bedrooms, plus cot; two sitting rooms; sun room; kitchen; bathroom. Garage. Multi-fuel burning stove and most modern conviences but no TV. Fully equipped including washing machine and telephone. Linen not supplied. Mountain stream and lovely walks on the doorstep. Sea, 45 minutes by car; Snowdon, one hour. Children welcome. Terms from £150. Apply: **Mrs J.H. Gervis, Nazeing Bury, Nazeing, Essex EN9 2JN (0199 289 2331) or Mrs G.E. Evans, Pant-y-Ceubren, Llanuwchllyn, Bala (016784 252).**

BEDDGELERT. Beudy Coed, Oerddwr, Beddgelert. Sleeps 4. Beautifully renovated shepherd's cottage one mile from Aberglaslyn Pass, situated in a secluded, elevated position overlooking the River Glaslyn. The views towards the mountain ranges are breathtaking. Ideal central location for exploring Snowdonia, walking, fishing, horse riding, yet only four miles away from Porthmadog's sandy beaches. Perfect setting for relaxing amongst the scenery. Accommodation to sleep four persons in double and twin-bedded rooms. Linen supplied. Lounge/diner with stone fireplace, colour TV, fitted carpets. Fully equipped kitchen; shower room. Patio area in enclosed garden with table and benches. Ample car parking. Pets welcome. Contact: **Mrs Madge Williams, Berllan, Borth-y-Gest, Porthmadog, Gwynedd LL49 9UE (01766 513784).**

BEDDGELERT. Bron Eifion, Rhyd Ddu, Beddgelert. Sleeps 6. Attractive semi-detached house on edge of small village in National Park at foot of Snowdon. Splendid mountain, valley and Pass walks from village including path up Snowdon. Lakes nearby. Excellent centre for seaside, historic castles and houses, riding, fishing and touring. Three bedrooms; two living rooms; bathroom; modern kitchen, fridge, airing cupboard, heaters. Well equipped. Mountain view, terrace, rough garden. Inn (serving meals) nearby. Cot. Sorry, no pets. High season £150 to £250 per week; low season £55 to £140 per week. Short Breaks by arrangement. Open all year. Apply: **Davies, 218 Clive Road, London SE21 8BS (0181-670 2756).**

BEDDGELERT. Meillionen, Beddgelert. Farmhouse situated in the heart of Snowdonia within one mile of picturesque village. Large house divided into two separate units. One consists of large kitchen/livingroom with colour TV, electric cooker, fridge and Rayburn; stone staircase leading to two double bedrooms and bathroom. Other unit consists of sittingroom, open fireplace; colour TV; kitchen with fridge and electric cooker; downstairs bathroom; three double bedrooms and single bed; cot and high chair also available. Bed and table linen not provided. Storage heaters in winter. Electricity on meter. Fishing, pony trekking and sports facilities nearby, also beaches within easy reach. SAE to **Mrs S.H. Owen, Cwm Cloch, Beddgelert, Caernarfon (01766 890241).**

BEDDGELERT. 2 Glanfa, Rhyd Ddu, Near Beddgelert. 150 year old, well-equipped stone cottage in the centre of a pretty village at the foot of Snowdon. In the heart of the National Park, it is an ideal centre for mountains or sea. Suitable for two families, sleeps eight in three bedrooms (two double and four single beds). Large livingroom with exposed beams, Welsh dresser, storage heater, radio and colour TV. Good-sized kitchen with fridge, electric cooker. Bathroom with electric shower. Cot and high chair available. Metered electricity. No pets. Near pub. Terms high season from £160 to £300; low season £75 to £120, with Short Breaks by arrangement in low season. Open all year. Apply **Mr and Mrs C.R. Vernon, 166 Court Lane, Dulwich, London SE21 7ED (0181-693 3971).**

BETWS-Y-COED. Jim and Lilian Boughton, Bron Celyn, Llanrwst Road, Betws-y-Coed LL24 0HD (01690 710333; Fax: 01690 710111). Our cosy 200-year-old converted coach house has been tastefully refurbished and offers accommodation for up to four persons. Upstairs: one double room with space for a cot, and one bunk-bedded room with full length/width bunk beds. All bed linen is provided but not towels. Downstairs: lounge with colour TV and wood-burning stove (ample supply of chopped timber available). Kitchen with fridge, electric cooker, microwave, toaster and water heater. Shower room and toilet. Electric storage heaters fitted throughout. Metered electricity (read arrival/departure). Open all year. Ideal centre for walking, climbing, fishing or simply just relaxing! Terms £120 to £300 per week. Short Breaks available.

BETWS-Y-COED. Mrs E. Thomas, Bryn Farm, Nebo, Llanrwst LL26 0TE (01690 710315). Working farm, join in. Farmhouse flat sleeping two. The perfect place for a peaceful holiday in lovely Conwy Valley close to the North Wales Coast and five miles from Betws-y-Coed in the heart of Snowdonia. The accommodation is private ad self-contained and consists of a living room with colour TV; fully equipped kitchen area with fridge and microwave; bathroom, toilet; double bedroom with electric blanket, duvets and bed linen provided free of charge. Also centrally heated during winter. Shop, bakery and Inn two miles. Open all year. Terms from £80 to £150 including heating and electricity. Bed settee also available for additional sleeping accommodation.

CAERNARFON. Mrs M. Hughes, Glan Llyn, Llanfaglan, Caernarfon LL54 5RD (01286 674700). Sleeps 4. Glan Llyn is a two bedroomed semi-detached cottage situated in a quiet area yet only two miles from historic town of Caernarfon and within easy distance of Caernarfon Golf Course and Caernarfon Bay for sea fishing. Ideally situated for touring North Wales, just seven miles from Snowdon and Anglesey and within easy reach of many seaside resorts. Accommodation comprises two double bedrooms; bathroom; lounge with TV; kitchen/diner with fridge, electric stove, electric fires or open fire. Bed linen supplied. Parking space. Cottage available all year round. Mid-week Breaks and Weekend Breaks available during off season. Reductions for winter breaks and weekend bookings during off season period; summer terms and full details on request.

CAERNARFON. Plas Y Bryn Chalet Park, Bontnewydd, Caernarfon LL54 7YE (01286 672811). Our  small park is situated two miles from the historic town of Caernarfon. Set into a walled garden it offers safety, seclusion and beautiful views of Snowdonia, and is ideal for touring the area, with village pub and shop within walking distance. Choice of two or three bedrooms with prices to suit all.

CAERNARFON. Mrs Ivy Atkin, Cwm Farm, Clynnogfawr, Caernarfon LL54 5DW (01286 660244). 300 acre mountain farm with private two acre fishing lake with islands and rowing boat. In elevated position overlooking Cardigan Bay with views of the Snowdon Mountains in the distance. Eight miles from Pwllheli and Criccieth, four miles from Clynnog and Bryncir. Large safe garden, plenty of parking space. House sleeps eight plus cot and high chair. Sittingroom with colour TV, inglenook fireplace and exposed beams; kitchen-cum-diner with oil-fired Rayburn cooker, microwave, fridge freezer and Calor gas cooker. Sun lounge with children's play area. Large downstairs bathroom; two double bedrooms and small bedroom with two single beds on main landing. Loft bedroom over bathroom, separate from main landing, with two single beds. Terms from £180 to £300 per week. No pets.

CHURCH BAY. Mrs Lindy Wood, The Lobster Pot Cottage, Church Bay, Holyhead, Anglesey LL65 4EY (01407 730241/730588; Fax: 01407 761247).

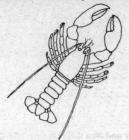

11 miles from Holyhead, the ferry port to Ireland, The Lobster Pot cottage/flat is above a renowned seafood restaurant in picturesque Church Bay, with working lobster tanks. The flat is small but cosy, well equipped with electric cooker, microwave, fridge, percolator, etc. It sleeps four in one double and one twin-bedded room. Gas wall fires, use of washing machine and tumble dryer and all linen included in tariff. Lawned gardens with barbecue. Well behaved pets welcome. Ideal for coastal walks, boating, bathing, bird watching. Nearby trout fishing, horse riding and golf. Terms from £110 to £240. Also The Anchorage, spacious house sleeping eight, ideal for two families. Rates from £208 to £360 per week. SAE please.

CONWY VALLEY. "Saronfa", Tal-y-Bont, Near Conwy. Sleeps 4.

This lovely cottage is situated in the beautiful Conwy Valley on the edge of the Snowdonia National Park. Modernised but retaining old world charm with two bedrooms (double and twin), cosy log fire, storage heaters, automatic washer, microwave, fridge freezer, etc. Secluded rear garden with views of mountains. Parking for two cars. Short distance from coastal resorts, the historic town of Conwy and the famous Bodnant Gardens. Shop, inn and country restaurant within walking distance. Owner supervised and cleanliness assured. Pets taken. Weekly terms from £102 to £210. Winter Breaks £16 per night including logs. **Mrs M.C. Waddingham, "Cefn", Tyn-y-Groes, Conwy LL32 8TA (01492 650233).**

Key to
Tourist Board Ratings

The Crown Scheme
(England, Scotland & Wales)

Covering hotels, motels, private hotels, guesthouses, inns, bed & breakfast, farmhouses. Every Crown classified place to stay is inspected annually. *The classification:* Listed then 1-5 Crown indicates the range of facilities and services. Higher quality standards are indicated by the terms APPROVED, COMMENDED, HIGHLY COMMENDED and DELUXE.

The Key Scheme
(also operates in Scotland using a Crown symbol)

Covering self-catering in cottages, bungalows, flats, houseboats, houses, chalets, etc. Every Key classified holiday home is inspected annually. *The classification:* 1-5 Key indicates the range of facilities and equipment. Higher quality standards are indicated by the terms APPROVED, COMMENDED, HIGHLY COMMENDED and DELUXE.

The Q Scheme
(England, Scotland & Wales)

Covering holiday, caravan, chalet and camping parks. Every Q rated park is inspected annually for its quality standards. The more √ in the Q – up to 5 – the higher the standard of what is provided.

CRICCIETH. Mrs L. Hughes Jones, Tyddyn Heilyn, Chwilog LL53 6SW (01766 810441). Freshly

renovated but keeping its antique features, charming farm cottage in tranquil, unspoilt countryside with sea on either side, sheltered by Snowdonia Mountains in distant background. Comfortably sized kitchen full of electrical gadgets; washing machine; spacious lounge with colour TV. Capricorn bathroom suite has full size Twingrip bath and shower. Victorian furnished bedrooms have Continental quilts. As well as flower and shrub beds, there is an olde worlde character to the front and back courtyards — ample parking space here. Also, but not in cottage vicinity, furnished home sleeping up to six persons. Passing through this farmland, the renowned Lon Goed walk has six mile roadway of oak and ash trees and in the flowered hedgerows too there are species of rare birds. Llanystumdwy, the home village of Earl Lloyd George with its commemorative museum, two fishing rivers, riding school, pets and rabbit farm, the church, cafes and a pub is one mile away. Write or phone for the moderate terms of the two holiday accommodation properties. Pets welcome. Highly Commended.

CRICCIETH. Mrs E.W. Roberts, Cae Canol Farm, Criccieth LL52 0NB (01766 522351). Sleeps 2 adults; 3 children. Pleasantly situated with lovely mountain views, this country cottage has two bedrooms sleeping four/five plus cot. Bathroom, toilet; spacious kitchen/diner, fully equipped with fridge, etc. Sittingroom with TV. Everything supplied except linen. Garden in front of cottage with plenty of parking space. Golf, tennis, boating, walks, shooting, fishing and horse riding all within easy reach of cottage. FREE fishing on private river — salmon and trout. Terms and brochure on request with SAE, please. Open all months of the year.

CRICCIETH. Mrs Williams, Ynys Graianog, Ynys, Criccieth LL52 0NT (01766 530234). Sleeps 8. Fully modernised farmhouse with large garden in a quiet rural area. Convenient for Lleyn Peninsula and Snowdonia. Fully equipped except linen. Available April to September. Also two stone cottages set in own grounds, three and four bedrooms. Open all year. Plenty of parking space.

CRICCIETH. Mrs B. Williams, Gaerwen Farm, Ynys, Criccieth LL52 0NU (01766 810324). Sleeps 7.

This 200 acre dairy/mixed farm is situated four-and-a-half miles inland from Criccieth and beaches. An ideal centre for enjoying climbing, fishing, pony trekking and quiet country walks with extensive views of Snowdonia and Cardigan Bay. Within easy reach of various historic places nearby. Accommodation is self-contained in furnished farmhouse, comprising TV lounge with inglenook fireplace and oak beams, electric fire; fitted kitchen with electric cooker, automatic washing machine, fridge/freezer and microwave; dining room; two double bedrooms, one twin-bedded room and one single bedroom, with duvets and bed linen; bathroom/shower with washbasin and toilet. Children most welcome, cot and babysitting available. Pets welcome. Car essential. Electricity provided. Weekly terms from £125 to £300. Short Breaks offered. SAE, please, for more details.

CRICCIETH. Betws-Bach & Rhos-Dhu, Ynys, Criccieth LL52 0PB (Tel & Fax: 01758 720047; 01766 810295). Wales Tourist Board Grade 5. A truly romantic,

memorable and special place to stay and relax in comfort. Old world farmhouse and period country cottage. Situated just off the B4411 road in tranquil surroundings. Equipped with washing/drying machines, dishwashers, microwaves, freezers, colour TV, old oak beams, inglenook with log fires, full central heating. Snooker table, pitch 'n' putt, romantic four-poster bed, sauna and jacuzzi. Open all year — Winter Weekends welcomed. Ideal for couples. Sleep two — six plus cot. Own fishing and shooting rights, wonderful walks, peace and quiet with Snowdonia and unspoilt beaches on our doorstep. For friendly personal service please phone, fax or write to **Mrs Anwen Jones.**

DOLGELLAU. Cefn Clawdd, Cross Foxes, Dolgellau. WTB 3 Dragons. Farm cottage in open valley

situated off A470 out of Dolgellau. Very accessible, 200 yards from main road, with hard road to farm. At foot of Cader Idris with panoramic views, little way along mountain path; Tal-y-Llyn Lake and Pass can be seen below. Tiny stream with trout fishing. Low beamed, low ceilinged old world cottage, solidly furnished, accommodates six in three double bedrooms; cot; bathroom, toilet; sittingroom; dining-kitchen with electric cooker, microwave, fridge, vacuum, twin-tub washer, clothes dryer. Shops five miles, sea eight miles. Car essential, parking. Pets by arrangement. Terms from £80 to £275 per week. Also converted wing attached to house, a separate unit sleeping four/five persons. Available all year. SAE, please, to **Mrs E. Wyn Price, Glyn Farm, Dolgellau LL40 1YA (01341 422286).**

DYFFRYN ARDUDWY. Mr O.G. Thomas, Bron Foel Uchaf, Dyffryn Ardudwy LL44 2HZ (01341 247570). Bron Foel is a spacious 18th century farmhouse full of character with outstanding views of Cardigan Bay and beyond. The lounge is spacious with oak beams and inglenook fireplace with wood supplied. Modern fitted kitchen with oil-fired Aga; three bedrooms — a double, a twin and a family room, all tastefully decorated. The house is set amidst ample grounds, in an elevated position to give privacy from the working farm. We are one and a half miles from the village of Dyffryn with Barmouth and Harlech a short distance away. Small pets and children welcome. Terms from £175.

FRON/CAERNARFON. Sleeps 5. Comfortable Economy 7 centrally heated, spacious holiday cottage situated five miles from Caernarfon. Sleeps five in double, twin and single rooms, cot and high chair available; large comfortable lounge with colour TV; well appointed kitchen/diner. Parking in garden. Children and well behaved dogs welcome. Situated in small mountain village within easy reach of many Welsh beauty spots, craft centres and beaches. Ideal for serious climbers or less ambitious walkers — lovely walks straight from the cottage. Out of season breaks (three days £85) and Senior Citizen discounts. Card meter electricity (£10 worth free, further cards available locally). Terms from £125 to £195 per week. For further details please contact **Mrs J. Morris, Cliff House, Beach Road, Happisburgh, Norwich NR12 0PP (01692 650775).**

CLIFF HOUSE
BEACH ROAD, HAPPISBURGH
NORFOLK NR12 0PP

GUEST HOUSE,
RESTAURANT and TEA SHOP
HOLIDAY FLATS
Telephone (01692)650775

LLANBEDR. Mrs L. Howie, Gwyn Fryn Farm, Llanbedr LL45 2NY (01341 241381). Stone built farm cottages set in 20 peaceful acres of beautiful scenery half a mile outside the village of Llanbedr. Our three bedroomed cottage has one double bedroom en suite and two twin rooms plus cot. The other cottage has a double bedroom. Both properties have oak beams, are warm, comfortable and of a high standard. Fully equipped fitted kitchens with microwaves and washing machines; colour TV, heating; parking. Children will love the animals — friendly ponies, goat, hens and ducks. Bed and Breakfast is also available in the farmhouse. Rooms with en suite facilities. Warm and welcoming.

LLANBEDR. Mrs G.P. Jones, Alltgoch, Llanbedr LL45 2NA (01341 241229). Sleeps 5 adults plus cot. Working farm, join in. Sheep farm situated two miles from Llanbedr village. Llanbedr is on the A496 between BARMOUTH and HARLECH. The house faces the Lleyn Peninsula in a quiet position with garden and plenty of parking space. Ideally situated for walking the Rhinog range, and paths to woodlands and moorlands for nature lovers. Good trout fishing and private lake. Three miles from the beach. The house sleeps five persons with modern conveniences including microwave, new kitchen units, large lounge with colour TV, central heating (free). Bed linen extra; cot and high chair available. Terms from £95 to £225 per week.

LLANBEDR. Mrs Beti Wyn Jones, Pensarn Farm, Llanbedr LL45 2HS (01341 241285). Working farm. Sleeps 4 adults, 2 children. Self catering, semi-detached cottage in beautiful surroundings, ideal for a peaceful and relaxing holiday. The accommodation consists of modern kitchen, lounge/diner, two bedrooms, bathroom and toilet on ground floor; one bedroom, shower/toilet upstairs. Night storage heaters. Ample parking space and garden. Children and pets welcome. It is situated one mile from the picturesque village of Llanbedr, quarter of a mile off the main Barmouth to Harlech road. Convenient for beach, mountains, golf course, fishing and pleasant walks up the River Artro to the Nantcol and Cwm Bychan Valleys. Terms from £120 to £180 per week.

FREE and REDUCED RATE Holiday Visits!
See our READERS' OFFER VOUCHER for details!

LLANBEDR. Mrs O. Evans, Werngron Farm, Llanbedr, Merioneth LL45 2PF (01341 241274). Working farm. Pleasant bungalow on working farm, set in own grounds and enjoying open views of unspoilt countryside. Llanbedr two miles, Harlech three, Barmouth 10. Good touring centre for north and mid Wales; within easy reach of sandy beaches, golf course, indoor swimming pool, pony trekking, freshwater coarse fishing, sea fishing, boat trips and lovely country and mountain walks. Sleeps six, plus cot, in three bedrooms — double, twin and bunks — all with own washbasins. Sittingroom with colour TV; diningroom; well equipped, all electric fitted kitchen; spacious sun lounge; bathroom/shower. Fitted carpets throughout, electric fires, oil central heating. Bed linen provided. Open all year. Terms from £170 to £195 per week plus heating and electricity.

LLANGOLLEN. Min-yr-afon, Llanarmon Dyffryn Ceiriog, Llangollen. Llanarmon Dyffryn Ceiriog is a

beautiful village set in breathtaking countryside, with the Berwyn Mountains rising to almost 3,000ft to the west. Not only famous for fishing, shooting and walking, it was the home of Welsh lyric poet John Ceiriog Hughes, born about 150 years ago. Nestling in this haven of Welsh beauty is Min-yr-afon, a three-bedroomed cottage. Carpeted throughout. Accommodation for six in one double, one single and one family bedrooms, with cot. Separate lounge with colour TV, downstairs bathroom and shower; diningroom. Fully equipped kitchen (electric cooker, fridge, toaster, kettle, cooking utensils, crockery, cutlery). Also washing machine, iron and ironing board. Linen not provided. Car parking available. Weekly terms from £80 to £195. Available January to December. Enquiries to **Mrs C. Edmonds, 7 Keymer Parade, Burgess Hill, West Sussex RH15 0AB (01444 236367 day; 01342 810908 evening).**

MACHYNLLETH. Tyhymaes, Dinas Mawddwy, Machynlleth. Holiday cottage in Cywarch Valley at the foot of Aran Fawddwy, near Cader Idris, not far from Aberystwyth and Barmouth. Ideal for walking, peaceful and safe for children to play in Snowdonia National Park. Well behaved house-trained dogs are welcome. Plenty of space for car parking. Everything supplied except linen and coal for fire. Electricity for light, cooking and hot water. Send SAE for prompt reply with full details: **Mrs Betty Humphreys, Pencae, Dinas Mawddwy, Machynlleth SY20 9JG (01650 531427).**

NEFYN. Ms P. Jones, Nant Bach, Llaniestyn, Pwllheli LL58 8SW (01758 730634). Sleeps 5 plus cot. Situated in a quiet valley with views of Garn Fadryn, ideal for exploring surrounding countryside. Pony trekking centre nearby, village of Nefyn for golf five miles. The cottage comprises two double, one single bedrooms, bathroom, lounge — it is compact, simple, clean and comfortable. Ideal economical holiday accommodation. Children welcome, cot and high chair available. Pets welcome. Ample parking. Cottage available all year. SAE brings prompt reply.

NORTH WALES/BORDERLANDS. "Alyn Cottages", Stoneleigh, Willow Court, Bangor-on-Dee, Wrexham LL13 0BT (01978 780679 24 hours; Tel & Fax: 01978 780770). Self catering accommodation in and around North Wales/Borderlands, South Cheshire and North Shropshire. For holidays and short breaks, we offer a friendly personal service with a wide choice of properties. All personally inspected and fully described in our free brochure, available by writing or phoning.

ALYN Cottages

CHOOSE FROM 200 SEASIDE & MOUNTAIN COTTAGES etc.

in superb locations in and around the beautiful Snowdonia National Park. Available all year round. Sleep 1 to 14 persons from as little as £95 per cottage per week in low season.

Central reservations: SNOWDONIA TOURIST SERVICES (Ref. FHG), PORTHMADOG, GWYNEDD LL49 9PG Telephone 01766 513829 (24 hours); 512660 up to 8pm or 513837 (Tel & Fax).

Please send me your FREE brochure.

Name .... Address ....

.... Postcode..........................

PORTHMADOG (Snowdonia). Felin Parc Cottages. Discover this idyllic 17th century riverside millhouse and charming wool manager's cottage in superb waterfall valley between Porthmadog and Beddgelert. Mill (WTB 4 Dragons) with large character beamed livingroom, period furnishings, open fire, central heating, colour TV. Luxury kitchen, modernised bathroom/cloakroom. Sleeps eight/10 in four bedrooms and overflow ping-pong annexe. Secluded terraces (barbecue/floodlighting) adjoin Mill pool and falls. Cottage (WTB 3 Dragons) sleeping four/six in two bedrooms, and self-contained gable annexe with similar facilities, is delightfully situated overlooking ancient fording bridge. Superb local scenery with Snowdon, Portmeirion, Ffestiniog Railway all nearby. Terms £150 to £550 weekly. Brochure, photographs: **Mr and Mrs O. Williams-Ellis, San Giovanni, 4 Sylvan Road, London SE19 2RX (0181-653 3118).**

PWLLHELI. Mrs M. Adams, Cae'r Ferch Uchaf, Pencaenewydd, Pwllheli LL53 6DJ (01766 810660). Cedarwood Chalet on a secluded smallholding consisting of three bedrooms, all with fitted wardrobes; large lounge with colour TV; luxury shower room with WC, additional WC in boiler room; kitchen/diner. The chalet is double glazed, centrally heated and open all year. The area is superb for walking and cycling, with quiet country roads throughout. The area is good for photography also. We are very central for all beaches and just a few miles from Snowdon. Charges are from £180 to £230 according to season. Dogs by arrangement only. Please write or ring for details.

PWLLHELI. Mrs C.A. Jones, Rhedyn, Mynytho, Pwllheli LL53 7PS (01758 740669). Working farm, join in. Sleeps 4. Rhedyn is a small dairy farm overlooking the beautiful Nanhoran Valley, and the farm cottage, accommodating four people, is offered for hire between April and November. It is two miles from Llanbedrog and Abersoch, both noted for their safe bathing. Children will enjoy watching the animals, and are made especially welcome. The house has two double bedrooms; bathroom and toilet; combined sitting/diningroom with TV; kitchen with immersion heater, washing machine, microwave oven. Calor gas stove and fridge. Linen supplied. Pets permitted. One mile from shops and two from the sea. Car essential, ample parking. SAE, for further details and terms.

PWLLHELI. S.P. Ellis, Gwynfryn Farm, Pwllheli LL53 5UF (01758 612536; Fax: 01758 614324). 4/5 Dragons Award. Our ORGANIC dairy farm is a haven for nature lovers away from the madding crowd yet only 15 miles from Pwllheli. Cottages for romantic couples/houses for four/eight persons, all personally supervised. Snowdon 25 miles, sea two miles — vary your activity to suit the weather or your mood. Beds made up, storage/central heating. Mini breaks October to March. Sample our hospitality. Gold Award Welcome Host. Children and pets welcome. Accommodation suitable for disabled visitors. Open all year. Caravan and camping facilities also available. Send for colour brochure.

SNOWDONIA. Caernarfon Bay Farm House and Cottages, Snowdonia. WTB 4 DRAGONS Tastefully converted farmhouse and cottages nestling peacefully in the hill surrounded by large old trees with magnificent views over Caernarfon Bay. The cottages have traditional inglenook fireplaces and exposed beams and come equipped with microwave, dishwasher, fridge, freezer and colour TV. All have central heating throughout. Children can play in the surrounding fields and hills in the freedom of 33 acres while parents can relax in a secluded and private location. Three-quarters of a mile from the village pub, beach five minutes by car; near Snowdonia. Sleep 2 – 9. Linen provided. Brochure available. Contact: **Ivor Davies, Cil Coed Uchaf, Clynnog Fawr, Caernarfon, North Wales LL54 5DA (01286 660661).**

SNOWDONIA (Caernarfon). Margaret Trottier, Ffridd Lwyd, Y Fron, Upper Llandwrog, Caernarfon LL54 7BD (01286 880718). Self catering high standard loft apartment for two. Well equipped kitchen, fridge, freezer. All electric with 50p meter. Lounge/diner with colour TV. Bathroom with shower. Bedroom with bedding provided. Parking space. Quiet mountain village opposite Nantlle Mountain Range. Short breaks or weekly bookings all year. Area of great interest, walking, climbing and National Trust properties. Leisure centre with extensive activities and abundant shopping facilities in Caernarfon. Pets accepted by special arrangements only. Weekly terms £115 October to March, £135 April to September.

TALSARNAU. Mrs A.M. Wells, Yr-Ogof, Ynys, Talsarnau LL47 6TL (01766 780058). Sleeps 4/5. This comfortable, old fashioned cottage is three miles from Harlech and just five minutes' walk to Ynys Beach. Convenient for shops. Lovely mountain views from cottage windows. Swimming pool at Harlech. Very attractive area with lovely walks. Also fishing nearby. All modern conveniences. Accommodation to sleep four/five persons in double and twin-bedded rooms; bathroom, toilet, also downstairs toilet; lounge with oak beams and colour TV; kitchen/diner with electric cooker, microwave, fridge etc. Everything supplied except linen. Extra charge for electricity used. Economy 7 central heating. Parking. Guaranteed clean home from home. Vacant May to September. Lower charges May to June. SAE, please for terms and further details or phone.

TYWYN. Coastal House, 35 Corbett Close, Tywyn. Lovely three bedroomed coastal house with garage, very close to the sea with easy access to sandy beach. Accommodation in one double, one bunk-bedded and one single rooms, blankets provided. Equipped as if it were your own home — new furnishings, washing machine, cooker, microwave, crockery, colour TV and stereo. Large bathroom with additional built-in shower room. Sole use of garden front and rear, patio set provided. Ten minutes' walk from Tywyn centre, within walking distance of Tal-y-Llyn Steam Railway, two minutes from pub with excellent meals, and eight doors from shop selling home-baked bread, pies, pasties etc. Very good walks in this beautiful area close to Snowdonia National Park. Pets are most welcome free of charge. Terms from £130 to £199 weekly. Further details from **Mr and Mrs Ian Weston, 18 Elizabeth Road, Basingstoke, Hampshire RG22 6AX (01256 52364 or 01256 412233 evenings).**

DYFED
Cardiganshire, Carmarthenshire and Pembrokeshire

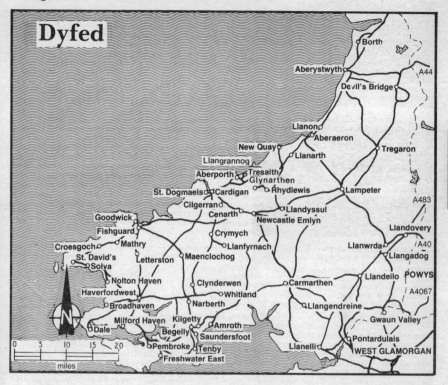

ABERPORTH. Mr and Mrs T. Williams, Ffrwdwenith-Uchaf Farm, Aberporth, Cardigan SA43 1RW

(01239 810 209). Sleeps 6. Furnished farm cottage situated on the Cardiganshire coast in a beautiful spot overlooking Cardigan Bay and within easy reach of many lovely sandy beaches. Two double bedrooms with three double beds and cot for child. Bathroom, sittingroom with colour TV, diningroom, kitchen with cooker and fridge. Hot and cold running water. Ideal for a quiet and away-from-it-all holiday. Cardigan five and a half miles, village shop one mile. SAE brings brochure giving full particulars. Visitors are requested to bring their own sheets, pillowcases and towels. Children welcome. Fresh milk daily. Weekly terms from £200 to £250.

ABERPORTH. Quality Cottages. Around the magnificent Welsh coast. Away from the madding crowd. Near safe, sandy beaches. A small specialist agency offering privacy, peace and unashamed luxury. Wales Tourist Board 1989 Award Winner. Residential standards — dishwashers, microwaves, washing machines, central heating, log fires, no slot meters. Linen provided. Pets welcome free. All in coastal areas famed for scenery, walks, wild flowers, birds, badgers and foxes. Free colour brochure. **S.C. Rees, Quality Cottages, Cerbid, Solva, Haverfordwest, Pembrokeshire SA62 6YE (01348 837871).**

BOSHERTON. Quality Cottages. Around the magnificent Welsh coast. Away from the madding crowd. Near safe sandy beaches. A small specialist agency offering privacy, peace and unashamed luxury. Wales Tourist Board 1989 Award Winner. Residential standards — dishwashers, microwaves, washing machines, central heating, log fires, no slot meters. Linen provided. Pets welcome. All in coastal areas famed for scenery, walks, wild flowers, birds, badgers and foxes. Free colour brochure. **S.C. Rees, Quality Cottages, Cerbid, Solva, Haverfordwest, Pembrokeshire SA62 6YE (01348 837871).**

CARDIGAN. Bwthyn, Llangoedmor, Cardigan. Sleeps 4. This bungalow is detached in its own quite

spacious grounds, garage alongside. Situated in a superb location one mile from market town of Cardigan, within easy distance to Cardigan Bay beaches. Excellent base for exploring beautiful Preseli Hills and the cathedral city of St. David's, also inland the scenic wooded Teifi Valley. Accommodation comprises living/diningroom; small but compact kitchen (electric stove, hot and cold stainless steel sink, fridge, kettle, all crockery/cutlery). Beautiful oak floored hall; extremely comfortable lounge; TV. Two double bedrooms (one twin-bedded); bathroom/toilet. Good carpets throughout (except kitchen). Guests supply own linen. Night storage heaters; Economy 7 for hot water. Regret no pets. No children under eight years. From £100 weekly. SAE **Mrs P.M. Davies, Llwynderwen, Llangoedmor, Cardigan SA43 2LF (01239 612427).**

CARDIGAN. Mrs J. Young, Cryngae Mawr, Blaenannerch, Cardigan SA43 2BQ (01239 811286). Working farm, join in. Converted barn retaining many

original period features. Secluded position surrounded by trees in peaceful setting within two mile drive of various sandy beaches. Situated in small, quiet 30 acre smallholding with Jersey cows, calves, donkey and tame sheep. Two-storey barn has one large double bedroom, two single bedrooms, toilet and washbasin upstairs, shower room downstairs. Well fitted kitchen with cooker, fridge-freezer and microwave; comfortable lounge with heating and colour TV. Linen provided at small extra charge. Sorry, no pets. Discount available for only two people. Further details available on request.

CARDIGAN. Llantood Farm Cottages. WTB Four/Five Dragons Award. Sleep 4/6. Situated on

200-acre working farm, three miles south of Cardigan, three miles coast, the Cottages are ideal for exploring Pembrokeshire National Park. The three cottages which sleep four, five and six respectively have been carefully renovated to the highest standards and provide luxury accommodation including central heating, woodburning stoves, colour TV, washing machine, microwave, fridge/freezer, inglenook and exposed beams. Each cottage has its own secluded fenced garden with patio table. Visitors welcome to explore the farm and our 30 acres of unspoilt woodland bordered by a small stream and observe wildlife. Pets welcome. Linen provided. Open all year. Terms from £130 to £330. Brochure: **Mrs G. Evans, Llantood Farm, Llantood, Cardigan SA43 3NU (01239 612537).**

CARDIGAN COAST (Tresaith/Llangranog). Mrs C. Davies, Brynarthen, Glynarthen, Llandysul SA44 6PG (01239 851783). Cottages sleep 6; Caravan sleeps 4. Brynarthen is a small working farm delightfully

BRYNTEG   BRYNARTHEN

situated amidst beautiful unspoilt countryside, minutes from sandy beaches, one mile off the A487 Cardigan/Aberaeron coastal road. Within the grounds are two charming traditional stone cottages and one caravan, each surrounded by pleasant lawns and gardens, ideal for those wishing to relax and take it easy. The superb cottages are personally maintained to a high standard and whilst retaining all their charm and character, are comfortably furnished to meet family needs. One is also ideal for the elderly or partially disabled. Each cottage sleeps six with three bedrooms, bathroom, fully equipped kitchen/diner, lounge with colour TV, video and fitted carpets throughout. The modern 28' caravan sleeps four with a double bedroom, bunk bedroom, shower room with instant hot water, fully equipped kitchen/diner and spacious lounge with colour TV and fitted carpets throughout. Laundry room. Play area. Sorry no pets. Terms from £100 to £395. Open all year. Brochure on request.

CARDIGAN near. Quality Cottages. Around the magnificent Welsh coast. Away from the madding crowd. Near safe sandy beaches. A small specialist agency offering privacy, peace and unashamed luxury. Wales Tourist Board 1989 Award Winner. Residential standards — dishwashers, microwaves, washing machines, central heating, log fires, no slot meters. Linen provided. Pets welcome free. All in coastal areas famed for scenery, walks, wild flowers, birds, badgers and foxes. Free colour brochure. **S.C. Rees, Quality Cottages, Cerbid, Solva, Haverfordwest, Pembrokeshire SA62 6YE (01348 837871).**

PLEASE SEND A STAMPED ADDRESSED ENVELOPE WITH ENQUIRIES

CRICCIETH. Quality Cottages. Around the magnificent Welsh coast. Away from the madding crowd. Near safe sandy beaches. A small specialist agency offering privacy, peace and unashamed luxury. Wales Tourist Board 1989 Award Winner. Residential standards — dishwashers, microwaves, washing machines, central heating, log fires, no slot meters. Linen provided. Pets welcome free. All in coastal areas famed for scenery, walks, wild flowers, birds, badgers and foxes. Free colour brochure. **S.C. Rees, Quality Cottages, Cerbid, Solva, Haverfordwest, Pembrokeshire SA62 6YE (01348 837871).**

CROFT FARM COTTAGES Near Cardigan

Featured in FARM HOLIDAY WHICH? 1995, Croft Farm is situated in unspoilt North Pembrokeshire countryside near sandy beaches, coastal path, Preseli National Park and many local attractions. Our slate cottages sleep 2–7. Wine, flowers, tea-tray and water welcome you. Each is fully equipped with central heating, colour TV, microwave and linen. The farmhouse also has en suite bathrooms, bedroom TVs, dishwasher and fridge freezer. Help feed Tabitha the pig, Pearl the goat and other friendly farm animals. Playground, garden, patio and barbecue for guests' use. Pets welcome.

Short Breaks from £55. Weekly cottages £425.

Brochure from Andrew & Sylvie Gow, Croft Farm, Croft, Near Cardigan, Pembrokeshire SA43 3NT   Tel/Fax: 01239 615179

GOODWICK. Mrs Rosemary Johns, Carne, Goodwick SA64 0LB (01348 891665). Working farm, join in. Sleeps 6. Part of old stone farmhouse in peaceful

surroundings on 200 acre dairy and sheep farm. The self catering accommodation which sleeps six comprises three bedrooms; large living/diningroom with colour TV; bathroom and fitted kitchen including washing machine. No linen supplied. Children are welcome and there is fenced garden where they can play safely. Cots, high chairs and babysitting available. The farm is three miles from Fishguard, two miles from the sea and within easy reach of many beaches by car. You can be sure of a warm welcome and visitors are invited to join in farm activities. Pets welcome if under control. Open all year.

HAVERFORDWEST. Nolton Haven Farm Cottages in the Pembrokeshire National Park. Situated

beside Nolton Haven's sandy beach which they overlook, these six stone, slate and pine cottages offer discerning guests the ideal situation to enjoy the superb Pembrokeshire coastline. The cottages are fully equipped with colour TV, microwave, fridge/freezer, etc. 30 yards to the beach, 75 yards to the local inn/restaurant. Pony trekking, surfing, fishing, excellent cliff walks, boating and canoeing are all available nearby. Colour brochure on request. Contact **Jim Canton, Nolton Haven Farm, Nolton Haven, Haverfordwest SA62 1NH (01437 710263).**

HAVERFORDWEST. Mrs E.M. Mathias, Court House Cottages, Wolfsdale, Camrose, Near Haverfordwest SA62 6JJ (01437 710310). Cottages sleep 6. Centrally situated for all St. Bride's Bay and close to Prescelli Hills, three homely, stone-built cottages, each sleeping six in three double rooms, plus cots. Well-equipped kitchen area, lounge/diner, colour TV, shower room and toilet. Electricity by 50p meter. Situated in quiet, unspoilt hamlet of Wolfsdale, the owners' 300-acre farm is nearby, and through it flows the Western Cleddau with good trout, sewin and salmon fishing. Lovely country walks, near beautiful sandy beaches and coastal paths. Car essential — ample parking. Shops half-a-mile. Open all year — weekly terms from £100. The market town of Haverfordwest, Cathedral City of St. David's, popular seaside resorts and many places of historic and geological interest within easy driving distance. Further details on request.

FREE and REDUCED RATE Holiday Visits!
See our READERS' OFFER VOUCHER for details!

QUALITY COTTAGES

AROUND THE MAGNIFICENT WELSH COAST

Away from the Madding Crowd · Near safe sandy beaches

A small specialist agency with over 34 years experience of providing quality self-catering offers privacy, peace and unashamed luxury.
The first Wales Tourist Board Self-Catering Award Winner. Highest residential standards.
Dishwashers, Microwaves, Washing Machines, Central Heating. No slot meters.
LOG FIRES   LINEN PROVIDED   PETS WELCOME FREE!
All in coastal areas famed for scenery, walks, wild-flowers, birds, badgers and foxes.
Away from the madding crowd.
Free colour Brochure: F.G. Rees, "Quality Cottages", Cerbid, Solva, Haverfordwest, Pembrokeshire SA62 6YE. Telephone: (01348) 837871.

LAMPETER near. Richard & Linda Burgess, Gaer Cottages, Cribyn, Lampeter SA48 7LZ (01570 470275). WTB Five Dragons Award. Nine traditional Welsh stone farm cottages nestling in beautiful unspoilt countryside just 10 miles from the coast, where there is an abundance of rugged cliffs, sandy beaches, fascinating coves and pretty fishing villages to explore. While the original character of each cottage has been maintained, the interior has been designed to provide excellent accommodation for all the family, furnished and equipped to the highest standard. Six of the cottages are single-storeyed and are therefore ideally suited to the elderly or disabled, with one cottage specially adapted to give the wheelchair user maximum independence and mobility. All are double glazed, centrally heated and have their own patio. Luxurious purpose built indoor heated swimming pool and games room. Pets welcome. Short Breaks available. Open all year. Please send for brochure.

LAUGHARNE. Mr and Mrs R. Aldridge, Sir Johns Hill Farm, Laugharne SA33 4TD (01994 427667 or 01994 427734). We offer a real farm holiday with lots of animals. Children are always welcome to help around the farm. They can ride the ponies, collect eggs or help feed our many animals and pets. Our farm is set in a very private location with magnificent views over the sea. We are 15 minutes' walk from the ancient township of Laugharne with its pretty restaurants and shops, castle and Dylan Thomas Boathouse. Our self catering cottages are superbly fitted and have video, colour TV, microwaves, etc. See what "Times Travel Supplement" thought. For full details, brochure and video please telephone.

LLANDOVERY. Tyncoed Farm, Myddfai Road, Llandovery. Sleeps 7+. This spacious and very comfortable old farmhouse is beautifully set overlooking the Towy Valley, with magnificent views from the house. Tyncoed is in a secluded and private position, yet very conveniently situated just off the A4069 Llandovery/Llangadog road. The farmhouse retains much character and charm with its original stone fireplace and oak beams. As it is on the fringe of the Brecon Beacons National Park, it makes a perfect base for touring this delightful rural area. Log fires and storage heaters. Fully equipped. Cot and high chair available. Terms from £120 to £220 per week. SAE, please for further details to **Mrs Lewis Jones, Llwynmeredydd Farm, Myddfai, Llandovery SA20 0JE (01550 720450).**

WHEN MAKING ENQUIRIES PLEASE MENTION
FARM HOLIDAY GUIDES

LLANGADOG (Brecon Beacons). Mrs D.J. Price, Gwydre Farm, Llanddeusant, Llangadog SA19 9YS (01550 740242). WTB Grade 5. Working farm. Sleeps 6 adults.

Gwydre is a comfortable, spacious and well equipped cottage on a working beef and sheep farm situated at 900 feet in the peaceful, beautiful Black Mountain area of the Brecon Beacons National Park. There are extensive views of farmland and mountains. Superb walking, from gentle strolls on country lanes to strenuous climbs on the Black Mountain. Fishing in nearby lakes and reservoirs and birdwatching. The cottage has an original inglenook fireplace and woodburner and consists of three bedrooms; two double beds, two single and a cot; portable TV. Bathroom with hot shower; separate toilet. Fully fitted kitchen with microwave, deep freezer and washing machine. Large lounge with colour TV and snooker table. Carpeted throughout. Full central heating. Electricity by 50p meter. Linen is supplied. Open April — October from £150 to £270 weekly.

LLANGOEDMOR. Glandwr, Llangoedmor, Near Cardigan. Glandwr Holiday House is in the Parish of Llangoedmor, situated on the B4570, one mile from market town of Cardigan. Glandwr is a charming, well-equippped semi-detached holiday house in its own grounds with a small drive. Ample parking space. Sunny position with lawn front and back. Lovely countryside views and walks. Comprising fitted kitchen/dining area, fully equipped with full size electric stove, microwave oven, all utensils etc., two fridges; comfortable sittingroom has 20″ colour TV. Two double bedrooms (double bed in each), single bedroom, all well equipped. Bathroom with over bath electric shower, washbasin, toilet; downstairs toilet. Fitted carpets. Central heating, electricity inclusive in charge. Available all year from £135 inclusive per week. Mini Breaks from £95. One well-trained pet £8 per week extra. All prices subject to change. Sandy beaches two to eight miles; fishing on River Teifi. High standard of comfort, service and heating. SAE to **Mrs B. Evans, Rhydfuwch Dairy Farm, Near Cardigan SA43 2LB (01239 612064).**

LLANGRANNOG. Quality Cottages. Around the magnificent Welsh coast. Away from the madding crowd. Near safe, sandy beaches. A small specialist agency offering privacy, peace and unashamed luxury. Wales Tourist Board 1989 Award Winner. Residential standards — dishwashers, microwaves, washing machines, central heating, log fires, no slot meters. Linen provided. Pets welcome free. All in coastal areas famed for scenery, walks, wild flowers, birds, badgers and foxes. Free colour brochure. **S.C. Rees, Quality Cottages, Cerbid, Solva, Haverfordwest, Pembrokeshire SA62 6YE (01348 837871).**

See also Colour Display Advertisement **MYDROILYN. Blaenllanarth Holiday Cottages, Mydroilyn, Lampeter SA48 7RJ (01570 470374). Wales Tourist Board** *APPROVED.* Stone farm buildings, recently converted into four cottages, providing a modern standard of comfort in a traditional setting. Sleep two/three (terms £90-£180) or four/eight (terms £145-£300). Gas, electricity and linen included in price. All have shower room and fully equipped kitchen. Colour TV; shared laundry room; facilities for children. Open Easter to October. Situated in a secluded rural area, with abundant wildlife and flowers, and only five miles from sandy beaches and picturesque harbours of Cardigan Bay. Within easy reach of National Trust coastal footpaths, sites of historic and cultural interest, steam railways, castles and breathtaking mountain scenery. Bird watching, fishing and pony trekking nearby. AA Approved. Full details from **Gil and Mike Kearney.**

NEWGALE. Quality Cottages. Around the magnificent Welsh coast. Away from the madding crowd. Near safe, sandy beaches. A small specialist agency offering privacy, peace and unashamed luxury. Wales Tourist Board 1989 Award Winner. Residential standards — dishwashers, microwaves, washing machines, central heating, log fires, no slot meters. Linen provided. Pets welcome free. All in coastal areas famed for scenery, walks, wild flowers, birds, badgers and foxes. Free colour brochure. **S.C. Rees, Quality Cottages, Cerbid, Solva, Haverfordwest, Pembrokeshire SA62 6YE (01348 837871).**

PEMBROKESHIRE. Charles and Joy Spiers, West Lambston, Portfield Gate, Haverfordwest SA62 3LG (01437 710038).

Delightfully restored cottage in 200 year old farmhouse, designed for your ease and comfort. No early morning tractors on this non working farm. Nearest beach within three miles; four more beaches within five miles. Wonderful coastal walks to regain your sanity! Sleeps four in two bedrooms. Well equipped kitchen contains fridge/freezer, electric and microwave cookers, automatic washer, and ironing equipment. Colour TV and cosy window with sea view. Charming oak beamed inglenook houses gas-fired cast iron stove. Shower and toilet room. Cot and high chair available. Bed linen, beach, bath, hand and tea towels provided inclusive. Pets by arrangement. Terms from £95 to £260 per week.

NORTH PEMBROKESHIRE. Mrs T. Jones, Penbanc, Tegryn, Llanfyrnach SA35 0BP (01239 698279). Working family farm with sheep, cows, calves, ponies, free range hens, ducks and geese; sometimes pigs. Traditional stone built farmhouse accommodation sleeps six plus cot; bathroom; kitchen; sittingroom with colour TV and woodburner, dining room. Small garden with picnic table. Plenty of books and games for wet days, also old piano. Petrol, stamps, milk and pub meals one mile; village store two miles. Centrally based for trekking, walking, touring, swimming, golf; coast 20 minutes by car (essential). Fishing — river, reservoir, sea or farm pool. Sandy beaches, rocky coves, coastal path. Island to visit. Plenty to do — castles, woollen mills, nature reserves, museums, crafts, leisure centres, theme park, zoo. Available May to September. Also seven-berth caravan available.

SOLVA. Quality Cottages. Around the magnificent Welsh Coast. Away from the madding crowd. Near safe, sandy beaches. A small specialist agency offering privacy, peace and unashamed luxury. Wales Tourist Board 1989 Award Winner. Residential standards — dishwashers, microwaves, washing machines, central heating, log fires, no slot meters. Linen provided. Pets welcome free. All in coastal areas famed for scenery, walks, wild flowers, birds, badgers and foxes. Free colour brochure. **S.C. Rees, Quality Cottages, Cerbid, Solva, Haverfordwest, Pembrokeshire SA62 6YE (01348 837871).**

ST. DAVID'S. Quality Cottages. Around the magnificent Welsh coast. Away from the madding crowd. Near safe sandy beaches. A small specialist agency offering privacy, peace and unashamed luxury. Wales Tourist Board 1989 Award Winner. Residential standards — dishwashers, microwaves, washing machines, central heating, log fires, no slot meters. Linen provided. Pets welcome free. All in coastal areas famed for scenery, walks, wild flowers, birds, badgers and foxes. Free colour brochure. **S.C. Rees, Quality Cottages, Cerbid, Solva, Haverfordwest, Pembrokeshire SA62 6YE (01348 837871).**

ST. DAVID'S. Ffynnon Ddofn, Llanon, Llanrhian, Haverfordwest. WTB 4 Dragons APPROVED.

Luxury cottage in quiet lane between St. David's and Fishguard, with panoramic views over many miles of this spectacular coastline. Ideal for walking; rocky coves and safe sandy beaches nearby. The cottage is fully carpeted, warm, comfortable and very well equipped, sleeping six in three bedrooms, plus cot. Washing machine, tumble dryer, freezer. Games room with table tennis and snooker, children's toys, with central heating and double glazing. Parking beside cottage. Shop one mile. Footpath to beach. Pets welcome. Open all year. Terms from £195, including heating and electricity. Brochure on request. **Mrs T.A. Rees White, Brickhouse Farm, Burnham Road, Woodham Mortimer, Maldon, Essex CM9 6SR (01245 224611).**

TENBY. Quality Cottages. Around the magnificent Welsh coast. Away from the madding crowd. Near safe, sandy beaches. A small specialist agency offering privacy, peace and unashamed luxury. Wales Tourist Board 1989 Award Winner. Residential standards — dishwashers, microwaves, washing machines, central heating, log fires, no slot meters. Linen provided. Pets welcome free. All in coastal areas famed for scenery, walks, wild flowers, birds, badgers and foxes. Free colour brochure. **S.C. Rees, Quality Cottages, Cerbid, Solva, Haverfordwest, Pembrokeshire SA62 6YE (01348 837871).**

TUFTON. Garden Farm, Tufton, Near Haverfordwest. Garden Farm offers a charming combination of

old character and modern facilities. There are two houses available, both detached. The farmhouse, WTB Grading 4 Dragons, sleeps up to 7 people. Centrally heated, fitted kitchen with microwave, dishwasher, fridge/freezer, full sized washer etc. Large dining room with inglenook wood burning fire and colour TV. Three bedrooms and bathroom upstairs. One bedroom downstairs. The Granary, WTB Grading 5 Dragons, sleeps up to 4 people with the bedrooms and bathroom downstairs and kitchen and living room containing colour TV upstairs to take advantage of the marvellous views. The kitchen is fully fitted with full sized cooker, microwave and fridge. The farm is situated 10 miles north of Haverfordwest and 9 miles east of Fishguard. It is within the National Park and only a short distance from the top of the Preseli Hills with magnificent views and walks. The nearby coastline is breathtaking and the scenery is some of the finest in the Bristish Isles. The farm is accessible at all times to visitors and supports a herd of pedigree Welsh Black Cattle and a flock of Beulah Speckleface Sheep. Contact: **Ann of Jennifer Barney, Yethen Isaf, Mynachlogddu, Clynderwen, Pembrokeshire SA66 7SN (Tel & Fax: 01437 532256).**

WHITLAND. Mrs Angela Colledge, Gwarmacwydd, Llanfallteg, Whitland SA34 0XH (01437 563260; Fax: 01437 563839). Gwarmacwydd is a country estate of over 450 acres, including two miles of riverbank.

Come and see a real farm in action, the hustle and bustle of harvest, cows being milked, newborn calves and lambs. Children are welcomed. On the estate are five character stone cottages, Tourist Board Grade 4. Each cottage has been lovingly converted from traditional farm buildings, parts of which are over 200 years old. Each cottage is fully furnished and equipped with all modern conveniences. All electricity and linen included. All cottages are heated for year-round use. Colour brochure available.

POWYS

BRECON. Lower Penllanafal, Llangorse, Near Brecon. WTB Grade 3. Sleeps 6 plus cot. Lower

Penllanafal is a superbly furnished cottage situated in beautiful countryside in National Park with views of Brecon Beacons. 50 yards off the road with its own private tarmac road leading up to a large yard by the cottage for parking. It has its own garden with lawn and orchard with stream. Sleeps six in two bedrooms; upstairs bathroom with toilet; comfortable lounge with easy chairs and colour TV; dining room with large table; fully equipped kitchen with electric cooker, fridge freezer. Heating by storage heaters, electric fires, open fires (logs provided). Bed linen provided. SAE for brochure. **Mrs S. Hamer, Middle-Penllanafal, Llangorse, Brecon LD3 7UN (01874 658307).**

BRECON near (Bwlch). Mrs Iris Lloyd, Talybryn, Bwlch, Near Brecon LD3 7LQ (01874 676278).

Sleeps 4. This luxury flat stands in 60 acres of farmland, situated off the A40, looking down on the River Usk. The hills hug the lovely old farmhouse, secluded and "away from it all". Available all year and always warm and comfortable with central heating. This is an area of natural loveliness with green meadows and lush pastures. Nature excels herself at every season here. There is accommodation for four in one double bedroom and one twin bedroom; bathroom and toilet; large sittingroom, colour TV; diningroom; fully fitted all-electric kitchen with all utensils etc.; sink unit and fridge. No meters. Regret no pets. Shops one mile, the beautiful Gower coast 38 miles. Car not essential (on bus route), though plenty of parking space. A warm welcome awaits you here. Brochure gladly sent on request with SAE, please. Farm Holiday Guide Diploma.

BRECON/BUILTH WELLS. Mr and Mrs Hennessy, Pant Gwyn, Merthyr Cynog, Brecon LD3 9SF

(01874 690267). Sleeps 2/4. The chalet is beautifully situated on a rural smallholding at 1300 feet midway between Builth Wells and Brecon. It is self-contained with kitchenette and attached bathroom with flush toilet. Many who like peace and quiet return. We provide a convenient centre for touring and walking in the National Park and the mid Wales area. The area also provides golf, fishing and pony trekking. There is no problem with access. Local pubs nearby. Children and pets welcome. Weekly terms are from £75 to £140.

See also Colour Display Advertisement CAERSWS. **Mrs Gwyneth Williams, Red House, Trefeglwys, Caersws, Montgomeryshire SY17 5PN (01686 430285). WTB 4 Dragons Award.** A highly furnished, self contained part of the farmhouse, situated on a mixed working family farm with panoramic views. Unspoilt scenery and the tranquillity of the Trannon Valley makes it an ideal, convenient base for Llanidloes (six miles) and Clywedog Reservoir, Powys Castle and the coast which are all close at hand. Fully equipped kitchen with washing machine and refurbished bathroom; other facilities include log fire, bed linen, garden furniture and ample parking. Lots of wildlife. We do all we can to ensure our guests' comfort and welcome them with tea on arrival. So come to Red House and enjoy a refreshing change. Terms from £100 to £250 per week. Open all year. SAE for brochure. OS Map Ref SN992 899.

LAKE VYRNWY (3 miles). Mrs J. Smith, Felin Wynfa, Llanfihangel, Llanfyllin SY22 5JB (01691 870228). WTB For Dragons. Cosy, beamed, self contained wing of former 17th century millhouse currently a 10 acre smallholding with sheep and poultry. Picturesque location beside a stream. Ideal walking, birdwatching area with a RSPB nature reserve a short distance away. Powis Castle, narrow gauge railway, Bala Lake and Pistyll Rhaeadr Waterfall are within a radius of 18 miles. Accommodation comprises well equipped kitchen/diner with microwave; sitting room; two bedrooms, one double leading through to children's room with bunk beds plus cot; shower room. Bed linen provided. Children welcome. Sorry no pets. Non-smokers preferred. Terms from £90 to £170 per week. Short Breaks available. Please write or telephone for brochure.

LLANDRINDOD WELLS. Mr and Mrs M.H. Kendrick, Cwmbrith Farm, Penybont, Llandrindod Wells LD1 5SR (01597 822391). Delightful modern bungalow built of red brick with green tiled roof, situated on 600 acre hill farm rearing sheep and cattle. Comprises lounge-cum-dining room, three double bedrooms, two with twin beds; bathroom; kitchen with electric cooker, fridge, stainless steel sink, etc. Storage heaters. No linen supplied. Children welcome. Car essential, parking. Three miles from shops and public transport. One and a half miles of fishing. Three miles from old spa town of Llandrindod Wells with all amenities, golf, lake fishing, two trout pools, bowling, tennis, pony rides, etc. Seaside at Aberystwyth 40 miles. Available all year round except Christmas. Terms from £125 weekly.

NEWTOWN. Mrs D. Pryce, Aberbechan Farm, Newtown SY16 3BJ (01686 630675). Working farm, join in. Sleeps 10. This part of quaint Tudor farmhouse with its lovely oak beams is situated in picturesque countryside on a mixed farm with trout fishing and shooting in season. Newtown three miles, Welshpool, Powis Castle and Llanfair Light Railway, 14 miles; 45 miles to coast. The sleeping accommodation is for 10 people in four double and two single bedrooms, also cot. Two bathrooms, two toilets. Sitting/diningroom with colour TV. Fully fitted kitchen with fridge, electric cooker, washing machine and dishwasher. Log fires and off-peak heaters. Electricity on meter. Large lawn with swing. Everything supplied for visitors' comfort. Linen available for overseas guests at extra cost. Car essential to obtain the best from the holiday. Farm produce available in season. Village shop one and a half miles away. Open all year. SAE please.

See also Colour Display Advertisement **TALGARTH. Mrs Bronwen Prosser, Upper Genfford Farm Guest House, Talgarth, Brecon LD7 0EN (01874 711360).** AA QQQ Recommended. The cottages are situated amongst the most spectacular scenery of the Brecon Beacons National Park. An excellent location for walking and exploring the Brecon Beacons, Black Mountains and Wye Valley. An Area of Outstanding Natural Beauty of historic and archaeological interest. The cottages are beautifully furnished and have fitted carpets, oil-fired Rayburn, oak-beamed lounges, antique furniture, open log fires, Calor gas heaters and colour TVs. Bed and Breakfast cottage available with bedrooms en suite having colour TV and beverage trays. Tea and home made cakes served on arrival at all cottages. Pets welcome and linen provided. A warm friendly welcome awaits you. Children enjoy our friendly pony "Topsy". Terms: Self Catering from £160 per week; Bed and Breakfast from £16. Weekend breaks available. Highly recommended. Nominated one of the top 20 proprietors for the finals of AA Landlady of the Year competition 1996 and is also one of the only two FHG Diplomas Winners from Wales for 1995/6.

WELSHPOOL. Mr and Mrs Jones, Lower Trelydan Farm, Guilsfield, Welshpool SY21 9PH (01938 553105). Working farm. Sleep 2/8. Newly converted luxury cottages, which have gained the Welsh Tourist Board highest award of Five Dragons. Set on a working farm in a beautiful quiet situation. Comfortable beds and furnishing, fitted carpets, modern kitchens and stylish bathrooms. Coupled with the orginal brickwork and pine arches. Attractive gardens with children's play area. Meal delivery service. Pub and shop within easy walking distance. Riding, fishing, sailing, golf, steam railway, canal, lakes and Powis Castle all nearby.

SOUTH WALES (formerly Glamorgan and Gwent)

Blaenau Gwent, Bridgend, Caerphilly, Cardiff, Merthyr Tydfil, Monmouthshire, Neath & Port Talbot, Newport, Rhondda Cynon Taff, Swansea, Torfaen, and Vale of Glamorgan

ABERGAVENNY. Llyweddrog Farm, Llanwenarth, Abergavenny. Sleeps 4 adults, 2 children. Stone

built farmhouse high on Sugar Loaf Mountain with panoramic views of Usk Valley. Partial central heating. Large fitted kitchen/diner and spacious lounge with open fire. Double, twin and bunk-bedded rooms. Situated between enclosed farmland and mountainside owned by National Trust — great for nature walks. Ideal base for exploring — Vale of Usk, Golden Valley, historic buildings, Roman remains, industrial heritage. Open May to October. Children welcome. Terms from £150 to £280 per week. Contact: **Mrs N.E. Smith, Penygraig Farm, Llanwenarth Citra, Abergavenny NP7 7LA (01873 853398).**

ABERGAVENNY. Troedrhiwmwm, Llanthony, Abergavenny. Sleeps 9. WTB Grade 4. Our traditional

14th century farmhouse on a working farm, furnished to a high standard, is located in the heart of the Black Mountains and commands spectacular views over Llanthony Priory and Valley. It is the perfect retreat for a relaxing and peaceful holiday; ideal for walking, birdwatching, pony trekking or exploring the beautiful surrounding countryside with its many old churches and castles. Guests are welcome to feed the hens, goats, pony, lambs and calves. The farmhouse has three bedrooms, spacious kitchen, fully equipped with microwave, etc. Lounge with large open fireplace and large garden/play area. Bed linen provided. Weekend and midweek breaks. Brochure available. For terms and full details contact: **Mrs Mary Thomas, Cwmbuchill, Llanthony, Abergavenny NP7 7NN (01873 890619).**

SWANSEA. Mr Richards, Bank Farm Holiday Park, Horton, Gower, Swansea SA3 1LL (01792 390228; Fax: 01792 391282). Fully furnished self catering bungalow available comprising two bedrooms, bathroom, kitchen and lounge. Electricity included in the price. Children and pets welcome. Private parking. Clean safe beach only half a mile away. Open March to December inclusive. Short Breaks available. Weekly terms from £85 to £310.

SWANSEA. H.H.M. Thomas & Son, Cwmcile Farm, Salem, Morriston (01792 845141). WTB 3

Dragon Award. Ty Rebecca is a 300 year old cottage with its history dating back to the Rebecca Riots where suspected rioters where apprehended by Captain John Napier in 1843, hence its name. Pleasantly situated overlooking the Lliw Reservoir on a working dairy and sheep farm. Visitors can view the milking and see the lambs. Cottage available April to October. Prices from £150 per week depending on season. Short lets available and enquiries taken for Bed and Breakfast (🌸🌸 *COMMENDED)* at the main farm house. Further details available on request.

WHEN MAKING ENQUIRIES PLEASE MENTION
FARM HOLIDAY GUIDES

CARAVAN AND CAMPING HOLIDAYS

NORTH WALES (formerly Clwyd and Gwynedd)

Aberconwy & Colwyn, Anglesey, Denbighshire, Flintshire, Gwynedd and Wrexham

CARAVANS

ABERGELE. Mr and Mrs T.P. Williams, Pen Isaf Caravan Park, Llangernyw, Abergele LL22 8RN (01745 860276). This small caravan site in beautiful unspoilt countryside is ideal for touring North Wales and is situated 10 miles from the coast and 12 miles from Betws-y-Coed. The eight-berth caravans are fully equipped except for linen and towels and have showers, flush toilet, hot and cold water, Calor gas cooker, electric light and fridge. Fresh eggs and milk can be obtained from the farm on which this 20 caravan site is situated. Children especially will enjoy a holiday here, there being ample space and facilities for fishing and pony riding. Pets are allowed but must be kept under control. Open March to October. Terms on application with SAE, please.

BALA. Mrs S.E. Edwards, Bryn Melyn, Rhyduchaf, Bala LL23 7PG (01678 520376). Sleeps 6. One six-berth caravan available on Bryn Melyn, a 56 acre mixed farm in the village of Rhyduchaf, two miles from Bala situated in beautiful countryside. The caravan has a bathroom, inside flush toilet, hot and cold water, electric light, gas cooker, gas heater, fridge, colour TV. Fully equipped with blankets, microwave, etc. Children welcome. Sorry, no pets allowed. Open from April to September. Electricity on slot meter (£1). Weekly terms from £85. SAE please for further details.

CRICCIETH. Mrs Margaret Roberts, Ynys-Wen, Llangybi, Pwllheli LL53 6TB (01766 810294). One only spacious six-berth caravan for hire on mixed working farm situated in its own private garden with swing and slide and beautiful views of Snowdonia and its majestic scenery.

The caravan has a large double bedroom with fitted wardrobes and separate bedroom with twin bunks. All bedding and bed linen is supplied. Large lounge area with colour television, gas heater and convertible bed settee. Separate bathroom with shower, toilet and washbasin. The Lleyn Peninsula, where we are situated, has many different beaches and coves. River and sea fishing, golf, horse riding, walking, etc., all close by. Rent includes electricity and gas. Terms from £80 per week. Further details sent on receipt of SAE.

PORTHMADOG. Mrs E.A.J. Williams, Tyddyn Deucwm Isaf, Penmorfa, Porthmadog LL49 9SD (01766 513683). Glorious six-berth caravan in own enclosure on working beef and sheep farm in peaceful countryside, overlooking Cambrian coast between Criccieth and Porthmadog in Snowdonia National Park. Elevated, sunny position. Walks on farm and nearby. Outstanding views of sea and mountains, also world famous Ffestiniog Narrow Gauge Railway which is nearby in Porthmadog. Very central for tourist attractions; near choice of good beaches, Caernarvon Castle, Snowdon, leisure centre, etc. Five minutes from restaurants, pubs, take-away. All modern amenities — electricity and gas, showers, etc. Three separate bedrooms (one double and two twin bunks), colour TV. Pets welcome by arrangement. Please state number in party. SAE, or telephone.

DYFED

Cardiganshire, Carmarthenshire and Pembrokeshire

CARAVANS

ABERPORTH. Mrs S. Jones, Manorafon Caravan Park, Sarnau, Llandyssul SA44 6QH (01239 810564). Sleeps 6. Quiet, peaceful site of 11 caravans, fully equipped except linen, all six-berth with end bedrooms. All essential facilities provided. Bathroom facilities with hot water on tap in each van; Calor gas cooker, electric lighting and heating. Toilets and washbasins, showers, shaving points. Calor and Camping Gaz sold. Available Easter to October. Children welcome. Dogs must be kept on lead. Horses welcome. Only half a mile from the pleasant Penbryn beach and nine miles from the market towns of Cardigan and Newcastle Emlyn. One and a half acres for campers and tourers.

ABERYSTWYTH. Mrs Anne Bunton, Cwmergyr Farm, Ponterwyd, Aberystwyth SY23 3LB (01970 890301). This luxury six-berth caravan is sited in its own enclosure on a 250-acre sheep farm in the beautiful Cambrian Mountains, 16 miles east of Aberystwyth, off the A44.

Accommodation consists of two bedrooms, bathroom (flush toilet, vanity unit and shower); kitchen (fridge and gas cooker); spacious lounge with colour TV and spectacular views; gas fire and hot and cold water throughout. Linen not supplied. No pets allowed. Car essential with ample parking. Within 15 mile radius there are sandy beaches, fishing, golf, pony trekking, steam railway, scenic drives and walks. An ideal location to explore mid-Wales. Children will love the stream and the farm animals. Open 1st April to 31st October. Terms £100 — £150 per week (all gas and electricity included).

BROAD HAVEN near. Sandra Davies, Barley Villa, Walwyns Castle, Near Broad Haven, Haverford-west SA62 3EB (01437 781254). Our comfortable, modern six-berth caravan is sited in the attractive, peaceful countryside of Walwyns Castle, which hosts a small nature reserve and several public footpaths. It is an ideal base for touring Pembrokeshire's beautiful coastline, visiting our famous bird islands and beautiful sandy bays ideal for swimming, surfing or sailing, all within easy reach by car.

Ample shared parking and storage for bicycles. The caravan has a double and twin room, shower/toilet; full size cooker, fridge; lounge and dining room with gas fire and colour TV. Bed linen is provided, beds made up for arrival. Terms from £85 to £150 fully inclusive of gas, electricity and linen.

HAVERFORDWEST near. Scamford Caravan Park, Keeston, Haverfordwest SA62 6HN (Tel & Fax: 01437 710304).  √ √ √ √ √ 25 Dragon Award luxury holiday caravans on peaceful park in attractive countryside, near Pembrokeshire Coastal Path and many lovely beaches. Every caravan has all mains services, fridge, gas fire, shower and colour TV. Also five touring pitches with electric hook-ups, free hot showers. Excellent children's playground — swings, sand pit, climbing frame and trampolines. Dog welcome. Some caravans "dog-free" for the sake of children with allergies. Telephone. Launderette, with ironing facilities. Plenty to do in the area — castle, farm parks, craft shops, boat trips, island bird sanctuaries, surfing, golfing, riding, etc., or spend a day at Oakwood Leisure Park. Weekly from £90. Colour brochure from resident owners **Jean and Maurice Gould.**

TENBY. Mrs J.N. Frazer, Highlands Farm, Manorbier-Newton, Tenby SA70 8PX (01834 871446). A spacious six-berth caravan situated in a quiet three-acre meadow. The caravan is fully serviced with electric lighting and TV, also gas cooker and room heater. There are two separate end bedrooms, fully fitted shower room, kitchen/diner and a lounge with panoramic views. The caravan is sited a couple of hundred yards from the main road providing a peaceful countryside setting ideal for children or a well behaved pet. A car is essential. Shopping facilities can be found in nearby Tenby or Pembroke. Please write or phone for details.

SOUTH WALES (formerly Glamorgan and Gwent)

CARAVANS

RHOOSE. Fontgary Holiday Leisure Park, Rhoose CF6 9ZT (01446 710386; Fax: 01446 710613). √ √ √ √ Fontgary Holiday Park is situated beside the Bristol Channel in the rural Vale of Glamorgan. High quality facilities include superb 25 metre indoor heated pool with funpool, poolside snackbar, carbaret lounge bars, shop, hairdresser, children's fun centre, games room and unique octagonal restaurant. Our superbly equipped health club is available for temporary membership. Children and pets welcome. This beautifully kept park is ideal for visiting the numerous attractions in the area. Luxury Dragon Award caravan holiday homes with colour TVs are available with a choice of either two or three bedrooms. Touring caravans welcome, sorry no tents. Send or telephone for your free colour brochure.

Key to Tourist Board Ratings

The Crown Scheme
(England, Scotland & Wales)

Covering hotels, motels, private hotels, guesthouses, inns, bed & breakfast, farmhouses. Every Crown classified place to stay is inspected annually. *The classification:* Listed then 1-5 Crown indicates the range of facilities and services. Higher quality standards are indicated by the terms APPROVED, COMMENDED, HIGHLY COMMENDED and DELUXE.

The Key Scheme
(also operates in Scotland using a Crown symbol)

Covering self-catering in cottages, bungalows, flats, houseboats, houses, chalets, etc. Every Key classified holiday home is inspected annually. *The classification:* 1-5 Key indicates the range of facilities and equipment. Higher quality standards are indicated by the terms APPROVED, COMMENDED, HIGHLY COMMENDED and DELUXE.

The Q Scheme
(England, Scotland & Wales)

Covering holiday, caravan, chalet and camping parks. Every Q rated park is inspected annually for its quality standards. The more √ in the Q – up to 5 – the higher the standard of what is provided.

ACTIVITY HOLIDAYS

NORTH WALES, CRICCIETH. Betws-Bach & Rhos-Dhu, Ynys, Criccieth LL52 0PB (Tel & Fax: 01758 720047; 01766 810295). Wales Tourist Board Grade 5. SELF CATERING: FISHING/SHOOTING. A truly romantic, memorable and special place to stay and relax in comfort. Old World farmhouse and period country cottage. Situated just off the B4411 road in tranquil surroundings. Equipped to Wales Tourist Board Grade 5 standard with washing/drying machines, dishwashers, microwaves, freezers, colour TV, old oak beams, inglenook with log fires, full central heating. Snooker table, pitch 'n' putt; romantic four-poster bed, sauna and jacuzzi. Open all year — Winter Weekends welcomed. Ideal for couples. Sleep two to six plus cot. Own fishing and shooting rights, wonderful walks, peace and quiet with Snowdonia and unspoilt beaches on our doorstep. For friendly personal service please phone, Fax or write to Mrs Anwen Jones.

DYFED, CRYMYCH. Riding Holidays in Pembrokeshire Coast National Park. SELF CATERING: RIDING. For riders with some experience. We offer fit and willing horses and escorted riding through spectacular mountain and moorland scenery. Small groups, indoor school, tuition, showjumps and cross-country fences. Own horses welcome. Self catering accommodation. Also NEW for 1997 season — TRAIL RIDING. For further details and brochures: **Chris or Gill Hirst, Ravel Farm, Brynberian, Crymych SA41 3TQ (01239 891316).**

FOR THE MUTUAL GUIDANCE OF GUEST AND HOST

Every year literally thousands of holidays, short-breaks and overnight stops are arranged through our guides, the vast majority without any problems at all. In a handful of cases, however, difficulties do arise about bookings, which often could have been prevented from the outset.

It is important to remember that when accommodation has been booked, both parties — guests and hosts — have entered into a form of contract. We hope that the following points will provide helpful guidance.

GUESTS: When enquiring about accommodation, be as precise as possible. Give exact dates, numbers in your party and the ages of any children. State the number and type of rooms wanted and also what catering you require — bed and breakfast, full board, etc. Make sure that the position about evening meals is clear — and about pets, reductions for children or any other special points.

Read our reviews carefully to ensure that the proprietors you are going to contact can supply what you want. Ask for a letter confirming all arrangements, if possible.

If you have to cancel, do so as soon as possible. Proprietors do have the right to retain deposits and under certain circumstances to charge for cancelled holidays if adequate notice is not given and they cannot re-let the accommodation.

HOSTS: Give details about your facilities and about any special conditions. Explain your deposit system clearly and arrangements for cancellations, charges, etc, and whether or not your terms include VAT.

If for any reason you are unable to fulfil an agreed booking without adequate notice, you may be under an obligation to arrange alternative suitable accommodation or to make some form of compensation.

While every effort is made to ensure accuracy, we regret that FHG Publications cannot accept responsibility for errors, omissions or misrepresentation in our entries or any consequences thereof. Prices in particular should be checked because we go to press early. We will follow up complaints but cannot act as arbiters or agents for either party.

NORTHEN IRELAND

BOARD ACCOMMODATION

ANTRIM

BALLINTOY. Mrs Rita McFall, Ballintoy House, 9 Main Street, Ballintoy (012657 62317). Two and a
half storey Listed Georgian building situated in the village of
Ballintoy. Within walking distance of Carrick-a-Rede Rope
Bridge and one and a half miles from Whitepark Bay. Boat
trips and fishing are available from Ballintoy harbour. One
double, one twin and one single bedrooms (two en suite), all
with tea making facilities. TV lounge. Three-course breakfast
served in a friendly atmosphere. Pets welcome. Bed and
Breakfast from £12 (en suite extra). Open all year.

**BALLYCASTLE. Mrs Oonagh McHenry, Torr Brae, 77 Torr Road, Torr Head, Ballycastle BT54 6RQ
(012657 69625).** A warm and friendly welcome awaits you
at Torr Brae with its spectacular view as shown of Torr Head
with the Mull of Kintyre visible in the background. Torr Head
is an ideal location for exploring the Causeway Coast and the
famous Glens of Antrim. This homely farmhouse offers large
en suite rooms, choice of breakfast and is fully centrally
heated. Residents' TV lounge. Tea/coffee making facilities in
rooms. Private parking. Stunning country walks, sea fishing,
golfing and tennis all available nearby. Children welcome at
reduced rate sharing. Bed and Breakfast from £15 to £18.
Vouchers accepted.

BUSHMILLS. Mrs E. Rankin, Ballyholme Farm, 198 Ballybogey Road, Bushmills (012657 31793).
Modern dairy farmhouse situated three miles from Portrush
and Bushmills. One double and one twin bedrooms with
washbasins. Home cooking. Children welcome. Central
heating. No smoking. TV in visitors' lounge. Supper provided
as required. Old fashioned cottage with interesting antique
artefacts nearby. Bed and Breakfast from £14.

COUNTY DOWN

BALLYNAHINCH. Mrs Sally Murphy, Bushymead Country House, 86 Drumaness Road, Ballynahinch BT24 8LT (01238 561171).

Bushymead Country House is built in classical style. It is a family run Bed and Breakfast; comfort, cleanliness and personal attention guaranteed. We are situated in the centre of County Down on A24 (Belfast to Newcastle route) close to Belfast, Lisburn, Downpatrick, Ards Peninsula and on the doorstep to Newcastle and the Mourne Mountains. Close to all tourist attractions — museums, forest, parks, golf, fishing, nature reserves, National Trust properties. All rooms have TV and tea/coffee making facilities. Winner of Best for Guests Award 1995, Welcome Host Awards, Irish Hospitality Award, N.I.T.B. Guest House Owners Award, Food Hygiene Certificate, 706/2 City and Guilds Full Catering. Advanced Bakery. Bed and Breakfast from £13 to £20. Special Break rates.

NEWRY. Mrs Caroline Gordon, Dairy Farm, 52A Majors Hill, Annalong, Newry BT34 4QR (013967 68433).

Modern bungalow on working dairy farm situated at the foot of the beautiful Mourne Mountains; 500 metre walk to village and harbour; Silent Valley two miles, Annalong is midway between Newcastle and the fishing port of Kilkeel. Ideal base for sightseeing, hill walking, fishing and bowls. Accommodation comprises three bedrooms — one double, one family and one twin-bedded rooms, all en suite with colour TV and tea/coffee making facilities. Evening meals by arrangement with the Harbour restaurant.

FERMANAGH

BLANEY. Mrs Hanna E. Bruce, Lough Erne House, St. Catherine's, Blaney, Enniskillin (013656 41216).

Family guesthouse in rural setting on shores of Lower Lough Erne. Convenient for all tourist amenities, boating marina adjacent, fishing available. One double, one single and one family bedrooms. Open all year. Meals available. Enniskillen 10 miles on A46 to Belleek.

BROOKEBOROUGH. Mrs E. Norton, Norfolk House, Killykeeran, Brookeborough (013655 31681).

Family-run country house situated in a peaceful area, ideal for walking. Cycling and fishing is available within walking distance. A warm welcome awaits guests, and a great breakfast. We are situated off the main Belfast Road, one mile Maguiresbridge, one mile Brookeborough, nine miles Enniskillen and close to all amenities. Accommodation comprises one double and one family rooms with en suite facilities, one twin-bedded and one single, all rooms have washbasins. Separate luxury guest room with oak beams. Colour TV. Separate dining room. Children welcome, reduced rates. Open all year. Bed and Breakfast £14.

EDERNEY. Mrs Elizabeth McCord, Greenwood Lodge, Erne Drive, Ederney (013656 31366). On the

outskirts of a peaceful village this comfortable family-run guesthouse has en suite rooms. All have tea/coffee facilities, central heating and TV; several are on the ground floor. Convenient for fishing, boating, golf, pony trekking and touring the Lakelands, Donegal and Omagh areas. Situated near Kesh, Castle Archdale, Necarne Equestrian Centre, Lakeland Airport and Belleek Pottery. Plenty of parking. Open all year.

IRVINESTOWN. Mr Joe Mahon, Mahon's Hotel, Irvinestown BT94 1GS (013656 21656; Fax: 013656 28344). Family run hotel established in 1883. All

rooms en suite with TV, radio and video channel. Entertainment at weekend. Games room, baby listening. Restaurant famous for home cooking. Beside new Ulster Equestrian Park. Private car park. Pets welcome. Central heating. Terms:- Weekend Breakaway £62.50 April to October, Midweek Breakaway £89.00, Week Breakaway £175, Single Day £29.50. Bed and Breakfast only from £25. Please write or telephone for further details. AA ** RAC.

KILLADEAS. Mr and Mrs J. Williams, Rossfad House, Kesh Road, Killadeas (01365 388505). Rossfad is a Georgian country house with spacious grounds adjoining Lower Lough Erne. Situated between Enniskillen and Castle Archdale, it is convenient for ferry crossings to Devenish and White Island, as well as good restaurants and a variety of sporting activities including boating, golf and pony trekking. Accommodation comprises one double en suite room and one family room, both south-facing with views of the lake. Open all year. Bed and Breakfast from £12.50 per night. Special rates for weekend and midweek breaks.

FOR THE MUTUAL GUIDANCE OF GUEST AND HOST

Every year literally thousands of holidays, short-breaks and overnight stops are arranged through our guides, the vast majority without any problems at all. In a handful of cases, however, difficulties do arise about bookings, which often could have been prevented from the outset.

It is important to remember that when accommodation has been booked, both parties — guests and hosts — have entered into a form of contract. We hope that the following points will provide helpful guidance.

GUESTS: When enquiring about accommodation, be as precise as possible. Give exact dates, numbers in your party and the ages of any children. State the number and type of rooms wanted and also what catering you require — bed and breakfast, full board, etc. Make sure that the position about evening meals is clear — and about pets, reductions for children or any other special points.

Read our reviews carefully to ensure that the proprietors you are going to contact can supply what you want. Ask for a letter confirming all arrangements, if possible.

If you have to cancel, do so as soon as possible. Proprietors do have the right to retain deposits and under certain circumstances to charge for cancelled holidays if adequate notice is not given and they cannot re-let the accommodation.

HOSTS: Give details about your facilities and about any special conditions. Explain your deposit system clearly and arrangements for cancellations, charges, etc, and whether or not your terms include VAT.

If for any reason you are unable to fulfil an agreed booking without adequate notice, you may be under an obligation to arrange alternative suitable accommodation or to make some form of compensation.

While every effort is made to ensure accuracy, we regret that FHG Publications cannot accept responsibility for errors, omissions or misrepresentation in our entries or any consequences thereof. Prices in particular should be checked because we go to press early. We will follow up complaints but cannot act as arbiters or agents for either party.

MAGUIRESBRIDGE. Mr Aubrey and Mrs Wendy Bothwell, Derryvree House, 200 Belfast Road, Maguiresbridge BT94 4LD (013655 31251). NITB

APPROVED. A warm and friendly welcome awaits you at Derryvree House, where guests can relax and enjoy a memorable family holiday at competitive rates. Situated on main Belfast/Enniskillen road. Large lounge with colour TV and turf fire. Central heating throughout. Spacious bedrooms, all with washbasins, and one room en suite. Tea/coffee making facilities. Children welcome. Packed lunches available. Enjoy good home cooking in our breakfast room. Trout fishing within walking distance at Colebrooke River. Convenient to Upper and Lower Lough Erne, Ardhowen Theatre and National Trust properties. Ideally located for touring Fermanagh's lakes and mountains. Open all year. Bed and Breakfast from £14 to £16 per person.

LONDONDERRY

COLERAINE. Mrs Heather Torrens, "Heathfield", 31 Drumcroone Road, Garvagh, Coleraine BT51 4EB (012665 58245). Winner of A.I.B. Agr-Tourism Farm Guest House 1995. 17th century farmhouse of great character and warmth set in large garden. Working beef and sheep farm. Ideally situated for business guest or holidaymaker.

From your peaceful rural base discover our many local attractions, Causeway Coast, etc; golf, horse riding and fishing nearby. En suite bedrooms. Tea/coffee facilities, TV, hair dryers, etc. Guest lounge with piano and log fire. Farmhouse hospitality and home cooking. Access/Visa cards. On A29 Garvagh to Coleraine Road. Open all year. Bed and Breakfast from £16.

COLERAINE. Mrs R. Butler, Darties House, 50 Gortycavan Road, Articlave, Coleraine BT51 4JY (Tel and Fax: 01265 848312). Country house on a working farm, situated on an elevated site giving panoramic views of the River Bann and the coastal towns of Portstewart and Castlerock. An excellent base for walking or touring the scenic North Coast. Sample the home baking when you arrive. One double and two twin rooms (one en suite, all with washbasins). Bed and Breakfast from £16.00 (additional charge for en suite). Weekend and mid-week breaks available. Directions: take Castlerock Road, two and a half miles from Coleraine, turn left onto the Gortycavan Road.

IRELAND

SELF-CATERING

COUNTY DOWN

BALLYNAHINCH. The Sycamores, 40 Hall Road, Ballynahinch. Sleeps 6. Spacious modernised house

in scenic countryside, large parking area, patio and garden. Accommodation comprises four bedrooms, two bathrooms and has fully equipped kitchen including microwave. Full central heating. TV and linen provided. Central for touring, 20 minutes from beaches and Belfast. Convenient for golfing, fishing, horse riding, swimming and forest parks. Pay phone. Terms from £190 low season, £250 high season. Contact: **Mrs Pat McKay, Laurel Hill, 21 Hall Road, Ballynahinch BT24 8XY (01238 562640).**

PORTAFERRY. Barholm Self Catering Accommodation, 11 The Strand, Portaferry, Co. Down BT22 1PF (012477 29598; Fax: 012477 29784). Modern

low cost self catering accommodation on the shore of Strangford Lough (an Area of Special Scientific Interest). Barholm, newly opened in April 1994, provides comfortable accommodation in beautiful surroundings, strategically situated near the ferry terminal and boat jetties and only 200 yards from the town centre. Services provided include family rooms, modern fully fitted kitchen facilities, dining room and lounge. Large groups catered for by prior arrangement. Study/lecture room available. Car parking, cycle store, utility and drying rooms. Portaferry has a lot to offer both the serious sportsman and the casual traveller seeking relaxation. Pets welcome. Bed linen and towels are supplied. Tariff: £9.95 Self Catering, £13.40 Bed and Breakfast, £24 Full Board. Please write, or telephone, for full colour brochure.

FERMANAGH

KINAWLEY. Mrs Helen Finlay, Pine Cottage, Tonywall, Kinawley BT92 4AV (013657 48518). Sleeps 6. Enjoy a self catering holiday in traditional,

whitewashed, thatched cottage, tastefully furnished with open fire and oil-fired central heating. Situated on working farm close to Knockninney beach and Carrick Craft cruiser hire base on the main Derrylin/Kinawley road. Cottage equipped with dishwasher and all modern conveniences. Children and pets welcome. Parking. Prices from £260 per week; weekends from £100.

KILSKEERY. Corkhill, 31 Old Junction Road, Kilskeery. Irish Tourist Board TWO STARS. Sleeps 7/9. Two storey farmhouse, newly renovated, situated eight

and a half miles from Enniskillen, three and a half miles from Irvinestown and seven and a half miles from Lough Erne. Peaceful, tranquil setting for a leisurely holiday break. Accommodation comprises one twin, one family and two single bedrooms plus bed/settee in lounge. TV, central heating and all modern conveniences. Children welcome, cot available on request. Pets welcome. Golf course nearby. Ideal base for touring Fermanagh and Tyrone. Prices from £150 to £250 per week. Weekend Breaks available from £60 low season only. Contact: **Thomas and Christina Brunt, 31 Old Junction Road, Kilskeery, Co. Tyrone BT18 5RH (013655 61865 or 013655 61495).**

REPUBLIC OF IRELAND

BOARD ACCOMMODATION

CARLOW

TULLOW. Mrs Maureen Owens, Sherwood Park House, Kilbride, Ballon, Tullow (0503 59117; Fax: 0503 59355). Working farm. Timeless elegance and a warm welcome await you at Sherwood. Our early Georgian house is on 100 acre mixed farm set in rolling parkland and tranquil countryside, just off N80, midway Dublin/Rosslare. Open fires, romantic bedrooms with brass and canopy beds. All bathrooms have both bath tub and shower. Excellent home cooking; bring your own wine. Golf, fishing, horse riding and beside renowned Altamont Gardens. Children welcome. Pets welcome if kept outside. Bed and Breakfast £23. AA QQQQ Selected.

CLARE

QUILTY. Mrs T. Donnellan, "Fionnuaire", Mullagh, Quilty (Tel & Fax: 00 353 65 87179). Working dairy farm in quiet location with sweeping views of scenic countryside and Atlantic Ocean. Fitted games and leisure room. Also available, guided walks, cycle tours (bicycle hire arranged). Guests welcome to participate in farm work. Music in village pubs within walking distance. Families especially welcome. Children catered for — farm pets, pony and play area. Bed and Breakfast per person with en suite room £16, without en suite £14. Evening Meal £12. Reductions for children sharing with parents, 50% discount. Self catering accommodation also available. Brochure and full tariff on request.

FHG PUBLICATIONS LIMITED publish a large range of well-known accommodation guides. We will be happy to send you details or you can use the order form at the back of this book.

CORK

BANTRY. Mrs Agnes Hegarty, Hillcrest Farm, Ahakista, Durrus, Bantry (00 353 27 67045). Seaside

dairy farm. Charming old-style farmhouse, newly renovated, retaining traditional character. Situated in picturesque peaceful setting overlooking harbour and Dunmanus Bay, quarter of a mile from Ahakista village on the Sheep's Head Peninsula. Magnificent sea and mountain scenery; swimming, fishing, boating and five minutes' walk to the sea. Irish pubs and restaurants close by. Bantry 12 miles, Durrus six miles. Ideal centre for touring the Peninsulas of West Cork and Kerry. Signposted in Durrus. Four guest bedrooms, three with bath/shower en suite, one with washbasin; two are family rooms. Ground floor room available. Tea/coffee making facilities and electric blankets in all bedrooms. Bathroom. Spacious dining room with stone walls; sittingroom with old world fireplace and log fire. Play/games room, antiques, swing, lovely garden with mature trees. Warm hospitality. Fresh farm vegetables and home baking. Babysitting. Bed and Breakfast from (Ir)£15.50; Dinner (Ir)£13.50; Evening Meal (Ir)£10.50. 25% reductions for children. Extensive breakfast menu. Award Winner of Farmhouse of the Year 1991/2. Also to let, modern seaside bungalow for self catering. Fully equipped and in superb location, from (Ir)£120 to (Ir)£280.

KERRY

KILLARNEY. Eden Villa Farm, Loreto Road, Killarney (064 31138; from UK 00 353 64 31138).

Lovely old country house in extensive gardens in peaceful farmland surroundings overlooking the lakes, mountains and Killarney town. One mile from Glen Eagle Hotel Complex, the National Park with forest and nature walks, pony trekking, boating and fishing nearby. Two double bedrooms and two single ones, electric blankets on beds. Bathroom with shower and two toilets. Lounge cum dining room. Tea on arrival to welcome you and also night snacks up to 10.30pm. Car essential. Three miles to Killarney town.

TRALEE. Mrs Mary O'Connor, The Abbey Tavern, Abbeydorney, Tralee (00 353 66 35145). This Irish country inn is ideally located for touring the lovely south-west and is within easy reach of Ballyheigue, Killarney, Dingle, Cork and the Ring of Kerry. Tralee and Banna Beach are both five miles away. Near Tralee, Killarney and Ballybunion Golf Courses. A warm welcome awaits all guests staying at the Abbey Tavern. Bed and Breakfast and partial Board available. Bar meals served all day. Self catering accommodation at the inn also available. Overnight stays welcome. Details on request.

TIPPERARY

LIMERICK near. Mrs Mary Sheary, "Eagles Nest", Greenhills, Birdhill, Near Limerick (00 353 61 379178). "Eagles Nest" farmhouse is situated one kilometre

off the N7 in peaceful surroundings in an area of great scenic beauty. Killaloe (three kilometres) is well known for its water sports and scenery. There are many country pubs within easy reach. Matt the Thrasher, situated in the village of Birdhill, is well known for its fine food and drink. Good golf and pitch and putt courses nearby. The farm is mainly dairy and also has a Charolais breeding herd. There are many pets on the farm. Guests may wander freely on the farmland. Supervised pony rides for children. Good old-fashioned cooking with ample portions, all freshly prepared with own organic produce used; no microwave cooking. Choice of breakfast menu. Complimentary tea/coffee, scones and home made jam on arrival. Bed and Breakfast £10.50; Evening Dinner £10; Evening Meal £6. 50% reduction for children. Open all year.

WATERFORD

DUNGARVAN. Mrs Kathleen Kiely, Ballyguiry Farm, Dungarvan (058 41194; from UK 00 353 58 41194). Working farm. Food and accommodation offered

in Georgian house built 1830. We practise mixed farming in the beautiful Brickey Valley, signposted on N25 road 4.5km southwards of Dungarvan. Some bedrooms en suite with TV and tea making facilities. Children's tennis court, pony, play area and sandpit on farm. Heritage centres, museums, scenic drives, beaches all within easy reach. West Waterford Golf Course (18 holes), bowling, swimming pool, coarse fishing, angling and trekking all available locally. Recommended in most travel guides. Good food, light refreshments on arrival. Pets welcome. Bed and Breakfast £15.

IRELAND

FOR THE MUTUAL GUIDANCE OF GUEST AND HOST

Every year literally thousands of holidays, short-breaks and overnight stops are arranged through our guides, the vast majority without any problems at all. In a handful of cases, however, difficulties do arise about bookings, which often could have been prevented from the outset.

It is important to remember that when accommodation has been booked, both parties — guests and hosts — have entered into a form of contract. We hope that the following points will provide helpful guidance.

GUESTS: When enquiring about accommodation, be as precise as possible. Give exact dates, numbers in your party and the ages of any children. State the number and type of rooms wanted and also what catering you require — bed and breakfast, full board, etc. Make sure that the position about evening meals is clear — and about pets, reductions for children or any other special points.

Read our reviews carefully to ensure that the proprietors you are going to contact can supply what you want. Ask for a letter confirming all arrangements, if possible.

If you have to cancel, do so as soon as possible. Proprietors do have the right to retain deposits and under certain circumstances to charge for cancelled holidays if adequate notice is not given and they cannot re-let the accommodation.

HOSTS: Give details about your facilities and about any special conditions. Explain your deposit system clearly and arrangements for cancellations, charges, etc, and whether or not your terms include VAT.

If for any reason you are unable to fulfil an agreed booking without adequate notice, you may be under an obligation to arrange alternative suitable accommodation or to make some form of compensation.

While every effort is made to ensure accuracy, we regret that FHG Publications cannot accept responsibility for errors, omissions or misrepresentation in our entries or any consequences thereof. Prices in particular should be checked because we go to press early. We will follow up complaints but cannot act as arbiters or agents for either party.

SELF-CATERING HOLIDAYS

CORK

BANTRY. Mrs Sheila O'Shea, Ard-na-Greine, Adrigole, Bantry (00 353 2760018). Ard-na-Greine is a furnished holiday house to let on private ground including a field suitable as children's playground. Situated in the Beara Peninsula overlooking Bantry Bay and within 200 yards of the shore of the peaceful sea inlet of Adrigole Harbour. Adrigole is adjacent to the Healy Pass on the Ring of Beara and is an ideal centre for touring; it is within easy reach of Gougane Barra, Glengarriff, the Lakes of Killarney, Ring of Kerry and the fishing town of Castletownbere. Adrigole lies at the foot of Hungry Hill (highest peak in the Caha Mountains) with their fishing lakes, waterfall and numerous walks. Accommodation consists of five bedrooms, bathroom with electric shower, sittingroom with colour TV, dining room, modern kitchen/breakfast room with electric cooker, fridge, automatic washing machine. Open fire, electric fires and off peak storage heating. Meter read on arrival. Linen not supplied. Terms from £150 to £250. International Reply coupon please.

BANTRY. Mrs Agnes Hegarty, Ahakista, Durrus, Bantry (00 353 27 67045). Irish Tourist Board *APPROVED.* **Working farm. Sleeps 6 adults; 2 children.** Charming seaside bungalow overlooking harbour and Dunmanus Bay in the "Sheep's Head" Peninsula. Magnificent scenery. Excellent bathing, fishing, boating and mountain climbing within 10 minutes' walk. Shops, Irish pubs and restaurants locally. Bantry 12 miles, Durrus six miles, Kilcrochane three miles. Ideal centre for touring West Cork and Kerry. Accommodation comprises three bedrooms (two double and one twin), all with washbasins; bathroom; shower room; large lounge with studio couch, open fireplace and colour TV; spacious fitted kitchen cum diningroom. Solid fuel cooker, electric cooker, fridge, kettle, toaster, fire, etc. Fully equipped for six adults. Central heating. Bed linen provided. Donkey on farm. Car park and lovely garden. Terms: April and May IR£180 per week; June and September IR£200 per week; July and August IR£280 per week; Christmas and Easter IR£200; rest of the year IR£120 per week. Also available Bed and Breakfast in family farmhouse plus Evening Meals. Superb hospitality, en suite rooms. Award Winner of Farmhouse of Year 1991/92.

CASTLETOWNBERE. Mrs Margaret O'Dwyer, Toormore Bungalow, Toormore, Castletownbere (00 353 27 70598 after 10am). Luxury double glazed bungalow in West Cork overlooking the fishing port of Castletownbere, Bere Island and Bantry Bay. Situated amongst peaceful surroundings with superb views of sea and mountains. One mile from town and sea. Ideal base for touring around the scenic Ring of Beara, Ring of Kerry, Killarney, Blarney, Glengarriff, etc. Golf, fishing, boating, sailing, swimming, cycling, horse riding, mountain climbing, water sports and shooting available locally. Four double rooms; sittingroom with open fire, living room with colour TV, bed settee; bathroom with shower; oak kitchen with all modern conveniences. Babysitting available. Oil and solid fuel central heating. Weekly from £150 to £300. Telephone or write for brochure. International Reply coupon please.

KERRY

ANNASCAUL. Mrs M. Sayers, Kilmurry Farm, Minard Castle, Annascaul (066 57173; from UK 00 353 6657173). Are you looking for a nice, peaceful holiday? All year round self catering accommodation is offered in the heart of Dingle Peninsula. One property accommodates six people (three double beds), the other sleeps four people (two double and one single beds). Fully equipped and carpeted. Bathroom, sittingroom, diningroom, kitchen with electric cooker, fridge, immersion heater. Linen at extra charge. Ideally situated, you can enjoy your meals looking out over Dingle Bay; also magnificent views of mountains all round. Beach within walking distance (safe for children). Minard Castle (famous for its part in "Ryan's Daughter"), and local pub and shops add enjoyment to your holiday. Car essential, parking. Suitable for disabled visitors. Weekly terms: April-May £150; June £160; July-August £220; September £150; October £120. Rest of the year on request. Pets £5. Electricity extra. Farmhouse also available, sleeps eight. International Reply coupon please.

IRELAND

See also Colour Display Advertisement **KILLARNEY. Killarney Lakeland Cottages, Muckross, Killarney (00 353 64 31538; Fax: 00 353 64 34113).** Superb complex of traditional and modern cottages situated on O'Shea's Farm on 12 acres of landscaped parkland on the edge of the Killarney National Park, providing an ideal base for touring in South West Ireland. Two, three and four bedroomed cottages, (sleep four/eight), colour/multi-channel TV, direct-dial telephone, dishwasher, laundry service, full central heating. Brochure available.

LAURAGH. Mrs M. Moriarty, Creveen Lodge, Healy Pass Road, Lauragh (064 83131; from UK 00

353 64 83131) Irish Tourist Board APPROVED. **Sleeps 6/8.** Attractive two-storey dormer-style farmhouse attached to proprietors' residence, 200 yards from roadside, with magnificent views of sea and countryside. The 80-acre mixed farm is conveniently situated for fishing, mountain climbing, Derreen Gardens, shops and old Irish pub: 16 miles south of Kenmare. Accommodation for six/eight persons in three double and one twin-bedded rooms, all with washbasins; cot. Sittingroom with large stone fireplace, TV; separate diningroom. Kitchen has gas and solid fuel cooker; oil-fired central heating and storage heating; washing machine and dryer. Everything supplied including linen. Solid fuel on sale. Children and pets welcome; high chair, and babysitting arranged. Car essential — parking. Available all year. April, May, June and September £140 per week; July and August £190 per week; rest of the year by arrangement. Gas and electricity extra.

TRALEE. Mrs Mary O'Connor, The Abbey Tavern, Abbeydorney, Tralee (066 35145 or (from Britain) 00 353 66 35145). Self catering flats, with optional Evening Meal, clean and reasonably priced, available from March to December, at this country village inn five miles from Tralee and five miles from Banna Beach; also within easy reach of Ballyheigue, Killarney, Dingle, Ring of Kerry. The flats have shower, toilet, livingroom/kitchenette with electric cooker, fridge, heater, etc. Linen and towels supplied. Cot on request. Also four bedroomed house available. Car essential, parking. Overnight stops welcome. Meals served all day. Also Bed and Breakfast and partial Board. Terms on request.

LEITRIM

DROMAHAIR. The Beech Cottage Riding Company, Beech Cottage, Dromahair (00353 71 64110). Riding School and holiday farm on a beautiful 19th century estate — The Magical Refuge. Special weekend offer: IR£89 per person sharing includes three nights accommodation in our luxurious apartments and five hours riding (showjumping and trekking available). Please phone for our full colour brochure.

CARAVAN AND CAMPING HOLIDAYS

KERRY

CARAVANS

See also Colour Display Advertisement **KILLORGLIN. West's Holiday Park, Killarney Road, Killorglin (066 61240; from UK 00 353 66 61240).** Caravan holiday homes to hire. Situated on the Killorglin/Killarney road, one mile from Killorglin on Ring of Kerry with Ireland's highest mountain in background, on the banks of River Laune renowned for trout and salmon fishing. On park facilities include circular indoor heated children's swimming pool, tennis court, river fishing (racquets and rods for hire), hairdryers, children's play area, table tennis, pool table, colour TV lounge, babysitting service, shop, payphone, etc. Central site for touring Kerry. Open Easter to end October. Further details on request.

KILKENNY

CARAVANS

BENNETTSBRIDGE. Nore Valley Caravan Park, Bennettsbridge (00 353 56 27229; Fax: 00 353 56 63955). This family-run site is located in a quiet, peaceful valley and is personally supervised at all times. A high standard of cleanliness is a priority throughout site and amenities. Situated on an open farm, patrons have free access to the farm and are encouraged to assist in animal feeding. You can enjoy home baked bread, scones, tarts, pizza and quiches daily or start the day with a cooked Irish breakfast available June to August. River walk through farm and woodland, crazy golf, pool room and children's play area. Local facilities include swimming, fishing, canoeing, golf and craft shop. Please write, fax or telephone for further details.

The
Countryman

Discover the countryside that belongs to us all.

There's always plenty to read in *The Countryman*. This little green book first appeared back in 1927. With nearly 200 pages in every issue, this bi-monthly magazine brings you stories and poems of country ways and insights into country life, as well as keeping a keen eye open for changes that threaten our glorious British countryside.

Our offices in the Cotswolds are a former coaching inn and readers are always welcome to visit the delightful garden with views of the Windrush valley across the stone roofs of the village.

Subscribe now, and for just £13.20 we will deliver the countryside direct to your door six times a year.

SUBSCRIPTIONS HOTLINE
CALL 0191 510 2290
quote ref FHG97

The Countryman makes the perfect gift for anyone who loves the countryside. If you make a gift subscription we send the recipient a greetings card to tell them you have thought of them.

ONE FOR YOUR FRIEND 1997

FHG Publications have a large range of attractive holiday accommodation guides for all kinds of holiday opportunities throughout Britain. They also make useful gifts at any time of year. Our guides are available in most bookshops and larger newsagents but we will be happy to post you a copy direct if you have any difficulty. We will also post abroad but have to charge separately for post or freight. The inclusive cost of posting and packing the guides to you or your friends in the UK is as follows:

**Farm Holiday Guide
ENGLAND, WALES and IRELAND**
Board, Self-catering, Caravans/Camping,
Activity Holidays.   **£5.50**

Farm Holiday Guide SCOTLAND
All kinds of holiday accommodation.   **£4.00**

**SELF-CATERING & FURNISHED
HOLIDAYS IN BRITAIN**
Over 1000 addresses throughout for
Self-catering and caravans in Britain.   **£5.00**

BRITAIN'S BEST HOLIDAYS
A quick-reference general guide
for all kinds of holidays.   **£4.00**

**The FHG Guide to CARAVAN &
CAMPING HOLIDAYS**
Caravans for hire, sites and
holiday parks and centres.   **£4.00**

BED AND BREAKFAST STOPS
Over 1000 friendly and comfortable
overnight stops. Non-smoking, The
Disabled and Special Diets
Supplements.   **£5.50**

**CHILDREN WELCOME! FAMILY
HOLIDAY & ATTRACTIONS GUIDE**
Family holidays with details of
amenities for children and babies.   **£5.00**

SCOTTISH WELCOME
Introduced by Katie Woods.
A new guide to holiday accommodation
and attractions in Scotland.   **£4.80**

**Recommended SHORT BREAK
HOLIDAYS IN BRITAIN**
'Approved' accommodation for
quality bargain breaks. Introduced by
John Carter.   **£4.80**

**Recommended COUNTRY HOTELS
OF BRITAIN**
Including Country Houses, for
the discriminating.   **£4.80**

**Recommended WAYSIDE AND
COUNTRY INNS OF BRITAIN**
Pubs, Inns and small hotels.   **£4.80**

**PGA GOLF GUIDE
Where to play. Where to stay**
Over 2000 golf courses in Britain with
convenient accommodation. Endorsed
by the PGA. Holiday Golf in France,
Portugal, Spain and USA.   **£9.80**

PETS WELCOME!
The unique guide for holidays for
pet owners and their pets.   **£5.50**

BED AND BREAKFAST IN BRITAIN
Over 1000 choices for touring and
holidays throughout Britain.
Airports and Ferries Supplement.   **£4.00**

**THE FRENCH FARM AND VILLAGE
HOLIDAY GUIDE**
The official guide to self-catering
holidays in the 'Gîtes de France'.   **£9.80**

Tick your choice and send your order and payment to FHG PUBLICATIONS, ABBEY MILL BUSINESS CENTRE, SEEDHILL, PAISLEY PA1 1TJ (TEL: 0141-887 0428. FAX: 0141-889 7204). **Deduct** 10% for 2/3 titles or copies; 20% for 4 or more.

Send to: NAME ....

ADDRESS ....

....

.... POST CODE ....

I enclose Cheque/Postal Order for £ ....

SIGNATURE .... DATE ....

Please complete the following to help us improve the service we provide. How did you find out about our guides:

☐ Press   ☐ Magazines   ☐ TV   ☐ Radio   ☐ Family/Friend   ☐ Other.